A Practical Introduction to
HOMELAND SECURITY and EMERGENCY MANAGEMENT

A Practical Introduction to
HOMELAND SECURITY and
EMERGENCY MANAGEMENT
From Home to Abroad

Bruce Oliver Newsome
University of California, Berkeley

Jack A. Jarmon
Rutgers University

Los Angeles | London | New Delhi
Singapore | Washington DC

Los Angeles | London | New Delhi
Singapore | Washington DC

FOR INFORMATION:

CQ Press

SAGE Publications, Inc.

2455 Teller Road

Thousand Oaks, California 91320

E-mail: order@sagepub.com

SAGE Publications Ltd.

1 Oliver's Yard

55 City Road

London EC1Y 1SP

United Kingdom

SAGE Publications India Pvt. Ltd.

B 1/I 1 Mohan Cooperative Industrial Area

Mathura Road, New Delhi 110 044

India

SAGE Publications Asia-Pacific Pte. Ltd.

3 Church Street

#10-04 Samsung Hub

Singapore 049483

Acquisitions Editor: Sarah Calabi

Editorial Intern: Katie Lowry

eLearning Editor: Allison Hughes

Production Editor: Melanie Birdsall

Copy Editor: Jared Leighton

Typesetter: C&M Digitals (P) Ltd.

Proofreader: Theresa Kay

Indexer: Wendy Allex

Cover Designer: Candice Harman

Marketing Manager: Amy Whitaker

Printed in the United States of America

Library of Congress Cataloging-in-Publication Data

Newsome, Bruce Oliver.

A practical introduction to homeland security and emergency management: from home to abroad / Bruce Oliver Newsome, Jack A. Jarmon.

pages cm
Includes bibliographical references and index.

ISBN 978-1-4833-1674-1 (pbk. : alk. paper)

1. Emergency management—United States. 2. National security—United States—Management. I. Jarmon, Jack A. II. Title.

HV551.3.N48 2016
363.34'60973—dc23   2015028428

This book is printed on acid-free paper.

15 16 17 18 19 10 9 8 7 6 5 4 3 2 1

BRIEF CONTENTS

DETAILED CONTENTS

PART III. PROVIDING SECURITY

PREFACE

Until September 11, 2001, the structure and strategy of U.S. national security essentially conformed to a design legislated in 1947. The trauma of the attacks on New York, Washington, DC, and Pennsylvania, on September 11, 2001 (9/11), shook the security establishment and the American people to their core. The 9/11 Commission unearthed findings that were the worst of fears to some, revelations to others. Among them was the following observation: "As presently configured, the national security institutions of the U.S. are still the institutions constructed to win the Cold War" (National Commission on Terrorist Attacks Upon the United States, 2004, p. 399). The commission recommended a quicker, more imaginative, and more agile government if the U.S. wanted to respond better to new threats.

The government had already started the largest reorganization of the security community since 1947. The founding of the Department of Homeland Security (DHS) in 2002 created a new cabinet-level department. Policymakers reasoned that the new cabinet department would improve information and intelligence sharing, enhance national preparedness and resiliency, and, at the same time, reduce bureaucratic overlap. The reorganization of personnel, material resources, and authorities brought together organizations—from departments as disparate as Agriculture and the Treasury—under a single department.

Meanwhile, the conflict arena continued to change. It involves asymmetric and nonasymmetric armed conflict, economic warfare, and climate disruptions. Poverty, migration trends, organized crime, terrorism, regional conflicts, disruptive technologies, and overuse and overreliance on an aging infrastructure all have impacted U.S. homeland security. Homeland security requires an *all-hazards strategy*.

Furthermore, the context is global. Despite U.S. material superiority in so many areas, the hyperconnectivity of today's world has reduced the United States' capacity to act unilaterally or to solve homeland insecurity purely from within U.S. borders.

This textbook is aimed at undergraduate, postgraduate, and professional students of homeland security, emergency management, counterterrorism, border security and immigration, cybersecurity, natural hazards, and related domains.

It offers a practical introduction to the concepts, structures, politics, laws, hazards, threats, and practices of homeland security and emergency management everywhere, while focusing mainly on the United States.

Moreover, it attempts to present the concept of homeland security as an evolving experience rather than simply an arm within the machinery of government. It is a profession and a conception that requires some forming from the ground up as well as from the top down.

PRACTICAL

This is a conceptual and practical textbook, not a theoretical work. It is focused on the knowledge and skills that will allow the reader to understand how homeland security and emergency management are practiced and should be practiced.

To illustrate key points, the authors use cases and vignettes about how different authorities practice and interact. This book will examine the relevant concepts, the structural authorities and responsibilities that policymakers struggle with and within which practitioners must work, the processes that practitioners and professionals choose between or are obliged to use, the actual activities, and the end states and outputs of these activities.

MULTIPLE DOMAINS

In this book, we will cover the full spectrum of homeland security from counterterrorism through border security and infrastructure security to emergency management.

Homeland security was traditionally part of national security, domestic security, or even international security but now incorporates older professions, such as emergency management, border control, immigration and customs, law enforcement, and counterterrorism. Consequently, homeland security crosses many domains and disciplines. It is, in fact, still contested as the situations and contexts change.

Traditionally more courses were taught with the title "national security" or "international security" than with the title "homeland security." Homeland security has been defined in legal, structural, and practical terms mostly by the U.S. government. It was justified largely as a response to the international terrorist attacks of September 11, 2001. Since then, according to Google Ngram, use of the term *homeland security* has risen from relative obscurity to surpass use of *national security*. However, national security is still an important concept, capturing the military end of security as well as much of national intelligence and counterintelligence.

In popular understanding, homeland security is usually equated with counterterrorism, but counterterrorism was always a minor part of departmentalized homeland security. (Counterterrorism is conducted mostly by the intelligence agencies, the Department of Defense, the Federal Bureau of Investigation [FBI], and the law enforcement authorities at state and lower levels, each of which lies outside of DHS.) Most of DHS's subdepartments and activities manage border security, immigration, tariffs and customs, maritime security within American waters, the security of infrastructure, natural risks, and emergencies in general. The trend in American homeland security has been away from counterterrorism to *all-hazards management*—a concept already normative in Canada and Europe.

INTERNATIONAL

Most books about homeland security concern only U.S. homeland security. However, U.S. homeland security is international. Therefore, this book draws attention to both the internationalization of United States, homeland security and the relevance of homeland security outside the United States, such as the Canadian focus on public safety, the European focus on local security, the Asian focus on internal security, and increasing international focus everywhere on emergency management at home.

Furthermore, without the cooperation of foreign states there is no *homeland security*. DHS deploys personnel at U.S. embassies and as liaison officers with foreign-partner authorities, as does the FBI, Department of Commerce, and the military—even the New York City Police Department has approximately 26 offices abroad.

Similarly, container security benefits from the collaboration of the foreign community—private and public. The U.S. Container Security Initiative requires diplomatic maneuvering to allow U.S. customs agents to reside and oversee the program at foreign ports. These programs do not work in isolation; they need international cooperation across many agencies of foreign governments. Container security covers not just border security but also maritime, air, and ground transport.

Cybersecurity is similarly international. US-CERT (Computer Emergency Readiness Team) is the operational arm of the National Cyber Security Division at DHS. Around the world, more than 250 organizations use the term CERT or the like. US-CERT acts independently of these organizations yet maintains relationships for information-sharing and coordination purposes.

Other international examples of homeland security or emergency management will be addressed throughout the book as well as threats with important national sources, such as Chinese cyber threats.

CHAPTER STRUCTURE

In each chapter, you should expect

- Learning objectives and outcomes

- An opening vignette

- Boxed case studies on current issues and controversies relevant to the chapter

- A final case study—a final main issue/case study or lessons learned from distinguished practitioners

- A chapter summary

- A list of key terms

- Questions and exercises—discussion questions and exercises that ask students to go back to the case studies to think critically about the material included

Each chapter provides insight from noted experts who not only excel in their subject but whose contribution to the field is historic.

Homeland security is a complex issue and subject to unprecedented pressures from diverse legacies and new events. Additionally, responding to the new order of world affairs has and will continue to be a process of trial, reorientation, missteps, and lapses. The aim of the authors and publisher of this work is that readers will gain a stronger grasp of the issues and skills relating to homeland security in a way that not only helps them to practice homeland security today but stimulates thought for the future as well.

INSTRUCTOR RESOURCES

study.sagepub.com/newsome

A password-protected **instructor companion site** supports teaching by making it easy to integrate quality content and create a rich learning environment for students.

- **Test banks** that provide a diverse range of pre-written options as well as the opportunity to edit any question and/or insert personalized questions to effectively assess the students' progress and understanding

- Editable, chapter-specific **PowerPoint**® slides offering complete flexibility for creating a multimedia presentation for the course

- A set of all the **graphics from the text**, including all of the maps, tables, and figures, in PowerPoint, .pdf, and .jpg formats for class presentations

ACKNOWLEDGMENTS

The authors thank Jerry Westby of SAGE for suggesting this title and Melanie Birdsall for managing the project to completion.

The authors thank Jared Leighton for copy editing.

The authors thank our many peers and interns who advised us, commented on drafts, collected data, or researched case studies for this book, particularly (in alphabetical order):

Tyler Andrews of Public Safety Canada

Jennifer D. Catlin of Bournemouth University

Connie Cheung of Public Safety Canada

Maire Cogdell of the University of California, Berkeley

Lawrence Conway of Public Safety Canada

Harrison Corbett of the University of California, Berkeley

Craig Dermody of the University of California, Berkeley

Robert Evans of Booz Allen Hamilton

Regan Forer of the University of California, Berkeley

Andrew Stephen Grant of the University of California, Berkeley

Emilie Hannezo of the University of California, Berkeley

Ashleigh Catherine Luschei of the University of California, Berkeley

Aditya Ranganathan of the University of California, Berkeley

Sean Rooney of the U.S. Department of Homeland Security

Larry Smarr of the University of California, San Diego

William James Stewart of the University of California, Berkeley

Eve Sweetser of the University of California, Berkeley

Forman Williams of the University of California, San Diego

Vivan Zhu of the University of California, Berkeley

The authors thank the esteemed practitioners and academics who wrote the final chapter case studies for this book.

Adm. Thad Allen (Ret.), Booz Allen Hamilton

Christian Beckner, George Washington University

Jessica Block, California Institute for Telecommunications and Information Technology

Michael Dinning, Volpe National Transportation Systems Center

Stephen Flynn, Northeastern University

Jeffrey K. Harp, U.S. Federal Bureau of Investigation

Melissa E. Hathaway, Hathaway Global Strategies LLC

Tom Kean, former Governor of New Jersey

Bob Kerrey, former Governor of Nebraska and U.S. Senator

Rey Koslowski, State University of New York, Albany

Sam Nunn, former U.S. Senator from Georgia

Jeffrey C. Price, Metropolitan State University of Denver

Bansari Saha, ICF International

Michael D. Tanner, Cato Institute

Sally Thompson, University of California, Berkeley

U.S. Federal Emergency Management Agency

PUBLISHER'S ACKNOWLEDGMENTS

SAGE gratefully acknowledges the contributions of the following reviewers:

Peter Allen, ICDC College Online Campus

Ryan Baggett, Eastern Kentucky University

Erick Kleinsmith, Lockheed Martin Center for Security Analysis

Jason K. Levy, PhD, Virginia Commonwealth University

Bruce Oliver Newsome, PhD, is an assistant teaching professor in international and area studies at the University of California, Berkeley. Previously he consulted to the Department of Homeland Security while employed by the RAND Corporation in Santa Monica, California. He earned his undergraduate degree with honors in war studies from King's College London, a master's degree in political science from the University of Pennsylvania, and a PhD in international and strategic studies from the University of Reading.

Jack A. Jarmon has taught international relations at the University of Pennsylvania, the John C. Whitehead School of Diplomacy and International Relations at Seton Hall University, and Rutgers University, where he was also associate director of the Command, Control and Interoperability Center for Advanced Data Analysis, a Center of Excellence of the Department of Homeland Security, Science and Technology Division. He was USAID technical advisor for the Russian government in the mid-1990s working for the Russian Privatization Committee and with such organizations as the U.S. Russia Investment Fund, European Bank of Reconstruction and Development, and various money center banks. His private-sector career includes global consultant firms, technology companies, and financial institutions. He was a manager with Arthur Andersen in Moscow and director of strategic alliances at Nortel Networks, Brampton, Ontario. Dr. Jarmon studied Soviet and Russian affairs at Fordham University and the Harriman Institute at Columbia University. He is fluent in Russian and holds a doctorate degree in global affairs from Rutgers.

CQ Press, an imprint of SAGE, is the leading publisher of books, periodicals, and electronic products on American government and international affairs. CQ Press consistently ranks among the top commercial publishers in terms of quality, as evidenced by the numerous awards its products have won over the years. CQ Press owes its existence to Nelson Poynter, former publisher of the *St. Petersburg Times*, and his wife Henrietta, with whom he founded *Congressional Quarterly* in 1945. Poynter established CQ with the mission of promoting democracy through education and in 1975 founded the Modern Media Institute, renamed The Poynter Institute for Media Studies after his death. The Poynter Institute (*www.poynter.org*) is a nonprofit organization dedicated to training journalists and media leaders.

In 2008, CQ Press was acquired by SAGE, a leading international publisher of journals, books, and electronic media for academic, educational, and professional markets. Since 1965, SAGE has helped inform and educate a global community of scholars, practitioners, researchers, and students spanning a wide range of subject areas, including business, humanities, social sciences, and science, technology, and medicine. A privately owned corporation, SAGE has offices in Los Angeles, London, New Delhi, and Singapore, in addition to the Washington DC office of CQ Press.

PART I

SCOPE

1

HOMELAND SECURITY DEFINITIONS AND STRUCTURE

In 2007, in response to protests for the removal of a statue at a Soviet-era war memorial in the capital city of Tallinn, Estonia suffered persistent cyber attacks. Government ministry websites were defaced and disabled as well as those of targeted political parties, news agencies, banks, and telecommunication companies. A minister of defense in this nation of 1.3 million charged that "one million computers" attacked his country.

Although there was no loss of life, the incident demonstrated the impact such an attack could have. The collapse of tightly networked infrastructure can paralyze a state and make it a helpless victim to a brand of *machtpolitik* that is prevailing in the post–Cold War arena of conflict.

Investigators tracked the assault back to Russia. Implicated in the attack was a shadowy organization known as the Russian Business Network. It is a known cybercrime organization reputed to have ties with the Russian government, which denies the allegation. Accusations persisted and concerns about issues of **collective security** were strongly voiced. However, as quickly the alarms sounded, they became muted due to a lack of verifiable attribution (determining the source of a threat or belligerent or harmful action). Adding to the indecision were voids of definition, precedent, framework for resolution, and any clear policy on an appropriate response. Officials offered assurances that such action would not be tolerated but struggled to say how. Despite the pronouncements, policymakers had little recourse.

The above example draws attention to the disorientation experienced by the legacy institutions and cultures since the end of the Cold War. The onset of the new conflict left policymakers and military planners to assess an unfamiliar battle terrain and to reimagine a future of new threats and the new institutions that

Learning Objectives and Outcomes

At the end of this chapter, you should be able to do the following:

- Define security, homeland security, national security, international security, and related domains

- Explain public safety, domestic security, and emergency management

- Explain the difference between homeland security and counterterrorism and intelligence

- Explain how security is described at different levels (international, national, state, local, etc.)

- Describe homeland security in law, popular culture, and practice, incorporating the Canadian primacy of "public safety" and the British primacy of "home affairs"

(Continued)

will have to be built to counter them. The security establishment created institutions and mechanisms to address the problems of an interstate system. Most of the security framework traces back to the time of World War II. During the period of the Cold War, countries across the earth generally fell within one of two orbits. The collapse of that order and the advancement in information/telecommunication technology created a more borderless environment. Taking advantage of the anonymity and ubiquity of the virtual world, new opportunities for criminal and terrorist activity arose and continue to expand. Some of these groups can be state sponsored and have the ability and jurisdictional immunity to wage new wars, resume old rivalries, and make convenient and fleeting alliances. Their groups take advantage of the dynamism of globalization by exploiting the lacunae in global governance and law enforcement as well as the complexities of attribution.

The events of the 2000s exposed a new field of conflict. A new web of international relations, issues of governance, the role of the state, and the organizing elements of politics and economics set a complicated context for security policy. The definitions of national security and threat acquired new meanings. The shift from *national security* to *homeland security* signals a break from the past. Adversaries are indistinct and enigmatic. The threats also include natural catastrophes and the overuse of and over-reliance on fragile infrastructures. The homeland security environment and modern technology move ahead of policy. The consequences of these historical times may mean, in addition to creating a homeland security framework of well-defined policies and clearly communicated missions, legitimate society will need to collaborate in nurturing an evolving security environment in a hyperconnected world, which is transforming at a pace never previously known.

In this chapter, we discuss the definitions of homeland security, how various domains implement policy, and the history and structures that have occurred as a result of both events and planning.

(Continued)

- Describe the reorganization of the national-security establishment as a result of the events of September 11, 2001

- Describe the creation of the Office of Homeland Security and its transition to a cabinet level department

- Describe the budgeting process as it is proposed by the executive office and moves through Congress

- Describe the Department of Homeland Security (DHS) organizationally, and review the lineup of mission responsibilities and stakeholders

- Describe the coordination effort by DHS with state and local authorities in the areas of intelligence gathering, law enforcement, and emergency management

- Describe the influence of weapon technology as it relates to the nature of warfare and homeland security

- Understand how geopolitics has changed since 9/11 and the end of the Cold War

WHAT IS SECURITY?

Security is the absence of risks. Thus, security can be conceptualized as the inverse of risk and any risk sources or associated causes, including threats, hazards, exposure, or vulnerability (Newsome, 2014, Chapter 2). *Security* as a term is often used in combination or interchangeably with *safety, defense, protection, invulnerability,* or *capacity,* but each is a separate concept, even though each has implications for the other. For instance, *safety* implies temporary sanctuary rather than real security, while *defense* implies resistance but does not guarantee security.

According to semantic analysts, *security* is "the state of being or feeling secure" (FrameNet, 2012b). The state of being *secure* means that we are "certain to remain safe and unthreatened"

COMPARATIVE PERSPECTIVES

Different Legal and Official Definitions of Security

NATO

The North Atlantic Treaty Organization (NATO) describes *security* as "the condition achieved when designated information, materiel, personnel, activities and installations are protected against espionage, sabotage, subversion, and terrorism, as well as against loss or unauthorized disclosure" (2008, p. 2-S-4). A *safe area* is "in peace support operations, a secure area in which NATO or NATO-led forces protect designated persons and/or property" (NATO, 2008, p. 2-S-1). The

▶ Cooperative Cyber Defence Center in Tallinn, Estonia

Source: NATO. Retrieved from http://www.nato.int/nato_static_fl2014/assets/pictures/2014_05.

defence area is "the area extending from the forward edge of the battle area to its rear boundary. It is here that the decisive battle is fought" (NATO, 2008, p. 2-D-3). Also central to the NATO mission is the concept of *collective security*. It is the notion that each state within the alliance agrees to the concept that security of one concerns the security of all.

United States

For the U.S. Department of Defense (DOD, 2010), *security* is "1. Measures taken by a military unit, activity, or installation to protect itself against all acts designed to, or which may, impair its effectiveness. 2. A condition that results from the establishment and maintenance of protective measures that ensure a state of inviolability from hostile acts of influences" (p. 419). The DOD dictionary does not define *safety*, *public safety*, *defense*, or *defense area*, but admits a *safe area* is "a designated area in hostile territory that offers the evader or escapee a reasonable chance of avoiding capture and of surviving until he or she can be evacuated" (p. 269). *Civil defense* is "all those activities and measures designed or undertaken to: a. minimize

BOX 1.1

the effects upon the civilian population caused or which would be caused by an enemy attack on the United States; b. deal with the immediate emergency conditions that would be created by any such attack; and c. effectuate emergency repairs to, or the emergency restoration of, vital utilities and facilities destroyed or damaged by any such attack" (p. 44).

Canada

The Canadian government has no official definition of *security* but the *Policy on Government Security* (effective July 2009) defines *government security* as "the assurance that information, assets and services are protected against compromise and individuals are protected against workplace violence. The extent to which government can ensure its own security directly affects its ability to ensure the continued delivery of services that contribute to the health, safety, economic well-being and security of Canadians" (Canadian Treasury Board, 2012, n.p.).

Public Safety Canada's internal *Security Policy* includes an effective operational definition of security; "security implies a stable, relatively predictable environment in which an individual or group may pursue its objectives without disruption or harm, or without fear of disturbance or injury" (n.p.). The Canadian government defines *public safety* as "the protection of all citizens by implementing measures that safeguard national security, improve emergency management, combat crime, and promote community safety" (Canadian Translation Bureau, 2015, n.p.).

Britain

The U.K. Ministry of Defence (MOD, 2009) uses the term *security* "to describe the combination of human and national security" (p. 6). The Development, Concepts and Doctrine Center says,

> Defence and security are linked, but different, concepts. Defence primarily refers to states and alliances resisting physical attack by a third party. Defence is about the survival of the state and is not a discretionary activity. Security is a contested concept that can never be absolute. It is therefore, to some extent, discretionary. It implies freedom from threats to core values both for individuals and groups. The decline in the incidence of inter-state war and the emergence of transnational threats, especially in the developed world, has resulted in greater political emphasis being placed on security rather than defence. Moreover, security has gradually evolved from the concepts of national and international security to the idea of human security. (2010, p. 76)

(FrameNet, 2012a). For criminologists, "security is the outcome of managing risk in the face of a variety of harms . . . [or] freedom from danger, fear, or anxiety" (Gibbs Van Brunschot & Kennedy, 2008, p. 10). For the Humanitarian Practice Network (2010), *security* is "freedom from risk or harm resulting from violence or other intentional acts" while *safety* is "freedom from risk or harm as a result of unintentional acts (accidents, natural phenomenon, or illness)" (p. xviii).

SECURITY DOMAINS

Security crosses many domains. A student is most likely to study security in disciplines like public administration; criminology and policing (in courses or fields titled "crime and justice," "transnational crime," "public safety," "public security," "counterterrorism," and "homeland security"); health and medicine ("public health" and "health security"); economics, political economy, or development studies ("economic security"); political science and international studies ("national security," "international security," "peace and conflict," "war studies," and "peace studies"); and military or defense studies ("strategic studies," "security studies," "security management," "defense management," and "military science"). Some courses ("counterterrorism" or "homeland security") are so truly interdisciplinary that they could be taught in any of these disciplines.

Consequently, a mix of disciplines, fields, and subfields (some of them ambiguous or contested) touch upon or converge in the study of security. Many people fret about insecurity but have disciplinary biases or formative experiences that constrain their study of security. Security crosses domains that academic disciplines and professional careers have tended to separate in the past.

COMPARATIVE PERSPECTIVES

BOX 1.2

Security—A Multidisciplinary Study

Studying security is a multidisciplinary project. It is not possible to think about security without recognizing that boundaries between realms such as health, crime, and the environment, for example, are often blurred, both in theory and in practice. This means that we must draw on a number of different fields of study to make sense of how balancing risk leads to security (or insecurity). While the primary target of much of the work on security has been criminal justice agencies, particularly law enforcement, the issues raised in addressing hazards from health and natural disasters include public health officials, engineers, scientists, and others . . . Although we bring to the project our backgrounds in sociology and criminology, we maintain that security is a subject that has yet to be adequately covered by a specific discipline or in a satisfactory interdisciplinary fashion. Furthermore, concerns over security are never far from issues that pervade the public and private domains. While public-health officials might concern themselves with flu epidemics and other transmissible diseases, for example, the goal of keeping populations healthy is ultimately a national and, increasingly, a global security issue for a vulnerable segment of the population, it also secures the public-health system by alleviating it from having to deal with the expenditures incurred if such epidemics were to occur. (Gibbs Van Brunschot & Kennedy, 2008, pp. 17–18)

The higher domains that concern everybody from the international to the personal level are national security, homeland security, international security, and human security, as described in the sections below, each structured by the U.S., Canadian, and British interpretations.

Human Security

The United Nations and most governments and nongovernmental organizations now recognize **human security** (freedom from fear or want). In 1994, the U.N. Development Programme published its annual report (*Human Development*) with a reconceptualization of human security as freedom from fear or want across seven domains:

1. Economic security

2. Food security

3. Health security

4. Environmental security

5. Personal security

6. Community security

7. Political security (human rights)

In 2001, Japan initiated the International Commission on Human Security. In May 2003, it published *Human Security Now*, which asserted human freedoms from pervasive hazards such as pandemic diseases. In May 2004, the U.N. Office for the Coordination of Humanitarian Affairs (OCHA) created a Human Security Unit. It defines *human security* as a concept that "(i) . . . concentrates on the security of the individuals, their protection and empowerment; (ii) drawing attention to a multitude of threats that cut across different aspects of human life and thus highlighting the interface between security, development and human rights; and (iii) promoting a new integrated, coordinated and people-centered approach to advancing peace, security and development within and across nations" (U.N. Office for the Coordination of Humanitarian Affairs, 2009, pp. 6-7).

Human security grew as a valued concept particularly among those who work on international or global development and humanitarian affairs. It is now included in military doctrines for stabilization, counterinsurgency, and counterterrorism after excessive focus on homeland security and national security in the 2000s. For instance, in the context of counterterrorism, human security has been defined as "freedom from fear or want for individuals or populations in terms of physical, economic, political, cultural and other aspects of security/absence of threat" (Beyer, 2008, p. 63).

COMPARATIVE PERSPECTIVES

Human Security and British Military Stabilization Operations

Security has traditionally been understood as National Security, concerning itself with territorial integrity and the protection of the institutions and interests of the state from both internal and external threats. However, increasingly, the understanding of security has been broadened to include the notion of Human Security, which emphasizes the protection of individuals who seek safety and security in their daily lives. Human security encompasses freedom from fear of persecution, intimidation, reprisals, terrorism and other forms of systematic violence as well as freedom from want of immediate basic needs such as food, water, sanitation and shelter. Importantly, where the state lacks the ability to meet the human security needs of the population individuals tend to transfer loyalty to any group that promises safety and protection, including irregular actors. Of note:

- There are obvious overlaps between national and human security. For example, the presence and activities of violent groups both exacerbates the fragility of the state and undermines the safety and security of the people.

- A stable state must protect the most basic survival needs of both itself and its people. This includes the provision of human security for the population in addition to the control of territory, borders, key assets and sources of revenue.

- A stable state exists within a regional context. As such it may import or export instability across its borders. Security issues that are outside of a host nation's direct influence will require regional political engagement. (U.K. MOD, 2009, pp. 1–6)

International Security

Most American political scientists acknowledge a field called *international relations*. Canadian, British, Australian, and similar academies are more likely to separate international relations or international studies as a discipline in its own right, but the place of international relations within or without political science remains contested everywhere.

Some academics recognize a field or subfield called *international security*. The American Political Science Association recognizes *international security and arms control* as a section. However, for ethical and practical reasons, the study of international security is not universally acknowledged. This is why Richard Betts advocated a political scientific subfield called *international politico-military studies*, which implies parity with other subfields, such as international political economy (Betts, 1997).

In the 1980s and 1990s, increased recognition of globalization and transnationalism helped to drive attention toward international security, but use of the term *international security* has declined steadily since its peak in 1987, despite a small hump from 1999 to 2001, while uses of *homeland security*, *economic security*, and *human security* have increased commensurately (according to Google Ngram). Some advocates of *international security* use it to encompass military, economic, social, and environmental hazards (Buzan, 1991). The concept of international security has revived since the 2000s as it has encompassed other forms of security. In particular, the supremacy of homeland or national security has collapsed as people realized the international sources of and solutions to homeland or national risks.

National Security

UNITED STATES The United States has institutionalized *national security* more than any other state, particularly since 1947 with the National Security Act, which established a National Security Council (NSC) and national security adviser to the executive. For DOD (2010), national security encompasses "both national defense and foreign relations of the United States" and is "provided by a military or defense advantage over any foreign nation or group of nations, a favorable foreign relations position, or a defense posture capable of successfully resisting hostile or destructive action from within or without, overt or covert" (p. 320).

▶ Soldier Meeting Children

Source: Human Security Report Project (2011). Best of the Marine Corps, May 2006, Defense Visual Information Center/Photo by Expert Infantry on Flickr.

Publicly stated, the function of national security and the responsibility of its establishment are to create and maintain a favorable environment for United States' national interests—in times of both war and peace (Jarmon, 2014). The term *American values* can be elusive. Former Secretary of State Dean Acheson defined the expression *American values* by asserting that it involved the fostering and preservation of "an environment in which free societies may exist and flourish" (Jordan, Taylor, Meese, & Nielsen, 2009, p. 233). The standards of freedom, however, are left open to another layer of interpretation. This objective to create and maintain a favorable environment for U.S. national interests, Andrew Bacevich (2008) argues, has given the U.S. national-security establishment justification for force projection—an approach that seems to clash semantically and conceptually with notion of defense and the namesake of the cabinet department charged with that responsibility.

After the investigations of the attack on the World Trade Center, the 9/11 Commission released its findings. Among them was the following observation: "As presently configured, the national-security institutions of the U.S. are still the institutions constructed to win the Cold War" (National Commission on Terrorist Attacks Upon the United States, 2002, p. 399). Many internationalists and foreigners consider national security an inaccurate and possibly xenophobic concept, especially given increasingly international and transnational threats. In practice, most Americans use *national security* and *international security* interchangeably or to describe the same domains whenever politically convenient while the newer term *homeland security* has supplanted *national security*.

The events of September 11, 2001, forced a reorganization of the national-security establishment and the creation of the Department of Homeland Security. The new post–Cold War era also forced American policymakers and planners to revisit their vision

COMPARATIVE PERSPECTIVES

Official U.S. Conceptualization of International Security

Senator John Kerry, speaking at the University of Virginia on February 20, 2013, days after his confirmation as U.S. Secretary of State . . .

I came here purposefully to underscore that in today's global world, there is no longer anything foreign about foreign policy. More than ever before, the decisions that we make from the safety of our shores don't just ripple outward; they also create a current right here in America. How we conduct our foreign policy matters more than ever before to our everyday lives, to the opportunities of all those students I met standing outside, whatever year they are here, thinking about the future. It's important not just in terms of the threats that we face, but the products that we buy, the goods that we sell, and the opportunity that we provide for economic growth and vitality. It's not just about whether we'll be compelled to send our troops to another battle, but whether we'll be able to send our graduates into a thriving workforce. That's why I'm here today.

I'm here because our lives as Americans are more intertwined than ever before with the lives of people in parts of the world that we may have never visited. In the global challenges of diplomacy, development, economic security, environmental security, you will feel our success or failure just as strongly as those people in those other countries that you'll never meet. For all that we have gained in the 21st Century, we have lost the luxury of just looking inward. Instead, we look out and we see a new field of competitors. I think it gives us much reason to hope. But it also gives us many more rivals determined to create jobs and opportunities for their own people, a voracious marketplace that sometimes forgets morality and values.

I know that some of you and many across the country wish that globalization would just go away, or you wistfully remember easier times. But, my friends, no politician, no matter how powerful, can put this genie back in the bottle. So our challenge is to tame the worst impulses of globalization even as we harness its ability to spread information and possibility, to offer even the most remote place on Earth the same choices that have made us strong and free.

of U.S. national security. The Department of Defense concept of force projection morphed into a "pushing out of the borders" strategy in homeland security. Some see the transition as a new vision for the future; others regard it as a variation on an old theme. Regardless, the security establishment and its apparatus continued to adjust to an era of indistinct borders and enigmatic foes.

Table 1.1 The U.S. National-Security Establishment					
President					

Secretary of State
 	
• Deputy
   ○ Operational Units
		Secretary of Defense
		
		• Deputy
		   ○ Operational Units
					National Security Council/National Security Advisor
					
					• Vice President
					• Secretary of State
					• Secretary of Defense
					• Chairman, Joint Chiefs of Staff
					• Director of National Intelligence
					• Director, CIA

Global Affairs Counselor Political Affairs Economic, Business, and Agricultural Affairs	Management Arms Control and International Security Public Diplomacy—Public Affairs	Secretary of the Army Office of the Secretary of Defense	Secretary of the Navy Inspector General Unified Combat Commands	Secretary of the Air Force Joint Chiefs of Staff	Advisors and Staff Nonstatutory Members Invited Attendees

Source: Jarmon (2014).

CANADA In 2003, the Canadian government established a Minister and a Department of Public Safety and Emergency Preparedness (Public Safety Canada). Public Safety Canada (PSC), as legislated in 2005, is not defined by national or homeland security but is responsible for only domestic civilian authorities: the correctional service, parole board, firearms centre, border services, the federal police, and the security intelligence service.

In April 2004, the Canadian government released its first national-security policy (*Securing an Open Society*), which specified three core national-security interests:

1. Protecting Canada and the safety and security of Canadians at home and abroad

2. Ensuring Canada is not a base for threats to our allies

3. Contributing to international security (Canadian Privy Council Office, 2004, p. vii)

The national-security policy aimed at a more integrated security system and declared objectives in six key areas:

1. Intelligence

2. Emergency planning and management

3. Public-health emergencies

4. Transportation security

5. Border security

6. International security (Canadian Privy Council Office, 2004)

The resulting institutional changes included the establishment of a National Security Advisory Council, an advisory Cross-Cultural Roundtable on Security, and an Integrated Threat Assessment Center.

In 2006, Public Safety Canada and the Department of National Defence (DND) created the Canadian Safety & Security Program "to strengthen Canada's ability to anticipate, prevent/ mitigate, prepare for, respond to, and recover from natural disasters, serious accidents, crime and terrorism" (Public Safety Canada, 2014b, n.p.)—a scope more like American homeland security, although no department of Canada's government has any definition of homeland security.

The federal government still lacks a federal definition of either *security* or *national security*, although the Defence Terminology Standardization Board defines "national security" as "the condition achieved through the implementation of measures that ensure the defence and maintenance of the social, political and economic stability of a country" (Canadian Translation Bureau, 2015, n.p.). DND recognizes *national security* as counterterrorism, infrastructure security, cybersecurity, and public safety and security generally—but not civilian border security (which falls under national law enforcement, for which the leading responsibility is Public Safety Canada) or military defense of Canada's borders or foreign interests. The *Policy on Government Security* (effective July 2009) defines the *national interest* as "the defence and maintenance of the social, political, and economic stability of Canada" (Canadian Translation Bureau, 2015). Public Safety Canada supports the Prime Minister in all matters relating to public safety and **emergency management** not covered by another federal minister. Public Safety Canada has defined its mission to achieve "a safe and resilient Canada," to enhance "the safety and security of Canadians" (2014a, p. 1), and to provide "leadership and guidance to federal government institutions, including in the preparation, maintenance, and testing of emergency management plans" (2012, p. 1).

The National Security Program is a coordinating and advisory mechanism within the Public Safety Portfolio that, when appropriate, works with other Canadian government offices on matters relating to international threats and threats to the territory of Canada. The areas of concern specifically include the following:

Critical infrastructure

Cybersecurity

Counter terrorism

Listing and de-listing of terrorist entities

Foreign investment risk

Radicalization leading to violence

Proliferation of weapons of mass destruction

It coordinates, analyzes, and develops policies and implements processes related to the above issues as it also advises the government on the impact of such policies and courses of action on individual rights and legislation.

Table 1.2 Public Safety Canada

Public Safety Portfolio

- Public Safety Canada (PS)
- Canada Border Services Agency (CBSA)
- Canadian Security Intelligence Service (CSIS)
- Correctional Service Canada (CSC)
- Parole Board of Canada (PBC)
- Royal Canadian Mounted Police (RCMP)
- RCMP External Review Committee (ERC)
- Commission for Public Complaints Against the RCMP (CPC)
- Office of the Correctional Investigator (OCI)

Organization Priorities

- Improve workplace culture through advancing the implementation of the departmental realignment, transformation activities, and Destination 2020 initiatives.
- Lead the federal government's efforts to advance the Canada's Cyber Security Strategy and cybercrime agenda in collaboration with provincial, territorial, private sector and international partners.
- Advance the Counter-terrorism Strategy by leading domestic efforts to prevent radicalization.
- Modernize the approach to emergency management in Canada to strengthen whole-of-society resilience and improve the government response.
- Achieve greater results in community safety by increasing the efficiency and effectiveness of crime prevention, policing and corrections systems.
- Continue to strengthen the fundamentals of financial and human resources management to ensure a nimble organization and a sustainable, productive and engaged workforce.

Source: Public Safety Canada (2015b). Report on Plans and Priorities 2015–16, 4–11, http://www.publicsafety .gc.ca/cnt/rsrcs/pblctns/rprt-plns-prrts-2015-16/rprt-plns-prrts-2015-16-en.pdf, Public Safety Canada, 2015–2016. Reproduced with the permission of the Minister of Public Safety and Emergency Preparedness Canada (2015).

Since its inception in 2003, Public Safety Canada's key role has been as a developer of policy and coordinator of programs across one of the largest and most decentralized democracies in the industrial world. PSC works with all levels of Canadian government (federal, provincial, and territorial), community groups, first responders, and the private sector on critical infrastructure issues, national emergency preparedness, and basic community safety. As mentioned above, the National Security Program is within its portfolio. In fulfilling its mission, it allies with other countries and international organizations. A major feature of the work of Public Safety Canada is its collaboration with the United States on infrastructure protection. A potential partnership is with the Department of Homeland Security's Regional Resilience Assessment Program (RRAP). The RRAP became operational in 2015. Its purpose is to identify vulnerabilities and set reliable measures and safety indices for evaluating the risks and addressing the vulnerabilities. It is a nonregulatory and voluntary arrangement that aims to enlist the participation of all levels of government, private-sector stakeholders, and academe.

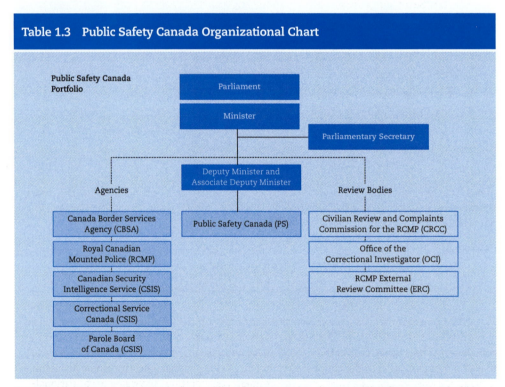

Table 1.3 Public Safety Canada Organizational Chart

Source: Public Safety Canada. (2015a). About Public Safety Canada, http://www.publicsafety.gc.ca/cnt/bt/index-eng.aspx, Public Safety Canada, 2015. Reproduced with the permission of the Minister of Public Safety and Emergency Preparedness Canada (2015).

BRITAIN In 2008, the British government published its first *National Security Strategy*. In May 2010, a new political administration, on its first day, established a National Security Council (a committee to the Cabinet) and appointed a national security adviser. The Cabinet

Office (2013) defines the National Security Council as "a coordinating body, chaired by the Prime Minister, to integrate the work of the foreign, defence, home, energy and international development departments, and all other arms of government contributing to national security." It is also the main forum for collective discussion of the government's objectives for national security. It attempts to set national-security priorities based on the threat analysis and how best to address them under the prevailing economic conditions and financial climate. The council meets weekly, and the chair is the Prime Minister. The membership includes the following officials:

- Prime Minister
- Deputy Prime Minister
- Chancellor of the Exchequer
- First Secretary of State
- Secretary of State for Foreign and Commonwealth Affairs
- Secretary of State for Defence
- Secretary of State for the Home Department
- Secretary of State for International Development
- Secretary of State for Energy and Climate Change
- Chief Secretary to the Treasury
- Minister for Government Policy

Other Cabinet ministers attend as required, which depends upon the need for their consultation when relevant matters to their subject fields and offices apply. Similarly, the chief of the defence staff and heads of intelligence agencies also attend when required.

Unfortunately, the Cabinet Office does not define national security. The U.K. Ministry of Defence (2009) defines national security as "the traditional understanding of security as encompassing 'the safety of a state or organization and its protection from both external and internal threats'" (p. 6).

The national-security strategy document, however, does pose a similar worldview as most governments. The shift away from interstate conflict and conventional military operations is the core theme of the report. Unlike the United States, the changing security environment does not require a reorganization of the national government. Rather, national security can be maintained through the existing apparatus and cross-government collaboration. According to the national-security strategy 2010 report, *A Strong Britain in an Age of Uncertainty*,

> The risk picture is likely to become increasingly diverse. No single risk will dominate. The world described above brings many benefits but can also facilitate threats. Therefore, achieving security will be more complex. During the Cold War we faced an existential threat from a state adversary through largely predictable military or nuclear means. We no longer face such predictable threats. The adversaries we face

▶ British Military Units on Parade

Source: U.K. Ministry of Defence, Copyright © Crown. Retrieved from www.defence images.mod.uk.

will change and diversify as enemies seeks means of threat or attack which are cheaper, more easily accessible, and less attributable than conventional warfare. These include gathering hostile intelligence, cyber attack, the disruption of critical services, and the exercise of malign influence over citizens or governments. (U.K. Cabinet Office, 2010, p. 18)

The Cameron government conducted Britain's first **National Security Risk Assessment** (NSRA) to outline national-security priorities. The findings and prioritization list based its results on degree of likelihood and the severity of impact on the economy, institutions, and infrastructure (see Table 1.4).

HOMELAND SECURITY

Canada

Public Safety Canada is formally defined by public safety and emergency preparedness (since 2003) and national security (since 2006) rather than homeland security, but its responsibilities include the national agencies for emergency management and border security, which in the United States fall under DHS. Public Safety Canada is responsible for criminal justice and intelligence too, which in the United States are outside of the DHS.

Britain

The British government has considered a department of homeland security but continues to departmentalize home, foreign, intelligence, and military policies separately. The Home Office is closest to a department of homeland security; it is officially described as "the lead government department for immigration and passports, drugs policy, counter-terrorism and policing" (U.K. Cabinet Office, 2013, n.p.).

United States

THE SECURITY PARADIGM BEFORE 9/11 During the Cold War, homeland security belonged to a scattered mix of federal, state, and local agencies. In all, the apparatus included more than two dozen departments and agencies, with assets distributed among all fifty states (Selbie,

Table 1.4 United Kingdom—National Security Priority of Risks

Tier One

- International terrorism affecting the United Kingdom or its interests, including chemical, biological, radiological, or nuclear attack by terrorists and/or a significant increase in the levels of terrorism relating to Northern Ireland
- Cyber attacks on United Kingdom cyberspace and large-scale cybercrime
- Major accident or natural hazard which requires a national response, such as severe coastal flooding affecting three or more regions of the United Kingdom or an influenza pandemic
- An international military crisis between states, drawing in the United Kingdom and its allies as well as other states and nonstate actors

Tier Two

- Attack on the United Kingdom or its overseas territories by another state or proxy using chemical, biological, radiological, or nuclear (CBRN) weapons
- Risk of major instability or overseas wars that creates an environment that terrorists can exploit to threaten the United Kingdom.
- A significant increase in the level of organized crime affecting the United Kingdom.
- Severe disruption of information received, transmitted, or collected by satellites, possibly as a result of a deliberate attack by another state

Tier Three

- Large-scale military attack on the United Kingdom by another state (not involving the use of CBRN weapons), resulting in fatalities and damage to infrastructure within the United Kingdom.
- Significant increase in the level of terrorists, organized criminals, illegal immigrants, and illicit goods trying to cross the border into the United Kingdom.
- Disruption of oil or gas supplies to the United Kingdom or price instability due to war, accident, major political upheaval, or deliberate manipulation of supply by producers
- Major release of radioactive material from a civil nuclear site within the United Kingdom that affects one or more regions
- A conventional attack by a state on another NATO or E.U. member to which the United Kingdom would have to respond
- Attack on a United Kingdom overseas territory as a result of sovereignty dispute or wider regional conflict
- Short- to medium-term disruption to international supplies of resources (e.g., food or minerals essential to the United Kingdom.)

Source: U.K. Cabinet Office (2010).

2001, p. 10). Border protection, public health, disaster management, law enforcement, and counterespionage were mostly themes and terrain separate from the notion, undertaking, and study of national security.

Several events in the 1990s, however, stirred concerns within government over the potential of terrorist attacks. The 1993 bombing of the World Trade Center, the bombing of the Murrah Federal Building in Oklahoma City in 1995, attacks on U.S. embassies in Kenya and Tanzania in 1998, and the 2000 assault on the USS *Cole* in Yemen created a conclusive body of evidence of a growing threat from networks of terrorists groups who could strike from anywhere in the world and within the United States. In 1999, the U.S. Commission on National Security/21st Century (2001), also known as the Hart-Rudman Commission, recommended overhauling the U.S. Government and civilian personnel system, redesigning executive branch institutions and reassessing and organizing congressional oversight. The commission noted that the era of U.S. invulnerability was closing. The proliferation of unconventional weapons and the asymmetric nature of warfare against terrorism had neutralized America's conventional military dominance.

As the Hart-Rudman Commission warned, at large in the world was access to the materials and expertise required to assemble weapons of mass destruction. The dissolution of the USSR elevated the potential threat from the proliferation of chemical, biological, radiological, and nuclear materials. The dismissal and dispersal of trained scientists and engineers from de-funded government programs led to the dissemination of technical personnel circulating the world in search of new homes for their skills. A global black market (currently in an estimated sum of 10 trillion USD [Nuewirth, 2011]) and the availability of information through open sources or via corruptible channels heightened fears of vulnerability. Against the backdrop of these events and circumstances, the security community began to consider the nation's ability to avert and mitigate the consequences of terrorist attacks. Those concerns concretized on September 11, 2001. Describing the time of the attack, the **9/11 Commission report** (formally known as the *Final Report of the National Commission on Terrorist Attacks Upon the United States*) began Chapter 8 with the line "THE SYSTEM WAS BLINKING RED" (9/11 Commission, 2002, p. 254). Finally, the 9/11 attack lifted the concept of homeland security to a new level of comprehension and created a sense of apprehension in government and among the public. With the suddenness of the attack, U.S. national interests were no longer in Europe, Japan, or in remote corners of the world. Commercial and critical infrastructure assets (such as seaports, energy and communication grids, the food supply, the health system, iconic structures, and anywhere an attack would mean a destruction or disruption of life and daily routine) required an effort for national security.

AN ERA OF NEW GEOPOLITICS At a Unity Luncheon in Atlanta, Georgia, in 2002, George Bush said, "It used to be that the oceans would protect us. But that was all changed on September 11th." The president was referring to the Global War on Terrorism and, by implication, announcing that the geopolitical rivalry was morphing into a new reality where the entire planet was a potential battle space. Using its own words, the Department of Defense (2006) concurred with Bush's assessment.

> Throughout much of its history, the United States enjoyed a geographic position of strategic insularity. The oceans and uncontested borders permitted rapid economic growth and allowed the United States to spend little at home to defend against foreign threats. The advent of long-range bombers and missiles, nuclear weapons, and more recently of terrorist groups with global reach, fundamentally changed the relationship between U.S. geography and security. Geographic insularity no longer confers security. (p. 24)

As technology was making the world smaller by crushing time and territory, it was also enabling state and nonstate adversaries with the same tools. The incorporation of the latest technological advancements has always been a challenge for all militaries. In the post–Cold War era, however, never has the pace of technological change been so great or **geopolitics** so complex. The term *revolution in military affairs* (RMA) is a recurring and loose theme to describe the process of integrating technological innovations in weapon systems. In the discourse over RMA, the primary focus is on the important changes created by computer technologies and communication systems (Dalby, 2009). The array of new generation weaponry was on display during the 1991 Gulf War. The use of "smart" weapons, which were supported by global positioning navigation systems and the latest information technology (IT), allowed allied forces to outmaneuver the opposition, destroy targets, and limit casualties (Dalby, 2009). This technology not only wrought changes in military arms but also in military organization and culture.

The **revolution in military affairs** began to gain notice during the 1970s. The increasing accuracy and effect of new munitions at the end of the Vietnam War and in Middle East conflicts was observable. One noted observer was the Soviet Chief of Staff Marshall Nikolai Ogarkov. In the 1980s, Ogarkov wrote about the "military technical revolution" he was witnessing. He viewed the trend as a threat to Warsaw Pact forces whose major advantage was in the number of military assets, not in the technological or computerized sophistication of its weapons. Experts often cite Ogarkov's writings and warnings to his government as the genesis of the current thinking on RMA (Chapman, 2003). However, his views were not singular to him. In 1970, two years before the invention of the microchip, General William Westmoreland, testifying in Congress, reported on the USSR's fear of the U.S.'s mounting advantage. He outlined his expectations for the nature of prospective military conflict, saying, "On the battlefield of the future, enemy forces will be located, tracked and targeted almost instantaneously through the use of data links, computer assisted intelligence evaluation, and automated fire control" (quoted in Chapman, 2003, p. 2).

Thus, RMA refers to the precision weapons and information technology of modern warfare needed to attain decisive military action without the need for large mobilized land forces. It is a system of systems, often referred to as C4ISR (command, control, communication, computers, intelligence, surveillance, and reconnaissance). C4ISR combines information collection, analysis, and transmission and weapons systems to create perfected mission assignment—or what others sarcastically have called "precision violence" or "just-in-time warfare" (Kaldor, 2001). The evolution of warfare technology creates a new fast-paced battlefield. Success on this battlescape ideally requires an integration of hyperaccurate reconnaissance, seamless intelligence, the most advanced standoff munitions (laser- or T.V.-guided missiles), and computers (Bolkom, 2000; Jordan et al., 2009, p. 318).

The key elements to having this advantage are enhanced command systems and situational awareness. Remote sensors and computer tracking of numerous targets allow for smaller, more flexible units to cover more distance by having the ability to interoperate and form into joint operations. This means a shift away from division-centric command structure to take advantage of precision navigation systems and precision air power (Jordan et al., 2009, p. 318). This sort of flexibility comes not only from the ability to adapt to technology but also from the ability to adapt change-management strategies operationally, organizationally, and according to regional and local environments (as in Afghanistan, where special forces units used horse transportation and laser targeting technology to track enemy movements). Theoretically, it also means no territory is remote and anywhere on earth is within reach at nearly any time. Geopolitics in this arena is no longer framed by an interstate system of borders and inviolate state sovereignty. Rather, it implies a field of global conflict involving state and nonstate actors, of disparate regional and strategic contests, and a struggle that targets political and economic objectives without the ideological passions of the past.

When Bush made his pithy comments, he was simultaneously discussing the new military arena, the "transformational military" his Secretary of Defense Donald Rumsfeld was advocating, and the terrestrial and earth-orbit technology that was driving events. The reorganization of the armed services into smaller brigade-sized units makes possible rapid deployment surges into global flash points and trouble spots. Therefore, the traditional organization of the service branches into separate missions and roles yielded to a new priority based upon joint operations (Dalby, 2009). However, despite the technological superiority of U.S. forces, the dependency on C4ISR systems makes the "transformed" military vulnerable. The ability to react faster because of superior intelligence gathering and synchronization methods comes with a risk. The disruption of the hi-tech military infrastructure can affect the delicate efficiencies of space-based communication and monitoring satellites and, in turn, the coordination of ground conditions and operations.

These same strategies also put homeland security on alert. As a way of compensating for the U.S. technological lead, peer competitors may choose to adapt strategies directed at nonmilitary targets. In commercial and private life, Americans have become highly dependent upon technology. The critical infrastructures of financial systems, energy grids, communication networks, commercial transportation, supply chains, and the food supply are strategic targets. These new asymmetric threat assumptions pertain to not only nonstate actors but also to near peer competition with established and rising states. As U.S. dependence on these systems has grown, economic, social, and security stability is targeted and made more vulnerable. The use of cyber terrorism, biochemical attacks, and the acquisition or development of WMDs can be part of strategies that, conjecturally and in reality, pose counter and pre-emptive strike options. An opposition force that is in a position of weakness, conventionally or technologically, will have these alternatives to consider. The overall national-security strategy must reflect these contingencies and provide for the systemic redundancy and resiliency needed to sustain and attack as well as have in place the capability to deter and retaliate.

RMA also makes the process of budgeting and planning for future conflict more complex. The advent of breakthrough or disruptive technology can erupt anytime and tilt the balance of power in one direction or another. Despite the degree of impossibility, national-security policy has to find a way to prepare for such events. Forecasting the future is even more challenging given the pace of technological advancement and the pattern of change, where the ability to defend is trailing the capability to attack.

NEW CONFLICT ARENA At the end of the World War II, the United States found itself at the center of world affairs. In order to counter the Soviet threat, the authors of **NSC-68** reassessed American foreign and defense policy and determined that conditions required a long-term military buildup in "righting the power balance." Today, the United States still holds

▶ C4ISR

Source: Photo on left by Information Technology/Photo by Bob Mical on Flickr; Photo in middle by Brandon Booth; Photo on right by NASA/JPL-Caltech.

center stage. However, the conflict arena is unfamiliar. It not only involves asymmetric and nonasymmetric armed conflict but also cyber war and climate disruptions. It is, in a very true sense, an **all-hazards** defense strategy. Poverty, migration trends, ecological disasters, organized crime, terrorism, regional conflicts, and disruptive technologies all have an impact on U.S. national security. Any attempt to reshape the future through foreign policy or national-security strategy must consider the new geography of violence and upheaval within a mutating security structure of continuous political tension.

Under such conditions, the policymaking process is complex. Nonetheless, the 9/11 Commission report emphatically made clear that the generation that experienced the 2001 catastrophe must match the effort of the earlier generation of Americans who restructured government to meet the challenges of the 1940s and 1950s. That security structure created a generation ago suits a world that no longer exists. The authors of the report also warn that incremental and *ad hoc* adjustments are inadequate. To date, the overhaul of the system has taken time and success is difficult to measure. The size of the bureaucracy, the scope of national security, and the forces of globalization all contribute to the enormity of the challenge. Despite the obstacles, the national-security strategy has to stipulate, as accurately as possible, the nation's preparation against any of the potential onslaughts.

Among the challenges is the fact that the new era of warfare occurs in areas of failed or frail states. In these jurisdictions, there are the virtual opposite conditions of legitimate, functioning states. They can hoist a national flag, issue a national currency, and declare a right to sovereignty, but control over territory and their monopoly on violence erodes as the administrative apparatus collapses and becomes corrupt (Kaldor, 2001). Modern warfare was an interstate battle between nations, which had no such issues, and hence, victory was basically achieved with the military capture of territory. However, the mere capacity to "kill people and break things" no longer is the essence of these new military conflicts. The purpose of the asymmetric war effort is to continue the violence. Rather than the Clausewitzean motive to "compel an opponent to fulfil our will," the objective, often, is to spread panic and create disorder so that the conditions for economic, political, and criminal exploitation remain apposite. Civilian targets surpass military targets as strike objectives while the military needs to respond as more than a combat force. To be effective, it requires diplomacy, law enforcement capabilities, technological skills, and the ability to administer humanitarian aid. Adapting national-security policy to meet the needs of the new conflict arena requires flexibility and foresight.

If the national-security interests of the United States included, as Dean Acheson asserted, "creating an environment in which free societies may exist and flourish," then those responsibilities required "the long war" of defeating terrorist networks, limiting the proliferation and development of WMDs, and influencing the options of fragile and failed states. It also infers that anywhere on the entire planet is a potential battlefield. The defense of the U.S. homeland must also take into account assaults of nature and the consequences of ecological disaster. How does the United States, then, defend itself in an all-hazards environment of potential natural- and human-inflicted catastrophes if the national-security establishment is often caught in the bureaucratic inertia of fighting the last war? This becomes the systemic challenge.

Adjustment to the new order of world affairs has and will continue to be a process of trial, reorientation, missteps, and lapses. Inhibiting progress are not only the present institutions and embedded interests but also a policymaking apparatus and a preference for large-scale maneuver warfare, which are rooted in a fluctuating interstate system. It is a system that has been reshaped by technology and the demands of an ever expanding and intensifying global economy.

These developments have given way to a different structure and level of interaction. For the national-security establishment, it involves a break from the state-centered international system and contending more with national and subnational governments, quasi-states, ethnic groups, rivalries among traditional allies, criminal gangs, diasporas, nongovernmental organizations, and the new phenomena in media. In the post–Cold War arena of conflict, the security framework of past power alliances and strategies based upon a notion of collective security has become outmoded. The principal that an attack on one member of an alliance presumes an attack on all members loses relevance in face of today's threats. The organizing principles of U.S. national-security strategy reflect less a threat from peer military competitors and more of an all-hazards approach to counter transnational forces that emanate from criminal enterprises, terrorists, pirates, and events caused by natural catastrophes. Yet, while these the emerging threats exist, the primary competitors of the Cold War are still major players. Russia and China are participants and innovators in this asymmetric war. They compete politically and economically with the United States and continue to prosecute the remains of a conflict born from the previous era but with variation in mission and a rationale adapted to the realities of the post–Cold War period. Adding to the enigma and burden of the American security establishment is the need for U.S. hegemony to support global commerce and defend the global commons. Hence, the role of the national security–homeland security establishment is more complex than in the past and subject to unprecedented pressures from varied and new sources.

THE ORIGIN OF THE U.S. DEPARTMENT OF HOMELAND SECURITY Justified mostly as a response to the international terrorist attacks of September 11, 2001 (9/11), on September 20, 2001, President George W. Bush announced that by executive order, he would establish an Office of Homeland Security within the White House. The actual order (13228) was issued on October 8. The office was established under the direction of Tom Ridge, formerly governor of Pennsylvania, with few staff and no budget for distribution. The Homeland Security Act of November 25, 2002, established, effective January 2003, a department (DHS) that absorbed 22 prior agencies—the largest reorganization of the U.S. government since the establishment of the Department of Defense in 1949. The Office of Homeland Security dissolved, and the new department, with a total of over 180,000 employees, became the third largest in the U.S. government.

Bush also sought stronger executive powers, partly in the name of homeland security. On October 29, Bush issued the first Homeland Security Presidential Directive (HSPD). He would issue a total of 25 before leaving office in January 2009; during his two terms, he issued 66 National Security Presidential Directives, almost all of them after 9/11. On September 24, 2001, Bush announced the "Uniting and Strengthening America by Providing Appropriate Tools Required to Intercept and Obstruct Terrorism" Act. This became the **USA PATRIOT Act**, which Congress approved with little deliberation (normally a bill of such length and consequence would be debated for years). The president signed it into law on October 26. The act was long and conflated many issues but primarily increased the government's surveillance and investigative powers in order to "deter and punish terrorist acts in the United States and around the world." The legislation also included the legal right to monitor credit card transactions, telephone calls, academic transcripts, drug prescriptions, driving licenses, bank accounts, airline tickets, parking permits, websites, and e-mails. The Patriot Act raised severe criticism. The expansion of government authority in redefining terrorist-related crimes and facilitating information sharing between local law enforcement and the intelligence communities were tested in the courts. Although the act provides for congressional oversight, opponents often warn and contest its potential threat for abuse and the danger it poses to individual privacy rights (Sauter & Carafano, 2005). To varying degrees, these arguments have successfully withstood challenges.

In the first executive order on October 8, 2001, in many executive justifications, and in popular understanding, homeland security was equated with counterterrorism, but counterterrorism was always a minor part of departmentalized homeland security. Before 9/11, 46 federal agencies had some counterterrorist responsibilities, according to the Congressional Research Service at the time (Perl, 2002, p. 9). DHS absorbed few of them. Then, as now, U.S. counterterrorism is conducted mostly by the intelligence agencies, the military services, the Federal Bureau of Investigation, and state and local law enforcement agencies, all of which lie outside of DHS, although they coordinate. Most of DHS's subordinate departments and activities manage border security, immigration, tariffs and customs, security within American waters, the security of infrastructure, natural risks, and emergencies in general.

The establishment of DHS popularized the term *homeland security*. From 2001 to 2008, according to Google Ngram, use of the term *homeland security* rose from relative obscurity to surpass use of *national security*. Almost all observers agree, however, that despite the years and waves of events and the massive investment, there is no single definition of homeland security. For some commentators, the term itself is embarrassing and misleading. For Benjamin Friedman, the term helps justify excessive, cost-ineffective investments in countering terrorism.

Similarly, we have no standard and effective homeland security strategy. For over a decade, iterations of these concepts have been illusive, and attempts to give them form appear in a sequence of official documents. However, no standard strategic statement has emerged. Critics complain that the effort to form a simple, clearly stated definition and an organizing homeland security strategy is hampered by a failure to (1) establish a set of national priorities, (2) identify resources for deployment and response to events, (3) align definitions with missions across an array of disparate federal and subfederal entities, and (4) address risk mitigation associated with

Table 1.5   Mission Areas of Homeland Security as Specified by the *National Strategy for Homeland Security* and Required by the Office of Management and Budget (OMB) for All Entities Submitting Budget Requests

2003 *National Strategy for Homeland Security*

- Intelligence and warning
- Border and transportation security
- Domestic counterterrorism
- Protecting critical infrastructure
- Defending against catastrophic events
- Emergency preparedness and response

2007 *National Strategy for Homeland Security*

- Prevent and disrupt terrorist attacks
- Protect the American people, critical infrastructure, and key resources
- Respond and recover from incidents that do occur

Source: Compiled from data from U.S. Homeland Security Council (2007).

the full range of threats. As a result, funding is inefficiently skewed and driven by availability and donor resources. Oversight is inadequate. A verdict by the Congressional Research Service in 2013 concluded,

> Definitions and missions are part of strategy development. Policymakers develop strategy by identifying national interests, prioritizing goals to achieve those national interests, and arraying instruments of national power to achieve the

COMPARATIVE PERSPECTIVES

BOX 1.5

Homeland security means domestic efforts to stop terrorism or mitigate its consequences. In that sense, the name of the Department of Homeland Security misleads. Much of what DHS does is not homeland security, and much of its budget does not count as homeland security spending, according to the Office of Management of Budget [sic]. I use the "odiously Teutono/Soviet" phrase "homeland security" with regret, only because it is so common. Only a nation that defines its security excessively needs to modify the word "security" to describe defense of its territory. In most nations, "security" or "defense" would suffice. (Friedman, 2010, p. 186) national interests. Developing an effective homeland security strategy, however, may be complicated if the key concept of homeland security is not defined and its missions are not aligned and synchronized among different federal entities with homeland security responsibilities. (Reese, 2013, n.p.)

The White House and DHS draft the primary documents that frame strategic homeland security policy (Reese, 2013). The Bush administration's 2002 and 2007 *National Strategies for Homeland Security* contained the accepted guiding principles during their tenure. The Obama administration's *2010 National Security Strategy* displaces the previous judgments put forth by the Bush White House, and added to the body of literature in 2011 with the release of the *National Strategy for Counter-Terrorism*.

The Department of Homeland Security produces strategic documents. However, DHS literature mostly focuses on departmental purview, not the more holistic issues of homeland security missions and responsibilities across the spectrum of federal and subfederal entities and jurisdictions.

The documents below form the list of official interpretations regarding the definition and mission statement of the American concept of *homeland security*. They all differ in focus, emphasis, and perceptions of what constitute clear and present threats. Although they converge on many points, each is sensitive to the historical moment and colored by political nuance.

- *2003 National Strategies for Homeland Security*

- *2007 National Strategies for Homeland Security*

- *2008 Department of Homeland Security Strategic Plan*

- *2010 National Security Strategy* (supersedes 2007 document)

- *2010 Bottom-Up Review*

- *2010 Quadrennial Homeland Security Review*

- *2011 National Strategy for Counter-Terrorism*

Rather than regard the domain of U.S. homeland security as a failure in the alignment of missions, resources, and national priorities, there are others who prefer to assess the situation more hopefully. They view homeland security as an evolving ecosystem rather than a complicated apparatus with custom parts tightly fitted to achieve a specific purpose. They reason that the lack of a common vision and vernacular allows the organism to find its own direction and form its shape. Under such design, whether intentional or inadvertent, homeland security forms more naturally from the ground up. This would be a counterconstruction of the national-security establishment, which is top-driven and highly centralized. Agreement is not always a blueprint for success. As Christopher Bellavita observes,

> Other important and often used terms—like terrorism, justice, disaster, or emergency management—also do not have single definitions. Yet we make progress

Table 1.6   Summary of Homeland Security Definitions

Document	Definition
2007 National Strategy for Homeland Security (White House)	A concerted national effort to prevent terrorist attacks within the United States, reduce America's vulnerability to terrorism, and minimize the damage and recover from attacks that occur
2008 U.S. Department of Homeland Security Strategic Plan 2008–2013 (DHS)	A unified effort to prevent and deter terrorist attacks, protect and respond to hazards, and to secure the national borders
2010 National Security Strategy (White House)	A seamless coordination between federal, state, and local governments to prevent, protect against, and respond to threats and natural disasters
2010 Quadrennial Homeland Security Review (DHS)	A concerted national effort to ensure a homeland that is safe, secure, and resilient against terrorism and other hazards where American interests, aspirations, and way of life can thrive
2010 Bottom-Up Review (DHS)	Preventing terrorism, responding to and recovering from natural disasters, customs enforcement and collections of customs revenue, administration of legal immigration services, safety and stewardship of the nation's waterways and marine transportation system, as well as other legacy missions of the various components of DHS
2011 National Strategy for Counter-Terrorism (White House)	Defensive efforts to counter terrorist threats
2012 Strategic Plan (DHS)	Efforts to ensure the homeland is safe, secure, and resilient against terrorism and other hazards

Source: Reese (2013, p. 8).

Table 1.7   Summary of Homeland Security Mission and Goals

Document	Mission and Goals
2007 National Strategy for Homeland Security (White House)	• Prevent and disrupt terrorist attacks • Protect the American people, critical infrastructure, and key resources • Respond to and recover from incidents • Strengthen foundations for the long term

Document	Mission and Goals
2008 U.S. Department of Homeland Security Strategic Plan 2008–2013 (DHS)	• Protect the nation from dangerous people • Protect the nation from dangerous goods • Protect critical infrastructure • Strengthen preparedness and emergency response capabilities • Strengthen and unify DHS operations and management
2010 National Security Strategy (White House)	• Strengthen national capacity • Ensure security and prosperity at home • Secure cyberspace • Ensure American economic prosperity
2010 Quadrennial Homeland Security Review (DHS)	• Prevent terrorism and enhance security • Secure and manage the borders • Enforce and administer immigration laws • Safeguard and secure cyberspace • Ensure resilience from disasters • Provide essential support to national and economic security
2010 Bottom-Up Review (DHS)	• Prevent terrorism and enhance security • Secure and manage borders • Enforce and manage immigration laws • Safeguard and secure cyberspace • Ensure resilience from disasters • Improve departmental management and accountability
2011 National Strategy for Homeland Security (White House)	• Protect the American people, homeland, and American interests • Eliminate threats to the American people's, homeland's, and interests' physical safety • Counter threats to global peace and security • Promote and protect U.S. interests around the globe
2012 U.S. Department of Homeland Security Strategic Plan 2012–2016 (DHS)	• Preventing terrorism and enhancing security • Securing and managing borders • Enforcing and administering immigration laws • Safeguarding and securing cyberspace • Ensuring resilience from disasters • Providing essential support to national and economic security

Source: Reese (2013, p. 11).

in understanding and using each of those ideas. The absence of agreement can be seen as grist for the continued evolution of homeland security as a practice and an idea. (Bellavita, p. 20)

One of the purposes of the study of homeland security is to offer some estimation of the objective reality and the institutions in place to execute policies and perform the missions related to *security*. In the process, the student will examine alternative definitions and issues and describe the entities charged with policy formulation and implementation while reviewing the origins and evolution of homeland security. It will be for the reader to decide how best to frame analysis. Is homeland security an organ of the state whose structure seeks to adapt to the changing environment of natural hazards and human conflict? Or is it best to assume it is an evolving social construction responding to stimuli?

THE U.S. HOMELAND SECURITY ESTABLISHMENT When the Homeland Security Act established the Department of Homeland Security, it not only set loose the greatest reorganization of government since 1949, it also stirred fears of governmental over-reach, abuse of power, and questions of whether a federal administrative body was up to the task of such a managerial test. The creation of the Department of Homeland Security was an effort to centralize responsibility and accountability under a single organizational body. It was also reasoned that information and intelligence sharing, enhanced national preparedness, and resiliency would improve under a central structure. Planners assumed the current arrangement of a scattered and uncoordinated network of command and control was a systemic weakness. Some success has been achieved. However, critics also note persistent weaknesses in program development, interoperability, execution, and even organizational culture.

The executive order of October 8, 2001, creating the **Homeland Security Council** (HSC) included a purpose statement that read as follows: "to develop and coordinate the implementation of a comprehensive national strategy to secure the United States from terrorist threats or attacks."[*] The president's Homeland Security Council included a membership of no more than 21 people, selected from the private sector, academia, officials, and nongovernmental organizations. Four Senior Advisory Committees for Homeland Security—State and Local Officials; Academia and Policy Research; Private Sector; and Emergency Services, Law Enforcement, and Public Health and Hospitals—form the core of the advisory body.

As defined, the Homeland Security Council is an advisory body that meets at the discretion of the President. Its function is to advise the President on all matters relevant to homeland security.

---

[*] The HSC was almost the same as the NSC; therefore, the change attracted criticism. "The creation of the HSC essentially **bifurcated** the homeland security process: there were now two agencies reporting to the President that had policy authority over national security issues" (Gaines & Kappeler, 2012, p. 209). In May 2009, President Barack Obama merged the staff of the NSC and HSC, although their separate statutes remain.

Membership includes the assistant to the president for homeland security and counterterrorism, vice president, director of the CIA, secretary of defense, secretary of the treasury, secretary of health and human services, attorney general, director of the FBI, secretary of transportation, and the administrator of the Federal Emergency Management Agency (FEMA). It is an entity within the Executive Office of the President. As with the NSC, membership includes statutory and nonstatutory members.

One of the outcomes of the attacks of 9/11 and in the recommendations by the 9/11 Commission report was the establishment of the Office of the **Director of National Intelligence**. The Intelligence Reform and Terrorist Prevention Act of 2004 created the position of the director of national intelligence (DNI). The legislation replaced the director of the CIA as the principal advisor on intelligence matters. The bill, in effect, created another layer of bureaucracy atop the intelligence community structure (Jordan et al., 2009, p. 128). How this will provide a centralized coordination process and a more efficient pattern of operation for intelligence gathering remains yet unanswered (Sarkesian, Williams, & Cimbala, 2008, p. 145). Critics claim that because of the reorganization, the NSA and the Defense Intelligence Agency (DIA), although having reporting responsibility to the DNI, are outside the agency's control. Combined, these two organizations, plus the NSA and DIA, account for 80% of the government's intelligence budget (Jordan et al., 2009). Altogether, they account for a major part and effort of the intelligence community. Part of the DNI's role includes control over the national intelligence budget, but the main collection agencies remain within DOD. As Senator John Rockefeller put it,

> We gave the DNI the authority to build the national intelligence budget, but we left the execution of the budget with the agencies. We gave the DNI tremendous responsibility. The question is, did we give the DNI enough authority to exercise his responsibility? (Senate Select Committee on Intelligence, 2007)

Although the CIA continues to be the major intelligence agency, the Director of National Intelligence is the chief coordinator, manager, and chief advisor to the president on intelligence matters. Additionally, not only must the DNI maintain a harmonized working relationship across the broad gamut of all U.S. intelligence-gathering agencies, the office must also build and maintain working relationships with foreign intelligence services. These ties are not restricted to allies but might occasionally include adversary states, too. The structure and operational success depends heavily upon the managerial and diplomatic skills of the director (Sarkesian et al., 2008, p. 148). Until an atmosphere of trust and familiarity settles in, the office and working arrangement will be subject to tensions.

Prior to the global war on terrorism, intelligence gathering had mostly been a matter for foreign policy rather than domestic policy (Samuels, 2006, p. 358). The events on 9/11, however, forced policymakers to reassess the current structure of agency collaboration, command, and control. The Bush administration recognized a need for effective information sharing and integration of intelligence from not only foreign and electronic surveillance operations but also links with local law enforcement. Because of constitutional restrictions about spying on U.S. citizens, the new powers raise serious legal questions.

▶ New York City—September 11, 2001

Source: 9/11 WTC Photo by 9/11 Photos on Flickr.

The FBI is the primary government agency tasked with counterintelligence; however, several other government offices also have responsibilities in the same area. The Office of Intelligence Analysis is an entity within DHS that oversees and coordinates operations throughout DHS, elements of the intelligence community, and between state and local authorities involved with counterintelligence. Additionally, states and major urban areas maintain their own intelligence operations. Known as fusion centers, subfederal level intelligence gathering stations focus on situational awareness and threat analysis to monitor and uncover terrorist threats. Not only do fusion centers concentrate on working to pursue, disrupt, and identify precursor crime and activity relative to emerging terrorist threats, they also work with private-sector personnel and public-safety officials on critical infrastructure protection, disaster recovery, and emergency response events.

These methods of police-led intelligence operations are unique to the traditions of counterintelligence. Proponents of the bottom-up approach to intelligence gathering hope that it can be a check against the reverse procedure of the top-down regimen, which can lead to a system of self-serving conveniences "enmeshed in meaningless operations, committed more to bureaucratic efficiency than to the purpose of intelligence" (Sarkesian et al., 2008, p. 155). The Cold War arms race and the invasion of Iraq are examples that some observers point to as clear cases where the blend of policy formulation and policy advocacy at the top have skewed the policymaking and policy-implementation process.

By employing the perspective of local authorities, many hoped that such an approach might ease that risk at the center and lower the potential for adverse outcomes based upon distorted analysis. According to a U.S. Senate subcommittee, however, these subfederal intelligence fusion centers have not fulfilled their promise. A 2012 report accused the majority of the nationwide network of 77 centers of producing "irrelevant, useless, inappropriate intelligence reporting to the DHS" (O'Harrow, 2012). The debate continues between the detractors and defenders of police-led intelligence.

Another way the central government works with local authorities is through the Defense Department's military commands. The homeland security remobilization involved the creation of the U.S. Northern Command. USNORTHCOM is one of the nine combatant commands under the Department of Defense and operates to centralize homeland defense activities. It provides military assistance to civil authorities in the continental United States, Alaska, Puerto Rico, the U.S. Virgin Islands, Mexico, and Canada. The Posse Comitatus

Table 1.8 The U.S. Homeland Security Establishment

President

Department of Homeland Security	Director of National Intelligence	Homeland Security Council
Management	Deputies	Homeland Security Advisor
Science and Technology	• Collection • Analysis • Acquisition	Vice President
Policy	• Policy plans and requirements	Secretary of Treasury
National Protection and Programs		Secretary of Defense
General Council	CIA Army NGO	Attorney General
Legislative Affairs	DIA Navy DEA	Secretary of Health and Human Services
Public Affairs	NSA USMC FBI	Secretary of Transportation
Inspector General	NRO USAF DOE	Administrator of FEMA
Health Affairs	INR USCG Treasury/TFI	Director, FBI
Operations Coordination	DHS/Intel	Director, CIA
Citizenship and Immigration Service		
Chief Privacy Officer		
Civil Rights and Civil Liberties		
Counter Narcotics Enforcement		
Federal Law Enforcement Training		
Domestic Nuclear Detection		
Transportation Security Administration		
U.S. Customs and Border Protection		
Immigration and Customs Enforcement		
U.S. Secret Service		
U.S. Coast Guard		
Federal Emergency Management Agency		
Intelligence and Analysis		

Source: Jarmon (2014).

Act, which restricts the role of the U.S. military in domestic affairs, regulates its operations. However, Congress can allow for exceptions to posse comitatus in the event of a national disaster or emergency.

Unlike its allies, who believed their government machinery and personnel adequate to meet the challenges of the global war on terrorism, the United States invested in a complete reorganization of its security establishment. The restructuring, critics claimed, did not address the salient problems of coordination and information sharing. Rather, the new department became a target for those citing its inefficiencies, tolerance of political patronage, and lack of effective policy guidance and success measurements.

THE BUDGETING PROCESS The Office of Management and Budget is critical to the budgeting process. It provides policy guidance, development, and execution assistance to the president government-wide. It also helps to establish order in the budgeting process amid the political turmoil, jurisdictional conflicts, and budget fights within government. By law, the president must present a budget to Congress by the first Monday in February each year. In the spring prior to that date, the OMB conducts a study of the economy and presents the president with its projections. Individual agencies revise current program budgets based upon the guidelines recommended by the OMB. After reviewing these projections, the OMB makes an analysis of programs and budgets. National-security policy formulation occurs as budget levels and projections are being prepared. This process lasts through the spring of the same year, and by the following summer, the president establishes guidelines and targets as a result of the findings. Agencies review the recommendations, make their projections, and resubmit them to the OMB. The president then makes the decision regarding agency budgets and overall budget policy. The final budget document is released after agencies conform to the president's decision and the OMB makes a final review.

Also required by law is the preparation of the **Quadrennial Defense Review** (QDR). The Department of Defense conducts studies and releases the QDR findings every four years. The Clinton administration authorized the first report in 1997. At the time, the document confirmed the U.S. orientation toward conventional war. Traditional doctrine and funding percentages among the branch services remained in place. The 2006 version, on the other hand, called for the preparation of a "long war" against terrorism. Defeating terrorism, preventing the development and acquisition of WMDs, homeland defense, and helping to democratize politically fragile states were the basic principles. Some of the issues future QDR reports will be addressing are potential economic and budget uncertainty, the balance between leverage and entanglement in foreign affairs, the future of the nation's nuclear arsenal, and the national priorities over investment decisions in infrastructure, security, and more. The government released the first Quadrennial Homeland Security Review in 2010. The QHSR serves as a similar tool for policy guidance as the QDR. Both documents set risk-informed priorities for operational planning.

In the budget process, agencies and departments simultaneously cooperate and compete to define needs and recommend funding limits. The absence of a centralized method for establishing policy and the approaches toward achieving goals forces the system to react in such a way. By meting out tasks and expectations, setting deadlines, and putting limits on the range of items for

Table 1.9 FY2012 Appropriations and FY2013 Requests for Homeland Security Mission Funding by Agency (in USD Millions)

Department	2012 Enacted	2013 Request	Total % (2013)
Agriculture	570.1	551.4	0.80
Commerce	289.6	304.1	0.44
Defense	17,358.4	17,955.1	26.05
Education	30.9	35.5	0.05
Energy	1923.3	1874.7	2.72
Health and Human Services	4146.8	4112.2	5.97
Homeland Security	35,214.7	35,533.7	51.57
Housing and Urban Development	3.0	3.0	—
Interior	57.6	56.7	0.08
Justice	4055.4	3992.8	5.79
Labor	46.3	36.6	0.05
State	2283.4	2353.8	3.42
Transportation	246.6	243.3	0.35
Treasury	123.0	121.1	0.18
Veterans Affairs	394.5	383.7	0.56
Corps of Engineers	35.5	35.5	0.05
Environmental Protection Agency	101.8	102.6	0.15
Executive Office of the President	10.4	11.0	0.02
General Services Administration	38.0	59.0	0.09
National Aeronautics and Space Administration	228.9	216.1	0.31
National Science Foundation	443.9	425.9	0.62
Office of Personnel Management	1.3	0.6	—

(Continued)

Table 1.9 (Continued)

Department	2012 Enacted	2013 Request	Total % (2013)
Social Security Administration	234.3	252.1	0.31
District of Columbia	15.0	25.0	0.04
Federal Communication Commission	—	1.7	—
Intelligence Community Management Account	8.8	—	—
National Archives and Records Administration	22.6	22.5	0.03
Nuclear Regulatory Administration	78.4	76.6	0.11
Security and Exchange Commission	8.0	8.0	0.01
Smithsonian Institution	97.0	100.1	0.15
U.S. Holocaust Memorial Museum	11.0	11.0	0.02
TOTAL	67,988.0	68,905.2	100

Source: Painter (2012).

deliberation, the overall process of federal budget procedures allows the system to work despite a highly charged political environment (Jordan et al., 2009, p. 193). As of 2012, the breakdown of homeland security funding was thus:

- Between federal and nonfederal
    - 30 federal entities receiving funds—48%
    - Department of Homeland Security—52
- Within the federal government
    - State and local entities—52%
    - Department of Defense—26%
    - Other federal agencies—22%

THE FUTURE OF DHS In a 2013 *New York Times* editorial, Thomas Kean and Lee Hamilton, Chair and Vice Chair of the 9/11 Commission report, wrote:

> Homeland Security personnel took part in 289 formal House and Senate hearings, involving 28 committees, caucuses and commissions. In 2009 alone, Homeland Security personnel spent the equivalent of 66 work-years responding to questions from Congress, at an estimated cost to taxpayers of $10 million. (n.p.)

▶ NewYork City—Ground Zero, 2014

Source: U.S. Customs and Border Protection.

DHS has absorbed more federal personnel and departments than any since the creation of the Department of Defense in 1947, but their total budget was reduced. The enabling legislation also prohibited unionization. The DHS was created quickly, without requisite bureaucratic input, and the executive's centralized control was enhanced by the quick appointment of partisan supporters to leadership positions. In 2006, the Office of Personnel Management found that job satisfaction was lowest in the DHS, of all federal departments and agencies (Gaines & Kappeler, 2012, p. 35). Richard Clarke (2008), the president's former special adviser on cybersecurity, complained that

> the chief criteria in designing and managing the major new government enterprise were appearance and politics, not problem solving. The largest federal department created in more than fifty years was slammed together with insufficient resources and regulatory powers. Worse yet, far from recruiting the best managers that government and industry could assemble, it was laced with political hacks and contractors to a degree never seen in any federal agency. (p. 204)

Other authors noted that many of the new subordinate missions (such as FEMA, Coast Guard, and Customs) were dissimilar to counterterrorism and contributed to "mission distortion within the DHS" (Gaines & Kappeler, 2012, p. 34).

> To a great extent, DHS is a work in progress. As homeland security matures as a federal imperative, the DHS will certainly continue to change. It is a natural part of organizational evolution, and if change does not occur, most likely the DHS will in some regards become less effective in pursuing its various missions. (Gaines & Kappeler, 2012, p. 37)

In such a polyvalent threat environment, cultural, diplomatic, economic, and technological issues also vex the policymaking process. As the authors of *American National Security*, the core text in the security studies field, state, "even given national security professionals committed to collaboration, it has become harder to get agencies to act in concert" (Jordan et al., 2009, p. 212).

Despite the effort to establish a system of responsibilities, accountability, guidelines, and time frames, nothing goes "according to the book." There is no "book." These influences plus the need to strike a balance politically and economically come together in a mill of government machinery where opinions constantly form and mature around homeland security strategy, personal biases, and real-world events.

COMPARATIVE PERSPECTIVES

BOX 1.6

Comment 1

Richard Clarke, *Your Government Failed You: Breaking the Cycle of National Security Disasters* (2008):

The creation and the subsequent dysfunction of the Department of Homeland Security is revealing of the reason why the U.S. government fails at national security. For several years, over two administrations of different political parties, people who were engaged in federal management and national security tried to resist a politically motivated drive to seen to "do something" about security through bureaucratic reorganization. When, after 9/11, that drive became irresistible, the chief criteria in designing and managing the major new government enterprise were appearance and politics, not problem solving. The largest federal department in more than fifty years was slammed together with insufficient resources and regulatory powers. Worst yet, far from recruiting the best managers that government and industry could assemble, it was laced with political hacks and contractors to a degree never seen in any federal agency. (p. 204)

Also according to Richard Clarke, White House Chief of Staff Andrew Card and White House Personnel Chief Clay Johnson, who engineered the design of the reorganization, had several clear objectives.

They wanted to cut federal expenditures. Thus, the budget for the new DHS was less than the combined budgets for the agencies that were transferred to it, which substantially weakened the department's ability to fulfill its mandates. Second, they emphasized political appointments in the department as opposed to recruiting career experts. Third, they sought to reduce the role of organized federal labor groups, so the enabling legislation prohibited unionization. Finally, they wanted to ensure that the new bureaucracy was created as quickly as possible, which eliminated requisite planning and criticism from bureaucrats who could identify problems or deficiencies with the new organizational plan. In essence, politics and ideology had a significant impact on the department during its early stages of development, which resulted in a number of problems in later years. (quoted in Gaines & Kappeler, 2012, p. 35)

Comment 2

Jeremy Shapiro, "Managing Homeland Security: Develop a Threat-Based Strategy" (2007):

> Policy discussions of homeland security are driven not by rigorous analysis but by fear, perceptions of past mistakes, pork-barrel politics, and an insistence of an invulnerability impossible that can not possible be achieved. It is time for a more analytic, threat-based approach, grounded in concepts of sufficiency, prioritization, and measured effectiveness. . . . [F]ive years into the apparently endless war on terrorism homeland security should evolve from a set of emergency measures into a permanent field of important government policy that, like any other, must justify its allocation of taxpayer funds though solid analysis. (pp. 1–2)

Should the DHS Be Abolished?

Michael D. Tanner and Christian Beckner

Yes, says Michael D. Tanner, a Senior Fellow at the Cato Institute.

> The creation of the DHS was a classic example of how Washington reacts to a crisis. In the wake of 9/11, the pressure was on Congress and the Bush administration to "do something," or at least look as if they were doing something. The result was a new Cabinet-level agency that cobbled together a host of disparate agencies, ranging from the Federal Emergency Management Administration (FEMA) to the Fish and Wildlife Service. Nearly every federal employee who wore a badge was simply swept up and dumped into the new bureaucracy. From a simple management or "span of control" perspective, lumping together so many unrelated functions is an invitation to failure.
>
> From a national-security standpoint, the DHS is part of the problem, not the solution. After all, the agencies primarily responsible for counter-terrorism, such as the FBI, CIA, and NSA, are not part of the DHS. This, of course, hasn't stopped the DHS from developing its own counter-terrorism infrastructure. But, if one of the primary intelligence gaps before 9/11 was the failure of agencies to share information and coordinate activities, it is hard to see how more duplication and fragmentation makes things better.
>
> Making matters worse, virtually every congressman wants to be part of protecting the homeland too. No fewer than 90 congressional committees and subcommittees oversee some aspect of the department.

(Continued)

(Continued)

With so much of Congress involved—and because no one wants to appear soft on protecting the homeland—spending has skyrocketed, tripling from $18 billion per year in 2002 to more than $54 billion last year [2014]. Money spreads to every congressional district without regard to actual security needs. Thus, the DHS has provided grants to such obvious terrorist targets as Bridgeport, Conn., Toledo, Ohio, and North Pole, Alaska.

Its workforce expanded from 163,000 employees in 2004 to 190,000 by 2014. And far from being efficient, the DHS is regarded as one of the most poorly managed agencies in Washington.

Government audits routinely find the DHS guilty of waste and mismanagement. The Government Accountability Office has for years included the DHS on its list of "high risk" government agencies. A 2010 National Academy of Sciences report accused the agency of failing to rigorously evaluate projects to see whether the benefits outweigh the costs. Many of the 22 agencies falling under the DHS umbrella are among the most dysfunctional in government, including FEMA, the TSA, and the Secret Service. (Tanner, 2015, n.p.)

No, says Christian Beckner, Deputy Director, Center for Cyber and Homeland Security at George Washington University.

First, and most importantly, the Department in many respects has become much more than the sum of its parts in the last decade, with respect to its operational mission performance. CBP, ICE, USCIS and the Coast Guard all work together to carry out the Department's border security and immigration missions. CBP, TSA and ICE all work together to prevent terrorist and other illicit travel (e.g. human trafficking) to the United States. FEMA and the Coast Guard have become closer since DHS was created in terms of their disaster response roles, and other operational components have been called on to support major disaster response efforts. ICE, the Secret Service, and NPPD all have significant cybersecurity responsibilities, and are working more closely together in support of their respective cyber activities. And all of the operational entities of DHS have some role (although admittedly not the lead federal role) in counterterrorism, and DHS information has played a critical role in disrupting several of the higher-profile terrorist plots targeting the United States over the past 7–8 years.

Second, the Department has played the critical federal role since its inception in integrating state and local law enforcement and first responders into supporting its missions. This is true not only with respect to FEMA and disaster response, but equally importantly with respect to counterterrorism, and increasingly in the last few years with respect to cybersecurity. (Of note on this issue, contrary to the CATO piece, fusion centers are not "operated by the DHS"—they are entities owned and operated by state and local governments, each with a small number of federal employees detailed by DHS and DOJ.)

Third, stories such as this promote a distorted perspective on the growth of DHS over the past thirteen years. The story says that "spending has skyrocketed, tripling from $18 billion per year in 2002 to more than $54 billion last year." This statistic likely refers to the OMB's government-wide crosscut of homeland security spending, but that annual analysis is not solely about DHS; OMB's numbers include items such as domestic force protection at the Department of Defense and biosecurity programs at HHS. In reality, the DHS budget has grown since its inception from $36 billion in FY 2002 to $55 billion in FY 2011—but this growth rate is far from a "tripling" of the budget. (Budget numbers taken from DHS's response to a Question for the Record by Sen. Ron Johnson from a 2011 Senate hearing. See numbered pages 1029–1031 of this very large PDF.)

It's also worth noting that most of this growth was not due to sprawling bureaucracy but due to increases to frontline operational capacity, in terms of personnel (notably the doubling of the size of the Border Patrol), technology and infrastructure. The reality is that the parts of DHS that I would consider to be "headquarters"— the Office of the Secretary and Executive Management (OSEM), the Office of the Undersecretary of Management, the Offices of Operations Coordination and Intelligence Analysis,

and the Science and Technology Directorate—account for only 1.7% of the DHS workforce, a large share of whom are carrying out government-wide Congressional mandates in areas such as IT management and financial oversight.

Fourth, anyone who proposes dismantling DHS should have the burden of proposing what they would do with its constituent parts, and how such an initiative would improve the performance of the Department's current missions. The five entities that have responsibility for immigration, border security and travel security (CBP, ICE, USCIS, Coast Guard, TSA), where the rationale for operational integration is strongest, account for 195,000 of the Department's 225,000 employees—around 87%. Is the author proposing that these five entities should not be within the same Cabinet department? If he is, he's making a proposal that will have a serious negative impact on the government's performance of these missions. If he is not, then he's not really proposing to break up DHS, but instead proposing a more moderate tinkering, perhaps by returning the Secret Service to the Treasury or making FEMA an independent agency again. I wouldn't recommend either of these; in particular, I think FEMA is now critically interlinked with many other parts of DHS. The reality is that there is no realistic option for a major overhaul of DHS that does not have significant operational impacts. (Beckner, 2015, n.p.)

Under these conditions, the term *homeland security* has many definitional variants filled with political nuance and professional and personal bias. Tensions exist due to the dilemmas regarding the choices between security versus freely flowing commerce, evolving policy versus embedded interests, domestic and foreign affairs, and—unavoidably—funding.

Finally, risk positions are complex. They are subject to culture and local capabilities. Attaining a balance between vulnerabilities and resources is at the core of homeland security strategy. In the international domain, countries craft policy and enact laws according to their estimation of specific threats, assessment of available resources, and notions about acceptable loss. There is no standard metric for calculating these factors or forming evaluations. Therefore, a final balance may also be struck between the imperative to have sharply defined and communicated definitions and mission statements that are top-driven and the need to develop a maturing security ecosystem from the ground up.

CHAPTER SUMMARY

This chapter has

- Discussed the various definitions of *security* and the various jurisdictional domains where they apply

- Touched upon the sundry disciplines, fields, and subfields that cover security as a topic

- Defined *human security* and the importance of the *stable state*

- Examined the difference and overlap of interpretations of the meaning between the terms *national security* and *international security*

- Discussed the differences in the missions and organizational structures of the national-security establishment in the United States, Canada, and Britain

- Discussed how the concept of homeland security influenced notions of national security in the United States, Canada, and Britain

- Discussed the impact of the revolution in military affairs on geopolitics, national security, and homeland security

- Reviewed the origins and rationale for the creation of the U.S. Department of Homeland Security

- Described the budgeting process of the U.S. Department of Homeland Security

KEY TERMS

All hazards *21*
Bifurcate *28*
Collective
  security *2*

Director of National
  Intelligence *29*
Emergency
  management *12*

Geopolitics *19*
Homeland Security
  Council *28*
Human security *7*

QUESTIONS AND EXERCISES

1. What is the definition of collective security and how has its meaning or nuance changed under the definitions of homeland security?

2. Describe the notion of security as it relates to the various primary domains.

3. What are the influencers that impact the setting of homeland security strategy as opposed to national-security policy?

4. How does Public Safety Canada align with the U.S. Department of Homeland Security? And how does it reflect Canada's federal system and unique geographical placement?

5. What is the difference between homeland security and national security in Britain?

6. In what ways does the security establishment in Britain correspond to that of the United States? And how does it set itself apart from its major ally?

7. What are the differences, similarities, and overlap between the National Security Council and the Homeland Security Council?

8. What do you believe the reasons are for no single, standard Department of Homeland Security strategy or definition of homeland security?

9. How has the revolution in military affairs influenced the security structure of the legacy national-security establishment and the development of homeland security?

10. How do we assess risk and what are the elements that shape strategy?

11. What is meant by a *homeland security ecosystem*?

2

POLICY AND LAW IN HOMELAND SECURITY

In January 2015, a former university football star received $385,000 as settlement in his lawsuit against the United States Government. Twelve years prior, Abdullah al-Kidd, who changed his name from Lavoni T. Kidd when he converted to Islam, was arrested by federal agents at Dulles Airport in Washington, DC, while boarding a flight to Saudi Arabia. The authorities planned to detain him as a material witness against a fellow University of Idaho student, Sami Omar al-Hussayen. Despite not being charged with any crime, he was held in custody for 16 days, repeatedly strip-searched, handcuffed, and put in leg irons as authorities moved him between jails. Prior to and during his detention, al-Kidd cooperated fully with federal officials. He further maintains the government never told him not to travel outside the United States or that he might need to testify against Al-Hussayen. Eventually, al-Hussayen was acquitted of all charges and deported to Saudi Arabia, and al-Kidd was never required to testify. Meanwhile, he and his attorneys claimed that in addition to having his civil rights violated, al-Kidd also lost a scholarship to study abroad and was denied employment opportunities because of his incarceration record.

Under the terms of the settlement, the federal government was forced to convey its regrets in the form of a letter, which included the following statement: "The government acknowledges that your arrest and detention as a witness was a difficult experience for you and regrets any hardship or disruption to your life that may have resulted from your arrest and detention" (Associated Press, 2015).

John Ashcroft, who was U.S. Attorney General at the time of al-Kidd's detention, asserted he was immune to lawsuits because of the nature of his job and responsibilities. However, in 2009, a three-judge panel of the 9th Circuit Court of Appeals opened the way for a lawsuit by al-Kidd against Ashcroft. It ruled the former Attorney General could be held liable for people who have been wrongfully detained and added that the use of material witnesses after the attacks on September 11, 2001, was "repugnant to the Constitution and a painful reminder of some of the most ignominious chapters of our national history" ("Appeals court rules," 2009).

Learning Objectives and Outcomes

At the end of this chapter, you should be able to

- Assess and prioritize homeland security risk

- Define the concepts of *just-war theory*

- Review the circumstances and justifications for appropriate responses to attack

- Describe the executive orders, acts, and other legislation that define homeland security in the United States, Canada, and Britain

- Explain how the relationship with the United States affects the policies of Canada and Britain

- Understand how civil-rights and national-security law cause tension in the United States, Britain, and Canada and what the implication is for homeland security

- Discuss the legal issues created by the detention center at Guantanamo Bay and how they relate to the concept of *jus in bello*

The announcement of the settlement against the federal government came the same week as the January 2015 terrorist attacks in Paris. Millions in France protested the murder of 17 unarmed citizens by Islamic extremists; however, the calls for a European version of the USA PATRIOT Act are largely met with disdain. Writing in newspaper *Le Monde*, Dominique de Villepin, the former French prime minister, commented, "The spiral of suspicion created in the United States by the Patriot Act and the enduring legitimization of torture or illegal detention has today caused that country to lose its moral compass" (Apuzzo & Erlanger, 2015).

The balance between security and civil liberty is a challenge for societies, their legislatures, and policymakers everywhere. The equilibrium is subject to traditions, cultures, and often events. In this chapter, we will examine this tension by covering the history of landmark decisions and the incidents and politics behind them. The chapter will also examine the perspectives from abroad and the influencers that produce impact.

ASSESSING HOMELAND SECURITY RISK

Risk positions are complex and influenced by history, culture, and capabilities. Achieving a balance between vulnerabilities and resources is the essence of a homeland security strategy. Nations shape policy and enact laws according to their perception of specific threats, their assessment of available resources, and notions about acceptable loss. There is no standard metric for calculating these factors or forming evaluations. Political estimations are highly subjective, and the consequences of attacks are vague and lack a rhythmic record and history. Quantifying the possibilities and outcomes of a distant event is a process surrounded by a heavy element of abstractness and a priori assumption.

To underscore the variance in risk positions from state to state and region to region, Gibbs Van Brunschot and Kennedy (2009) use the example of the complications of Somalia's choices in addressing the threat of terrorism and the influence of al-Qaeda against the realities of that country's most oppressive drought in 60 years. With respect to terrorism, policymakers consider the risk position within context of the entire threat spectrum and the most immediate dangers to their population. The government must weigh the deployment of scant resources and pleas for international assistance according to the priorities and pressures from the most harmful exposures. Could Somalia, under these circumstances, afford to put the threat from terrorism above the problem and risk of starvation?

> With limited resources available to apply to terrorist threats, the risk associated with that particular type of vulnerability must be evaluated in light of resources available to address vulnerabilities. Resources may be social (including resources based on various group memberships or, in the case of states, particular political alliances), cultural (including characteristics that relate to determinations of status), and economic (money, trade, and physical reserves). When dealing with states, the realms of social and cultural capital include foreign policies. (p. 165)

While many areas of the world face the oppressive threats of natural disasters, endless violence from civil war, frail or barely existent infrastructures, developed countries, on the other hand, face threats of a different nature. The international legal norms and codes are not keeping pace with technology. Therefore, the laws governing issues related to state sovereignty and electronic intrusions such as the theft of intellectual property and cyber attacks as acts of war lag behind the momentum of technological development and the pace of change. The demands of a de-bordered global system and the pressures of the global economy can only tolerate an efficient security regime if it enables business. Therefore, security is often seen as a barrier to trade. This is a standing dilemma for the developed world. These countries also face an unfamiliar "battlescape" of terrorists, criminals, traditional foes, and even allies. Fueling the conflict are spreading poverty, an increase in natural disasters, environmental threats, and a growing string of frail and failed states, which can become a natural safe harbor for terrorism and crime. Policymakers and legislatures reconsider their options as they contend with the globalization process. They also revisit some traditional ideals, about the reasons for going to war, the conduct of war, and conditions for peace, which in past eras were often referred to as the principles of a just war.

THE JUST WAR

In Western civilization, **just-war theory** has been the guiding moral canon on the use of armed force. Great 17th- and 18th-century philosophers such as Augustine, Aquinas, Suarez, and Vattel contributed to the body of work that eventually formed the basis of international laws. They were the principles included and formed the legal and moral foundations of The Hague and the Geneva Conventions. Among these great minds is **Hugo Grotius**, whose *De jure belli ac pacis* (*The Law of War and Peace*) created a structure for the international legal system and established

DEFINITION

the distinctions between states of war and states of peace (Stahn, 2006). He argued that even if presuming a war was undertaken rightly, it must also be fought rightly in order to be just. Only when it serves right does Grotius maintain that war is justifiable—a general principle open to both subtle and brutal corruption.

As evidenced by today's conflicts, in the intermediate times and conditions between war and peace, understanding of international law is vague. The complexities of international law and global conflict in the current arena compels legal scholars, policymakers, and military planners to reassess which organizing frameworks are effective, what constitutes an appropriate response, and what actions and policies should be considered legal. The global conflict zone is less an environment of competing nation states than it was 400–500 years ago and more a world of mobile and adaptive terrorist groups, criminal gangs, entrepreneurial hackers, and insurgents motivated by idealistic causes, patriotic fervor, religious inspiration, or financial gain to create altering circumstances and occasions. An obvious question becomes, In such an environment, are the previous principles of just-war theory any longer relevant? A U.S. air force captain, writing about the just-war doctrine, remarked in 2006,

> The concept of victory and reasonable aspirations of success associated with countries laying down their arms, surrendering on battlefields, and negotiating terms to end all hostilities have all but vanished in today's world. Aquinas and Augustine place supreme confidence in rationalism and its ability to win over the irrational. This simply is not the case today. (Braun, 2006, p. 33)

The three pillars of just-war theory are *jus ad bellum*, *jus in bello*, and *jus post bellum*. These principles address the just and moral reasons for entering into war, moral conduct during the

DEFINITION

Just-War Doctrine

jus ad bellum

- **Just reason or cause** for declaring and engaging in war, including self-defense, the protection of innocents, or the effort to right an egregious wrong

jus in bello

- **Just and moral conduct during war** refers to restraint of undue force, avoidance of attacks upon noncombatants, the absence of revenge as motivation for violence, and the ban of the use of torture

jus post bellum

- **Justice in the peace agreements** restricts the exaction of unjust gains and revenge and affords security and protection of an occupied population as well as the application of human rights

BOX 2.2

prosecution of war, and the justice of the terms and conditions of peace agreements at the conclusion of hostilities.

The post–Cold War conflict arena has challenged long-standing principles of declaring, waging, and demobilizing from war. The legal framework of war and peace is not as antipodal as it once was in simpler times. In the era of globalization, policy and law trail the forces of technology. Borders lose their meaningfulness as global commerce overwhelms them with trade. In cyberspace, there are no borders or boundaries. Terrorist groups and criminal gangs are not rooted to geographic territories and, therefore, have no states to defend. They can attack, dissever, and reorganize, often at will. Their battlefields can be anywhere in the world, including cyberspace. The option to "kill or capture our way to victory" is no longer a strategic opportunity (Paul, 2010, p. 106). General David Petraeus commented to the International Security Assistance Force in Afghanistan that it is a truth in the 21st century's arena of conflict that leaves some strategists and academics to pine for simpler times.

HOMELAND SECURITY POLICY

United States

The Bush doctrine of preemptive war was a critical démarche from a standing foreign policy that sought multilateralism and was reticent about committing its citizen-soldier force. America's security establishment, whose purpose was the projection of power for the prevention of war, faces a tripartite mission: covering conflict conditions, transitioning stages to peacetime, and stabilization. Since World War II, this has included regions where the nation's national interests are under debate, such as Vietnam, Grenada, Afghanistan, and Iraq. The new agenda required the military to be not just-war fighters but also aid providers, local diplomats, and law enforcement authorities. At the same time, a massive reorganization of the national-security establishment was taking place with the creation of DHS and an emerging homeland security establishment was taking form. As the world's greatest economic and military power, the United States holds center stage in international affairs, and hence, other governments adjust their policies correspondingly— sometimes in support, other times in resistance, and often somewhere in between.

History can offer precedence, but history is also interpretative. The justification for the invasion of Iraq and Afghanistan could compare with the Kennedy administration's use of preemptive tactics during the Cuban missile crisis. The Israelis preemptively bombed the Iraqi nuclear facility at Osirak in 1981 under a *jus ad bellum* plea of self-defense. In more recent history, the developers and launchers of the cyber weapon Stuxnet would most likely present the same case to justify their action against Iran at the nuclear facilities at Natanz. The justification for the attack on Estonia's e-government operations in 2007 and Georgia in 2008 might have similar defenders. Policymakers and legal academics cannot avoid asking, are these comparable acts of war, acts of self-defense, or false equivalents? Were these acts of aggression just causes?

Other legal questions and complications about the role and mission of national armed forces arise and scale on various levels and issues. Anwar al-Awlaki, an American-born al-Qaeda leader, was placed on a list of individuals targeted for assassination by the U.S. government. The action was unprecedented. Many considered his death in September 2011 by a drone strike a military success.

However, to others it was a political murder of an American citizen by the U.S government. Both views are legally valid. Regardless of the real-life military and political consequences, the internal moral and legal conflict of al-Awlaki's elimination bespeaks of the inconsistencies and rising challenges that a centuries-old just-war doctrine bequeaths, particularly in an environment as entwined, multivarious, and as powerfully transformative as the present era.

HOMELAND SECURITY IN LAW AND POLICY

The September 11, 2001, terrorist attacks rallied world public opinion and sympathy for the United States. The earlier decisions by the United States to reject the Kyoto Treaty, refusing to sign the chemical weapons ban and the Anti-Ballistic Missile Treaty, and declining to join the International Criminal Court had costs for the United States publicly. Protests to these policy decisions were muted by the tragedy of 9/11. In the immediate wake of the attacks in New York, Pennsylvania, and Washington, DC, support was broad, unprecedented, and, perhaps, eventually squandered. The U.S. rush to war revived some anti-American sentiment of many in the Arab world as well as among the country's closest allies (Epstein, 2004). Moreover, according to Richard Clarke, former Bush White House advisor, these actions may have undermined the Global War on Terrorism (GWOT).

> We're fighting Islamic radicals and they are drawing people from the youth of the Islamic world into hating us. Now, after September 11, people in the Islamic world said, "Wait a minute. Maybe we've gone too far here. Maybe this Islamic movement, this radical movement, has to be suppressed," and we had a moment, we had a window of opportunity, where we could change the ideology in the Islamic world. Instead, we've inflamed the ideology. We've played right into the hands of al-Qaeda and others. We've done what Osama bin Laden said we would do. (NBC News, 2004)

The wars in Iraq and Afghanistan may have also inhibited the effort to build a secure and holistic supply chain through the implementation of multilateral treaties and state-to-state agreements. U.S. legislation, known as **Public Law No. 110-53**, created a voluntary program for putting into action private-sector preparedness standards. One of its sections called for DHS to put in place a system that scans all containers for nuclear devices. Six hundred ports around the world would be required to scan containers bound for the United States. Over 1,400 radiation portal monitors (RPM) have been deployed thus far. The U.S. strategy involved "pushing out its borders." The legislation and its enactment raised protests from such trading partners as the European Union, Singapore, and political blocs within India. Much of the protest concerned the complaint of it being an unnecessary expense and impediment to trade. Others voiced an alarm of it being a veiled attempt by the United States to impose its hegemony ("Are US security measures," 2007). Experts also warn that such factors as the probability of detection, the nuisance of false alarms, the technology's risk of being defeated or compromised, costs, and unforeseen conditions may only lead to system failure. Both Michael Chertoff and Janet Napolitano eventually declared the program unnecessary. They contended that 100% scanning was far too time consuming (Jarmon, 2014). The events and protests demonstrate, however, how hyper-connected the globalization process is, the impact potential in a clash between local politics and world affairs, and intricacies and risks within the notion of *American exceptionalism*.

Meanwhile, Europe experienced its own terrorist incidents. On March 11, 2004, terrorists detonated 10 bombs on four trains at separate Madrid train stations. One-hundred-ninety-two people died and over 2,000 were injured. Authorities linked the attack to a circle of Islamic militants called the Moroccan Islamic Combatant Group, which was alleged to have ties with al-Qaeda. Eventually, 28 people from a local radical Islamic terrorist cell (unaffiliated with the Moroccan Islamic Combatant Group) were tried and 21 were convicted. The act was viewed as retribution against the Spanish government for its support of the U.S. wars in Iraq and Afghanistan. The damage was placed at 212 million euros in direct economic loss (Reinares, 2010, p. 83). The tourism industry suffered only a short-term loss and recovered relatively quickly (International Institute for Strategic Studies, 2007). However, although there was only a .03% decline in Spain's GDP for the year, the incident's impact on Spanish elections was significant. The incumbent party was removed from power, and the opposition, whose political stance with the United States was less approving, took its place. The political impact was the objective of the bombing plotters. Although they were arrested, they also succeeded.

The following year, in London, four attacks occurred on the city's transit system. In the morning of July 7, 2005, explosives ripped through three underground trains, killing 39 people. An hour later, 13 people died when another bomb exploded on the upper deck of bus in the vicinity of Tavistock Square. In addition to the dead, 700 people were injured. In contrast to Spain, the attack on London's underground in 2005 cost the industry 1.08 billion dollars in tourism and transport revenues. The bombing also resulted in a 10% permanent increase in operational costs due to security investment. The annual cost level to secure London's metro since the attack is 115 million dollars (Roucolle & Lowes, 2006).

The attacks in Britain and Spain did not match the financial and economic impact of the attack on New York during the 9/11 incidents. Politically, it is futile to try to separate out the differences in consequence between the attacks on the World Trade Center and the events in Washington, DC, and Pennsylvania. But in financial terms, the comparisons between New York, London, and Madrid are quantifiable.

Spain's experience with the Basque separatist organization Eta (Euskadi Ta Askatasuna [Basque Homeland and Freedom]) provided it with a substantial body of law and institutional capacity to combat terrorism (Archick, 2006, p. 36). By the time of the 2004 attacks, Spain's counterterrorism effort was organized and functioning. Consequently, there was no broad reorganization of government. Homeland security institutions stayed intact while the government focused efforts on providing additional resources for coordinating agency interoperability and addressing specific threats (Archick, 2006).

Similarly, the years of political unrest in Northern Ireland willed to the United Kingdom a security infrastructure well adapted to terrorism-related threats. As in the case of Spain, the British government felt no need to reorganize its security establishment on a grand scale. Rather, interagency cooperation and information sharing, which already was established through policy implementation and practice, continued—however, in greater earnest. The British determined that the dual-use mechanism that combines emergency management operations with counterterrorism programs serves the nation well by avoiding the frustrations of an overblown bureaucracy and as a cost-effective means of aligning countermeasures with threats. The

Table 2.1   New York, London, Madrid Terrorist Attacks and Consequences

New York, 2001

- **$531 million** in lost fares, tax collection, and expenses for recovery and rescue as a result of 9/11/2001
- **$1.1 billion** of capital injection to rebuild and secure transit system

Madrid, 2004

- **212 million euros** in direct economic loss
- **.03%** decline in Spain's GDP for the year, but the impact on national elections was direct and significant

London, 2005

- **$1.08 billion** in lost tourism and transport revenues as a result of 2005 London bombings, which recovered to the 2004 level after three months
- **10%** permanent increase in operational costs due to investment into security
- **$115 million** annual cost level of security in London Metro System

government determined that the arrangement of intergovernmental cooperation gives the system the flexibility to address natural catastrophes and terrorism.

American allies have not felt the need to overhaul their security regimes as has the United States. Because the projection of military force did not necessarily align with imperatives of national interest, these governments did not deem a remobilization of assets or a reorientation in strategic defense policy necessary. While the United States retooled its domestic security and border protection apparatus and created a new cabinet department complementary to the Department of Defense, its allies maintained their current security structure. The response of programs, initiatives, and legislation in the United States, which occurred as a result of the 9/11 attacks are not, however, solely confined to U.S. jurisdiction. These efforts require capacity building in the form of bilateral agreements, treaties, information-sharing mechanisms, and often the stationing of U.S. officials on foreign territories. America's closest allies can be most crucial and are where the most impact is felt, particularly when the United States views pushing out its borders as its best defense option.

United States

In obvious contrast to the threat of natural disasters, civil war, and famine, as discussed in Somalia's example, the U.S. response to the September 11, 2001, tragedy was a state of war. The consequence was a mixture of disbelief and outrage. Despite the warnings from the 1999 Hart-Rudman Commission of the strong likelihood of an attack on American soil resulting in heavy casualties, America was unprepared. The proliferation of the technological and material means, the growing number of potential actors, and the appeal of a target-rich, predominant United States created an eminent but neglected threat. Making the threat more perilous was the observance by the commission that the structures and assets that formed the homeland security apparatus were scattered across all fifty states and over two-dozen departments and agencies (Selbie, 2001, pp. 9–10). Yet the shock expressed by many in government and the public was palpable across the world. Until that moment, few were aware that the world was engaged in a new kind of conflict.

The response by the public and most elected officials was a reaction of horror and vents of anger against an enigmatic foe. The outrage was justifiable, but some of the calls for reprisal and extreme security measures were without basis and practicality. Retaliation appeared a national agenda item. Some called for the United States to resort to the nuclear option. In step with the prevailing mood of an enraged public and a disposition toward a fortress mentality, the U.S. Congress proposed a bill authorizing the physical inspection of all inbound containers onto U.S. territory. Such legislation, if enacted, would have disrupted the national and global supply chain. Many warned it could bring commerce to a virtual halt.

President George W. Bush told a joint session of Congress on September 20, 2001, "This is not, however, just America's fight. And what is at stake is not just America's freedom. This is the world's fight. This is civilization's fight" ("Text: President Bush address," 2001, n.p.). He also, at this time, announced the formation of the Office of Homeland Security. In the same address, Bush proclaimed, "Either you are with us or you are with the terrorists" ("Text: President Bush address," 2001, n.p.). The remark was meant to mobilize as much as it was intended to polarize. Critics claimed the administration was using the attacks as justification for the further projection of U.S. power. Robert Kagan, a neoconservative foreign policy theorist, made remarks that chimed with Bush as well as those of his detractors when he said, "America did not change on September 11. It only became more itself" (Bacevich, 2008, p. 10).

Stridently, the drumbeat toward war with Iraq began in the absence of hard evidence of Saddam Hussein's involvement and with little public resistance or debate. In March 2003, the United States attacked Baghdad under the assumption Saddam Hussein maintained an arsenal of weapons of mass destruction. The assertion, however, that Iraq was secretly stockpiling and producing WMDs or had any connection with the 9/11 attack was never substantiated.

The American response to the 9/11 terrorist attacks also underscored the natural tension between the national-security and foreign-policy arms of the U.S. government (Jordan, Taylor, Meese, & Nielsen, 2009, p. 120). This tension first found voice and legislative action during the 1960s and early '70s. The **War Powers Resolution** of 1973 was intended as a restraint on the president's authority to take the country to war.* It requires the president to notify Congress 48 hrs prior to committing U.S. forces and restricts the period of action to 60 days. This joint resolution of Congress largely resulted from public and congressional opposition to the extended Vietnam War and the sense of a creeping presidential prerogative in foreign affairs. The charges of an "imperial presidency" became a subject of popular debate. The legislation

---

*This is not to be confused with the War Powers Act of 1941, which was an emergency law increasing the federal government and the president's authority to prosecute the World War II.

was eventually signed into law over-riding the veto of President Richard Nixon. However, the resolution has carried little effect. Each of Nixon's successors through George W. Bush have called the law unconstitutional and no president has faced any successful legal actions despite conflicts in Grenada, Lebanon, Libya, Panama, Kosovo, the Nicaraguan harbors, and the Persian Gulf, to name several.

Immediately after 9/11, the resolution was tested again when George W. Bush sought the power to take action against those responsible for the attacks and the broader authority to act preemptively against possible future attacks. With open support from an enraged public, the U.S. Senate passed a resolution on September 14, 2001, granting the president the power to retaliate, but not to launch preemptive action. Attacks against the Taliban and al-Qaeda in Afghanistan occurred with overwhelming approval from Congress and the Senate. Bush acted quickly to appoint a homeland security advisor to serve in the same capacity as the national-security advisor. As with its counterpart in the National Security Advisory Council, the office would not be subject to congressional oversight. However, while the Homeland Security Advisory Council still exists within the executive branch, Congress demanded the Office of Homeland Security be elevated to the Department of Homeland Security in order to give Congress the power of budgetary oversight and confirmation appointment.

The creation of the Department of Homeland Security occurred on November 25, 2002, with the enactment of the Homeland Security Act. By elevating the former office to the cabinet level, the Congress also inherited a new source of distributed political influence and opportunity. The addition to the ranks of federal agencies absorbed personnel from 22 organizations totaling over 180,000 employees. Commensurate in size was also the scale in largesse from the opportunity for lucrative federal contracts. As natural catastrophes fell under the panoply of homeland security, the term *disaster capitalism* eventually appeared in some literature (Bellavita, 2008, p. 18). At the time of the creation of the U.S. Department of Homeland Security, Republican Congressman John Mica of Florida expressed his cynicism bluntly when he said, "Anyone who thinks you can combine 22 agencies and 200,000 people and it's going to be more efficient and economical needs to have their head examined" (Evans, 2012, n.p.).

The growth of the federal government created an environment and legacy of jurisdictional overlap and conflicting legislation. Currently, more than 100 congressional committees and subcommittees claim jurisdiction over homeland security. The all-hazard attack surface, which placed iconic structures, public squares, and critical infrastructure facilities on the potential target list, drew under the homeland defense panoply the Departments of Agriculture and Transportation, the EPA, the United States Coast Guard, and other offices and entities. As more agencies and departments take on responsibilities, the result is an uncoordinated array of congressional purview, mission creep among agencies, and additional layers of staff to fill roles on committees, subcommittees, bureaus, offices, centers, and so forth.

Despite this and the misgivings of other officials, over a decade later, the U.S. Department of Homeland Security is in the process of building a new headquarters. It is the largest construction project in the District of Columbia since the completion of the Pentagon in 1943. The 20-year construction plan's estimated costs are between $3.9 and $4.5 billion. The new headquarters' site is on the campus of a former federal insane asylum. St. Elizabeths Hospital is an abandoned mental institution that was once the home of poet Ezra Pound and John Hinckley. Some critics of DHS might make note of the situational irony. Others, such as the cochairs of the 9/11 Commission, Lee Hamilton and Thomas Kean, point more to the problems of a department plagued by a welter of congressional oversight and a patchwork system of supervision and accountability as the underlying causes of dysfunction (Kean & Hamilton, 2013).

In addition to the attacks on 9/11, the USA PATRIOT Act (or Patriot Act) owes its origin to the findings of the Hart-Rudman Commission (The U.S. Commission on National Security/21st

---

Table 2.2   The USA PATRIOT Act: Crimes, Penalties, and Procedures

New Crimes Under the Patriot Act

- Terrorist attacks on mass transportation facilities
- Biological weapon offenses
- Harboring terrorists
- Affording terrorists material support
- Misconduct associated with money laundering
- Fraudulent charitable solicitation
- Conducting affairs of an enterprise that affects interstate or foreign commerce through the patterned commission of terrorist offenses

New Penalties Under the Patriot Act

- Establishes new maximum penalties for acts of terrorism
- Raises the penalty for the conspiracy to commit certain terrorism offenses
- Envisions sentencing some terrorists to lifelong parole
- Increases the penalties for counterfeiting, cybercrime, and charity fraud

New Procedural Adjustments Under the Patriot Act

- Increases the rewards for information on terrorism cases
- Expands Posse Comitatus Act exceptions
- Authorizes "sneak and peek" search warrants
- Permits nationwide and perhaps worldwide execution of arrest warrants in terrorism cases
- Eases government access to confidential information
- Allows attorney general to collect DNA samples from prisoners convicted of any federal crime of violence or terrorism
- Lengthens the statute of limitations applicable to any crimes of terrorism
- Clarifies the application of federal criminal law on American installations and in residences of U.S. personnel overseas
- Adjusts federal victims' compensation and assistance programs

Source: Doyle (2002).

Century) and the 9/11 Commission report (*Final Report of the National Commission on Terrorist Attacks Upon the United States*). As the government pushed ahead with its reorganization and its plans to incorporate the recommendations of these panels, the Patriot Act was igniting debate. As discussed in Chapter 1, the law gave federal officials greater authority to monitor and intercept communications for the purposes of law enforcement and foreign intelligence gathering. It further vested the Treasury Department with increased powers to combat foreign money-laundering operations. In an effort to secure the borders, the Patriot Act also hardened the restrictions to entry and allowed for the detention and removal of individuals suspected of engaging or plotting to commit acts of terrorism. In summary, the act created new crimes and established new penalties and procedures in the prosecution of terrorist suspects and in the name of national and homeland security.

These new provisions of the law increased the tensions between the imperatives of homeland security and the protection of civil rights. The arguments over the delicate balance between security and individual freedoms are recurring ones. They have their antecedents in the courts, in legislatures, and on the public square. In the mid-1970s, the Church Commission recommended curtailing the power and practice of intelligence agencies conducting unauthorized searches and surveillance of domestic dissident groups. The investigations of the U.S. Senate Select Committee to Study Governmental Operations with Respect to Intelligence Activities led to the Foreign Intelligence and Surveillance Act of 1978. The act set procedures and restrictions on intelligence gathering and, until the enactment of the Patriot Act, covered that section of the law unmodified.

▸ Department of Justice Building

Source: U.S. Department of Justice Office of the Inspector General.

In 1986, the Iran–contra scandal revealed an abuse of powers by senior officials in the Reagan Administration. National Security Council staff facilitated the sale of arms to Iran despite a weapons embargo to that nation. They planned to use proceeds to support the Nicaraguan contras in their struggle against the anti-American Sandinista government. The operation was in violation of the Boland Amendment to the Defense Appropriation Act of 1983, which limited U.S. assistance to the contras. The revelations churned up anger among the administration's opposition and unleashed a new round of congressional oversight over the intelligence community. Protecting the homeland and safeguarding freedoms are two national imperatives that can often clash. Effective policies and laws that intend to uphold one tend to threaten the other. The reality is a long-range dynamic influenced by shifting public concerns and altering events, which eventually impact legislation, policies, organizations, and action.

> The result of this interplay tends to be a somewhat cyclical process in which institutions and policies to increase security are strengthened during times of perceived danger, weakened (often through enhanced congressional oversight) when liberty is unduly restricted or abuses take place, and then strengthened again if the institutions appear to be ineffective at accomplishing their missions. (Jordan et al., 2009, p. 133)

Moreover, in such a polyvalent threat environment, cultural, diplomatic, economic, and technological issues also vex the policymaking process; "even given national security professionals committed to collaboration, it has become harder to get agencies to act in concert" (Jordan et al., 2009, p. 212).

DEFINITION

American Exceptionalism

A former assistant secretary of state likes to use a comment from a young British diplomat to illustrate the meaning of *U.S. exceptionalism*. In a casual conversation with an official who was temporarily assigned to work with the State Department, he asked, "What's the difference between working at the British Foreign Office and the U.S. Department of State?" Without pausing, the U.K. envoy replied, "'When something happens in the world, the Americans ask, 'What should we do?' In the British Foreign Office, when something happens in the world, we ask, 'What will the Americans do?'" (quoted in Koh, 2003, p. 1488).

There are various definitions at work within the concept of American exceptionalism. Some variants are less flattering than others. Alexis de Tocqueville coined the phrase to mean "the perception that the United States differs qualitatively from other developed nations, because of its unique origins, national credo, historical evolution, and distinctive political and religious institutions" (Koh, 2003, p. 1481). Andrew Bacevich, in his book *The Limits of Power*, refers to it as a "providential purpose" expressed by America's behavior and evolution. Since 9/11, that has meant, according to Bacevich, "using any means necessary—suasion where possible, force as required" (Bacevich, 2008, p. 3). Still, to others, the notion is a myth—yet myths have power. In the final

reckoning, it is many things to many people. However, despite the interconnectedness of the global economy, the realization that the United States cannot enact security policies and programs without the cooperation of foreign partners is sometimes obscure to public officials and policymakers.

Before 9/11 and the creation of the Department of Homeland Security, the defense of the United States was the purview of a national-security establishment, which saw its role more as an instrument of American power and national interests abroad, rather than a structure to defend against an attack on U.S. territory. The terrorist attacks in 2001, however, brought about broad transformation in the areas of national-security policy, diplomacy, domestic politics, and U.S. law. The sea change produced an awkward syncretism for policymakers trying to align an establishment in place to fight the last war with the reality of post–Cold War threats. Despite these rifts, the projection of American power still echoed in George W. Bush's second inaugural speech. "The survival of liberty in our land increasingly depends on the success of liberty in other lands" ("President Bush's second inaugural," 2005).

A legal conflict also erupted over new issues, concepts, and definitions. Human rights, sovereign rights, rights of privacy, property rights, American constitutional rights, and international norms clashed. The American exceptionalism that allowed the United States to justify unilateral involvement in the name of liberty and the spread of democracy outside its borders was no longer the focus. Now it implied the priority of scanning inbound cargo to the United States, the rationalization of extralegal creations such as Guantanamo Detention Center, monitoring the transfer of funds, and tracking the movement of U.S. citizens and the exchange of their communications.

The United States provides humanitarian relief and protection forces all over the world. Its navy maintains the security of the global supply chain. The nation's foundation of universities and research institutes is an international magnet and force for advancement in the sciences and arts. However, as a result of a reckoning from the financial crisis, the public's fatigue of war, and underinvestment in its infrastructure, the United States may now turn its aspirations inward. As it reassesses its national interests and continues to prosecute the Global War on Terrorism, the vexing question it raises for itself and the rest of the world is still, what will the Americans do?

Guantanamo and *jus in bello*

Many of these policy dilemmas and legal questions converge over the opening and continuance of the **Guantanamo Detention Center** at Guantanamo Bay in Cuba. Following the 9/11 attacks, Congress passed the **Authorization for Use of Military Force (AUMF)**, giving the president the power to "use all necessary and appropriate force against those . . . [who] planned, authorized, committed, or aided the terrorist attacks" against the United States. Individuals suspected and captured during military operations in Afghanistan, Iraq, and elsewhere were brought to the detention center at Guantanamo Bay for further interrogation and possible prosecution or release.

From the beginning, the authorization and the facility raised controversy. Nearly 800 detainees have been processed. Some of them were reportedly between the ages of 13 and 16 (Amnesty International, 2003). Domestic and international critics protest the treatment of detainees and question the quality of the access they have been granted to the federal courts.

Since 2002, the majority have been released to other countries for further questioning or release. The remainder (1) are facing criminal trial, (2) have been cleared for release or transfer and are awaiting disposition, or (3) are being detained in order to prevent their return to rejoin hostilities. Under this third category, detention is considered nonpenal, but detainees are denied prisoner of war status (Styen, 2004, p. 13).

The rules of the Geneva Convention apply to their treatment. Therefore, the use of torture, cruel and inhuman punishment, and degrading treatment in any circumstance is prohibited.

President Obama pledged to close Guantanamo during his first administration. In 2009, he issued an executive order to close the facility within one year. However, congressional opposition prohibited the use of funds for the transfer or release of detainees to the United States and assured that the detention camp remained open through 2013 and beyond (Garcia, Elsea, Mason, & Liu,

▶ Guantanamo Detention Center

Source: U.S. Department of Defense (n.d.). Photo by U.S. Army Sgt. Sara Wood.

2013). Legal experts warn of the complex issues that could arise if prisoners from Guantanamo transfer to the territory of the United States. The transfer could trigger questions over constitutional protection rights as well as immigration laws (Garcia et al., 2013). In addition, there is debate over which forum—federal trial court, military court-martial system, or military commission—would be the appropriate jurisdiction for prosecution.

The Guantanamo Detention Center has been a vortex of clashes over legal jurisdictions, executive powers, international laws and norms, human rights, provisions of the Patriot Act versus civil rights, and the writ of **habeas corpus** versus the law of war. Despite the broad international support after the attacks on 9/11, many saw a rush to judgment in the period following the attacks. They argued against the hastily enacted Patriot Act, which gave the president "vast powers to override civil liberties" (Steyn, 2004, pp. 6–7). In voicing his criticism over the conduct of the U.S. government in its prosecution of the wars in Afghanistan, Iraq, and the Global War on Terrorism, Johan Steyn, Justice of Her Majesty's High Court of Justice, recounted an earlier historical period.

I must acknowledge that, despite the Magna Carta, in harsher times England resorted to the expedient of sending prisoners beyond the reach of the rule of law. One of the charges made against Edward Hyde, the First Earl of Clarendon, in his impeachment in 1667 was that he attempted to preclude habeas corpus by sending persons to "remote islands, garrisons, and other places, thereby to prevent them from the benefit of the law," that is by sending persons to places where the writ of habeas corpus would not be available. In 1679 this loophole was blocked . . . For more than three centuries such stratagems to evade habeas corpus have been unlawful in England. (2004, p. 8)

DEFINITION

Habeas Corpus

A writ of *habeas corpus* (also known as the "great writ") is the principle ordering a detainee to be brought before a court or judge, especially so that the court may ascertain whether his detention is lawful. It ensures that a prisoner can be released from unlawful detention, which infers lacking sufficient cause or evidence.

The Guantanamo Detention Center is one outcome of the post-9/11 legislation and has been the salient issue in questions regarding homeland security policy and law. The struggle for a final disposition on the detention camp's future underscores the political divide in government as well as the debate about its legality in the court system. The Global War on Terrorism has been described as an "unending war." If so, the detention policies will have to consider what rights and privileges captives are entitled. The determination will not only affect the quality of U.S. democracy but will also set a precedent and standard for others. The treatment of enemy belligerents will involve a harmony of judicial rulings, executive policies, and legislative enactments, which in the current cycle of history appear to be lacking.

Canada

Because of a shared history and shared border, Canada has its special relationship with the United States. Until the break up of the Soviet Union, the U.S.–Canadian border was the longest in the world. Since the creation of the international border between the Russian Federation and Kazakhstan, it has become the longest undefended border in the world over which the greatest trade partnership exists. Therefore, Canada's special relationship with the United States is not based on mutual defense but, more importantly, on mutual trade and commerce. There are more than 680 billion dollars in trade exchanges between the United States and Canada annually. Eighty percent of Canada's global trade is with the United States while over 20% of U.S. trade flows into Canada. These statistics are at the core of American–Canadian relations. Canada's economic and political vital interests are inextricably linked to the United States. The proximity of geography and history is underscored by the fact that 90% of Canadians live within 160 km of the U.S. border (Selbie, 2001, p. 14). Yet, despite these strategic reasons, Canada has always worked to preserve its separate identity from the United States, even though its relationship with America is central to its economic life (Gibbs Van Brunschot & Kennedy, 2009, p. 179). In contrast to Britain, Canada did not support the U.S. military invasions of Afghanistan and Iraq (although classified and declassified documents revealed Canada clandestinely supported the war in Afghanistan) (Núñez, 2002, p. 14). During the Vietnam War, Canada did not support U.S. involvement in that conflict. In both cases, it chose, rather, to emphasize its neutrality and independence despite the pressures from Washington.

The "peaceable kingdom" has often tended to embrace nonalignment positions and worked to support multilateralism, reflecting its neutrality and self-determination. As a sign of its independence, Canada declined to merge its forces with USNORTHCOM. Instead, it joined the alliance by creating **Canada Command** to serve as a separate member of a defense pact, rather than submitting to a U.S.-only command. The aim remains to build a cooperative effort whose mission is responsible for the defense of the land and sea approaches to North America. However, appearances may be everything.

Since 1957, **NORAD** (North American Aerospace Defense Command) has been a U.S.–Canada binational command for air defense. The Soviet bomber threat made vital a collective-security mechanism for continental defense. After 9/11 and as early as 1989, tracking of small aircraft was added to the threat column. A May 2006 NORAD agreement renewal expanded the command structure to include a maritime warning mission. The new accord added U.S. and Canadian maritime approaches, maritime areas, and inland waterways as part of the defense domain. Although there appears to be some overlap between NORAD, Canadian

Command, and USNORTHCOM, the arrangement satisfies the diplomatic wants of both countries and, in particular, eases the pressure on Canadian officials who incur criticism and backlash from political circles who might rankle at the notion of Canadian military subordination to Washington (McDonald, 2003, p. 24). The refusal to extend the command structure under USNORTHCOM in favor of NORAD is in line with Canada's grander strategy of sovereignty and neutrality.

As one of the world's most decentralized federations, Canada's security, crisis management, and infrastructure protection onus devolves to the provincial and local authorities (Selbie, 2001, p. 10). However, the events of 9/11 created a public willingness and sense of urgency for cooperation. The threat of terrorism, the porous U.S.–Canada border, and the potential impact on trade with the United States pressured the Canadian government to commit to more deeds and displays of solidarity. Currently, there are over 80 treaty-level defense agreements, 250 memoranda of understanding, and about 145 bilateral agreements that relate to or mention defense matters (Selbie, 2001, p. 10).

Two key legal transactions occurred in the wake of the 9/11 attacks: the Canadian 2001 Anti-Terrorism Act and the 2001 **Smart Border Accord**. The Canadian 2001 Anti-Terrorism Act criminalized (1) participating in or facilitating in terrorist activities, (2) knowingly harboring or concealing a terrorist, (3) instructing other persons to commit a terrorist act directly or on behalf of a group, and (4) knowingly collecting funds in support of terrorist crimes. The Anti-Terrorism Act is similar in concept and passage as the Patriot Act. Both statutes were hastily enacted and intended to address the threat posed by terrorist attacks. The aim of the drafters was to give government agencies additional tools and powers to prevent and combat terrorism. Similarly, both also drew criticism and protest. Both legal systems, nonetheless, are rooted in

Table 2.3   Canadian Anti-Terrorism Act of 2001: Crimes and Procedures

New Crimes Under the Anti-Terrorism Act of 2001
• Knowingly collect or provide funds, directly or indirectly, in support of terrorist activities
• Knowingly participate in, contribute to, or facilitate the activities of a terrorist group
• Instruct anyone to carry out a terrorist act or an activity on behalf of a terrorist group (leadership offence)
• Knowingly harbor or conceal a terrorist

New Procedural Adjustments Under the Anti-Terrorism Act of 2001
• Allows for preventative arrest to avert a potential terrorist attack
• Provides for investigative hearings of individuals who may have information about a terrorist event
• Requires the attorney general and the minister of public safety and emergency preparedness to report annually on their opinion about whether these provisions should be maintained

Source: Compiled with data from Gibbs Van Brunschot & Kennedy (2009).

the British common law tradition. However, the Anti-Terrorism Act and the Patriot Act vary in the way each mirrors the dissimilarities between the United States and Canada with respect to constitutional, legislative, and bureaucratic structures (Wispinski, 2006). Similar to the Patriot Act, the Canadian Anti-Terrorism Act created new crimes and new procedures for prosecuting suspects of terrorism.

Key differences exist but are mostly because of preexisting legal frameworks in the respective counties. The differences also relate to the divergent approach of legislators in the way they perceive problems based upon the separate notions about national security, civil liberties, immigration policies, and sovereign rights. For example, American military analysts in the past charged Canada with underinvesting in its military and having immigration laws that are too liberal (McDonald, 2003; Núñez, 2002). Canada and the United States are two immigrant nations with different attitudes and policy tendencies toward immigration. While Canada seeks younger, skilled workers in order to address an imminent demographic problem, the United States favors family unification as the basis for selection (Rekai, 2002). As the two countries attempt to harmonize their diverse immigration policies, the tension may play out along their mutual border.

The second significant legislative event was the 2001 Smart Border Accord between Canada and the United States. The agreement's goal is to facilitate low-risk trade over the border as it implements a multilevel security system. Bilateral cooperation, deployment of information technology, and risk management targeting are important pillars of the plan designed to simultaneously lubricate trade as it secures it.

The accord is often referred to as the **30 Point Plan**, whose elements are included in Table 2.4.

The June 2005 Security and Prosperity Partnership of North America superseded the Smart Border Accords. The new agreement called for enhanced technology implementation and testing. However, Rey Kosloski of Albany University argues,

> Smart borders are not just a matter of deploying hardware and software; they require international cooperation—and lots of it. Existing smart border agreements lay out an agenda for extensive international cooperation, but even more cooperation will be necessary to collect the necessary data for the smart border concept to work in practice. (Koslowski, 2005, p. 544)

Studies since the activation of the Smart Border Accord and its successor program have unveiled some discouraging financial data. Although no major terrorist incident has occurred, the cost to commerce and the administrative costs of **border thickening** have levied a price. Border thickening refers to the impermeability of borders due to layers of security procedures in place to ferret out suspicious individuals or shipments (Moens & Gabler, 2012, p. 25). There is quantitative evidence that this security "hardening" process takes its toll on tourism, commercial trade, and the taxpayer. According to a preliminary study by Canada's Fraser Institute, the Smart Border Accords and the 2005 Security and Prosperity Partnership of North America "added many new programs and costs to border crossing but that did not deliver significant efficiencies" (Moens & Gabler, 2012, p. 25). In addition, the report claims overnight and day trips by Americans into Canada have fallen by 53% over the past decade. Idling cost for road traffic at the borders has increased while trusted shippers programs, designed to accelerate trade, have

Table 2.4 Smart Border Accord (30 Point Plan)

Biometric identifiers	Joint facilities
Permanent resident cards	Customs data
Single alternative inspection system	Container targeting at seaports
Refugee/asylum processing	Infrastructure improvements
Managing of refugee/asylum claims	Intelligent transportation systems
Visa policy coordination	Critical infrastructure protection
Air preclearance	Aviation security
Advance passenger information/passenger name record	Integrated border and marine enforcement teams
Joint passenger analysis units	Joint enforcement coordination
Ferry terminals	Integrated intelligence
Compatible immigration databases	Fingerprints
Immigration officers overseas	Removal of deportees
International cooperation	Counterterrorism legislation
Harmonized commercial processing	Freezing of terrorist assets
Clearance away from the border	Joint training and exercises

Source: U.S. Department of State (2002).

significantly added to administrative cost for business. Lastly, in the estimated total cost to the national economy from public expenditures on planning and maintaining security programs, the authors of the report state,

> Given all the separate and incidental costs for a myriad of programs, we cannot aggregate a total for any one year. However, we estimate the total cost to the Canadian economy by aggregating all of the individual program costs and concluded that "border thickening" costs Canadian taxpayers between $500 million and $1 billion annually. (Moens & Gabler, 2012, p. 26)

The Obama administration and the Harper government announced in 2011 a new initiative called *Beyond the Borders Action Plan*. It trumpets the setting of "joint priorities for achieving a new long-term security partnership in four key areas, guided by mutual respect for sovereignty and our separate constitutional and legal frameworks that protect individual privacy" (U.S. White House, 2011d, n.p.). The plan promises an enhancement of existing programs and mechanisms, pilot projects and advanced technological tools, and expanding law enforcement frameworks. In response to complaints by commerce, it plans to reduce some unnecessary regulatory issues in order to accommodate the passage. The plan also includes a standing strategic orientation and momentum from previous orders, directives, and initiatives—preemptive defense. "We intend to pursue a perimeter approach to security, working together within, at, and away from borders of our two countries to enhance our security and accelerate the legitimate flow of people, goods, and services between our two countries" (U.S. White House, 2011c, n.p.). So claims a White House statement.

International cooperation in joint border infrastructure development and joint inspections requires sizable investment and diplomatic pressure. As the United States implements a strategy of pushing its borders outward, with such programs as the Smart Border Accord and other initiatives like Customs-Trade Partnership Against Terrorism, Container Security Initiative, and the Automated Targeting System (discussed later in the book), it has and will continue to encounter political resistance. The financial and budgetary conditions and the resources of statecraft figure prominently. With respect to Canada's trade and collective-security relationship with the United States, its policies have drawn criticism from its trade and defense partner. As discussed above, American officials and security analysts at times appear impatient with Canada's liberal immigration policies and what the United States deems an underinvestment in defense (McDonald, 2003, p. 10). Canada often finds that as the "junior partner" it often is subject to the directives and programs of a U.S. Congress and policy establishment that works with a "security first" approach with respect to U.S.–Canada cross-border trade issues (Moens & Gabler, 2012).

Yet the strategic and cultural ties between these two nations are tightly bound and are overarching factors. Nevertheless, Canada may need to establish some cross-border objectives relative to the needs of the national economy and cost them out. The United States, on the other hand, may need to reevaluate some of its security programs to determine whether they are necessary to homeland security or the result of pressure from imbedded special interests in Washington. The evaluation should also extend to questions concerning whether these strategies contribute to a global good or, in effect, inhibit commerce and diplomacy to some unconstructive and harmful degree.

Britain

Britain's "special relationship" with the United States is important to U.S. capacity-building efforts and an important driver of Britain's foreign policy (Gibbs Van Brunschot & Kennedy, 2008, p. 157). A major factor in Britain's relevance on the world's stage is, perhaps, found in the triangulated relationship Britain sees itself forming between the United States and the rest of Europe. Gibbs Van Brunschot and Kennedy (2009) recount a speech by Prime Minister Tony Blair delivered two months after the 9/11 attacks in which he said,

> I hope, too, we have buried the myth that Britain has to choose between being strong in Europe or strong with the United States. Afghanistan has shown vividly how the relationships reinforce each other; and that both the United States and our European partners value our role with the other. So let us play our full part in Europe, not retreat to its margins; and let us proclaim our closeness to the United States and use it to bring Europe closer to America. (p. 173)

In the war on terrorism, Britain aligned policy with Washington. For its support of the wars in Iraq and Afghanistan, the government came under harsh domestic political pressure. Although it did not follow the U.S. approach of reorganizing its security establishment, it moved to put in place a central coordinating system that mirrors, on a smaller scale, the concept of DHS. In 2004, the British government unveiled a cross-departmental strategy to combat terrorism, protect public and critical infrastructure, and enable the system to restore itself in the event of a high impact event. **CONTEST**, as it is known, seeks to also address the underlying causes of domestic terrorism and terrorism abroad. The four pillars of the strategy are (1) prevent, (2) pursue, (3) protect, and (4) prepare. As its framers envision it, CONTEST is an efficient and coherent way to combine existing resources and prevailing expertise across the government-wide spectrum of offices charged with the various aspects of counterterrorism, preparedness, emergency management, and response.

The United Kingdom Cabinet and ministerial committee system has at its leadership level the prime minister as the chair of the cabinet. The PM is supported in the Cabinet by an array of committees and subcommittees with which the Cabinet Office coordinates policy and strategy on issues related to security. The Defence and Overseas Policy Committee, the Intelligence Services Committee, and the Civil Contingency Committee play key roles. In the event of an event, COBR (named for the Cabinet Office briefing room where it meets) convenes to plan and coordinate emergency response. Despite being promoted as an effective approach to the alternative of an additional and cumbersome bureaucracy, the array of government offices and committees that fall under CONTEST is an impressive list. Table 2.5 lists the government entities involved in the United Kingdom's homeland security effort.

The British government has signed collaborative agreements with the United States. Among the most prominent U.S. initiatives are the Container Security Initiative and the agreement on **Cooperation in Science and Technology for Critical Infrastructure Protection and Other Homeland/Civil Security Matters**. The Container Security Initiative requires U.S. teams of inspectors at foreign ports to screen and clear all in-bound cargo onto U.S. territory. Host nations must agree to their stationing. If there are disputes between DHS representatives and local authorities in the risk level of any container, the U.S. official has the right and duty to ban the cargo from entry. The Cooperation in Science and Technology agreement provides a framework for the United States and the United Kingdom to share research relative to homeland security. It stipulates the "facilitation of systematic exchange of technologies, personnel, and information derived from or applied to similar or complementary operational research, development, testing, or evaluation programs." The agreement is similar to other accords established between the United States and Germany, France, Israel, Estonia, Sweden, Mexico, and Canada.

Key legislation enacted by Britain since 9/11 includes the Anti-Terrorism Crime and Security Act. After the commercial airplane attacks on 9/11, the British Parliament passed legislation to harden aviation security. It included expanding the list of prohibited articles allowed onboard aircraft, authorizing the forcible removal of passengers, and enhanced screening methods and searching of passengers and baggage.

Other legislative events include the 2002 National Immigration and Asylum Act. The law strengthened immigration procedures to more vigorously limit the opportunities for abuse of asylum seekers and prevent illegal immigration. Its measures required both air and sea carriers to consult databases for suspicious individuals seeking entry onto U.K. territory.

In 2004, the year prior to the London transit bombings, parliament passed the Civil Contingencies Act. Similar to but less controversial than the USA PATRIOT Act, this legislation

Table 2.5 United Kingdom: Departments, Ministries, Committees, and Offices Involved in Counterterrorism

Centre for the Protection of the National Infrastructure	HM Treasury
Crown Prosecution Service	Home Office: The Office for Security and Counter-Terrorism
Department for Business, Innovation and Skills	Joint Terrorism Analysis Centre
Department for Communities and Local Government	Ministry of Defence
Department for Education	Ministry of Justice
The Department of Energy and Climate Change	The National Offender Management Service
Department for Energy	National Security Council
Department for Environment, Food and Rural Affairs	The National Counter-Terrorism Security Office
Department for International Development	Northern Ireland Office
Department for Transport	Scotland Office
Department of Health	Secret Intelligence Service
Devolved Administrations	Security Service
Foreign and Commonwealth Office	U.K. Border Agency
Government Communications Headquarters	Wales Office
Government Office for Science	

Source: Compiled with data from U.K. Secretary of State for the Home Department (2011).

faced resistance from civil rights advocates. The law gave the government the right to confiscate property, restrict public gatherings, and deny access to and evacuate populations from areas deemed contaminated or otherwise dangerous. It also gave the government the right to declare a state of emergency without the approval of Parliament (Archick, 2006, p. 47).

In 2008, Parliament enacted the Counter-Terrorism Act to add further powers and terms to existing laws created to combat terrorism. The additional provisions allowed for authorities to extend the precharged detention times of terrorist suspects and emend the law regarding postcharged interrogation. Under these revisions, silence during questioning could result in inferences, which could be used in court. The 2008 legislation also allowed for inquests without a jury in certain cases, the imposition of harsher sentences on offenders with terrorist connections, and the requirement of those convicted of terrorist offences to report to authorities changes in their addresses or other relevant living conditions (Gibbs Van Brunschot & Kennedy, 2009, p. 183).

Efforts by the United Kingdom to reinforce its homeland security regime and pursue capacity-building initiatives have generally kept apace with the perception of the threat vector. However, Britain, as with most of Europe, has felt the impact of the 2008 financial crisis. Resources and budgets are strained. As stated above, "With limited resources available to apply to terrorist threats, the risk associated with that particular type of vulnerability must be evaluated in light of resources available to address vulnerabilities" (Gibbs Van Brunschot & Kennedy, 2009, p. 165). As a result, the balance in domestic policy as it relates to security investment and other public goods has become more delicate.

There is the opinion that Britain assumes a unique place in world affairs, which relies upon its bonds with the United States. "Britain knows it brings to the table particular qualities that make it a leading power—particularly its relationship with the United States" (Gibbs Van Brunschot & Kennedy, 2009, p. 174). In contrast to Canada, whose ties with its giant neighbor make it appear as a junior partner forced to assert its national identity, Britain attempts to leverage its unique connection. It feels it has a place in the world as the global community's elder statesman. In 2001, Tony Blair emphasized the point when discussing security issues in an address, saying, "Grinding poverty, pandemic disease, a rash of failed states, where problems seldom leave their stain on one nation but spread to whole regions" (quoted in Gibbs Van Brunschot & Kennedy, 2009, p. 175). Part of the United Kingdom's homeland security strategy is to be at the center of collaboration. Yet an inescapable factor is the Anglo–American relationship. It not only plays out in the international arena but also impacts homeland security policy in Britain.

▶ High Angle View of Hundreds of People Who Are Coming to Pay Their Tribute to the Victims of the London Terror Attacks, Outside Kings Cross Underground Station in London. A week earlier, multiple terrorist bombing attack targeted the public transport system and claimed over 50 lives. An Al-Qaeda affiliated Islamic terror cell has proclaimed responsibility for the bombings.

Source: iStockphoto.com/onebluelight.

In summary, the United Kingdom *2009 National Security Strategy* speaks for all developed countries in its assessment and attempt to define and address the challenges of homeland security.

> We include not just the threats from hostile states, but also non-state threats such as terrorism or serious organized crime, and serious hazards to the U.K., such as flooding; not just traditional areas through which we may be threatened, such as military action; but new ones such as cyber space; not just traditional drivers of threats such as nationalism or interstate rivalry; but wider drivers such as climate change, competition for resources or international poverty. (Lewin 2011, p. 13)

Canada and Britain, because of their obvious ties with the United States, based on a common language, history, culture, and geopolitical positioning, have always been natural allies. Britain was an unflagging supporter of the U.S. war in Iraq and Afghanistan. Canada, while not committing troops to the military operations, maintains its strong ties with the United States and its guardianship of the U.S.–Canada trade partnership. The Smart Border program is one prime example of collaboration.

The Patriot Act has created controversy as the debate over its infringement of civil rights wears on. The legislation, passed immediately after the 9/11 attacks, gave to the executive branch extraordinary powers, which some legal experts regard as necessary given the new rules of conflict while others claim them to be too extreme. Similarly, Canada and Britain responded with their own brand of legislation, which enjoyed both a level of support and protest from domestic political circles. Canada's Anti-Terrorism Act and the United Kingdom's Civil Contingencies Act ignited debate and resistance from civil liberty groups. The arguments continue to be tested in the courts, in parliaments, and on the public square. Table 2.6 is a brief history of terrorist events and the legislation they prompted.

Table 2.6 Legislation and Events, 2001–2008

Year	Events	United States	Britain	Canada
2001	WTC/Pentagon attacks	USA PATRIOT Act and Smart Border Accord	Anti-Terrorism, Crime and Security Act	Anti-Terrorism Act and Smart Border Accord
2002		DHS established by law	Nationality, Immigration and Asylum Act	
2003				
2004	Madrid train bombings		Civil Contingencies Act	Public Safety Act
2005	London Underground bombing			
2006	Toronto bomb arrests	Safe Port Act		
2007		Public Law 110-53		
2008	Global financial crisis		Counter-Terrorism Act	

U.S.–European Union Collaboration

From its beginning, the Obama Administration has worked to continue the momentum of the Bush presidency in sustaining U.S. cooperation with the European Union on matters concerning counterterrorism, border controls, and transport security. This collaboration has cultivated the transatlantic dialogue as well as enabled a more vibrant multilateral structure for formulating antiterrorist policy and programs, which previously were the domain of bilateral agreements (Archick, 2014).

As in the United States, the European Union struggles with the delicate balance between establishing a reliable security regime and assuring citizens of their basic civil liberties. An additional layer of complexity exists for the E.U. as it attempts to form a union among 28 member states with diverse legal systems and traditions. Since the creation of Europe's borderless Schengen Area in 1995, E.U. citizens have the right to live and travel freely in any E.U. country. The **Schengen Agreement** essentially abolished most security checks within the European Union Area.

In order to counterbalance the de-bordering process, the E.U.'s **Justice and Home Affairs (JHA) Council** is a mechanism for building a framework for security cooperation and common policies. The JHA works to make uniform security measures without infringing on sovereignty rights and, at the same time, promote the free movement of trade among its members. It meets every three months. Justice ministers generally address issues concerning cooperation in civil law, criminal law, and fundamental rights. Home affairs ministers, on the other hand, primarily oversee migration, border management, and police cooperation. The effort produced a new generation of antiterrorist legislation and a common legal definition of terrorism.

However, despite the spirit of cooperation, dissimilar positions among members and between E.U. institutions regarding the limits of data privacy protection or intelligence sharing can complicate the process of synchronizing national laws and establishing E.U.-wide policies. In spite of the obstacles, these efforts have produced results. Negotiators reached agreements on information-sharing arrangements, extradition agreements, and mutual legal assistance treaties.

As well, the attempts at capacity building between the United States and the E.U. have made substantial progress. Since 2001, accords concerning container and passenger transport security (including biometrics, visa policy, and sky marshals) and programs to track and interdict the financing of terrorist activity have been struck (Archick, 2006). Key members of the Obama administration's cabinet meet with European counterparts annually to discuss judicial and enforcement issues relative to counterterrorism matters. A working group of senior officials sustain these negotiations on a more regular basis. Additionally, the administration maintains the relationship through reciprocal liaison links between the FBI, the Secret Service, and Europol. Of specific concern is the number of radicalized Western European and American Muslims returning home from conflicts in the Middle East, particularly Syria and Iraq. According to the Obama White House, U.S. officials from the Department of Justice and the Department of Homeland Security consult with E.U. counterparts to "address a wide range of measures focused on enhancing counter-radicalization, border security, aviation security, and information sharing" (U.S. White House, 2014, n.p.) to address potential threats posed by these foreign fighters.

However, challenges remain. The disclosure by Edward Snowden about the NSA's surveillance programs (particularly the tapping of German Chancellor Angela Merkel) created tensions. Other differences remain over detainee policies, terrorist designation lists, and varying security standards concerning border control and the continuance of legitimate transatlantic commerce.

SUMMARY

Within the notion of homeland security are inherent contrasts in legal norms, jurisdictional divides, concepts of just wars, and understandings of hard power, to name a few. Uniquely, America's defense establishment since the World War II was designed to defend the country's interest abroad through the **projection of force**. The word *defense* was shorn of meaning when referring to the actual defense of U.S. territory. That responsibility was mostly a matter of law enforcement in the minds of military planners. The spirit and effect of the **Posse Comitatus Act** of 1878, which was designed to create a clear division between the military and domestic police forces, applied operationally, bureaucratically, and culturally. Interoperability was a mute point.

Meanwhile, allies of the United States respond to the new threat matrix and, simultaneously, to American policy. Through various administrations and changing domestic political environments, the doctrine of preemptive wars and security programs that extend U.S. borders influenced homeland security frameworks in other countries. This occurs during attempts to anneal policy as, at the same time, debate and resistance rise over civil liberties and American over-reach. The former protesters and fears about American hegemony were not assuaged by a wounded United States that challenged the world community by demanding, "You are either with us or with the terrorists."

A U.S. Department of Defense maintained more than 700 foreign bases to protect U.S. interests and guarantee the spread of democracy. Now, a new U.S. Department of Homeland Security created programs that effectively pushed out its borders by stationing inspectors in overseas ports, formed and funded joint research initiatives, and built a network of surveillance alliances.

However, the attacks on 9/11 changed the calculus and dynamic of national security everywhere. Instantly, the world was in an asymmetric war with an enigmatic enemy, which may as well be described as a war with itself. As the United States maneuvered to reorient its national-security establishment's mission, it discovered the bureaucracy it had created as an organizing framework to mobilize assets, industry, technology, allies, and population was also organized around entrenched interests, embedded mindsets, and the Cold War. Traditional Cold War foes and allies found themselves in a similar trap.

The end of the Cold War cleared the field for events like the 9/11 attacks. The conclusion of the superpower hostilities left behind a string of failed states and quasistates. Across the globe, once the aegis of mutual assistance programs, treaty organizations (with the exception of NATO, which expanded), and military pacts was tossed aside, new tensions emerged unleashing a massive wave of migration from Europe as well as in Africa, Asia, and South and Central America (Koppel & Szekely, 2002, p. 12). The end of the "orderly" Cold War system of power alliances blurred the divide between east and west and reduced the roles and importance of borders. These developments ushered in a new era of cross-border crime and terrorism (Jarmon, 2014). It also enabled other threats, which included creeping abject poverty, a lawless cyber realm, and a reckoning of the global overuse and neglect of vital resources. Governments attempt to adjust policy and laws effectively and justly. However, the forces of globalization and advancing technology have created challenges for the state-centered system. Governments attempt to keep pace, and the enterprise of building an efficient homeland security framework that protects the daily routine and enables commerce is a work in progress.

How Has Homeland Security Policy and Law Changed Since 9/11?

Tom Kean

As I write this, it is 13 years since the attack on 9/11 and over 10 years since I chaired the National Commission on Terrorist Attacks Upon the United States. Since then, many things have changed and some things remain the same. On that day, we were attacked by 19 terrorists who came from other parts of the world to do us harm. They evaded our immigration authorities to get into this country, and they remained unidentified while they prepared the final details of their plot. During that period, many got driver licenses and credit cards in their own names and still were not detected by any agency of the U.S. government.

In the years since, we have hardened our defenses, creating the Department of Homeland Security, reorganizing our intelligence agencies, and creating the TSA to improve airport security. This has worked, and it is now hard to imagine that many foreign nationals getting into our country and living here while they plan their attack.

Today, the threat has changed, and so we must change. We must not fight yesterday's battles. The new attacks will be different than the one carried out on 9/11, and we must be prepared.

Over the last few years, we have destroyed much of al-Qaeda's leadership. They no longer have the capacity to plan large-scale attacks. For that reason, we must prepare for smaller attacks planned by lone-wolf terrorists. The highest danger in this regard is American citizens recruited over the Internet who therefore have the ability to move around our country at will. We must devote more effort to disrupt this Internet recruiting and to work with these countries' Muslim communities to disrupt plots before they can be carried out.

The conflict in Syria has generated the threat of young Muslims recruited to fight, a number from Europe and some from the United States. The Americans, in particular, can come home and, if they have accepted jihad, plan attacks in the homeland. We must do everything possible to identify those individuals before they return home.

When we wrote our report, nobody was worried about cyberspace. Now, it may be our greatest vulnerability. Still, the Congress has been unable to agree on a bill. Our public and private sectors remain largely uncoordinated. This could be our next 9/11. We must take the cyber threat much more seriously.

Finally, one thing remains unchanged. Much of our intelligence remains classified, so we have no idea of the internal workings of our intelligence agencies. Congressional oversight is vital. Nevertheless, at present, it remains dysfunctional. When we wrote our report we noted that the Department of Homeland Security reported to 88 different congressional committees. This means that leaders in the department spent too much of their time testifying and not enough protecting the country. Now, the number is 94. Because of this dysfunctional congressional oversight, our country is less safe.

On December 16, 2002, Former New Jersey Governor Tom Kean was named by President George W. Bush to head the National Commission on Terrorist Attacks Upon the United States. The Commission's work culminated on July 22, 2004, with the release of the 9/11 Commission report. He currently serves as cochairman, with Congressman Lee Hamilton, of the National Security Preparedness Group.

FINAL CASE STUDY

CHAPTER SUMMARY

This chapter has explained

- What is involved in assessing security
  - How it differs from state to state and region to region
  - How priorities are set

- Western traditions of the rules of war
  - What is meant by *jus ad bellum*
  - What is meant by *jus in bello*
  - What is meant by *jus post bellum*

- The security environment in the United States, Britain, and Canada

- The debate and tension between security and the guarantee of civil liberties

  - The legal implications of the Guantanamo Detention Center

- How policies and law in Britain and Canada align with or diverge from the United States

- What factors influence the security framework in each country

- What are the specific laws in each country and how have they redefined crime and reset penalties and prosecution procedures

- What are the specific security programs in each country

- How do programs mirror one another, converge, overlap, and differ

KEY TERMS

30 Point Plan *59*
Authorization for Use of Military Force (AUMF) *55*
Border thickening *59*
Canada Command *57*
CONTEST *62*
Cooperation in Science and Technology for Critical Infrastructure Protection

and Other Homeland/Civil Security Matters *62*
Guantanamo Detention Center *55*
Habeas corpus *56*
Hugo Grotius *44*
Justice and Home Affairs (JHA) Council *66*
Just-war theory *44*

NORAD *57*
Posse Comitatus Act *67*
Projection of force *67*
Public Law No. 110-53 *47*
Schengen Agreement *66*
Smart Border Accord *58*
War Powers Resolution *50*

QUESTIONS AND EXERCISES

1. What is meant by *just-war theory*?

2. What are the distinctions between *jus ad bellum*, *jus in bello*, and *jus post bellum*?

3. How have the elements of the just-war theory changed after 9/11

and been altered by the Global War on Terrorism?

4. How is the U.S. DHS's effort to "push its borders out" similar to the DOD's "projection of force"?

5. How is the U.S. DHS's effort to "push its borders out" different from the DOD's "projection of force"?

6. What are the main drivers in Canada's relationship with the United States?

7. How does Britain assess its role with the United States in the context of international relations?

8. What are the legal issues that erupt if *belligerent combatants* are detained on the territory of the United States?

9. What are the main arguments and issues that clash between the Patriot Act and civil liberties?

PART II

HAZARDS AND THREATS

3

TERRORISM

In September 18, 2010, Sami Samir Hassoun, a 25-year-old Lebanese citizen legally resident in Chicago, placed a backpack that he thought contained a bomb into a trash can on the crowded sidewalk by Wrigley Field—the Chicago Cubs baseball stadium—where a concert was taking place.

The device was a fake, supplied by an FBI **undercover officer**. The **sting** was led by a local Joint Terrorism Task Force (JTTF) of FBI agents, City of Chicago police officers, and other federal, state, and local law enforcement personnel.

They had become involved after an informant had reported that Hassoun was hoping to profit from acts of violence in Chicago. Hassoun later admitted telling an informant of an idea to bomb the commercial area surrounding Wrigley Field. The informant later introduced Hassoun to the undercover officer who posed as an accomplice. Hassoun said he was willing to use a car bomb and to attack Chicago police officers. On three occasions in August 2010, Hassoun videotaped potential targets around Wrigley Field, focusing on popular bars and restaurants. As he filmed, he commented on the tactical advantages and risks of an attack at the various locations.

On the night of September 18, Hassoun took a shopping bag and a backpack containing the fake bomb from undercover officers. The officers said the device was surrounded by ball bearings and that the blast could destroy half a city block. A few minutes after midnight, after he had helped to set the device's timer, Hassoun placed the backpack into the trash container.

Hassoun pled guilty to attempted use of a weapon of mass destruction and attempted use of an explosive device. On May 30, 2013, a federal judge sentenced him to 23 years in prison (Federal Bureau of Investigation, 2013).

Learning Objectives and Outcomes

At the end of this chapter, you should be able to

- Define terrorism

- Describe the frequency and distribution of terrorism

- Describe the outcomes and costs of terrorism

- Explain the sorts of targets that terrorists choose

- Describe terrorist profiles

- Explain counterterrorist organizations and strategies

DEFINITIONS

Terrorism is the use and threat of violence to terrorize. Terrorism is a highly contested concept, which means that it is difficult to study, legislate against, and cooperate against. Thus, this section is dedicated to explaining the many disputes.

Some terrorism scholars can be remarkably unambitious with their definitions. For instance, Walter Laqueur (1977) once wrote that "a comprehensive definition of terrorism . . . does not exist nor will it be found in the foreseeable future" (p. 5). However, Michael Stohl (2012) has noted "significant agreement that a definition of terrorism should include the following components: 'There is an act in which the perpetrator intentionally employs violence (or its threat) to instill fear (terror) in a victim and the audience of the act or threat'" (p. 45).

By careful inductive and deductive argument, Peter Sproat (1991) has provided the most complete behavioral definition of terrorism.

> [Terrorism is distinguished by] motive (political rather than private), intention (to instill fear rather than merely to destroy), and status (that allows certain legal violent activities of the state at home, which, if committed abroad, would qualify as terrorism to exist as legitimate punishment), while enabling particular arbitrary and/or indiscriminate actions to be labeled as domestic state terrorism. Thus, terrorism can be identified as the deliberate threat or use of violence for political purposes by either non-state actors or the state abroad, when such actions are intended to influence the victim(s) and/or target(s) wider than the immediate victim(s); or the use of such purposive violence by the state within its own borders when such actions either fail to allow the victim prior knowledge of the law and/or [fail to] distinguish between the innocence and guilt of the individual victim. (p. 21)

The definition above might seem so long as to be impossible to operationalize. An **operational definition** is one that is useful for coding some event as either terrorist or not, such as when we want to count terrorist events replicably and transparently, as the Global Terrorism Database (GTD) does. Maintained since 2001 at the University of Maryland, the database covers events since 1970. An event must fulfill the following criteria before admittance into the database:

1. international

2. violent

3. committed by sub-national perpetrators

4. meet at least 2 of the following 3 criteria:

    a. political, economic, religious, or social goal

    b. intention to convey a message to a broader audience

    c. occurrence outside the context of legitimate warfare

Unfortunately, different persons, institutions, governments, and even departments within governments have different definitions of terrorism. The disputes about how to define terrorism are normally disputes about how to account for each of the following four things: actors; behaviors and activities; targets; and motivations, ideologies, and intents. The subsections below review these definitions and disputes. Along the way, you will compare different legal and official definitions.

ACTORS

Nonstate Actors

Some definitions allow for states or state governments to commit terrorism but governments, including the U.S. government, tend to define terrorism as a nonstate activity. This is rational; states self-interestedly prefer to define crimes that exclude states as criminals; they are incentivized to define terrorism as a political activity directed against them by nonstate actors. Consequently, many domestic laws define terrorism as a purely nonstate activity, even though international law does not (see Comparative Perspectives, Box 3.1).

Bruce Hoffman (1999) has given this state-centric view its most academic justification. He objects to definitions in which "governments on practical, political, and legal grounds could be considered terrorists" (p. 35). He prefers to restrict the definition by the actor's legal status or motivations. He has admitted that states sometimes commit the same acts as nonstate terrorists but uses the term **war crime** to describe the state's action and maintains that international law holds such states accountable. He admits definitions that define terrorism as a form of illegitimate violence. "But this is not an entirely satisfactory solution either, since it fails to differentiate clearly between violence perpetrated by states and by non-state entities, such as terrorists" (p. 33). Hoffman resolves this problem by defining terrorism as an exclusively nonstate activity.

Colin Wight (2012) reaches the same position. He does not admit to Hoffman's influence but accepts the traditional premise (traceable back to Max Weber, 1864–1920) that states monopolize legitimate violence within their own territory and concludes that states cannot be accused of illegitimate violence at home. Wight effectively accepts state-level equivalents of terrorism, without admitting them as terrorism.

> This is the main problem with the use of the term **state terrorism**; it begins to look like every state activity is, or potentially can be, a form of state terrorism. I do not doubt, or deny, that states engage in activities intended to spread fear and terror among populations. Often the target audience of such state activity will be the citizens of that state themselves and often they are citizens of another state. Yes, such state actions are morally reprehensible and should be challenged and rejected whenever possible. What I do not accept is that we need to call this terrorism and nor do I understand what we gain in doing so. (p. 56)

Michael Stohl (2012) counters this argument by pointing out that the legitimacy of violence is not essential to the definition of the state or the definition of terrorism (p. 47).

Different Legal and Official Definitions

U.N.

For U.N. agencies, terrorism is "a concept generally understood to mean a criminal act or acts intended to inflict dramatic and deadly injury on civilians and to create an atmosphere of fear, generally in furtherance of a political or ideological (whether secular or religious) purpose" (U.N. Office for the Coordination of Humanitarian Affairs [OCHA], 2004, p. 31).

NATO

NATO's (2008) standard definition (since 1989) of terrorism is "the unlawful use or threatened use of force or violence against individuals or property in an attempt to coerce or intimidate governments or societies to achieve political, religious or ideological objectives" (p. 2-T-5).

United States

The U.S. Department of Justice (which administers the Federal Bureau of Investigation) defines terrorism as "the unlawful use of force or violence against persons or property to intimidate or coerce a government, the civilian population, or any segment thereof, in furtherance of political or social objectives" (U.S. FBI, n.d., n.p.).

According to the current U.S. criminal code (Title 18, Part I, Chapter 113B, Section 2331), terrorism must

A. involve violent acts or acts dangerous to human life that are a violation of the criminal laws of the United States or of any State, or that would be a criminal violation if committed within the jurisdiction of the United States or of any State;

B. appear to be intended—

   i. to intimidate or coerce a civilian population;

   ii. to influence the policy of a government by intimidation or coercion; or

   iii. to affect the conduct of a government by mass destruction, assassination, or kidnapping.

By contrast, other legislation (Title 22, Section 2656f[d]) that requires annual reports on terrorism from the U.S. Department of State, defines terrorism as "premeditated, politically motivated violence perpetrated against noncombatant targets by subnational groups or clandestine agents, usually intended to influence an audience."

The U.S. Department of Homeland Security (DHS, 2011) defines terrorism as the

premeditated threat or act of violence against noncombatant persons, property, and environmental or economic targets to induce fear, intimidate, coerce, or affect a government, the civilian population, or any segment thereof, in furtherance of political, social, ideological, or religious objectives. (p. A2)

(Continued)

(Continued)

The U.S. Department of Defense (2010) defines terrorism as "the calculated use of unlawful violence or threat of unlawful violence to inculcate fear; intended to coerce or to intimidate governments or societies in the pursuit of goals that are generally political, religious, or ideological" (n.p.).

Canada

Paragraph 83.01(1)(b) of Canada's Criminal Code defines a "terrorist activity" as "an act or omission, in or outside Canada,

 i. that is committed

  A. in whole or in part for a political, religious or ideological purpose, objective or cause, and

  B. in whole or in part with the intention of intimidating the public, or a segment of the public, with regard to its security, including its economic security, or compelling a person, a government or a domestic or an international organization to do or to refrain from doing any act, whether the public or the person, government or organization is inside or outside Canada, and

 ii. that intentionally

  C. causes death or serious bodily harm to a person by the use of violence,

  D. endangers a person's life,

  E. causes a serious risk to the health or safety of the public or any segment of the public,

  F. causes substantial property damage, whether to public or private property, if causing such damage is likely to result in the conduct or harm referred to in any of clauses (A) to (C), or

  G. causes serious interference with or serious disruption of an essential service, facility or system, whether public or private, other than as a result of advocacy, protest, dissent or stoppage of work that is not intended to result in the conduct or harm referred to in any of clauses (A) to (C), and includes a conspiracy, attempt or threat to commit any such act or omission, or being an accessory after the fact or counselling in relation to any such act or omission, but, for greater certainty, does not include an act or omission that is committed during an armed conflict and that, at the time and in the place of its commission, is in accordance with customary international law or conventional international law applicable to the conflict, or the activities undertaken by military forces of a state in the exercise of their official duties, to the extent that those activities are governed by other rules of international law.

European Union

The European Council's Framework Decision on Combating Terrorism (2002), Article 1, defined terrorism as

 1. seriously intimidating a population, or

 2. unduly compelling a Government or international organisation to perform or abstain from performing any act, or

 3. seriously destabilising or destroying the fundamental political, constitutional,

economic or social **structures** of a country or an international organization, shall be deemed to be terrorist offences:

a) attacks upon a person's life which may cause death;

b) attacks upon the physical integrity of a person;

c) kidnapping or hostage taking;

d) causing extensive destruction to a Government or public facility, a transport system, an infrastructure facility, including an information system, a fixed platform located on the continental shelf, a public place or private property likely to endanger human life or result in major economic loss;

e) seizure of aircraft, ships or other means of public or goods transport;

f) manufacture, possession, acquisition, transport, supply or use of weapons, explosives or of nuclear, biological or chemical weapons, as well as research into, and development of, biological and chemical weapons;

g) release of dangerous substances, or causing fires, floods or explosions the effect of which is to endanger human life;

h) interfering with or disrupting the supply of water, power or any other fundamental natural resource the effect of which is to endanger human life;

i) threatening to commit any of the acts listed in (a) to (h).

Britain

British legislation formerly relied almost wholly on **political violence** to define terrorism.

- Prevention of Terrorism (Temporary Provisions) Act (1989): "'Terrorism' means the use of violence for political ends, and includes any use of violence for the purpose of putting the public or any section of the public in fear" (S.20[1], c. 4).

- Reinsurance (Acts of Terrorism) Act (1993): Terrorism is "acts of persons acting on behalf of, or in connection with, any organisation which carries out activities directed towards the overthrowing or influencing, by force or violence, of Her Majesty's Government in the United Kingdom or any other government de jure or de fact" (S.2[2], c.18).

The Terrorism Act of 2000 significantly revised the definitions in the acts of 1989 and 1993 and would be incorporated into the Terrorism Act of 2006.

1. In this [Terrorism] Act [2000] "terrorism" means the use or threat of action where—

   A. the action falls within subsection (2),

   B. the use or threat is designed to influence the government [the Act of 2006 allowed also an international governmental organization] or to intimidate the public or a section of the public, and

   C. the use or threat is made for the purpose of advancing a political, religious or ideological cause.

(Continued)

(Continued)

2. Action falls within this subsection if it—

   A. involves serious violence against a person,

   B. involves serious damage to property,

   C. endangers a person's life, other than that of the person committing the action,

   D. creates a serious risk to the health or safety of the public or a section of the public, or

   E. is designed seriously to interfere with or seriously to disrupt an electronic system.

3. The use or threat of action falling within subsection (2) which involves the use of firearms or explosives is terrorism whether or not subsection (1)(b) is satisfied.

States

The U.N. General Assembly has spent decades arguing without agreeing on an acceptable definition of terrorism for all international laws and activities due to disputes primarily over whether terrorism should be confined to nonstate actors or state actors, whether terrorism can also be freedom fighting, and whether violations of human rights count as terrorism. The International Law Commission (since 1954) has failed to agree on a definition of terrorism. The International Law Commission's *Draft Code of Offences Against the Peace and Security of Mankind* (1954), Article 2, Section 6, included the offense of "undertaking or encouragement by the authorities of a state of terrorist activities in another state, or the toleration by the authorities of a State of organized activities calculated to carry out terrorist acts in another state." However, this article was eliminated from the final text.

The General Assembly's Committee on International Terrorism (1972 to 1979; 35 member states) failed to reach a consensual definition. The Organization of the Islamic Conference allows any "people's struggle including armed struggle against foreign occupation, aggression, colonialism, and hegemony" (Easson & Schmid, 2011, p. 137), as reaffirmed at a summit in Kuala Lumpur, Malaysia, in February 2002, but most Western governments object to this resolution.

While some states and the U.N. have failed to define terrorism as a state activity, many authorities, particularly human rights lawyers, do not want states to be allowed to perform activities that would be punishable if perpetrated by nonstate actors, so they have admitted the concept of *state terrorism* (terrorism by the state).

State-Sponsored Actors

State terrorism (terrorism by the state) is often differentiated from **state-sponsored terrorism** (terrorism by an entity sponsored by the state). As you have read above, many states and state-centric academics have resisted the concept of state-sponsored terrorism for fear of being accused of being a sponsor, but

> if the concept [of terrorism] is to have meaning it will also have to apply to acts falling within the definition regardless of who carries them out. Thus, support for groups using terrorism must be clearly noted as instances of state-sponsorship of terrorism whether it be by friend or foe. (Wardlaw, 1989, p. 185)

Some authors disagree with official use of the concept of state-sponsored terrorism because it is widely used to condemn other states for reasons unrelated to terrorism. It is used by autocratic or repressive states as an accusation against states that sponsor groups working for human rights or democratization. Most states are hypocritical; they accuse others of state-sponsored terrorism for sponsoring their domestic opponents but routinely sponsor their own favorites abroad. The United States has certainly sponsored groups that have engaged in terrorism, such as the many groups resisting Soviet occupation of Afghanistan, who turned into terrorists after Soviet withdrawal, not to mention various anticommunist groups in South America who certainly engaged in illegitimate activities against their opponents. The United States has claimed that it cannot be responsible for activities that it would not condone just because it supported legitimate activities by the same groups.

In the United States, the Arms Export Control Act of 1976 authorizes the president to restrict the sale of arms and the provision of services to any state fostering terrorism. The Omnibus Antiterrorism Act of 1996 prohibits the sale of any arms or the granting of any aid to any country that the president decides is not cooperating with U.S. **antiterrorism** efforts. The International Trade and Security Act of 1985, Section 505, authorizes the banning of imports from any country supporting terrorism. (The embargo on trade with Libya was legislated in Section 503 specifically.)

Annually, since 1979, the United States has issued lists of state sponsors of terrorism. Such a designation criminalizes any exports to the designated country of dual-use technology (technology that could be used for military purposes) or secret or otherwise excluded technology. The U.S. list started in 1979 with Iraq, Libya, South Yemen, and Syria. Iraq's fortunes give evidence for criticisms of issue linkage; Iraq was removed from the list in 1982 to allow U.S. companies to sell arms during Iraq's war with Iran, then considered the greater threat, but returned to the list in 1990 when Iraq invaded Kuwait. South Yemen was removed in 1990 following its incorporation into Yemen. Just before 9/11, the U.S. government listed Cuba (since 1982), Iran (since 1984), Iraq (since 1990), Libya (since 1979), North Korea (since 1988), Sudan (since 1993), and Syria (since 1979) as terrorist states. Afghanistan was designated noncooperative in countering terrorism. This list was separate from the list of terrorist organizations, which grew from 29 in January 2001 to 43 by 2009. Iraq was removed in 2004 following the U.S.-led invasion in 2003. Libya was removed in 2006 following its regime's renunciation of terrorism and nuclear weapons. North Korea was removed in 2008 after meeting foreign inspection requirements of its nuclear weapons program.

BEHAVIORS AND ACTIVITIES

Defining terrorism by activities alone conveniently avoids the disputes over the actors. Some academics have ignored the actor and defined terrorism as illegitimate or indiscriminate violence. For instance, William McGurn (1987) has defined terrorism as "a strategy rather than an ideology" (p. 14). The simplicity of a definition composed of only indiscriminate violence remains attractive to more recent definers (Mockaitis, 2011, p. 17). However, such a definition is impractically loose because of the difficulties of knowing what is truly illegitimate or indiscriminate. For many, illegitimacy means activities criminalized by law, but this allows for authorities to criminalize anything as terrorist, such as legitimate protest, just because the actor is objectionable.

Consequently, some academics have differentiated terrorism as any illegitimate violence that also tries to terrorize. For instance, *state terrorism* is different from state **oppression** or **repression** because the former is trying to terrorize a wider audience (Stohl & Lopez, 1984, p. 8).

Ted Honderich (2014) objected to any definition in terms of the actor or the victim and simply condemned the behavior. He argued that some legitimate causes could trump the identity of the victim, such as in war, when indirect harm to civilians is regrettable but allowable. He further argued that no victim can be truly innocent when benefiting from the acts of others even if not directly participating or when every person has the capacity for wrong. He argued that terrorism is not war, so terrorists cannot claim that civilian harm is allowable under the laws of war. Thus, he defined terrorism as an illegitimate sociopolitical behavior. "Terrorism is (i) violence, (ii) smaller in scale than war, (iii) social and political in aim, (iv) illegal, and (v) *prima facie* wrong since it is indeed killing, maiming and destruction" (p. 88).

However, Peter Sproat (1991) has pointed out that although states can be held accountable for war crimes, war crimes do not capture all state terrorism. The main rule of war is to leave noncombatants alone, but the state can be terrorist if it uses illegitimate violence to instill fear. Western interpretations of terrorism as both anti-Western and substate neglect state terrorism and leave definitions of terrorism predicated on the nature of the targeted regime (pp. 20, 23).

Similarly, Michael Stohl (2012) agreed that any actor could commit terrorism—the behavior, not the actor, is defining. He has proposed an "actor-neutral definition of terrorism: 'Terrorism is the purposeful act or the threat of the act of violence to create fear and/or compliant behavior in a victim and/or audience of the act or threat'" (p. 46). "To deny the existence of state terrorism as a concept ignores significant scholarship and creates further impediment to understanding the context, conditions and implications of the decision calculus of audiences and the political process" (p. 50).

TARGETS

Terrorism is sometimes defined by its target, where the main dispute is between definitions that restrict the targets to unofficial or civilian targets and those that do not restrict. The origins of this dispute go back to disputes about the legitimacy of unofficial or civilian resistance to official or military invaders. The first term to consider is *guerrilla*. This is a Spanish word meaning *small wars*.

International Conventions and Laws Relating to Terrorism

Although the U.N. has failed to agree on a definition of terrorism in general, member states have agreed to various international conventions, and laws have succeeded in defining certain proscribed activities, especially related to civil aviation and maritime security, such as

- the Convention on Offenses and Certain Other Acts Committed on Board Aircraft, signed in Tokyo on September 14, 1963;

- the Convention for the Suppression of Unlawful Seizure of Aircraft, signed at The Hague on December 16, 1970;

- the Convention for the Suppression of Unlawful Acts Against the Safety of Civil Aviation, signed at Montreal on September 23, 1971;

- the Convention on the Prevention and Punishment of Crimes Against Internationally Protected Persons, including Diplomatic Agents, adopted by the General Assembly of the United Nations on December 14, 1973;

- the International Convention Against the Taking of Hostages, adopted by the General Assembly of the United Nations on December 17, 1979;

- the Convention on the Physical Protection of Nuclear Material, agreed at Vienna and New York on March 3, 1980;

- the Protocol for the Suppression of Unlawful Acts of Violence at Airports Serving International Civil Aviation, supplementary to the Convention for the Suppression of Unlawful Acts Against the Safety of Civil Aviation, signed at Montreal on February 24, 1988;

- the Convention for the Suppression of Unlawful Acts Against the Safety of Maritime Navigation, agreed in Rome on March 10, 1988;

- the Protocol for the Suppression of Unlawful Acts Against the Safety of Fixed Platforms Located on the Continental Shelf, agreed in Rome on March 10, 1988;

- the International Convention for the Suppression of Terrorist Bombings, adopted by the General Assembly of the United Nations on December 15, 1997; and

- the International Convention for the Suppression of the Financing of Terrorism, adopted by the General Assembly of the United Nations on December 9, 1999.

It entered the English language during the Spanish **insurgency** against Napoleonic rule in the early 19th century. The Spanish guerrilla's alignment with the ultimately victorious British-led alliance gave the word a formative positive meaning. Some authors subsequently claimed that guerrillas were legitimate, even though terrorists are never legitimate.

For the most part, guerrillas uphold the distinction between combatants and civilians, primarily targeting combatants either by direct ambush or by means of espionage and sabotage. . . . This distinguishing feature of guerrilla warfare indicates, at least intuitively, that, though nonconventional, this kind of warfare warrants some legitimacy, even though it does not render its participants eligible for the protection of international conventions and the war rights of soldiers specified in them. (Meisels, 2014, p. 75)

During the Cold War, many communists advocated guerrilla warfare, so left-wing commentators have tended to treat the word positively. In the "first world" (the noncommunist developed world), some left-wing terrorists called themselves *urban guerrillas* as distinct from the primarily rural **insurgents** of the developing world ("third world").

The loose term *irregular warfare* was in first-world official use at the time. It is normally used to describe any activities outside of conventional warfare. It primarily covers terrorism, insurgency, and official covert actions.

Academics who have defined terrorism in ways that exclude states as perpetrators have erred in distinguishing between official and unofficial targets. For instance, Walter Lacqueur (1977) influentially defined terrorism as violence against the government (p. 79), but this definition would fit insurgents too. Some definitions differentiate terrorism from other violence by the deliberate targeting of innocents (McGurn, 1987, p. 13), but definitions of genocide or indirect retribution also differentiate by the deliberate targeting of innocents. Bruce Hoffman (1999) conveniently but inaccurately proposed that terrorists, unlike insurgents, do not target militaries. Similarly, both Rohan Gunaratna and Stuart Gottlieb defined terrorism as political violence "against noncombatants" (Gunaratna, 2014, p. 14; Gottlieb, 2014, p. 1). Tamar Meisels (2014) went to the extreme of claiming that while militaries and guerrillas usually discriminate by selecting legitimate, official targets, terrorists do not discriminate. "For terrorists, however, the killing of noncombatants is not a regrettable by-product or side effect; innocent victims are not an 'occupational hazard.' Instead, they are the be all and end all of this form of belligerency" (p. 76).

These are not accurate or legally useful claims. They are often motivated to help states and state-centric theorists to avoid defining terrorism as a state activity. In practice, the same actor could target both military and civilian targets. Historically, terrorism and insurgency have always overlapped; increasingly, terrorism and insurgency look alike. The same actors could choose to attack officials one day, civilians the next. Some avowed terrorists pursue civilian targets, while others refuse civilian targets, such as terrorists with tangible political objectives, who tend to minimize civilian harm in order to maintain civilian support. Thus, the target is not sufficient for defining terrorism.

Insurgents are defined more by their aims than by their targets or behaviors; *insurgents* aim to separate from or overthrow a government. The RAND Corporation, an independent, nonprofit, and federally funded research and development center, has provided a more operational definition wherein insurgents are essentially revolutionary or secessionist, without defining their targets.

We define an insurgency as an internal conflict in which (1) a group or groups are trying to overthrow the government or secede from it, (2) more than 1,000 [people] have died over the course of the war, and (3) more than 100 have died on each side. (Jones & Libicki, 2008, p. 9)

BOX 3.3

Competing American Definitions of Insurgency

Insurgency is "the organized use of subversion and violence by a group or movement that seeks to overthrow or force change of a governing authority" (DOD, 2010, p. 233).

Thomas Mockaitis (2011) criticized the DOD definition as "far too broad to be useful, and it leaves out the important element of terror." He defined insurgency as "an organized movement to overthrow a government *from within the borders of the state* through a combination of subversion, terror, and guerrilla warfare" (p. 14). He claimed that the Irish Republican Army, which Britain and the United States designated terrorist, was an insurgent group because of its clear aim to separate from Britain, whereas **al-Qaeda** was terrorist because its "demands are cosmic, not concrete" (p. 18).

MOTIVATION, IDEOLOGY, AND INTENT

The fourth and final category of definitions reviewed here are those that define terrorism by the perpetrator's motivation, ideology, or intent. The long-term debate about whether one man's terrorist is another man's freedom fighter is essentially a dispute about whether legitimate motivations can justify illegitimate activities.

Traditionally, terrorism has been regarded as politically motivated violence. If terrorism means to influence constituencies and governments, it is political. In the 1970s, a decade when terrorism was globally salient for the first time, Paul Wilkinson (1977), an early British-Israeli writer on terrorism, influentially defined terrorism as a form of political violence, requiring "either the deliberate infliction or threat of infliction of physical damage for political ends" or "the systematic use of murder and destruction, and the threat of murder and destruction in order to terrorize individuals, groups, communities, or governments into conceding to the terrorists' political demands" (pp. 30–31). Then, the main dispute was about the legitimacy of political violence; otherwise, the assertion of terrorism as political violence seemed stable. Terrorism as political violence remains popular. Reviewers of 73 definitions from 55 articles concluded that "terrorism is a politically motivated tactic involving the threat or use of force or violence in which the pursuit of publicity plays a significant role" (Weinberg, Pedahzur, & Hirsch-Hoefler, 2004, p. 789).

Defining terrorism by political motivations leaves several operational difficulties, such as judging the perpetrator's motivations and deciding how political the motivations must be before they become terrorist. Official authorities can claim that their political opponents are terrorist given their political motivations. Some academics have tried to solve this conflation by condemning extreme ideologies. For instance, Thomas Mockaitis (2011) wrote that "the term *terrorism* is best reserved for extremist organizations whose ideology is so utopian as to be unachievable. . . . Unlike insurgent groups, they seldom negotiate with the state to achieve limited results when their ultimate goal is thwarted" (p. 17). This is clearly not accurate or operationally useful and is open to manipulation by those who want to assert an opponent is either reasonable or unreasonable.

Dominic Bryan (2012) points out that defining terrorism by political motivations "is not very distinguishing. If we take the broadest definition of politics as being activities relating to relationships of power, then even acts of violence that relate simply to the person, such as armed robbery, assault or rape have, in the broadest sense, a political dimension" (p. 21).

Political motivations or ideologies are necessary but not sufficient for terrorism. The intent to terrorize also is necessary. For Sproat (1991), terrorist violence is certainly distinctly political, but, although all terrorism is political violence, not all political violence is terrorism; the distinguishing characteristic of terrorism is its intent to terrorize (p. 21).

Already by the 1980s, some authors had included the intent to terrorize as a fundamental part of their definitions. For some, terrorism's audience is more important than the victim. Stohl and Lopez (1984) defined terrorism as a terrorizing form of "political violence" (p. 4) or "the purposeful act or threat of violence to create fear and/or compliant behavior in a victim and/or audience of the act or threat" (p. 7) while Wardlaw (1989) said it was

> the use, or of threat of use, of violence by an individual or a group, whether acting for or in opposition to established **authority**, when such action is designed to create extreme anxiety and/or fear-inducing effects in a target group larger than the immediate victims with the purpose of coercing that group into acceding to the political demands of the perpetrators. (p. 16)

In the 1990s and 2000s, the intent to terrorize became a fundamental operational (but not legal) differentiator of terrorism from other political activities. The U.N. OHCA (2004), the U.S. DHS (2009), and the U.S. Department of Defense (2012a) all define terrorism as intended to terrorize or create fear, although laws ignore this intent (see Comparative Perspectives, Box 4.1).

Not all political violence is terrorism, and, increasingly, not all terrorism is political or violent. As terrorism started to include cyber and other nonviolent activities and to be motivated by more religious than political ideologies, defining terrorism as political violence seemed old-fashioned. Subsequent definitions tended to emphasize the perpetrator's intent to terrorize more than his or her political motivations. Bruce Hoffman emphasized the political less and emphasized the terrorizing intent more.

> Distinguishing terrorism from other crime allows us to see that terrorism is political, violent, designed to have psychological repercussions, conducted by an organization with structure, perpetrated by non-state entity. (Hoffman, 1999, p. 43)

> Terrorism is fundamentally the use (or threatened use) of violence in order to achieve psychological effects in a particular target audience. (Hoffman, 2001, p. 420)

Later, Paul Wilkinson also chose to emphasize terrorism as a terrorizing form of political violence.

> Some commentators in the media, some politicians and members of the public continue to use "terrorism" as a synonym for political violence in general, when in reality it is a special form of violence. It is a deliberate act by a group or by a

government regime to create a climate of extreme fear to intimidate a target social group or government or commercial organization with the aim of forcing it to change its behavior. (Wilkinson, 2010, p. 129)

It is a special type of violence, not a synonym for political violence in general. It is the use and credible threat of extreme violence to create a climate of fear to intimidate a wider target than the immediate victims of the terrorist attacks. (Wilkinson, 2012, pp. 11–12)

For most authorities, terrorism must be terrorizing for political purposes. The Humanitarian Practice Network (2010) says "terrorism [is] acts intended to inflict dramatic and deadly injury on civilians and to create an atmosphere of fear, generally in furtherance of a political or ideological objective" (p. xix). For some authors, terrorism is not necessarily political. Weinberg and Pedahzur (2003) write, "Terrorism is a kind of violence intended to influence or modify the behavior of one or various audiences by arousing fear, sowing confusion, promoting the indiscriminate retaliations, stimulating admiration, and arousing emulation" (p. 3). However, some authors have pushed back against the differentiation of terrorism by any intent to communicate terror, pointing out that almost all violence is communicative, from capital punishment to strategic bombing (Bryan, 2012, p. 21).

It is my contention that in using the label "terrorist" or "terrorism," we immediately make assumptions about the acts of violence, as well as their reception by victims, witnesses and the wider society. And of course, we differentiate those acts of violence labeled terrorism from those acts of violence that are not given that label, thus sometimes excluding reasonable comparisons. . . . And yet at the other end of the spectrum, whilst many of the acts of violence defined as terrorism are undoubtedly terrifying for those caught up in it, can we really argue that the wider population are terrified? Worried, horrified, even scare, but terrified? Any possibility of collapsing the meaning of the word terrorism to a definition based on the intended psychological outcome of the act is clearly not plausible. (Bryan, 2012, pp. 8, 23)

TERRORISM FREQUENCY AND DISTRIBUTION

Trends

Compared to other pure risks, terrorism is an infrequent, dynamic, and uncertain behavior that does not reward trend analysts. Infrequent events are unreliable populations for statisticians. Terrorists are adaptive, so past behaviors may not indicate future behaviors.

Understanding terrorism requires good intelligence or good theory, but good intelligence is usually kept out of the public domain or is politicized. Meanwhile, terrorism has not attracted many rigorous researchers. Consequently, terrorism scholars tend to have highly subjective opinions and anonymous official sources. Early on, before terrorism studies became "popular," two genuine social scientists found that research into terrorism is "not research-based in any rigorous sense; instead it is often too narrative, condemnatory, and prescriptive" (Schmid & Jongman, 1988, p. 179). One review found that only 3% of articles published from 1971 to 2003 used inferential analysis. The reviewers complained of "limited and questionable data" and rare use of "statistical analysis" (Suttmoeller, Chermak, Freilich, & Fitzgerald, 2011, pp. 81–82). Another social scientist reviewed more than 60 forecasts of terrorism, published from 2000 to 2010, and found little discernible theory or methods (Bakker, 2012).

Official forecasts of risks or security often mention terrorism but are not focused on terrorism. For instance, the U.S. National Intelligence Council's (2012) latest forecast, with a horizon of 2030, included some forecasts of terrorism but was focused on other risks. Few think tanks forecast terrorism in any systematic way. In 2005, the RAND Center for Terrorism Risk Management Policy (since 2002, mostly in Arlington, Virginia) published a forecast of mostly al-Qaeda terrorism up to the year 2020 (Chalk, Hoffman, Reville, & Kasupski, 2005). In 2011, the Center for Strategic and International Studies (Washington, DC) published a forecast of al-Qaeda terrorism up to 2025 (Nelson & Sanderson, 2011).

Unlike the mostly opinion-based commentary on terrorism, one should be evidence-based. Fortunately, in the 2000s, a superior dataset emerged, although no dataset is perfect. The Global Terrorism Database is a freely available dataset with global breadth and meaningful depth, although its data go back only to 1970, are not normally updated to the most recent year, and do not capture all events. (See the operational definition above to understand what the database recognizes as *terrorist*.) These data show that terrorism is very infrequent compared to other crimes, conflicts, and natural events of much more severe consequence. Like any events-based database, the GTD understates the frequency and overstates the impact of the average terrorist event. It captures the more spectacular minority of all events, such as events that kill lots of people, while most terrorism kills no one and is not recorded anywhere except at local levels, such as politically motivated vandalism of infrastructure.

The GTD observes 87,708 terrorist attacks from 1970 to 2008, for an average of 2,308 per year or more than six per day. Only 500 attacks occurred per year from 1970 until the frequency started to grow in 1974, reaching about 2,700 in 1979. The frequency remained elevated but in slight decline for a few years before proceeding upward again, despite lesser steps back, until peaking at over 5,000 attacks in 1992. The frequency fell rapidly in the 1990s as governments countered terrorism more effectively while seeking settlements. In 1998, terrorist attacks fell to a low not seen since the 1970s. The frequency remained relatively low until September 11, 2001.

While the overall frequency of terrorism declined in the 1990s, religious motivations were increasing, and religious terrorism is associated with increased lethality. Bruce Hoffman (1999) identified a surge in religious terrorism during the 1990s. David Rapoport (2004) retrospectively dated religious terrorism back to the **Islamist** revolution in Iran in 1979, although religious terrorism can be dated back to the ancient Israelite zealots (p. 61). Religious terrorists tend to have less realistic motivations, faith in unearthly judgments, contempt for external norms and conventions, and contempt for those outside their particular religion (**infidels**), so they tend to be more murderous than secular terrorists. Terrorists can come from any religion, but the most active since the 1990s have been violent Muslim terrorists, usually known as **jihadis** or *Islamists*, although each term is inaccurate and controversial.

The attacks of September 11, 2001 (9/11), collectively amount to the deadliest single terrorist attack ever, with nearly 3,000 dead. Jihadis, mostly from Saudi Arabia, sponsored by al-Qaeda (Arabic: the base), hijacked four airliners. They flew an airliner into each of the two towers of the World Trade Center, New York, setting fires that eventually caused each tower to collapse. They flew another airliner into the Pentagon, the headquarters of the U.S. Defense Department, in Washington, DC. The fourth airliner crashed into the ground in Pennsylvania during an attempt by passengers to gain control of the cockpit.

The U.S. Global War on Terror (officially from September 11, 2001, to 2009) correlated with increased terrorism by frequency and average lethality, almost all of it outside of the United States, most of it in countries subject to United States, military interventions. In the early 2000s, the attack frequency remained steady, around 1,000 per year, although with increased lethality per average attack, until a dramatic rise from 2005 onward, as terrorism became mixed up in other conflicts, mainly in Iraq, Afghanistan, Pakistan, North Africa, and East Africa. Previously, compared to war, murder, and suicides, terrorism accounted for a relatively trivial proportion of violent deaths, but the Institute for Economics and Peace (2012) concluded that "terrorism has emerged as a significant source of conflict since 2001" (p. 37).

Terrorism frequency and lethality appeared to flatten from 2008 to 2010, but it has increased every year since 2011, with a 61% increase in terrorism deaths from 2012 (11,133) to 2013 (17,958). Terrorism deaths were 5 times as great in 2013 as in 2000 (Institute for Economics and Peace, 2014b).

For the first years after 9/11, expectations about the future of jihadi terrorism were dominated by highly partisan and unscientific opinions until more evidence-based studies started to rise, as neatly summarized below in a scientific study that was published by RAND in 2008.

> There has been some discrepancy about the effectiveness of U.S. strategy against al Qa'ida. In 2007, for example, vice president Dick Cheney stated that the United States had "struck major blows against the al-Qaeda **network** that hit America." Pakistan's president Pervez Musharraf claimed that "Pakistan has shattered the al Qa'ida network in the region, severing its lateral and vertical linkages. It is now on the run and has ceased to exist as a homogenous force, capable of undertaking coordinated operations." The National Security Strategy of the United States boldly stated, "The al-Qaida network has been significantly degraded." These arguments were regularly repeated after 2001. "Al Qaeda's Top Primed to Collapse, U.S. Says," read a Washington Post headline two weeks after Khalid Sheikh Mohammed, the mastermind behind the September 11 attacks, was arrested in March 2003.
>
> Our analysis suggests that these claims were overstated. A growing body of work supports out conclusion. For example, the 2008 Annual Threat Assessment of the Director of National Intelligence reported that, "Using the sanctuary in the border area of Pakistan, al-Qa'ida has been able to maintain a cadre of skilled lieutenants

capable of directing the organization's operations around the world." It also noted that "Al-Qa'ida is improving the last key aspect of its ability to attack the US: the identification, training, and positioning of operatives for an attack in the Homeland." The 2007 national intelligence estimate, The Terrorist Threat to the US Homeland, similarly noted that the main threat to the U.S. homeland "comes from Islamic terrorist groups and cells, especially al-Qa'ida, driven by their undiminished intent to attack the Homeland and a continued effort by these terrorist groups to adapt and improve their capabilities." Bruce Riedel, who spent 29 years at the CIA, acknowledged that "Al Qaeda is a more dangerous enemy today that it has ever been before. (Jones & Libicki, 2008, pp. 103–104)

This same study went on to neatly summarize the evidence for al-Qaeda's growing capacity:

> Al Qa'ida was involved in more terrorism in the first six years after September 11, 2001, than it had been during the previous six years. It averaged fewer than two attacks per year between 1995 and 2001, but it averaged more than ten attacks per year between 2002 and 2007. . . . After 2001, al Qa'ida significantly increased its number of attacks, which spanned a wider geographic area across Europe, Asia, the Middle East, and Africa. . . . Al Qa'ida also became involved in two major insurgencies against U.S. forces. The first was in Afghanistan, where it assisted the Taliban, Gulbuddin Hekmatyar's Hezb-i-Islami, Jalaluddin Haqqani's network, and a variety of other organizations in their struggle against Hamid Karzai's government. The second was in Iraq.
>
> Public-opinion polls also showed notable support for al Qa'ida. In a poll released in 2007 by the University of Maryland's Program on International Policy Attitudes, for example, 25 percent of Egyptians interviewed said that they supported al Qa'ida's attacks on Americans and shared its attitudes toward the United States. Another 31 percent of Egyptians opposed al Qa'ida's attacks on Americans but shared many of its attitudes towards the United States. Furthermore, 40 percent of Egyptians, 27 percent of Moroccans, 27 percent of Pakistanis, and 21 percent of Indonesians had positive feelings toward Osama bin Laden. . . . More than 25 percent of those interviewed in a number of Muslim countries—such as Indonesia, Pakistan, Jordan, and Nigeria—had either a lot or some confidence in bin Laden. (Jones & Libicki, 2008, pp. 110, 112, 114–115)

The year 2011 was a year of optimism for **counterterrorism**, particularly for Americans. In December 2010, street-led revolutions started in North African countries, spreading to Middle Eastern Arab countries, becoming known as the Arab Spring. These revolutions were seen to marginalize al-Qaeda because ordinary citizens were overthrowing harsh governments without the help of al-Qaeda, which previously had claimed to represent ordinary Muslims in a campaign against pro-Western, un-Islamic regimes. On May 2, 2011, Osama bin Laden and some supporters were killed in a compound in Pakistan by U.S. special operators. On August 27, 2011, bin Laden's Libyan-born operations chief (Atiyah Abd al-Rahman) was killed in Pakistan.

However, the year of optimism (2011) was soon tarnished by realization that the Arab Spring had replaced stable states with unstable or failing states, principally Libya and Syria, where jihadis were congregating and basing themselves for operations elsewhere. Soon these same jihadis had traveled overland to destabilize states as far away as Mali and South Sudan. Although Osama bin Laden was dead, al-Qaeda survived, led by Egyptian-born Ayman al-Zawahiri, who quickly proved, by publicly releasing messages that urged Muslims to congregate in Libya and Syria, that his ambition and command were no less than bin Laden's.

Geographical Distribution

Since 1970, terrorism has ranked most frequent in Latin America, the Middle East and North Africa, Western Europe, South Asia, Sub-Saharan Africa, Southeast Asia, North America, Eastern Europe, and East and Central Asia. Terrorism has been most frequent in South American and South Asian countries; from 1970 to 2008, Colombia (6,911 attacks), Peru (6,041), El Salvador (5,330), and India (4,799) each have seen more terrorist attacks than Iraq (4,168), although most of Iraq's terrorism has occurred in the last decade. The next most frequent states (in order) are Northern Ireland (a province of the United Kingdom), Spain, Pakistan, the Philippines, Turkey, Sri Lanka, Chile, and the United States.

In the 2000s, the Middle East and North Africa became the region with the most frequent terrorism, followed closely by South Asia. Terrorism is less frequent, by orders of magnitude, in the other regions—Southeast Asia, Sub-Saharan Africa, Russia and surrounding states, Western Europe, South America, and North America. In fact, terrorism is increasingly widely distributed; in 2002, deaths from terrorism occurred in only 28 countries, but in 2012, the count was 59 countries (Institute for Economics and Peace, 2014a, p. 42).

Most terrorists arise within the same countries where they will attack. Transnational or international terrorists are less numerous but are usually more motivated, capable, and difficult to counter. Transnational terrorists tend to migrate into and proliferate in permissive areas, where governance is weak, governments are distracted by other conflicts, borders are porous, local populations lack capacity to resist, and local populations are divided by ethnic, cultural, or religious differences that terrorist entrepreneurs can exploit (U.K. Prime Minister's Strategy Unit, 2005, p. 29).

Deadliest Groups

According to the Global Terrorism Database, for the years 1970–2008, South American countries were homes to four of the top five deadliest terrorist groups: Shining Path in Peru (11,647 fatalities); Liberation Tigers of Tamil Eelam in Sri Lanka (9,534); Farabundo Marti National Liberation Front in El Salvador (8,508); Nicaraguan Democratic Force (7,268); and Revolutionary Armed Forces of Colombia (4,835). Al-Qaeda is the sixth deadliest terrorist group (4,299 fatalities through 2008) and has achieved this rank with more recent and fewer attacks. All the other deadliest terrorist groups in the top 20 are Middle Eastern or African, except the Irish Republican Army (ranking 12th at 1,829 fatalities).

THE OUTCOMES AND COSTS OF TERRORISM

This section reviews the political outcomes of terrorism, the human costs of terrorism, the direct economic costs of terrorism, and the costs of reactions to terrorism.

Political Outcomes

Some academics have claimed that terrorists almost always fail (Abrahms, 2006; Mueller, 2006), but they tend to judge victory by whether the terrorists cause a government or a state to fail, which is impractical. While terrorists may desire such an outcome, most of their goals usually are lowlier and more achievable, such as simply drawing attention to an issue or causing harm.

James Lutz and Brenda Lutz (2012) note that "the suggestion that terrorist activities cannot threaten state security ignores at least some cases where it has led to changes in the structure of states" (p. 61), such as fascist takeovers of European and South American states between the world wars, colonial withdrawal, and separatism. Many of these successes are undercounted, such as by states that claim nominal rule over a province that is effectively autonomous. Even where states do not change their structures, they almost always change their policies. They may even forego actions for fear of terrorist retaliation (Lutz & Lutz, 2012, p. 64). Much of the triumphalism about the supposed ineffectiveness of terrorism concerns the supposed strengths of democracies (Adams, 2006), but democracies routinely autocratize or reduce civil liberties in response to terrorism (Lutz & Lutz, 2012, p. 65).

In 2008, the RAND Corporation published a seminal study of "how terrorist groups end." Of 648 terrorist groups that were active at some point between 1968 and 2006, a total of 268 ended during that period, another 136 groups splintered, and 244 remained active. Of the 268 that ended, 43% reached a peaceful political accommodation with their government. Most of these had sought narrow policy goals. The narrower the goals, the more likely the government and terrorists were to reach a negotiated settlement. In 10% of cases, terrorist groups ended because they achieved their goals. Forty percent were eliminated by local police and intelligence agencies. Seven percent were eliminated by military force (Jones & Libicki, 2008).

Human Costs

Most terrorist attacks are meant to damage infrastructure or a symbolic target rather than to kill people. The Global Terrorism Database (1970–2008) reports that 58.7% of terrorist attacks killed nobody, 32.2% killed one to five people, 3.7% killed six to nine people, 3.9% killed 10–25 people, 0.9% killed 26–50 people, 0.3% killed 51–100 people, and 0.1% killed more than 100 people.

Most terrorists lack the capacity or motivation for mass-casualty attacks. However, mass casualty attacks, although still a minority of all attacks, have increased in frequency over the last two decades. Mass-casualty terrorist events (at least five dead) and high-casualty terrorist events (at least 15 dead) have increased dramatically in frequency. Religious terrorists seek to maximize lethality, at least among "infidels." Religious terrorism has increased most dramatically in unstable and religiously contested countries like Iraq. These religious terrorists tend to be unusually committed and agile and have migrated to wherever a new religious conflict arises or can be started, such as in civil wars in Libya and Syria since 2011.

Two Different Presentations of the Same Data

1. "A recent RAND study focusing on how terrorist campaigns end found that roughly 10 percent of the 268 terrorist groups that have come and gone since 1968 disbanded after achieving all or some of their political objectives. A much larger percentage ended after being incorporated into the mainstream political process, which, for some of these groups, represented a partial victory in its own right" (McCormick & Fritz, 2014, p. 149).

2. "Of the 648 groups identified in the RAND-MIPT Terrorism Incident database, only 4 percent obtained their strategic demands" (Abrahms, 2014, p. 154).

Mass-casualty events have increased as a proportion of all events, while attacks of all types have also increased over the last two decades, although with more volatility. Consequently, terrorist lethality in general has increased. Total global deaths from terrorism per annum reached nearly 10,000 in 1991, falling to about 6,000 in 1995, but peaking in 1997 close to 11,000. Annual deaths declined rapidly after 1997 to less than 2,000 in 1999, then started to climb again to 3,800 in 2002 and to 10,000 in 2007, at the height of the Iraq war. If terrorist deaths in active war zones or counterinsurgent zones were removed, the trend in terrorist deaths during the 2000s would have been downward (Institute for Economics and Peace, 2012, p. 37). One estimate of the global fatalities from terrorism during the 2000s, ignoring the casualties of wars and insurgencies that can be cross-counted as terrorism, is around 5,000 per year (Russett, 2010, p. 11). Although deaths fell to 7,000 in 2010, and the foreign coalition nominally withdrew from Iraq in 2011, deaths rose to more than 11,000 in 2012, 17,800 in 2013.

On September 11, 2001, terrorist attacks caused the destruction of four airliners, the collapse of both towers of the World Trade Center and secondary damage to surrounding structures in New York, and the destruction of part of the Pentagon building in Washington, DC. These events are normally considered one attack; it caused the greatest loss of life from any terrorist attack ever— just under 3,000 people. More than 2,100 of the dead were Americans; nearly 900 were foreign, from about 90 countries.

The September 11 death toll of nearly 3,000 is exceptional. Without 9/11, 2001 would not have been a particularly deadly year for terrorism. September 11 accounted for about half of all terrorism-related deaths globally that year (less than 6,000). In 2002 and 2003, terrorism killed 2,000 each year, globally, while war-related deaths increased dramatically. Terrorism lethality rose dramatically as terrorists reacted to the severe counterterrorism effort and took advantage of the associated instability, mostly in Afghanistan, Iraq, Pakistan, North Africa, East Africa, and Southeast Asia. In 2013, 82% of all deaths from terrorist attacks occurred in five states (in order): Iraq, Afghanistan, Pakistan, Nigeria, and Syria.

Nevertheless, terrorism remained an elevated but low risk. From 9/11 through 2012, nonterrorist Americans murdered more than 600 times more Americans (180,000) within the United States than terrorists murdered both in the United States and abroad (less than 300 U.S. citizens, excluding United States military combatants). Fewer Americans were killed by terrorism in that period than were crushed to death by furniture. In 2001, road traffic killed more than 10 times more Americans than terrorism killed. During the seven calendar years (2000–2006) around 9/11, the rate of road traffic deaths in low- to middle-income countries ran 200 to 220 times greater than the rate of terrorism deaths globally. Terrorism killed about 80 times fewer Americans than road traffic accidents killed. During that same period, road traffic killed 300 times more Britons than terrorism killed. Even in Iraq, during the peak in the insurgency and counterinsurgency there, terrorism killed about the same proportion of the Iraqi population as the proportion of the British population that was killed by road traffic.

Political and popular obsessions with terrorism declined in the late 2000s, when economic recession and natural catastrophes clearly emerged as more urgent. In Britain, the independent reviewer of terrorism legislation admitted that the most threatening forms of terrorism deserve special attention but pointed out that terrorism risks had declined and were overstated.

> Whatever its cause, the reduction of risk in relation to al-Qaida terrorism in the United Kingdom is real and has been sustained for several years now. Ministers remain risk-averse—understandably so in view of the continued potential for mass casualties to be caused by suicide attacks, launched without warning and with the express purpose of killing civilians. (Anderson, 2012, pp. 21–22)

He took the opportunity to describe terrorism, in the long run, as "an insignificant cause of mortality" (five deaths per year, 2000–2010) compared with total accidental deaths (17,201 in 2010 alone), of which 123 cyclists were killed by road traffic, 102 military personnel were killed in Afghanistan, 29 Britons drowned in bathtubs, and five Britons were killed by stings from hornets, wasps, or bees (Anderson, 2012, p. 27).

Direct Economic Costs

Terrorist attacks are infrequent and mostly not lethal but disproportionately costly in economic terms, even before 9/11. For the years 1970 to 2001, terrorist attacks accounted for 18% of insured events and killed 0.3% of the people killed in insured events but made up 37% of all insurance claims. By comparison, weather events accounted for 53% of all insured events, 54% of associated deaths, and 46% of insurance claims (Suder, 2004, p. 190).

Yet terrorism has not produced the costliest events. Just before 9/11, each of the top 10 costliest disasters or catastrophes for insurers had been natural events. Hurricane Andrew (August 1992) was the costliest of those—$20.5 billion in 2001 dollars of insured losses, more than $40 billion in total economic losses. The costliest of the terrorist attacks (a bombing of the city of London on April 24, 1993) cost $907 million (2001 dollars) in insured-property losses and killed one person. The first bombing of the World Trade Center (February 26, 1993) cost $725 million in insured-property losses and killed six people. The bombing in Oklahoma City in 1995 cost $145 million in insured-property losses and killed 168 people.

September 11 remains the costliest terrorist attack in history. All in all, the insured losses from 9/11 amounted to $40 billion or about 0.4% of U.S. gross domestic product (GDP) that year.

On top of insured losses, the federal government spent $8.8 billion in aid in response to 9/11. The direct material cost of 9/11 was about $22 billion, including insured damage to property ($10 billion), insured interruption to business ($11 billion), and insured event cancellation ($1 billion). The human deaths of 9/11 (nearly 3,000) and disabilities cost less than $5 billion in insured lives and workers' compensation. The human effects of 9/11 amounted to less than $10 billion in lost earnings.

The insured losses from 9/11 were about twice as great as the third most costly event for insurers (Hurricane Andrew in 1992) but much smaller than the most costly event (Hurricane Katrina in 2005—more than $40 billion in insured losses, $29 billion in federal aid, and $100 billion in total losses).

Terrorism does threaten political, social, and economic functionality in ways that typical road traffic accidents cannot, but terrorism is not as costly in direct economic costs. For 2000, the U.S. National Highway Traffic Safety Administration estimated $230.6 billion in total costs for reported and unreported road traffic accidents, excluding the other costs of traffic, such as environmental and health costs due to emissions from automobile engines.

Reactive Costs

The costs of the reactions to terrorism are typically greater than the direct harm. These reactions include economic distortions, policy changes, new regulations, new laws, and military interventions. A study across more than 200 countries, from 1968 to 1979, suggests that for every doubling of terrorist attacks within a state, the state should expect a 6% decrease in bilateral trade (Suder, 2004, pp. 49–50, 145).

After 9/11, international inflows (such as imports and foreign tourists) fell for a short while due to foreign fears and increased U.S. barriers; for instance, international tourist arrivals in the United States fell by 9% from September to December 2001. The local economic costs due to post-9/11 distortions of economic behavior were greatest (up to 10% of GDP). The reactive costs were greater: U.S. spending on security increased by 1.35% of GDP in the year after 9/11, or nearly 7 times greater than the direct physical costs. Overall spending on homeland security (public and private) rose from $56 billion in 2001 to about $99.5 billion in 2005. U.S. military spending doubled from 1999 to 2009. U.S. intervention in Afghanistan and Iraq cost $1 trillion in direct war appropriations by the end of 2009 and more than $1.4 trillion by the end of 2012, excluding perhaps more than $3 trillion in indirect costs; more than 6,000 U.S. soldiers had died, more than 40,000 had been wounded, and more than 100,000 civilians had died (Gaines & Kappeler, 2012, p. 27). These countries remain unstable and dependent on foreign support, despite nominal foreign coalition withdrawal from Iraq in 2011 and from Afghanistan in 2014.

TERRORIST TARGETS

The U.S. Government Accountability Office (2005c) has classified the *targets* of terrorism as "the general public, targets of symbolic value, organizational, governmental, and societal infrastructure, cyber and physical infrastructure, and economic sectors and structures" (p. 110).

Different terrorists have different intents and capabilities but some targets are more likely than others, if only for reasons of availability. In unstable or hostile environments, where operations need to be more self-sufficient and are short of local supplies, operational targets tend to proliferate, including logistical nodes, communications, vehicles, and personnel of all types.

Terrorists attack mostly commercial properties and private persons. Private targets are more numerous than public targets and often less protected, so their availability and accessibility encourages terrorist attacks, even when terrorists prefer to attack higher political or symbolic targets. Transnational and religious terrorists are more motivated to hold out for a hard public target but still tend to attack more private than public targets. For instance, in 2001, international terrorists struck 544 U.S. or American targets, of which 408 were commercial, 101 were private or local public, and 35 were national government, diplomatic, or military. The commercial, private, and local targets were 14.5 times more frequent than national official targets. From 1970 to 2008, 40% of terrorist attacks struck private citizens and property (22%), businesses (16%), or the news media (2%). Another 17% of terrorist attacks struck transport, utilities, educational institutions, religious, and other mass sites. Forty-three percent of terrorist attacks struck national government (14%), military (14%), police (12%), or diplomatic (3%) sites (Global Terrorism Database, n.d.). In the last decade, attacks on private citizens and property have increased absolutely and proportionately.

Religious terrorists are the minority of all terrorists, but they are growing, absolutely and proportionately, and they tend to target private citizens above all else, sometimes holding out for a spectacular economic or official target, generally combining such targets with mass casualties of private citizens. This trend was seen clearly in the first year of the foreign occupation of Iraq. In the first months (from March to October 2003), terrorist and insurgent attacks increased slowly, with a roughly equal split of targets between civilians and infrastructure. However, as foreign religious terrorists and insurgents immigrated in the months following October 2003, the frequency of attacks on civilians increased while attacks on infrastructure decreased (Paul, Clarke, & Grill, 2010).

Even when terrorists target official or symbolic targets, bystanders are more likely to be harmed because of the difficulties terrorists face in accessing the inside of the official area rather than the perimeter, where more passersby are exposed.

TERRORIST PROFILES

Profiling the typical terrorist is very difficult. This section helps you understand terrorist profiles by introducing what we know about terrorist psychosocial profiles, demographic profiles, and American terrorists in particular.

Psychosocial Profiles

Studies of terrorist psychology and motivations are too diverse and numerous to properly review here. Few are purely evidence-based anyway. One review found that "little empirical work exists that allows us to effectively understand the processes that result in extremists or extremists groups radicalizing to commit violent terrorist activities" (Suttmoeller et al., 2011,

p. 82). Another review found that most "existing research is not empirical" (Borum, 2004, p. 65) and that "research on the psychology of terrorism largely lacks substance and rigor" (Borum, 2004, p. 3). Nevertheless, by reviewing the empirical data this same review was able to conclude with the following useful observations:

- Mental illness and traditional psychoanalytic profiles, although once popular for explaining terrorism, are not empirically valid.

- Perceived injustice, need for identity, and need for belonging are push factors.

- Childhood abuse and trauma are prominent in terrorist biographies.

- Terrorist ideologies are pull factors and justify extreme behaviors.

- Social connections are necessary to most entrants into terrorism and to their acceptance of the in-group identity, perceived grievances, and ideologies.

- Imprisonment and incarceration are common situational opportunities for socialization of radical ideologies and for the acquisition of new perceived grievances.

- Terrorists recruit in deprived subpopulations, but deprivation does not seem to cause terrorism.

- Terrorists are more likely to be young adult, unmarried, middle class, urban, higher educated males, but almost all people of this profile are not terrorists. (Borum, 2004)

Another useful review of terrorist motivations concluded with five primary psychological, social, and situational explanations:

1. Frustration-aggression. Classes of society that are chronically frustrated (by perhaps political under-representation or economic disadvantage) are more likely to turn to aggressive solutions. For instance, many jihadis explicitly turn to terrorism in pursuit of conservative religious revolutions that would be impossible to achieve peacefully.

2. Relative deprivation. All classes in society may be developing positively, but one class may feel that it is not doing as well as another class; more frustrating, it may feel that the other class is doing better at its expense. For instance, many Muslim-European groups have claimed that jihadi terrorism in Europe is caused by European societies marginalizing the Muslim minority.

3. Identity crisis. Some classes may feel alienated from their home society and identify with an alternative interpretation of society or with a foreign or transnational opposition. For instance, most jihadi terrorists in Europe and America have been residents who claim higher loyalties to transnational religious movements than to nationality.

4. Narcissistic rage. Narcissistic personality types and cultures are attracted to terrorism because it offers further inflation of the in-group's self-righteousness and intolerance of out-groups. For instance, much terrorism is justified as vengeful; religious terrorism is particularly genocidal toward infidels.

5. Moral disengagement. Terrorism implies extreme reverse morality, such as indiscriminate or illegitimate killing, terrorizing the majority for the sins of a minority. For instance, many terrorists claim that they can attack a government through its citizens because citizens are responsible for electing or supporting governments, but really no civilian is responsible for their government. Many religious terrorists claim that their God controls all things, so anybody who suffers harm from terrorism, even fellow believers, must have been judged by God as unworthy in some way. (Borgeson & Valeri, 2009)

Demographic Profiles

Identification of terrorist **hazards** (potential terrorists) relies on demographic attributes, behaviors, experiences, or situations (altogether also known as *correlates* or *risk factors*). Some of these correlates are politically sensitive because they suggest racial or religious profiling. They are also impractical on their own because most people with the same factors never will be prosecuted for any crime. Yet terrorists, particularly the most dangerous terrorists, are more likely to show certain profiles, even though most people with the same profiles will not turn to crime, and these profiles are not in themselves diagnostic of terrorism. Evidence-based profiles of the types of people more likely to join in terrorism are justified descriptively, although discrimination among individuals is not justifiable ethically. Politicians and judicial authorities are often under political pressure to negatively or positively discriminate toward certain demographic profiles, but these profiles are best used to understand terrorism so that policies and practices can be adjusted to reduce the risk, rather than being used to investigate certain people as potential terrorists.

Empirically, foreign-born residents, second-generation immigrants, and religious converts are more likely to turn to crime, including terrorism, especially jihadi terrorism—the riskiest form of terrorism in the developed world. Certain religious and other sympathies tend to be correlated with certain ethnicities or places of residency, so these other attributes could be considered risk factors, although these second-degree risk factors become more politically and socially controversial. The American cases are summarized below.

- Converts to Islam account for

  o 33% of the nine Muslim Americans who killed other people in America after 9/11 through 2013,

  o 35% of Muslim-American domestic terrorist indictees after 9/11 through 2012, and

  o 42% of those convicted for significant violent jihadi plots against the United States after 9/11 through 2009.

- First-generation immigrants account for

  o 44% of the nine Muslim Americans who killed other people in America after 9/11 through 2013,

  o 33% of the Muslim-American indictees after 9/11 through 2012, and

  o 46% of those convicted for significant violent jihadi plots against the United States after 9/11 through 2009.

- Second-generation immigrants (born in-country to parents who had immigrated) account for

  o 22% of the nine Muslim Americans who killed other people in America after 9/11 through 2013 and

  o 16% of those convicted for significant violent jihadi plots against the United States after 9/11 through 2009. (The data on the whole population Muslim-American indictees does not include this attribute.)

AMERICAN TERRORISTS

To better understand American terrorists in particular, this section reviews the frequency of terrorism in America or against American targets up to 9/11, secular American terrorism since 9/11, religious American profiles since 9/11, Muslim-American terrorist attacks since 9/11, intercepted plots by American Muslims since 9/11, and Muslim-American terrorism indictees since 9/11.

Frequency

The United States, for its size, population, and importance, has not suffered much terrorism over the long term. According to the Global Terrorism Database, for the years 1970 through 2011, the United States comes 13th for number of terrorist attacks by nation-state, behind Chile. Terrorist attacks in America represent about 3% of all attacks globally during that period. During that time, the United States suffered at home 2,362 terrorist attacks, or 57.6 on average per year. Counting attacks at both home and abroad, about 11 Americans per year have been killed by acts of terrorism, compared to 15,000 Americans per year killed in other murders within the United States.

Terrorism in the United States has declined over the long term. The United States suffered 1,357 terrorist attacks at home in the 1970s, the peak decade for frequency but not lethality. In the 1980s, Americans abroad suffered more casualties to terrorism, usually by Middle Eastern or North African nationalist or transnationalist Arab terrorists, some with state sponsorship and with more secular left-wing political than religious ideologies. The deadliest attack on Americans before 9/11 occurred on October 23, 1983, in Lebanon, when a suicide bombing by a local Shiite group on a building that was accommodating U.S. Marines killed 307 people. U.S. targets suffered several similar bombings that year and subsequent years in the Lebanon.

Subsequent years were dominated by terrorism sponsored by Libya, which was retaliating against U.S. sanctions. The bombing of a nightclub, popular with U.S. servicemen, in West Berlin on

April 5, 1986, killed three and injured 230 people. On December 21, 1988, a small explosive device, hidden in luggage, exploded on Pan Am Flight 103 over Lockerbie, Scotland, on its way from Frankfurt via London to New York, killing all 259 aboard and 11 on the ground. The bomb had been loaded onto the plane, probably in Frankfurt, from a connecting flight from Malta. Investigators accused two employees of Libyan Arab Airlines, whom Libya surrendered for trial in 1999. Only Abdel Basset Ali al-Megrahi was convicted by a Scottish court in 2001, but in 2009, he was released on compassionate grounds (he was suffering from cancer) around the time when reports emerged of tainted evidence and witnesses as well as linkages with British–Libya political and economic deals. Libya reached a civil-international legal settlement in 2002 but always claimed that its officials had been acting without government orders.

Six times as many Americans were killed in the 1980s than in the 1990s. Just 87 Americans were killed by terrorism abroad in the 1990s; 176 Americans were killed at home but most (168) of these were killed by one attack—the bombing by an American citizen with Christian-fundamentalist and antifederal motivations, Timothy McVeigh, of a federal building in Oklahoma City on April 19, 1995.

The continental United States suffered its first foreign-terrorist, mass-casualty attack on February 26, 1993, when foreign-born jihadis trained or sponsored by al-Qaeda left a bomb in a van parked in the underground parking lot of the North Tower, World Trade Center, New York. It killed six people but did not cause a catastrophic failure, as the bombers had hoped. The impact on U.S. public awareness of jihadi threats and on U.S. official assessments of the threats was limited.

Jihadis attacked more U.S. targets abroad. On August 7, 1998, al-Qaeda–sponsored terrorists detonated vehicle-borne explosives outside the U.S. embassies in Nairobi, Kenya (212 killed, including 12 Americans, and 4,000 injured), and Dar-es-Salaam, Tanzania (11 killed and 85 injured). Osama bin Laden claimed that the attacks were revenge for U.S. intervention in Somalia. The United States responded with some remote unmanned air strikes on al-Qaeda sites.

On January 3, 2000, al-Qaeda–sponsored suicide bombers attempted to bring their explosives-laden boat alongside the USS *The Sullivans* (a guided-missile destroyer) while it was visiting Aden Harbor, Yemen, but their boat sank. On October 12, 2000, other bombers detonated explosives on a boat alongside the USS *Cole* (another guided-missile destroyer) in Aden, killing 17 U.S. sailors and injuring 39.

On September 11, 2001, hijackers deliberately piloted hijacked airlines into each of the towers at the World Trade Center, New York, the Pentagon building in Washington, DC, and the ground in Pennsylvania. By its own admission, al-Qaeda perpetrated this attack, including some perpetrators who had been involved in 1993.

Terrorism against U.S. targets and Americans surged in frequency after 9/11, but few Americans died as a result at home, although many Americans were killed in wars and counterinsurgencies overseas. For the years 2000 through 2013, 3,042 people died due to terrorism within the United States, although 2,996 of these died on 9/11. (In the same period, 64 times more people died in the United States due to other homicides: 195,948 homicides.) For the years 2002 through 2011, the Global Terrorism Database reports 168 terrorist attacks and 30 related fatalities within the United States—most of the attacks were not jihadi, but most of the fatalities occurred during the few jihadi attacks. According to the State Department, from 2002 through 2011, foreign terrorists killed 238

Americans abroad. In 2011, foreign terrorists killed 17 U.S. citizens globally (0.1% of all victims killed by terrorism that year) and injured 14 U.S. citizens globally, all of them in Afghanistan, Iraq, or Israel (ignoring U.S. military combatant deaths). In 2013, the United States experienced nine terrorist attacks, which killed six people (Institute for Economics and Peace, 2012, 2014b).

Secular American Terrorist Profiles Since 9/11

Historically, most American terrorists are not jihadi. Before 9/11, American right-wing terrorists were responsible for the most lethal attacks within America, led by the Oklahoma City bombing of 1995. American right-wing terrorists typically have antifederal, antiabortion, fundamentalist Christian views. The risks from right-wing terrorism were highest in the 1990s, during a growth in armed antifederal groups that tended to call themselves militias, few of which were violent. The right-wing threat soon resolved into a lone-wolf strategy, particularly after 1995, in which ideologues were expected to share a collective purpose but act alone in order to protect the collective from exposure.

American left-wing terrorism is very rare but tends to respond to wider disputes between extreme left- and right-wing positions. For instance, on August 15, 2012, Floyd Lee Corkins II (aged 28) entered the Family Research Council in Washington, DC, with intent to harm staff, whom he accused of homophobia. (He shot only the guard who apprehended him.)

Some American terrorists are categorized as ethnonationalist in that they attack certain races, ethnicities, or nationalities. Such terrorism is very difficult to separate operationally from other, much more frequent organized violence between rival gangs of different ethnonational identities or more spontaneous acts of violence where the perpetrator and the victim are of different ethnonational identities.

In the 2000s, jihadi terrorists clearly emerged as the riskiest. In the same decade, officials recognized the increased risk due to environmental terrorists or ecoterrorists, who typically attack property developments, car dealerships, and commercial organizations associated with exploitation of natural resources. Their attacks can be very costly in terms of property damage but are not normally meant to harm people; the people who are harmed are typically security guards or firefighters trying to save the property.

Responding to a survey in 2004, 59% of American police executives (n = 1,744) reported ethnic-supremacist terrorists in their area, 58% reported antiabortionists, 48% reported right-wing groups, 39% reported ecoterrorists, 28% reported Islamists, 17% reported left-wing groups, and 11% reported foreign terrorists. More police reported fears that ecoterrorists (44%) and Islamists (40%) would act than reported their presence. They had less fear that the other groups would act: anti-abortionists (37%), ethnic supremacists (34%), right-wing groups (28%), left-wing groups (12%), and foreign terrorists (7%) (Anarumo, 2011).

U.S. federal authorities do not usually publicly reveal which terrorist hazards they are tracking, although the National Counterterrorism Center has maintained a database with more than 1.1 million names of suspected terrorists as of December 2013, of which about 25,000 were Americans. This is the Terrorist Identities Datamart Environment (TIDE), also known inaccurately as the watch list. Names within TIDE are coded at different levels of risk, of which 47,000 names were on the no-fly list, of whom 800 were Americans.

Religious American Profiles Since 9/11

About 78.4% of American adults are Christian, 1.7% are Jewish, 0.7% are Buddhist, 0.6% are Muslim (somewhere over 2 million in a national population of 314 million), 0.4% are Hindu, and 16.1% are religiously unaffiliated. By comparison, Europe is 76% Christian and 5% Muslim (more than 38 million Muslim residents). Christianity and Islam are the two largest religions by population globally, and one or the other is dominant in most countries. About 32% of the global population is Christian; 23.4% is Muslim.

American Muslims are relatively more integrated than in most other countries, although Muslims, like Christians, tend to socialize within their own faith. According to a 2011 Pew Research Center survey, about half of U.S. Muslims say that all (7%) or most (41%) of their close friends are followers of Islam, and half say that some (36%) or hardly any (14%) of their close friends are Muslim. By contrast, Muslims in other countries nearly universally report that all or most of their close friends are Muslim (global median of 95%). Even Muslims who also are religious minorities in their countries are less likely than U.S. Muslims to have friendships with non-Muslims. For example, 78% of Russian Muslims and 96% of Thai Muslims said that most or all of their close friends are Muslim (Bell et al., 2013).

Most U.S. Muslims (63%) say there is no inherent tension between devout religious practices and living in a modern society. A nearly identical proportion of American Christians (64%) agree. Around the world, about half of Muslims (global median of 54%) share the view that modern life and religious devotion are not at odds. Most American Muslims (59%) say there is generally no conflict between science and religion. Globally, about half of Muslims agree (median of 54%). Fewer Americans (37%) and American Christians (39%) view religion and science as generally compatible. On the question of natural evolution, 45% of American Muslims believe humans and other living things have evolved over time while 44% disagree. American Muslims are about as likely to believe in evolution as U.S. Christians (46% of whom say they believe in evolution). Slightly more Americans overall (52%) and slightly more Muslims worldwide (median of 53%) accept evolution (Bell et al., 2013).

Most American Muslims say suicide bombings and other forms of violence against civilian targets are never justified (81%) or rarely justified (5%) to defend Islam from its enemies. Worldwide, most Muslims reject this type of violence, with a median of 72% saying such attacks are never justified and 10% saying they are rarely justified. Just 1% of U.S. Muslims and a median of 3% of Muslims worldwide say suicide bombings and other violence against civilian targets are often justified, while 7% of U.S. Muslims and a global median of 8% of Muslims say such attacks are sometimes justified to defend Islam (Bell et al., 2013).

Terrorist Attacks Executed by Muslim Americans Since 9/11

After 9/11 through 2014, more than 200,000 murders occurred in the United States. During the same period, 19 Muslim Americans carried out 17 violent attacks, of which 10 collectively killed 50 other people (more than half of all terrorist-related deaths in America in that period). Of the 19 perpetrators, four were first-generation immigrants, seven were second-generation immigrants (including immigrants as minors and children born to immigrants), six were American converts to Islam, and two were American Muslims without known immigrants in their immediate ancestry.

The frequency of American-Muslim violent attacks (1.3 attacks per year, 2002–2014) is about the same as the equivalent in the European Union (Kurzman, 2015).

BOX 3.5

Violent Attacks by Muslim Americans in the Homeland, 2002–2014

1. On July 4, 2002, Hesham Hadayet, an Egyptian-born immigrant, shot to death an Israeli airline employee and passenger before being shot to death at Los Angeles airport.

2. On January 5, 2002, Charles Bishop, a 15-year-old boy, flew a stolen small plane into an office building in Tampa, Florida, killing himself. He left behind a note supporting the 9/11 attacks, Osama bin Laden, and entreating God, so he is coded as a Muslim American in some datasets (Kurzman, 2013, p. 3).

3. In October 2002, around Washington, DC, John Allen Muhammed and Lee Boyd Malvo, both converts to Islam, shot to death 10 people. They had attempted extortion and are not recognized as terrorists by the Global Terrorism Database but are recognized elsewhere because they admitted to racially motivated targets and an intent to terrorize people.

4. On March 3, 2006, Mohammed Taheri-Azar, a 23-year-old who had grown up in America with Iranian immigrant parents, drove his car into students at Chapel Hill, North Carolina. He admitted murderous intent and jihadi inspirations.

5. On July 28, 2006, Naveed Haq, born in America to Pakistani-Muslim immigrant parents, shot to death an employee of a Jewish center in Seattle.

6. On February 12, 2007, Suleman Talovic, a Bosnian-Muslim immigrant, shot to death five others and himself at a shopping center in Salt Lake City, Utah.

7. On October 21, 2007, Tahmeed Ahmad, a 22-year-old who naturalized as a minor with immigrant parents from Kuwait, wielded knives against military police at Homestead Air Reserve Base, Florida.

8. On June 1, 2009, Abdulhakim Muhammad, a convert to Islam (he was born Carlos Leon Bledsoe), shot to death a soldier at a military recruitment center in Little Rock, Arkansas.

9. On November 5, 2009, U.S. Army Major Nidal Hasan, born in America to Palestinian immigrant parents, shot to death 13 soldiers and civilian staff at Fort Hood, Texas.

10. On May 1, 2010, Faisal Shahzad, a 30-year-old naturalized U.S. citizen born in Pakistan, left a vehicle in Times Square, New York City, with explosives that failed to detonate, for which he was later convicted.

11. Overnight October 16 to 17, 2010, Yonathan Melaku, a 22-year-old who had naturalized with his parents from Ethiopia, fired shots at the National Museum of the Marine Corps in Triangle, Virginia. Later in October, he fired on the Pentagon in Arlington, a U.S. Marine recruiting center in Chantilly, the Marine Corps museum again, and a U.S. Coast Guard recruiting center in Woodbridge in November. He was arrested on June 21, 2011, with explosive materials in Arlington National Cemetery.

12. On November 30, 2012, an explosive device was placed outside the back door of the

(Continued)

Social Security office in Case Grande, Arizona; it exploded harmlessly. An Iraqi refugee, Abullatif Aldosary, was arrested. His motives remain unclear.

13. On April 15, 2013, two ethnic Chechen brothers, who had been born in Kyrgyzstan before immigrating as children to the United States, placed two bombs at the Boston Marathon that killed three people. On April 18, they prepared six more explosive devices, shot to death a police officer, and hijacked a car with intent to attack Times Square, New York City, but the driver escaped and called the police. In the subsequent firefight, police shot to death the elder brother (Tamerlan Tsarnaev, aged 26) and wounded the younger (Dzhokhar A. Tsarnaev, aged 19), who escaped until he surrendered nearby on April 19. In May 2015, he was sentenced to death.

14. From April to June 2014, Ali Muhammad Brown (a 29-year-old male American) shot to death four people in Washington State and New Jersey.

15. On September 25, 2014, Alton Nolen (a 30-year-old male American convert to Islam) entered a food-processing plant that had recently terminated his employment, beheaded one woman with a knife and attacked another woman before being shot by another employee.

16. On October 23, 2014, Zale Thompson (a 32-year-old male American convert to Islam) attacked two policemen with a hatchet before being shot to death.

17. On December 20, 2014, Ismaaiyl Abdullah Brinsley (a 28-year-old male American) shot his former girlfriend in Baltimore before shooting to death two police officers in their car in New York City.

Intercepted Plots by Muslims, 2002–2009

In addition to the actual attacks by Muslim Americans after 9/11, more jihadi plots of violence were intercepted by American authorities on or over American territory. Many times more plots have been intercepted or discouraged than were executed, but the true quantity and quality is difficult to establish because of secrecy surrounding some of the investigations and controversies about the investigations. Many of the cases turned out to involve **confidential human sources** (also known as **confidential informants**) and *undercover officers*, often supplying mock weapons in order to test the suspect's intent to carry out a plot. These undercover operations were justified officially as safe ways to gather incontrovertible evidence of the suspect's intent, but critics characterize these operations as "stings" or *entrapment*, which would be inadmissible. No counterterrorist case since 9/11 has involved a successful defense on the grounds of entrapment, but the stings have declined in frequency, while prosecutors in most districts have clearly specified that investigators should collect more evidence of intent while showing that the suspect's intent is independent of those gathering the evidence.

A good period of examination is the period after 9/11 through 2009, after which the frequency of intercepted plots declined. Depending on one's viewpoint, the period 2001 to 2009 gives an exaggerated measure of the American jihadi threat due to official stings or a realistic measure of potential jihadi terrorists.

While acknowledging the difficulties of counting true plots, some authors have counted 23 "most significant" intercepted plots after 9/11 through 2009—a frequency of 2.6 per year (Bullock, Haddow, & Coppola, 2013, pp. 91–92). These plots resulted in 61 convictions. Twenty-seven (42%) were formal converts to Islam or had replaced their formal religion with sympathies to Islam, while 34 (58%) had been raised as Muslims. Eighteen (30%) were U.S. citizens by birth and whose parents were U.S. citizen by birth, 10 (16%) were U.S. citizens by birth with immigrant parents, 28 (46%) were immigrants (including naturalized citizens, refugees, asylum seekers, and illegal residents), and five (8%) were residents of foreign countries.

Intelligence leaders have tended to claim more intercepted plots than are described in the public domain. On June 18, 2013, the director of the National Security Agency (General Keith B. Alexander) told the U.S. House of Representatives' Intelligence Committee that the NSA's communications intelligence had helped to prevent "potential terrorist events over 50 times since 9/11" (Sullivan, 2013, n.p.). He said at least 10 of the disrupted plots involved terrorism suspects or targets in the United States, but he identified only one (the plot against New York's subway in 2009). At public conferences in June and July, he said that communications intelligence had "contributed to our understanding" of "54 different terrorist-related activities," which he described as 42 terrorist plots and 12 individuals identified as having provided material support to terrorist groups. Of the 54 activities, Alexander said 13 were based in the "homeland nexus," 25 in Europe, 11 in Asia, and five in Africa. However, in later clarifications, only one terrorist plot was described as ending in an arrest thanks to communications intelligence alone, and this was an attempt to send money to a U.S.-designated terrorist group abroad.

Muslim-American Indictees Since 9/11

From 2002 through 2014, about 250 American residents were indicted for violent terrorism, a frequency of 20 per year. After an outlying peak of 50 indictments for terrorism in 2009, 26 were indicted in 2010, 21 in 2011, 14 in 2012, 16 in 2013, and 25 in 2014 (Kurzman, 2015).

Of these 250, 175 (70%) were U.S. citizens (133 citizens by birth, 42 naturalized citizens), 31 were refugees, 27 were legal residents, two were foreign students, and 15 were illegal residents. Two-hundred-forty (96%) were male, 10 female. Ninety-two (37%) were converts to Islam compared to 158 born Muslims. Twenty-seven (11%) had been incarcerated prior to their terrorist plotting. Another 476 were indicted for support of terrorism, such as financing; after a peak of 88 in 2001, the frequency declined steadily to 27 in 2010, eight in 2011, six in 2012, eight in 2013, and eight in 2014.

Most of the indictees are American persons without clear foreign radicalization; they are usually classified as **homegrown violent extremists** by officials. The terrorists with most lethal intent tend to have foreign connections. For instance, Anwar al-Awlaki (1971–2011) was born in the United States to Yemeni parents but left the United States in 2002 and eventually settled in Yemen, where he was involved in several terrorists plots, mainly against the United States (including the attempt to blow up an American airliner on Christmas Day 2009 with explosive underpants hidden on a Nigerian volunteer), until his death in 2011 (reportedly due to a missile fired from a U.S. unmanned aerial vehicle). Meanwhile, in 2008, Nidal Malik Hasan (b. 1970), who was born in the United States to Palestinian parents and then served in the U.S. Army as

Chronological List of Intercepted Violent Plots by Muslims in the Homeland, 2001–2009

1. In December 2001, Richard Reid, a British-Jamaican convert to Islam, attempted to detonate explosives in his shoe on a commercial flight.

2. In 2002, Jose Padilla, a U.S. citizen convert to Islam, was arrested after returning to the United States after terrorist training with intent to murder, for which he was convicted in 2008. Initially, he was accused of a plot involving a radiological explosive device, but this accusation was dropped.

3. In 2002, six men, all born in Yemen and naturalized U.S. citizens, were arrested for attending terrorist training in Pakistan. They were convicted in December 2003.

4. In 2003, Lyman Farris, a naturalized citizen from Pakistan, was apprehended after plotting, with al-Qaeda sponsorship, to bring down the Brooklyn Bridge and derail a train.

5. In 2003, the Virginia Jihad Network was broken up while plotting undetermined attacks. Nine members, including seven Pakistani Americans and two American converts to Islam, were convicted in 2004.

6. In 2003, Nuradin Abdi, a Somali national with asylum based on false statements, was arrested for various terrorist offenses, including plots with Farris. He was convicted in 2007.

7. In 2004, Dhiren Barot, an Indian-born British national who had converted to Islam, was arrested in Britain after surveying targets in New York for al-Qaeda. He was convicted in 2007.

8. In 2004, Shahawar Matin Siraj, a Pakistani immigrant, and James Elshafay, an American with Egyptian and Irish immigrant parents, were arrested after an informer encouraged and recorded their plot to bomb a subway train station in Manhattan.

9. In 2004, Yassin Aref, a refugee from Iraqi Kurdistan, and Mohammed Hossein, a Bangladeshi immigrant, were arrested by the FBI after agreeing to participate in the financing of the import of a surface-to-air missile on behalf of a terrorist group. (The plot was entirely created by the FBI.)

10. In 2005, three American converts to Islam and a Pakistani citizen were arrested while plotting to attack Jewish and U.S. military targets in and around Los Angeles.

11. In 2005, Michael Reynolds was arrested after agreeing to meet an FBI informer about a plot to blow up natural gas pipelines. He had drawn attention to himself by advertising in an online forum for recruits to an attack in opposition to the U.S. invasion of Iraq.

12. In 2006, five U.S. citizens, a Haitian immigrant, and an illegal resident from Haiti, all of them members of a cult with sympathies toward Islam, were arrested after agreeing to help informers who were pretending to represent al-Qaeda.

13. In 2006, Lebanese authorities arrested Assem Hammoud on evidence gathered in cooperation with the FBI that he was plotting with Pakistani terrorists for suicide

BOX 3.6

attacks on trains between New Jersey and New York.

14. In 2006, Derrick Shareef, an American convert to Islam, was arrested by the FBI after agreeing with an informant to attack a shopping mall in Rockford, Illinois.

15. In 2007, six Muslim Americans (four ethnic Albanians from the former Yugoslavia, of which three brothers were illegal immigrants; a naturalized ethnic Palestinian immigrant from Jordan; and a Turkish permanent resident) were arrested for plotting an attack on Fort Dix, New Jersey.

16. In 2007, four men (three from Guyana, of which one was naturalized in the United States, and one from Trinidad and Tobago, all converts to Islam) were arrested after telling an informer that they planned to blow up fuel tanks at John F. Kennedy Airport, New York.

17. In 2008, Christopher Paul, an American convert to Islam who had received terrorist training in Pakistan before 9/11, was arrested for plotting bomb attacks, partly with Farris.

18. In 2009, four men (three U.S. citizens, one Haitian immigrant, all converts to Islam) were arrested in New York after implementing a plot to bomb a synagogue and shoot down aircraft, all with fake weapons provided by FBI informers.

19. In 2009, Najibullah Zazi, a childhood immigrant from Afghanistan, and two high school friends (one another immigrant from Afghanistan, the other from Bosnia) were arrested close to implementing a long-planned al-Qaeda–sponsored plot to blow themselves up on subway trains in New York.

20. In 2009, Hosam Maher Husain Smadi, a 19-year-old illegal resident from Jordan, was arrested after implementing an FBI-inspired plot to bring down a skyscraper in Dallas with what an FBI informer had persuaded him were truck-borne explosives.

21. In 2009, Michael Finton, an American convert to Islam, was arrested after implementing another FBI-inspired plot to blow up a federal courthouse in Springfield, Illinois, with what an informer had led him to believe were truck-borne explosives.

22. In 2009, Tarek Mehanna, a U.S. citizen with immigrant parents from Egypt, and Ahmad Abousamra, a Syrian-American dual national, were indicted for seeking terrorist training abroad for attacks in the United States. Abousamra fled the United States; Mehanna was convicted of material support to al-Qaeda.

23. On Christmas Day 2009, a Nigerian man attempted to detonate explosives hidden in his underwear while aboard a commercial flight. He had been prepared by al-Qaeda in the Arab Peninsula.

a psychiatrist, started communicating with Awlaki by e-mail. On November 5, 2009, Hasan opened fire with a pistol in the Soldier Readiness Center at Fort Hood, Texas, killing 13 and wounding 29. On May 1, 2010, Faisal Shahzad (b. 1979), a naturalized U.S. citizen born in Pakistan, left a vehicle in Times Square, New York City, with explosives that failed to detonate, for which he was later convicted. He claimed to have been inspired partly by Awlaki.

COUNTERTERRORISM

Counterterrorism is any attempt to control terrorism. Counterterrorism is often used interchangeably with antiterrorism, although in technical circles *antiterrorism* means purely defensive measures, whereas counterterrorism means both offensive and defensive measures. The subsections below review organizational issues, different strategic options, and U.S. counterterrorism since 9/11.

Organizational Issues

The organizational issues are mainly choices between centralized or decentralized structures, choices between hierarchies or networks, and efforts to improve **interagency coordination**.

CENTRALIZED VERSUS DECENTRALIZED STRUCTURE *Structures* are patterns of authorities and responsibilities. The *authorities* are those departments or persons assigned to determine how security and risk should be managed. The *responsible parties* are supposed to manage security and risk as determined by the authorities.

Structure is important because security receives improper attention when the responsibilities or authorities are unclear or dysfunctional. Structure is important also to outsiders who want to know with whom to communicate. Imagine a stakeholder who wants to contribute to your security but cannot find the best authority within the organization (or cannot find an interested authority). The wasted time and effort and frustrations count as unnecessary transaction costs, could damage your reputation, and reduce the chances of future opportunities. Structure is important to the efficiency of an organization since clearer authorities and responsibilities reduce the transaction costs and redundant activities associated with confused or redundant authorities.

Traditionally, official bureaucracies that aim at the benefits above have favored centralization, but centralization implies remoteness, rigidity, and less transparency, so recent trends have been toward decentralization. Designers should be careful, too, not to vacillate between

- highly centralized management, which should be materially efficient but is remote from lower managers and possibly unaware of managerial practices at lower levels, and

- decentralized management, which could be more efficient for the system as a whole, if junior managers are self-motivated and skilled, but also hide dysfunctional practices from higher managers.

Additionally, organizational designers need to be careful that they do not vacillate between

- lots of well-specified authorities that are overwhelmed by responsibilities and inefficiently dispute each other, and

- poorly specified authorities that are unaccountable or unsure (Newsome, 2007, pp. 18–22; Newsome, 2014, pp. 137–139).

HIERARCHIES VERSUS NETWORKS In the 1990s, some strategists criticized official bureaucracies as too centralized and slow while nonstate actors were moving away from conventional *hierarchies* (with clear steps up to higher authorities) to more agile and socially penetrative *networks*, which are defined by more connections and less hierarchical connections between nodes (Arquilla & Ronfeldt, 1996, 2001). After 9/11, much discussion of al-Qaeda's success credited its network structure. The Bush administration pledged to intervene overseas and to adopt more network structures in order to counter al-Qaeda's "flexible transnational network structure, enabled by modern technology and characterized by loose interconnectivity both within and between groups" (U.S. White House, 2003, p. 8).

However, others denied that al-Qaeda was as much a network as it was a **hierarchy**. Al-Qaeda always had a hierarchical core, with departments responsible for recruitment, finances, procurement, and public relations. Al-Qaeda sought to inspire groups remotely but also to direct them, even if they retained much of their autonomy (Spencer, 2014, pp. 14–15).

Some denied that official hierarchies were inferior, so they opposed counterterrorist movements toward more network structures. For instance, Mette Eilstrup-Sangiovanni and Calvert Jones (2008) stated that conventional "law enforcement agencies enjoy several advantages over clandestine networks, such as centralized information processing, monitoring of activities, formal training, and reliable organizational memory" (p. 11). By contrast, Phil Williams (2011) argued that "these structures—even a decade after the attacks on New York and Washington—continue to operate through standard procedures that inhibit cooperation with other agencies even at the domestic level, let alone with bureaucratic organizations in other nations" (p. 33).

INTERAGENCY COOPERATION A more popularly and politically recognized problem for counterterrorist organizations is **interorganizational coordination**, which is separate organizations positively working together, more popularly but narrowly known as *interagency cooperation*.

Organizations are often stereotyped as insular and self-interested, even when they are agencies of the same government. Each agency wants the glory and the credit for successful counterterrorism but the ability to blame other agencies for unsuccessful counterterrorism. The result is separate and sometimes contradictory activities unless agencies are encouraged or forced to cooperate. In 2004, the 9/11 Commission (The National Commission on Terrorist Attacks Upon the United States) reported that agency insularity and interagency malcoordination led to many examples of lost or misplaced pieces of intelligence that collectively could have warned of the plot that led to 9/11.

Coordination between organizations implies benefits, such as mutually improved security and reduced collective costs. Security coordination implies deliberate cooperation, more than commercial relationships, political alliances, or rhetorical friendships. For instance, after 9/11, the United States signed many bilateral agreements with other governments in which both governments stated their shared commitment to fighting terrorism. Sometimes, the United States promised money to help the other government develop its counterterrorist capacity; however, few of these early agreements specified how the two governments were supposed to coordinate their counterterrorist activities, measure their coordination, or hold each other accountable for their coordination. Meanwhile, other governments with whom the United States had made no new agreements coordinated better (Newsome, 2006).

Coordinating security between organizations is not easy, even when objectively each organization has a self-interest in coordination. Commercial competition inhibits coordination, although security against third-party threats does not need to affect commercial competitiveness. Many private actors assume that official authorities will protect them, but officials cannot be expected to follow every private actor or activity, particularly in remote locations. Some private actors inflate their self-reliance without realizing the benefits of coordination or the interdependency of risks. Table 3.1 summarizes the possible impediments and approaches to coordination.

As an example from Table 3.1, consider structural or geographical separation as a barrier to coordination between organizations. A commonly understood solution is to exchange *liaison officers*. For instance, the British national government sends government liaison officers to local Emergency Control Centers, the Ministry of Defense appoints joint regional liaison officers to each of the Emergency Control Centers, and local governments appoint a host-organization lead officer to manage mutual aid. Organizations are supposed to appoint (news) media liaison officers too (Newsome, 2014, pp. 145–146).

Strategic Options

Counterterrorist strategies do not have a good reputation, in part because official strategies are often unclear, vacillatory, or clearly different in plan than in practice. Generally, strategies change greatly before governments are satisfied, starting with hard military and legal responses,

Table 3.1   Impediments and Approaches to Security Coordination

Impediments		Approaches
Category	Examples	
Material	Resource constraints	Resource pooling, risk sharing, shared controls, review risk assessments, and efficiency of controls
	Physical separation	Liaison officers and communications
Cultural and social	Linguistic or cultural differences	Multicultural employees or experts
	Self-reliance culture	Set coordination as a corporate objective
	Internally oriented culture	Develop external orientations
	Pursuit of relative gains	Reward absolute gains

Impediments		Approaches
Category	**Examples**	**Approaches**
Structural and strategic	Competing objectives	Cooperative objectives
	"Buck-passing" (passing one's own responsibilities to another)	Accountability to a third party
	Redundant authorities	Consolidate authorities
	Ambiguous responsibilities	Define responsibilities
Procedural and personnel	Ill-defined or incompatible processes	Standardize a process
	Lack of expertise	Train or employ experts
Political	Political issue linkage	Prohibit changes outside of major policy changes
	Politicization	Nonpartisanship
	Political sensitivities	Compartmentalized information assurance

Source: Based on Newsome (2006) and Newsome and Floros (2008, 2009).

proceeding through socioeconomic and sociopsychological interventions, before reaching political settlement (Jones & Libicki, 2008). Paul Shemella (2011) wrote that "good strategy in general is rare and, in the cause of fighting terrorism, exceedingly rare" (p. 131).

The main categorical choices for counterterrorism strategy in the literature have been among the following five:

1. Political strategies (mostly about reaching political settlements)

2. Legal strategies (to better proscribe the activities that contribute to terrorism)

3. Economic strategies (mostly about alleviating poverty or improving greater socioeconomic opportunities)

4. Military reactions (mostly about violently interrupting terrorist capacity, where the term *military* has been used to mean violence by any official actor, not just the military)

5. Sociopsychological interventions (mostly about dissuading at-risk subpopulations or individual hazards from joining in terrorism)

Just after 9/11, L. Paul Bremer III (2002), chair of the U.S. National Commission on Terrorism, described Western counterterrorist strategy as mature by the 1980s with three principles:

1. No concessions are granted to terrorists.

2. States that use or sponsor terrorism should be ostracized.

3. It is important to use the rule of law against terrorists. They are criminal. (p. 55)

Western counterterrorism changed greatly after 9/11. In risk management terms, the United States focused narrowly on *risk prevention* by fighting terrorists abroad and preventing terrorists from accessing the homeland. Britain's counterterrorism strategy has been described as a broad risk management approach, although in practice Britain's approach was closer to the U.S. plan than the British plan. More principled states, such as Canada, focused on *risk preemption*, meaning interventions at home to stop hazards being activated as terrorists by terrorist entrepreneurs, their ideologies, and social contagion at radical religious sites or in prisons. This is not to say that other governments were not engaged in risk pre-emption, just that Canada was more focused on it (Svendsen, 2010).

Daniel Byman (2009) identified seven counterterrorist strategic options:

1. *Unilaterally crushing terrorists*—the dominant U.S. and Israeli strategy up to then; although self-reliant, it is alienating

2. *Multilaterally crushing terrorists*—the evolving coalition strategy in Afghanistan, this strategy shares risks but is less agile for individual members

3. *Containment of terrorists in certain areas*, such as the remote mountains of Afghanistan and Pakistan, although these are also bases for their missions elsewhere

4. *Defense*, such as the Israeli barrier between the Palestinian West Bank from Israel, although this is expensive and alienating

5. *Diversion*, as illustrated by the many Muslim countries that encouraged their radicals to wage a religious war against the Soviets in Afghanistan rather than at home

6. *Delegitimation of the terrorist's motivations, goals, methods, or ethics*, such as by claiming that a terrorist who claims to fight for religious morality also breaks religious edicts against theft, murder, and so on

7. *Transforming terrorist breeding grounds* by eliminating their grievances, improving their conditions, representing them, or diversifying them

Paul Shemella (2011) listed ten means that governments could use to counter terrorism:

1. Diplomacy

2. Information, specifically information that counters extremism

3. Military forces

4. Economic sanctions

5. Financial isolation

6. Intelligence

7. Law enforcement

8. Emergency services, especially medical services

9. Civil society organizations, such as charities, trade unions, and religious organizations

10. Moral factors, primarily legitimacy (p. 131)

He recommended that governments interrupt the terrorist's ten "centers of gravity":

1. Legitimacy

2. Funding

3. Training

4. Weapons

5. Mobility

6. Communications

7. Leadership

8. Unit cohesion

9. Sanctuary

10. Ideology (p. 131)

U.S. COUNTERTERRORISM SINCE 9/11

This section reviews the strategy of the George W. Bush administration (2001–2009), the strategy of the Barack Obama administration (2009–2017), U.S. efforts to build foreign capacity, and U.S. efforts to counter the financing of terrorism.

The Bush Administration's Strategy, 2001–2009

The George W. Bush administration characterized its response to 9/11 mostly by the phrase *war on terror* (also, Global War on Terror, or GWOT). Many critics pointed out that the phrase was illiterate and impractical (one cannot make war on a concept, only on actors). Britain, the strongest foreign partner, preferred the phrase "campaign against terrorism." The Global War on Terror formally ended in 2008, although the phrase continued to be used to describe various ongoing activities.

The Bush administration's clearest articulation of its counterterrorist objectives is known by the four *D*s:

1. Defeat the terrorists

2. Deny the terrorists' sanctuaries

3. Diminish their support

4. Defend the homeland (U.S. White House, 2003, p. 15)

In practice, the Bush administration's strategy was mostly military.

> The current U.S. strategy against al-Qaeda centers on the use of military force. Military force was not, of course, the only instrument that the United States used against al-Qaeda. The U.S. Department of State engaged in a range of diplomatic counterterrorism initiatives, including through its Antiterrorism Assistance Program. The FBI and local police agencies historically tracked and arrested terrorists in the United States. The U.S. Department of Homeland Security implemented numerous policies at ports of entry and critical infrastructure to secure the United States from terrorist attacks. The U.S. Department of Treasury targeted terrorists' financial networks. And the CIA collected, analyzed, and conducted operations against terrorist groups abroad. While a range of instruments was used, the military component was paramount in two respects. First, U.S. policymakers and key national-security documents referred to operations against al Qa'ida as the global war on terror. . . . Second, the U.S. military spent the bulk of counterterrorism resources. (Jones & Libicki, 2008, pp. 105–106)

In practice the Bush administration's strategy and activities were often contradictory and counterproductive, such as by killing or detaining a few alleged terrorists while providing grievances for many more.

> Despite initial success in capturing some al Qa'ida leaders, the United States failed to significantly weaken the organization. There was an increase in the number of attacks that involved al Qa'ida either directly or indirectly, an expansion of al Qa'ida's geographic reach, and an evolution of its organization structure. Part of the reason was an overreliance on military force and the perception that there was a battlefield solution to a "war" on terror. But military force has rarely been effective against terrorist groups in the past. (Jones & Libicki, 2008, p. 120)

In particular, the military interventions in Afghanistan in 2001 and in Iraq in 2003 were criticized as increasingly unrelated to counterterrorism and counterproductive.

Ironically, the Iraq intervention stemmed in part from the Bush administration's sense of frustration with the inability to quickly capture or kill bin Laden. Frustrated in dealing with an elusive enemy, the U.S. government reverted to what it does best, which is to use large-scale conventional forces in conventional warfare against a static and fixed, state-bound enemy. (Williams, 2011, p. 31)

These U.S. interventions encouraged jihadis to extend their network into the same countries and to shift from terrorism to insurgency, to which American targets were more exposed abroad than they would have been at home.

Al Qa'ida also played a role in connecting Afghan and Pakistani insurgent groups to the broader jihadi network, including in Iraq. With al Qa'ida's assistance, Islamic militants in Iraq provided information, through the Internet and face-to-face visits, on tactics to the Taliban and other insurgent groups. This included suicide tactics and various kinds of remote-controlled devices and timers. In addition, a small number of Pakistani and Afghan militants received military training in Iraq. Iraqi fighters met with Afghan and Pakistani extremists in Pakistan; and militants in Afghanistan increasingly used homemade bombs, suicide attacks, and other tactics honed in Iraq. (Jones & Libicki, 2008, p. 120)

The interventions in Afghanistan and Iraq remained popular at home for years, until the formal justifications (counterterrorism, counterproliferation of weapons of mass destruction, and democratization) were proven to be unsound, the occupations became mired in insurgencies, and rushed and flawed democratization (Iraq's first national election was in 2004) clearly produced corrupt tyrannies of the majority led by former exiles who had been favored by the United States.

At home, the Bush administration attempted to counter terrorism mainly by improving defenses at the borders and strengthening surveillance and investigatory powers within the borders. From the start, the Bush administration's legal and regulatory changes were characterized by secretive new executive orders or interpretations of old orders, an enormous and underdebated main piece of legislation (the USA PATRIOT Act of October 26, 2001) that eased investigations and prosecutions but also curbed human rights and intruded into privacy, and the extrajudicial rendition, detention, and torture of suspects, with few checks or balances.

When the consensus turned critical, the legal part of the strategy was easiest to criticize as counterproductive.

The USA PATRIOT Act gave expansive powers to the federal government in terms of spying on suspected terrorists. White House and U.S. Justice Department memoranda routinely, if not explicitly, approved the use of torture when dealing with so-called enemy combatants. Foreigners are routinely prohibited from coming to the United States, and American travelers are routinely subjected to intrusive inspections and restrictions. The average citizen seems oblivious to or unconcerned with these limitations on their freedoms. Perhaps such measures can be justified should they result in America being safer. There is little evidence, however, that draconian measures have resulted in a reduction of terrorist acts in the United States, led to the capture of any terrorists, or in any way made Americans safer. Indeed, they likely made America more vulnerable to attack as extremists view some of these practices as an attack on their faith, culture, and sovereignty. Such acts certainly have had an adverse impact on how other countries across the globe view the United States. (Gaines & Kappeler, 2012, p. 9)

The Obama Administration's Strategy, 2009–2017

Around the end of the 2000s, evolving administrations in Britain and the United States explicitly downgraded foreign interventions and elevated the strategies of terminating and turning negative risks, starting in the United States, led by President Barack Obama since January 2009.

> Against this backdrop, we began our tenure with some thoughts about what we needed to do to be more effective. In general, we believed, we had to be more comprehensive, more genuinely strategic in our approach. We had to invigorate our diplomacy to strengthen the foreign partnerships that are vital to our success. We knew, moreover, that while the military, intelligence community, and law enforcement agencies were firing all cylinders, civilian agencies—here in the U.S. but also in governments around the world—were not yet sufficiently engaged. And we recognized that kinetic action was not enough to reduce the threat as much as we wanted to.
>
> With that in mind, we put a high priority on two key areas: capacity building, so countries around the world could do a better job dealing with the threats within their borders and regions; and, recognizing that we had to address what Deputy National Security Advisor John Brennan labeled the "upstream factors" of radicalization, we resolved to strengthen our work on countering violent extremism—or CVE—so we could blunt the attraction of violence and reduce the number of recruits to our enemies' cause. (Benjamin, 2012)

In June 2011, the Obama administration (U.S. White House, 2011b) published a strategy that sounded much like Britain's CONTEST strategy, with extensions to activities abroad.

- Protect the American people, homeland, and American interests . . .

- Disrupt, degrade, dismantle, and defeat al-Qa'ida and its affiliates and adherents . . .

- Prevent terrorist development, acquisition, and use of weapons of mass destruction . . .

- Eliminate safe havens . . .

- Build enduring counterterrorism partnerships and capabilities . . .

- Degrade links between al-Qa'ida and its affiliates and adherents . . .

- Counter al-Qa'ida ideology and its resonance and diminish the specific drivers of violence that al-Qa'ida exploits . . .

- Deprive terrorists of their enabling means (pp. 8–9)

In September 2011, the U.S. Department of Homeland Security (DHS) published a new strategy toward its "national preparedness goal" that is essentially the same as the British CONTEST strategy.

- Preventing, avoiding, or stopping a threatened or an actual act of terrorism.

- Protecting our citizens, residents, visitors, and assets against the greatest threats and hazards in a manner that allows our interests, aspirations, and way of life to thrive.

- Mitigating the loss of life and property by lessening the impact of future disasters.

- Responding quickly to save lives, protect property and the environment, and meet basic human needs in the aftermath of a catastrophic incident.

- Recovering through a focus on the timely restoration, strengthening, and revitalization of infrastructure, housing, and a sustainable economy, as well as the health, social, cultural, historic, and environmental fabric of communities affected by a catastrophic incident. (2011, p. 1)

Although the formal strategy changed a lot, some U.S. activities certainly did not change from the Bush to Obama administrations, such as the extrajudicial detention of terrorists at Guantanamo Bay and the extrajudicial killing of terrorists abroad.

Strategy became more contested over theoretical and empirical questions, such as whether democratization promotes freedom from extremism or just permits extremist majorities to gain power; whether poverty, unemployment, or corruption cause terrorism or are just economic explanations for the availability of recruits; whether focusing on Islamic extremism is a realistic response to risk or neglectful of more frequent non-Muslim violence; whether engagement with Muslim minorities helps to integrate or alienate Muslims; whether promoting gender rights undermines or provokes extremists; and whether a general strategy should be prepared in advance or should be reactive to particular cases (see Gottlieb, 2014).

These disputes remained unresolved when the U.S. government started its Summit on Countering Violent Extremism, originally scheduled for October 2014 but postponed to February 18, 2015 (over three days), with representatives from 60 countries. The name of the summit actually disagreed with the government's new international strategy, rebranded as "Preventing Violent Extremism." *Countering* was criticized for focusing on countering extremist messages, while *preventing* was marketed as a more inclusive approach to "ensuring inclusive governments," "building secure and resilient communities," and "amplifying" moderates (Hudson, 2015). The State Department, particularly the undersecretary of state for civilian security, democracy, and human rights (Sarah Sewall), was the leading manager of this change. In a speech on January 20, 2015, Sewall said,

Where there is weak governance or a lack of quality education, economic opportunity, or respect for human rights, citizens are most at risk to being alienated by or from their governments and each other. This is not just about ideological affinity; it is about alienation and anger that drives communities to align or tolerate the violent extremists. (n.p.)

However, other officials have complained off the record that the new strategy is not practical (Hudson, 2015).

Building Foreign Capacity

Perhaps the clearest changes in the Obama strategy were the wariness of formal military intervention abroad and the emphasis on building foreign capacity.

We know that in terrorism, small numbers can have outsize and even enormous impacts, and that with strong leadership or an influx of funding, groups can revive, expand and cause great damage. This is a moment for leaning into the problem of violent extremism, for continuing to degrade terrorist groups and to shape the environment they operate in to our and our partners' advantage. . . .

Make no mistake: The United States will continue to use all the tools at its disposal to protect itself from terrorism. But as we go forward—capacity building, countering violent extremism, counterterrorism diplomacy—these are the growth areas of the future. Propagating what we and others have learned throughout the international community and establishing a durable coalition of like-minded partners is vital. (Benjamin, 2012)

The United States spends directly on its own missions and aids foreign counterterrorism. Most of that aid is distributed by the DOD and wrapped up in general military aid, so the true cost of counterterrorism aid is difficult to separate. Other counterterrorism aid is distributed through the Departments of State, Homeland Security, Justice, and Treasury, and the Federal Deposit Insurance Corporation.

In 2011, with 30 founding members (29 countries and the E.U.), the United States launched the Global Counterterrorism Forum (GCTF). The State Department's Bureau of Counterterrorism is the lead department of U.S. government. The GCTF has mobilized over $175 million to strengthen counterterrorism-related rule-of-law institutions and has developed best practice documents in rule of law, combating kidnapping for ransom, and prison deradicalization and disengagement. By 2012, the GCTF was also developing two international training centers in the Middle East and North Africa region to provide training in the forum's two areas of strategic priority: countering violent extremism and strengthening rule-of-law institutions.

Countering Terrorist Financing

Most terrorism is not remarkably expensive while most terrorist organizations spend much more money on other things than terrorism, so counterfinancing is not necessarily intended to prevent terrorism, although it is important to the prevention of truly catastrophic terrorism. A practical ambition for counterfinancing is to provide intelligence useful to other investigations.

The main departments of the U.S. government involved in counterfinancing are Treasury, State, Homeland Security, and Justice, whose main investigating agency is the FBI. The Bank Secrecy Act of 1970 obliges financial institutions to file suspicious activities reports (SARs) and currency transaction reports (CTRs), such as a deposit of more than $10,000 in cash. The Money Laundering Suppression Act of 1994 required all money transmitting businesses, including nonbanks, to register with the Department of Treasury and provided for uniform laws across the states to regulate "businesses that provide check cashing, currency exchange, or money transmitting or remittance services, or issue or redeem money orders, travelers' checks, and other similar instruments." These regulations were to include reporting of foreign bank drafts. Few of these state-level regulations were implemented, so the USA PATRIOT Act of October 2001 encouraged the states to implement them on the grounds of counterterrorism and to counter foreign money laundering.

The USA PATRIOT Act also imposed additional "special measures" and "due diligence" on financial businesses, including an obligation to file suspicious activity reports to the Department of the Treasury and to verify customer identification and to record all transactions in case of future official investigation of the financial chain to a crime. The act specified new crimes, such as laundering the proceeds from or supporting terrorism or cybercrime, even if the crimes were perpetrated abroad.

In 2012, the Department of State provided $20.45 million to multiple federal agencies for Anti–Money Laundering and Counterterrorist Finance (AML/CTF) training and technical assistance programs for participants from multiple countries. The State Department's Bureau of Counterterrorism designed and implemented innovative courses and workshops to assist foreign governments to identify AML/CTF deficiencies, strengthen domestic abilities to address the terrorist financing threat, and to develop their awareness of and ability to confront kidnapping for ransom.

The Department of Treasury's Financial Crimes Enforcement Network (FinCEN) provided analytical exchanges with foreign financial intelligence units (FIUs). The Department of Justice Asset Forfeiture and Money Laundering Section provided expertise in the drafting of laws and regulations. The Internal Revenue Service's Criminal Investigations Office focused on developing forensic accounting techniques and an investigative "follow the money" technique, used to examine financial records and data to help determine hidden assets and money movement. The Federal Bureau of Investigation conducted international training in countering terrorist financing, money laundering, financial fraud, and complex financial crimes.

DHS's Immigration and Customs Enforcement (ICE) Homeland Security Investigations (HSI) conducted capacity-building efforts through the HSI-led Cross-Border Financial Investigations Training (CBFIT) and Resident Cross-Border Financial Advisor programs (R/CBFIA). The ICE HSI Trade Transparency Unit (TTU) conducted presentations on trade-based money laundering to hundreds of personnel from foreign law enforcement, customs authorities, and foreign military charged with border enforcement functions as well as representatives from the financial sector from various countries around the world. The presentations and discussions resulted in numerous beneficial contacts and potential case leads.

BOX 3.7

International Counterasset Regimes

- The U.N. counterassets regime, as authorized by U.N. Security Council Resolutions 1267 (1999), 1333 (2000), and 1390 (2002), authorizes the U.N. to maintain a Consolidated List of proscribed individuals and groups and obliges member states to freeze assets of, prevent transit by, and prohibit military assistance to those on the Consolidated List.

- The U.N. counter–state assistance regime, as authorized by the U.N. Security Council Resolution 1373 (of September 29, 2001) obliges states to deny assistance to terrorists and establishes a Counterterrorism Committee, to which all states are supposed to report their performance.

- The E.U. action plan (September 21, 2001) provides for increased cooperative countermeasures.

- The E.U. Framework (June 13, 2002) elevates theft and extortion for terrorism.

- The G7 finance minster's action plan (October 2001) freezes assets of terrorists and intervenes in terrorist financing.

- The OSCE Bishkek International Conference on Enhancing Security and Stability in Central Asia (December 2001) included measures against financing.

FINAL CASE STUDY

How Should We Assess the Terrorist Threat in Formulating Policy?

Bob Kerrey

Here are the two central challenges for the men and women whose job it is to protect us against terrorists. First, terrorism is not an ideology or a religion; it is a highly effective tactic that has always been used in war. Second, the terrorist looks like us. He or she does not wear a uniform or dress in any way that makes it obvious he or she is our enemy. They are usually young, religious, and have loving mothers and fathers. And like our heroes, they are willing to die for a cause they have been persuaded to believe.

At the moment, the religion of most terrorists is Muslim, though that has not always been the case. There have been Christian terrorists, Jewish terrorists, Hindu terrorists, Buddhist terrorists, pagan terrorists, and I suppose even atheist terrorists. In truth, it will be difficult to "defeat" terrorism if we are unable to understand that for a Muslim living in Iraq, Afghanistan, Pakistan, or Palestine who has experienced the terror of a drone, we just might fit the definition as well.

I know these are provocative things to say. However, I believe we must say them in order to demonstrate the meaning of freedom and to defeat an enemy that is using terrorism against us. You can be sympathetic and understanding without descending the slippery slope of moral relativism.

For make no mistake: We did not declare war on terrorists; they declared war on us. And unlike us, they do not feel remorse over civilian casualties. For them, civilian casualties are not accidents; this is their intent.

In a political environment, blind stridency and cautious language prevails in the debate about what our response should be to these threats. In an academic environment, blind stridency and caution should be banished. This may be our only hope to find sustainable answers to this threat.

Here are just some of the questions you should consider and discuss: In the work of identifying terrorists, what are the trade-offs between freedom and the order that makes freedom possible? What is the right balance between providing for the common defense and ensuring domestic tranquillity? When should an accused terrorist be tried in our federal courts, and when should they become sources of actionable intelligence? How are the responsibilities borne by United States military and economic leadership different than those of other nations? How much diplomatic risk should we take in trying to resolve conflicts that could reduce the basis for some terrorist groups?

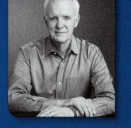

Bob Kerrey is a former governor (1983–1987) and U.S. senator (1989–2001) from Nebraska. During the Vietnam War, he served with the United States Navy's SEAL team and was awarded the Congressional Medal of Honor for "conspicuous gallantry." He was a member of the 9/11 Commission, president of the New School in New York City from 2001 to 2011, and is currently a managing director of Allen and Company as well as chairman of the Minerva Institute, a member of the U.S. Department of Defense's Policy Board, and chairman of the Holland Children's Movement.

CHAPTER SUMMARY

This chapter has explained

- How terrorism is defined, in terms of
  - actors,
  - behaviors and activities,
  - targets, and
  - motivations, ideologies, and intents.
- The actual frequency and distribution of terrorism

- The outcomes and costs of terrorism, including
  - the political outcomes,
  - the human costs,
  - the direct economic costs, and
  - the reactive costs.
- The sorts of targets that terrorists choose

- Terrorist profiles, including
  - psychosocial profiles,
  - demographic profiles, and
  - American terrorists.

- Counterterrorism, including
  - organizational issues,
  - strategic options, and
  - U.S. counterterrorism.

KEY TERMS

Al-Qaeda *83*
Antiterrorism *79*
Authority *84*
Confidential human
  source *102*
Confidential informant *102*
Counterterrorism *88*
Hazard *96*
Hierarchy *107*
Homegrown violent extremists *103*
Infidel *86*

Insurgency *81*
Insurgent *82*
Interagency coordination *106*
Interorganizational
  coordination *107*
Islamist *86*
Jihadi *87*
Network *87*
Operational definition *73*
Oppression *80*
Political violence *77*

Repression *80*
State terrorism *74*
State-sponsored
  terrorism *78*
Sting *72*
Structure *77*
Terrorism *73*
Undercover officer *72*
War crime *74*

QUESTIONS AND EXERCISES

1. What is the difference between nonstate terrorism, state terrorism, state-sponsored terrorism, oppression, and war crimes?

2. What is the difference between terrorism and other political violence?

3. What is the difference between terrorism and insurgency?

4. What is a good operational definition of terrorism?

5. Why has the United Nations struggled to define terrorism in international law?

6. Look at the different national legal definitions of terrorism. What is operationally different about U.S., Canadian, European Union, and British legal definitions?

7. Why was terrorism decreasingly frequent in the 1990s?

8. How would you characterize trends in terrorism lethality and frequency since 9/11?

9. Why is terrorism forecasting poor?

10. Give five pyschosocial observations associated with terrorists.

11. Give three demographic observations about Western jihadi terrorists.

12. How would you contrast the motivations of terrorists who kill Americans in America versus abroad?

13. Why are some U.S. federal indictments of terrorists controversial?

14. What is different about the targets associated with religious terrorism compared to nonreligious terrorism?

15. Why should we separate the direct costs and reactive costs of terrorism?

16. What are the five main categories of counterterrorist strategy?

17. What is contradictory about U.S. counterterrorism?

18. How does the United States attempt to build foreign counterterrorist capacity?

19. How does the United States attempt to counter the financing of terrorism?

4

TRANSNATIONAL CRIME

In October of 2000, an accomplice in a plot to steal several hundred million dollars from the Bank of Sicily and the European Union turned himself in to authorities. Before his defection, he was part of a group of 20 people who set out to create a digital clone of the bank's online component in order to divert $400 million of E.U. funds. These funds, allocated for regional projects in Sicily, were to be laundered through financial institutions in Switzerland, Portugal, and even the Vatican bank.

Though thwarted, this plot illustrates the nature of transnational organized crime today. The conditions for criminal exploitation involved a large financial transaction (in this case, a state-to-state initiative), a purposely opaque financial system, jurisdictional voids, disregard for borders, deregulation, the secrecy, anonymity and ubiquity of electronic commerce, and the collusion of criminal elements and insider personnel. Elements of the explanation and incentives for these new opportunities are globalization and technology. FBI Director Robert Mueller, at the time, described the technology accompanying the current age of globalization as "a double-edged sword. Entrepreneurs and engineers are not the only ones that recognize the vast potential of the Internet. Criminals and terrorists do too" (Bedi, 2005, n.p.). Yet, cybercrime is only one realm of opportunity for transnational crime.

Despite the array of resources legal authorities have at their disposal, the room for maneuver within the security paradigm for transnational criminals appears almost without bounds. Authorities are hindered by cumbersome legal codes, the physical realities of the conflict zone, and the expanse of possibilities in the virtual world. The very nature of the global supply chain resembles the character of cyberspace in its vastness, complexity, intentional opaqueness, resistance to governance, and the unending fluctuation and process of globalization, which all work to the benefit of transnational crime.

Learning Objectives and Outcomes

At the end of this chapter, you should be able to

- Define transnational crime

- Describe the structure of transnational crime organizations

- Understand the motives of transnational crime organizations and how those motives differentiate them from terrorists

- Understand the similarities between transnational crime organizations and international terrorism with respect to modi operandi

- Understand how transnational crime exploits the mechanisms of globalization and technology in similar ways as legitimate actors

(Continued)

DEFINITION OF TRANSNATIONAL CRIME

The definition of transnational crime varies and is as illusive in meaning as the term *terrorism*. The United Nations Office on Drugs and Crime (UNODC) defines *transnational organized crime* to allow for a broader interpretation of the term in order to apply the designation to the emerging forms of illegal activity that surface over time. (A more complete discussion is found on the website of the United Nations Convention Against Transnational Organized Crime: http://www.unodc.org/unodc/treaties/CTOC.)

Rather than attempt to assign a definition to transnational organized crime, most authorities find it more practical to offer up a definition of an *organized-crime group*. The National Institute of Justice defines transnational organized-crime organizations as "groups or networks of individuals working in more than one country to plan and execute illicit business ventures" (National Institute of Justice, 2007, n.p.)

Underscoring the legal and academic complexities of defining organized crime, the Obama administration offers a more detailed analysis, yet, despite the specificity, it is ultimately as amorphous.

> There is no single structure under which transnational organized criminals operate; they vary from hierarchies to clans, networks, and cells, and may evolve to other structures. The crimes they commit also vary. Transnational organized criminals act conspiratorially in their criminal activities and possess certain characteristics which may include, but are not limited to:

(Continued)

- Identify and discuss the various transnational crime groups and the potency of their threat
  - Russian organized crime
  - Italian Mafia
  - Japanese yakuza
  - Chinese triads
  - Organized-crime groups and the Central Asian drug trade
  - Organized-crime groups and the South America drug trade
- Examine the role of failed states in facilitating organized crime and terrorism
- Describe the current anticrime methods, regimes, and capacity-building efforts to counter crime worldwide

DEFINITION

BOX 4.1

Transnational Organized Crime, UNODC

A group of three or more persons that was not randomly formed; existing for a period of time; acting in concert with the aim of committing at least one crime [. . .]; in order to obtain, directly or indirectly, a financial or other material benefit. (U.N. Office on Drugs and Crime, 2015, n.p.)

- In at least part of their activities they commit violence or other acts which are likely to intimidate, or make actual or implicit threats to do so;

- They exploit differences between countries to further their objectives, enriching their organization, expanding its power, and/or avoiding detection/apprehension;

- They attempt to gain influence in government, politics, and commerce through corrupt as well as legitimate means;

- They have economic gain as their primary goal, not only from patently illegal activities but also from investment in legitimate businesses; and

- They attempt to insulate both their leadership and membership from detection, sanction, and/or prosecution through their organizational structure. (U.S. National Security Council, n.d.)

The lack of consensus on the definition of the term notwithstanding, there are at least 52 categories of activity that are generally recognized as falling under the transnational organized-crime rubric. They range from intellectual theft, drug trafficking, and environmental crime and run the gamut of nuclear smuggling to counterfeit toys.

In recent years, the impact of transnational crime has reached unprecedented levels. The United Nations Office on Drugs and Crime (2011a) estimates that in 2009, the proceeds from transnational organized crime (TOC) equaled 3.6% of global gross domestic product (GDP),

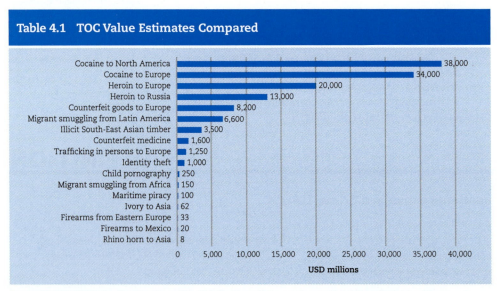

Table 4.1 TOC Value Estimates Compared

Source: UNODC (2010a) estimates. From *The Globalization of Crime: A Transnational Organized Crime Threat Assessment,* by United Nations Office on Drugs and Crime, © 2010 United Nations. Reprinted with the permission of the United Nations.

or the equivalent to $2.1 trillion. The report continues to approximate that the socioeconomic costs of TOC surpass its illicit revenue stream by a ratio of 2:1. In advanced countries, such as the United States and Britain, the ratios may even be higher. Not only does TOC take its toll on the victims from whom it diverts income and the society upon which it imposes the need for remedial and law enforcement regimes, it also comes with a cost when it reinvests its earnings. Investments from these ill-gotten gains displace legitimate economic activity and can ruin the effectiveness and credibility of institutions, local economies, and even national economies. The situation can be particularly acute for financial firms.

These crimes and the criminals who engage in such activity destabilize governments and nourish violence. The toll on human suffering is incalculable. Between 12 and 27 million people represent the transnational-crime forced-labor pool (Council on Foreign Relations, 2013). The numbers eclipse those from the peak period of the African slave trade, and the violence perpetrated in these areas undermines the legitimacy of legal authorities. Counterfeit medicines impact community health by further sickening the already ill and introducing more virulent strains of viruses and other pathogens. Illegal dumping, poaching of protected animal species, and deforestation destroy

Map 4.1 The Intersection of Transnational Organized Crime and Instability

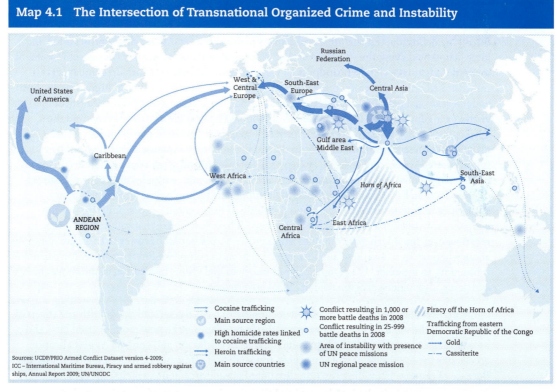

Sources: UCDP/PRIO Armed Conflict Dataset version 4-2009; ICC – International Maritime Bureau, Piracy and armed robbery against ships, Annual Report 2009; UN/UNODC

Source: UNODC (2010a). From *The Globalization of Crime: A Transnational Organized Crime Threat Assessment,* by United Nations Office on Drugs and Crime, © 2010 United Nations. Reprinted with the permission of the United Nations.

the delicate ecosystem and contribute to the increase in natural disasters. Meanwhile, as officials work to marshal support and public resources to combat TOC, large swathes of populations rely on criminal elements for employment, markets, and even basic services that elected authorities fail to provide.

In addition to these facts, accurate statistics on transnational crime are rare and often politicized (Council on Foreign Relations, 2013). Peter Andreas (2003b) suggests that the numbers presented as data on the level of organized-crime activity, particularly in counterfeit goods, are often driven by agencies whose agenda is to draw public attention for the purpose of influencing budgets and policy (pp. 81–82). He cites an Organisation for Economic Co-operation and Development (OECD, 1998) report, which claims, "Many of the anti-counterfeiting organizations are lobby groups and have an incentive to present exaggerated figures that may bias the true picture" (p. 27). However, victims of fraud, computer hacking, and piracy often have incentives to suppress numbers in order to preserve investor confidence, avoid higher insurance rates, protect careers, and avoid costly lawsuits. In many cases, particularly those involving cybercrime, organizations are unaware their security has been breached. Revelations are usually revealed through third parties and often after some time has elapsed (McGurk, 2012). Some extrapolation of these conflicting and skewed quantitative measurements, it would reason, reveals a truer statistic. The absence of hard data, unfortunately, creates a blurred picture and has impact on the public and policy decisions.

Finally, by definition, transnational crime spans national borders. TOC eludes prosecution and interdiction by defying the sovereign and jurisdictional boundaries that provide law enforcement institutions legitimacy and a **monopoly of force** to control these activities. In combat against transnational crime, therefore, there exists a conflict among sovereign rights, human rights, local and international politics, and legal jurisdictions and codes. Legal authorities and institutions evolve over generations. However, their evolution lags behind the march of events and the development of technology. Policy and protocol trails in the wake of developments on the ground, and these institutions in place to defend the public find themselves challenged by a state-centered system and obsolete laws, which can overlap and often conflict. These conditions hinder institutional and bureaucratic efforts as the statal system struggles under the pressures of globalization. Even if they overmatch their opponents technologically and in weaponry, authorities face disadvantages legally and politically. These conditions not only apply to the geopolitical world but also extend to virtual space. There is software that can track suspects in real time over the Internet as communication moves across borders. However, there are questions about whether the use of these applications is legal, and a compliant foreign partner (or partners) is necessary to interdict. The rampant rise of transnational crime, in addition to the above threats and perils, also underscores the void in global governance.

Globalization and the emergence of new technologies have accelerated the growth and diversity of TOC. All the while, crime organizations thrive by adapting the new modern "tool kits" and by adjusting organizationally to horizontal models of command and control. As globalization accelerates the expansion of world markets, transnational crime has little difficulty keeping pace. Because of the ease in evading territorially rooted law enforcement agencies, the difficulties of the state in controlling the growth of transnational organized crime have become salient in the argument that national governments are losing control and the proposition that the state is losing relevance.

THE STRUCTURE OF
TRANSNATIONAL CRIME ORGANIZATIONS

For many years, the accepted wisdom among criminologists concluded organized crime was a cartel or confederation with formal and informal aspects that created both a business organization and a government. In whatever manner of linkage or depth of connection, the amalgamation included presidents, boards, executives, managers, foremen, and workers as well as judges, legislators, and administrators. Law enforcement officials and academic observers long assumed that it was the structure and apparatus of organized crime that perpetuated it, not its personnel or the force of an individual persona or central leader. That assessment is now under revision as technology and globalization change the methods and pragmatism of those determined to break the law and those assigned to defend it.

Today, the pace of events force and the advancements in technology allow for actors to respond to changeable and unpredictable conditions with the power of a thousand minds and the speed of a keystroke. Therefore, the single, pyramid-based structure of traditional organized crime has morphed into a less crystalline configuration of fluid networks and functional cooperation. "Criminals are 'sovereign-free' actors in that they trail their activities across several jurisdictions to minimize law enforcement risks, with no single jurisdiction having effective 'ownership' of a particular criminal case" (Jamieson, 2001, p. 378).

A primary facilitator of this **jurisdictional arbitrage** (using legal discrepancies between jurisdictions or states in order to have advantage over government law enforcement agencies) is the obvious technological revolutions in transportation and information/communication. The impact of technology has been one of the key drivers in the global economy and, as well, an enabler of growth in criminal markets. Whether the markets are above or below ground, populations are more accessible for servicing, exploitation, or plunder due to the modern machinery resulting from advancements in science. As **economic globalization** and technology have lowered the costs of the movement of goods and the transmission of information and funds, they have accelerated commerce and opened the field of play to new actors and opportunities for creating wealth. Yet it has also allowed criminals to take advantage of the same mechanisms that benefit the movement of capital and the initiation and execution of business planning. Therefore, as with legitimate actors, organized crime competes in the illicit marketplace with similar functional arms. Distribution, transportation, and finance units contribute specialized and diverse staffs to their corporate, albeit corrupt, mission. In this environment, ethnicity may be a secondary element to function, skill, and a prevailing opportunity—just as it is in the corporate world. In this respect, the concept and image align with traditional assessments of organized crime but only at the surface level.

The de-bordering of global commerce has de-bordered crime. The new pattern challenges old structures and tests traditional beliefs. Criminal groups are highly entrepreneurial and often operate semiautonomously or autonomously across national boundaries. Rather than subsidized foreign branches, these units conduct their business with nothing more than a seal of approval from their native home office (Varese, 2012, p. 249). The origin for transnational crime depends more on the feasibility of the local opportunity rather than a strategic decision made at headquarters. Often times a "foreign expedition" may be the effort of a restless or exiled affiliate. The consequence can be a short-term niche or a vast network of dispersed contacts of international associates, corrupt officials, and unwitting or unwilling partners.

Technology alone is not the only mechanism responsible for the expansion of transnational crime. Liberal economic policies that encourage deregulation, privatization, and unencumbered trade boost commerce but also blur distinctions between legal and illegal activity. The policies encouraged by the world's most industrial countries and foisted by the International Monetary Fund and the World Trade Organization mostly benefited the first world and have exacerbated third-world debt and deepened the chasm between rich and poor. While contributing to the fertile territories for furtive commerce and arrant crime, such guidelines for economic growth have also made transnational crime more difficult to prosecute and dislodge.

Rather than view transnational organized crime as a counterforce to authority and a driver of events, the United Nations Office on Drugs and Crime suggest that it may be more accurate to regard TOC as a range of actors responding to market forces. The groups themselves become less important than the markets. As criminal groups emerge and disappear, the laws of supply and demand are resistant and make insignificant the structure and substance of the criminal element. Market dynamics abide as market entrants come and go. This state of affairs applies to all markets, whether legitimate or not. However, in the case of illegal activity, law enforcement tends to focus its efforts on controlling the actors and has neither the resources nor the authority to address the market conditions (UNODC, 2010a).

Furthermore, justice systems are rooted locally while commerce and crime are global phenomena. Hence, the growth of economic globalization has outpaced the evolution of global governance. The seas cover three quarters of the earth's surface, and no regime or hegemon has the means or authority to control this anarchic realm. The financial system has unlimited points of access, and participants trade anonymously. They move money rapidly and in high volumes, unencumbered by intrusive regulations and assisted by offshore accounts that obscure ownership and origin of capital. The Internet is boundless and as ungovernable as the seas. Its ubiquity and anonymity provide perfect cover for fraud, electronic theft, and terrorism. As long as institutional weaknesses persist and human nature is susceptible to its lure, TOC will continue to be a source of permanent

DEFINITION

BOX 4.2

Transnational Organized Crime

Like organized crime, the global economy is interdependent yet sovereign-free; the market place recognizes no ethical responsibilities. Organized crime is far more than a crime—it is a social phenomenon, a network of relationships based on reciprocal benefits that extends to the heart of society and of institutional and economic life. Its pervasiveness demands responses that are equally wide-ranging. In some communities—especially those undergoing turbulent change or where social infrastructure are weak—it provides a substitute set of institutions, employment, higher-than-average earnings, and social mobility, and therefore exerts a strong attraction, especially to the young. Risks and physical danger may be an added attraction. (Jamieson, 2001, p. 385) conflict and a challenge to democracy. Its structure is reactive to illegal market conditions, the mechanisms of globalization, and the accessibility of corrupt authorities.

HOW MOTIVES OF TRANSNATIONAL CRIME ORGANIZATIONS DIFFER FROM TERRORISTS

Organized-crime groups are traditionally politically conservative. Rather than aiming to destabilize a political system, criminals try to profit off it. Therefore, while terrorists seek the destruction of the state, criminals have a vested interest in the state's survival even while it challenges their authority. Organized crime, typically, has long-term financial interests, and in order to allow their parasitic relationship to thrive, a functioning host is crucial. In the past and in many emerging and transitioning states, organized criminals are established members of the elite. They use state institutions and structures to manipulate the system, rather than bring it down. Along the path to power and pelf is a simple axiom: "Whereas violence eliminates an adversary, corruption creates an accomplice whose utility continues over time" (Jamieson, 2001, p. 380). Crime organizations, such as the Japanese yakuza and the American Cosa Nostra, have a disposition toward strong loyalty to the state.

On the other hand, terrorists have no such concern or claim. Historically, and as mentioned above, terrorists challenged the authority of the state and often sought its overthrow. Terrorism worked against the very institutions and structures that were the apparatus of functioning economies and pluralistic governance. Their limited horizons, either economic or political, put them outside any prospect for legal inclusion in or illegal collusion with the greater society (Jarmon, 2014).

As a result of their different worldviews, there have been basic differences in the respective **modi operandi**. Crime concerns itself with wealth accumulation, whereas terrorists are more concerned with funds disbursement. Organized criminals follow the same accounting and management systems as do legitimate businesses. Profit and accumulation are the reasons for their existence,

COMPARATIVE PERSPECTIVES

Crime Versus Terrorism

Longstanding transnational crime groups and their more recently formed counterparts have a very different relationship to the state and to terrorism. The older crime groups, often in long-established states, have developed along with their states and are dependent on existing institutional and financial structures to move their products and invest their profits. With the exception of Colombia, rarely do large established crime organizations link with terrorist groups, because their long-term financial interests require the preservation of state structures. Through corruption and movement into the lawful economy, these groups minimize the risk of prosecution and therefore do not fear the power of state institutions. (Shelley, 2005, p. 101)

BOX 4.3

and therefore, money laundering for the criminal is more an important core business process than it is for the traditional terrorist. Furthermore, terrorists have the additional revenue source of donations from sympathizers and sponsoring states. In some cases, these contributions are not only substantial but also legitimate. An example of such revenue streams is the Irish Northern Aid Committee for support of the Irish Republican Army. The Palestine Liberation Organization imposes a 5% tax on Palestinians living abroad and **diaspora** communities of Albanians contributed 3% of earnings to the Kosovo Liberation Army before its official disbandment in the late 1990s (UNODC, 2004, p. 33). In the past, terrorists have tread a narrow line, assuring their sympathizers their donations support causes and not crimes.

Another way criminals differed from terrorists was in their avoidance of attention. Although the accounts of flamboyant mob bosses basking in notoriety and thriving amid media attention is rich in lore, in reality, criminals prefer their operations to be as invisible as possible. Any activity that would draw the attraction of authorities could undermine the organization. On the other hand, terrorists aspire to create public panic in order to bring attention to their cause. The same tactic for the criminal yields few benefits. The Sicilian **Mafia**, in 1993, hoped to intimidate public opinion against the Italian Parliament's anti-Mafia agenda. A plan to car bomb the Uffizi Galleries in Florence failed, and the motives behind the plot, once revealed, created a backlash in the press and on the street. Forcing political change through violence and public hysteria is not a common practice of crime, which relies on a functioning economy and a passive public in order to corrupt, plunder, and prosper.

However, despite the differences of the past, the new era of competition and technology have linked crime and terror with a revised pragmatism. Terrorism once tended to be parochial. Today, globalization has opened borders and spurred mass migration flows. Groups take their identities, cultures, prejudices, and visions of the world with them. The foreign communities they establish reflect these collective perspectives and become recruiting grounds and sources of funding. Hence, terrorist cells become international as the global system opens up and creates new opportunities. As state regulations wither away and technology overwhelms territorial borders and old protocols, mergers occur, and alliances form between legal, illegal, and—sometimes— terrorist business partners. Crime can be another way of exacting vengeance over a perceived injustice. In frequent cases, these joint ventures include a combination of crime and terrorism, particularly when the establishment is a target.

SIMILARITIES BETWEEN TRANSNATIONAL CRIME ORGANIZATIONS AND INTERNATIONAL TERRORISM WITH RESPECT TO MODI OPERANDI

Regardless whether they seek to destroy or corrupt and loot, terrorists and criminals have the same opponent: the state. Law enforcement agencies are the natural enemies of both groups. In order to survive, they often resort to the same methods and infrastructure of networks. Murder, smuggling, counterfeiting, money laundering, and intimidation tactics are common enterprises familiar to both. Terrorists often need funding and resources. Criminals, despite their conservative political tendencies in stable societies, often benefit from political instability in frail states. Crime satisfies both needs while also filling societal voids through black-market operations, protection rackets, and even social services. These opportunities often offer moments and terrains of intersection for crime and terror to merge and collude. When these intersections occur a **crime–terrorist nexus** forms to create a security challenge with little previously history. The merging of criminal and political violence is a relatively new variant that signals a departure from traditional patterns of criminology.

Generally, the loci for interaction between crime and terrorism are mutually convenient and advantageous. Neighborhoods, penal institutions, conflict zones, and **failed states** are naturally shared spaces (Shelley, 2005). In areas where there is a low regard for the state, institutions, or the elite class, there exist favorable circumstances and impetuses for both criminals and terrorists to connect and form contracts. The interactions result in professional and personal familiarity and the development of expertise. The consequence is a denser and more complex web of illegal operations, arrangements, and—perhaps—longer term plans. The overhanging threat to legitimate society is a mutant criminal infrastructure bearing far less resemblance to the paradigm of the past era. Unlike the Italian Mafia, the Japanese yakuza, Chinese triads, and much of Russian organized crime, which are **hierarchical organizations**, the current structures are loose, flexible networks of affiliates who are rootless and thrive on the ability to become invisible. "Organized crime

Table 4.2 Comparative Perspective: Crime Versus Terrorism

Crime	Terrorism
Opposes the state as a rival for power and wealth	Opposes the state to seek its overthrow
Benefits from frail economic and political conditions	Benefits from frail economic and political conditions
Recruits and exploits similar populations as terrorists	Recruits and exploits similar populations as TOC
Politically conservative	Politically radical
Has long-term time horizons	Has short-term time horizons
Seeks only wealth accumulation	Concerned with wealth distribution
Prefers anonymity	Openly assumes responsibility for its crimes
Uses diaspora and foreign ethnic communities for cover and exploitation	Uses diaspora and foreign ethnic communities for cover and exploitation
Globalization has forced their organizations to be less pyramidal and more horizontally structured	Globalization has forced their organizations to be less pyramidal and more horizontally structured
Relies upon criminal activity for financial support	Relies upon crime, state sponsorship, and private donations as sources for financial support

researchers often stress how few classical, large-scale pyramidal or bureaucratically organized groups still exist in today's underworld" (Bovenkerk & Chakra, 2004, p. 7), claims a 2004 United Nations report. Meanwhile, law enforcement struggles to reorient to the changing landscape, which is encumbered by old protocols and obsolete legal codes. Furthermore, security and law enforcement agencies are most comfortable working against an adversary whose organizational structure mirrors their own. Sadly, for traditional practitioners, this model is disappearing.

Despite the fact that transnational crime and international terrorism appear to be on opposite sides of the political aisle and motivated by different ambitions, they often collaborate under the right circumstances. Those situations usually involve drug and human trafficking. Examples of cooperation include the ultranationalist Grey Wolves of Turkey and the Kurdish Workers' Party. In Lebanon, Christians, Shiites, Sunnis, and Druze were partners in the drug trade as well. South America has been the site of joint ventures between Hezbollah and Chinese criminal gangs, who partnered to exploit the underground market in consumer goods, arms, and pirated software. The conclusion that may be drawn is that terrorism and transnational crime easily meld under the lure of power and wealth. Operationally, they use the same modes whether acting in collaboration or when conducting separate activities.

HOW TRANSNATIONAL CRIME EXPLOITS THE MECHANISMS OF GLOBALIZATION AND TECHNOLOGY IN SIMILAR WAYS AS LEGITIMATE ACTORS

TOC benefits from globalization and technology much the way global businesses do. Access to technological innovation and the formation of global goods and financial markets have offered opportunities to criminal organizations. Exploiting markets, taking advantage of capital and exchange-rate spreads, and moving funds and personnel are not limited to the world of licit business. Transnational crime groups can find sources of lucre, move their assets, and mobilize forces, associates, and sympathizers. They can also form alliances with strategic partners.

In many cases, the interdependencies among criminal groups assist in expanding markets and taking advantage of local conditions, such as labor pools and legal or regulatory loopholes. As with transnational corporations, TOC inherits efficiencies through linkages with foreign groups. Trained personnel, tested trafficking routes, developed corruption networks, and existing contacts for distribution or administration are already in place. There are many examples of Russian organized crime working with Colombian drug cartels to open markets in Eastern Europe. Money laundering, drug trafficking, and smuggling are attractive enterprises for Chinese triads, Mexican crime groups, and the Russian Mafia operating in the United States and Canada. As with legitimate businesses, they cooperate under joint-venture arrangements or subcontract agreements. When market conditions no longer serve the purposes of these accords, they cease cooperation and compete against one another using the same methods and mechanisms.

According to a 1998 report by the European Institute for Crime Prevention and Control, interdependencies between foreign crime groups are a way for them to respond to transforming markets and legal or regulatory change. The report goes on to say, "The concept of interdependencies among crimes and activities . . . is a useful theoretical tool in understanding how organized crime has altered its modes of operation and therefore in improving control strategies" (Adamoli, Di Nicola, Savona, & Zoffi, 1998, p. 8).

International businesses recruit and operate worldwide. Wherever there are local laws promoting investment or offering tax havens, transnational corporations will seek them out. In much the same way, TOC takes advantage of corruptible states and officials, frail legal and security infrastructures, consumers of products, and employment opportunities. Diasporas and local affiliates offer channels and cover for illicit activity. Transnational crime and transnational corporations take advantage of discrepancies between legal jurisdictions. Crimes and enforcement are not standard in all states; neither are regulations. As the chain of offenses expands, foreign criminal groups can form joint ventures and increase their market share. At later points in time, they may dissever and become competitors. In the meantime, they have the ability to shift from one activity (or product line) to another and add or pull back from markets, depending upon the atmosphere of risk and reward.

Neoliberal economic policies have specifically provided transnational crime with broader horizons of opportunity. The deregulation of markets and the privatization of formerly public services and holdings have offered up "more spaces for illegal activity including those that involve financial and capital instruments" (Mittelman, 2000, p. 213). The liberalizing of trade has also liberalized interpretation of what is legal and what is not. Several years ago, bribery was not only considered a cost of doing business, it was tax deductible in some European countries. It was not until an OECD treaty went into effect that certain "side payments" lost their tax status (Mittelman, 2000, p. 213). TOC pays bribes as well but without the tax benefits. In either case, the taxpayer is the ultimate victim. The taxpayer is burdened by the loss of state revenues and the increased security cost at one end and, at the other end, as government resources are diverted from public services to supporting security regimes. Another example is the dismantling of U.S. usury laws, which allowed financial institutions to charge much higher interest rates on credit cards. Their cost, previously outlawed, sometimes rivaled loan-sharking rates. In the late 1970s, those rates became comparable, although the consequences of missing payments were quite dissimilar.

As the economy becomes more politicized, it becomes less democratic. The lack of accountability in the market has translated to an uneven distribution of wealth and growth in top income. It has marginalized populations and made them ripe for exploitation as labor sources and consumers who are desperate for basic services. The global economy has also created industries that only crime can service and supply. The mass migration phenomenon is an opportunity for human trafficking. The lowering of state barriers, the complexity of corrupt officials, and the tectonic impact of technology facilitate the "sector's" growth.

James Mittelman (2000) writes, "What drives organized crime groups increasingly are efforts to exploit the growth mechanisms of globalization" (p. 208). Therefore, TOC (and many terrorist entrepreneurs) does not confine activity to the familiar crimes such as illegal arms, narcotics, kidnapping, extortion, fraud, murder for hire, and so forth. Their body of work includes imputing "taxes" for security, regional safe havens, and use of trafficking routes (Rollins, Wyler, & Rosen, 2010, p. 8). They also collect licensing fees from associate groups and enter into partnerships in order to compete in vertical crime markets (Mittelman, 2000, p. 213). Many organized-crime groups even understand the concept of good corporate citizenship. The Russian Mafia and Colombian drug cartels are noted for establishing charities, maintaining schools and hospitals, and providing public services.

In summary, the deregulation of the economy has imposed the discipline of the market on many spheres of activity. However, the market is not perfect and its "invisible hand" does not move flawlessly and seamlessly, smoothing over areas of disruption where entry and access to information are on a level playing field. In many places and instances, it is influenced by the lack of political accountability, the privatization of formerly public functions, the "tyranny" of credit-rating agencies, and the constant pressure from rent seekers. In many parts of the world, criminals, corrupt government officials, and the elite form a web of collusion to take advantage of a vast global marketplace that lacks governance. Whether illicit or legal, both groups follow the logic of the global economy. Using the same mechanisms, legitimate and criminal actors maximize profits, reduce risks, and align products with market demand. They achieve their goals with relative ease, and often, the legality and ethical merit of their practices are indistinguishable.

TRANSNATIONAL CRIME GROUPS AND THE POTENCY OF THEIR THREAT

Transnational crime is not novel to the post–Cold War era. Its history dates back centuries to the "emergence of transoceanic commerce and the restrictions on mercantilist restrictions" (Andreas, 2003a, p. 21). Many early American fortunes were made thanks to smuggling during the colonial period. The East India Company's opium trade was supported by the might of the British military. Napoleon recruited British smugglers to assist against the English blockade attempts. More recently, the Soviet Union required an underground economy to relieve the pressures of a dysfunctional command market plagued by product shortages and an underdeveloped service sector. What changed over time are methods, laws, the nature of the complicity of states, and the public's varying tolerance or demand for the products and services transnational crime can provide.

The asymmetrical structure of the conflict between legitimate and criminal forces is also a departure from the past. The rapid pace of scientific advancement and the unpredictability of a disruptive technological breakthrough were not factors in eras past. In the present environment, disruptive technologies can appear at any moment, and despite the advantage of state-funded programs, individual actors may be beneficiaries of the next bleeding-edge technology. The commoditization of precursor materials for small-scale nuclear arms, biochemical weapons, and radiological devices is another element of the threat matrix. Also, information and expertise are as accessible as *matériel*. A small group with limited financial resources can become a peer force under the right circumstances and confluence of events, timing, expertise, and personnel. A *Washington Post* article from 2004 claimed there exists a sophisticated black market in "weapons designs, real-time technical advice, and thousands of sensitive parts" (Warrick & Slevin, 2004, p. A1). The authors of the piece also reported that much of this equipment may have been manufactured at secret factories. In the context of the new security paradigm, asymmetric threats become nonasymmetric.

Ideas, goods, and funds exchange at an unprecedented pace owing to the revolutions in transportation and information and communication technology. Moreover, thanks to the hyper-connections of the global system, so can panic. Markets crash on one exchange and the reverberation is felt around the world. Instability can move with the same speed as malware might over the Internet. Like many technologically dependent environments, systems and structures can be fragile. Political parties and careers can fall as a result of a single event. The 2004 Madrid bombings had only a relatively slight and temporary economic impact. However, they forced the ouster of the government in the following elections and a change in foreign policy, which eventually led to the withdrawal of Spain's support for Operation Iraqi Freedom. The 2008 financial crises affected the U.S. presidential elections and pushed the political stability in Western Europe into turmoil. These incidents demonstrate the butterfly effect on politics and public opinion that events of all dimensions can have in a hyper-connected world.

In many instances, when the objective is chaos and there is a breakdown of law and order, outlaw elements can succeed and prosper. Whether by chance or intent, the system is subject to these events and outcomes. A small or seemingly insignificant group can tip the balance from relative stability to uproar. However, transnational crime, as with transnational corporations, eventually prefers stability to operate. Chaos may provide an initial opportunity, but enterprises mature and expand under conditions of certainty. In narco-states (usually substate jurisdictions rather than sovereign entities), governments are either directly involved or simply paid to not interfere with trade. These territories give crime all the legitimacy it needs. TOC can eventually become part of the economic infrastructure and nearly impossible to dislodge. As with legitimate actors, it also seeks to expand its market based upon the risk and return.

Today's transnational crime environment reflects these trends. Narcotics trafficking is still a staple of organized crime. The market for illegal drugs is sturdy and growing. However, because criminal organizations are also influenced by opportunity–risk ratios, their activity diversifies with changing environments that globalization and technology invite. Harsher laws and sentencing for illegal drugs offenses have persuaded many groups to consider and invest in computer and economic crime (Adamoli et al., 1998, p. 24). The volume of transactions over the electronic financial network, which spans multiple jurisdictions and institutions, makes tracking funds sometimes impossible. This is despite the technological improvements and success in instituting transparency reforms. The territory of cyberspace, for the same basic reasons, is a fertile field for fraud and intellectual-property theft.

The mass migration of people from economically depressed areas across borders toward urban centers creates a rich opportunity for international smugglers. Ecological crimes, such as illegal dumping of hazardous materials and poaching of endangered species, are also very lucrative. The new panoply of opportunity forces transnational crime to become more specialized, decentralized, and flexible as it evolves into new markets and expands its scope.

Russian Organized Crime

Russian organized crime most likely evolved from the prerevolutionary criminal *arteli*. However, the earliest records of organized crime emerge in the 1920s and 1930s from gulag accounts. Known as *vorovskoi mir* (thieves world), Russian organized crime existed alongside legitimate society regardless of ideology, political regime, or war. The Russian word *vori* (thieves) was

Table 4.3 Prominent Transnational Organized-Crime Groups

Organization	Major Subgroups	Activity
Russian organized crime	Solntsevskaya Bratva Tambov gang	Known to operate in nearly 60 countries. Many operations and personnel originally funded by the KGB. Russian organized crime is a broad merger of criminals, thugs, government officials, and members of elite society. Activities are vast and reach is almost boundless.
Italian Mafia	Cosa Nostra Camorra 'Ndrangheta Sacra Corona Unita	Known as the Italian or Italian-American Mafia. The most prominent organized-crime group in the world from the 1920s to the 1990s. They have been involved in violence, arson, loan sharking, gambling, drug trafficking, fraud, and political and judicial corruption.
Japanese yakuza	Yamaguchi-gumi Inagawa-kai Smiyoshi-kai	Involved in multinational criminal activities, with a reputed membership of nearly 85,000 associates worldwide. Yakuza have been particularly adept in the area of official corruption and their influence on Japanese domestic politics is considerable.
Chinese triads	Kung Lok 14K Sun Yee On United Bambo Wo Hop To Big Circle Boys Wo Shing Wo Butterfly Gang Kokang	Loosely connected and lacking a central hierarchical command structure, triads accompanied the Chinese diaspora. Today, they control secret markets and are involved in money laundering and drug trafficking. Their association with official corruption is well documented within the PRC and abroad. Their operations are global.

Organization	Activity
Chinese Fuk Ching	Chinese organized criminal group in the United States. They have been involved in smuggling, street violence, and human trafficking.
Taiwanese Heijin	Taiwanese gangsters who are often executives in large corporations. They are often involved in white-collar crimes, such as illegal stock trading and bribery, and sometimes run for public office.
Thailand Chao Pho	Organized-crime group in Thailand. They are often involved in illegal political and business activity.
Thailand Red Wa	Gangsters from Thailand. They are involved in manufacturing and trafficking methamphetamine.

Organization	Activity
Jamaican posses	Instrumental in bringing the cocaine trade out of South America and into North America
Peruvian Shining Path (Sendaro Luminoso)	South American terrorist group that protects drug traffickers and conducts negotiations with growers for financing more terrorism
Revolutionary Armed Forces of Colombia (FARC)	While it continues to claim it is a political organization, its interests are increasingly economic. Beyond its borders, FARC formed trafficking networks with Mexican and Caribbean crime organizations. In 2000, revenues from illicit narcotics equaled $500 million annually.
Irish Republican Army	Counterfeiting, smuggling, extortion, and simple robbery have been the new trade of the IRA since the fade of their traditional forms of financing.
Hells Angels	Allies with South American drug cartels to transport cocaine. Reports claim the group operates a fleet of cargo ships, is technologically proficient, and holds Swiss bank accounts as well as major real estate investments.
Turkish Babas	Forms linkages with the Iranian Mafia to bring narcotics out of Afghanistan and transport supplies through Turkey into Europe.
Iranian Mafia	Major participant in the drug trade in Central Asia. They network with the large Iranian immigrant community in Turkey to facilitate narcotics trafficking.
Kurdish Workers Party (PPK)	Operates similarly to Turkish Babas but are also a terrorist group that resorts to suicide bombings. They have been accused of forcing women into service by holding their children as hostages and security.

Sources: Data compiled from Adamoli et al. (1998) and National Institute of Justice (2007).

more than a term for simple criminals. *Vori* referred to an entire world with its own dress, language, code of behavior, and rudimentary court system (Varese, 2001, pp. 146–147). The gulag prison system was its homeland, where extended terms were required for membership into its brotherhood. It was a fraternity that lived by strict, self-regulating rules and demanded tests of commitment to its set of laws. Steve Handelman, in his 1995 work, *Comrade Criminal*, writes, "No tradition was more compelling than the underworld code" (p. 32). Today, Russian organized crime is less hierarchical, and its operations and membership are vaster. Its infiltration of government, business, and political life is deep. Its structure is more fluid. As a result of globalization, crime is a major Russian export.

Its rigid control system began to show signs of future unraveling during the 1940s. Rifts erupted during World War II between those members who supported the "Great Patriotic War" and traditionalists who felt any allegiance to an authority other than the *vorovskoi mir* code was sacrilege. Gradually, the traditionalists faded into the background. The official numbers of *vori* in the 1950s and their strict traditions were becoming faint, but overall numbers increased during the 1960s and '70s (Handelman, 1995, pp. 167–169). The stagnating Soviet economy was the reason for its revival. Systemic bottlenecks and the burden of the Cold War arms race strained the economy. The massive industrial-based economy was trying to function without a competent service sector. It was constricting and losing ground to its rivals in the West. The sclerotic Soviet administrative system, therefore, had to rely on *tolchkatki* (literally, pushers or brokers) and *vori* services to grease and add support to an apparatus that its economy had outgrown (Jarmon, 2014). Many experts agree that the Russian Mafia took shape and formed its present bonds with government and the state bureaucracy during this period of economic frustration and unmet expectations (Finckenauer & Voronin, 2001, p. 6). The interconnection of the administrative system with the underground economy developed more deeply and robustly from the 1980s to the 1990s. As the communist era faded, the new political environment opened up new commercial opportunities. Yet it also created the current composition and machinery of Russian organized crime. New "Russian businessmen" appeared. They used connections and former positions to control financial institutions, resources, and previously government-owned enterprises to dominate regional economies. Their ambitions and networks soon extended beyond their origins and Russia's borders. Ethnic crime syndicates, such as Chechens, also became prominent entrants in the criminal market.

The most powerful Russian organized-crime groups draw their influence from the ranks of the old Soviet **nomenklatura**. The Communist Party elites, which dominated the center of political life in the USSR., continued to hold sway after the fall of the Soviet Union. Known simply as the *nomenklatura*, their numbers approximated 1.5 million. Throughout the period of communist domination, it freely looted its own state. The only restraint on its authority was an internal system of punishment and reward. Georgi Arbatov, an official of the Central Committee and himself a former member, wrote about the reality of the *nomenklatura's* place within this "classless society."

> [It was] organically connected with corruption. . . . an enormous and parasitic apparat [that] gives or takes away, permits or prohibits, takes care of everything, can fire anybody, demote anybody, often even throw him in prison or, on the contrary, raise him up. (quoted in Handelman, 1995, p. 98)

During the Cold War, the Soviet Union financed clandestine operations around the world. Through the same conveyance network, these assets were often siphoned into private offshore accounts of the *nomenklatura* elite. KGB channels into terrorists groups, foreign communist organizations, and commercial covers underwrote these operations. They also helped support party member lifestyles.

By the latter half of the 20th century, the Union of Soviet Socialist Republics could no longer support the corruption and inefficiency of the system it built and tried to export. Its collapse created a vacuum of legal codes and security structures. The state was bankrupt. In order to support itself, the military sold excursions in tanks to foreign visitors and office parties. Moscow police relied on passing motorists to patrol the city due to a lack of official police vehicles in operating condition. The collapse set loose a massive economic and political shockwave. During the Yeltsin administration, the country defaulted on its debt. However, once the ruble stabilized, the *nomenklatura* stood in position to take advantage of the new order. Until the current unrest with its neighbor, capital flight remained at a rate of 6 billion USD per month. Reinvestment is risky and lacks incentive. Yet modest growth persisted, mostly driven by revenues from the energy sector. Since Russia's incursion into Ukraine, however, the economy has seriously faltered. Capital flight has increased precipitously and the economy anticipates a period of contraction.

With the breakup of the Soviet Union, communism had given way to crony capitalism. Many post-Soviet "businessmen" expropriated key industries and the embryonic banking sectors (Finckenauer, 2007, p. 20). Using the connections with associates abroad and its relationships with the *vori, nomenklatura* capitalists became exporters of strategic raw materials, international investors, real estate developers, money launderers, arms dealers, extortionists, and illegitimate owners of legitimate businesses. Corrupt officials in the Russian army returning from missions in Central Asia reportedly provided supply vehicles for use as transports for illegal narcotics (Handelman, 1995).

Crime commercialized with the aid of police and official collusion. Its penetration into legitimate commerce gives it a unique feature: It is more difficult to dislodge and more problematical to contain. The Russian word **krysha** (roof) became a term for protection. "Protection services" are a core business operation for Russian organized crime and a source of revenue for what has become known as the *police mafia*. The early failures of promising democratic institutions in Russia provided a void that crime was eager to fill. Criminal organizations established order in return for protection money. In addition to exacting fees, they sometimes also took over public services normally under the purview of the government. Citizens in some areas relied upon the local crime syndicates to provide funding for schools, hospital repairs, and charities (Handelman, 1995, p. 24).

According to Finckenauer and Voronin (2001), organized crime in Russia even attempts to take a share of monopolies normally reserved for the state. The regulation of business markets, territorial districting, taxation (protection fees), and tariffs are a few of the areas contested. Hence, the weakened rule of law has created the surge in privatized forms of violence. As a result of this relationship, which was formed during the transition from a command economy to a demand economy, "organized crime in Russia evolved to its present ambiguous position of being both in direct collaboration with the state and, at the same time, in conflict with it" (p. 5).

ROC's access to the warehouse of Russia's wealth of raw and strategic materials makes for a particularly ominous threat. Groups act opportunistically and no longer operate under the strict control structures of their antecedents or the current Japanese yakuza and Italian-American Cosa Nostra. It has broken away from its highly structured command-and-control organizational model toward a more horizontal configuration. Keeping it in check are internecine competition and no apparent central command with any grand strategy or objective. It is mostly a fluid arrangement of "entrepreneurial spirits" acting in their economic self-interest. Today, ROC is multiethnic. Its members are cosmopolitan and often educated in the West. They are second-generation elites and have effective, operational connections into the Russian banking system and energy sector (Galeotti, 2012, p. 4). Its rise is part of the "new Russia" that emerged from the disintegration of the Soviet Union. Whether the initial entrants into the illicit markets operate legitimate businesses or criminal ones, it is clear that Russian transnational crime forms part of the DNA of Russia's current economic and political apparatus. The global impact on transnational crime and implications for interstate relations are significant.

COMPARATIVE PERSPECTIVES

BOX 4.4

Russian Organized Crime Versus the Rise of Traditional Crime Groups

During the privatization period, new businesses and reconstituted government agencies staked out areas of the criminal market. Official corruption within the organs of government is simply a way of doing business. Beyond Russia's borders, it is yet another fact of life. Globalization has facilitated the growth in scope and the extent of the reach of Russian organized crime. The intertwinement of elite society and crime in Russia has produced a global threat. Few places in the world are endowed with such a bounty of resources and opportunities for plunder. The ambitions and reach of Russian organized crime cannot be confined to its borders.

In the decade since the collapse of the Soviet Union, the world has become the target of a new global crime threat from criminal organizations and criminal activities that have poured forth from over the borders of Russia and other former Soviet republics such as the Ukraine. The nature and variety of the crimes being committed seems unlimited—drugs, arms trafficking, stolen automobiles, trafficking in women and children, and money laundering are among the most prevalent. The spillover is particularly troubling to Europe (and especially Eastern Europe) because of its geological proximity to Russia, and to Israel, because of its large numbers of Russian immigrants. But no area of the world seems immune to this menace, especially not the United States. (Finckenauer & Voronin, 2001, p. 1)

Italian Mafia

There are parallels between the Italian Mafia and Russian organized crime. The most salient are the similarities of their beginnings. The voids in governance and a weak legal apparatus provided the vacuum for extrastate organizations to fill. As with Russia after the collapse of the Soviet Union, mid-19th-century Sicily (the birthplace of the Mafia) lacked a middle class and a developed civil society (Shelley, 1994, p. 666). Italy was transitioning out of a feudal economic system and experiencing the same societal traumas as Russia did during its transition from socialism. The disintegration of the economic machinery left a crisis of authority in both instances. Organized criminality may have plundered and exploited the situation it found for itself, but it also provided a public service. When the state could no longer exert its power or provide functioning institutions, crime intervened. The Mafia supplied commerce with protection, organized markets, and a functioning legal code. As these extrastate institutions become more efficient, the legal authorities find it more difficult to dislodge and replace them.

The origins of the term *Mafia* may even echo these themes. The meaning of the word is not easily traceable. However, a widely accepted interpretation of *Mafia* refers to an organization, individual, or state of mind that "can get things done" (Ianni & Reuss-Ianni, 1972, p. 25). Because of the uneven transition to a market economy in the 19th century, southern Italy's demand for any system where property rights and some administrative or financial codes of practice was irresistible. The availability of disbanded personal protection units (known as *bravi*), discharged army personnel, and bandits brought together the elements and conditions for the rise of the Mafia (Varese, 2001, p. 258). In other words, it became an organization the public can trust "to get things done" when state authorities seem ill-equipped to provide protection for property rights as ownership spreads and the velocity of commercial transactions increase.

A formalized Mafia does not exist. Rather, a coalition of families (*cosche*) called Cosa Nostra ("our thing") in Sicily, and 'Ndrangheta (loosely derived from the Greek word for heroism) in southern Italy, dominate, operationally and historically, the criminal culture. Similar groups include the Camorra and the Sacra Corona Unita, who are associated with the area around Naples. All are hierarchically structured and demand from members loyalty, solidarity, and a readiness to engage in violence. At the core of their society is **omerta**—the code of silence. In brief, *omerta* emphasizes noncooperation with authorities.

Its role in the development of the Italian state has been significant since its earlier founding during the transition period toward democratic reforms and development. From the time of its beginnings and through today, the mafia has become institutionalized in Italy. Its holdings are primarily in tourism and construction. However, its control over Italy's economy is a national issue. The proceeds from the narcotics trade have allowed it deeper access into legitimate economic activity (Shelley, 1994, p. 662). The pragmatism and tarnish of the earlier period survive today. The effects run deep and thrive where conditions bid opportunity. In the mid-1990s, Louise Shelley (1994) wrote,

> Organized crime while now an issue in national politics affects many more aspects of the society. A central element of the economic life, particularly in the southern region of the country, its economic power now extends beyond its traditional territories. (p. 663)

Between 1815 and 1870, the side effect of the revolutionary movement in Italy was the emergence of the mafia. Its expansion endured through the 20th century and reached into North America. By the turn of the century, and in the decades prior to World War I, nearly two million immigrants entered the United States from Sicily and southern Italy and existed in city slums where they mingled and competed with other street and criminal ethnic gangs (Mastrobuoni & Patacchini, 2010). Following World War I, they were joined by a second wave of immigration from Italy as Fascist prosecutions made life difficult and the lure of opportunity in America provided enticement.

In the years following World War I, Cosa Nostra influence grew, mostly under its "boss of bosses" Lucky Luciano. Although convicted for murder in 1936, he served only 10 years of a 30- to 50-year sentence. His cooperation in the war effort during the allied invasion of Sicily resulted in a commuted sentence and deportation to Italy. By the late 1950s, the Cosa Nostra power was waning. The raid on 60 underworld bosses in upstate New York in 1957 drew public attention and led to investigation proceedings in Washington. The U.S. Senate's McClellan Committee, in 1957, studied the extent of organized crime in America. In 1963, a former Cosa Nostra member turned government informer, Joe Vallachi, provided details on the activity and organizational structure of organized crime. His testimony before a congressional committee identified 25 families with an estimate of 5,000 Cosa Nostra members (Mastrobuoni & Patacchini, 2010, pp. 9–10).

In both Italy and North America, the Italian Mafia never achieved the same comparative level of influence as its criminal counterparts in Russia, Japan, China, and South America. One reason is its strict recruitment requirements. Membership is limited to descendents of Mafia family members and men born in either Sicily or Calabria. Therefore, they lack the experienced manpower required to compete in emerging black markets. Hampered by law enforcement investigations and competitive losses to Mexican, Chinese, Russian, and other emerging crime groups, the power of the Italian Mafia in the United States has been in decline. However, its descent has been more than offset by the rise of criminal networks from other parts of the world.

Japanese Yakuza

Despite the translation of its name, "born to lose" (the literal meaning is 9, 8, 3—a losing hand in a popular card game), yakuza ties with Japan's political elite are long-standing and have proven quite profitable. Its modern beginnings date to the close of World War II. However, the yakuza's link to samurai traditions following Japan's civil war is a connection to the country's past. In the 18th century, they organized into "families" for mutual protection. Although these connections were not based on bloodline, the kinships ran deep, and bonds were unshakable. By the 19th century, yakuza were becoming politically active. Groups sought the cooperation of government officials as their interests became more criminal, particularly in the area of gambling.

As Japan rose from the ashes of World War II, the yakuza emerged as a player and shaper of the inner workings of Japanese politics. The surrender of Japan in 1945 and the start of reconstruction coincided with the precipitous rise in yakuza membership. Estimates were as high as 184,000 during the early 1960s. Today most estimates place their numbers around 85,000. They became not only power brokers in Japanese politics but also king makers. The center-right Liberal Democratic Party (LDP) formed during this time and, until relatively recently, prevailed with the backing of the yakuza. Yet despite the shared history between the LDP and the yakuza, the arrangement is not a case of mere political tropism. As public policy shifts in its tolerance of crime and corruption so does the backing of the yakuza and, as a consequence, the fortunes of politicians. The yakuza will switch party affiliations and even handpick candidates when political practicality dictates.

In 2007, the yakuza turned away from the party it had supported for decades. The LDP lost its backing when yakuza leadership determined that the party was leading the effort to crackdown on their illicit gambling and sex trade operations. The Yamaguchi-gumi and the Inagawa-kai, two of the largest yakuza organized-crime groups, cut their support of previous political allies in favor of the major opposition party: the Democratic Party of Japan (DPJ). The turn of events shook Japanese politics. Up until that time, the LDP dominated. The decision to trade alliances brought the DPJ into power, and in return, legislation to enact criminal-conspiracy laws (*kyobozai*) derailed. Jake Adelstein, a former reporter for Japan's largest paper, *Yomiuri Shinbum*, reports a source saying at the time, "We've worked out a deal with a high ranking member of the DPJ. We help them get elected and they keep the *kyobozai* off the books for a few years" (Adelstein, 2010). The right-wing LDP advanced and thrived in domestic politics as the yakuza expanded and worked its vast criminal network. Once the yakuza withdrew its support, the LDP was swept from office. Although the yakuza may not have been the sole reason for the change in government, most agree their influence was felt, and the shift in Japanese politics was unprecedented and on a grand level.

This vast, native mafia network not only insinuates itself politically but also is firmly entrenched in the mechanisms of the commercial infrastructure. Yakuza status in Japanese society is accepted and, at varying times, regarded as effectively legal. Their enterprises entwine with legitimate commerce. Politically conservative, they often display gang pins on their business suits and are self-described patriots.

> Until the 1990s, the yakuza were tolerated, even accepted in Japanese society as fraternal organizations, like Kiwanis clubs. They put their logos on office doors, held press conferences, and intimidated the general public with impunity. (Miller, 2002, p. 8)

Their organization was so well embedded that during the Kobe earthquake in 1995, yakuza relief response was quicker than the government's. Their recovery efforts may have also netted them as much as $24 billion, according to some accounts (Miller, 2002). The cooperation and corruption practices between the yakuza and the police are a fine line. The yakuza often assist in cases, and members have a history of admitting to crimes and turning themselves into authorities. In exchange for bribes, police drop charges or turn a blind eye to the groups' operations.

When it is not interfering in politics or involved in corruption, the yakuza engages in loan sharking, prostitution, corporate blackmail, drug production and trafficking, and illegal gambling. However, as new opportunities arise, they respond. When the global financial markets roared, the yakuza went all in. Due to their connections in government and industry, the yakuza found a comfortable and profitable niche in the securities and financial markets during the 1990s. Their infiltration was so entrenched that it posed a threat to the accountability and reputation of Japan's economy. Market manipulation became rampant to the point that, in order to preserve its standing, the Osaka Stock Exchange threatened to de-list as many as 50 companies accused of having direct ties to the yakuza.

More so than the Italian-American Mafia, the yakuza maintain close ties with the corporate community and national political life. Although their influence in politics is not as strong it was immediately after World War II, their stature in these circles is still considerable. Times have shifted for the yakuza and have forced changes. The hierarchic structure has come under pressure. Emerging rivalries have brought discord and a greater reliance on the use of violence. However, their tentacles into legitimate society are more basal than the connections their Italian-American Mafia counterparts enjoy. They are less involved in ordinary street crime or as susceptible to internecine violence. Their activities have brought them connections with South American drug cartels, the Sicilian Mafia, and the Chinese triads (Miller, 2002, p. 16). Their operations in Southeast Asia extend back to the 1970s. Their influence grows and corrupts. Their presence in the world of transnational crime is enduring.

Chinese Triads

The origin of triads is open to popular and scholarly debate. Most believe their beginnings spring from the 17th century, during the attempt to overthrow the Qing Dynasty. According to this view, monks and scholars organized these groups with political and patriotic objectives as their purpose (Lintner, 2004, p. 87; Miller, 2002, p. 8). Others trace the triads' starting date as far back as the 12th century. The exact dates and motivations for their appearance have become vague over time and by tradition. Not all triads evolved into criminal gangs. However, the ones who did currently command a significant share of international trade in contraband goods and property. Today, their impact is undeniable and their reach is global. Triad criminal gang activity spans the gamut of trafficking in illegal drugs, weapons, human beings, and endangered animals and plants. They are also adept in financial fraud, software piracy, high-tech theft, prostitution, and loan sharking.

More than their counterparts in the Cosa Nostra who value power and respect above the accumulation of wealth (Paoli, 2004, p. 23), triad members' motives are purely financial. Despite the importance of devotion and fealty to the organization, "the dollar is their only loyalty" (Curtis, Elan, Hudson, & Kollars, 2002, p. 20). In order to achieve their goals, members form and enter into loose confederations that offer affiliates autonomy and the option to engage in any activity or associate with any group that bring a profit (Berry, Curtis, Elan, Hudson, & Kollars, 2003, p. 3). Similar to the Japanese yakuza, high-ranking triad figures have established reputations as legitimate businessmen. Underscoring their looser organizational structure, the leadership usually function as mediators of disputes and sources of financing, rather than filling roles as operation managers. Even with the centuries of traditions, codes, hierarchal structure, and fixed rituals, triads and other Chinese criminal groups function with the flexibility to adjust to conditions of host countries where opportunity for profit exist and particularly where there are substantial ethnic Chinese populations (Berry et al., 2003). Their exploitation of Chinese communities through extortion and protection schemes is their usual entrée into other illegal markets. These opportunities increase as émigré communities continue to disperse and expand.

In China, as with many countries, secret societies have long been part of the tradition and history. As Chinese populations moved across the globe, triads took the form of political movements, labor associations, and aid organizations serving Chinese communities in unfriendly host countries, territories, and neighborhoods (Berry et al., 2003; Miller, 2002, p. 8). Criminal gangs, however, were a natural devolvement. Triads initially ingratiated themselves as protection and predatory forces of Chinese-owned businesses and ultimately became transnational crime organizations. As they established themselves, their experience and success with official corruption became rooted and well known within the PRC and with other governments.

The conclusion of the Cold War and the arrival of economic globalization unlocked China's hermetic society and opened the ruling Communist Party to opportunities for further exploitation and corruption. The easing of state control in China fostered an environment for free enterprise and corruption in much the same but limited way as it did in Russia. The word *baohusang*, or "protective umbrella," came to mean a government official who accepts bribes to provide cover and protection for criminals and their operations. The practice has a history. Mao Zedong reportedly maintained ties with criminal figures to help finance and achieve political goals (Miller, 2002, p. 7). Sun Yat-sen and Chiang Kai-shek also had underworld connections (Chin & Godson, 2006, p. 6). Deng Xiaoping, the father of China's economic reforms, declared in 1984 that "some of them [triad members] were good and patriotic" (Lintner, 2004, p. 90). During the reform period, the allure of a market economy proved so tempting that the government later altered its policy in the 1990s in order to curb the rampant crime it had inadvertently encouraged.

In the noninterventionist environment of global free trade and lax governance, the differences between crime and bureaucracy are often indistinct. Criminals and politicians frequently mingle and many times assume both roles. As many as 15 to 20 criminal triad gangs freely operate out of Hong Kong, the center of activity and the largest site in the world for cash transactions (Shelley, 2005, p. 60). Some reports claim that as many as one third of the politicians in Taiwan are gangsters (Jarmon, 2014). Illustrations of linkages between transnational crime and officialdom are well known.

One example occurred around 2000. Using his connections within the Communist Party of China (CPC), a businessman on the mainland went about setting plans to build a smuggling empire. Lai Changxing's operations included the trade of crude oil, cars, electronic equipment, rubber, appliances, and tobacco, and more. Unfortunately for him, his connections failed, and he was forced to escape conviction and sentencing by fleeing to Canada. Lai divulged to reporters that China had a network of spies in North America specifically placed to steal industrial and military secrets.

His assertions later proved factual. An operation named Sidewinder involved Chinese "businessmen," their criminal counterparts, and PRC intelligence agencies. Authorities accused the group of stealing software from Lucent Technologies in order to help create a joint venture with a Chinese data-network supplier. Developments such as these illustrate the potential that exists between crime and the state and how triads might enjoy an important, and perhaps elevated, place in the new order. They also demonstrate how in China, as in Russia and, to a degree, in Western countries, the relationship between the state and crime can be simultaneously supportive and in conflict.

Chinese triads are highly adaptive. They follow the ethnic track of Chinese populations throughout the world. Once established, they use their influence among these communities to launch other criminal activity, exploiting the general populations of their new surroundings. They often form temporary or lasting alliances with other ethnic crime organizations, depending upon the pragmatism of prevailing conditions. Triads and other Chinese crime organizations operate in either small or syndicated groups. They may frequently dissever upon the completion of a "project" only to re-form after a time to attempt other exploits, thus making detection difficult (Berry et al., 2003, p. 3). Triads exist in many forms, from the local gang to transnational networks. They are diversified and flexible structures, which often use the cover of legitimate business to secure their footing and impede the efforts of law enforcement agencies. They are also adept at exploiting the weaknesses in jurisdictional sovereignty and the inconsistencies in governance. They have been successful in the recruitment of public officials in many parts of the world. With the aid of official corruption, a global network of affiliates, and an ability to regulate its structure to adapt to changing conditions for crime, they have come to be considered one of the most serious threats to society by law enforcement authorities on every habitable continent.

Organized-Crime Groups and the Central Asian Drug Trade

The illicit narcotics trade has been a reliable source of income for criminals and self-financing terrorists worldwide. The plains of Central Asia and the jungles of South America are founts of the global drug trade. The revenues from heroin and cocaine amount to over $150 billion per year (see above).

The opium poppy plant was on course to surpass oil and natural gas deposits as the source of the most lucrative revenue in Central Asia. There seemed to be no limit to the supply and demand for illegal opiates. However, according to a 2014 United Nations study, the use of heroin and opium has appeared to level and stabilize at between 12.8 and 20.2 million users, globally (UNODC, 2014). The United Nations Office on Drug and Crime estimates that 6,883 T of opium flow annually into the world market, approximately 5,500 T of which (80% of global opium production) is produced exclusively from Afghan opium. The UNODC also estimates that from this flow, 560 T of heroin is produced and eventually winds its way along routes that extend globally (UNODC, 2014). As the heroin trade ceaselessly travels from its source into Europe and North America, it passes through a string of frail and fragile states. Political instability, rampant crime and corruption, and a weak security infrastructure assist the movement of narcotics and other contraband.

For populations on the edge or below the poverty line, narcotics trafficking offers economic relief. Where official salaries can be as low as $10 to $30 per month, the drug trade can be an irresistible force. The illegal industry is a magnet for organized crime, corruption, and locals forced to scratch out an existence in a harsh landscape. There are areas of Central Asia and the Trans-Caucasus region, where as much as 80% of the population engages in some form of trafficking (Falkenberg, 2013). Such factors as a common language, pervious borders, the social turmoil of regional conflicts, economic instability, and easy access to the source converge to facilitate trade (Curtis, 2002, pp. 8–9).

There are two primary heroin-trafficking routes, which connect Afghanistan to the enormous markets of Russia and Western Europe. The Balkan and northern routes account for a combined total of a $33 million drug market. The Balkan path snakes through Iran (often via Pakistan), Turkey, Greece, and Bulgaria across Southeast Europe and onward to Western Europe. It uses a combination of land and seaborne connections to move both opium and heroin. The northern route is mostly heroin. It passes mainly through Tajikistan and Kyrgyzstan (or Uzbekistan or Turkmenistan) to Kazakhstan and Russia.

A prime mover in the drug trade is the Albanian mafia. During the 1990s, the Albanian organized-crime groups controlled heroin-trafficking routes. Their primary accomplice was the Kosovo Liberation Army (KLA). Prior to the end of the Kosovo War, the KLA maintained links to former mujahideen fighters in Afghanistan. Through these connections, the narcotic trade helped finance weapons purchases and insurgency operations. Hostilities ended in 1999, and the KLA officially disbanded. However, linkages survived, including the connection with drug-trafficking and money-laundering operations (*The threat posed*, 2000). Many members of the KLA joined other armed groups or entered into politics. Balkan groups still controlled an important portion of the heroin trade in Europe. Criminal organizations from Turkey, Bulgaria, Romania, Italy, Greece, and Central Asia formed networks with their Balkan affiliates.

Their activities caused a leading official at INTERPOL to conclude,

> The Albanian Republic itself, is definitely a cause of concern to the international community, especially when one takes into account the geo-political instability in the region and . . . the links between drug trafficking and terrorism in Central Asia. (*The threat posed*, 2000, p. 44)

Personal connections formed in earlier years remain. Accusations are strong that opium cultivation and heroin production persist in the region. INTERPOL and other international organizations further claim the drug-running operation by the Albanian mafia "is one of the best in the world" (Rusche, 2006, p. 8). Of Kosovo's 2 million inhabitants, 98% are ethnic Albanians. The province's annual income in 2006 equaled a mere 50 million euros. However, some estimates maintain that income from illegal sources may have amounted to 400 million euros during the same time period (Rusche, 2006, p. 3). The 1:8 ratio of legal income to illegal proceeds suggests that a *drug state*, or what is sometimes referred to as the *Colombia syndrome*, is taking form. Its numbers, strategic location, and networks with other transnational criminal gangs make the Albanian mafia a major force in Southeast Europe. Among its strategic targets are not only the criminal markets but also the key spheres of politics and legitimate business.

The key organization of Albanian society is the clan. The same clan structure extends to the Albanian mafia, which is based on kinship that demands strict discipline of family members and

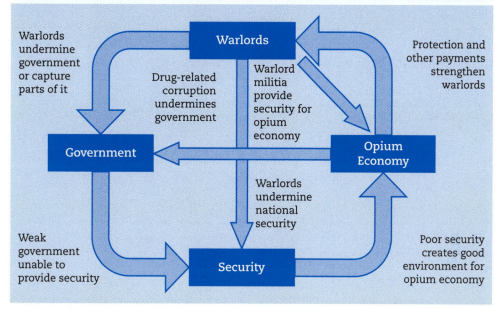

Figure 4.1 Narcotics and Security in Afghanistan

Warlords undermine government or capture parts of it

Drug-related corruption undermines government

Protection and other payments strengthen warlords

Warlord militia provide security for opium economy

Warlords undermine national security

Weak government unable to provide security

Poor security creates good environment for opium economy

Warlords

Government

Opium Economy

Security

Source: World Bank (2005, p. 120).

is a cloak of insulation from outsiders. The medieval code of *Leke Dukadjinija* prevails in society and over attempts to introduce international legal norms and provisions (Rusche, 2006, p. 5). *Leke Dukadjinija* requires vendetta and clan revenge against traitors and those who fail to honor contracts. The institution is binding and influences everyday life at all levels. Criminal activity and groups benefit from its code of loyalty and distrust and disdain for the foreigner. The adhesion *Leke Dukadjinija* brings to the group translates into collective devotion and resistance under siege. Along the Balkan route, a similar culture and safe haven for crime survives in Chechnya.

Chechnya is another prime example of organized crime flourishing in the societal wreckage of a failed state. The clan culture of the Albanians and the Chechens requires obligations of mutual defense in times of siege. Connections between organized crime and terrorism are seamless and often bound by kinship. Similar to Albanians, Chechens have established links with other foreign Muslims. However, in addition to these ties, they maintain a close bond with their diaspora in Europe, particularly in Russia. Within the criminal underground in Russia, their presence is significant, owing to an organizationally loose but socially cohesive network (Jarmon, 2010). Their access to high-ranking officials allowed Chechen gangs to capture a principal role in the Russian drug trade. They are one of the most active groups involved in narcotics trafficking in Central Asia, the Caucasus, and many regions within Russia (Curtis, 2002, p. 23). The proceeds from their illegal trade funds not only further criminal activity but also terrorist operations. The Chechen history of activity in the global narcotics trade complements the Albanian experience, thanks to the strategic advantages of geography, connections made through their networks, and a similar culture that relies on clannish solidarity and scorn for outsiders.

Map 4.2 Global Heroin Trade Routes

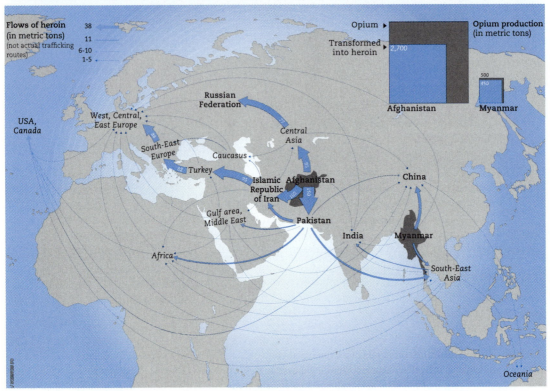

Source: U.N. Office on Drugs and Crime (2010b). From *World Drug Report 2010* by the United Nations Office on Drugs and Crime (UNODC). Copyright © 2010 United Nations. Used by permission of the United Nations.

Chechnya and Albania are at an intersection of drug traffic between Central Asia and Europe. However, in addition to drug trafficking, these organizations are also active in protection racketeering, extortion, kidnapping, auto theft, arms dealing, counterfeiting, bank fraud, and illegal trade in oil and precious metals. They have a well-earned reputation for ruthlessness but also understand the modern tools of the information age. They represent the new generation of criminal organizations by having the organizational suppleness and skills to operate semiautonomously and, if necessary, dissever, disappear, and reform. The Balkan wars and the war in Chechnya during the 1990s opened up new opportunities to form linkages and for plunder. The results may be felt by legitimate society for a long time.

Organized-Crime Groups and the South American Drug Trade

Globally, there are 16 to 17 million users of cocaine, which is approximately similar to the number of people who use opiates. Therefore, the illegal-drug market is economically significant for

Map 4.3 Heroin Flows to the Russian Federation and Eastern Europe, 2009

Source: U.N. Office on Drugs and Crime (2010b). From *World Drug Report 2010* by the United Nations Office on Drugs and Crime (UNODC), Copyright © 2010 United Nations. Used by permission of the United Nations.

both hemispheres. It also utilizes the same distribution mechanisms and attracts the same scale of enterprise and human element.

According to the United Nations Office on Drugs and Crime, the North American market is responsible for more than 40% of cocaine consumption out of a total global estimate of 470 T. The 28 European Union and four European Free Trade Association countries accounted for more than a quarter of total consumption. These two regions represent more than 80% of the total value of the global cocaine market. The combined total market for cocaine is between $85 and $88 billion a year worldwide.

The cocaine-trafficking route generally makes its way from Colombia to Mexico or Central America by sea and then continues by land to the United States and Canada. A seaborne route services the European market via container ships. Colombia is the main source of cocaine for both Europe and North America. Distributors in the United States also receive shipments directly from Peru and Bolivia. Cultivation has declined since 2012, mostly due to aerial spraying and other government eradication programs (UNODC, 2014).

The source countries of cocaine are subject to what analysts refer to as the **balloon effect**. During the decades of the 1980s and 1990s, cocaine cultivation occurred mainly in Bolivia and Peru. Successful government crop-eradication programs forced producers to relocate operations to Colombia. Over time, Colombia has been losing its dominance for the same reasons that initially drove the trade out of the earlier centers of production. Recent data suggest that the decline may be forcing coca cultivation back again to Bolivia and Peru (Beittel, 2012, p. 27). As law enforcement exerts pressure at a point along the production–distribution route, producers react by moving operations. The programs have an effect on local economies, but the global market is undisturbed.

The main narco-player of the Colombian connection is the Revolutionary Armed Forces of Colombia (Fuerzas Armadas Revolucionarias de Colombia or FARC). Its roots go back to the Cold War, when it operated as the armed wing of the pro-Soviet Colombian Communist Party (Martin, 2003, p. 145). Today, FARC engages in every aspect of the drug trade from cultivation to production and refining to trafficking (Chalk, 2011a, p. XII). It is designated by the U.S. State Department as a foreign terrorist organization (FTO). Yet its motives have become more economic than political.

FARC became a formidable guerrilla force by the 1990s. As a result of military victories, the Colombian government ceded territory to FARC as "demilitarized zones" in 1998, which FARC converted into drug-producing regions. Since then, the government has made attempts to retake these areas. Losses forced FARC to enter into peace negotiations. However, despite the setbacks, FARC is still a serious security risk and continues to be active in the cocaine trade. Despite its claims of being a political organization, it employed such tactics as kidnapping, robbery, assassination, and the conscription of children (Chalk, 2011a). According to the 2010 Congressional Research Service report, it not only forced farmers to grow coca in its territory, it also taxed harvesters and buyers of coca paste. FARC further added to its revenue stream by collecting protection money from laboratory processors and leasing airfields to traffickers (Rollins et al., 2010, p. 8). To finance its narcotics and paramilitary operations, FARC formed trafficking networks with Mexican and Caribbean crime organizations. The organization sometimes accepts weapons as payment for narcotics, in addition to cash. It is also not the only criminal-terrorist organization in the region.

The National Liberation Army (Ejercito de Liberacion Nacional or ELN) also operates in Colombia and has Cold War roots similar to FARC. Less Marxist-Leninist and more ideologically

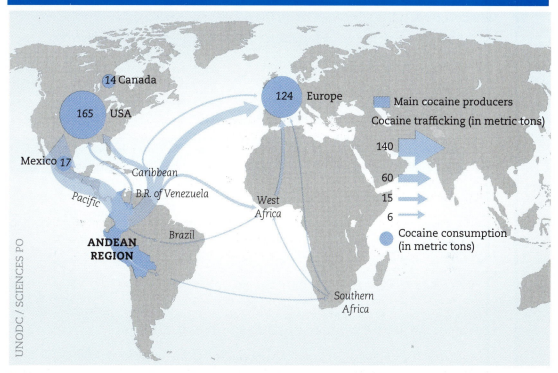

Map 4.4 Global Cocaine Trade Routes

14 Canada

124 Europe

165 USA

Mexico 17

Caribbean

B.R. of Venezuela

Pacific

West Africa

Brazil

ANDEAN REGION

Southern Africa

Main cocaine producers

Cocaine trafficking (in metric tons)

140

60

15

6

Cocaine consumption (in metric tons)

UNODC / SCIENCES PO

Source: U.N. Office on Drugs and Crime (2009, 2011b), whose calculations were informed by U.S. Office of National Drug Control Policy, *Cocaine Consumption Estimates Methodology* (2008), and U.N. Office on Drugs and Crime (2010b). From *World Drug Report 2010* by the United Nations Office on Drugs and Crime (UNODC). Copyright © 2010 United Nations. Used by permission of the United Nations.

associated with Che Guevara and Castro's Cuba than with the party line of the former Soviet Union, it often attacks government infrastructure sites, such as transportation and energy facilities. A particularly favorite target is the Cano-Limon pipeline. Like FARC, ELN has suffered losses politically and in manpower. However, it still represents a potent force as it redirects terrorist efforts against the state and the rural population and orients more toward cocaine production and trafficking (Chalk, 2011a). In an attempt to regain popularity and regenerate some of its lost vigor, ELN agreed to a truce with its FARC rivals and expressed interest in being included in the peace negotiations between the Colombian government and FARC. At the same time, reports claim ELN has entered pacts with various criminal organizations in order to pursue their drug-trafficking interests more earnestly (Looft, 2012).

Despite their history of competition, ELN and FARC, together, controlled much of the countryside in the 1990s and into the early years of this century. The government has struggled, with some success, to reassert its authority after nearly collapsing a decade and a half ago. The **Colombian syndrome**—the fusion of crime with politics—thrives, and the global cocaine market remains stable in spite of periodic declines in production and demand. With the facilitation of

The Tri-Border Area of South America

Where the border territories of Argentina, Brazil, and Paraguay intersect is one of the most lawless places on earth. It is a geographic area where transnational criminals can gather, ply their trade, and if necessary, conspire with terrorists. Known as simply the **tri-border area** (TBA), it has been recognized for providing a sanctuary for money laundering and drug and arms trafficking and a haven for organized crime and official corruption.

Map 4.5 Map of the Tri-Border Area

Source: Hudson (2003).

In the early 1970s, Brazil and Argentina established a free-trade zone to take advantage of Iguazu Falls' potential as an energy-producing facility and tourist attraction. What eventually evolved was a magnet and hive of illegal activity. A 2003 Federal Research Division Report of the Library of Congress describes the area as, "in effect, a mutually beneficial nexus among these three sectors [official corruption, organized crime, and terrorists groups]. The TBA serves as a microcosm for examining this relationship" (Hudson, 2003, p. 6).

Outlaw groups use the TBA as a staging locale for illegal trade in small arms, drugs, and counterfeit goods and the human trafficking of immigrants and minors for prostitution. Foreign criminal groups that mingle with indigenous associates represent crime organizations from

BOX 4.5

▶ Iguazu Falls in the Tri-Border Area of Argentina, Paraguay, and Brazil

Source: Photo on left by Dvortygirl on Flickr; photo on right by Samantha Beddoes on Flickr.

Chile, China, Colombia, Corsica, Ghana, Libya, Italy, Ivory Coast, Japan, Korea, Lebanon, Nigeria, Russia, and Taiwan. The list of obstacles that effective law enforcement confronts is the same as in other regions where security regimes are weak: inadequate training, poor equipment, lack of vigorous public support, and low pay that cultivates widespread profiteering by officials. In the TBA, however, conditions have matured, and an infrastructure for crime has become institutionalized.

In the mid-1970s, the TBA began feeling the effects of the Lebanese Civil War. Instability in that part of the Middle East drove many Muslims out and forced them to seek asylum in South America. The area is host to between 20,000 and 60,000 ethnic Arabs (six million was the estimated total of Muslims living in Latin American cities in 2005) (Neumann, 2011). Due to the feeble security framework, the population soon became vulnerable to

crime and their home a refuge for criminals and political extremists (Shelley et al., 2005, p. 60). Other Islamic terrorist groups include the Egyptian Al-Jihad, Al-Gama'a al-Islamiyya, and Hamas.

The area is accessible by sea and has passable outlet into the Atlantic. Small and medium cargo vessels navigate the water routes. Three population centers serve as modern communication and transportation hubs. Puerto Iguazu in Argentina, Foz do Iguacu, Brazil, and the Paraguayan city of Ciudad del Este also provide the region with international banking services. A network of over 100 hidden airstrips adds to the underground infrastructure (Steinitz, 2003, p. 8). The area is a cauldron of crime, terrorism, and corruption.[*]

Forty thousand people and 20,000 vehicles cross the bridge between Ciudad del Este and Foz do Iguacu daily. Only 10% are spot-checked,

---

[*]The Paraguayan President, Julius Stroessner, was an original developer of the free trade zone project and has been accused of turning the TBA into a haven for fugitives. Such individuals include the Nazi war criminal Josef Mengele, a former resident. Stroessner was also suspected of being involved in drug-trafficking operations.

(Continued)

(Continued)

while citizens, tourists, and potential criminal suspects travel with and without documentation. The customs systems of Paraguay and Brazil suffer from both a lack of coordination and a culture of corruption. Adding to the morass, few members of the nonindigenous communities are legally registered. Their movements can occur undetected, and efforts to interdict and extradite are easily obstructed. Corruption in the Immigration Department is at the source of a serious problem. Some observers claim that official corruption is so inured in the structure, process, and criminal pattern within the TBA that the Drug Trafficking Investigating Commission of Brazil's congress concluded that only a complete

▶ Friendship Bridge, *Ponte de Amizade*, Between Ciudad del Este and Foz do Iguacu

Source: Photo by Cesar I. Martins on Flickr.

restructuring and rearming of the police might address the problems.

With a population of approximately 320,000, Ciudad del Este swarms with over 5,000 businesses. Its economy is a source for cheap Asian-made products and counterfeit goods that make it ideal for money laundering and other illegal transactions (Methods and Motives, p. 60). The city ranks only behind Hong Kong and Miami in volume of cash transactions. It is an attraction for criminal activities and elements worldwide. The corrupt security infrastructure is also a locus of human rights violations.

While formal financial institutions have long provided an adequate means of laundering and transferring funds, the centuries-old **hawala** system is an informal banking system that adds another layer of service. It has been used extensively throughout the Arab world for over a thousand years. *Hawala* bankers work simply and effectively out of small shops, accepting cash, checks, or valuable goods at one location and arranging for a reciprocal payment at a receiving location. These transactions occur minus the intrusion of legal reporting or government disclosure requirements (Schneider, 2010, p. 21). *Hawala* means "transfer" in Arabic, but the official world refers to it as an **informal value transmission system (IVTS)**. Mostly immigrant workers seeking a way of transferring funds for minimal transaction fees use it for legitimate reasons (Ballard, 2005, pp. 323–324). However, in addition to being an integral part of the black market, it can also be a banking haven for money laundering and terrorist financing.

Collaboration is not only within ethnic communities but also between mixed groups with mutual interests, including crime and terrorism. Reports tell of arrangements between Hezbollah, Hong Kong triads, Chechen groups, and Chinese Mafia.

In addition to the arrival of Mideast refugees, which began in the 1970s, there has been a steady stream of Chinese immigrants into Paraguay and the TBA since the 1980s. A large Cantonese population of nearly 30,000 is part of the Ciudad del Este community and provides excellent cover for crime groups (Hudson, 2003, p. 69). These crime organizations feed off the local Chinese community, and their businesses run large-scale smuggling and protection operations. Many believe these Chinese groups are the main criminal force in the TBA.

When law enforcement does achieve success, the balloon effect (see above) may be set in motion. The three free-trade zones of Macao in Colombia, Margarita Island in Venezuela, and Chile's Iquique are additional havens. Many assume Islamic terrorist groups have moved into other regions in Venezuela, Chile, and Uruguay. Crime analysts also contend that a second tri-border area developed between Brazil, Bolivia, and Peru due to a combination of increased criminal activity and the limited success of law enforcement countermeasures. The pressure from security forces and the overflow from Muslim communities have shaped the landscape, culturally, socially, and in terms of the criminality of the region.

The TBA, Chechnya, the Balkans, parts of Africa, and the border areas around Central Asia are geographic spaces where crime, terrorism, and corruption can not only comfortably nest but also overwhelm official society. As mentioned above, such areas have become microcosms for further analysis. Understanding economic drivers, the origins of political discontent, and even the backlash or other reactions to globalization creates the framework for addressing the growing transnational crime challenge. Assessing the dynamic taking place in the TBA is a means of analyzing the security threat and understanding its ability to inhabit organs within the state, influence the rhythms of legitimate society, engulf geographic territories, and affect daily life.

Mexican cartels, these two groups and smaller Peruvian and Bolivian organizations control the movement of drugs onto the North American continent. Shipments to Western Europe reach their markets with the assistance of West African syndicates based in Ghana and Guinea-Bissau. Italian crime groups extend the network into other world markets.

The native regions of cocaine cultivation and production are ungoverned areas. Drugs, arms, and human beings move virtually without restriction. Narcotic trafficking is not only lucrative but, in many instances, an economic essential. In South, Central, and Meso-America, purposely opaque financial systems and state corruption provide cover and logistical support for illegal trafficking and money laundering over a vast exploitable terrain. It is another part of the world where criminals and, occasionally, terrorists can operate and even wage war against legitimate society.

THE ROLE OF FAILED STATES IN FACILITATING ORGANIZED CRIME AND TERRORISM

The category of the failed state includes both sovereign states and substates. These are areas without the adequate economic infrastructure or resources to fulfill the needs of their citizens. Often thanks to economic globalization policies, such as structural-adjustment programs, privatization strategies, and other IMF– and World Bank–imposed economic-reform projects, many population segments have succumbed to poverty due to onerous debt payments, reduced social services, and lack of regulation. Many aid recipient nations pay more than 50% of government revenues toward debt service. The burdensome financial liability has led to bankruptcy, unemployment, and poverty and has forced many in the developing world to seek opportunity in developed countries.

The debt trap being experienced by the developing world in parts of Asia, Africa, and South America has set in motion a mass global migration on a scale never before known. The world's cities are swelling with new residents seeking opportunities. As this grand resettlement trend occurs, ethnic groups and religious sects travel the earth without losing contact with identities, cultures, belief systems, and devotions or hatreds. As urban centers swell and the economic prospects of these populations go unmet, the people in these poverty areas become vulnerable to the services and enticements of crime.

The instruments of technology and globalization allow them to connect with their communities and worldviews. They also bring with them criminal elements and political extremists. For transnational organized crime, these populations represent exploitable consumer markets and labor pools. Product piracy, drug trafficking, human trafficking, and prostitution have become more lucrative as the demand and labor pool (forced or unforced) grows and less risky as official corruption becomes embedded and concerns for financial and economic accountability wither away.

As well as marketplaces, these failed states and lawless communities provide cover for criminal operations. The same spaces often offer legal protection through official corruption. *Kryshi* and *baohusang* thrive on these conditions to further their interests and erode the rule of law. The Chechen Mafia can establish an IVTS or *hawala* to transfer funds through its diaspora communities in Central Europe and Russia without detection. Chinese and Balkan criminal gangs can recruit and traffic in the international sex trade by exploiting economically helpless populations. Every year hundreds of billions of dollars in wealth is created by the cultivation, production, shipment, and distribution of heroin, cocaine, cannabis, and methamphetamine with the help of these failed states and their crumbling and corrupt security regimes.

CURRENT ANTICRIME METHODS, REGIMES, AND CAPACITY-BUILDING EFFORTS TO COUNTER CRIME WORLDWIDE

Part III of the book discusses several U.S. government, United Nations, and other capacity-building programs that address security issues relating to the supply chain, cybersecurity, and physical security. To avoid overlap and redundancy, a detailed discussion is deferred until later in the book. However, a quick survey of those programs is worth a discussion here.

The U.S. Department of Homeland Security's Customs Border Protection (CBP) Agency's Customs-Trade Partnership Against Terrorism (C-TPAT) Program was primarily designed by the business sector. While mainly it was in response to the terrorist attacks in New York

Source: U.N. Office on Drugs and Crime (2010b). From *World Drug Report 2010* by the United Nations Office on Drugs and Crime (UNODC). Copyright © 2010 United Nations. Used by permission of the United Nations.

City in September 2001, C-TPAT was also a program to address the threat to the global maritime supply chain from not only disruption but by abuse of smugglers. It is a voluntary program, and the security measures generally reflect the common practices and standards of global shippers, which were already in place at the time of 9/11. Critics charge it was as much an attempt by the shipping and trade community to avoid regulation as it was an effort to harden supply chain security. However, after its initial phase, standards and requirements for certification have become more rigorous and the validation process more rigid. The program lies within a layered defense strategy that draws together the cooperation of the private-sector trade community to work with CBP. The ultimate aim is security and frictionless trade. Enrollees of the program become trusted shippers and receive benefits by agreeing to C-TPAT security measures and standards. Upon certification, participants enjoy the advantages of reduced inspections and shorter delay times of U.S.-bound shipments. The program is United States–centric. However, through coordination with the World Customs Organization, a capacity-building element extends it.

The World Customs Organization established the Framework of Standards to Secure and Facilitate Global Trade (SAFE Framework) to effectively expand C-TPAT and other CBP programs beyond the sphere of U.S.–bound trade. After being adopted in 2005, the initiative was shortly put into force. Participating members of SAFE operate in their own self-interest or with the support of states. Mostly isolated efforts at self-regulation are the norm. The ambition to even define cybercrime is faint, let alone the effort to establish a political framework for cyber arms control. A few noted and effective cybersecurity exceptions exist.

The U.S. Computer Emergency Readiness Team (n.d.) (US-CERT, also known as CSIRT [Computer Security Incident Response Team]) "leads efforts to improve the Nation's cybersecurity posture, coordinate cyber information sharing, and proactively manage cyber risks to the Nation while protecting the constitutional rights of Americans" (n.p.). Its partners include private-sector cybersecurity vendors, academia, and federal agencies. Information Response Team refers to groups of computer experts who handle computer security incidents. The Morris Worm (named after its author, Robert Tappan Morris, a Cornell graduate student) was what sparked the need for and creation of the first team, formed in 1988. As a result of the panic set off by this early generation of malware, the federal government contracted with Carnegie Mellon University to help monitor activity and manage the response mechanisms to cyber threats. The Carnegie Mellon site remains a chief coordinating center. Currently, more than 250 organizations using the name CERT or CSIRT focus on cybersecurity threat issues and response. In addition to advisory services to resolve problems and mitigate risks, CERT/CSIRT serves as a central point for reporting cyber threats and providing education. By 2003, US-CERT was established as a U.S. government partner. Located in Washington, DC, it is the operational arm of the National Cyber Security Division at the Department of Homeland Security. US-CERT works with these partners to control the abuse and misuse of technology across cyberspace. According to its website, US-CERT's (n.d.) mission is to "improve the Nation's cybersecurity posture, coordinate cyber information sharing, and proactively manage cyber risks to the Nation while protecting the constitutional rights of Americans" (n.p.). Moreover, it "partners with private sector critical infrastructure owners and operators, academia, federal agencies, Information Sharing and Analysis Centers (ISACs), state and local partners, and domestic and international organizations" (n.p.). Although it acts independently, US-CERT maintains relationships for information sharing and coordination purposes.

The amount of money laundered through the global financial system is as hard to imagine as it is difficult to calculate. Expert estimates put the yearly total figure in the vicinity of 2% to 5% of world GDP (Schroeder, 2001, p. 5). To combat international money laundering, the G-7 founded the **Financial Action Task Force (FATF)** in 1989. It is an independent, intergovernmental organization created to control threats to the international banking system. After the September 11, 2001, attacks, it broadened its scope to identifying terrorist financing activity. Its role was further expanded after the 2008 financial crisis. Determining that the world banking system was put in peril by the distressed conditions of many financial institutions, the FATF revamped its mandate and broadened its recommendations to the international banking community. Its objectives involve setting standards and promoting regulatory codes, operational measures, and transparency laws to battle money laundering and terrorist financing. The FATF basically toils against any related threats to the reliability of the international financial system. Working with its 34 national members and two regional partners, it is a policymaking body. It also helps to synchronize anti–money laundering and transparency laws on the national level with mutual legal assistance treaties to heighten and equalize risks for transnational crime across jurisdictions. It also serves to facilitate investigations as well as extraditions.

▶ Money Laundering

Source: U.S. Department of Homeland Security (2014); U.S. Customs and Border Protection.

Thanks to the perception of it as a rule-making authority and benevolent problem solver, FATF has been successful in generating the necessary political will to bring about national legislative and regulatory reforms in these areas. Despite being voluntary, nations agree to compliance. The FATF has established itself as a monopoly authority (Kerwer & Hülsse, 2011, p. 63). The threat of being blacklisted by the FATF carries enough weight that its influence over members is effectively coercive. The exclusion from participation in the FATF also means a nonmember cannot be party to the standard-setting process. The combination of these strictures has even capably pressured some states into putting aside their roles as traditional tax havens.

The FATF also works with two other categories of participants. Nonstate, associate members are regional organizations. Observer members are international organizations that have a specific anti–money-laundering function along with a broader mission. These organizations include the African Development Bank, European Bank for Reconstruction and Development, International Monetary Fund, INTERPOL, Organisation for Economic Co-operation and Development, World Customs Organization, and 20 other commissions, committees, offices, and financial institutions.

One exception to the usual absence of force monopoly involves the battle against maritime piracy. Maritime piracy's estimated cost to the global economy is about $7 billion a year (*Update of efforts to combat piracy*, 2013). Organized crime is the main source of piracy in South America. Colombia, in particular, is cited because of FARC's active participation. These incidents are usually part of a larger effort to control territory for the purpose of maintaining drug-trafficking routes, rather

Table 4.4 The 36 Members of the FATF

Argentina	Greece	New Zealand
Australia	Gulf Co-operation Council	Norway
Austria	Hong Kong, China	Portugal
Belgium	Iceland	Russian Federation
Brazil	India	Singapore
Canada	Ireland	South Africa
China	Italy	Spain
Denmark	Japan	Sweden
European Commission	Republic of Korea	Switzerland
Finland	Luxembourg	Turkey
France	Mexico	United Kingdom
Germany	Netherlands	United States

than as opportunities for direct financial gain. Generally, reports claim these incidents as terrorist activity. Kidnapping and extortion may occur; however, cargo and crew seizures are far more rare. The key areas of piracy in the world are in the Gulf of Guinea off the West African coast, along the Horn of Africa, and in Southeast Asia.

Petroleum tankers are the main attraction for pirates in the Gulf of Guinea. Nigerian criminal gangs are especially active. In addition to fuel theft, vessel and hostage taking are other sources of lucre. Pirates also attack drilling platforms and floating pumping stations. While these incidents are not included in data related to piracy, these attacks are conducted by the same criminal and terrorist elements and are part of the same theater of operations. Their exclusion from piracy statistics translates to an under-reporting of actual incidents by perhaps as much as one half (Tull, 2011, p. 28).

A counterforce to pirate exploits is U.S. Naval Forces Africa (NAVAF), which partners with regional law enforcement authorities and the private sector to secure the coastlines and sea-lanes. An initiative called African Partnership Station (APS) is NAVAF-led and involves national representatives from regional states. Another U.S. military partner is the U.S. Africa Command (AFRICOM), which also offers training and equipment assistance to APS. A driver of U.S. strategic interests in the Gulf of Guinea is the oil production. Currently, the United States receives 18% of its petroleum imports from this region and is projected to increase that percentage to 25% by 2015 (Tull, 2011, p. 32).

Ecological destruction and economic marginalization spawned the violence and lawlessness, which drew the involvement of criminals and terrorists and the ire of political activists. Therefore, it is not simply an eruption of violence due to rampant criminality, it is also, partly, a rebellion. The prospects for a near-term resolution are not promising.

The seas around the Horn of Africa have offered up a rich bounty for Somali pirates for the past decade. Ten percent of the world's oil and 50% of world container cargo passes through the Gulf of Aden. Hence, the economic implication of a secure sea-lane in the region has global consequence. Pirate activity spiked between 2007 and 2008 after a period of steady growth in the prior years. The rise in piracy drew international attention and resulted in the deployment of international naval forces organized to conduct counterpiracy operations. Under the command of the Combined Maritime Force, the Combined Task Force 151 coordinates operations with NATO's Operation OCEAN SHIELD and the European Union's Operation ATLANTA to create safer commercial shipping lanes. Following some measurable success in 2009, the number of attacks rebounded in 2010 as pirate activity flowed deeper into the Indian Ocean and away from the more heavily patrolled waters along the Gulf of Aden (Caldwell & Pendelton, 2011). Since 2011, however, the number of successful pirate attacks has diminished thanks to the coordinated efforts of international actors and the deployment of privately contracted armed security personnel aboard ships.

▶ Combined Maritime Force

Source: iStockphoto.com/tantawat.

Fifty percent of the world's oil and a quarter of its commerce pass through the Straight of Malacca and the South China Sea. The waters of Southeast Asia have teemed with piracy due to regional conditions of extreme poverty and frail government and security apparatuses. Lloyd's Market Association temporarily designated the area a war-zone risk in 2005 (Loewen & Bodenmüller, 2011, p. 42). Circumstances are similar to those in the Gulf of Guinea. Despite the absence of an overarching antipiracy strategy, the strategic importance of these sea-lanes has generated international pressure on the straight states. The creation of agreements on transnational crime and terrorism; improved security regimens of Indonesia, Malaysia, and Singapore; and capacity-building measures aided by Japanese financial support and the U.S. Seventh Fleet have made the sea territories much safer in recent years. However, the original cause of piracy lingers. The challenges of economic inequity, social disparity, and political corruption persist. In order to maintain the current order for the long term, these conditions will have to be addressed.

A final footnote to the study of transnational organized crime concerns the dialogue. The difficulties of global governance are not only due to the scattered and uncoordinated landscape of security regimes, legal codes, and national and parochial self-interests, they are also due to a "terminological inconsistency" (Cornish, Livingston, Clemente, & York, 2010, p. 36).

Standardizing appropriate responses to threats also means establishing a common dialogue. Barriers to interoperability occur when politicians, lawyers, military experts, computer scientists, network operators, law enforcement, and segments of civic society hijack the discussion and debate with a parlance based upon a specific specialty or worldview. Therefore, not only absent is a common framework for ethics and values in establishing and enforcing laws but also a standardization for language. Dismantling the silos that inhibit the prosecution of transnational crime also means abandoning comfort zones, participating in multidisciplinary forums, and establishing milieus of operational cohesiveness across agencies, national borders, and bureaucratic divides.

In summary, the definition of transnational organized crime is often lacking in specificity. Its organizational structure is flat more often than it is hierarchal. TOC operations are fluid. Many times, criminals function within the bounds of the law as well as act outside it. They mimic the affairs and business models of legitimate companies as easily as they meld with terrorism. Inconsistent legal codes, jurisdictional gaps, and overburdened or corrupt law enforcement authorities allow transnational organized crime to fall between the cracks of a system that lacks global governance. The fields of operation for transnational crime are vast. Cyberspace and the global supply chain offer innumerable opportunities and a limitless number of breach points.

The legacy security infrastructure in place to react is too often hindered by bureaucratic cumbrances and turf battles, obsolete legal codes, diplomatic protocols, and a lack of interoperability and information sharing. Failed states and substate jurisdictions create cover and safe havens. The criminalization of politics allows some territories to function as courtesan states actively inviting crime. Others countries export it. In areas of the world on the edge of abject poverty, crime can offer economic relief, if not survival. The cost of all this to the world economy is over $2 trillion per year, and the indirect socioeconomic costs are much higher and extend over long periods of time.

Technology and intensifying globalization drives events at a faster pace and TOC is quick to adapt. Their associates are not a pool of mere thugs. The staffs are educated, multicultural, and often well connected politically and sometimes socially. Diasporas assist ethnic crime groups with global reach as the greatest mass migration in history continues its trend toward urban centers.

Yet successful anticrime programs and initiatives exist. Multilateral agreements and collaborative military and law enforcement operations can be effective in reestablishing order. The advantages that legitimate states have in resources and technological research and advancement have an impact. Also key is the involvement of the private sector and its effort to protect its physical and intellectual assets and shield its commercial infrastructure and supply chain. The challenges are great but so are the opportunities for partnership. At the base of the problem is the disproportionate dispersion of wealth and lack of economic opportunity for so many dispossessed. As long as crime creates an alternative to legitimate justice, nonaccessible markets, and relief from the desperation of poverty, it will always have a role in human affairs. It is a utopian fantasy to believe crime can be eradicated. However, methods of controlling it and undermining its causes and incentives are possible through legal, military, and humanitarian collaboration.

The Future of Transnational Crime

Jeffrey K. Harp

The FBI participated in the development of the 2011 White House *Strategy to Combat Transnational Organized Crime*, along with U.S. law enforcement, intelligence, and other agencies. The strategy provides a framework for the U.S. government to collaboratively address the TOC threat through established investigative approaches, intelligence collection and analysis, and other methods, such as diplomacy and financial tools. The FBI has embraced the strategy's broad definition of TOC to include Eurasian, Balkan, Asian, Italian, and Mexican and South American criminal enterprises, such as Los Zetas; international gangs such as Hells Angels and MS-13; and human-trafficking and smuggling organizations.

To effectively combat TOC threats, the FBI established three international organized-crime task forces (OCTFs) in Madrid, Spain; Bangkok, Thailand; and Prague, Czech Republic. They were modeled on earlier success with the OCTF in Budapest, Hungary, which was set up early in 2000. FBI task force personnel partner with local law enforcement and intelligence agencies in their host countries to share resources and intelligence and provide law enforcement assistance. By leveraging these relationships, the FBI has generated valuable intelligence and joint operations that assist in the FBI's mission to combat TOC on a global scale.

The FBI's National Gang Task Force targets Central American gangs such as MS-13 through several initiatives. One of its most successful programs is the Transnational Anti-Gang (TAG) Initiative. By directing vetted anti-gang units in El Salvador, Guatemala, and Honduras, the TAG units have been instrumental in successfully investigating transnational cases with direct links to the United States.

By utilizing these focused intelligence efforts, the FBI has been able to drive successful operations that have significantly impacted Los Zetas. These include Operation Fallen Hero, in which the FBI, in conjunction with Homeland Security Investigations (HSI), successfully identified eight Los Zetas members responsible for the shooting of two HSI agents in Mexico, four of whom have been extradited. The FBI led a four state, multiagency money-laundering investigation in which over 400 of Miguel Treviño Morales's quarter horses were seized; auction proceeds netted over $8 million.

The FBI participates in the DOJ-sponsored Top International Criminal Organizations Targets (TICOT) List and the Treasury's Office of Foreign Asset Control (OFAC) efforts. Current investigations target OFAC and TICOT List targets and their criminal activities, which include money laundering, trafficking in contraband, and corruption activities, as they impact the United States and other countries. Partnerships with foreign law enforcement allow for the leveraging of intelligence and the use of sophisticated investigative techniques, including undercover and electronic surveillance methods.

(Continued)

(Continued)

Recently, the FBI has significantly altered the role it plays in the Southeast European Law Enforcement Center (SELEC), based in Bucharest, Romania. This multilateral platform established bilateral relations with the law enforcement and customs liaison officers representing the 13 SELEC member countries of the Balkan region. The FBI shifted its focus at SELEC from training to identifying opportunities for joint international operations and investigations with a U.S. nexus. The mission change resulted in numerous joint cases and a significant increase in intelligence collection and dissemination.

As highlighted in the strategy, the FBI supports the Strategic Alliance Group (SAG), a criminal law enforcement group consisting of partners from Australia, Canada, New Zealand, the United Kingdom, and the United States (FBI, HSI, DEA). The FBI participates in SAG to share and exchange threat information and investigative tools and to take part in working groups focused on criminal proceeds, cyber issues, and intelligence.

The U.S. White House (n.d.) has explained its number one priority is to "protect Americans and our partners from the harm, violence, and exploitation of transnational criminal networks" (n.p.). Along with this important priority, it has also committed to helping partner countries strengthen governance and transparency, break the corruptive power of transnational criminal networks, and sever state–crime alliances. By using the tools that the FBI and other U.S. law enforcement agencies bring to the table, the United States will be in a better position to break the economic power of transnational organized criminal networks and to protect strategic markets and the U.S. financial system from TOC penetration and abuse. The White House has made it clear that TOC networks pose a great threat to national security. By targeting their infrastructures, depriving them of their enabling means, and preventing the criminal facilitation of terrorist activities, the United States will succeed in significantly reducing the viability of all TOC groups. Through the building of international consensus, multilateral cooperation, and public–private partnerships, law enforcement will not only succeed in eliminating the TOC impact on the U.S. economy but will positively impact the entire global economic outlook.

Jeffrey K. Harp has served as the assistant special agent in charge in the San Francisco Division of the Federal Bureau of Investigation, overseeing the Special Weapons and Tactics (SWAT) Team, the Evidence Response Team, Foreign Language Programs, Surveillance, and Intelligence Collection. Mr. Harp graduated from the University of Illinois with a dual bachelor of science degree in forestry and natural-resource management (1987). He completed his MBA at Indiana University. Following training at the FBI Academy, in 1995, he was assigned to the Los Angeles Field Office, where he was a member of the SWAT Team and the counterterrorism team. In January 1998, Mr. Harp was selected to serve on the FBI's Hostage Rescue Team (HRT), where he spent four-and-a-half years as an operator on an assault team, specializing in aircraft hijackings and international security and working closely with U.S. Military Special Operations Group. He was promoted to the position of supervisory special agent at FBI HQ in June 2002, where he was responsible for establishing and overseeing FBI detainee operations in Guantanamo Bay, Cuba, and Afghanistan as well as managing military liaison at each of the Combatant Commands. In January 2005, Mr. Harp was promoted to the position of field supervisor in San Francisco, where he managed the Joint Terrorism Task Force and supervised the SWAT Team. In April 2008, Mr. Harp was selected to be the director's FBI representative as a legal attaché in Sofia, Bulgaria. Mr. Harp returned to San Francisco Division in April 2009.

Source: Courtesy of Jeffrey K. Harp.

This chapter has explained

- The various definitions of transnational crime

- The structures of transnational crime organizations

- What motivations drive transnational crime organizations

- How these motivations differ from those of terrorists groups

- The *modi operandi* of transnational crime organizations and how they may be similar to international terrorist groups

- How transnational crime organizations operate similar to multinational companies

- The origins, evolution, and impact of current major transnational crime organizations

  o Russian organized crime

  o Italian Mafia

  o Japanese yakuza

  o Chinese triads

  o Organized-crime groups and the Central Asian drug trade

  o Organized-crime groups and the South America drug trade

- The impact of failed and fragile states in the struggle against transnational organized crime

- How increasing mass migration has influenced the rise of transnational crime

- The current anticrime regimes, programs, and efforts to combat transnational organized crime

  o Various supply chain countermeasures

  o Cybersecurity methods and regimes

  o Anti–money-laundering efforts

  o Antipiracy naval forces and programs

- How greater international cooperation and collaboration on standardizing legal codes and establishing effective global governance needs to be addressed

KEY TERMS

Balloon effect *150*
Baohusang 144
Colombian syndrome *151*
Crime–terrorist nexus *131*
Diaspora *130*
Economic globalization *127*
Failed state *131*
Financial Action Task Force (FATF) *159*

Hawala (also informal value transmission system, IVTS) *154*
Hierarchal organization *131*
Jurisdictional arbitrage *127*
Krysha 139
Mafia *130*
Modus operandi (plural: modi operandi) *129*

Monopoly of force *126*
Neoliberal economic policy *133*
Nomenklatura 138
Omerta 141
Tri-border area *152*
Vorovskoi mir 135

QUESTIONS AND EXERCISES

1. Why do definitions of transnational organized crime differ?

2. Discuss the economic and social costs due to transnational organized crime.

3. How has technology and globalization affected the organizational structure of TOC?

4. What traits does the global supply chain share with cyberspace? How do these features facilitate TOC and create a challenge for legitimate society?

5. What does it mean when a transnational organized-crime group is described as "sovereign free"? How is this aspect of TOC a problem for traditional law enforcement?

6. How is transnational crime similar to international terrorism?

7. How is transnational crime dissimilar to international terrorism?

8. In what ways does TOC reflect the way global corporations operate and conduct business?

9. What are the main factors that facilitate the cultivation, production, and distribution of illegal narcotics? Identify the actors, social conditions, and geographic locations that are most prominent.

10. What similar social conditions contributed to the rise of the Mafia in Italy and Russian organized crime?

11. How is Russian organized crime different from other crime groups in scale and potential?

12. Why is money laundering more central to transnational crime operations than to terrorist groups?

13. What are the risks to TOC groups with terrorist organizations as partners?

14. What might be the impact of mass global migration on TOC?

15. Discuss reasons for the tri-border area being described as a "microcosm for further analysis."

16. What collaborative anticrime programs and initiatives exist?

17. How do anticrime regimes exert their rule-making authority?

5

MATERIAL HAZARDS AND WEAPONS

Theft of HEU [highly enriched uranium] and plutonium is not a hypothetical worry; it is an ongoing reality. Since the end of the Cold War, there have been approximately twenty documented cases of theft and smuggling of plutonium or HEU, some in kilogram-plus quantities. One alarming recent case was a seizure of stolen HEU in Moldova in mid-2011, in which the smugglers claimed to have access to nine kilograms of HEU that they were willing to sell for $31 million. Moldovan officials report that "members of the ring, who have not yet been detained, have one kilogram of uranium." This case appears to involve a real buyer—still at large—and the possibility that there are kilograms of weapons-grade HEU in the smugglers' hands, making it potentially the most serious case in years. (Bunn, 2014, pp. 180–181)

MATERIAL HAZARDS AND WEAPONS IN GENERAL

This first section defines material hazards, describes terrorist use of related weapons in the past, reviews forecasts of terrorist use in the future, and describes international and U.S. responses.

Defining Material Hazards and Weapons

Hazards are things in a nonharmful state; **threats** are in a harmful state. A *weapon* is anything that can be used to inflict harm. When in a disabled state or not wielded in a harmful manner, a weapon should be regarded as a hazard; if it is being used with the intent to harm, it should be regarded as a threat.

Many things are hazards, such as a rock that you could trip over or a human being who could attack you. This chapter will focus on the main material hazards, some of which lie all around

Learning Objectives and Outcomes

At the end of this chapter, you should be able to

- Define material hazards in general, review past malicious use of such hazards, forecast their use, and review official responses

- Define chemical hazards, describe industrial chemical hazards, describe chemical weapons, forecast malicious use, and describe response options

- Define and describe biological hazards, forecast malicious use, and describe response options

- Define nuclear hazards, describe the availability of these hazards, review past nuclear accidents, forecast malicious use, and describe response options

- Define radiological hazards, describe past malicious use, and describe practical responses

- Define chemical explosives, describe explosive materials, describe their effects, and review official responses

- Define and describe energy weapons

- Define firearms, review firearm violence, review terrorist use of firearms, and review official responses us, particularly in developed countries, urban areas, and even our homes. These materials are hazardous by themselves and could be weaponized.

As will be explained in later sections, the seven main categories of material hazards are as follows:

- a **chemical hazard**, or any chemical that could cause harm by its **toxicity** (causing biochemical harm to a living thing);

- a **biological hazard**, or any biological material that could cause harm by its toxicity or **pathogenicity** (causing disease in a living thing);

- a **nuclear hazard**, which emits harmful electromagnetic energy and could explode from nuclear reactions (rather than chemical energy);

- a **radiological hazard**, which emits harmful electromagnetic energy;

- a **chemical explosive hazard**, or a chemical compound or mixture of chemicals that could rapidly release energy in the form of gas and heat;

- an **energy hazard**, which could transfer harmful energy—such as electromagnetism, light, heat, or sound—directly to the target; and

- a **firearm**, a weapon from which a projectile could be propelled by an internal explosion.

The categorical material hazards above are often collected together in an acronym for convenience. Up until a couple decades ago, the conventional focus was on chemical, biological, nuclear, and radiological hazards (CBNR or CBRN, depending on the order). CBNR has been updated to CBNRE due to increased risks from **chemical explosives**. Given the emerging importance of **energy weapons**, we should admit a second *E*—making the acronym CBNREE. Firearms are not conventionally added to the acronym, but if they are included, the acronym would become CBNREEF, an awkward but realistic description of the hazards any society must manage.

Note the overlap between some of these categories. For instance, most **explosive** weapons use chemical explosives. However, *chemical weapons* rely on toxicity for their harmful effects while *chemical explosive weapons* rely on **blast**. Nevertheless, the ingredients of chemical explosives are usually also toxic, and chemical weapons can be distributed explosively.

In popular culture and judicial prosecutions, these hazards commonly conflate or are confused with *weapons of mass destruction* (WMD). The U.S. Department of Homeland Security (DHS, 2009) defines a WMD as a "weapon capable of a high order of destruction and/or of being used in such a manner as to destroy large numbers of people or an amount of property" (p. 112). Based on this definition, only **nuclear weapons** and high-yield chemical explosives warrant descriptions as weapons of mass destruction; most CBNREEF weapons threaten fragile organisms or tissues without destroying built structures. However, judicial prosecutors are incentivized to accuse indictees of using WMDs, even when the accused were using homemade chemical explosives, because the accusation has proven more persuasive to juries.

Historical Terrorist Use of CBNREE

Contrary to popular culture, CBNR weapons are rarely used. While popular culture commonly imagines terrorist use of CBNR weapons to contaminate mass-transit systems, the water supply, or the food supply of densely populated areas, terrorists almost always attack with explosives or **small arms**.

In fact, the most lethal terrorist attack ever (9/11) used knives and aircraft as weapons. For the terrorist, firearms and chemical explosives are familiar, mature, portable, cheap, easy-to-use technologies. By contrast, the terrorist would need new intents and capabilities to acquire and use CBNR weapons.

Terrorist activation of CBNR hazards is much less frequent than accidental activation by the officials that control them. CBNREEF hazards have gone missing from failed states, such as Iraq in 2003 and Libya in 2011, although most states closely guard CBNR weapons. Attempted terrorist uses have been very rare and lack the mass casualties suggested by popular fiction. Almost all terrorist violence has involved explosives and firearms. Few terrorists could be bothered to acquire CBNR weapons so long as chemical explosives and firearms are more readily available. Moreover, CBNR weapons face severe national and international restrictions. CBNR weapons are extremely difficult for nonofficial actors both to obtain and to contain as hazards deployable as threats when and where needed. Biological or chemical terrorist attacks are exceedingly rare in history and never have caused as many casualties as some of the single-explosive devices that terrorists have used. Nuclear weapons have been used against an enemy only twice (by the United States against Japan in 1945).

Yet some terrorists have considered them. Journalistic reports and leaked official intelligence suggest that al-Qaeda considered biological, chemical, and radiological weapons from an early stage. Written and video evidence collected from Afghanistan in late 2001 proves that its operatives experimented with bacterial and chemical agents but concluded that the weapons would be too hazardous to use without certain harm to others. In 2005, the RAND Center for Terrorism Risk Management Policy forecasted al-Qaeda's "desire to use chemical, biological, radiological, and nuclear (CBRN) weapons but little ability to execute large-scale unconventional attacks" (Chalk, Hoffman, Reville, & Kasupski, 2005, p. 16).

Forecasts of Use

Historically, forecasts of terrorism, from general survey respondents to academics and responsible officials, have assessed CBNR risks to be high. From 2000 to 2012, 25 of 60 publications that forecasted terrorism focused on CBNR terrorism (Bakker, 2012, p. 74). In June 2003, the U.S. government reported to the U.N. Security Council its estimate of a "high probability" that al-Qaeda would attempt an attack with a WMD within the next two years. The 2010 U.S. *National Security Strategy* declared that there was no greater danger than a terrorist with a **weapon of mass destruction**. In May 2011, the first U.S. *National Strategy for CBRNE Standards* declared that "CBNRE agents remain a grave threat to US citizens" (U.S. National Science and Technology Council, 2011, p. 4). The U.S. Government Accountability Office (GAO) agreed with the Department of Homeland Security that "the likelihood of terrorists smuggling WMD into the United States in cargo containers is low, [but] the nation's vulnerability to this activity and the consequences of such an attack—such as billions of losses in U.S. revenue and halts in manufacturing production—are potentially high" (Caldwell, 2012b, p. 1).

Similarly, the U.K. Cabinet Office (2008) declared that British jihadi terrorists "have aspirations to use chemical, biological and radiological weapons" (p. 10). The British Home Office ruled that "al-Qaida is the first transnational organization to support the use of CBRN weapons against civilian targets and to try to acquire them" (U.K. Home Office, 2010, p. 6). The U.K. Ministry of Defence (2010) has forecasted that by 2040 "nuclear weapons are *likely* to proliferate" (p. 12) and "terrorists are likely to acquire and use chemical, biological and radiological weapons *possibly* through organised crime groups" (p. 12; emphasis in original).

Historically, CBNR risks have been assessed higher than later events would justify. Remember: Most terrorism is conducted using conventional explosives that are not usefully classified separately under the CBNR class. This leaves the risk manager with a dilemma: CBNR risks tend to be overestimated, but this overestimation is official. Moreover, past frequencies may not be a useful guide to assessing the future. However, terrorism is adaptive, and there are terrorists who are interested in CBNR weaponry. Consequently, many officials err on the side of caution, inflating the risks on the assumption that terrorists will use CBNR weapons eventually with unforeseen frequency or returns or on the assumption that the public wants to see overt controls regardless of the objective risks. Indeed, many officials are correctly focused on the public's sensitivity to CBNR terrorism, in which case our sensitivity to the risks is inflated by the public's fears. The public may suffer real negative returns from stress and panic even without an objective CBNR threat.

Responses

INTERNATIONAL RESPONSES In 2004, the U.N. Security Council passed Resolution 1540, the only international instrument designed to prevent terrorists from acquiring CBNR weapons and their delivery systems. It obliges states to adopt legislation to prevent terrorist acquisition of CBNR weapons and delivery systems and to report their fulfillment; however, many states have never reported as obliged.

In 2002, the G8, the eight states with the leading economies, along with 25 state partners, launched a 10-year, $20 billion program to prevent CBNR materials from reaching terrorists or the states that sponsor terrorists (the Global Partnership Against the Spread of Weapons and Materials of Mass Destruction, also called the Global Partnership). For the first 10 years, the work was focused on destroying nuclear submarines and chemical weapons in Russia; the rest of the activity occurred in other former Soviet states. By the end of 2012, the program had surpassed its initially budgeted funding and duration and had expanded geographically to other states and to prevent the proliferation of radiological and biological hazards too.

U.S. NATIONAL RESPONSES On November 17, 1990, President George H. W. Bush signed an executive order that found that chemical and biological weapon proliferation was a threat to U.S. national security and declared a national emergency to counter this threat. On November 14, 1994, President Bill Clinton signed Executive Order 123998, which refined the ruling and extended it to nuclear weapons. The National Defense Authorization Act of 1997 directs the Secretary of Defense to develop and maintain at least one rapid-response team capable of detecting and controlling CBNR threats.

On June 5, 2000, the National Commission on Terrorism (a congressionally mandated bipartisan group) reported with recommendations that included more capacity to counter CBNR terrorism. On May 8, 2001, President George W. Bush signed an executive order that ordered the Federal Emergency Management Agency (FEMA) to establish an Office of National Preparedness against CBNR terrorism.

The *National Strategy for Homeland Security* specified the following relevant objectives for the DHS, which would become operational from January 2003 with FEMA as one of its subordinate agencies.

- Prevent terrorist use of nuclear weapons through better sensors and procedures

- Detect chemical and biological materials and attacks

- Prepare healthcare providers for catastrophic terrorism

- Develop a broad spectrum of vaccines, antimicrobials, and antidotes

- Augment America's pharmaceutical and vaccine stockpiles

- Prepare for chemical, biological, and radiological decontamination (U.S. Office of Homeland Security, 2002)

In early 2011, the U.S National Science and Technology Council's Committee on Homeland and National Security established a subcommittee on CBNRE Standards, with representatives from every major U.S. government department and from the executive office of the president. In May 2011, this new subcommittee, in collaboration with the DHS, the Department of Commerce, and the Office of Science and Technology Policy at the White House, published a *National Strategy for CBRNE [Protection] Standards*, which is supposed to be effective by 2020.

The DOD administers a joint-service Chemical and Biological Rapid Response Team (CB-RRT) that would support civilian authorities in a chemical or biological disaster. The DOD has authorized 55 National Guard Weapons of Mass Destruction Civil Support Teams.

In May 2004, the National Nuclear Security Administration (reporting to the Office of Defense Nuclear Nonproliferation) established the Global Threat Reduction Initiative to identify, secure, remove, and dispose of nuclear and radiological hazards globally. Since then, it has converted highly enriched uranium to low-enriched uranium or verified the closure of reactors in 25 countries, removed all weapons-usable uranium from 17 countries, physically upgraded radiological sources at more than 1,700 buildings (including in the United States), and provided radiological Alarm Response Training to more than 3,000 first responders across the United States (U.S. National Nuclear Security Administration, 2014).

Similar is the Global Threat Reduction Program, whose main administrator is the Department of State. It funds efforts to prevent terrorists and proliferating states from acquiring WMD-related expertise, materials, technologies, and equipment.

CHEMICAL HAZARDS

This section defines chemical hazards, describes industrial hazards, and reviews chemical weapons, forecasts of their use, and official responses.

Definition

A chemical hazard is any chemical that could harm by its *toxicity* (causing biochemical harm to a living thing). A **chemical weapon** is any chemical used with intent to harm by its toxicity. International conventions define chemical weapons as "a toxic chemical and its precursors [and] ammunition or [a] device, specifically designed to cause death or other harm through the toxic properties of those toxic chemicals" (Chemical Weapons Convention Implementation Act of 1998).

Chemical weapons are conventionally categorized in five classes:

1. Irritants

2. Choking or pulmonary agents

3. Blister agents

4. Blood agents

5. Nerve agents

Irritants, such as tear gas and pepper spray, are normally nonlethal; however, victims with preexisting respiratory disorders might suffer lethal reactions, while others might suffer other life threatening responses due to panic or stress.

Choking or pulmonary agents liquefy upon contact with the skin—particularly moist membranes—either blinding the victim, or upon inhalation, suffocating the victim by causing the pulmonary system to fill with fluid. Pulmonary agents include chlorine gas, sulfur mustards (mustard gases), and phosgene, all of which have been used since World War I as chemical weapons and are in routine industrial use. Phosgene is used in the production of plastics at the rate of 1,000,000,000 lbs per year in the United States alone (Tucker, 2002, p. 124).

Blister agents cause blisters upon contact with the skin but are unlikely to make contact with the skin except when falling to earth in a gaseous state when aerosolized and released from above. Blister agents tend to be denser than air and settle in low areas as a liquid; they can remain in this liquid state for weeks and then return to a gaseous state with heat and agitation. This persistent contamination of terrain is the main reason why blister agents are useful to both the military and to terrorists.

Blood agents interfere with the red blood cells' ability to release oxygen, without which any muscular function would fail. Blood agents—such as hydrogen cyanide, cyanogen chloride, and cyanogen bromide—are lethal when inhaled in high concentrations but are not normally concentrated enough to be lethal unless directly applied to the victim.

Nerve agents can enter the body through the skin or inhalation and block vital nervous-system muscular functions, such as breathing and heartbeat. Nerve agents include sarin, soman, and tabun. Commercial insecticides are chemically similar, so in theory, they could be concentrated as nerve agents.

Industrial Hazards

In 2000, the U.S. Environmental Protection Agency counted at least 15,000 facilities in the United States that stored or produced hazardous chemicals; 2,000 that had capacity to leak chemicals that could affect at least 100,000 people; and 123 chemical plants that had the capacity to kill millions (Tucker, 2002, p. 124).

Many of these sites are poorly regulated; storage sites, unlike manufacturing sites, do not need to be inspected, leaving the operators free to expose the public to shocking risks without public oversight until an emergency. For instance, in January 2014, 7,500 gal of 4-methylcyclohexane methanol (MCHM), a coal-cleaning agent, leaked into the Elk River in West Virginia from a 35,000-gallon above-ground storage tank on a site owned by Freedom Industries, just 1.5 mi upstream from pipes feeding water into a public water-treatment plant, which could not remove the toxin (an irritant that induces vomiting and diarrhea when consumed). Nine counties with a collective population of 300,000 banned their residents from drinking or washing with tap water for five days until the toxin could be removed. Freedom Industries filed for bankruptcy within days of the emergency.

Most leaks affect the natural environment without harming people. For instance, in February 2014, coal ash, a natural by-product of burning coal containing arsenic and heavy metals, leaked into the Dan River, North Carolina, from storage ponds at a site owned by Duke Energy. The U.S. Fish and Wildlife Service reported that coal ash contaminated the riverbed for 70 mi without affecting human consumption. Although water treatment plants can remove these toxins, river life is still harmed.

In theory, someone could make malicious use of industrial chemicals. For instance, on February 28, 2000, someone (still unidentified) opened a valve in a storage tank, leaking 200 gal of anhydrous ammonia that formed a poisonous cloud that spread to downtown Pleasant Hill, Missouri, and forced more than 250 residents to evacuate. Possibly this person had malicious intent, was sourcing ammonia for the production of methamphetamines, or was a careless site employee who never admitted his or her mistake.

America's worst chemical accident occurred in 1989, when an explosion due to an accidental release of gases at a Phillips chemical plant in Houston, Texas, killed 23 and injured 120 people.

The most lethal industrial chemical release in the world was from the Union Carbide factory in Bhopal, India, in 1984, which killed 2,500 people (activists claim more) and sickened 200,000 people. Within a few hours, 30 to 40 MT of methyl isocyanate had escaped from a holding tank, causing a toxic cloud to spread over an area of 10 sq mi, including densely populated shantytowns. Originally reported as an accident, Union Carbide's own investigation blamed an act of sabotage by a disgruntled employee, a conclusion that some chemical weapons experts accept (Hoffer, 2011, p. 103).

Use

Chemical weapons are easily packaged and stored in the same packages as conventional ordnance, down to the smallest projectiles. Historically, most states have acquired chemical weapons at some point, although most procurers have now disposed of most of their acquisitions. However, because they are difficult and expensive to dispose of, poor or corrupt governments tend to keep stocks indefinitely, pending foreign assistance or intervention.

More chemical weapons have been produced than used; most of their use occurred in earlier wars. Most uses do not count as terrorism and are not typical of terrorist use. Official uses indicate the potential results when the attackers are highly organized and the targets are concentrated.

Around 124,000 tons of chemicals were used as weapons during World War I, resulting in 91,000 deaths and 1.2 million injured persons. Iraq and Iran used chemical weapons against each other during their war (1980–1988); perhaps as many as 45,000 soldiers were exposed to mustard gas alone during that war.

In March 1988, Iraq deployed chemical weapons against a rebellious town in Kurdistan, killing 3,000 to 5,000 people—still the largest deployment of chemical weapons against civilians (Gaines & Kappeler, 2012, pp. 249–250).

In 1990, Tamil Tigers used chlorine gas against a Sri Lankan fort, where it killed 60 soldiers; however, the gas also drifted back over the perpetrators. The attack also generated considerable international condemnation. The Tamil Tigers did not repeat the method.

From 1989 to 1995, a cult (Aum Shinrikyo) in Japan used chemical weapons against 12 targets. These attacks included the murder of three members of a dissenting family, by injections of potassium chloride, in November 1989. Beginning in 1993, there were several releases of the nerve agent sarin. One incident led to the collateral death of eight people from vaporized sarin who had the misfortune of living adjacent to judges who were the intended targets. Aum Shinrikyo made attempts on other lives using VX (another nerve agent) and phosgene gas. An informer was successfully eliminated as a result of an attack. On March 20, 1995, the cult released sarin on five subway trains in Tokyo, killing 13 who had unfortunately suffered copious direct exposure to the liquid state and prompting more than 6,000 others to seek hospital treatment, including hundreds with long-term motor or memory problems. Aum quickly attempted three mass releases of hydrogen cyanide before Japanese authorities shut it down in May (Danzig et al., 2012).

In February 2002, Italian police in Rome arrested nine Moroccans in possession of 4 kg of potassium ferrocyanide planned for release into the water supply to the U.S. Embassy. In 2003, al-Qaeda developed a device to produce hydrogen cyanide gas in crowded urban spaces. On April 26, 2004, Jordanian authorities announced that they had broken up a jihadi plot to use chemical weapons against different targets and had seized blistering agents and nerve gas.

In 2003, a supermarket employee in the United States deliberately contaminated ground beef with an insecticide that sickened nearly 100 people.

In 1981, Iraq started production of hundreds of tons of blister and nerve agents and tens of thousands of chemical warheads for artillery shells, ballistic rockets, and aerial **bombs**. Some were expended during the ongoing war with Iran until 1988; a few were expended against Iraqi Kurds. Thousands of warheads remained in poorly managed stores. After the invasion of Iraq in 2003 and through 2011, U.S. troops found around 5,000 chemical warheads (mostly in artillery shells) in Iraq, all manufactured before 1991, some in an unidentified and distressed state. Six-hundred-twenty-nine American military personnel have reported to military medical authorities that they may have been exposed to chemical weapons in Iraq. The Department of Defense revealed the number after a national newspaper reported a few cases. Most soldiers were exposed to mustard gas, a few to nerve agents (Chivers, 2014a, 2014b).

Iraqi insurgents started to deploy chemical warheads as soon as 2004, although possibly by accident, mistaking chemical shells as conventional explosive shells. In at least 15 harmful attacks from October 2006 to June 2007, insurgents in Iraq packaged liquid or gaseous chlorine with explosives. Conventional explosives mostly burnt or dispersed the chlorine without adding to the harm, although many people died or were injured in each attack (Bullock, Haddow, & Coppola, 2013, pp. 85–87; U.K. Home Office, 2010, p. 6).

In June 2014, the Islamic State in the Levant/Syria (ISIL/ISIS) overran the abandoned chemical weapons establishment at al-Muthanna, which had not been cleared completely of chemical hazards. In September, Iraqi government forces claimed that ISIS had started to deploy chlorine gas against them. In one medically confirmed case, on September 15, ISIS fighters detonated an explosive device surrounded by containers of chlorine, which drifted over a defensive position held by Iraqi forces in Duluiyah, north of Baghdad, sickening 11 police officers (Morris, 2014).

Forecasts of Terrorist Use

In 1999, a special commission to the U.S. president and Congress played down the utility to terrorists of chemical weapons (Gilmore Commission, 1999). However, terrorists do not need access to official chemical weapons. One recent study of past terrorist use concluded that chemical weapons are more accessible than biological weapons and are within the reach of any intentional group because terrorist chemical weapons can be synthesized with knowledge from a public library and materials obtained ostensibly for other purposes, while biological precursors are less available and more difficult to weaponize (Danzig et al., 2012).

Responses

Chemical weapons are proscribed in international conventions and laws since 1874 (the Brussels Convention). The First Hague Peace Appeal in 1899 specifically proscribed asphyxiating gases, although this prohibition broke down in 1915, during World War I. The Geneva Protocol of 1925 prohibited the use of poisonous gases but not development or storage. The Chemical Weapons Convention of 1993 essentially proscribes any handling of chemical weapons, from development to storage (except for research purposes), although around 10 countries have not signed or ratified the convention while many others are noncompliant.

Chemical weapons are strongly specified in most of the counter-WMD programs described above. For instance, the U.S. Global Threat Reduction Program contains the only U.S. chemical-security program on improving chemical-security best practices, raising awareness of chemical

COMPARATIVE PERSPECTIVES

BOX 5.1

Three Different Estimates of the Risks of Terrorist Chemical Weapons

The reality is that effective use by terrorists of a chemical weapon presents numerous difficulties. The first of these is the sheer volume of agent that must be used to achieve lethal concentrations over a large area. Sunlight, wind, distance from the release point, and time rapidly diminish an agent's concentration and thus its effectiveness. . . . However, what terrorists can do is use toxic industrial chemical agents found in our own backyard to attack us. (Hoffer, 2011, p. 102, 104)

Although chemical agents do not require sophisticated delivery systems (crop duster airplanes, commercial spray devices, or improvised explosives devices might be sufficient), the acquisition of war chemical agents for a large-scale attack by terrorists would be technically very difficult, if not impossible. Terrorist intentions and terrorist capabilities do not always coincide. However, it is plausible that, as in the case of Aum Shinrikyo, a resolute terrorist group with powerful resources could carry out an attack using toxic industrial chemicals (TICs). (Carpintero-Santamaria, 2012, p. 79)

In summary, chemical weapons do indeed pose a threat. However, many problems are associated with their use that will be difficult for terrorists to overcome. It appears that if chemical weapons are used, they will be used with small concentrated targets resulting in relatively few casualties. (Gaines & Kappeler, 2012, p. 267)

security, promoting the elimination of hazardous chemicals, and improving the management of dangerous chemicals in laboratory and industry settings. The *National Strategy for Homeland Security* specified that the then-prospective Department of Homeland Security should "detect chemical and biological materials and attack" and "develop . . . antidotes" (U.S. Office of Homeland Security, 2002, p. x).

A strict risk assessment would encourage officials to focus less on chemical weapons than commercial chemicals.

The historical record indicates that most incidents of chemical terrorism have involved the use of household or industrial chemicals. Although such compounds are far less toxic than military-grade agents, the Bhopal disaster demonstrates the deadly potential that could result from the sabotage of a commercial chemical plant or a series of railroad tank cars. It therefore makes sense to devote more resources to addressing forms of chemical terrorism that would be less catastrophic but are more likely, such as industrial sabotage, rather than focusing exclusively on worst-case scenarios involving the large-scale release of a military nerve agent. Improving the security of chemical plants and the transportation infrastructure will require cooperative efforts by government and the private sector.

With respect to consequence management of a chemical terrorist attack, greater emphasis and funding should go to training and exercising local and state first responders, particularly Hazmat teams, and improving their capabilities for crowd decontamination, medical triage, and treatment of large numbers of casualties. (Tucker, 2002, p. 131)

BIOLOGICAL HAZARDS

This section defines biological weapons, describes the hazards, reviews official forecasts, and reviews official responses.

Definition

A *biological hazard* is any biological material that could harm by its toxicity or *pathogenicity* (causing disease in a living thing). The United Nations International Strategy for Disaster Reduction (2009) defines "biological hazards" as "processes of organic origin or those conveyed by biological vectors, including exposure to pathogenic micro-organisms, toxins and bioactive substances, which may cause the loss of life or injury, property damage, social and economic disruption or environmental degradation" (p. 1).

A **biological weapon** is any biological material used with intent to harm. The U.N. Office for the Coordination of Humanitarian Affairs (2004) defines a biological weapon as "a weapon of mass destruction based on pathogenic biological agents" (p. 3). However, this definition is too narrow; **biological agents** could be toxic rather than pathogenic, and not all weapons are weapons of mass destruction.

The U.S. Centers for Disease Control and Prevention (CDC, 2007) defines a "bioterrorism attack" as "the deliberate release of viruses, bacteria, or other germs (agents) used to cause illness or death in people, animals, or plants" (n.p.).

Hazards

The U.S. Army categorizes four types of *biological warfare agents*: **pathogens** (organisms that cause disease, such as pathogenic bacteria), **biotoxins** (biological materials that are toxic), **bioregulators** (any chemicals, such as hormones, that regulate biological processes), and **prions** (infectious proteins that causes other proteins to take on their dysfunctional form).

The CDC (n.d.) lists more than 20 bioterrorism agents and diseases. Table 5.1 shows them listed in alphabetical order, each with its agent type, vector type, and CDC hazard code (A, B, or C, where A is worst; this is a judgmental scale, judged by ease of communication from person to person and by rate of lethality).

Most biological harm is caused by natural pathogens, such as influenza, and by avoidable diseases, such as most forms of heart disease, stroke, and cancers. Some of these routine natural risks are not normally considered within homeland security. Other biological hazards, particularly those that can be weaponized, are normally considered within homeland security. The following

Table 5.1 Bioterrorism Agents

Disease and/or Agent	Agent Type	Main Vectors	Category
Anthrax (*Bacillus anthracis*)	Bacterium	Human, animal, animal product, food, and weaponized form	A
Botulism (*Clostridium botulinum* toxin)	Bacterial toxin	Food and weaponized toxin	A
Brucellosis (*Brucella* species)	Bacteria	Human, animal, and food	B
Cholera (*Vibrio cholerae*)	Bacterium	Water and food	B
Cryptosporidium parvum	Bacterium	Water	B
E. *coli* O157:H7 (*Escherichia coli*)	Bacterium	Food	B
Epsilon toxin of *Clostridium perfringens*	Bacterial toxin	Weaponized toxin	B
Glanders (*Burkholderia mallei*)	Bacterium	Animals (primarily equines), food, and water	B
Melioidosis (*Burkholderia pseudomallei*)	Bacterium	Animals, food, and water	B
Plague (*Yersinia pestis*)	Bacterium	Fleas	A
Psittacosis (*Chlamydia psittaci*)	Bacterium	Birds	B
Q fever (*Coxiella burnetii*)	Bacterium	Animals (primarily ruminants), food, dust, ticks, humans	B
Ricin toxin from *Ricinus communis* (castor oil beans)	Biological toxin	Weaponized toxin	B
Salmonellosis (*Salmonella* species)	Bacteria	Food	B
Shigellosis (*Shigella dysentriae*)	Bacterium	Food	B
Smallpox (variola major)	Virus	Human	A
Staphylococcal enterotoxin B	Bacterial toxin	Food and weaponized toxin	B
Tularemia (*Francisella tularensis*)	Bacterium	Animals (primarily rodents), ticks, biting flies, dust, water	A

Disease and/or Agent	Agent Type	Main Vectors	Category
Typhoid fever (*Salmonella* Typhi)	Bacterium	Food, water, feces	B
Typhus fever (*Rickettsia prowazekii*)	Bacteria	Lice, fleas, ticks	B
Viral encephalitis, caused by alphaviruses, such as Venezuelan equine encephalitis, eastern equine encephalitis, and western equine encephalitis	Virus	Mosquitoes	B
Viral hemorrhagic fevers caused by filoviruses (Ebola and Marburg) and arenaviruses (such as Lassa and Machupo)	Virus	Animals and humans	A
Emerging viral diseases caused by Nipah virus, hantavirus, and others	Virus	Animals and humans	C

Source: U.S. CDC (n.d.).

subsections will focus on salmonella, *botulinum*, *anthracis*, and ricin as the greatest biological threats historically, in order of frequency of use.

SALMONELLA **Salmonella** is a bacterium that when ingested causes a digestive-tract disease with symptoms of severe fever, diarrhea, and abdominal cramps for several days. The disease is at least temporarily incapacitating and can kill the infirm. The CDC estimates about 1.2 million illnesses in the United States each year, of which about 42,000 are confirmed by laboratories and 400 to 450 are fatal. Salmonella is naturally occurring in intensively farmed animals and vegetables and untreated water, although it can be easily killed by heat. In 1984, followers of a cult (Bhagwan Shree Rajneesh, later known as Osho) in Oregon hoped to use salmonella bacteria to incapacitate voters in a nearby town so that their own candidates would win the county elections. Using salmonella obtained from a hospital, they contaminated salad bars at 10 local restaurants, sickening 751 people.

BOTULINUM *Botulinum* is a biotoxin produced by rare but robust bacteria that occur naturally in the soil, from where it could be ingested with food, passed through wounds, or injected with contaminated needles. *Botulinum* is effectively a nerve agent that causes a paralyzing disease known as **botulism**. The CDC receives reports of around 150 cases per year. From 1993 to 1995, Aum Shinrikyo, a Japanese cult, attempted to use biological weapons, including *botulinum* and *anthracis*, against six targets. The attacks failed even when the attempted murder victims directly ingested the bacterium, so Aum switched to chemical weapons. Aum dispersed *botulinum* by sprayer from a car in 1993 and on the subway system in Tokyo in March 1995, five days before the lethal attack with sarin.

ANTHRACIS *Anthracis* is a highly stable and lethal bacterium. *Anthracis* survives for decades as a dormant endospore but replicates rapidly once inhaled, ingested, or injected. The cells produce biotoxins that cause a disease known as **anthrax**, with symptoms of ulcers on contaminated skin, fevers and chills, shortness of breath, coughing, and nausea, along with aches when inhaled and abdominal pain and vomiting when ingested. Anthrax is usually fatal; death is more likely when it is ingested and most likely when it is inhaled.

Progressive prevention is achieved by vaccinating animals where outbreaks have occurred in the past (although underregulated or underdeveloped areas remain unaffected, from where endospores can spread via infected hides and other animal products). People who work with *anthracis* can be vaccinated. Infected patients can be treated with antibiotics.

Spores can be destroyed by burning, boiling, or oxidizing agents, such as chlorine dioxide. Spores can be contained for research purposes, but some risk managers prescribe destruction over containment because of the lingering possibility that containment could fail. For instance, in June 2014, the Centers for Disease Control and Prevention revealed that 84 people had possibly been exposed to *anthracis* at three laboratories in Atlanta, Georgia, due to improper handling. The affected persons were treated with vaccines or antibiotics.

Anthracis endospores are easily stored, and anthrax is equally lethal to humans and most animals; for this reason, it has attracted military interest as a weapon that would threaten both human and agricultural populations.

The most lethal case of weaponized *anthracis* occurred on April 2, 1979, when a Soviet biowarfare site in Sverdlosk (now Ekaterinburg), Russia, accidentally released aerosolized *anthracis*. At least 68 people died; another 30 victims were saved. Soviet weaponization had violated the Bioweapons Treaty of 1972, so the Soviets blamed infected meat. After the dissolution of the Soviet Union in 1991, Russia admitted the true cause but continues to be evasive about the true effects.

On September 18, 2001, letters containing *anthracis* spores were mailed to five news-media offices and two U.S. senators representing the Democratic Party. About 50 people were exposed, mostly by handling the mail, of whom 22 were infected, mostly by inhaling spores, and five were killed. The U.S. Postal Service and corporate internal mail services were disrupted for weeks. The FBI initially blamed Steven Hatfill, a bioweapons expert, but six years later admitted its mistake and paid him $5 million compensation. A later suspect, Bruce Edwards Ivins, a consultant scientist at the federal biodefense labs at Fort Detrick, Maryland, committed suicide on July 27, 2008. In October and November of 2001 alone, U.S. authorities identified 550 hoax anthrax threats, such as harmless powders mailed in envelopes together with notes describing the contents as *anthracis*. Similar hoaxes continue to be mailed every month, but the more threatening bioweaponized letters since then have used ricin.

RICIN **Ricin** is a toxic protein obtained from natural sources, such as castor oil beans. It has been used to kill but only by injection into the blood stream; much larger quantities would be required to kill by ingestion. Soviet-manufactured pellets of ricin are believed to have been surreptitiously injected into a Bulgarian dissident in 1978 before he died after four days of illness. Ricin could be equally lethal if inhaled, but aerosolizing ricin is difficult.

Criminal interest in ricin has tended to be infrequent and amateurish. In 1992, a U.S. federal court convicted four antifederal residents of Minnesota of producing ricin with intent to harm a deputy U.S. marshal. In 1993, a U.S. citizen was detained by Canadian border control officers with a packet of ricin that he claimed to carry for his own protection. In November 1999, a U.S. citizen was arrested in Colorado after threatening to poison two judges; he was found with materials for making ricin. In August 2002, Ansar-al-Islam, an Iraqi Sunni terrorist group, tested ricin in an aerosol form. In January 2003, British police raided houses in London and Manchester where Algerian and British jihadis were preparing ricin for terrorist use. (One policeman was stabbed to death in the fourth raid.) In February 2008, an American man fell ill in a hotel room from ricin that he had produced for unknown purposes. In June 2009, a British man was arrested for planning racist attacks involving ricin. In November 2011, four members of an antigovernment group in Gainesville, Georgia, were accused of plotting to disperse ricin from a moving plane or car, although this was one plot among more credible alternatives using conventional weapons.

Ricin has been most disruptive when sent by mail. In October 2003, a postal facility in Greenville, South Carolina, discovered an envelope containing a small container of ricin with a note threatening the trucking industry. In February 2004, three U.S. Senate office buildings were closed after mail addressed to the senate majority leader tested positive for powdered ricin, although later tests suggested that nontoxic by-products of the castor bean plant in the paper could have triggered the initial test. On April 16, 2013, granulated ricin was found in a letter addressed to a junior senator before it cleared the screening facility ahead of delivery to Capitol Hill. On April 17, a similar letter addressed to the U.S. president also tested positive for ricin at the screening facility; some senate office buildings were shut after a staffer there accepted a letter by hand without screening. On May 29, letters sent to the mayor of New York, Michael Bloomberg, were confirmed to contain ricin. Similar letters were sent to Mark Glaze, the director of Mayors Against Illegal Guns, a group founded by Bloomberg. These letters criticized the mayor's support for gun control. Two days later, similar letters addressed to the president were intercepted. Later, a woman was arrested and pled guilty for sending the letters and trying to frame her husband.

Forecasts

Biological terrorism is rare and very difficult for terrorists to achieve unless they can access the sort of sophisticated technologies, which some states are known to have developed, for containing the bioweapon securely until required for quick release in an aerosol form. Bioweapons are legally proscribed by the Bioweapons Treaty of 1972, but some countries (including the United States) are known to have omitted information about some of their sites and programs from their mandated reports to the U.N. The United States is most worried about former Soviet bioweapons that proliferated in the 1990s after the dissolution of the Soviet Union.

In 2000, the U.S. National Commission on Terrorism concluded that biological weapons were the most attractive of the CBNR weapons to terrorists because the terrorist should be able to escape in the time before the biological agents become apparent to officials and terrorize the public, which could cause significant harm through psychological stress and socioeconomic distortion. The chair of the Commission, L. Paul Bremer III (2002), maintained that view after 9/11 (p. 58).

The U.S. *National Strategy for Countering Biological Threats* presented a more nuanced view of future threats.

> Biological weapons and their use or proliferation by States or non-State actors (biological threats) present a significant challenge to our national security. The development and use of biological weapons involves the diversion of resources that are globally available. Distinguishing illicit intent within the expanse of legitimate activity presents a unique challenge. It is quite possible that we would not obtain specific warning of an imminent threat or impending attack in time to stop it. . . . We are fortunate that biological threats have not yet resulted in a catastrophic attack or accidental release in the United States. However, we recognize that:
>
> 1. the risk is evolving in unpredictable ways;
>
> 2. advances in the enabling technologies will continue to be globally available; and
>
> 3. the ability to exploit such advances will become increasingly accessible to those with ill intent as the barriers of technical expertise and monetary costs decline.
>
> Accordingly, we cannot be complacent but instead must take action to ensure that advances in the life sciences positively affect people of all nations while we reduce the risks posed by their misuse. (U.S. National Security Council, 2009, p. 2)

The U.S. National Security Council (2009) noted evidence collected in Afghanistan from 2001 that al-Qaeda had sought bioterrorist capacity and concluded that, although al-Qaeda has lost most of its capacity, "it is prudent to assume that its intent to pursue biological weapons still exists" (p. 2).

On February 23, 2013, Bonnie D. Jenkins, the State Department's special envoy and coordinator for threat reduction programs, told an academic conference on bioterrorism at Tufts University in Massachusetts that the "United States Government recognizes that bioterrorism is a significant threat not only to the United States, but to the entire world. Biological agents do not acknowledge international borders and sovereign nations" (n.p.).

However, she also stated that

> it is important when addressing the threat posed by bioterrorism to note that the mechanisms we use to address it are equally applicable to emerging infectious diseases. This "dual benefit" to our efforts to counter bioterrorism means that it is absolutely imperative that we work together across the health and security communities as we address biological threats, no matter the cause. (Jenkins, 2013, n.p.)

Most experts on biological warfare recognize that public capacity to counter biological hazards is greater than capacity to counter other hazards, especially chemical hazards. Of all the material hazards, humans have the longest experience countering biological hazards. Humans have always countered natural pathogens and biotoxins. More recently, humans have weaponized some biological agents, although they struggle to keep them safe until they ready for mass lethality when needed. Biological agents have very short storage lives, even when refrigerated, except for *anthracis*. Biological agents are most effective when injected or ingested, but this method is not practical beyond the murder of individual persons. For mass effects, they must be dispersed at very high concentrations, close to the intended target, in a form that can be readily inhaled or ingested. Most practical forms of mass dispersal would destroy biological organisms. Subsequent exposure to sunlight, humidity, and temperature changes would complete the destruction of most within days. In theory, biological agents can be aerosolized for delivery, but this would involve advanced technical skills and specialized equipment of the sort that even superpowers have struggled to acquire. Postal mail is a cheap, low-tech delivery system with mass effects but without the same potential for lethality (Carpintero-Santamaria, 2012, p. 80). Unfortunately, popular culture and potential suppliers of counters to biological hazards exaggerate the risk (Hoffer, 2011, pp. 104–105).

Responses

INTERNATIONAL The Convention on the Prohibition of the Development, Production, and Stockpiling of Bacteriological (Biological) and Toxin Weapons and on Their Destruction (signed April 10, 1972; effective March 26, 1975) essentially proscribes signatory states from acquiring or encouraging others to acquire biological weapons except for defensive research. The convention is comprehensive but has been widely ignored even by signatories. (In March 2015, the 173rd state signed the convention.) Its main implication for countering bioterrorism is in its prohibition of states encouraging acquisition by others.

In 2005, all 194 member states of the World Health Organization (WHO) agreed to the International Health Regulations (IHR), which obliged them (effective 2007) to prevent and respond to acute public-health risks, whether sourced naturally or from terrorism, that have the potential to cross borders and threaten people worldwide.

On September 19, 2011, the United States and the WHO signed a memorandum of understanding to help developing nations strengthen their capacity to address all public-health emergencies of international concern. It had six effective objectives:

1. Enhance the existing global alert and response systems

2. Support implementation of the IHR

3. Strengthen global, regional, and national public health networks

4. Enhance knowledge generation, innovation, and tools for improved management of public health risks and events that may constitute a public health emergency of international concern

5. Enhance global, regional, and national inter-sectoral co-operation for preparedness and management of public health risks and events that may constitute a public health emergency of international concern . . .

6. Strengthen global health leadership and collaboration. (*Memorandum of understanding*, 2011, p. 2)

U.S. President Barack Obama (2011) told the United Nations General Assembly that "we must come together to prevent, detect, and fight every kind of biological danger—whether it is a pandemic like [influenza] H1N1, or a terrorist threat, or a treatable disease" (n.p.).

The IHRs required states to acquire national core public-health capacities by mid-2012, although more than 60% of states requested the allowable two-year extension until mid-2014. In support of this critical need to identify and strengthen implementation gaps, the G8 Global Partnership assisted the funding of five WHO IHR Regional Stakeholders Meetings, attended by partners from different sectors such as health, agriculture, travel, trade, education, and defense.

In 2012, the G8, under the presidency of the United States, expanded the scope of the Global Partnership against WMDs to biological hazards and created a Biosecurity Sub-Working Group, working with the World Health Organization, the World Organization for Animal Health (OIE), the Food and Agriculture Organization (FAO), the Biological Weapons Convention Implementation Support Unit, and INTERPOL. The resulting Global Partnership biosecurity deliverables document specified five "deliverables" to be reviewed annually and assessed after a period of five years.

1. Secure and account for materials that represent biological proliferation risks.

2. Develop and maintain appropriate and effective measures to prevent, prepare for, and respond to the deliberate misuse of biological agents.

3. Strengthen national and global networks to rapidly identify, confirm and respond to biological attacks.

4. Reinforce and strengthen biological non-proliferation principles, practices, and instruments.

5. Reduce proliferation risks through the advancement and promotion of safe and responsible conduct in the biological sciences. (U.S. Department of State, 2012, n.p.)

UNITED STATES The Biological Weapons Antiterrorism Act of 1989, as amended by the Omnibus Antiterrorism Act of 1996, made it a federal crime to threaten, attempt, or conspire to use a biological weapon and directed the secretary of Human and Health Services to issue regulations identifying potential agents and governing their management.

U.S. federal spending on countering bioterrorism dramatically increased after the anthrax attacks in late 2001. The National Institute of Health (NIH) spent less than $50 million on research into countering bioterrorism in 2001; this amount increased to $93 million in 2002, although this spending still accounted for just 0.4% of the NIH budget (Knobler, Mahmoud, & Pray, 2002, p. 22).

The U.S. Congress voted large sums to develop capacity for screening mail before delivery to legislative and executive offices. Such mail is separated at a U.S. Postal Service facility in the capital before being sent to a facility in Maryland that heats and irradiates the mail before final delivery. As of 2012, the U.S. Postal Service admits to spending $12 million per year on screening.

In June 2002, U.S. President George W. Bush signed into law the Public Health Security and Bioterrorism Preparedness and Response Act, which enhanced federal powers to regulate biological industry, food, water, and preparedness for biological terrorism.

The *National Strategy for Homeland Security* specified the following relevant objectives:

- Detect chemical and biological materials and attacks . . .

- Develop a broad spectrum of vaccines, antimicrobials, and antidotes . . .

- Implement the Select Agent Program [which attempts to regulate the carriage and transfer of biological organisms and toxins] (U.S. Office of Homeland Security, 2002, p. x)

Capacities to counter bioterrorism were specified in the *National Strategy to Combat Weapons of Mass Destruction* (December 2002) and two Homeland Security Presidential Directives in 2004 (HSPD-9, *Defense of United States Agriculture and Food*, January 30, 2004; HSPD-10, *Biodefense for the 21st Century*, April 28, 2004).

In April 2003, the Center for Counterproliferation Research at the National Defense University published a proposal for a "national biodefense strategy." In October 2007, President Bush signed Homeland Security Presidential Directive 21, which explicitly referred to *Biodefense for the 21st Century* as the basis for a "National Strategy for Public Health and Medical Preparedness (Strategy)," to be led by the secretary of Health and Human Services. The U.S. government produced no national strategy for biodefense until 2009.

In the middle 2000s, much federal funding was allocated to local preparedness against bioterrorism; however, some of the allocations looked inefficient when small cities acquired the same capacity as large cities with dense biological industry. Local authorities held their counter-bioterrorist capacity in readiness for terrorist attacks when it could have been used to mitigate day-to-day threats to health. At the same time, biological risks increased due to globalization, emerging diseases, antibiotic resistance, and other reasons that had nothing to do with terrorism.

Since then, federal authorities have focused on biological hazards as a spectrum of hazards that can be countered similarly, whether the sources are natural or terrorist. President Barack Obama signed a foreword to this effect in his administration's first *National Strategy for Countering Biological Threats*.

> Advances within the life sciences hold extraordinary potential for beneficial progress, but they also empower those who would use biological agents for ill purpose. Economic, political, and religious forces have given rise to a form of fanaticism that seeks to harm free societies. We know that some of these fanatics have expressed interest in developing and using biological weapons against us and our allies. Addressing these unique challenges requires a comprehensive approach that recognizes the importance of reducing threats from outbreaks of infectious disease whether natural, accidental, or deliberate in nature. (U.S. National Security Council, 2009, n.p.)

The National Security Council (2009) stated that the United States "must reduce the risk that misuse of the life sciences could result in the deliberate or inadvertent release of biological material in a manner that sickens or kills people, animals, or plants, or renders unusable critical resources" (p. 1). However, the NSC admitted that past U.S.

> efforts targeted to prevent such threats have received comparatively limited policy focus or substantive guidance at the National level. Although it is entirely feasible to mitigate the impact of even a large-scale biological attack upon a city's population, doing so incurs a significant cost and effort. We therefore need to place increased priority on actions to further reduce the likelihood that such an attack might occur. (p. 1)

The strategy was defined by seven objectives, whose first letters spelled out the goal ("protect"—as in "protect against the misuse of the life sciences to develop or use biological agents to cause harm").

1. Promote global health security: Activities that should be taken to increase the availability of and access to knowledge and products of the life sciences that can help reduce impacts of outbreaks of infectious disease whether of natural, accidental, or deliberate origin.

2. Reinforce norms of safe and responsible conduct: Activities that should be taken to reinforce a culture of responsibility, awareness, and vigilance among all who utilize and benefit from the life sciences to ensure that they are not diverted to harmful purposes.

3. Obtain timely and accurate insight on current and emerging risks: Activities that serve to improve threat identification, notification, and assessment capabilities as well as our understanding as to the global progress and presence of the life sciences to help identify and understand new and emerging challenges and inform appropriate actions to manage the evolving risk.

4. Take reasonable steps to reduce the potential for exploitation: Activities that are targeted to identify, sensitize, support, or otherwise safeguard knowledge and capabilities in the life sciences and related communities that could be vulnerable to accidents or misuse.

5. Expand our capability to prevent, attribute, and apprehend: Activities that are intended to further hone the Nation's ability to identify and stop those with ill intent to reduce the risk of single, multiple, or sequential attacks.

6. Communicate effectively with all stakeholders: Activities that should be conducted to ensure the Federal Government is advancing cogent, coherent, and coordinated messages.

7. Transform the international dialogue on biological threats: Activities targeted to promote a robust and sustained discussion among all nations as to the evolving biological threat and identify mutually agreed steps to counter it. (U.S. National Security Council, 2009, p. 4)

In September 2011, the Centers for Disease Control and Prevention published *A National Strategic Plan for Public Health Preparedness and Response*, with eight objectives:

1. Prevent and/or mitigate threats to the public's health . . .

2. Integrate public health, the healthcare system, and emergency management . . .

3. Promote resilient individuals and communities . . .

4. Advance surveillance, epidemiology, and laboratory science and service practice . . .

5. Increase the application of science to preparedness and response practice . . .

6. Strengthen public health preparedness and response infrastructure . . .

7. Enhance stewardship of public health preparedness funds . . .

8. Improve the ability of the public health workforce to respond to health threats (pp. 4–7)

The Global Threat Reduction Program, administered by the State Department, leads the U.S. government's international biosecurity effort. It works to improve the security of dangerous biological materials in countries that have a significant terrorist presence or bioscience capacity or have high-risk endemic pathogens.

NUCLEAR HAZARDS

This section defines nuclear weapons, reviews their availability, reviews past accidents, reviews forecasts of their use, and describes official responses.

Definition

A *nuclear hazard* emits harmful electromagnetic energy and could explode from nuclear reactions (rather than chemical energy). A *nuclear weapon* derives its explosive power from nuclear reactions rather than chemical energy. Any nuclear explosion produces immense heat, blast, and electromagnetic energy. If detonated on or near the surface, it would distribute radioactive material over a yet wider area. A single nuclear weapon detonated in a city could destroy built structures for dozens of miles, kill hundreds of thousands of people directly, render the city uninhabitable for decades, and distribute radioactive material globally (depending on weather and climatic conditions).

Availability

Nuclear weapons have been used aggressively only twice, during World War II, both times by the United States against Japan in August 1945 before Japan's surrender. Since then, around 2,300 nuclear explosions have been detonated as tests; most were underground while some were on the surface or in the air. These tests resulted in awful environmental consequences and unexpected harm to thousands of personnel who were supposed to be out of range or protected (see Table 5.2).

Perhaps 125,000 nuclear warheads have been produced, most of which have been reconstituted or deleted. We count warheads because one platform or vehicle, such as an aircraft or **missile**, could carry multiple warheads, some of which might be independently targeted. The United States produced about 70,000 of those warheads. The United States was the first nuclear weapon state, followed shortly by the Soviet Union, Britain, and France. Some states have acquired nuclear weapons since the end of the Cold War while the earlier holders have reduced their holdings. Today, nine states are known to have nuclear weapons, with a total stock of around 19,000 warheads (see Table 5.3).

In one sense, the reduction in the global total of warheads is misleading because current warheads are much more powerful than earlier warheads and because the more recent holders are less trustworthy stewards. For instance, a hydrogen bomb is around 250 times more powerful than the atom bombs dropped on Japan, and North Korea's small but uncertain inventory is more concerning to other states than France's larger inventory.

Separate to the 19,000 extant nuclear weapons, nuclear materials of the type that could be used in nuclear weapons (highly enriched uranium, separated plutonium, and the plutonium content in fresh mixed-oxide fuel) are contained within hundreds of sites in 25 countries as of January 2014. In addition, some nuclear power stations produce material that can be used in nuclear weapons. These sources are generally well defended, but there have been instances where the sites have been penetrated (see Chapter 8) and site officials have trafficked their contents.

Since 1992, 27 states have removed practically all weapon-usable nuclear materials from their territories (see Table 5.4), bringing the number of states with 1 kg or more of weapon-usable nuclear materials down to 25 (see Table 5.5), as reported by the Nuclear Threat Index in January 2014.

The index does not measure the countries with materials that could be used in radiological weapons, only in nuclear weapons. In 2011, the world carried around 2,000 metric tons of weapons-usable nuclear materials, of which only 13% was in active warheads. Ten percent was still in retired warheads, and 43% was in other government-owned forms. In total, 85% of the material was held by military and other authorities not subject to International Atomic Energy Agency (IAEA) security guidelines. The total amount included an estimated 1,440 metric tons of highly enriched uranium and 495 MT of separated plutonium (Nuclear Threat Initiative, 2014, p. 10).

Surprising quantities of nuclear materials are not accounted for, even in stable countries. **Orphan sources** are radioactive sources without proper controls. In 1977, the U.S. GAO reported that several thousand kilograms of nuclear materials were unaccounted for since 1955. Illegal trafficking of nuclear weapons materials surged during the 1990s from the former Soviet Union and Pakistan. Although international agreements and oversight helped to secure or destroy most nuclear weapons from the Cold War, some remain unaccounted for.

Some of this material turns up in the hands of smugglers. Between 1995 and 2008, the IAEA reported 1,562 incidents of confirmed illicit trafficking or smuggling of nuclear and radioactive materials. For instance, in 2003, a smuggler heading for Turkey was captured with 180 g of nuclear material. In 2006, another smuggler nearly escaped Georgia with 5 times that amount. In

Table 5.2 Nuclear Weapon Tests by State and Decade

Country		1945–1949	1950–1959	1960–1969	1970–1979	1980–1989	1990–1999	2000–2010	2010–2013	TOTAL
United States	Frequency	8	188	471	278	177	29	0	0	1151
	Total Yield	203.04	147,963.50	52,260.62	23,328.03	7,691.46	2,965	0	0	234,210.65
USSR	Frequency	1	85	253	335	298	8	0	0	980
	Total Yield	22	26,980.59	241,905.51	47,710.84	7,744.90	2,965	0	0	327,328.84
China	Frequency	0	0	10	16	8	11	0	0	45
	Total Yield	0	0	6,449.2*	22,857*	1,254*	858.52*	0	0	31,418.72
United Kingdom	Frequency	0	21	5	5	12	2	0	0	45
	Total Yield	0	6,108.5*	159.5	450	1,525	105	0	0	8,348
France	Frequency	0	0	30	61	89	18	0	0	198
	Total Yield	0	0	5,770*	9,995	5,550	1,120*	0	0	22,435
India	Frequency	0	0	0	1	0	2	0	0	3
	Total Yield	0	0	0	12	0	Not available	0	0	12*
Pakistan	Frequency	0	0	0	0	0	2	0	0	2
	Total Yield	0	0	0	0	0	Not available	0	0	Calculation undeterminable
North Korea	Frequency	0	0	0	0	0	0	2	1	3
	Total Yield	0	0	0	0	0	0	Not available	Not available	Calculation undeterminable

Source: Data in author's possession from David Jepsen, Section Leader, Nuclear Monitoring Earth Monitoring and Hazards Group, Minerals and Natural Hazards Division, Geoscience Australia.

*Not all yield information is available.

Table 5.3 Estimated Nuclear Warheads by State, 2012–2014

State	Warheads in 2014	Warheads in 2013	Warheads in 2012
United States	7,300 (about 6,800 ballistic missiles; about 500 air-delivered warheads)	7,700	8,000
Russia	8,000 (about 7,000 ballistic-missile warheads; about 1,000 air-delivered)	8,500	10,000
Britain	225 ballistic-missile warheads		
France	300 (about 240 on ballistic missiles, 50 air-delivered, and 10 spare)		
China	250 (about 188 ballistic-missile warheads, 40 air-delivered, 22 spare)		
India	90–110 aerial bombs		80–100 aerial bombs
Pakistan	100–120 aerial bombs		90–110 aerial bombs
Israel	80 aerial bombs		
North Korea	6-8 aerial bombs	10 aerial bombs	

Source: Stockholm International Peace Research Institute (2013, 2014).

July 2013, the IAEA disclosed that each year it receives about 100 reported incidents of theft and other unauthorized activities involving nuclear and radioactive material.

These amounts are too small to be weaponized as nuclear weapons but could be used in radiological weapons (see the next section). According to the Union of Concerned Scientists, an actor would need about 40 to 50 kg of enriched uranium and considerable skills and protective equipment to construct the most basic fissile nuclear weapon. Lighter quantities of rarer species (about 12 kg of highly enriched uranium or 4 kg of plutonium) would be sufficient given higher skills. According to a more skeptical academic, the actor would need more than 100 kg of highly enriched uranium or more than 400 kg of 20% enriched uranium to make a crude nuclear weapon (Hoffer, 2011, p. 110).

Any of these materials has a high radioactive signature, so the handlers would need rare protective materials and skills to survive the handling as well as heavy shielding materials to dampen the signature during transport of the device to its intended place of detonation.

Unofficial use of nuclear weapons is a frequent scenario in popular fiction. However, no nonstate actor is known to have acquired nuclear weapons; the technical challenges remain formidable. Because weapons-grade material does not occur naturally, no nonstate actor would be able to acquire the huge and highly technical capacity necessary to produce such material without official detection or cooperation. Terrorists would need to buy or steal it, but holders of such material are

Table 5.4 States That Have Practically Eliminated Weapons-Usable Nuclear Materials Since 1992

Year	States
1992	Iraq
1996	Colombia
1997	Spain
1998	Denmark, Georgia
1999	Brazil, Philippines, Slovenia, Thailand
2005	Greece
2007	South Korea
2008	Bulgaria, Latvia, Portugal
2009	Libya, Romania, Taiwan
2010	Chile, Serbia, Turkey
2012	Austria, Mexico, Sweden, Ukraine
2013	Czech Republic, Hungary, Vietnam

Source: Nuclear Threat Initiative (2014). Reprinted with permission from the Nuclear Threat Initiative.

strictly proscribed from proliferation; materials have signatures that can be traced back to the source. Stealing a weapon from a secured official site, transporting it, and hiding it without detection is practically impossible.

Radiation is easier to detect than chemical or biological signatures and amateurs tend to be sloppy in their containment of the radiation, so some signature is likely. While some of the less energetic radiological material, in small quantities, is easily shielded for transport by a person, the more hazardous materials, such as those emitting lots of gamma radiation, are very difficult to shield. Shield materials, such as lead, must be large and heavy enough to imply that a radiological device must be carried in a large vehicle.

Even possession of a nuclear weapon does not mean that it is usable since most warheads have locking mechanisms that require codes and expertise to unlock. Even after procurement of the nuclear material itself, the actor would need to mill and shape the weapons-grade material, for which they would need rare technical experts and facilities, without which the technical specialists would expose themselves directly to radiation that would kill them within hours. Assuming that the actor could acquire and prepare the material into a weaponizable form, they would still need to deliver it to the target. By then, the weapon would weigh around one ton. Most nuclear weapons are configured to be delivered by a large missile or aircraft. Thermonuclear weapons are most destructive when

Table 5.5 States Retaining at Least 1 Kg of Weapons-Usable Nuclear Material	
State	**Estimated Weight of Material**
United States	500 or more MT
Russia	500 or more MT
United Kingdom	100–499 MT
France	100–499 MT
Kazakhstan	10.00–99.99 MT
Japan	10.00–99.99 MT
China	10.00–99.99 MT
Pakistan	2.00–9.99 MT
India	2.00–9.99 MT
Germany	2.00–9.99 MT
South Africa	0.50–1.99 MT
Netherlands	0.50–1.99 MT
Israel	0.50–1.99 MT
Belgium	0.50–1.99 MT
Poland	100–499 kg
Italy	100–499 kg
Canada	100–499 kg
Switzerland	21–99 kg
North Korea	21–99 kg
Belarus	21–99 kg
Uzbekistan	5–20 kg
Iran	5–20 kg
Norway	Less than 5 kg
Australia	Less than 5 kg
Argentina	Less than 5 kg

Source: Nuclear Threat Initiative (2014). Reprinted with permission from the Nuclear Threat Initiative.

they explode a short distance (thousands of feet) above the ground. This detonation requires highly sophisticated technology of its own (Hoffer, 2011, pp. 109–111; Mueller, 2012, p. 86).

Past Accidents

Nuclear accidents are rated on a 7-point scale, known as the International Nuclear and Radiological Event Scale (INES), which was introduced by the International Atomic Energy Agency in 1990 for use by member states when reporting accidents (see Table 5.6).

The utility of the INES scale is contested for four main reasons:

1. Most accidents occurred before the IAEA introduced its rating system in 1990.

2. The IAEA relies on member states to report their accidents and rarely investigates their codings.

3. Many of the facts are secret or in dispute.

4. The IAEA does not publicize most of the information it receives.

The IAEA does not maintain a dataset on accidents older than six months or so, mainly to avoid public comparisons of each nation's reporting rate.

The INES scale is logarithmic, meaning that each step up the scale indicates an event 10 times worse than the step below, similar to the moment magnitude scale that is used to describe the comparative magnitude of earthquakes.

According to the IAEA, at least 33 nuclear accidents have occurred from 1952 through 2011, a rate of 0.56 accidents per year (see Table 5.7).

This reporting rate is not a true accident rate because the reporting rate might reflect different reporting vigor or rigor. We probably know of more accidents in recent years thanks to greater national transparency and international accountability. So although the rate of accidents appears to have increased in the last couple decades, in reality the accident rate has probably fallen even while the reporting rate has increased. Moreover, many more radioactive sources are in official and commercial practice today than previous decades, so the real accident rate per source has fallen dramatically.

Yet the list of known accidents is probably an underestimate of all accidents due to official secrecy, particularly in earlier decades of military secrecy. Apart from the two aggressive uses of nuclear bombs in 1945 and the thousands of nuclear weapon tests since then, no nuclear weapon has detonated accidentally, but the true rate of near-accidental detonations is uncertain. This illustrates the uncertainty we still deal with in assessing the true future-risk based on past frequencies.

For instance, the U.S. military reports 32 *broken arrows*, the military's term for accidents involving nuclear weapons, between 1950 and 1980. The last of these occurred in September 1980, when the liquid fuel tank in a Titan II intercontinental ballistic missile exploded due to a leak caused by the impact of a dropped wrench at a U.S. Air Force base in Damascus, Arkansas.

Table 5.6 International Nuclear Event Scale

Level	Definition	People and Environment	Radiological Barriers and Control	Defense in Depth	Example
7	Major accident	Major release of radioactive material with widespread health and environmental effects requiring implementation of planned and extended countermeasures	—	—	Chernobyl, Ukraine, 1986
6	Serious accident	Significant release of radioactive material likely to require implementation of planned countermeasures	—	—	Kyshtym, Russia, 1957
5	Accident with wider consequences	Limited release of radioactive material likely to require implementation of some planned countermeasures. Several deaths from radiation.	Severe damage to reactor core. Release of large quantities of radioactive material within an installation with a high probability of significant public exposure. This could arise from a major criticality, accident, or fire.	—	Windscale, Britain, 1957; Three Mile Island, Pennsylvania, 1979
4	Accident with local consequences	Minor release of radioactive material unlikely to result in implementation of planned countermeasures other than local food control. At least one death from radiation	Fuel melt or damage to fuel resulting in more than 0.1% release of core inventory. Release of significant quantities of radioactive material within an installation with a high probability of significant public exposure.	—	Fukushima, Japan, 2011

Level	Definition	People and Environment	Radiological Barriers and Control	Defense in Depth	Example
3	Serious incident	Exposure in excess of 10 times the statutory annual limit for workers. Nonlethal deterministic health effect (e.g., burns) from radiation.	Exposure rates of more than 1 Sv/h in an operating area. Severe contamination in an area not expected by design, with a low probability of significant public exposure.	Near accident at a nuclear power plant with no safety provisions remaining. Lost or stolen highly radioactive sealed source. Misdelivered highly radioactive sealed source without adequate procedures in place to handle it.	Sellafield, Britain, 2005
2	Incident	Exposure of a member of the public in excess of 10 mSv. Exposure of a worker in excess of the statutory annual limits.	Radiation levels in an operating area of more than 50 mSv/h. Significant contamination within the facility into an area not expected by design.	Significant failures in safety provisions but with no actual consequences. Found highly radioactive sealed orphan source, device, or transport package with safety provisions intact. Inadequate packaging of a highly radioactive sealed source.	Atucha, Argentina, 2005
1	Anomaly	Overexposure of a member of the public in excess of statutory annual limits		Minor problems with safety components with significant defense-in-depth remaining. Low activity lost or stolen radioactive source, device, or transport package.	Breach of operating limits at a nuclear facility. Theft of a moisture-density gauge.

Source: IAEA (2008). Adapted and reprinted with permission from the International Atomic Energy Agency, INES: *The International Nuclear and Radiological Event Scale User's Manual*, 2008 Edition, IAEA, Vienna (2013).

Table 5.7 Major Nuclear Accidents

Year	Country	Site	INES Level	Description
2011	Japan	Fukushima	5	Reactor exploded after cooling failed due to damage caused by tsunami
2011	Japan	Onagawa	—	Reactor fire due to damage caused by tsunami
2006	Belgium	Fleurus	4	Worker harmed by radiation at a commercial irradiation site
2006	Sweden	Forsmark	2	Degraded safety functions for common cause failure in the emergency power supply system at nuclear power plant
2006	USA	Erwin	—	35 L of highly enriched uranium solution leaked during transfer
2005	Britain	Sellafield	3	Radioactive material released but contained within the installation
2005	Argentina	Atucha	2	Worker irradiated beyond annual limit at a power reactor
2005	USA	Braidwood	—	Nuclear material leak
2003	Hungary	Paks	3	Fuel pellets spilled when partially spent fuel rods ruptured during cleaning
1999	Japan	Toakimura	4	Workers fatally irradiated at a nuclear facility
1999	Peru	Yanangio	3	Radiation burns caused by radiography source
1999	Turkey	Ikitelli	3	Loss of a Cobalt-60 source
1999	Japan	Ishikawa	2	Control rod malfunction
1993	Russia	Tomsk	4	Explosive mechanical failure due to overpressure
1993	France	Cadarache	2	Radiation spread to an area not expected by design
1989	Spain	Vandellòs	3	Fire resulted in loss of safety systems at nuclear power station
1989	Germany	Greifswald	—	10 fuel rods damages by overheating
1986	Ukraine/USSR	Chernobyl	7	Material escaped into the atmosphere from a reactor core

Year	Country	Site	INES Level	Description
1986	Germany	Hamm-Uentrop	—	Fuel pebble became lodged in the pipe used to deliver fuel to the reactor
1981	Japan	Tsuraga	2	Overexposure of more than 100 workers
1980	France	Saint-Laurent des Eaux	4	One channel of fuel in the reactor melted without release outside the site
1979	USA	Three Mile Island	5	Reactor core damaged
1977	Czechoslovakia	Jaslovské Bohunice	4	Radioactivity released after fuel integrity damaged and fuel cladding corroded
1969	Switzerland	Lucens	—	Explosion due to loss of coolant at experimental reactor
1967	Britain	Chapelcross	—	Fuel element caught fire after graphite debris partially blocked a fuel channel
1966	USA	Monroe	—	Sodium cooling system malfunctioned
1964	USA	Charlestown	—	Accidental criticality due to error by worker
1959	USA	Santa Susana Field	—	Partial core meltdown
1958	Canada	Chalk River	—	Uranium fuel rod caught fire and was torn in two due to inadequate cooling
1958	Yugoslavia	Vinča	—	Six scientists overexposed during undetected power buildup during a subcritical counting experiment
1957	Russia	Kyshtym	6	Radioactive material released into the environment following an explosion in a waste storage tank due to cooling failure
1957	Britain	Windscale Pile	5	Radioactive material released into the environment following a fire in a reactor core
1952	Canada	Chalk River	5	Power excursion beyond double the reactor's rating due to a reactor shut-off, rod failure, and several human errors

Source: IAEA (2008). Adapted and reprinted with permission from the International Atomic Energy Agency, *INES: The International Nuclear and Radiological Event Scale User's Manual,* 2008 Edition, IAEA, Vienna (2013).

The U.S. military list has been criticized as incomplete. Until long after 1980, the military did not admit the hundreds of minor accidents and technical failures to either Congress or the public. The accident and failure rates were highest between 1958 and 1968, when U.S. nuclear weapons were held at their most ready state. Strategic Air Command held ready thousands of nuclear weapons and nearly 2,000 bombers with capacity to carry nuclear bombs, some proportion of which were held fully fueled and loaded with bombs so as to be ready for launch within 15 min, fully armed in the air.

The closest the United States came to an accidental detonation of a nuclear weapon probably occurred on January 23, 1961, but this event is not on the IAEA's list, and the truth was not revealed for over 52 years after. On that day, a B-52 bomber on a routine flight broke up over North Carolina. A mechanical switch inside the cockpit released the two Mark 39 hydrogen bombs over Goldsboro. One fell to the ground unarmed, but the second fell with three of its four safety mechanisms in a state that would have allowed detonation. Two of these mechanisms had been damaged by the aircraft's breakup, and one was activated by the fall; a single low-voltage switch prevented detonation. The United States admitted the accident at the time but claimed no chance of detonation. The final investigative report was declassified and published on September 23, 2013, after a Freedom of Information Act request by a journalist based in London.

In 1968, Strategic Air Command terminated its airborne alert. Nuclear warheads were subsequently carried within the United States by ground transportation. No more aircraft carried nuclear warheads over the United States until August 2007, when a B-52 bomber mistakenly flew from North Dakota to Louisiana loaded with six cruise missiles, each armed with a 150-kt nuclear warhead. The U.S. Air Force reported that it had intended to carry the missiles but not the warheads (Schlosser, 2013).

Forecasts of Malicious Use

In 1999, a special commission reported to the U.S. president and Congress that terrorist acquisition of a nuclear weapon would face "Herculean challenges" (Gilmore Commission, 1999).

Al-Qaeda has certainly intended to procure nuclear weapons. In 1999, Osama bin Laden told American journalists that all Muslims were religiously obliged to acquire all weapons possible to kill Americans. In 2001, a defector from al-Qaeda testified that al-Qaeda's agents had tried to acquire uranium in Sudan (supposedly ultimately sourced in South Africa) in late 1993. At the time, U.S. officials reported his testimony as incontrovertible and damning (Bremer, 2002, pp. 58–59), but the defector was reporting hearsay and his credibility is doubtful.

In 2001, al-Qaeda's agents are supposed to have met with two disaffected Pakistani nuclear scientists about nuclear weapons (U.K. Home Office, 2010, p. 6). In November 2001, Osama bin Laden told a Pakistani journalist that al-Qaeda had nuclear weapons as a deterrent against U.S. use of WMDs. Since then, public information about al-Qaeda's ambitions has been suggestive but not conclusive. For instance, at the international Nuclear Security Summit in April 2010, U.S. President Obama said, "We know that organizations like al Qaeda are in the process of trying to secure nuclear weapons or other weapons of mass destruction and would have no compunction at using them" (CNN, 2010).

In 2006, the Weapons of Mass Destruction Commission concluded,

> It is unlikely that terrorist groups today could develop and manage the substantial infrastructure that would be required to produce enriched uranium or plutonium for weapons. However, nuclear weapons and weapon materials could be stolen by terrorists either from storage or during transportation. (p. 40)

In April 2010, the United States hosted an international Nuclear Security Summit that recognized the increased risks associated with smuggling of and terrorist interest in nuclear materials. President Obama opened proceedings with the following warning:

> The single biggest threat to U.S. security, both short-term, medium-term and long-term, would be the possibility of a terrorist organization obtaining a nuclear weapon. . . . This is something that could change the security landscape in this country and around the world for years to come. If there was ever a detonation in New York City or London or Johannesburg, the ramifications—economically, politically and from a security perspective—would be devastating. (CNN, 2010)

John Arquilla, a primary theorist of network warfare, argued in 2013 that al-Qaeda would inevitably acquire nuclear weapons if given the time and that, as a network, it cannot be deterred by conventional nuclear deterrence.

More likely, nuclear weapons will proliferate within and between less trustworthy states. The U.K. Ministry of Defence (2010) has forecasted that by 2040 "nuclear weapons are likely to proliferate" (p. 12). Some analysts have described nonstate use of nuclear weapons as inevitable.

> The development of a new generation of tactical nuclear weapons, not yet subject to restrictive international treaties, is in any case already underway. Its widespread use in armed conflict will open a new page in nuclear arms control.
>
> There is also an increasing likelihood that non-state actors will use nuclear weapons, although for the time being they appear not to have access to this technology. But technological "democratization" will, sooner or later, given them this opportunity. For non-state actors, nuclear weapons are unlikely to become a tactical tool to achieve their goals: they will use them in the last resort, when they face a threat to their survival. (Veselovsky, 2013, n.p.)

Global Zero, established in 2008, campaigns for global elimination of nuclear weapons as a control on the risks associated with nuclear war and accidents, not just terrorism. It tends to assess the risks higher than official assessments.

> World powers have come disastrously close to nuclear exchanges many times before—from the 1962 Cuban Missile Crisis [US–Soviet Union] to the 1999 Kargil War [India–Pakistan]. And every day, terrorists are working to build, buy or steal a nuclear weapon. We've been staggeringly lucky so far. (e-mail communication, October 18, 2012)

Responses

In 2006, the United States and Russia created the Global Initiative to Combat Nuclear Terrorism (GICNT), with themselves as cochairs, 85 member states, and four international observers (International Atomic Energy Agency, European Union, INTERPOL, and United Nations Office on Drugs and Crime). By 2012, the GICNT Working Groups in Nuclear Forensics, Nuclear Detection, and Response and Mitigation each had developed best practices and guidance documents.

The U.S. State Department administers a Preventing Nuclear Smuggling Program (PNSP), which assists in reducing the amount of nuclear and radioactive material currently on the black market and helps to integrate these efforts with other U.S. and international threat reduction efforts. PNSP projects range from improving prosecutions of smugglers, enhancing nuclear forensics capabilities, amnesty for orphan sources, strengthening smuggling response protocols, and improving border security.

Many countries deploy systems that can detect radiological materials, usually with earth-orbiting satellites and inspections at border crossings. Some of these systems are unobtrusive portals large enough for vehicles and containers to pass through. When such portals are installed at port exits or over highway checkpoints, practically all vehicles can be screened unobtrusively before access to the interior. Handheld detectors can be carried by officials inside vehicles and containers during intrusive inspections.

The U.S. *National Strategy for Homeland Security* charged the forthcoming DHS with leading the official effort to counter nuclear terrorism within the United States. The primary relevant objective was listed as "prevent[ing] terrorist use of nuclear weapons through better sensors and procedures" (U.S. Office of Homeland Security, 2002, p. 38). The DHS subsequently worked with the Department of Transportation to acquire such sensors and procedures throughout the national transportation infrastructure. However, in September 2002 and September 2003, journalists from ABC News shipped depleted uranium supplied by the Natural Resources Defense Council inside containers about the size of a soda can from foreign Muslim countries into the United States. The depleted signature was of sufficient scale that it should have been detected by official defenses, but, in each case, officials inspected the container without detecting the nuclear material.

RADIOLOGICAL HAZARDS

This section defines radiological hazards and reviews past historical use and practical responses.

Definition

Radiological material radiates harmful electromagnetic energy, of which the most harmful forms are the various ionizing radiations—charged particles of sufficient energy to harm (alpha and beta particles)—and gamma rays. Ionizing radiation is carcinogenic and can burn and sicken the victim in extreme cases.

Radiological material is not necessarily useful for a nuclear explosion, which is impossible without a critical mass of unnatural nuclear materials. Radiological material could be obtained from nuclear weapons or in much smaller quantities from more accessible sources, such as food irradiators, radiation therapy systems, and certain oil exploration equipment.

A **radiological weapon** distributes radiological material. The most efficient method of dispersal would be a small explosive charge (a **dirty bomb**) that would blow radioactive material over a wider area, rendering the area uninhabitable for decades, short of a very burdensome clean up. The greater the explosive blast, the more effective the dispersion of radioactive material, although the ultimate effects would depend on the strength and direction of wind, air temperature, secondary materials, and the topography of the surrounding area (Carpintero-Santamaria, 2012, p. 82).

Accidental radiological incidents indicate the potential returns. On September 13, 1987, in Gioânia, Brazil, two unauthorized men entered an abandoned medical site and salvaged a radiation therapy unit used to treat cancer; they dismantled it, exposing radioactive cesium chloride, and sold everything to a scrap yard, where the radioactive material was displayed and distributed as an exotic or supernatural material for its blue glow. After many people became sick, officials confirmed and secured the source on September 29. About 112,000 people were examined, 1,000 people were identified with unnatural levels of radiation, 249 people were found to be significantly contaminated, 129 internally, of whom 20 people showed signs of radiation sickness and four died from having handled it while consuming food or inhaled the powder; others suffered burns that required amputations. Several houses and all their contents and thousands of tons of topsoil were removed. This incident indicates how a small radiological weapon, using commercially available hazards, could be used to disrupt the lives of hundreds of thousands of people in an urban area, particularly if the incident leads to panic, even though few people would be killed.

Another delivery mechanism would be to damage a nuclear power station in order to release large enough amounts of radioactive material without necessary explosive distribution. Such power stations are well protected from outside attack and have incorporated safeguards to prevent a nuclear-core meltdown even if terrorists should gain control of the reactor. However, the large pools and storage containers used to hold spent nuclear fuel are outside of the reactor and can be accessed more easily. Terrorists could empty a pool or breach a container, leading to a high-temperature fire that would release large quantities of radioactive material into the environment. In the United States, such nuclear waste is held at around 66 commercial and 55 military sites (Hoffer, 2011, p. 108). The risks from nuclear fuel were illustrated in March 2011, when an earthquake and tsunami crippled the nuclear power station at Fukushima, 130 mi northeast of Tokyo, Japan, sparking triple nuclear meltdowns, contaminating the ocean for thousands of miles, and forcing more than 160,000 residents to flee from nearby towns.

Historical Terrorist Use

In November 1995, Chechen jihadi terrorists planted a radiological explosive device with **dynamite** and cesium-137, used in gauges and cancer treatments, in a park in Moscow. They alerted the news media without detonating the device. In December 1998, Chechen authorities found a similar device in Argun, Chechnya.

In 2002, Jose Padilla, an American convert to Islam by the adopted name of Abdullah al-Muhajir, was arrested. Official accusations centered on an alleged plot to detonate a radiological device in the United States, but eventual charges never mentioned such a device. In March 2003, the

U.S. DHS reported a credible threat to the nuclear power plant at Palo Verde, Arizona. In August 2003, Canadian police detained 19 Pakistani-born men who had filed a flight path over a nuclear plant and taken flying lessons. In 2004, jihadi terrorists in Britain considered radiological weapons. In 2006, the leader of al-Qaeda in Iraq appealed for nuclear scientists to join him in order to attack U.S. military bases (U.K. Home Office, 2010, p. 6).

The more frequent malicious use of radiological material is to poison individual persons. In August 1995, an employee at the Center for Cancer Research, Massachusetts Institute of Technology, Boston, was probably deliberately poisoned when he ingested a small amount of phosphorous-32, without developing any symptoms. In November 2006, Alexander Litvinenko, a former Soviet/Russian spy, was living in asylum in Britain after revealing nefarious official Russian activities when he fell ill and died. British investigators found traces of polonium-210 in his body, at a restaurant where he had met with Russian agents, and in the seat in which one of them had flown to Britain. Russia has refused to extradite the suspects.

Practical Responses

Radiological sources should be contained and protected from illegitimate use. Alternatives to radiological equipment should be sought, such as nonradiological medical treatments. Large radioactive sources, such as power stations, should be located far from urban areas.

In the event of radiological release, the most effective response is avoidance of exposure. Exposure time should be minimized, the distance to the source should be maximized, and shields should be placed between the target and the source. The first preference should be evacuation. Those who cannot be evacuated should be ordered to shelter inside a structure of higher material density and with apertures sealed; personnel could be issued protective clothing.

For those already exposed, they can be cleaned of contamination, thereby reducing the chance of ingestion or inhalation of radioactive materials, but they would continue to be exposed to radiation from the source until they are removed or that source is contained. In anticipation of—or immediately after—exposure, people can be defended with orally administered potassium iodate, a stable form of iodine that can bind to the thyroid gland and prevent uptake of radioactive iodine by the gland. Otherwise, once exposed the victim cannot be cured of radiation exposure, although he or she can be treated for the health consequences. These consequences tend to be slow-onset cases with high uncertainty, so much uncertainty that some later health problems may not be provably blamed on radiation.

CHEMICAL EXPLOSIVES

This section defines chemical explosives and reviews the different types of chemical explosives, explosive effects, and official responses.

Definitions

Given the complexity of chemical explosives, the subsections below define several terms: chemical explosive, improvised explosive device, vehicle-born improvised explosive device, body-borne improvised explosive device, and explosively formed projectile.

CHEMICAL EXPLOSIVES A *chemical-explosive hazard* is a chemical compound or mixture of chemicals that could release energy rapidly in the form of gas and heat. The rapid release of gas is experienced mostly as *blast*, where energy is moving rapidly through the surrounding space as a wave of compressed air, which can crush, blow over, or blow apart materials and people. The rapid release of heat might burn or start fires.

Chemical explosives are produced commercially for use in demolition and mining. They are used militarily as propellants of projectiles, such as bullets, and as explosive warheads within projectiles, such as high-explosive shells. **High-yield explosives** or **high explosives** are more efficient chemical explosives and are typical of military applications. Chemical-explosive weapons are separate from chemical weapons, which do not need to be explosive to be harmful.

Many authorities do not recognize or declare any threshold between high-yield and low-yield explosives. Some authorities prefer to separate **military-grade explosives** from **commercial-grade explosives**. In the definitions and policy documents issued by the U.S. DHS and British Civil Contingency Secretariat, the *E* in CBNRE refers to explosives. In Public Safety Canada's standard it refers to high-yield explosives, which makes more sense because we would not want to separate anything but high-yield explosives as special when almost all military and terrorist weapons use chemical explosives of some sort or another. However, legislators and prosecutors are incentivized to include all explosives under CBNRE so as to make prosecution easier. Indeed, some terrorist plotters have been indicted for intent to use WMDs even though their only intended weapons were homemade explosives.

High-yield explosives can be so efficient that a small volume—smaller than a human fist—would be energetic enough to cause a catastrophic failure in a pressurized airliner if properly placed. Such explosives tend to be expensive and restricted to trusted military clients, but military ordnance can leak into the hands of insurgents and terrorists. Some of the most restricted forms have leaked into the hands of terrorists through disreputable governments, such as when Libya supplied Semtex to the Irish Republican Army. Additionally, a Libyan agent used Semtex to destroy Pan Am Flight 103 over Lockerbie, Scotland, in December 1988. Semtex is physically plastic for easier handling and use and lacks the chemical signatures that would alert explosives detection dogs and other sensors.

IMPROVISED EXPLOSIVE DEVICES In the past, all explosive devices were known as bombs or mines, but these terms have narrower meanings in military use, so the trend in recent decades has been to refer to **improvised explosive devices (IEDs)** as distinct from industrially produced military munitions. The terrorist's usual weapons are improvised from reconfigured ordnance or publicly accessible chemicals, such as agricultural fertilizers and fuel oils, and some detonating system, usually electrical. In the 2000s, more than half of terrorist attacks used explosives. Insurgents also increasingly rely on explosives, particularly during insurgencies in areas with unsecured military munitions, such as in Iraq following foreign invasion in 2003. Their skills and materials have disseminated whenever foreign insurgents have migrated. From 9/11 through 2010, high-casualty bombings alone (each at least 15 dead) killed more than 26,000 people globally; 60% of them were in Iraq. Although the rate in Iraq fell in late 2007 after political deals and military changes, the rate remains high and steady—500 to 1,000 deaths to high-casualty bombings every six months. Meanwhile, from 2007 on, high-casualty bombings increased in frequency in Pakistan. Some of the skills proliferated as far afield as Mexico, where illegal drug cartels used them to make war on each other and official authorities. From 2003 to 2007, the coalition in Iraq suffered 13.7 IED attacks per day, which accounted for around 2,000 or about two thirds of all U.S. combatant deaths during the first four years of the occupation of Iraq. The frequency of IED attacks in Afghanistan doubled from 2008 to 2009, accounting for about 80% of U.S. combatant deaths (Marshall & Cole, 2011, p. 7).

VEHICLE-BORNE IMPROVISED EXPLOSIVE DEVICES Small portable devices are more attractive to the terrorist or insurgent in rural areas and in tightly controlled urban areas where vehicles are subject to searches. Large devices take time to collect and prepare and usually must be transported in a large vehicle. Officials refer to these systems as **vehicle-borne improvised explosive devices (VBIEDs)**. The vehicles are usually cars, but attackers have used motorbikes, bicycles, and even wheelbarrows for proximate threats; truck-borne IEDs have been used to destroy large buildings, although large trucks are practically impossible to fill with explosives unless the actor is operating in a corrupt or failing state with insecure official stocks of explosives.

BODY-BORNE IMPROVISED EXPLOSIVE DEVICES Human beings can transport explosives and detonate themselves or be detonated remotely by others. Although commonly termed **suicide bombers**, not all are suicidal, so they are properly called *human-borne bombs*, **human bombs**, or **body-borne IEDs** (BBIEDs). *Suicide bombers* implies that they have conscious intent to kill themselves in the process; however, some bombers are duped into carrying bombs that are detonated remotely by a controller, while others might have intended to drop their explosives before detonation but ended up detonating them prematurely.

BBIEDs are effective because humans can adapt to defensive measures before detonation. However, humans can carry fewer explosives unobtrusively than would fit inside a typical vehicle, so BBIEDs are acquired to attack better defended but fragile targets at proximate range. They have been used

- to assassinate very important human targets (For instance, on March 10, 2009, a Tamil Tiger killed a Sri Lankan minister and 14 others at an open-air festival in Akuressa.)

- to kill guards ahead of other attackers (On April 5, 2010, human bombers approached local guards at the U.S. Consulate in Peshawar, northern Pakistan, before other attackers struck.)

- to harm groups of densely packed civilians in the open (On March 2, 2004, around 12 suicide bombers and a couple vehicle-borne explosive devices struck crowds celebrating a Shia festival in Karbala, Iraq, killing around 180 and injuring more than 500.)

- to harm smaller groups of people inside enclosed spaces (On November 9, 2005, suicide bombers from al-Qaeda in Iraq struck inside three hotels in Amman, Jordan, killing more than 60 and wounding more than 100.)

Human bombs are very rare and make up a small proportion of all terrorist attacks, but the frequency has increased greatly in the last decade. Human bombs are more likely than any other type of attack to be deadly or to cause serious debilitating wounds. Robert Pape (2005) counted just 315 suicide attacks from 1983 to 2003. The annual frequency peaked at more than 500 in 2007, most of them in Iraq. From 2003 through 2010, Iraq suffered 1,003 documented suicide bombings. Suicide attacks also increased in Afghanistan, from two in 2003 to 123 in 2006.

From 1980 to 2003 (excluding 9/11), 12 people died per human bombing globally. In Iraq, from 2003 through 2010, the rate was 12.5 fatalities per human bombing, with 12,484 civilian and military fatalities in total. The death rate per casualty was 28.6% for civilians only, similar to the death rate for casualties due to small arms. Few of the casualties were soldiers; 79 events killed 200 soldiers. Human bombs caused 42,928 (19%) of the civilian casualties, including 30,644 (26%) injured civilians and 12,284 (11%) deaths in Iraq during that period (Hicks, Dardagan, Bagnall, Spagat, & Sloboda, 2011).

EXPLOSIVELY FORMED PROJECTILES One type of chemical-explosive weapon behaves more like a firearm (as described in the last section of this chapter), in that it produces *explosively formed projectiles* (EFPs), but is often inaccurately conflated with an IED, when, in fact, an EFP weapon might or might not be improvised. The EFP weapon consists of a cone-shaped piece of ductile material, such as copper or lead, with its point facing into an explosive material, away from the target. When the explosive detonates, it causes the ductile material to collapse and project toward the target as a long thin projectile travelling at a very fast speed. EFPs are normally acquired to attack armored vehicles. EFPs can be produced industrially or improvised; the Iraqi insurgency proved the proliferation of the materials and skills necessary for improvisation of EFPs, although any IED would fail to achieve the yield of an industrially produced device.

Materials

The subsections below explain in more detail the explosive materials, including military munitions, commercial explosives, ammonium nitrate–based mixtures, alternatives to ammonium nitrate, potassium chloride, hydrogen peroxide, and commercially available fuels.

MILITARY MUNITIONS Military munitions contain explosives for either propellant or destructive purposes. Military munitions are attractive to malicious users because their propellants or warheads normally contain explosive materials that are more energetic (higher yield) than commercially available alternatives. Military explosives are distinguished by superior energy and stability, a combination that malicious actors struggle to achieve otherwise. For instance, **trinitrotoluene (TNT)** has been in use for more than 100 years in both commercial and military sectors because it is both reasonably energetic and stable—stable enough that it needs much more energetic materials to detonate.

Explosive devices must be packaged in some way for transport or delivery. The most likely components are a case or casing, a detonator, and a main explosive charge or filling. *Bombs* are usually delivered by aircraft and finish their journey in free fall. Some bombs are guided by fins or active propulsion; in the latter case, they are likely to be known colloquially as *missiles*, although all projectiles are missiles in the general sense. **Mines** or **land mines** are explosive devices placed in or on the ground before they are armed, with expectation that they would be detonated by something passing over or near them. Small devices that can be carried, armed, and thrown in one hand are best differentiated as **hand grenades.** (They were once known as bombs too.) Portable mines and **grenades** are easier to hide and carry but are not normally lethal unless the victim is within a few dozen yards; thus, most landmines require the victim to step on to the device before detonation while hand grenades are usually thrown at the target.

Military munitions can be converted into other forms of explosive devices: munitions can be drained of their explosive content so that they can be packaged differently; munitions can be placed with other devices that are easier to detonate, in the hope that the other munitions would detonate sympathetically; or military munitions can be used with different detonation systems. For instance, an aerial bomb could become a land mine if equipped with a different detonator.

COMMERCIAL EXPLOSIVES IEDs can be based on commercially available materials too, such as chemical explosives used in industrial mining operations, fuels, or agricultural fertilizers. The resulting explosives tend to be less stable and/or energetic than military explosives. The user would need larger devices for the same yield, which implies a greater burden in gathering, transporting, and using such materials, although in poorly regulated or permissive societies this burden may not be observed by authorities.

Some explosives are commercially available, although usually subject to strict licenses. These include *dynamite* (nitroglycerin absorbed into a porous material) and **pentaerythritol tetranitrate (PETN)**. They are normally packaged in sticks weighing a few pounds.

Explosives can be supplied as **detonating cords** (inside a thread or plastic coating) or as *blast caps* or **blasting caps**, which are small containers of very sensitive explosive used to detonate a main charge sympathetically. These quantities are useful for detonating other explosives but are not normally sufficient to harm unless held against the human body. Insurgents have used detonating cords to execute prisoners but have not relied on cords or caps for IEDs. Cords and caps can be mixed with other explosives in improvised devices to make up the weight or in an attempt to accelerate the collective detonation. In theory, malicious actors could collect enough cords or caps to form large bombs, but this would be unnecessarily burdensome.

Commercial explosives are normally licensed only for commercial demolitions or mining, but commercial supplies were sold corruptly to the jihadi terrorists who attacked railway trains in Madrid, Spain, on March 11, 2004, with the resulting loss of 191 lives.

AMMONIUM NITRATE–BASED EXPLOSIVES Ammonium nitrate (AN) is a commonly available compound that can be used as the main ingredient in several explosive mixtures. It is most available as an agricultural fertilizer. Agricultural fertilizer can be explosive by accident. For instance, on April 16, 2013, an explosion during a fire at an ammonium nitrate fertilizer plant in the small town of West, Texas, killed 15 people, injured around 200, and leveled 75 homes. The fire may have been started deliberately.

A common explosive that is sold as a compound and can be made from commercially available materials is a mix of **ammonium nitrate and a fuel oil (ANFO)**; diesel is an example of the fuel used. ANFO has an explosive yield up to 1.4 times the yield of TNT when properly processed. Ammonium nitrate is typically supplied in 110-lbs (50-kg) bags. Terrorists have used ANFO for large bombings in tightly controlled developed states where military ordnance is practically impossible to acquire, such as

- The IRA's bombing of Bishopsgate, London, on April 24, 1993 (2,000 lbs, one dead)

- The Oklahoma City bombing, April 19, 1995 (4,000 lbs, 168 dead)

- The jihadi plot against London nightclubs and a shopping center (1,000 lbs, arrests made on March 30, 2004)

- The jihadi plot against the Toronto stock exchange, 2006

- Anders Behring Breivik's VBIED, central Oslo in Norway, July 22, 2012 (2,000 lbs, eight dead; Breivik had collected 3 MT of ammonium nitrate)

Insurgents and terrorists have used ANFO extensively in Afghanistan, where large military munitions are less available than in Iraq. Most Afghan ANFO IEDs weigh around 40 lbs (18 kg) but can surpass 1,000 lbs (454 kg). Most Afghan IEDs using military explosives weigh 5 to 10 lbs.

Most AN in Afghanistan is manufactured in Pakistan. In November 2009, the North-West Frontier provincial government banned ammonium and nitrate fertilizers. In January 2010, the Afghan and Pakistan national governments banned ammonium nitrate. Seizures in Afghanistan of AN doubled in the first seven months of 2012 (about 480 T) compared to 2011, but IEDs also reached a new record high (16,600). ANFO was used in about 65% of the IEDs reported by coalition forces in Afghanistan in 2012.

Explosive alternatives to ANFO include **ammonium nitrate and sugar (ANS)** and **ammonium nitrate aluminum (ANAL**, an unfortunate acronym).

ALTERNATIVES TO AN In April 2013, Sandia National Laboratories, New Mexico, released a formula for a fertilizer (essentially AN with an iron sulfate additive that splits the AN into iron nitrate and ammonium sulfate and gives the powder a green tint) for free, although critics claim that urea or even urine would reverse the reaction.

AN can be replaced by urea-based alternatives that are less explosive, but farmers prefer AN for its higher agricultural yield. Urea-based IEDs are less energetic and are more difficult to detonate. For instance, on May 1, 2010, Faisal Shahzad, a Pakistani-born naturalized U.S. citizen, attempted an attack in Times Square, New York, with a VBIED packed with propane, gasoline, fireworks, gunpowder, and urea-based fertilizer, but it failed to explode; vendors noticed smoke and alerted police.

POTASSIUM CHLORATE Another commercially available compound of explosive potential is potassium chlorate ($KClO_3$), which is used to bleach paper and to make matches and fireworks. As an ingredient, it is less explosive than ammonium nitrate, so it requires more chemistry and material to form IEDs of the same yield. Jihadi terrorists, associated with Jemaah Islamiyah, used IEDs made from potassium chlorate, aluminum, and sulfur to attack a nightclub and a bar in Bali on October 12, 2002. Their largest VBIED contained about 2,000 lbs of explosive. Potassium chlorate IEDs became common in eastern Afghanistan and western Pakistan, using commercial Chinese and Indian supplies, after crackdowns on AN in 2009. Lashkar-e-Jhangvi, a Pakistani jihadi group, used potassium chlorate for two bombings in early 2013.

HYDROGEN PEROXIDE Hydrogen peroxide is the main ingredient in triacetone triperoxide (TATP), a sensitive liquid explosive, and hexamethylene triperoxide diamine (HMTD), a more stable explosive. Although unstable, TATP has been used frequently by terrorists, including

- A British convert to Islam, Richard Reid, who attempted to light an IED in his shoe on an airliner on December 22, 2001

- The four suicide bombers who killed themselves and 52 other people on London transport on July 7, 2005

- The British jihadis who plotted to bomb U.S.-bound airliners out of London in August 2006

- Danish jihadis who plotted to bomb targets in Vollsmose in September 2006 and Copenhagen in September 2009

- German jihadis who plotted to bomb targets in Sauerland in September 2007

- A British convert to Islam, Nicky Reilly, who attempted to blow himself up in a restaurant in a shopping center in Exeter on May 22, 2008, but succeeded in burning only himself

- The American jihadis who plotted to bomb the New York subway in September 2009

COMMERCIALLY AVAILABLE FUELS Commercially available fuels, such as diesel and propane, are easily used as inflammatory materials but are not normally explosive until combined with other materials, contrary to popular cultural depictions of readily exploding automobiles and oil drums. Terrorist attempts to use available fuels have tended to fail. For instance, in July 2006, two British-Indian jihadis attempted to attack the Tiger Nightclub in Leicester Square, London, with two cars packed with propane, gasoline, and nails but failed to detonate them; the same perpetrators attempted to bomb Glasgow Airport in Scotland with a similar vehicle but succeeded in burning only themselves. On May 1, 2010, Faisal Shahzad's attempt to attack Times Square, New York, included propane and gasoline in his VBIED, but neither of these materials exploded.

Effects

Explosive devices are attractive to attackers who want to limit their own exposure to countermeasures, since explosives can be prepared in advance and timed to detonate after the deliverer has departed or detonated remotely. Most explosive attacks cause minor damage and do not kill anyone. If people are harmed, more people are injured or distressed than are killed. The typical rate of deaths among all injured victims is 10%. Experienced and well-trained terrorists with plenty of foreign supplies and local targets can raise the lethality rate dramatically without leaving identifying evidence. For instance, the lethality rate per military casualty from terrorist explosions was at least 22% in Northern Ireland.

Blast is lethal and destructive at proximate range but is baffled by built structures, so it is most threatening to humans if the device is detonated close to them, in the open or inside built structures with limited apertures, or if the blast causes the structure to collapse on top of occupants. Most built structures would survive typically sized terrorist IEDs, although blast can blow windows and other fragile materials into buildings as flying hazards to the occupants. Unless the device is very large (as would fill a truck) and driven alongside or inside the built structure or the target is very vulnerable (such as a pressurized airliner), most built structures would not fail catastrophically.

Yet large IEDs, if properly placed near critical structural elements, could cause a catastrophic failure in almost any structure. For instance, on April 18, 1983, a terrorist drove a van into the foyer of the U.S. embassy in Beirut before detonating the explosive load, causing higher floors to collapse, although the bulk of the structure did not; 63 people died. On October 23, 1983, another terrorist drove a truck into the lobby of a similarly sized building nearby in Beirut, which was being used by the U.S. Marine Corps to accommodate marines on a peacekeeping mission. The blast caused the building to collapse, killing 242; 58 French personnel were killed in a simultaneous attack on French barracks.

Much smaller explosives could cause fragile or pressurized structures to fail. For instance, on December 21, 1988, a half pound of Semtex, hidden inside a radio-cassette player, destroyed Pan American Flight 103 over Lockerbie, Scotland, killing 270.

Blast and heat can start fires, dramatically raising the death toll. For instance, on October 12, 2002, a van-borne device on a narrow street in Bali caused the partial collapse of and fires in neighboring structures, including a nightclub. A suicide bomber also struck a bar. The total death toll was 202, mostly from fire in the nightclub. On February 27, 2004, a small bomb aboard a superferry out of Manila, the Philippines, killed no one directly but started a fire that soon killed at least 116 people.

Civilians are much more likely than military personnel to be harmed by terrorist attacks, partly because soldiers have more defensive capacity, such as armored vehicles and personal armor. The economic effects also tend to be quite severe; explosive devices can damage infrastructure and distort economies. Even fake or unexploded IEDs cause authorities to close roads or public areas until the device is properly identified and safely cleared, often by hand, a process that typically lasts hours per device. The United States spent $17 billion on protective acquisitions and counter-IED activities in fiscal years 2002 to 2010.

Official Responses

Homeland Security Presidential Directive 19 of February 12, 2007, established a national policy and called for the development of a national strategy and implementation plan on the prevention and detection of, protection against, and response to terrorist use of explosives in the United States (HSPD-19; Combating Terrorist Use of Explosives in the United States). Under the HSPD-19 framework, DHS, DOJ, and DOD have created a joint program office to coordinate the execution of policy and programs to counter the terrorist use of explosives in the United States. DHS established the Office for Bombing Prevention to lead DHS's participation.

ENERGY WEAPONS

An *energy weapon* directly transfers energy to the target, such as by electromagnetism, light, heat, or sound.

Some energy weapons are commercially accessible to everyone. For instance, handheld laser lights, sold commercially as pointers for instructional purposes, are powerful enough to dazzle pilots of commercial airliners as they come in to land. Although targeting such a device by hand from the ground is too erratic to cause blindness in a pilot, it is disruptive enough to potentially prevent a pilot from safely landing the plane.

Since around 2000, more powerful lasers, some with target-tracking technologies, have been available for military purposes, such as blinding optical sensors. Some handheld military lasers can damage image intensifiers and thermal imagers from a range of about one mile. Lasers of such power could easily blind a human eye, but such use seems to be illegal under existing international law, and they are usually configured by their electromagnetic band to avoid damage to human eyes. However, some Russian and Chinese lasers have been marketed for military use in dazzling human eyes.

Some energy weapons have been developed as short-range nonlethal alternatives, such as microwave weapons that cause unpleasant heat sensations and sonic weapons that knock people over with a sonic blast rather than blast produced from chemical energy. However, these weapons remain expensive and historically have struggled to incapacitate humans reliably without killing them. Given the immaturity and exoticism of some of their technologies, their users ironically face greater ethical, legal, and technical uncertainties than users of kinetic weapons.

The most destructive—but not the most lethal—energy weapon is electromagnetic. The smallest nuclear explosion produces enough electromagnetic energy to destroy unshielded electronic equipment miles away. The prohibitions on the use and proliferation of nuclear weapons would suggest that such an electromagnetic weapon is unlikely, although presumably ambitious and thoughtful nonstate threats are likely to consider an electromagnetic weapon. The effects would be greatest against civilian targets in highly developed, highly populated places, as military electronics tend to be shielded.

FIREARMS

This section defines firearms and reviews firearm violence, terrorist use of firearms, and official responses.

Definition

Firearms are weapons from which projectiles are propelled by an internal explosion. This internal explosion is normally produced from chemical energy. One round of ammunition is typically composed of a chemical propellant charge behind the projectile. More exotic weapons can launch similar projectiles using electromagnetic rails or compressed air, but these tend to be experimental or specialist weapons for rare purposes.

By this definition, firearms include the largest artillery, but these are largely military hazards that are rarely present as hazards for civilian authorities. Only a few types of artillery are reviewed in this chapter, although more antiaircraft, antishipping, and antivehicle weapons are reviewed in later chapters.

More frequent hazards in both military and civilian use are *small arms*—portable firearms, such as rifles, pistols, and revolvers. Sometimes portable rocket launchers or self-propelled missile launchers are considered small arms; these include **rocket-propelled grenades (RPGs)**, some of which are small enough to install as attachments to rifles, although the most produced model is a legacy Soviet design that is fired from the shoulder (RPG-7). Some shoulder-launched missiles (known inaccurately as bazookas) are designed to destroy tanks or bring down aircraft (**man-portable air defense systems, or MANPADs**).

Firearm Violence

Criminal violence using firearms necessarily derives from both human intent and human use of a firearm. Firearms add to the threat significantly. Although most people with access to firearms would not commit a crime with firearms, when people both develop real intent to harm (themselves or others) and have access to firearms, they are likelier to cause more harm than they would with just their hands. Most suicides and violent crimes are impulsive. If the impulse were to pass without access to firearms, the person must find another usually less capable way to harm themselves or others. Of course, a person with sufficient intent could acquire another weapon (such as kitchen knives, which are legal purchases almost everywhere) with which to commit murder, but naturally, any capability that is available and more harmful would make the threat more harmful. Countries with stricter restrictions on public ownership of firearms have fewer lethal crimes than countries with looser ownership of firearms even if the countries have similar rates of violent crime.

According to WHO estimates, intentionally violent injuries caused 1.6 million deaths in 2004; 51% of these were by suicide, 37% were by interpersonal violence, and 11% were in wars and other mass conflicts.

The United Nations Office on Drugs and Crime (2010a) estimates that the global market for illicit firearms is $170 million to $320 million per year, equivalent to 10 to 20% of the licit market (p. 129).

Firearms are most available to private residents in the United States; Americans own the most firearms per capita (0.88 firearms per capita), the most firearms in total (270 million firearms), and a higher proportion of types (such as semiautomatic rifles) that are restricted to military or law enforcement personnel in most democratic countries. In 1994, the U.S. Congress passed a federal ban on *assault weapons* (semiautomatic weapons that resemble fully automatic rifles), but the law expired in 2004.

American firearm ownership is bimodal: most Americans own either no firearms or several firearms. Very few Americans with access to firearms are firearm criminals. Indeed, while the rate of privately owned firearms is around 88,000 per 100,000 Americans, the rate of murders by firearms is 2.97 per 100,000 Americans. However, Americans suffer more violence in general and more firearm crimes in particular than residents of most other democracies. Even though the frequency of homicide has declined in America since the 1980s, the proportion of homicides caused by firearms has remained the same (around 80%). This proportion is higher than anywhere else in the world except Mexico, where firearm crime is inflated by conflicts over illegal narcotics. The United States suffers a lot more violence than Switzerland (second most guns per capita in any democracy and the third most guns per capita in any country, after Yemen).

Today, the United States suffers a median rate of violent crime (all types, including homicides) similar to the rate in other western democracies, such as Britain, France, and Germany, but the homicide rate is much greater in America than in these other countries. For instance, in 2010, the United States, with a population around 5 times greater than Britain's population, experienced 244 times more murders by firearms than Britain, with only 41 murders by firearms. Firearms killed 0.01% of Americans in 2010, although about two thirds of these were suicides or accidents, and one third resulted from crimes.

Most violent crimes, including homicides, have declined in America since the 1980s. Private firearm ownership also has declined from a high of 54% of households in 1994 to lows of 40%, according to Gallup surveys; nevertheless, firearm crimes have not declined as a proportion (around 80%) of crime. Firearm crimes started to rise after a trough in 2000. In 2010, the last year for which data on American firearms deaths are available, more than 31,000 Americans were killed in America by firearms, or about 10 per 100,000 residents. About 19,000, or about 61%, of these deaths were suicides (more than 6 per 100,000); 11,078 deaths were homicides committed with firearms (3.6 per 100,000 residents); just 3 to 4% of the firearms deaths were due to accidents. The deaths and injuries attributable to firearms cost America $68 billion in medical costs and lost work in 2010 (Newsome, 2014, pp. 165–167).

Terrorist Use of Firearms

Most terrorist attacks involve bombings, followed by small arms. Small arms are portable and simple to use, yet their projectiles tend to be more lethal (about 30% probability of lethality per wound) than whatever projectiles are picked up and carried by a blast (about 10% probability of lethality per wound).

Unlike abandoned explosive devices, users of small arms can adapt to the target, seeking to expose the targets and evade their defenses. Consequently, small-arms attacks tend to include a higher proportion of dead among all casualties. Most violent deaths in Iraq since 2003 have been by firearms, many of them murders of unarmed victims at proximate range, which helps to explain the high rate of lethality—around 50% of all civilian casualties.

Small arms have become more attractive to highly motivated terrorists in South Asia too. For instance, on March 3, 2009, 12 attackers from Lashka-e-Taiba, a jihadi group based in Pakistan, attacked the Sri Lankan cricket team's bus as it passed Liberty Square in Lahore, Pakistan. Eight people, six policemen and two civilian drivers, were killed; nine people were injured. The attackers escaped on motorcycles, although some were arrested later.

The supply-side barriers to small-arms attacks include the unavailability of weapons, the user's aversion to killing at proximate range, and the user's fears of defensive countermeasures. For instance, Anders Behring Breivik took time and some international intrigue to acquire his armament (a shotgun, a carbine, and a pistol), with which he killed 69 people on an island near

Oslo, Norway, on July 22, 2011. Later, in court, he admitted spending more time preparing psychologically with violent movies and video games, saying, "It's easy to press a button and detonate a bomb. It's very, very difficult to carry out something as barbaric as a firearm-based action" (Pidd, 2012, n.p.).

Few attacks use a mix of weapons at the same time; these multiweapon or multimethod attacks are more challenging but more effective. The attackers might use explosives to perforate a perimeter, then access the interior with small arms, or use an explosion to draw reaction forces that can be attacked with small arms. For instance, on April 2, 2005, attackers detonated seven vehicle-borne explosive devices at the perimeter of the prison at Abu Ghraib, Iraq, before pedestrian attackers with small arms crossed the perimeter. On September 14, 2012, suicide bombers perforated the perimeter of Camp Bastion, a foreign coalition base in Afghanistan, so that gunmen could enter the base with small arms. On July 22, 2013, vehicle-borne suicide bombers, supported by mortars, breached the perimeter of Abu Ghraib prison again while pedestrians with portable weapons intercepted reaction forces. Five hundred to 600 prisoners escaped; dozens of prisoners and security forces were killed.

The firearm is the deadliest weapon in American terrorism. Since 9/11, 19 Muslim-American terrorists carried out 17 violent attacks, of which nine involved firearms, three used IEDs, three used bladed weapons, one used a car, and one used a plane. About 75% of the 200,000 murders in the United States during the same period were murders by firearms (Kurzman, 2013, 2015).

Official Responses

Most Americans are genuinely scared of firearm crime; these fears drive much of the defensive demand for guns. Sensitivity to firearm crime is countered by the freedoms to own and bear arms. Some cities and states have legislated against firearm ownership or carriage, but national political interest in firearm control did not change significantly until after a series of mass murders with firearms occurred in 2012, the severest of which was the killing of 20 children and six adults at an elementary school in Sandy Hook, Newtown, Connecticut, on November 30, 2012. The perpetrator, 20-year-old Adam Lanza, had shot to death his mother earlier at home and later shot himself to death inside the school. At the end of 2012, the Obama administration pushed for more restrictive federal legislation. This event illustrates the potential for *shocks* (unusual events) to change popular or political sensitivity. The administration announced 23 separate executive actions, including a new ban on assault rifles, a ban on high-capacity magazines, and wider checks on the buyer's background, although these actions were blocked in Congress.

The Obama administration's initiative quickly trailed off but was revived later in 2013. On September 16, 2013, 34-year-old Aaron Alexis, employed by the U.S. Navy as a contractor maintaining computers at Navy facilities from 2012 to 2013, used firearms in his backpack to kill 12 people at the Washington Navy Yard before being killed by police. President Obama used the case to again call for firearm controls, although the case caused as much concern about how he could maintain the secret-level clearance despite a history of mental illness and three arrests (2004, 2008, 2010), including twice for discharging his pistol after altercations. In March 2014, the DOD announced changes to its clearance system and site security.

How Could We Improve Nuclear Security?

Sam Nunn

Obviously, in an age of terrorism, the airline industry depends on this safety and security system for its economic viability, and countries depend on it to protect their citizens. Shouldn't the security of potentially the most dangerous material on the planet have an equally effective approach?

We also need to think broadly about nuclear security as it is affected by nonproliferation, arms reductions, and nuclear energy. For example, let's think about these questions and challenges:

- What are the security implications of continuing to increase nuclear material stockpiles without limits?

- What are we doing about the spread of technology for peaceful nuclear power programs that can also be used for nuclear weapons, and can we close gaps by building consensus around new approaches to the nuclear fuel cycle?

- Can we think and act boldly by beginning to bring the production of all enrichment and reprocessing under strict international monitoring?

The intersection of all of these areas is the nuclear material and whether it is managed responsibly. Nuclear security is not a stand-alone issue; it is a continuing and perpetual mission, one that can be made easier or harder depending on the policy decisions made in these related areas.

My bottom line is this: The world needs a nuclear materials security system in which

1. All nuclear weapons–usable materials are covered—civilian and military

2. All states adhere to internationally recognized standards and best practices

3. States demonstrate to each other that they have effective security in place by taking reassuring actions, such as inviting peer reviews of their facilities using outside experts

4. States reduce risks by decreasing their material stocks and the number of facilities that house them

Former senator Sam Nunn served as senator from Georgia from 1972 to 1997. He is currently cochairman and CEO of the Nuclear Threat Initiative, a nonprofit, nonpartisan organization working to reduce the threats from nuclear, biological, and chemical weapons.

Source: Courtesy of the Nuclear Threat Initiative.

This chapter has

- Defined material hazards in general and reviewed past malicious use of material hazards, forecasts of terrorist use, and international and U.S. responses

- Defined chemical hazards, described industrial hazards and chemical weapons, and reviewed forecasts of malicious chemical-weapon risks and reviewed international and U.S. responses

- Defined biological hazards, described the hazards, and reviewed forecasts of future malicious use and official responses

- Defined nuclear hazards, described the availability of these hazards, and reviewed past

accidents, forecasts of malicious use, and official responses

- Defined radiological hazards and reviewed past malicious use and practical responses

- Defined chemical explosive hazards, described the materials used to make the hazards and threats, described the effects of explosives, and reviewed official responses

- Defined energy weapons and reviewed past use

- Defined firearms and reviewed firearm violence, terrorist use of firearms, and official responses

KEY TERMS

Ammonium nitrate (AN) *206*
Ammonium nitrate aluminum (ANAL) *207*
Ammonium nitrate and fuel oil mixture (ANFO) *206*
Ammonium nitrate and sugar mixture (ANS) *207*
Anthracis 180
Anthrax *180*
Biological agents *177*
Biological hazard *168*
Biological weapon *177*
Bioregulator *177*
Biotoxin *177*
Blast *168*
Blasting cap *206*
Body-borne IED *204*
Bomb *174*
Botulinum *179*
Botulism *179*
Chemical explosive *168*

Chemical explosive hazard *168*
Chemical hazard *168*
Chemical weapon *172*
Commercial-grade explosive *203*
Detonating cord *206*
Dirty bomb *201*
Dynamite *201*
Energy hazard *168*
Energy weapon *168*
Explosive *168*
Firearm *168*
Grenade *206*
Hand grenade *206*
Hazard *167*
High explosive *203*
High-yield explosive *203*
Human bomb *204*
Improvised explosive device (IED) *203*

Land mine *205*
Man-portable air defense system (MANPAD) *211*
Military-grade explosive *203*
Mine *205*
Missile *188*
Nuclear hazard *168*
Nuclear weapon *168*
Orphan source *188*
Pathogen *177*
Pathogenicity *168*
Pentaerythritol tetranitrate (PETN) *206*
Prion *177*
Radiological hazard *168*
Radiological weapon *201*
Ricin *180*
Rocket-propelled grenade (RPG) *211*
Salmonella *179*
Small arms *169*

QUESTIONS AND EXERCISES

1. How are weapons of mass destruction and CBNREE weapons different?

2. Why does the public tend to inflate CBNREE risks?

3. Why has terrorist use of CBNREE weapons been rare?

4. Which of the CBNREE weapons is most frequently stocked by governments and used by terrorists?

5. How do international authorities counter CBNREE weapons?

6. What is the difference between chemical weapons and chemical explosives?

7. Why are chemical weapons more accessible than biological weapons?

8. Give four categorical examples of biological weapons.

9. Why would the sources of anthrax attacks be mainly official but the sources of ricin attacks be mainly private?

10. Why are nuclear weapons difficult to acquire?

11. How are nuclear and radiological weapons different?

12. How have radiological materials been used to kill?

13. How should potential victims reduce their exposure in case of a radiological release?

14. What is a high-yield explosive?

15. In what situations would you expect more IEDs?

16. Why would malicious actors prefer military explosives when making IEDs?

17. Why would malicious actors prefer commercially available materials when making IEDs?

18. What commercially available materials can be used as the explosive content of IEDs?

19. To whom are BBIEDs normally targeted?

20. When would terrorists prefer BBIEDs or VBIEDs?

21. What is an energy weapon?

22. Why are energy weapons rare?

23. Why would a malicious actor prefer firearms over IEDs?

24. What are the usual scenarios for firearm use?

6

NATURAL RISKS

In September 2012, the World Economic Forum surveyed more than 1,000 experts and found them slightly more pessimistic for the next decade of global risks. This shift in opinion arose because persistent economic weakness decreases our ability to tackle environmental challenges. Respondents viewed the failure of climate change adaptation as the environmental risk with the most knock-on effects for the next decade (Howell, 2013).

In 2013, the World Economic Forum identified the following six natural risks:

1. Extreme weather events

2. Natural catastrophes of other kinds

3. Man-made environmental catastrophes

4. Major biodiversity loss and ecosystem collapse

5. Water crises

6. Failure of climate change mitigation and adaptation (World Economic Forum, 2014, p. 13)

The World Economic Forum asked experts to choose the greatest risks over the next decade from a list of 31. The experts' top 10 global risks included four natural risks.

1. Fiscal crises in key economies

2. Structurally high unemployment/underemployement

3. Water crises

4. Severe income disparity

5. Failure of climate change mitigation and adaptation

Learning Objectives and Outcomes

At the end of this chapter, you should be able to understand the definitions, trends, distribution, and returns of

- Natural hazards and threats in general

- Climate change in general

- Weather events in general

- Droughts and heat waves

- Storms, hurricanes, cyclones, and typhoons

- Tornadoes

- Floods

- Geological and geomorphic hazards (such as subsistence)

- Seismic hazards (mostly earthquakes)

- Volcanic hazards (such as ejected lava or ash)

- Fires (both human-caused and wild)

- Cosmic hazards (such as solar storms and meteors)

6. Greater incidence of extreme weather events . . .

7. Global governance failure

8. Food crises

9. Failure of a major financial mechanism/institution

10. Profound political and social instability (World Economic Forum, 2014, p. 9)

NATURAL HAZARDS AND THREATS IN GENERAL

This section defines natural hazards and threats, reviews trends in natural risks, and describes the distribution of natural hazards and threats.

Defining Natural Hazards and Threats

Hazards are things in a nonharmful state; **threats** are in a harmful state. **Natural risks** are risks that arise from natural sources; these sources are natural in that they exist without human creation, although human activities are often necessary to activate hazards as threats. Where humans activate the threat from a **natural hazard**, many authorities would regard the threat as a **human-made threat** or a *human-manufactured threat*, even though their effects are often indistinguishable.

Unfortunately, we have no standard list of natural risks. The International Risk Governance Council's list of natural forces (wind, earthquakes, volcanic activities, drought, flood, tsunami, wildfire, avalanche) is incomplete (see Table 6.1).

Similarly, the Canadian government's taxonomy categorizes natural risks as meteorological, geological, and ecological, separate from health and "emerging phenomena and technologies," which include many natural risks (see Table 6.2).

Munich Reinsurance Group (2011) counts geophysical events (earthquakes, tsunami, volcanic eruptions, dry-earth movements), meteorological events (storms), hydrological events (floods, wet mass movements), and climatalogical events (extreme temperatures, droughts, and wildfires). Munich Re orders natural events from Class 0 to Class 6 (see Table 6.3).

In this chapter, natural hazards and threats are separated into eleven classes:

- climate change in general,
- weather events in general,
- droughts and heat waves,
- storms, hurricanes, cyclones, and typhoons,
- tornadoes,
- floods,

- geological and geomorphic hazards (such as subsistence),

- seismic hazards (mostly earthquakes),

- volcanic hazards (such as ejected lava or ash),

- fires (both human-caused and wild), and

- cosmic hazards (such as solar storms and meteors).

Table 6.1 The International Risk Governance Council's List of *Hazardous Agents*	
Category	**Subcategories**
Physical	Ionizing radiation, nonionizing radiation, noise (industrial, leisure, etc.), kinetic energy (explosion, collapse, etc.), temperature (fire, overheating, overcooling)
Chemical	Toxic substances, genotoxic/carcinogenic substances, environmental pollutants, compound mixtures
Biological	Fungi and algae, bacteria, viruses, genetically modified organisms, other pathogens
Natural forces	Wind, earthquakes, volcanic activities, drought, flood, tsunami, wildfire, avalanche
Sociocommunicative	Terrorism and sabotage; human violence (criminal acts); humiliation, mobbing, and stigmatizing; experimentation with humans; mass hysteria; psychosomatic syndromes
Complex combinations	Food (chemical and biological); consumer products (chemical, physical, etc.); technologies (physical, chemical, etc.); large construction, such as buildings, dams, highways, bridges; critical infrastructures (physical, economic, and socio-organizational and -communicative)

Source: Renn (2008, p. 6); International Risk Governance Council (2005).

Trends

Natural risks are so pervasive and extensive that they can be underestimated; events can be frequent and individually trivial but add up or compound as highly consequential aggregates. Yet these events may be ignored in comparison to infrequent but disastrous events. For instance, people are more likely to remember the once-in-a-lifetime flood that killed hundreds of people in a day, rather than the thousands of people killed per year in minor accidents involving water.

Due to human activities, many types of natural disaster are becoming more frequent and costly (such as storms), even though human activities have practically terminated other natural hazards (such as some pathogens).

Table 6.2   The Canadian Government's Taxonomy of Threats and Hazards

Group	Category	Subcategories
Intentional	Criminal	Terrorist, extremist, individual criminal, organized criminal, corporate or insider saboteur, corporate spy
	Foreign state	State-sponsored terrorist, spy, war belligerent
Unintentional	Social	Migration, social unrest and civil disobediences
	Technical and accidental	Spill, fire, explosion, structural collapse, system error yielding failure
Health	Pandemics and epidemics	Human health, animal health
	Large-scale contamination	Contaminant of drugs and health products; contaminant of food, water, or air; contaminant of the environment
Emerging phenomena and technologies	—	Biological science and technology, health sciences, (re)emerging health hazards, chemical components, emerging natural hazards, material science and engineering, information technologies
Natural	Meteorological	Hurricane; tornado or wind storm; hail, snow, or ice storm; flood or storm surge; avalanche; forest fire; drought; extreme temperatures
	Geological	Tsunami, earthquake, volcanic eruption, land or mudslide, land subsidence, glacier or iceberg effects, space weather
	Ecological and global phenomena	Infestations, effects of overexploitation, effects of excessive urbanization, global warming, extreme climate change conditions

Source: Public Safety Canada (2013, p. 65). *All Hazards Risk Assessment Methodology Guidelines, 2012–2013,* page 65, http://www.publicsafety.gc.ca/cnt/rsrcs/pblctns/ll-hzrds-ssssmnt/index-eng.aspx#ahra_business, 2012-2013. Reproduced with the permission of the Minister of Public Safety and Emergency Preparedness Canada (2015).

The simplest cause of increased natural risks to humans is increased exposure. In the last 200 years, the human population has grown from one billion to seven billion; in the previous 800 years, the population had increased by just 700 million. The modern population has concentrated in larger cities and spread into more hazardous areas. Simultaneously, people with higher standards of living put more demand on natural resources and commodities (Swiss Re Group, 2013, p. 5).

Accidents are usually **rapid-onset hazards**, whereas long-term exploitation of the natural environment without sufficient periods for natural relief or recovery is associated with **slow-onset**

Table 6.3	Munich Re's Natural-Event Scale						
	Class	Property Damage	Overall Losses (USD Millions)				and/or Fatalities
			1980s	1990s	2000s	2010+	
0	Natural event	None	—	—	—	—	None
1	Small-scale–loss event	Small scale	0.63	0.91	1.18	>1.33	1–9
2	Moderate-loss event	Moderate	5.08	7.28	9.40	>10.60	>10
3	Severe catastrophe	Severe	29	42	54	>61	>20
4	Major catastrophe	Major	114	164	212	>230	>100
5	Devastating catastrophe	Devastating	305	437	504	636	>500
6	Great natural catastrophe	"substantial economic loss," and insured losses reaching "exceptional orders of magnitude"					Thousands

Source: Munich Reinsurance Group (2011).

hazards, such as desertification, exhaustion of fresh water, salination of soils, toxic contamination of soils, erosion of soils, and changes in **weather** and climate (see Table 6.4). Slow-onset hazards have long-term effects, and some are irreversible. These slow-onset hazards are getting worse, although some optimists forecast rapid solution by future technologies, such as genetically engineered crops that would need less water or could tolerate more salty or acidic soils.

The trends are accelerating in both frequency and costs. In 2005, a new record was set for losses to natural catastrophes, only to be surpassed in 2011, due mainly to earthquakes and floods in Japan, New Zealand, Thailand, and thereabouts. Subsequent years have been less costly globally, but more of the economic costs were concentrated in the United States (see Table 6.6).

Distribution, Exposure, and Capacity

Some populations are disproportionately exposed to more natural hazards. In addition, some populations lack capacity to control the risks. Within the population of all exposed targets, some of these targets may have superior capacity to control the risks, while other targets have inferior capacity. A natural event, such as a storm, could be unremarkable for people living far away (not exposed) or for people with capacity to control the risks but could be disastrous for people exposed without such capacity. Thus, natural risk is a combination of the natural hazard, exposure to the hazard, and the incapacity to control the risk.

Table 6.4 Lethality of Different Categories of Natural Disasters, 1900–1999

Onset Type	Natural Disaster Type	Percentage of Natural Disaster Deaths
Slow	Famines and droughts	86.9
Rapid	Floods	9.2
Rapid	Earthquakes and tsunami	2.2
Rapid	Storms	1.5
Rapid	Volcanic eruptions	0.1
Rapid	Landslides	Less than 0.1
Rapid	Avalanches	Negligible
Rapid	Wildfires	Negligible

Source: Wisner, Blaikie, Cannon, and Davis (2004, p. 3).

Table 6.5 Frequency and Cost of Class 6 Natural Catastrophes, 1950–1999, and of Class 1 to Class 6 Natural Events, 2000–2014, by Decade

Decade	1950–1959	1960–1969	1970–1979	1980–1989	1990–1999	2000–2009	2010–2014
Number of events	20	27	47	63	91	7,675	4,475
Overall economic losses (USD billions)	42.7	76.7	140.6	217.3	670.4	934.0	945
Insured losses	—	6.2	13.1	27.4	126.0	301.5	279

Source: Data from Munich Reinsurance Group (2011).

The Alliance Development Works produces an influential annual review of natural risks globally by calculating risk as a product of exposure and capacity. They write,

> Our core statement is that a country's exposure to a natural hazard and the effects of climate change is not the only factor responsible for the disaster risk, but that rather, it is also the social framework conditions and capacities to take action that are reflected in susceptibility, coping capacities and adaptive capacities. These three components describe a society's vulnerability and can shed light on whether the occurrence of an extreme natural event can result in a disaster. . . . Thus it is owing to the social, economic, ecological and institutional conditions in a society that one country will be vulnerable while another will not. (Beck et al., 2012, p. 18)

Table 6.6 Frequency and Cost of Class 1 to Class 6 Natural Events by Year, 2000–2014

Year	Number of Events	Economic Losses (USD Billions)	Insured Losses (USD Billions)
2000	Circa (c.) 850	30	7.5
2001	c.700	36	11.5
2002	c.700	55	11.5
2003	c.700	60	15
2004	640	150	48
2005	675	220	100
2006	850	50	15
2007	960	83	26
2008	750	200	45
2009	850	50	22
2010	960	150	38
2011	820	380	105
2012	905	170	70
2013	890	135	35
2014	980	110	31

Source: Data from Munich Reinsurance Group (2011).

Using the formula described above, the Alliance Development Works ranks countries annually by their natural risks (see Tables 6.7 and 6.8).

As explained in the three subsections below, risks tend to be lower in the developed world and higher in the developing world (due to increased exposure and incapacity, each of which is associated with sociopolitical inequities as well as geographical coincidence).

DEVELOPED WORLD North and Central America suffer almost as many natural disasters as Asia, despite being a smaller region, mainly due to denser development in the path of routine weather hazards. Europe is the densest developed of these regions and suffers the most harmful natural event per resident and unit land area. Most of these events are weather events (see Table 6.9).

The United States is the most materially developed and insured country and is also a large country with exposure to extreme climates and seismic fault lines, so it suffers the costliest natural disasters in economic and insured terms (see Table 6.10), although it also has great capacity for defense and response.

Table 6.7 Countries Ranked by Their Natural Risks: 50 Riskiest Countries in 2014

Rank	2014	
	Country	World Risk Index
1	Vanuatu	36.50
2	Philippines	28.25
3	Tonga	28.23
4	Guatemala	20.68
5	Bangladesh	19.37
6	Solomon Islands	19.18
7	Costa Rica	17.33
8	El Salvador	17.12
9	Cambodia	17.12
10	Papua New Guinea	16.74
11	Timor-Leste	16.41
12	Brunei Darussalam	16.23
13	Nicaragua	14.87
14	Mauritius	14.78
15	Guinea-Bissau	13.75
16	Fiji	13.65
17	Japan	13.38
18	Vietnam	13.09
19	Gambia	12.23
20	Jamaica	12.20
21	Haiti	12.00
22	Guyana	11.81
23	Dominican Republic	11.50
24	Niger	11.45

Rank	2014	
	Country	World Risk Index
25	Benin	11.42
26	Chile	11.30
27	Chad	11.28
28	Cameroon	11.20
29	Madagascar	11.20
30	Senegal	10.96
31	Honduras	10.80
32	Burundi	10.59
33	Sierra Leone	10.57
34	Indonesia	10.55
35	Togo	10.47
36	Cape Verde	10.32
37	Albania	10.17
38	Zimbabwe	10.01
39	Djibouti	9.93
40	Afghanistan	9.71
41	Burkina Faso	9.62
42	Cote d'Ivoire	9.29
43	Myanmar	9.14
44	Mozambique	9.03
45	Mali	8.85
46	Ghana	8.77
47	Uzbekistan	8.67
48	Guinea	8.53
49	Suriname	8.42
50	Kyrgyzstan	8.33

Source: Garschagen et al. (2014, p. 64).

Table 6.8 Countries Ranked by Their Natural Risks: 50 Least Risky Countries in 2014

Rank	2014	
	Country	World Risk Index
121	Bulgaria	4.21
122	New Zealand	4.20
123	Bahamas	4.19
124	Uruguay	4.00
125	Libyan Arab Jamahiriya	4.00
126	Australia	3.93
127	United States	3.88
128	Russia	3.85
129	Kazakhstan	3.74
130	Paraguay	3.74
131	Argentina	3.68
132	Slovenia	3.64
133	Portugal	3.61
134	Austria	3.58
135	Slovakia	3.57
136	United Kingdom	3.54
137	Czech Republic	3.46
138	Latvia	3.45
139	Belgium	3.41
140	Kuwait	3.34
141	Poland	3.28
142	Spain	3.20
143	Canada	3.14
144	Belarus	3.12
145	Ukraine	3.11
146	Lithuania	3.01
147	Germany	3.01
148	Mongolia	3.00

Rank	2014	
	Country	World Risk Index
149	Denmark	2.93
150	Cyprus	2.76
151	Oman	2.74
152	France	2.59
153	Luxembourg	2.52
154	Seychelles	2.51
155	Switzerland	2.48
156	Estonia	2.43
157	Israel	2.38
158	Norway	2.31
159	Egypt	2.29
160	Singapore	2.25
161	Finland	2.24
162	Sweden	2.19
163	United Arab Emirates	1.91
164	Bahrain	1.78
165	Kiribati	1.72
166	Iceland	1.56
167	Grenada	1.44
168	Barbados	1.21
169	Saudi Arabia	1.17
170	Malta	0.62
171	Qatar	0.08

Source: Garschagen et al. (2014, p. 66).

In the 1960s, U.S. presidents declared 167 major disasters, in the 1970s, 331, in the 1980s, 237, in the 1990s, 460, in the 2000s, 550, and in 2010, a new annual record of 81 (the average per year during these years is 44.5). In 2011, earthquakes and flooding catastrophes in the United States alone caused more than $120 billion in insured losses, although these losses were dwarfed by related events in other regions that year. The year 2012 was less costly ($60 billion in insured losses and $140 billion in total economic losses from natural catastrophic events) than 2011 for the United States but still above the average for the preceding 10 years.

DEVELOPING WORLD The developing world includes countries mostly in the southern hemisphere, South America, Africa, and Asia. The developing world by definition is developing its capacity in comparison with the developed world. It is also exposed to significant hazards. Developing countries tend to be located in areas with high exposure to great storms, on great river floodplains, in low-lying coastal areas, and on top of seismic fault lines and lack developed-world infrastructure or the capacity to develop such infrastructure. Moreover, developing countries tend to suffer more industrial and terrorist disasters, due partly to increased exposure and partly to weak capacity to control the risks and respond to events (see Table 6.9).

Asia is the largest region and suffers the costliest and most frequent natural disasters. Due to lower take-up of insurance, the developing world suffers less of the insured costs, even though it suffers most of the deaths due to **natural threats**. Over 95% of all deaths due to weather, seismic, industrial, and terrorist disasters from 1970 to 2001 were caused by weather and seismic activity in the developing world (see Table 6.10).

SOCIOPOLITICAL INEQUITIES The elevated risks in the developing world are issues for the developed world, ethically and materially, since the developed world effectively shares the risks by responding charitably or by suffering consequences, such as migration or political violence, that flow out of the developing world at increased rates after disasters.

Whether developed or not, within any area, the poor or the marginalized tend to be disproportionately exposed or vulnerable to natural hazards. Their exposure or vulnerability can turn a hazard into a disastrous threat for them, even while it remains just a hazard for others. Since hazards are concentrated in space, such as on floodplains or seismic fault lines or in the normal path of hurricanes or monsoons, people with capacity reduce their exposure by moving away, leaving the poor to live in more hazardous areas, or by acquiring defensive responses, such as reinforced structures.

Table 6.9   Distribution of Natural Disasters in 2014 by Continent

Region	Events	Fatalities	Overall Economic Losses	Insured Losses
Asia	37%	75%	46%	17%
North America, Central America, and the Caribbean	20%	5%	29%	58%
Europe	16%	4%	16%	21%
Africa	10%	10%	1%	<1%
Australia and Oceania	8%	1%	1%	3%
South America	9%	5%	7%	1%

Source: Munich Re Group (2011).

Table 6.10 The Frequency of, Deaths Caused by, and Value of Insurance Claims Due to Disasters, 1970–2001

Region	Weather	Seismic	Industrial	Terrorist	TOTAL
North America	23 disasters 2,000 deaths $66 billion	1 disaster — $17 billion	1 disaster 2,000 deaths $2 billion	3 disasters 3,000 deaths $50 billion	28 disasters 7,000 deaths $135 billion
Europe	5 disasters — $5 billion	— — —	2 disasters — $2 billion	6 disasters — $6 billion	13 disasters — $13 billion
Japan	3 disasters 3,000 deaths $3 billion	1 disaster 1,000 deaths $1 billion	— — —	— — —	4 disasters 4,000 deaths $10 billion
Central and South America	5 disasters 21,000 deaths $5 billion	5 disasters 130,000 deaths $5 billion	— — —	— — —	10 disasters 151,000 deaths $10 billion
Developing Asia, Africa, and Middle East	14 disasters 650,000 deaths —	15 disasters 420,000 deaths $3 billion	2 disasters 8,000 deaths —	8 disasters 1,000 deaths $8 billion	39 disasters 1,079,000 deaths $11 billion
TOTAL	50 disasters 676,000 deaths $79 billion	22 disasters 551,000 deaths $26 billion	5 disasters 10,000 deaths $4 billion	17 disasters 4,000 deaths $64 billion	94 disasters 1,241,000 deaths $173 billion

Source: Suder (2004, p. 190).

Further, a demographic might marginalize certain groups deliberately. Such a demographic could leverage political or military power to push others into hazardous areas. Another consequence of this marginalization would be inferior access to the resources that the higher authority could offer to others as controls on the risks—controls such as flood defenses or emergency services. Further, after a negative event, that same higher authority is likely to react by focusing on its favored groups, so the risks would fall for favored groups but remain the same for unfavored groups (see Figure 6.1) (Wisner et al., 2004, pp. 6–8).

Natural threats are often visualized as quick, discrete events. However, interacting with social, economic, and political factors, they can have strange and obscure long-term socioeconomic effects, which often compound other risks, with consequences that are not captured by typical

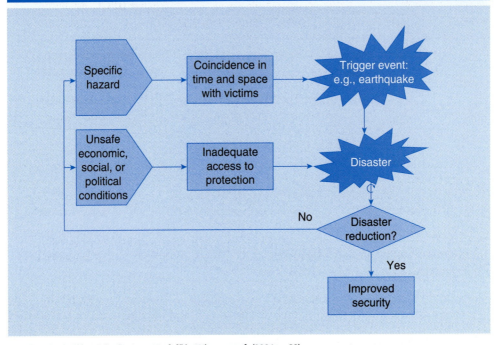

Figure 6.1   A Model of Natural Disasters

Source: Adapted from the "Access Model" in Wisner et al. (2004, p. 89).

measures (human casualties and economic losses). For instance, in 1992, Hurricane Andrew struck Florida, directly killing 65 people and causing about $45 billion in economic losses, with profound negative socioeconomic consequences. Hurricane Andrew coincided with a weak political and economic state; weak regulation had left the state with substandard preparations for a hurricane and contributed to feverish speculation on the housing market, leading to a housing bubble. The hurricane's destruction and the market bubble compounded each other, leading to spikes in abandoned properties, deferred rebuilding, and unemployment. More obscure were the effects on families: Impoverishment, unemployment, homelessness, dependency, and uncertainty contributed to domestic stresses, including increased violence within the home (Wisner et al., 2004, pp. 15–16).

CLIMATE CHANGE

The U.S. National Oceanic and Atmospheric Administration's National Weather Service (2009) defines **climate** as "the composite or generally prevailing weather conditions of a region, throughout the year, averaged over a series of years" (n.p.). The subsections below define climate change and global warming, review the consequences, and review controls on climate change.

Definitions

CLIMATE CHANGE The Intergovernmental Panel on Climate Change (IPCC, established in 1988 by the U.N. General Assembly) defines **climate change** as

> a change in the state of the climate that can be identified (e.g., by using statistical tests) by changes in the mean and/or the variability of its properties, and that persists for an extended period, typically decades or longer. Climate change may be due to natural internal processes or external forcings such as modulations of the solar cycles, volcanic eruptions, and persistent anthropogenic changes in the composition of the atmosphere or in land use. (Field et al., 2014, p. 5)

The United Nations Framework Convention on Climate Change (signed 1992) defines climate change as "a change of climate that is attributed directly or indirectly to human activity that alters the composition of the global atmosphere and that is in addition to natural climate variability observed over comparable time periods" (Core Writing Team et al., 2007, p. 30).

GLOBAL WARMING Climate change is measured most clearly in terms of increasing average temperature. This warming is partly natural and cyclical but is also driven by artificial emissions of greenhouse gases that trap heat in the atmosphere.

Carbon dioxide is the greatest contributor to global warming, followed by black carbon (incompletely burnt organic material in the atmosphere). Fossil fuels release carbon dioxide when burnt. A few of the main contributors to emissions are electrical power stations, generators, and automobiles. The energy sector accounts for more than two thirds of greenhouse gas emissions. Fossil fuels are consumed in the manufacture of many plastics and other constructive materials, which, when burnt, release carbon dioxide and other toxic compounds.

Methane (sold mostly as natural gas) is another core greenhouse gas. Methane is burnt as a fuel and is a by-product of drilling for other fossil fuels. About half of all methane emissions by the oil and gas industry occur during upstream oil and gas operations. Commonly, unnecessary emissions leak from aging pipelines, especially in Europe, Russia, and the United States.

While power stations and heavy industrial uses are responsible for most emissions, 12 to 16% of greenhouse gas emissions come from animal agriculture. Animals naturally emit carbon dioxide as a product of respiration; ruminants emit unusually large volumes of methane too.

Global warming is self-reinforcing: melted ice and snowcaps (atop the globe's poles, mountains, and glaciers) are no longer reflecting solar rays, and thawed permafrost releases natural greenhouse gases.

Long-term trends (induced from marine fossils) suggest that the Earth warmed quickly at the end of the last ice age (11,300 years ago) but entered a slow cooling trend until the industrial revolution (from the late 1700s), when human consumption of fossil fuels caused an unprecedented jump in global temperature—a greater jump toward warmer temperatures in the course of a century than the temperature had fallen over the several millennia before.

Given the carbon dioxide already in the atmosphere, this long-term trend suggests that by 2100 A.D. the Earth's average temperature would surpass any previous millennia (Marcott, Shakun, Clark, & Mix, 2013).

The global annual temperature has increased at an average rate of 0.06 °C (0.11 °F) per decade since records began in 1880. The rate has accelerated to 0.16 °C (0.28 °F) per decade since 1970. In 1990, the United Nations' Intergovernmental Panel on Climate Change forecasted an exponential rate; global temperatures increased at about half that rate in the 1990s but rose sharply in the late 1990s before stabilizing in the 2000s and rising again from 2008, marked by unusually severe heat waves and droughts across the globe each year.

In 2001, the Intergovernmental Panel on Climate Change forecast global warming to increase by 1.5 to 5.8 °C by the end of the 21st century. In 2009, states, nongovernmental organizations, and intergovernmental organizations met at Copenhagen, Denmark, in the latest attempt to agree on an international response to climate change. Most participants pledged to activities that are intended to limit global warming to 2 °C (3.6 °F), although even if this target were achieved global weather would be altered, perhaps irreversibly. In fact, by 2012, these measures already appeared insufficient to achieve that goal. Instead, many governments and their advisers estimated that warming by 3.5 °C (6.3 °F) was probable by sometime between 2060 and 2080 A.D.; warming by more than 6 °C (10.8 °F) is possible.

In 2012, the global temperature was 0.57 °C (1.03 °F) warmer than the 20th century's average (13.9 °C or 57 °F). The year 2012 was the 36th consecutive year with a global temperature above the 20th century's average and the 10th warmest year since 1880.

Swiss Reinsurance (a commercial reinsurer) developed six future scenarios based on possible trends in politics, economics, technology, and the natural environment. In no scenario would global warming be limited to 2 °C or less; instead, they forecasted warming of 3 to 5 °C (Swiss Re Group, 2013, p. 11).

In September 2013, the Intergovernmental Panel on Climate Change reported that the global temperature had risen by almost 1 °C from 1880 to 2012 and forecasted a rise of 1.5 to 4.5 °C (2.7 to 8.1 °F) by 2100 A.D. It concluded that human activities were "extremely likely" (a probability of more than 95%) to have caused this change, having previously estimated (in 2007) the chance as "very likely" (more than 90%). At the end of March 2014, the IPCC published forecasts assuming a rise of 2 to 4 °C.

In May 2014, the U.S. federal government released its third national climate assessment by more than 300 experts, guided by a federal advisory committee of 60, which forecast global warming of 1.4 to 4.5 °C (2.5 to 8.0 °F) by 2100 A.D. (Melillo, Richmond, & Yohe, 2014).

Consequences

As the climate warms, we can expect more slow-onset natural hazards. We must also expect declining crops, extinct species and environmental damage, migration, social instability, and political instability. A consulting group (Mercer) has estimated the costs of climate change at $2 trillion to $4 trillion by 2030. The OECD's Climate Change Expert Group has estimated costs at 5 to 20% of gross domestic product (GDP) (Howell, 2013, pp. 18–19). The costs of globally coordinated long-term reduction of greenhouse gases are estimated at 1 to 2% of global GDP, while the costs of subglobal, immediate adaptation to climate change are estimated at 5 to 10% until 2050 (Swiss Re Group, 2013, p. 13).

The subsections below examine the effects on sea levels, biodiversity, agriculture and food supplies, and society.

RISING SEAS AND DECLINING COASTLINES Melting ice and snowcaps contribute to rising sea levels and warming seas. Rising sea levels threaten to flood coastal land everywhere; the effects are proportionally greater for low-lying and poorly protected states like Mauritius.

In 2008, the Intergovernmental Panel on Climate Change forecasted that the otherwise permanent floating ice on the Arctic Ocean (which has remained intact for at least the last 130,000 years) would melt away by 2100. In 2010, it brought the estimate forward to 2050. In 2012, it lowered the event horizon to 2025.

Glaciers also affect sea levels. For instance, Greenland alone has 7 m (23 ft) of sea level rise contained in its glaciers. A 3-m rise in the North Atlantic would flood the current southern quarter of Florida (including all of the Miami metropolitan area, currently home to nearly six million people). The OECD (2008) studied 136 port cities and estimated that the population exposed to coastal flooding could triple by 2070 A.D. due to urbanization and climate change. Local adaptation is highly variable; for instance, Californian and Dutch cities have the capacity for more defenses against rising sea levels, but most large coastal cities, such as Cape Town, Lima, and Manila, do not (Sandler, 2009).

Rising seas and increasingly frequent or severe storms (all linked with climate change) compound each other. For instance, from 2004 to 2009, the United States lost more than 360,000 ac of freshwater and saltwater wetlands to fierce storms, sea level rise, and human development along U.S. coasts. This represented a 25% increase in the rate of loss in the same areas from the previous survey, which covered a 6-year period from 1998 to 2004. About 80,000 ac of wetlands disappeared each year from 2004 to 2009, compared with 60,000 ac per year from 1998 to 2004. Wetlands in the Gulf of Mexico declined fastest, in part because of several unusually large hurricanes in the period, including Katrina, Rita, and Ike. Human development was a major factor, especially on the Atlantic Coast. Urban development leads to more **precipitation** runoff. Meanwhile, sea levels are rising—for instance, 4 mm per year as measured in Virginia. Wetlands are the locations for human recreation, representing billions of dollars in U.S. economic activity, and are nurseries for marine life that is fished for human consumption, again worth billions to the U.S. economy. Saltwater wetlands control flooding risks by buffering high tides or seawater being pushed inland by storms. Freshwater wetlands soak up the runoff from the precipitation associated with storms. Wetlands serve as at least transient habitats for marine life and for three quarters of the nation's waterfowl and migrating birds. Nearly half of endangered species depend on wetlands (Dahl & Stedman, 2013).

In May 2014, the U.S. federal government's third national climate assessment forecast a sea level rise of 1 to 4 ft by 2100 A.D.

BIODIVERSITY Biodiversity is the variety of species. Increased exploitation of the natural environment, agricultural pesticides, hunting for food, artificial selection, and global warming each reduce natural biodiversity. Warming climate allows diseases and their vectors, such as mosquitoes, to spread further north and south, away from equatorial regions where they are endemic. Warming seas threaten marine species that reside in cold waters or rely on food originating in cold waters.

The historical extinction rate is one species per million per year. The Intergovernmental Panel on Climate Change estimates that the proportion of all species that are at increased risk of extinction is at least 20% (given lower greenhouse gas emissions scenarios) and as high as 70% (worst scenarios) (Core Writing Team et al., 2007, p. 54). The International Union for Conservation of Nature and Natural Resources (2008) estimates that 35% of bird species, 52% of amphibian species, and 71% of coral species have traits that put them at an increased risk of extinction from global climate change.

AGRICULTURE AND FOOD SECURITY Global warming will help agriculture in areas that traditionally were too cold or dark for intensive agriculture. However, climate change will be negative for agriculture in most places; seawater will flood coastal land, droughts and storms will be more frequent and severe, global warming will permit pests to spread further north and south, and biodiversity will decline.

Food insecurity is probably the most immediate impact of climate change and is already driving human migration and conflict. Rising sea levels promise to flood productive coastal land with seawater. The more extreme weather patterns associated with climate change promise to hit farmers with more frequent and severe droughts and storms. Global warming promises to permit the spread of warm-climate pests, such as locusts, further north and south.

Climate change affects food security globally but hits hardest in the traditionally insecure areas: those with low natural capacity for agriculture, low economic capacity for food imports, and more exposure to rising oceans and declining rainfall.

SOCIAL CHANGES Climate change compounds other threats to agriculture and food supply. In response, humans will migrate and engage in conflict over access to agriculture and food.

In 2008, the U.S. National Intelligence Estimate argued for the first time that climate change would impact U.S. national security as it destabilized foreign economies and societies and caused more destabilizing migration.

Controlling Climate Change

No international organization has lead authority to control climate change, although regional organizations and the U.N. have brokered some international agreements. The highest authority is the Intergovernmental Panel on Climate Change, which the U.N. General Assembly established in 1988. It counts hundreds of scientists as members. It issues its major reports every 5 or 6 years. These are summaries of knowledge and judgments on climate change. The panel has no executive authority.

Prevention is preferable, both ethically and materially, to making restitution after the event. Yet current self-interests help to drive inaction. Current generations enjoy the benefits of a high-emission lifestyle and pass most of the costs to future generations. Those currently most exposed to the hazards of global climate change have the least resources to adapt and are least responsible (primarily because they consume less).

The world has no institutions that could scale up to control hundreds of millions of climate refugees or to prevent the extinction of thousands of species per year. Collective action is imperative yet is curbed for similar reasons. Local adaptation is ineffective and inefficient at the global level; for instance, local flood defenses benefit locals while global reductions in greenhouse gases would benefit everyone (Sandler, 2009).

Three broad strategies are available for controlling climate change: reducing emissions, removing carbon dioxide, and managing solar radiation.

REDUCING EMISSIONS In June 2013, the International Energy Agency's report urged nations to take four steps by 2015 to keep alive any hope of limiting climate change to 2 °C.

1. Aggressive energy-efficiency measures

2. Limit output of inefficient coal plants and mandate that all future coal plants be highly efficient supercritical ones

3. Reduce the release of methane in oil and gas operations

4. Phase out fossil-fuel subsidies (p. 10)

Objective trends and subjective judgments suggest that we can expect some but insufficient controls on emissions. The United States, historically the leading national emitter, has been comparatively resistant to reductions of emissions, mainly because of the economic costs. In fiscal years 2009 and 2010, federal agencies spent just $100.9 million on climate engineering research, spread across 52 different programs, with no coordinating authority (U.S. Government Accountability Office, 2010a).

REMOVING CARBON DIOXIDE The rate of artificial emissions of greenhouse gases could be controlled further but is unlikely to decline for decades. Consequently, many experts have argued for removal of carbon dioxide from the atmosphere. Plants do this naturally, but flora are in decline, again mostly due to human activities. Artificial removal of carbon dioxide is technologically possible but is currently impractical due to expense and disruption.

More than 500 billion tons of carbon have been burned since the beginning of the Industrial Revolution. In 2012, global emissions of carbon dioxide from energy use rose 1.4% to 31.6 billion tons, a record year; this rate of increase could mean a temperature increase over preindustrial times of as much as 5.3 °C (9 °F), according to the International Energy Agency's report in June 2013.

Carbon dioxide reached a new record in 2013, rising at the fastest rate since 1984. The average amount of CO_2 in the air was raised to 396 parts per million (ppm)—2.9 ppm higher than in 2012 and 142% the level in 1750 (before the Industrial Revolution). Methane had reached 253% the level in 1750 while nitrous oxide reached 121%. The report observed more rapid ocean acidification, which occurs as oceans absorb carbon from the atmosphere, than at any time. The oceans take up about 4 kg of CO_2 per person per day (World Meteorological Organization, 2014).

In September 2013, the Intergovernmental Panel on Climate Change endorsed a "carbon budget"—a limit on the amount of carbon dioxide that could be produced by industrial activities and the clearing of forests—of 1,000,000,000,000 MT of carbon, if planetary warming were to be kept below 2 °C (3.6 °F) above the level of preindustrial times. At the current increasing rate of consumption, the last ton would be burned sometime around 2040. More than 3,000,000,000,000 MT of carbon are still left in the ground as fossil fuels.

On November 12, 2014, the United States and China, which produce 45% of the world's carbon dioxide, concluded a summit in Beijing with a Chinese pledge to stop the growth of emissions by 2030 and a U.S. pledge to reduce emissions by 26 to 28% by 2025, based on 2005 levels. Chinese President Xi Jinping said that by 2030, 20% Chinese energy production would come from zero-emission sources, such as wind and solar.

SOLAR-RADIATION MANAGEMENT Theoretically, the Earth could be cooled by placing materials in the atmosphere that reflect sunlight; this possibility is known as *solar-radiation management*. In 2009, Russia injected particles into the atmosphere as an experiment in reflecting sunlight, but otherwise, the field is theoretical (GAO, 2010a, p. 15). In the United States, the National Academy of Sciences started to research the possibility with funding from NASA, the National Oceanic and Atmospheric Administration, and the Central Intelligence Agency. On September 10, 2013, the academy held a conference on the possibility.

A major volcanic eruption or meteor impact could throw enough material into the atmosphere to cool the earth, but we would be reckless to hope for such events as they are likely to harm many people immediately, after which their climatic effects could throw the earth into a long winter that would make civilization impossible to sustain.

WEATHER EVENTS

The U.S. National Weather Service (2009) defines *weather* as "the state of the atmosphere with respect to wind, temperature, cloudiness, moisture, pressure, etc. . . . at a given point in time (e.g., today's high temperature)" (n.p.). The subsections below review the global frequency of major weather events and review the returns from weather events.

Frequency

Most natural disasters are weather related, and they are increasing in frequency and scale. Globally, weather-related disasters are about 3 times more frequent and 169 times more deadly than terrorist disasters (see Table 6.10). Most disasters or catastrophes are caused by natural storms, including floods and landslides caused by storms.

Weather events are increasing in frequency and consequence, explained partly by natural changes, partly by **human-caused** changes in the climate, and partly by increasing exposure as human populations grow into more exposed areas and exploit more natural resources. Climate change is associated with more extreme weather of all types, as appropriate to the season (such as cold, heat, precipitation, and drought). Although long-term trends are clear, individual major weather events remain frustratingly difficult to predict until they are too imminent to control.

Weather disasters or catastrophes are becoming more frequent and costly in the United States Weather disasters in North America tend to be the costliest materially but least deadly because of the high levels of development and insured property there. (Seventy-five percent of weather-related insurance claims were paid out in North America.) Munich Reinsurance America reports 30,000 deaths and $1 trillion (2011 values) in damages due to weather catastrophes from 1980 to 2011. The U.S. National Climatic Data Center counts, during the 1980–2012 period, 123 weather-related events that each caused at least $1 billion in damages and costs (nearly four per year) (Swiss Re Group, 2012).

Returns

Weather and climate are of consequence to all of us. At all times, they affect agriculture and thence the supply of food and the prices that consumers pay for their food, the demand for and price of energy used to heat or cool homes and offices, travel and communications, and even heavy industries or mechanized activities, such as drilling for oil in drought-prone areas or storm-prone seas.

Extreme weather events, such as storms, directly cause losses, damage, deaths, and injuries. Most disasters occur in the developing world, where they are more deadly but less financially costly because of lower development and capacity. The estimated economic loss due to the floods in Thailand in 2011, for example, was $30 billion, whereas the economic cost of Hurricane Katrina in the southern United States in 2005 was $125 billion (Howell, 2013, p. 18).

Slow-onset and persistent weather events, such as drought, heat waves, cold fronts, inland flooding due to precipitation, and coastal flooding due to sea level rises, tend to be the deadliest.

Drought and Heat Wave

This section defines drought and heat wave and reviews the frequency of these events and their returns.

DEFINITION **Drought** is defined by below-average precipitation for some period. A **heat wave** is defined by hotter temperatures than average for some period. Both are slow-onset and persistent threats; they are not normally coded until they persist for more than 1 week. The persistence of these threats helps to explain their high lethality and economic costs.

The U.S. National Weather Service (2009) defines drought as "a deficiency of moisture that results in adverse impacts on people, animals, or vegetation over a sizeable area" (n.p.). It defines a heat wave as "a period of abnormally and uncomfortably hot and unusually humid weather. Typically a heat wave lasts two or more days" (n.p.).

FREQUENCY A **flood** is a rapid-onset threat that lasts days to weeks, but a drought or heat wave is a slow-onset threat that last weeks to decades.

The southwest is the driest, warmest region of the United States. Over millennia, the southwestern United States has experienced drier periods lasting years, sometimes decades and even longer than a century during the middle Holocene (around 6,000 years ago) and the medieval period (around 1,000 years ago). The Native American population in the West expanded in the wet years, but during the long, dry medieval period, they almost disappeared, including the so-called Anasazi collapse in the Southwest about 800 years ago.

Within cycles measured in centuries are cycles measured in decades. The Pacific Decadal Oscillation is a cycle of change in the temperature of surface water in the North Pacific Ocean, every 20 or 30 years, with a shift from drier and warmer to wetter and milder or vice versa.

El Niño and La Niña are slow weather cycles caused by oceanic current oscillations in the Southern Hemisphere, primarily on and around the Pacific Ocean. They affect cycles of wet and drought, each 10 to 12 years long, in the southwest United States. They contributed to the wider American droughts of the 1930s (known colloquially by its effects as the Dust Bowl), 1950s, and 2000s to 2010s.

On top of these cycles, global warming is intensifying and lengthening droughts. In October 2010, the U.S. National Center for Atmospheric Research (NCAR) reported that

> the United States and many other heavily populated countries face a growing threat of severe and prolonged drought in coming decades . . . possibly reaching a scale in some regions by the end of the century that has rarely if ever been observed in modern times. (n.p.)

The NCAR warned that such persistent drought would most affect parts of the world that already suffer cycles of persistent drought, including the American Southwest, the great plains of Brazil and Argentina, the Mediterranean rim, North and Central Africa, southern South Asia and East Asia (including parts of China), and Australia.

Related trends are decreasing snowpack and increasing wildfire frequency. Climate change suggests a longer, more severe drought just after the southwestern American population has expanded most rapidly (Hockensmith, 2014). In May 2014, the U.S. federal government released its third national climate assessment, which forecast longer and more intense droughts across the southwestern United States, southern Great Plains, and Southeast due to global climate change.

RETURNS Heat waves kill more people than droughts, but droughts have longer and greater economic effects. In an average year, around 1,500 Americans die during heat waves (see Table 6.11), although the toll is not generally noticed in an average year unless the deaths are concentrated in a particularly short hot period. The victims tend to be the old, young, or otherwise vulnerable, so death can be blamed on multiple factors, leaving many contests about how to fairly count the deaths due to heat waves alone. The returns are controlled by improving the forecasting of droughts, encouraging at-risk subpopulations to remain in cool environments, and improving the availability of social services and medical services for at-risk populations.

Droughts have more severe economic effects. For instance, in summer 2012, a drought across North America affected global prices of corn, soy, and meat. The ongoing drought in California affected national supplies because California has the largest area set-aside for crops.

BOX 6.1

Droughts in California

California is the wealthiest, most populous, largest state and suffers frequent droughts. The so-called Great Drought in 1863–1864 contributed to the demise of the cattle rancho system, especially in Southern California. The 1928–1935 droughts established hydrologic criteria widely used in designing storage capacity and yield of large Northern California reservoirs. The 1976–1977 drought, when statewide runoff hit an all-time low, showed that state water agencies were unprepared for major cuts in their supplies. Forty-seven of the state's 58 counties declared local drought-related emergencies at that time. The 1987–1992 drought was notable for its 6-year duration; 23 counties declared local drought emergencies. The 20th century was an unusually wet and mild century, but the 2000s were a dry decade, and the drought continued into the 2010s. The year 2013 is the driest year in California since records began in the 1840s. According to the width of tree rings, California had not been drier since 1580. In January 2014, the state declared a statewide drought emergency after three consecutive years of below-average rainfall. Every county was in drought. The state governor (Jerry Brown) called on Californians to reduce water usage by 20% or risk mandatory rationing. Some cities and counties cut some supplies.

The returns are controlled by collecting data on past droughts in order to better forecast where and when droughts would occur, storing water ahead of droughts, planning to reduce usage during droughts, reducing water-intensive flora, improving the water retention of soils, and reducing unnecessary water loss from reservoirs, irrigation systems, pipes, and outlets.

Storms, Hurricanes, Cyclones, and Typhoons

This section defines storms and reviews their distribution and frequency regionally, the human returns, the economic returns, and the environmental harm.

DEFINITIONS Storms are weather systems defined by precipitation and wind. They are produced when warm, moist air rises as it meets cold air. A *thunderstorm* is defined by unusually heavy rains, wind, and lightning. In the United States, a thunderstorm is judged severe if its winds reach 58 mph or more, it precipitates hail of 0.75 in. or more in diameter, or it produces tornadoes (narrower vortices of air).

A *tropical depression* is a low-pressure system of clouds and winds of less than 34 kn (39 mph). A depression could develop into a *tropical storm* with winds from 34 to less than 64 kn (39 to less than 74 mph). A **hurricane** is a cyclonic tropical storm with winds sustained at 74 mph or higher. A hurricane is called a **cyclone** across most of the Pacific and Pacific Rim but is called a **typhoon** in the Western Pacific and Southeast Asia. In the United States, the National Hurricane Center categorizes hurricanes in five levels by wind speed (see Table 6.12).

The cyclone is a spiral of winds extending hundreds of miles outwards from the *eye* (the calmer center, up to 30 mi across). These systems arise over warm oceans and typically stay over water, but if they head inland, they push seawater inland (a **storm surge**) and bring high winds and heavy rain.

Table 6.11 Droughts and Heat Waves in the United States, 1966–2013

Year	Number of Events	Number Killed	Total Damages (Millions of USD)
1966	2	262[1]	0
1972	1	10[1]	0
1973	1	22[1]	0
1980	1	1,260[1] to 10,000[2]	2,000[1] to 20,000[2]
1983	1	188[1]	0
1986	1	48[1] to 100[2]	1,300[2] to 1,750[1]
1987	1	80[1]	0
1988	1	7,500[2]	40,000[2]
1989	1	0[1]	1,000[1]
1990	1	11[1] to 502[2]	1,000[2]
1991	2	0[1]	1,335
1993	1	16[2] to 48[1]	1,000[2]
1995	1	670[1]	0
1995–1996	1	0[1]	5,000[1]
1998	1	130[1] to 200[2]	4,275[1] to 7,500[2]
1999	1	0[1]	1,100[1]
1999	1	257[1]	1,000[1]
2000	2	0[1]	1,100[1]
2000	1	35[1] to 140[2]	4,000[2]
2001	1	56[1]	0
2002	1	0[1]	3,300[1]
2002	1	14[1]	10,000[2]
2005	1	33[1]	1,000[2]
2006	2	188[1]	6,000[2]
2007	1	15[2]	300[1] to 5,000[2]

Year	Number of Events	Number Killed	Total Damages (Millions of USD)
2008	1	0[1]	2,000[1]
2009	1	0[1]	5,000[1]
2011	2	22[1] to 95[2]	8,000[1] to 12,000[2]
2012	2	0	20,000[1]
2013	1	123	30,000[2]

Sources:

[1] EM-DAT: The International Disaster Database by Centre for Research on the Epidemiology of Disasters (CRED). At least one of the following criteria has to be fulfilled: 10 or more people reportedly killed, 100 people reportedly affected, a call for international assistance, or a declaration of a state of emergency.

[2] National Centers for Environmental Information (2015).

DISTRIBUTION AND FREQUENCY The world experiences about 100 tropical storms every year, most in the Pacific Ocean and around the Pacific Rim's sea and lands. Global warming suggests that an increasing proportion of future storms will be larger and more energetic, although the frequency of all tropical storms will remain about the same. A warmer atmosphere combined with a warmer ocean means more similar winds in the lower and upper atmospheres and thus a more stable climatic system. However, warmer temperatures lead to more water and energy in the atmosphere.

Increasing human development leads to increased exposure. The proportion of the world's gross domestic product annually exposed to tropical cyclones has increased from 3.6% in the 1970s to 4.3% in the 2000s (Beck et al., 2012, p. 32).

The subsections below review the Pacific Rim and the Atlantic Rim separately.

Pacific Rim. Cyclones or typhoons are most likely in the South Pacific, where they affect small island territories.

Tropical storms sometimes travel from the South Pacific west to Southeast Asia, where they affect very large nation-states with multiple islands, some of them very large. The Philippines are struck by about 14 major tropical storms per year, Vietnam by about 10.

Tropical storms sometimes travel north to Japan and China. According to China's Office of State Flood Control and Drought Relief, seven typhoons hit China each year. Rarely, tropical storms travel east to the western United States. Hawaii has been hit by six major cyclones since 1851, all of them occurring between the years 1938 and 1992.

Atlantic Rim. The U.S. National Hurricane Center has identified, for the years from 1492 through 1996, a total of 467 Atlantic cyclonic storms (more than one every year), each of which certainly or probably killed around 25 or more people.

The United States recognizes a hurricane season from June 1 through 30 November 30. The earliest hurricane in any calendar year occurred on March 7, 1908, and the latest occurred on December 31, 1954. The latest hurricane in any calendar year to leave the Atlantic and strike the United States was Sandy on October 29, 2012. Of Atlantic storms that killed 25 or more people, about 40% occurred in September, 30% in August, 20% in October, and less than 5% in any other month. The longest lasting recorded hurricane lasted 20 days (Hurricane Ginger in 1971); the longest lasting recorded major hurricane lasted 11.5 days (1899).

Atlantic storms tend to develop in the equatorial South Atlantic. Very rarely, hurricanes travel into South America. Most hurricanes pass east of the Caribbean and up the eastern seaboard of North America, gradually losing energy as they advance northward. Occasionally, they travel northwestward through the Caribbean, where they first encounter the Lesser Antilles (whose sovereign states include Antigua and Barbuda, Barbados, Grenada, Saint Kitts and Nevis, Saint Lucia, Saint Vincent and the Grenadines, and Trinidad and Tobago). The effects tend to be most consequential on a local level in the Lesser Antilles, where a whole state-island can be devastated, but in absolute scale, the effects tend to be greater in the large and populous states of the Greater Antilles (Puerto Rico, Dominican Republic, Haiti, Jamaica, and Cuba).

From the Caribbean, the storms normally veer north up the Atlantic but could pass into the Gulf of Mexico to threaten Mexico and the southern United States. Occasionally, while heading north up the eastern seaboard, storms will veer inland. By then, most hurricanes have degraded to storms (often called **nor'easters** by Americans) but still are associated with damaging high winds, rainfall, and flooding. Very rarely, hurricanes travel past the United States and veer into Canada or travel across the Atlantic to Europe's Atlantic seaboard. During events with at least 25 certain deaths, 29% of deaths have occurred in the Greater Antilles, 21% in the Lesser Antilles, 16% in the U.S. mainland, 12% in Central America (including Mexico), and 22% on the oceans. Less than 1% of all deaths have occurred in all of South America, the Bahamas, Bermuda, Canada, Cape Verde Islands, and Ireland.

Several nor'easters can be expected to make landfall per year. Dozens of hurricanes can be expected every summer, of which few will make landfall. From 1851 to 2010, 284 hurricanes (less than 1.8 per year) hit the United States, of which 96 (0.6 per year) were major. During that period, an average six hurricanes made landfall per decade, but they surged in the 1940s and 1950s (around 10 per decade). The frequency and intensity fell from 1960 to 2000 (five per decade) but rose again in the 2000s (seven, of which three killed 25 or more people). Additionally, the exposed areas were much more densely populated and valuable. Table 6.13 shows the distribution of hurricanes by state.

Landfall is frustratingly difficult to predict. The National Hurricane Center admits to an error, in the year 2000, of more than 130 mi between its forecast of landfall and the actual landfall 48 hrs later. This mean error dropped to around 70 mi in 2011. Its target is 60 mi by 2020. That accuracy is sufficient for predicting states affected but still impractical for local emergency managers, since a few dozen miles can separate the center of a dense city from countryside or the center of a Caribbean island from open sea.

HUMAN RETURNS

Atlantic Rim. Hurricanes cause most of their damage by pushing sea water inland (the *storm surge*). Rain contributes to the flooding while the sustained high winds damage structures.

Table 6.12   U.S. Official Categories of Hurricane (as modified in 2012)

Category	Winds	Description of Damage	Frequency of U.S. Landfalls, 1851–2010
1	74–95 mph (64–82 kn; 119–153 kph)	**Very dangerous winds will produce some damage.** Well-constructed frame homes could have damage to roof, shingles, vinyl siding and gutters. Large branches of trees will snap and shallowly rooted trees may be toppled. Extensive damage to power lines and poles likely will result in power outages that could last a few to several days.	113
2	96–110 mph (83–95 kn; 154–177 kph)	**Extremely dangerous winds will cause extensive damage.** Well-constructed frame homes could sustain major roof and siding damage. Many shallowly rooted trees will be snapped or uprooted and block numerous roads. Near-total power loss is expected with outages that could last from several days to weeks.	75
3 (major)	111–129 mph (96–112 kn; 178–208 kph)	**Devastating damage will occur.** Well-built frame homes may incur major damage or removal of roof decking and gable ends. Many trees will be snapped or uprooted, blocking numerous roads. Electricity and water will be unavailable for several days to weeks after the storm passes.	75
4 (major)	130–156 mph (113–136 kn; 209–251 kph)	**Catastrophic damage will occur.** Well-built frame homes can sustain severe damage with loss of most of the roof structure and/or some exterior walls. Most trees will be snapped or uprooted and power poles downed. Fallen trees and power poles will isolate residential areas. Power outages will last weeks to possibly months. Most of the area will be uninhabitable for weeks or months.	18
5 (major)	157 mph (137 kn; 252 kph) or higher	**Catastrophic damage will occur:** A high percentage of framed homes will be destroyed, with total roof failure and wall collapse. Fallen trees and power poles will isolate residential areas. Power outages will last for weeks to possibly months. Most of the area will be uninhabitable for weeks or months.	3

Source: U.S. National Hurricane Center (2013).

Table 6.13	Hurricane Strikes on the U.S. Mainland by State, 1851–2010					
State	Category 1	Category 2	Category 3	Category 4	Category 5	TOTAL
Florida	43	34	29	6	2	114
Texas	27	18	12	7	0	64
Louisiana	21	16	16	3	1	57
North Carolina	25	14	11	1	0	51
South Carolina	17	7	4	2	0	30
Alabama	17	5	5	0	0	27
Georgia	15	5	2	1	0	23
Mississippi	4	6	8	0	1	19
New York	6	1	5	0	0	12
Connecticut	5	3	3	0	0	11
Massachusetts	6	2	3	0	0	11
Virginia	7	2	1	0	0	10
Rhode Island	3	2	4	0	0	9
Maine	5	1	0	0	0	6
Maryland	1	1	0	0	0	2
New Hampshire	1	1	0	0	0	2
Delaware	2	0	0	0	0	2
New Jersey	2	0	0	0	0	2
Pennsylvania	1	0	0	0	0	1

Source: U.S. National Hurricane Center (2013).

Storm surges are greater, with more intense hurricanes, higher tides, shallower seafloors, and lower inland elevation. The states along the Gulf of Mexico and Florida are most exposed to storm surges, but most of the Atlantic and Gulf coasts of the United States are less than 10 ft above sea level. Hurricane Katrina (2005) swept seawater inland to a depth of dozens of feet.

According to estimates by the U.S. National Hurricane Center, Atlantic storms from 1492 to 1994 killed between 300,000 and 500,000 people, around 600 to 1,000 per year.

Deaths have increased each century at an exponential rate, similar to population growth, due to the increasing exposure associated with wider human habitation. In the 1700s, the death rate rose even quicker (more than 50,000 certain deaths in the 1700s, compared to around 10,000 in the 1600s) because of increased rates of maritime transport and settlement in the Atlantic rim. Most of the deaths occurred from 1760 to 1790, and most of these were maritime losses. More than 90% of all maritime/offshore deaths and 100% of all 12 offshore events with more than 1,000 dead each occurred before 1790. In the 1800s, the security of maritime transport improved dramatically.

Deaths due to events each with 25 or more dead fell in the 1800s to around 30,000, but the total was in line with the cross-centuries base rate. In the 1900s, known deaths surged to more than 71,000 people. Deadly Atlantic storms with at least 25 known dead were most frequent from 1909 to 1933 (each year had five such events), probably because of rapidly increasing human habitation in the most exposed areas at a time when the capacity and knowledge for risk mitigation was still poor. For the same reasons, such events surged again in the 1950s and 1960s and yet again in the 2000s.

One hundred forty-four events (one every 3.5 years) killed more than 100 people per event. Thirty-nine events (one nearly every 13 years) each killed more than 1,000. Five events (one every 101 years) each killed more than 8,000 people.

The deadliest Atlantic storm killed around 22,000 people. The extremity of this event can be appreciated further when one considers the low population density in that area (Lesser Antilles) and at that time (October 1780) and that the event killed more people than have died due to Atlantic storms during any other decade.

The second deadliest hurricane globally centered on Galveston, Texas, around September 8, 1900. It killed 8,000 to 12,000 people. These deaths account for about one third of all hurricane-related deaths in the United States.

Three other storms have killed around 8,000 people (Dominican Republic, 1930; Haiti and Cuba, 1963; and Honduras, 1974). Five events have killed more than 8,000 people each, together accounting for 10 to 18% of all estimated deaths caused by Atlantic cyclones. The 10 deadliest events killed at least 74,000 people; these events account for less than 0.2% of all tropical cyclones but 15 to 25% of all estimated cyclone-related deaths.

Pacific Rim. Cyclones rarely cross the Pacific to reach North America or even Hawaii. Hawaii suffered peak damage of $1.8 billion in 1992 (2010 USD) and peak lethality of four deaths (in each of 1957 and 1992). California's worst cyclone (in 1939) killed 45 people.

In 1991, Tropical Storm Thelma killed 5,000 people, mostly in the Philippines. In December 2012, a typhoon killed more than 1,900 Filipinos. On November 8, 2013, Typhoon Haiyan/Yolanda killed around 6,000 people in the Philippines.

On October 15–16, 2013, Typhoon Wipha traveled the length of Japan's Pacific coast from the southwest to the northeast, killing one person in Tokyo and around 60 people on Izu Oshima island, south of Tokyo, after the typhoon triggered landslides.

On September 30, 2013, Typhoon Wutip killed around 70 Chinese and Vietnamese fishermen in the South China Sea, then made landfall on Vietnam's coast with winds gusting up to 133 kph.

Deadliest Hurricanes in the United States

From 1851 through 2010, 52 hurricanes killed 25 or more people in the United States, 24 hurricanes killed more than 100 people, and five killed more than 1,000.

The deadliest hurricane in the United States was the Galveston event of September 8, 1900, when 8,000 to 12,000 people died. The second deadliest hurricane in the United States struck Florida in 1928 (2,500 to 3,000 dead). Hurricane

Katrina (2005) is the third deadliest hurricane in the United States: it killed 1,200 people, displaced around one million, left all of those remaining without food and water for days to weeks, and left some people with injuries that were impossible to treat locally because every hospital in New Orleans was affected. (Six months later just one third of their beds were available.) Only two other hurricanes killed more than 1,000 Americans, both in 1893.

Vietnam closed schools, ordered all boats ashore, and evacuated 70,000 people to shelters. On October 5, Typhoon Nari hit Vietnam, which had evacuated residents in the way but still lost five people. Both typhoons had bypassed the Philippines and were Category 1 typhoons still when they hit Vietnam. Typhoon Haiyan hit Vietnam on November 11, 2013. Although weakened by its passage over the Philippines, Haiyan affected thousands of people. Thousands of homes still were damaged from Wutip and Nari.

ECONOMIC RETURNS Cyclonic storms in the United States caused most of the world's top 10 costliest disasters, mostly because of the high insured value of U.S. property compared to most other places where storms hit.

In the United States, nine of the top 10 costliest natural disasters were caused by cyclonic storms (an earthquake at Northridge, California, in 1994 is in the top 10). Of the 284 hurricanes to hit the United States from 1851 to 2010, 113 were Category 1, 75 were Category 2, 75 were Category 3, 18 were Category 4, and three were Category 5. A Category 4 or 5 hurricane strikes the United States about once every eight years.

Of the 30 costliest or deadliest hurricanes to hit the United States, two were Category 5 hurricanes. Hurricane Katrina of August 2005 (the deadliest) was a Category 3 hurricane. Hurricane/Storm Sandy of October 2012 (the costliest) dropped from Category 3 to Category 2 by the time it hit the United States.

The 10 costliest storms (including hurricanes) in United States history all have occurred since 1989 (see Table 6.14), partly because such events are growing in frequency and scale, human habitation in coastal areas has increased, and costs tend to go up with increased population, property value, and insurance. If the costs were adjusted for current inflated money value, population, and housing value, then the costliest would date back to 1926. Nevertheless, four of the 10 costliest storms in the United States have occurred since 1992 and eight of the 30 costliest storms have occurred since 2000.

Table 6.14 The 10 Costliest Hurricanes or Storms, 1989–2012

Year	1989	1992	2004	2004	2005	2005	2005	2008	2011	2012
Weather system's official name	Hugo	Andrew	Ivan	Charley	Katrina	Wilma	Rita	Ike	Irene	Sandy
Cost of damage (2010 USD in billions)	9.7	45.6	19.8	15.8	105.9	20.6	11.8	27.8	15.8	75.0
Normalized cost of damage[1]	16.1	58.6	21.6	17.2	113.4	22.1	12.6	29.5	15.4	72.0

Source: U.S. National Hurricane Center (2015).

[1] 2010 USD in billions, normalized by inflation, changes in personal wealth and coastal population to 2005.

Hurricane Katrina (August 2005) was the costliest since Hurricane Andrew in 1992 or the costliest since 1926 if adjusted for inflated money value, population, and housing value. Katrina was costlier in direct damage and responsive federal funding ($29 billion) than terrorism on September 11, 2001 ($8.8 billion).

The U.S. National Hurricane Center makes the point that a storm's strength is less important to its effects than its path. Consequently, categories are very misleading to the general public, which tends to react more calmly toward a low category heading for landfall than a high category passing the coast.

Small changes in route can dramatically change the effects. For instance, Hurricane Katrina passed through and around New Orleans (population close to 500,000 in 2005), but if its path had shifted a few dozen miles to the east or west, it would have missed the city. Hurricane Sandy hit the most densely populated areas of New Jersey and New York. In 1992, Hurricane Andrew (Category 5) caused around $25 billion (current dollars) in losses in the state of Florida. A 20-mi shift northward would have resulted in 2 to 3 times as much damage; a 40-mi shift southward would have resulted in negligible losses at a state level, although it would have devastated parts of the Florida Keys. Remember that in 2011, the mean distance between the National Hurricane Center's forecasted impact point and the actual impact point 48 hrs later was 70 mi.

The year 2012 was another bad one for weather in the United States. In January, a winter storm knocked out power to 25,000 homes in the Pacific Northwest. In February, tornadoes leveled property in Illinois, Indiana, Kansas, and Nebraska. In April, tornadoes damaged nearly 1,000 homes in the Dallas metropolitan area, Texas. In June, wildfires destroyed 165,000 ac and 700 homes in

Colorado and a derecho windstorm cut power to tens of thousands of people in Ohio and the mid-Atlantic states. Finally, in October, the northeast states were hit by Hurricane/Storm Sandy.

ENVIRONMENTAL HARM Hurricanes tend to cause great environmental damage by pushing seawater inland, causing rivers to flood, and destroying vegetation and associated habitats. For instance, Hurricane Katrina damaged a sensitive coastal environment, a central breeding or feeding ground for some marine birds, reptiles, and mammals. Sixteen national wildlife refuges were damaged; Breton in Louisiana lost more than half of its area.

Tornadoes

This section defines tornadoes; reviews their distribution, frequency, and returns; and explains how they are forecasted.

DEFINITION Tornadoes are vertical vortices of air, observed as rotating funnels of apparent cloud, sometimes touching the ground. Tornadoes are much smaller and more short-lived than hurricanes but are more sudden and energetic for their size.

The U.S. National Weather Service (2009) defines a tornado as

> a violently rotating column of air, usually pendant to a cumulonimbus, with circulation reaching the ground. It nearly always starts as a funnel cloud and may be accompanied by a loud roaring noise. On a local scale, it is the most destructive of all atmospheric phenomena. (n.p.)

DISTRIBUTION AND FREQUENCY Tornadoes arise within severe convective storms, which can occur anywhere on the earth, but tornadoes are much more likely in the middle latitudes, between about 30° and 50° North or South. Here, cold, polar air routinely meets warmer, subtropical air, generating convective storms. In addition, air in the mid latitudes often flows at different speeds and directions and at different levels of the troposphere, facilitating the development of rotation within a storm cell. These latitudes are not as densely populated as more northerly and southerly latitudes; they include high precipitation, fertile lands that attract agricultural development, and spotty urban development. In theory, the frequency of tornadoes should increase with global warming since tornadoes arise from warm, humid weather.

The United States is a large country in the middle latitudes. It experiences the most tornadoes of any country, an average of about 1,200 tornadoes per year. About 20 can be expected to be violent, of which one would be expected to reach the maximum rating of EF5 on the enhanced Fujita (EF) scale. These rates are steady, even though improved instruments mean more frequent observation. Canada comes second, with around 100 per year. Tornadoes are most common per land area in Britain, but almost all are so small that they are unnoticed by the general population. Tornadoes are relatively frequent in other countries of northern Europe, the Middle East and Caucasia, Bangladesh, China, Japan, Australia, New Zealand, South Africa, and Argentina.

BOX 6.3

The Costs of Hurricane/Storm Sandy

Hurricane Sandy killed around 100 people in the Caribbean before it landed in the United States on October 29, 2012. By then, it had dropped from a Category 3 to a Category 2, but it remained unusually large (1,100 mi across). It killed more than 110 people in 10 states and knocked out power to 8.5 million people. In late November, the governors of New Jersey and New York estimated the damage at $70 billion. Sandy cost $20 to 25 billion in insured losses, according to Swiss Re's initial estimates, and more than $60 billion in total losses, the second costliest storm since 1900 in constant 2010 dollars and the sixth costliest after adjusting for inflation, property values, and population, according to the National Hurricane Center. For comparison, Typhoon Haiyan's strike on the Philippines on November 8, 2013, killed many more people (more than 6,000) and affected a wider area but caused lower value damage ($5.8 billion of damage, according to an estimate released by the Philippine Secretary of Socioeconomic Planning Arsenio Balisacan on November 19).

In January 2013, the governors of New Jersey and New York requested nearly $80 billion in federal aid; the U.S. Congress approved over $60 billion ($9.7 billion for immediate relief from flooding, followed by $17 billion for general relief, $5.4 billion for aid through FEMA directly to individuals and local communities for rebuilding, and $33.6 billion for long-term rebuilding). The total federal aid was equivalent to more than half of the federal spending cuts agreed upon days before and due to come into effect at the end of January and was larger than the annual budgets of many states.

In October 2013, a year after first onset, billions of federal aid remained unspent, leaving thousands of homes unrepaired and vacant. Delays in repairs and rehousing cause extra costs as victims suffer more costs of temporary housing. For instance, the Small Business Administration had authorized $2.4 billion in disaster loans to more than 36,000 households and businesses but had paid out only about one quarter. FEMA gave $1.42 billion to help storm victims pay rent, replace lost possessions, and make emergency repairs. FEMA gave another $2.7 billion to help municipalities clean up debris, repair critical infrastructure, and reopen damaged hospitals. The federal flood insurance program paid $7.8 billion to nearly 132,000 policyholders who sustained damage during the storm (Caruso, 2013).

In the United States, most tornadoes occur in southern states during humid summers. Within the United States, three regions experience the most tornadoes: the Florida peninsula; the states on the Mexican Gulf Coast ("Dixie Alley"); and the south-central plains states ("Tornado Alley"), where Texas, Oklahoma, Arkansas, Missouri, and Kansas suffer the most tornadoes of any states in the United States.

Tornadoes generally arise during thunderstorms, which are most common during humid summers, although they can occur at any time of the year, even during northerly winter thunderstorms. In the United States, tornado season is generally described as March to August, starting in the south, or wherever is warmest and most humid, and moving northerly as the summer matures. Florida and the Gulf Coast experience thunderstorms almost daily as well as several tropical storms or hurricanes per year, although the tornadoes they spawn tend to be weaker than those produced by nontropical thunderstorms. The Gulf Coast experiences tornadoes most frequently in the late fall (October through December), followed by February to April. The south-central plains states experience most tornadoes in late spring and occasionally the early fall, and these tornadoes tend to more destructive.

Since humidity builds up during the day and thunderstorms normally gain most of their energy from solar heating and latent heat released by the condensation of water vapor, 80% of tornadoes occur between noon and midnight. Tornadoes are least likely around dawn, when temperatures are lowest and radiation deficits are highest. However, tornadoes have occurred at all hours of the day; nighttime occurrences give the least warning.

EFFECTS In the United States, since 2007, tornadoes are measured on the enhanced Fujita scale from EF0 to EF5. EF3, EF4, and EF5 are also known as strong to violent tornadoes (see Table 6.15).

Wind speeds over 200 mph are rare and are used to specify the highest category of tornado (EF5). Wind speeds can approach 300 mph—about 100 mph faster than in the most intense hurricane—although tornadoes are much smaller than hurricanes. The most energetic tornadoes are a mile or two in diameter, whereas hurricanes are hundreds of miles wide.

Most tornadoes descend from cloud level without touching ground. When tornadoes do strike land, they affect anything they touch, although most landfalls are very narrow and last seconds. Large tornadoes tear apart structures as they encounter them and also pick up debris as hazardous projectiles. These projectiles are more likely to be thrown to the ground when the tornado changes course or dissipates.

The landfall and path of a tornado is chaotic. Tornadoes follow the path of least resistance, such as valleys and barren ground, and do not typically fall in cities, but a large tornado can crash

Table 6.15 Enhanced Fujita Scale for Rating Tornadoes

Scale	Estimated Wind Speed		
	mph	kph	mps
EF0	65–85	104–137	29–37
EF1	86–110	138–177	38–49
EF2	111–135	178–217	50–60
EF3	136–165	218–266	61–73
EF4	166–200	267–322	74–90
EF5	>200	>322	>90

Source: U.S. National Weather Service (2015).

BOX 6.4

Deadliest Tornadoes in the United States

Most tornadoes are not energetic enough to kill people. In fact, more deaths are caused by smaller tornadoes that cluster in time and space than are caused by the rarer strong tornadoes. For instance, on April 27, 2011, 199 tornadoes struck southern states, killing 317 people.

The deadliest tornado in the United States occurred on March 18, 1925, when 695 people died from a tornado that traveled more than 200 mi across Missouri, Illinois, and Indiana. Other tornadoes that day raised the total tornado-related deaths to 747, the deadliest day due to tornadoes ever in the United States. The second deadliest American tornado killed 317 (on May 6, 1840, in Louisiana and Mississippi).

Deaths due to tornadoes have fallen in the United States because of enhanced warnings and heightened preparedness. The deadliest tornado since World War II occurred April 9, 1947, when a tornado in Woodward, Oklahoma, killed 181 people. On May 22, 2011, in Joplin, Missouri, 162 people died. On June 8, 1953, in Flint, Michigan, a tornado killed 116. On May 20, 2013, another EF5 tornado crossed Moore, Oklahoma, killing at least 24 people and injuring more than 240 others within less than an hour, with a tail 17-mi long and more than a mile wide.

through properties before it is deflected. For instance, on September 24, 2001, a tornado touched Alexandria, Virginia, touched down again on the Mall in Washington, DC, and then touched down in College Park, Maryland.

FORECASTING In principle, human effects would be easy to avoid if the public were given notice and took shelter in substantial structures without exposure to glass windows and other fragile materials, but tornadoes are often sudden, and they cluster in time and space with thunderstorms. In the 1980s, U.S. forecasters could forecast about 25% of tornadoes within a couple days. In the 1990s, with the deployment of Doppler radar systems nationally, they could forecast about 75%. Although weather forecasters can forecast an increased likelihood of thunderstorms, and thence tornadoes, with a spatial accuracy at the state level, they cannot predict landfalls with accuracy useful for local emergency managers until minutes before the tornado arrives.

The warnings do not change the general public's behavior much since few people could avoid home or work for a whole day just because of an increased probability of tornadoes in the general area, although they could be more mindful. Most victims are caught during their normal daily activities, after perhaps only minutes of warning that is local enough to be actionable. For instance, on March 1, 2011, federal forecasters warned that on March 3, a line of storms with potential for tornadoes would hit the eastern states. On March 3, tornadoes struck Alabama, Georgia, Indiana, Kentucky, Mississippi, and Ohio, killing 38 people. The tornadoes traveled close to but avoided major cities such as Atlanta, Cincinnati, Louisville, and Nashville.

Floods

This section defines flood and reviews the risk and common controls.

DEFINITION A *flood* is an overabundance of water on land that is normally dry. Most floods are precipitation-related. Precipitation that does not soak into the ground runs off and collects in tributaries that run toward larger and larger rivers. If any of these routes overflow, the land is flooded.

Flash floods are rapid-onset floods, sometimes within minutes. Flash floods are likelier in dry areas with infrequent but intense precipitation. A flash flood can occur somewhere remote to the rainfall and in areas that have been dry for years. For any of these reasons, people are likelier to be surprised by flash floods than by a permanent river that steadily overflows its banks.

Coastal floods are caused by strong winds and high tides. Contained bodies of water, such as lakes, might flood because of seismic or volcanic destruction of the barriers, such as dams or levees that contain the water. Seismic activity underneath bodies of water can lift up the water and cause a wave that floods inland; this sort of *tsunami* is described under seismic risks.

The U.S. National Weather Service (2009) defines flood as "any high flow, overflow, or inundation by water which causes or threatens damage" (n.p.).

RISK Floods are the most frequent emergencies in the United States and are increasingly frequent due to increasing human habitation on flood plains, particularly where human development of the land interrupts natural runoff. Each year from 2001 to 2010, flooding caused $2.7 billion in costs on average.

Floods are mostly local events with discrete cycles of frequency that should be investigated locally without any implication for flooding risks elsewhere. Floods are associated with rare, large events such as hurricanes, which push seawater inland and dump precipitation that can saturate the land and overburden the rivers.

Even rarer are atmospheric rivers. An *atmospheric river* is an unusually large atmospheric trail of moisture moving northeast from the tropics across the Pacific Ocean for thousands of miles to the west coast of the Americas, where it delivers unusually severe rain for two or three days. Almost all major floods in California follow atmospheric river storms. Fortunately these are infrequent—every 100 to 200 years. The last such storm occurred in 1861–1862, when the Central Valley, including the state capital (Sacramento), was under around 10 ft of water. Today, Sacramento is much larger, and the Central Valley has more major cities. The U.S. Geological Survey modeled the 1861 flood with today's development and estimated $725 billion in damage to the state (Hockensmith, 2014).

In May 2014, the U.S. federal government's third national climate assessment forecast more severe flooding in the United States, even in places suffering declining average rainfall, due to climate change (Melillo, Richmond, & Yohe, 2014).

CONTROLLING FLOOD RISKS Flood risks are controlled at local levels by digging ditches and dykes, building levees, diverting rivers, planting flora that soak up water and bind soils, preparing rescue services with waterproof and buoyant equipment, and discouraging developments on flood plains.

One expert's lessons and best practices are copied at the end of this chapter as the final case study.

GEOLOGICAL AND GEOMORPHIC HAZARDS

The subsections below define geological and geomorphic hazards and review their causes and past events.

Definitions

Geological hazards are those on or in the natural surface of the earth. For disciplinary reasons (just because geologists traditionally study these things), all sorts of seismic, volcanic, and geomorphic hazards are normally categorized together as geological, even though they have very different sources. Sometimes even cosmic hazards are considered geological just because geologists study them. However, geological risks are easier to understand if separated as geomorphic, seismic, and volcanic.

Geomorphic hazards are those that physically change the earth, such as landslides, rivers, and glaciers. Glaciers are very slow-onset hazards compared to landslides, so sudden land movements tend to be meant when talking about geomorphic hazards.

Earth movements are sometimes differentiated as dry and wet. **Wet movements** are triggered by precipitation or flooding, such as avalanches and mudslides. Precipitation or water movements do not trigger dry movements. **Dry movements** include wind erosion, rock falls triggered by wind erosion, landslides triggered by earthquakes, and **subsidence** triggered by underground mining.

Causes

Rapid-onset land movements are activated by natural forces, such as fire, precipitation, or seismic activity, and by human activities, such as drilling, tunneling, or excavation. Humans increase their exposure to geomorphic hazards by living or working in less stable areas as well as by destabilizing these areas with their activities.

Burnt land tends to be less stable due to the weakening of the organic structure. Therefore, landslides are more likely after wildfires, particularly if precipitation follows quickly and the terrain is grass dominant (whose roots are very shallow and weak). Land can remain unstable for years before more deeply rooted vegetation reestablishes and binds the soil. If wildfires are more frequent than the lifecycle of deep-rooted vegetation, some sort of earth movement or soil erosion by wind and precipitation is inevitable.

Past Events

Geomorphic risks must be assessed at local levels, given highly technical assessments of the geology, compound events (such as flooding and wind erosion), and potential activations (such as earthquakes). An illustration of an unpredicted event with severe consequence is the wet movement on the night of March 22, 2014, when a hillside above the north fork of the Stillaguamish River collapsed and settled over hundreds of acres, including the village of Oso, northeast of Seattle, in Washington State, completely destroying the village and killing around 50 people.

Major geomorphic events globally are listed in Table 6.16.

Table 6.16　Earth Movements, 1970–2013, by Decade and Region

Region	1970–1979	1980–1989	1990–1999	2000–2009	2000–2013	TOTAL
Europe	17 disasters	13 disasters	13 disasters	5 disasters	1 disaster	49 disasters
	1,178 deaths	200 deaths	430 deaths	43 deaths	3 deaths	1,854 deaths
Russia/Soviet Union	1 disaster	4 disasters	7 disasters	3 disasters		15 disasters
	13 deaths	176 deaths	409 deaths	158 deaths		756 deaths
Oceania	3 disasters	3 disasters	5 disasters	5 disasters	1 disaster	17 disasters
	113 deaths	87 deaths	399 deaths	93 deaths	60 deaths	752 deaths
Japan	3 disasters	5 disasters	4 disasters	1 disaster	1 disaster	14 disasters
	127 deaths	292 deaths	118 deaths	44 deaths	3 deaths	584 deaths
Central and South America	15 disasters	36 disasters	30 disasters	31 disasters	10 disasters	122 disasters
	5,355 deaths	3,006 deaths	1,946 deaths	904 deaths	454 deaths	11,665 deaths
Developing Asia, Africa, and Middle East	12 disasters	45 disasters	68 disasters	85 disasters	35 disasters	245 disasters
	322,509 deaths	3,596 deaths	5,882 deaths	6,428 deaths	3,934 deaths	342,349 deaths
North America	2 disasters		1 disaster	1 disaster		4 disasters
	431 deaths		0 deaths	15 deaths		446 deaths
TOTAL	53 disasters	106 disasters	128 disasters	131 disasters	48 disasters	466 disasters
	7,453 deaths	7,357 deaths	9,181 deaths	7,685 deaths	4,454 deaths	358,406 deaths

Source: Centre for Research on the Epidemiology of Disasters, 2015. Events fulfill at least one of the following criteria: 10 or more people reportedly killed, 100 people reportedly affected, a call for international assistance, or a declaration of a state of emergency.

Seismic

The subsections below review the definitions, causes, frequency, distribution, and returns of seismic risks.

DEFINITION The term **seismic** refers to movements of the earth originating from natural forces below the surface of the earth. Seismic energy can travel to the surface and can be experienced as vibrations and movements (often described as quaking, shaking, or trembling) that affect the geology, persons, and structures at the surface (**earthquake**).

The rapid-onset effects, such as shaking or erupting of the earth, are most dramatic but not the main causes of death or damage. Instead, secondary hazards, such as falling debris from damaged structures, flooding from failed levees or dams, tsunami, landslides, fires, leaking toxic gases, contaminated water, and blocked communications compound on one another until we face collective destruction or deaths or disruption amounting to a disaster. Tertiary effects include psychological stress and social displacement.

Earthquakes beneath a body of water cause waves (known by the Japanese word *tsunami*) that in turn cause floods inland or damage vessels on the water. A *wave* is energy that is traveling through water; it is not a body of water that is traveling. As a wave travels through the water, the water is seen to move up and down, although the wave rather than the water is traveling laterally. When the wave approaches shore, the elevated water can flood the land as the wave continues to travel inland. A tsunami is such a long and fast wave (miles across and traveling at up to 450 mph in deep water) that it would be difficult to observe except at shore, where it would be observed as a very rapid low tide followed by a very rapid high tide. When a wave approaches the coast, where the seafloor rises, the wave tends to slow and rise higher. Water is sucked from the shore to feed the rising wave. Thus, the first warning would be an unusually rapid falling sea level. As the tsunami hits land, it resembles an unusually rapid incoming tide. This elevated water can rise more than 100 ft above normal and travel inland for miles.

CAUSES A tectonic earthquake is brought about by the collision of different tectonic plates, whose edges often stick together, resulting in the build-up of potential energy. When the force of collision eventually overcomes the force of friction, energy is released in the form of a quake.

Most earthquakes are natural events with no practical controls on their activation, although human activities, such as drilling or excavating, can activate the hazards. For instance, high-pressure hydraulic fracturing (*fracking*) of the earth is used to extract natural gas trapped in shale rock but has been linked with earthquakes (as well as pollution of groundwater and the air). The practice originated in the United States, but the link was clearest in 2012 around Blackpool, England, where natural earthquakes are extremely rare, but several earthquakes followed the first commercial fracking there. The British government subsequently banned fracking, although in December 2012, it lifted the ban, subject to new controls.

FREQUENCY Earthquakes and volcanic eruptions are rapid-onset hazards. Humans have a poor record of predicting them; in fact, earthquakes are practically unforecastable, although we know a great deal about historical events.

The U.S. Geological Survey's National Earthquake Information Center estimates several million earthquakes globally per year, most of them not detected because of their weak energy or remoteness to recording instruments. The National Earthquake Information Center traditionally located about 20,000 per year, but thanks to more numerous and more sensitive instruments globally, since the year 2000, the center has located closer to 30,000 per year.

The U.S. Geological Survey lists 127 earthquakes that killed 1,000 or more people from 1900 through 2012 worldwide (see Table 6.17). The U.S. Geological Survey identifies 48 deadly earthquakes in the United States since its founding (1787), a frequency of one deadly earthquake every less than 4.9 years.

Table 6.17 Earthquakes With 1,000 or More Deaths Since 1900, by Decade and Region

Region	1900–1909	1910–1919	1920–1929	1930–1939	1940–1949	1950–1959	1960–1969	1970–1979	1980–1989	1990–1999	2000–2009	2000–2013	TOTAL
Europe	1 disaster 72,000 deaths	1 disaster 3,261 deaths		1 disaster 1,404 deaths	1 disaster 1,000 deaths		1 disaster 1,100 deaths	2 disasters 2500 deaths	1 disaster 2,375 deaths	1 disaster 1,185 deaths			9 disasters 84,825 deaths
Russia										1 disaster 1,989 deaths			1 disaster 1,989 deaths
Oceania										1 disaster 2,183 deaths			1 disaster 2,183 deaths
Japan			2 disasters 145,820 deaths	1 disaster 3,000 deaths	4 disasters 8,282 deaths							1 disaster 20,896 deaths	9 disasters 183,500 deaths
Central and South America	4 disasters 7,882 deaths			1 disaster 30,500 deaths	3 disasters 14,450 deaths	1 disaster 1,000 deaths		3 disasters 98,000 deaths	3 disasters 11,500 deaths			1 disaster 316,000 deaths	16 disasters 479,332 deaths
Developing Asia, Africa, and Middle East	7 disasters 88,450 deaths	5 disasters 11,100 deaths	6 disasters 256,200 deaths	10 disasters 106,510 deaths	7 disasters 135,190 deaths	4 disasters 15,026 deaths	7 disasters 46,754 deaths	12 disasters 322,509 deaths	6 disasters 39,642 deaths	10 disasters 48,277 deaths	10 disasters 464,015 deaths	1 disaster 2,200 deaths	86 disasters 1,535,873 deaths
North America	1 disaster 72,000 deaths												1 disaster 72,000 deaths
TOTAL	13 disasters 181,332 deaths	6 disasters 14,361 deaths	8 disasters 402,020 deaths	13 disasters 141,414 deaths	15 disasters 158,922 deaths	5 disasters 16,026 deaths	8 disasters 49,509 deaths	17 disasters 423,009 deaths	10 disasters 53,517 deaths	14 disasters 59,136 deaths	10 disasters 464,015 deaths	3 disasters 339,096 deaths	**122 disasters 2,302,357 deaths**

Source: U.S. Geological Survey (2015).

Earthquakes last from a few seconds to several minutes. Earthquakes are associated with aftershocks, which are subsequent earthquakes triggered by the first earthquake. Each earthquake releases some of the tension from the fault but also leaves the fault in a new state, whose tensions take dozens of aftershocks to resolve. The final aftershock might come days to months after the first event. Some aftershocks are best considered separate earthquakes if their power is similar to the initial event. Occasionally, an earthquake can trigger a more powerful earthquake, although the chance is low (about 5% globally). Smaller aftershocks can be riskier than the initial event if they are powerful enough to damage structures before they can be repaired or response systems can recover.

DISTRIBUTION Events are unpredictable, but locations are broadly predictable. Seismic hazards are located along the collision or fault lines between tectonic plates. One line directly affects habitable ground along the Pacific coast of the Americas. Another line affects directly Japan, Taiwan, the Philippines, Indonesia, and New Zealand. Other lines directly affect Burma, Northern India, Pakistan, Bangladesh, Western China, Central Asia, Iran, Turkey, and Southeastern Europe. Nowhere on the planet is free of earthquakes, although they are extremely rare and inconsequential in some areas, such as Northwest Europe.

The largest cities located on fault lines are Tokyo (Japan), Taipei (Taiwan), Manila (the Philippines), Singapore, Jakarta (Indonesia), San Francisco (USA), Mexico City, and Santiago (Chile). Some of these cities (such as San Francisco and Tokyo), thanks to strong regulation and national and local capacity, are much better protected and prepared than other cities (such as Manila and Jakarta).

From 1970 to 2001, 15 seismic disasters occurred along the line from Southeast Asia to Turkey, more than twice as many as occurred elsewhere, and these 15 events killed more than three quarters of the people killed by all the seismic disasters in the world during that period. The only seismic disaster in North America during that period accounted for 65% of all the insurance claims (see Table 6.10).

Most earthquakes in the United States occur in the western coastal states, followed by the Rocky Mountain states, and then the eastern states, with every few in between. In order, the 10 likeliest American states to experience earthquakes are Alaska, California, Hawaii, Nevada, Washington, Idaho, Wyoming, Montana, Utah, and Oregon.

California experiences about one quarter of the earthquakes in the United States and experiences most of the economic losses and fatalities. More than 2,000 fault lines run through California; probably, others remain unidentified. For instance, the deadly earthquake that focused on Northridge, southern California, in 1994, originated from a previously unidentified fault. California experiences more than 100 earthquakes per day, although most do not affect anything other than local instruments.

Tsunami are of most concern in the Pacific Ocean, traveling westward, from the fault line along the Americas, toward Japan, Southeast Asia, and Australasia, or eastward toward the Americas. In between are the Polynesian and Micronesian islands, which have plenty of volcanic activity of their own and are exposed to tsunami traveling both eastward and westward.

RETURNS

Magnitude. Seismic events are conventionally measured by energy (**magnitude**) at their epicenter (the point on the surface of the earth above the **focus** of the earthquake) and by their extent (usually the maximum distance from the epicenter at which the energy were observed). Magnitude was traditionally measured on the **Richter scale** but is now measured more often on the **moment magnitude scale** (see Table 6.18).

Table 6.18	Conventional Scales for Assessing Earthquakes				
Richter Magnitude Scale	Moment Magnitude Scale	Modified Mercalli Intensity (MMI) Scale	Abbreviated MMI Description		Frequency, Global
	1.0–3.0	I	Not felt except by a very few under especially favorable conditions.		Earthquakes of less than 2.0 magnitude (microearthquakes) are not normally felt by humans
	3.0–3.9	II	Felt only by a few persons at rest, especially on upper floors of buildings. Delicately suspended objects may swing.		
		III	Felt quite noticeably by persons indoors, especially on upper floors of buildings. Many people do not recognize it as an earthquake. Standing motorcars may rock slightly. Vibration similar to the passing of a truck. Duration estimated.		
<4.3	4.0–4.9	IV	Felt indoors by many, outdoors by few during the day. At night, some awakened. Dishes, windows, doors disturbed; walls make cracking sound. Sensation like heavy truck striking building. Standing motorcars rocked noticeably.		Thousands of 4.5 or higher magnitude earthquakes per year
4.4–4.8		V	Felt by nearly everyone; many awakened. Some dishes, windows broken. Unstable objects overturned. Pendulum clocks may stop.		

Richter Magnitude Scale	Moment Magnitude Scale	Modified Mercalli Intensity (MMI) Scale	Abbreviated MMI Description	Frequency, Global
4.9–5.4	5.0–5.9	VI	Felt by all, many frightened. Some heavy furniture moved; a few instances of fallen plaster. Damage slight.	
5.5–6.1		VII	Damage negligible in buildings of good design and construction; slight to moderate in well-built ordinary structures; considerable damage in poorly built or badly designed structures; some chimneys broken.	
6.2–6.5	6.0–6.9	VIII	Damage slight in specially designed structures; considerable damage in ordinary substantial buildings with partial collapse. Damage great in poorly built structures. Fall of chimneys, factory stacks, columns, monuments, and walls. Heavy furniture overturned.	
6.6–6.9		IX	Damage considerable in specially designed structures; well-designed frame structures thrown out of plumb. Damage great in substantial buildings, with partial collapse. Buildings shifted off foundations.	
7.0–7.3		X	Some well-built wooden structures destroyed; most masonry and frame structures destroyed with foundations. Rail bent.	
7.4–8.1		XI	Few if any (masonry) structures remain standing. Bridges destroyed. Rails bent greatly.	8.0 magnitude earthquakes (great earthquakes) occur once every year
>8.1		XII	Damage total. Lines of sight and level are distorted. Objects thrown into the air.	

Source: U.S. Geological Survey (2015).

The magnitude scales are infinite (meaning they have no upper limit). They are also logarithmic, which means that each event is 10 times more energetic with each 1.0 step upwards on the scale.

The U.S. Geological Survey (2015) estimates globally, since 1900, per year,

- 1.3 million earthquakes of 2.0–2.9 magnitude,

- 130,000 of 3.0–3.9 magnitude,

- 13,000 of 4.0–4.9 magnitude,

- 1,319 earthquakes of 5.0–5.9 magnitude,

- 134 of 6.0–6.9 magnitude,

- 15 of 7.0–7.9 magnitude, and

- one of 8.0 magnitude or greater.

Intensity. Earthquakes can be judged by their effects (**intensity**) on the Mercalli scale. The modified Mercalli intensity scale is finite, from Roman numeral I to Roman numeral XII, and is purely judgmental. Magnitude can be measured with replicable instruments, but intensity must be judged by human coders (see Table 6.18).

Human Deaths. From 1900 through 2012, the world has experienced 127 earthquakes that each killed at least 1,000 people, a frequency of 1.12 such earthquakes per year (see Table 6.17).

BOX 6.5

Notable Earthquakes in the United States

The United States experiences thousands of earthquakes every year, although most are too small to be felt by humans. (They are observed only by automated instruments.) From 2000 through 2012, the United States National Earthquake Information Center located 49,685 earthquakes in the United States of any magnitude that could be recorded by official instruments, an average of 3,822 per year. Of these, 381 per year were of 4.0–4.9 magnitude, less than 56 per year were of 5.0–5.9 magnitude, 5.6 per year were of 6.0–6.9 magnitude, 0.6 per year were of 7.0–7.9 magnitude, and none was larger.

The earthquake of greatest moment magnitude (9.2) to strike the United States occurred on March 28, 1964, in Prince William Sound, Alaska, and lasted about 3 min. The earthquake killed 15 people directly and generated a tsunami that killed another 113 (total deaths: 128). The tsunami reached a maximum recorded height of 67 m and reached down the Pacific coast of the rest of the United States (where 15 people were killed) and caused damage on Hawaii. The earthquake and tsunami together caused more than $300 million in damages, excluding costs in Canada.

The greatest magnitude earthquake to hit the United States east of the Rockies since 1897 occurred on August 23, 2011, with an epicenter in Louisa County, Virginia. This earthquake had a magnitude of 5.8 and an intensity of VII. Damage was minor and not deadly but widespread, with total costs close to $300 million, centered on the capital area.

From 1970 to 2001, seismic disasters killed around 551,000 people—138 times as many as were killed by terrorist disasters during the same period and not far off as many as were killed by weather (see Table 6.10).

From 2000 to 2012, nearly 600,000 people around the world were killed by earthquakes (even after adjusting down from Haiti's inflated estimate of deaths in 2010). Earthquakes killed more people in the most recent 13 years than were killed in the preceding 30. Earthquakes of great magnitude are not more common; they are just becoming more consequential because of increased human population in general and increased development in earthquake zones in particular.

In 2012, the world experienced 17 earthquakes that killed people (according to the U.S. Geological Survey), each with a magnitude from 4.9 to 7.6, causing 768 total deaths, including 306 in northwestern Iran on August 11, 2012; 113 in the Negros-Cebu region of the Philippines on February 6, 2012; 81 in and around Sichuan province, China, on September 7, 2012; and 75 in the Hindu Kush region of Afghanistan on June 11, 2012.

Globally, 22 earthquakes each killed more than 50,000 people, the earliest in 856 A.D. in Iran, the most recent on January 12, 2010, in Haiti, a frequency of 1 in every 52.5 years (according to the U.S. Geological Survey).

The five deadliest earthquakes ever, according to the U.S. Geological Survey (2015), are as follows:

1. More than 830,000 people dead in China on January 23, 1556

2. Officially 242,769 people dead, although most estimates are higher (as high as 655,000 dead), from a 7.5 magnitude earthquake in the Tangshan area of China on July 27, 1976

3. Around 200,000 dead from a 7.8 magnitude earthquake in Haiyuan and surrounding counties of China on December 16, 1920

4. 142,800 dead from a 7.9 magnitude earthquake in Kanto province, Japan, on September 1, 1923

5. 110,000 dead from a 7.3 magnitude earthquake in Ashgabat, Turkmenistan, on October 5, 1948

The sixth deadliest earthquake occurred on January 12, 2010, near Port-au-Prince, Haiti, killing less than 100,000 people. (In 2011, the government of Haiti estimated 316,000 deaths, but foreign aid organizations do not agree.) The death toll and damage were severe because the earthquake was of major magnitude (7.0) and its epicenter was near a populous capital (about 16 mi away), but mostly because the quality of construction was very poor. The International Federation of Red Cross and Red Crescent Societies estimated three million affected. USAID estimated 1.5 million displaced. Haiti was already a focus of international humanitarian work after hurricanes and political violence. (A U.N. Stabilization Mission has been present since 2004, and Hurricane Ike had struck Haiti in 2008.) Hundreds of thousands of Haitians were already displaced or destitute before the earthquake and remain so.

The deadliest tsunami in recorded history occurred on December 26, 2004. The earthquake (around 9.2 on the moment magnitude scale) was the largest since 1964 and the third largest since 1900. Its epicenter was near the island of Sumatra, Indonesia. The tsunami spread mostly east and west (because of the north–south axis of the fault line) and reached the South African and North and South American coasts, although most of the energy hit India and Southeast Asia. The tsunami reached nearly 100-ft high and inundated land, causing at least 230,000 deaths, of which at least 170,000 died in Indonesia; 35,000 in Sri Lanka; 18,000 in India; and 8,000 in Thailand. Since the impacted areas were not particularly well insured or developed, this was not the costliest seismic event; it caused $14 billion in direct damage.

The tsunami that struck Japan on March 11, 2011, was the costliest in economic terms but not the deadliest, although it killed around 18,500 people directly. The quake struck 109 mi off of Japan's Fukushima coast, at a depth of 18.6 mi.

The four deadliest earthquakes in the United States include the following:

1. Around 3,000 people killed in San Francisco on April 18, 1906

2. 165 killed in Hawaii, Alaska, and California by a tsunami started by an earthquake in the Aleutian Islands on April 1, 1946

3. 128 killed in Alaska, Oregon, and California, mostly by a tsunami, due to an earthquake in Prince William Sound, Alaska, on March 28, 1964

4. 115 killed by an earthquake in Long Beach, California, on March 11, 1933 (U.S. Geological Survey, 2015)

The other earthquakes in the United States each killed less than 80 people. The U.S. Geological Survey lists 48 deadly earthquakes in the United States since 1811, the most recent on December 22, 2003 (in Central California leaving two dead).

Economic Costs. Four of the five costliest natural events in recorded history are seismic events. (The other is a hurricane.)

The tsunami that struck Japan on March 11, 2011, was the costliest natural event ever and the 20th-deadliest earthquake since 1900. The tsunami reached more than 130 ft high in narrow coastal valleys and travelled 6 mi inland. The tallest seawalls in Japan at that time were 12 m (39-ft) high. The earthquake was also the greatest ever to be recorded in Japan. (It measured more than 9 on the moment magnitude scale.) The tsunami caused most of the deaths and damage; it killed more than 18,500 people, of which more than 92% drowned, and damaged or destroyed nearly 1.1 million built structures and 230,000 automobiles. Japan quickly estimated the total economic cost at more than $300 billion; the World Bank estimated $235 billion. By either estimate, this event was the costliest natural event ever. (The tsunami also damaged the nuclear power plant at Fukushima. This event is described in Chapter 5.)

Japan suffered the world's second costliest earthquake on January 17, 1995, near Kobe, with the loss of almost 6,500 people and $100 billion in damages (World Bank estimate).

The third costliest earthquake in the world occurred on May 12, 2008, near Chengdu in Sichuan province, China; it caused 70,000 deaths and $29 billion in direct damage.

Volcanic

The subsections below define volcanic activity and review the risks.

DEFINITION A **volcano** is an aperture in the surface of the earth from which **magma**, gas, or steam sometimes escapes from beneath the surface. *Volcanic events* occur on the surface, after the force of pressure from magma or steam or gases overcomes the force of pressure from whatever (usually bedrock or solidified **lava**) is preventing its escape. Under the surface, volcanic activity may be observed as seismic activity. True volcanic activity occurs when gases, water (usually as steam), and magma (as lava) escape the earth.

RISKS Volcanic hazards tend to be colocated with seismic hazards, so the distribution of seismic hazards (see the section above) is a guide to the distribution of volcanic hazards.

The actual volcanic eruption lasts only seconds or minutes, although the build-up, such as the growth of a new volcano, can last months, and the aftereffects, such as the release of lava, also can last months. Indeed, some vents effectively leak lava, steam, or gases continuously.

If the volcanic eruption is explosive in very short periods of time (seconds or minutes), it can cause harm by blast. Most harm is caused over longer periods of time by escaping ash, gases, steam, and lava, which burn and poison the environment.

Most volcanic events have very localized effects. Large events can send ash and gases high into the atmosphere, where they can spread around the world, affect climate, and interrupt communications. For instance, in June 1991, Mount Pinatubo, a volcano in the Philippines, blasted around 20,000,000 T of sulfur dioxide and ash into the stratosphere, where the sulfur dioxide formed sulfate particles that reflected sunlight back into space. These particles enveloped the Earth for almost two months and deflected enough sunlight to cool the planet by about 1 °F.

The risks to communications from volcanic events was highlighted from March through May 2010, when the Eyjafjallajökull volcano in Iceland erupted with very little lava and few tremors but colossal emissions of ash that disrupted air transportation and weather patterns regionally.

Fires

The subsections below define fires and review the distribution of fires in space, their frequency over time, their returns, and controls.

DEFINITIONS A **fire** is the combustion of a material by rapid oxidation, releasing energy in the form of light and heat and producing oxidized compounds and waste products.

A **wildfire** (also known as a forest fire, vegetation fire, or, in Australasia, bushfire) is an uncontrolled fire on wildland. *Wildland* is land that has not been significantly developed or altered by human beings. Literally, a wildland fire occurs on wildland; this is usefully distinguished from urban fires and from *wildland-urban interface (WUI) fires*, also known as *interface fires* or *intermix fires*, which occur where wildland and human-developed lands meet.

Most wildfires are **spot fires** that burn out naturally without spreading from the ignition spot. Most moving wildfires are slow *surface fires* or **ground fires**, spread by contact from fuel to fuel on the ground. Wildfires spread quicker when they reach into the crowns of trees and become **crown fires**. Generally, surface or ground fires are less energetic, less devastating, and more frequent than crown fires. *Grassland fires*, which move across land whose flora are predominantly grasses, tend to be quickest to spread but also quickest to burn out.

Fires spread quickest when hot embers rise into the atmosphere and are blown onto new fuels. When driven by winds, fire can spread from vegetation to vegetation much quicker than any animal can run and have been known to overtake automobiles.

Changes in weather, from calm or moist winds to energetic dry winds, can be very sudden. The resulting surge in fire activity due to increased wind or drier wind is known as a **blowup**.

DISTRIBUTION

Ignition. A fire is caused by lightning, human accident (such as abandoned cigarettes or camp-fires), broken power lines, and arson. Humans cause almost all fires, accidentally or deliberately. Human activities are the only practical sources of ignition in developed lands. Sometimes, human and natural activities interact to cause the fire. For instance, in April 1906, an earthquake struck the San Francisco urban area, damaging power lines that caused a fire that raged for days, killing around 3,000 people altogether.

Wildfires became dramatically more frequent and intense and consequential to human life and property from the late 19th century as human populations developed wildlands at an unprecedented pace. Human penetration into wildlands brought more unnatural ignition sources and exposed more humans and property. Human suppression of wildfires in the first half of the 20th century lowered the frequency of all wildfires; in some areas, fire suppression has practically eliminated fires to date.

Fire risk increases with increasing human population and housing density. As land and public capacity for fire management are developed further, wildlands disappear entirely and wildfires practically disappear too. Wildfires are most likely in intermediate-density housing, where wildlands and housing are mixed up, and at the interface between dense housing and wildlands. In both areas, humans and wild fuels are most likely to meet. In the United States, this interface is known as the wildland–urban interface and is given special attention for fire management.

> From 2001 through 2011, an average of 85 percent of wildfires in the United States were caused by people (121,849 lightning-caused and 717,527 human-caused). The two areas with the highest percentage of wildfires caused by humans are the Eastern (99 percent) and Southern (96 percent) areas. However, in terms of average annual number of acres burned by human-caused wildfires in 2001–2011, the Southern area is highest nationwide, with more than 1 million acres, followed by the Southwest region, with about 380,000 acres of human-caused wildfires annually. (Stein et al., 2013, p. 16)

California, the Mediterranean Basin, Chile, Australia, and South Africa all show increasing frequency of wildfires and of human-caused wildfires where human development has increased; the frequency is highest at intermediate population densities.

Humans cause 95% of wildfires in California, where urban areas and wildlands are very large and the climate is prototypically Mediterranean (at least in the coastal south) (Syphard, Radeloff, Hawbaker, & Stewart, 2009, pp. 760, 763). Data from the California Department of Forestry and Fire Protection and the U.S. Forest Service for the 1970s show that in Alameda County, the most densely developed county on the San Francisco East Bay but still with large areas of wildlands, lightning caused fires just 1.8 times per decade per 100,000 ha of protected wildlands, while humans caused fires about 900 times. In the larger and less densely developed Santa Clara County, lightning caused 5.3 fires per decade per 100,000 ha of protected wildlands while humans caused about 500. In the nearby Plumas and Sequoia National Forests, lightning caused more than 200 wildfires per decade per 100,000 ha while humans caused less than half as many (Keeley, 2005, pp. 288, 291–292).

Lightning strikes are more likely sources of ignition in true wildlands, but even there, they are relatively infrequent and inconsequential. Lightning occurs only during thunderstorms, which are not as frequent in the Mediterranean-type climates as in the more temperate climates, which are less vulnerable to fire due to damper conditions and different vegetation. In Mediterranean-type areas, lightning causes mostly spot fires that do not spread. Lightning is more likely to ignite fires that spread through grasslands than woodlands. Grasslands dominate where wildfires or grazing are frequent enough to prevent shrubs taking over, but grassland fires do not tend to spread further. From 1950 to 2000, lightning-ignited wildfires exceeded 1,000 ha on only three occasions in the United States (Keeley, 2005, pp. 291–293).

Vegetation and Climate

Mediterranean and Similar Climates

Wildfires are most likely in Mediterranean-type climates, which include the lands around the Mediterranean Sea (the Mediterranean Basin), the coastal southwestern United States, western

Mexico, central Chile, southwestern Australia, and the Cape Region of South Africa. The true Mediterranean climatic areas make up less than 5% of the Earth's nonglaciated land surface yet suffer the most frequent wildfires per unit area. The climate allows for sufficient precipitation, sunshine, and warmth to allow dense and varied flora (20% of the world's flora) but also hot, dry summers that dry out that vegetation producing readier fuels. Mediterranean climates are dominated by evergreen, woody, sclerophyllous shrubs that are highly flammable, although adapted to survive (Syphard et al., 2009, p. 759).

Wildfires are almost as likely in surrounding areas that are not strictly Mediterranean in climate but are practically little different from the perspective of fire ecologists. These areas effectively include the entire west of North America and South America, Australia, South Africa, and the Mediterranean Basin, extending up into southern Switzerland.

These climates and flora are attractive for agriculture, residency, and tourism, so human development historically has penetrated into the same areas where wildfires are most frequent while leaving significant wildlands undeveloped where interior climates are less attractive. (About 23% of Chile was practically free of vegetation in 2005. The Mediterranean area of North Africa borders the Sahara Desert, and the Mediterranean-type southwestern United States also borders deserts.) Consequently, human civilization has tended to develop with stark interfaces between developed lands and wildlands, where opportunities for humans to start wildfires and to suffer exposure to wildfires are greatest (Syphard et al., 2009, p. 763).

Grasslands

Wildfires are more likely where certain vegetation dominate. Grasslands are dominated by grasses and other herbaceous species that dry out easily, are more susceptible to fire, extend the length of the fire season, and have short, weak roots that leave the soil more likely to slide after a fire, although their fires tend to be rapid and less energetic. Human-caused clearance of forests and agricultural grazing favor grasses and cereals, which account for 40% of land cover in southwestern Australia and South Africa and 20% in North America and Chile (as of 2005; Syphard et al., 2009, p. 763). Alien grasses, with ecological and agricultural consequences, dominate some of the grasslands. The western United States has large areas of alien cheatgrass (*Bromus tectorum*) and buffelgrass (*Pennisetum ciliare* or *Cenchrus ciliaris*), which are prone to frequent fires.

Deciduous and Mixed Forest

Deciduous trees annually shed leaves and limbs, which become ready fuels once they have dried out; so deciduous forests tend to experience more frequent ground fires than nondeciduous forests experience.

Human exploitation of natural forests has favored deciduous hardwoods, so natural deciduous forests have seen most human intervention. This exploitation has increased human ignition of and exposure to wildfires in some areas while eliminating wildfires elsewhere.

In Mediterranean-type regions, where pine and oak crown fires are natural, human penetration has dramatically increased the frequency of human ignition and exposure while fire suppression allowed forests and natural fuel loads to increase in density, so that when an uncontrolled wildfire broke out, it tended to be more intense and costly.

Eastern North America is naturally damper than the rest of North America and has seen more extensive human intervention, to the extent that human development has practically eliminated wildlands in whole states, such as New Jersey and Maryland, or replaced the endemic oak and pine woodlands with mesophytic hardwood woodlands, which are less vulnerable to crown fires.

Shrubland

In true Mediterranean climates, adapted shrubs are endemic. Fuels grow to unnatural volumes where humans prevent ground fires that would burn away such fuels or where humans clear forests without removing the dead vegetation. In the early 20th century, new national and state parks were closed to agricultural grazing, allowing natural shrubland to return, which is associated with less frequent fires. In the late 20th century, declining pastoral use of land and increasing conservation of land at the state and city level, particularly around urban coastal areas of California, led to recolonization by endemic shrubs there too, and they effectively serve as more fire-resistant buffers at the interface between large urban areas and true wildlands. Data from 1945 to 2002 suggest that the protected wildlands of Santa Clara County on the San Francisco East Bay have a fire rotation interval (the time interval between complete burns) of around 100 years, presumably with a lengthening interval given recent changes in the vegetation and the human management of fire (Keeley, 2005, pp. 285, 289).

By contrast, in the Mediterranean as a whole during the 20th century, vegetative cover and fuels increased and wildfires increased in frequency and extent in wildlands that transitioned from low-fuel grazed and cleared grasslands to high-fuel natural shrublands as humans stopped their pastoral use of wildlands and concentrated in enclosed agricultural and urban areas (Hessl, 2011, pp. 396–397).

Coniferous Forest

Most coniferous (needle-leafed) trees do not shed leaves or limbs normally until they die, and they also favor higher, damper elevations. So coniferous forests are not the most prone to wildfires, but a crown fire in a coniferous tree is very energetic, so crown fires tend to be devastating. Needle-leaf forests account for 21% of land cover in North America and less than 10% in Chile, Australia, South Africa, and the Mediterranean Basin (as of 2005).

Prehistoric frequencies of wildfires suggest the natural frequency of wildfires in areas unaffected by human activities. Prehistoric environments similar to northern hemisphere coniferous forests suffered severe crown fires once every 3 to 35 years. Wetter, higher latitude coniferous forests and temperate shrublands and boreal forests suffered such fires every 105 to 1,585 years. The fire in Yellowstone National Park (primarily in the state of Wyoming) in 1988 suggests a natural severe fire that occurs in a natural temperate environment every 200 to 300 years. It burned for more than 3 months and was extinguished only by the first snows (in mid-September) despite the previous efforts of 25,000 firefighters at a cost of $120 million; the fire consumed more than 1,400,000 ha (Pausas & Keeley, 2009, pp. 594, 599).

Tropical Forest

Wildfires are not natural in tropical forests, but human penetration and human clearance of natural tropical forests have increased the frequency of essentially unnatural fires. Combined with occasional periods of drought, wildfires in tropical forests can be devastating, such as in Indonesia in 1997, which released as much carbon into the atmosphere as 13 to 40% of global annual emissions from fossil fuels (Pausas & Keeley, 2009, p. 599).

FREQUENCY

Wildfire Season. Wildfires start annually after the winter snows and spring meltwater have retreated and after some period of warm and dry weather has dried out the natural fuels. They occur most frequently in late summer, after prolonged drought. In some wetter climates, wildfires are not equally likely year after year but occur infrequently during irregular cycles of heat and drought. By contrast, in climates with reliable hot, dry summers after wet, warm spring seasons (when vegetation growth spurts), wildfires tend to be more frequent.

Global Climate Change. In 2007, the Intergovernmental Panel on Climate Change Working Group II predicted that climate change would increase the frequency and intensity of wildfires in most areas, particularly where more frequent and longer droughts would increase the frequency of wildfires and lengthen the wildfire season.

However, global warming will increase the rate of decomposition in wetter climates and, thus, reduce the natural buildup of fuels there (Pausas & Keeley, 2009, p. 600). Moreover, some areas can expect more precipitation due to climate change, even as other areas experience more precipitation. Already, arid regions with slow growing and sparse vegetation are likely to see such decreased growth due to increased drought that wildfires would disappear there. Eastern North America, Northern Europe, and tropical Africa should experience more precipitation and fewer wildfires. Western North America, the Mediterranean rim (including Portugal, Spain, Switzerland, Italy, and Greece), Russia, and Australia would experience more severe droughts. Additionally, climate change is associated with more frequent and severe thunderstorms and longer thunderstorm seasons, which means more lightning strikes—natural sources of ignition—in addition to the increasing frequency of human-caused ignitions associated with increased human penetration. For areas of increasing wildfire frequency, the effects would be severe for a few decades before fuels diminish, vegetation changes, and local human responses counter the frequency (Hessl, 2011, pp. 395–396, 399–401).

North America. Most of western North America suffered more frequent consequential fires in the late 19th century due to human penetration, agricultural grazing, and logging of wildlands, without much public capacity for fighting fires. The frequency probably peaked in the 1930s, before more effective wildfire management and firefighting.

In the eastern United States and Canada, wildfires became less frequent after about 1850 despite a warming trend, presumably because of increased precipitation, the artificial replacement of endemic oaks and pines with hardwoods, and the extensive urbanization of whole states and islands so as to eliminate wildlands altogether.

In the last third of the 20th century, North America suffered an increasing frequency of wildfires of all sorts due to warmer, longer seasons, and increased human penetration. For the years 1970 to 2003, researchers identified 1,166 large (more than 400 ha) wildfires on federally managed land in the western United States (about 61% of all western U.S. forested areas). Compared to the period 1970–1986, in the period 1987–2003, wildfire frequency was 4 times greater, the wildfire season was 64% longer (an extension by 78 days), the period from discovery to control increased from 7.5 days to 37.1 days, and the area burnt was 6.5 times greater. The greatest increase in frequency occurred around 2,130-m elevation. The increased frequency was earliest and most pronounced in the western United States, where the frequency and extent of wildfires increased as early as 1970, more due to longer, drier summers than to human activities.

Global warming is a strong cause: averaged spring and summer temperatures increased by 0.87 °C from 1970 to 1986 and from 1987 to 2003, with the latter period being the warmest since records began in 1895. Global warming and cyclical weather patterns due to Pacific sea surface temperature variations (El Niño, La Niña, and the Pacific Decadal Oscillation) contributed to severe droughts in 2000 and 2002 that promoted more wildfires in the southwest United States (Hessl, 2011, pp. 396–399; Westerling, Hidalgo, Cayan, & Swetman, 2006, pp. 940–941).

Global warming has contributed to the increased frequency and to the outbreak of wildfires in areas without precedent, such as the tundra of western Canada and the western United States, where wildfires have broken out after five millennia of absence. These areas have experienced longer, drier summers, with some thawing of permafrost.

Wildfires are likely to increase in frequency and intensity in most areas of the United States due to climate change. Given a global increase in carbon dioxide to twice natural levels, North America would experience a 10 to 50% increase in fire season severity; models for Canada forecast a 46% increase in seasonal severity and area burnt. If carbon dioxide rates triple, Canada can expect a 74 to 118% increase in seasonal area burnt. However, most of eastern North America, where the climate would become more mesic, would suffer less severe seasons (Hessl, 2011, pp. 395–396).

The record number of wildfires in the United States in any year was 249,370 (in 1981). By comparison, in 2009, the United States suffered 1,348,500 fires in human-developed areas or vehicles (according to the National Fire Protection Association). According to the U.S. National Interagency Fire Center, the United States suffers more than 92,000 wildfires in an average year, most of them small spot fires that harm no humans or built structures (see Table 6.19). Local fire departments responded to an average of 36,700 fires annually in forests, woodlands, or other wildlands from 2004 to 2008 (Stein et al., 2013, p. 7).

In the United States, the Insurance Institute for Business and Home Safety (IBHS) estimates that 38 states face significant risks associated with wildfires; the risks are greater in western states.

In 2000, nearly a third of U.S. homes (37 million) were located in the WUI. Between 1990 and 2000, more than one million homes were added to the WUI in California, Oregon, and Washington combined. California has more homes in the WUI than any other state—3.8 million. More than two thirds of all land in Connecticut is in the WUI (Stein et al., 2013, p. 12).

Table 6.19 Wildfire Frequency and Damage by Year in the United States		
Year	Wildfires, Count	Area Burnt (Millions of Acres)
2014	63,312	3.60
2013	47,579	4.32
2012	67,774	9.33
2011	74,126	8.71
2010	71,971	3.42
2009	78,792	5.92
2008	78,979	5.29
2007	85,705	9.23
2006	96,385	9.87
2005	66,753	8.69
2004	65,461	8.10
2003	63,629	3.96
2002	73,457	7.18
2001	84,079	3.57
2000	92,250	7.39
1999	92,487	5.63
1998	81,043	1.33
1997	66,196	2.86
1996	96,363	6.07
1995	82,234	1.84
1994	79,107	4.07
1993	58,810	1.80
1992	87,394	2.07
1991	75,754	2.95
1990	66,481	4.62

Source: U.S. National Interagency Fire Center (2015).

RETURNS

Social Effects. The effects of fires are routinely measured by tangible measures, such as deaths, land area burnt, houses burnt, firefighters responding, insured losses, and indirect economic costs.

Fires can be ranked or categorized by judgmental schemes, such as the Australian *bushfire levels.* The U.S. *fire regimes* categorize fires by ecological type as well as effects (see Table 6.20).

The largest recent fire was the Yellowstone National Park fire in 1988—1,400,000 ha. Historically, wildfires burn less than 4,000,000 to 5,000,000 ac (1,600,000 to 2,000,000 ha) of land in the United States in an average year, but the annual burn surpassed 8,000,000 ac in 2004–2007 and 2011–2012 (see Table 6.19).

The deadliest wildfires occurred in the United States in the late 19th and early 20th centuries, when firefighting capacity was poor and human habitation was increasing rapidly in the western states. In 1871, more 1,200 people were killed by the Pestigo wildfire in Wisconsin. In 1881, 300 were killed in Michigan. In 1894, more than 400 were killed in Minnesota and, in 1918, another 400 in Minnesota.

Fires in human-developed areas and vehicles kill about 3,000 Americans and injure another 17,000 every year, excluding 75,000 to 85,000 injured firefighters (data for 2009).

Wildfires can damage human health and take human lives even when people do not come into direct contact with the fire itself. People living near or downwind of a wildfire can be exposed to pollutants travelling through the air, which can exacerbate respiratory irritation, allergies, and bronchitis and impair judgment.

Natural Ecology. Natural biodiversity is unaffected by most wildfires since endemic vegetation has evolved to survive and even thrive after typical wildfires. Wildfire is fundamental to the ecology of 94% of wildlands across the conterminous United States. The indigenous vegetation has adapted to protect itself by developing thick bark or water-filled skins or deep tubers that are protected underground. Many species of flora, such as the lodgepole pine, require fire to regenerate. Such fire-dependent species distribute seeds with hard shells that open only under heat or smoke so that they are most likely to germinate when nourished by ash and relieved of non–fire resistant pests and smothering tree canopies. Black carbon can nourish the soil for thousands of years. Animals can escape by fleeing to burrows or damp or rocky areas, although some fires move quicker than any animal can travel naturally (Stein et al., 2013, p. 1).

However, wildfires are becoming so hot or frequent as to interfere with naturally evolved fire ecology. In the past, most wildfires travelled along the ground without killing mature trees, but larger wildfires can travel through the canopies or crowns of trees, which do not survive. Such wildfires can be so hot as to destroy even those seeds that had evolved to survive traditional fires. Wildfires can be so frequent that natural propagation is interrupted. For instance, in parts of the Australian bush, many species of tree need around 20 years to propagate, but wildfires are occurring more frequently, before trees can mature and produce seeds. When wildfires become unnaturally frequent, only grasses and a few other herbaceous species can survive, so endemic shrubs and trees tend to be replaced by alien grasses (Syphard et al., 2009, p. 760).

Table 6.20 U.S. Fire Regimes

Fire Regime Group	Severity	Description or Definition	Examples	Wildland (Percentage of Total)	Frequency (Years)
I	Low to mixed	Low-severity fires that leave most dominant overstoryed vegetation intact; can include mixed-severity fires, replacing up to 75% of overstory	Lower elevation Ponderosa pine forests in the West; Pine and oak forests in the Southeast	25	0–35
II	High	High-severity fires that consume at least 75% of overstory vegetation	Grassland areas across the central United States; chaparral stands throughout the West	19	0–35
III	Mixed to low	Generally mixed-severity fires; can also include low-severity fires	Mixed deciduous-conifer forests of the upper Midwest and Northeast; Western Douglas-fir forests	22	35–200
IV	High	High-severity fires that consume or kill most of the aboveground vegetation	Lodgepole pine in the Northern Rockies; isolated areas of the Great Lakes and New England regions	12	35–200+
V	Any	Infrequent fires that consume or kill most of the aboveground vegetation	Wetter forests in much of Maine, northern Pennsylvania, and parts of the West	16	200+

Source: Stein et al. (2013, p. 3).

Wildfires also contribute to global warming. Wildfires emit about as much carbon as 26% to 31% of the carbon emissions stemming from combustion of fossil fuels and industrial use of fossil fuels. In addition to carbon dioxide, which is the largest contributor to global warming, wildfires produce black carbon (burnt, solid material specks) that is the second largest contributor to global warming. Biomass burning contributes about 40% of global black carbon emissions (Hessl, 2011, p. 393).

Wildfires can compound with other risks. Wildfires can damage the vegetation that binds soils and are associated with land movements, soil erosion, and pollution. For instance, soil erosion and flash flooding following the fire around Buffalo Creek, Colorado, in 1996 resulted in more than $2 million in flood damage as well as more than $20 million in damage to Denver's water supply system (Lynch, 2004).

Economic Effects. The few fires that spread cause almost all of the significant damage. Fires can burn persons and property. Emitted smoke can injure persons. Costs are incurred from direct damage and from fighting the fire as well as the costs of managing the risks between wildfire events.

The costs include

- property damage,

- costs to human health,

- lost business,

- lost tax revenues,

- the costs of fighting fires,

- the costs of evacuations,

- the costs of restoring burned areas, and

- compound natural risks, such as mudslides during later rains.

Since the Yellowstone fire of 1988, the growing capacity of public firefighting and increasing regulation have reduced the risks of urban fires, and wildfire disasters are less frequent and less deadly on average, but keeping wildfires out of developed land is increasingly costly due to increasing human habitation and property values. By the mid-2000s, wildfire fighting regularly cost more than $1 billion per year (Westerling, Hidalgo, Cayan, & Swetman, 2006, p. 940). The U.S. Forest Service alone spent more than twice as much on fire suppression in an average year ($1.2 billion) from 2001 to 2010 as in an average year ($580 million) from 1991 to 2000. State forestry agency spending (including federal funding expended by state agencies) on wildfire protection, prevention and suppression also has more than doubled in the 2000s compared to the 1990s to more than $1.6 billion annually. These figures do not include the cost to local fire departments (Stein et al., 2013, p. 7).

In 2002, a fire around Hayman, Colorado, burnt 138,000 ac and caused documented direct costs, not including suppression costs or costs to rehabilitate burned areas, of $115.9 million. These included the following costs:

- Total insured private property losses: $38.7 million

- Loans and grants from Small Business Administration and FEMA: $4.9 million

- Damage to transmission lines: $880,000

- Loss in recreation concessionaire revenue on two U.S. Forest Service ranger districts: $382,000

- Lost value of water storage capacity: $37 million

- Lost value from timber: $34 million

In 1998, 6 weeks of large wildfires (500,000 ac) across 18 counties in northeastern Florida caused total documented costs of $522 million to $762 million. These included the following costs:

- Commercial timber (softwood) losses: $322 million to $509 million

- Suppression and disaster relief: $50 million to $100 million

- Property losses (including 340 homes): $10 million to $12 million

- Tourism and trade losses: $140 million

- Health care (asthma treatment): $325,000 to $700,000 (Stein et al., 2013, p. 8)

California is the wealthiest and most populous state and has developed most rapidly since World War II, so it has suffered the most frequent wildfires since then. On September 26, 1970, California suffered its worst wildfire (known as the Laguna or Kitchen Creek Fire after its initial area in eastern San Diego County) to date, after downed power lines ignited chaparral. It burnt 175,000 ac, destroyed 382 homes, and killed eight people.

On October 20, 1991, the San Francisco Bay Area suffered its worst interface fire since 1923 when a wildfire blew in from above the Caldecott Tunnel into the hilly urban areas of northern Oakland and southern Berkeley, destroying more than 3,300 homes over more than 1,500 ac and killing 25 people at a cost of more than $1.5 billion.

During October 2003, several wildfires ravaged San Diego County; together they were known as the Cedar Fire, the second largest wildfire in the history of the state of California. It burnt over 280,000 ac, destroyed 2,232 homes, killed 14 people (including one firefighter), and injured 104 firefighters. The main source was a man who set a fire in wildland; he was eventually charged with arson. The conditions for wildfire were extreme following a hot, dry late summer and the arrival of strong, dry Santa Ana winds.

CONTROLS Wildfire risks are controlled by removing fuels, banning ignition sources, banning human ingress or certain activities, clearing vegetation, and growing fire-resistant vegetation.

Hazards are controlled by clearing fuels (mostly dead vegetation) manually or by igniting occasional controlled or prescribed fires. (Wildfire managers normally intervene before peak dry season or human visitation and wait for calm, moist winds blowing toward natural breaks or low-fuel areas, such as rocky outcrops.) Rarely, controlled fires become uncontrolled. For instance, on July 2, 1999, the Bureau of Land Management lit a prescribed fire to clear 100 ac near Lewiston, California. The wildfire grew to about 2,000 ac and destroyed 23 residences before it was contained 1 week later.

If areas cannot be burnt (for instance, where trees are grown commercially for logging), the risks are controlled by maintaining standard separation distances between forests and by clearing occasional corridors or lanes. (The lanes interrupt the travel of fire and are useful also for ingress by emergency responders during a wildfire.)

The most efficient way to reduce the risk is to prevent an ignition. Likely ignitions include playing with matches, burning leaves or trash, tossing cigarettes, leaving campfires unattended, or driving an automobile through dry grass.

In addition to reducing human-caused ignitions, community wildfire prevention includes taking actions to protect homes and property from future wildfires. Such actions focus on modifying the vegetation in and around structures and ensuring that all structures are constructed with fire-resistant materials (Finney & Cohen, 2003).

The property owner can reduce exposure by not residing in wildlands, by building within developed areas, or by maintaining separation between the perimeter and the property. The area around the home can be planted with fire-resistant vegetation and cleared of fuels such as dry vegetation or wooden structures. If the vegetation includes grasses, deciduous trees, and other vulnerable vegetation, they should be cut short and their detritus removed. Clearing should include removal of materials from gutters and drains. According to the IBHS, the cleared area should extend at least 5 ft from the property, but FEMA recommends 30 to 100 ft. Vulnerability can be reduced by avoiding wooden materials in construction. Dual-pane tempered glass is more resistant to the heat that could start fires within by radiation. Screens help to prevent the ingress of embers into air vents and rafters.

Trees, shrubs, and other vegetation are removed or reduced from within and around a community to reduce the intensity and growth of future fires and to create a relatively safe place for firefighters to control and contain wildfires. Because vegetation continues to grow, mechanical and prescribed fire treatments must be repeated over time to keep fuels from accumulating.

Ignitability of structures can be reduced if homeowners adopt practices that the U.S. Department of Agriculture collectively describes as *Firewise Communities* (www.firewise.org), such as reducing flammable hazards in the *ignition zone* around individual structures (also known as *defensible space*) and using fire-resistant building materials (especially on roofing, decks, and vents) (Stein et al., 2013, pp. 17–18).

Where fires start, firefighters can be sent to extinguish them directly. Spot fires are, by definition, fires that do not spread, yet they should be extinguished on prospect of a blowup. Firefighters may be sent to put out such spot fires as a precaution, although in peak season, spot fires are too frequent.

Oxygen is necessary to fire, so a key solution to burning is to eliminate oxygen by sucking out the gas or blanketing the burning material with an inert gas or material. On the ground, firefighters can manually remove fuels from a fire and throw dirt on the fire. From the air, aircraft can release water or more chemically complex retardants onto the fire.

In advance of a moving fire, firefighters on the ground can remove fuels to create a firebreak. Where an area is accessible by road, bulldozers, excavators, and other useful machines could be delivered to help. Clearing fuel from the perimeter helps contain larger fires that cannot be extinguished. Wildfire fighters like to base themselves in a burnt area or on some sort of fuel-free area, such as a highway. Most fires could not pass such a control, but where the fire is large enough and the wind vectoring is in the right direction and at sufficient strength, embers have been known to float across the widest highways and start spot fires of sufficient frequency to overwhelm firefighters.

Where a wildfire cannot be contained, persons in the path must be evacuated and most of their property abandoned until sufficient firefighting resources and calmer, moister weather help to contain the fire.

COSMIC RISKS

Cosmic risks are those sourced from the **cosmos**—everything outside of the earth and its atmosphere. Cosmic threats include solar storms and cosmic objects (such as asteroids, comets, and earth-orbiting objects).

The two subsections below examine solar storms and cosmic objects.

Solar Storms

This section defines solar storms, reviews their frequency and returns, and explains the available controls.

DEFINITIONS **Solar storms** or **geomagnetic storms** are disturbances in the earth's normal electromagnetic field by waves of cosmic electromagnetic energy (**solar winds**) emitted during solar activity. The sun emits electromagnetic energy all the time; these emissions surge with certain solar activity, such as **solar flares**, which are unusually large thermonuclear explosions on the sun's surface. Solar flares are classified as A, B, C, M, or X (most severe), with intervals of 1 to 9 within each class, except that X is allowed infinite intervals; the most powerful solar flare ever recorded was rated X28.

FREQUENCY Solar storms coincide with peak solar activity, which follows a cycle, currently around every 11 years, although the cycle can be much shorter. Solar storms occurred in 2000 and 2003. Solar Cycle 24 was supposed to peak in 2013, although in January 2013, NASA forecasted that this peak would be the mildest in at least 100 years. Later in 2013, experts revised their forecast of the peak to 2015.

The most recent strong solar storm occurred in March 1989, affecting mostly Québec, Canada; such events occur every 50 years or so.

The largest recorded solar storm occurred around August to September 1859. This event is known as the *Carrington Event* after the main observer. Historical auroral records suggest that such extreme storms occur every 150 years (Lloyd's, 2013).

RETURNS The effects of solar storms are worse at latitudes tilted toward the sun and wherever electrical systems are most concentrated and exposed. The largest known solar storm (the Carrington Event of 1859) occurred at the start of the electrical age. It shorted telegraph systems, electrocuted telegraph operators who were in contact with telegraph interfaces, and ignited telegraph paper.

The less severe events of 1882, 1921, and 1960 caused radio signal disruption and electrical fires.

The event of March 1989 disrupted earth-orbiting satellites and radio signals and caused the failure of the electricity transmission system in Québec, Canada, leaving around six million people without power for 9 hrs.

Solar storms in 2000 and 2003 damaged satellites, but no electrical transmission systems on Earth.

A severe storm on the scale of the 1859 storm today would short-circuit and damage unshielded electrical systems on a global scale, including electrical transmission systems; electricity generators and transformers; computers and other devices with electronic circuits; electronic access controls; electronic payment systems; and electric ignitions in automobiles, radios, and earth-orbiting satellites, followed by months to years of repair, at a cost of billions to trillions of dollars.

The United States, particularly at higher latitudes, would suffer the most harm due to its large population and developed infrastructure. Lloyd's of London estimated that a Carrington-level event would directly disrupt power to 20 to 40 million Americans, over a period from 16 days to 2 years, for a total economic cost of $0.6 trillion to $2.6 trillion. The duration of the outage would depend largely on the availability of spare replacement transformers. The acquisition of new transformers would take at least five months. The most affected people live in the densely populated and electrified Atlantic corridor, running north to south from New York City to Washington, DC. The Midwest states, such as Michigan and Wisconsin, would be widely affected too, as well as regions along the Gulf Coast (Lloyd's, 2013).

Longer electricity transmission lines over large provinces in North America, China, Australia, and Africa are more vulnerable, but increased interconnectedness has reduced their vulnerability. In fact, weather and falling objects damage electrical transmissions systems much more frequently.

CONTROLS Geomagnetic risks are controlled by shielding from electromagnetic radiation, shutting down electrical power, disconnecting electrical systems, staying away from electrical transmissions, and investing in alternative systems, particularly at times of peak solar activity.

Shielding consists usually of metal casings, which are simple enough to design and produce but add weight and cost; effectiveness varies with the quality and thickness of material. Generally, most military electronic systems and major civilian electronic systems, such as earth-orbiting satellites, are shielded, but almost all consumer electronics are neither shielded nor accommodated within shielded structures, including most computer servers. Some data protection services offer digital data storage inside facilities that are shielded from Carrington-level events, but most do not. Critical financial data and official data could be lost in unshielded equipment.

Radio signals, which are critical to emergency services and aircraft safety, cannot be shielded at all, even though radios can. Thus, the effects of a large solar storm must be controlled by shutting down routine services or relying on old-fashioned nonelectrical communications.

Cosmic Objects

The subsections below define cosmic objects, review their frequency and returns, and explain how they can be controlled.

DEFINITIONS *Cosmic objects* are objects that reside outside the earth's atmosphere. They include

- asteroids,

- comets,

- near-Earth objects (asteroids and comets in orbits closer to Earth), and

- Earth-orbiting objects, including around 3,000 artificial Earth-orbiting satellites and the junk left over from other objects launched from Earth.

Comets are cosmic objects composed mostly of water ice with embedded dust particles. **Asteroids** are cosmic rocks or lumps of metal that are usually smaller than comets. **Near-Earth objects** are comets and asteroids that have been nudged by the gravitational attraction of nearby planets into orbits that pass closer to Earth than the vast majority of other orbiting cosmic objects. All near-earth asteroids come from the asteroid belt around the sun.

Parts of comets and asteroids can veer toward a collision with the Earth. If they enter Earth's atmosphere they are known as **meteors**. Few cosmic objects become meteors, and most meteors burn up in the atmosphere without anyone on Earth noticing. If they survive the atmosphere and impact Earth, they are known as **meteorites**. **Artificial Earth-orbiting satellites**, which are vehicles for communications systems and sensors that are launched from Earth into an orbit around Earth, also can fall to Earth.

FREQUENCY The cosmos is mostly space; the vast majority of cosmic objects are not in orbit around the Earth and never will be, but tens of thousands of objects could collide with Earth.

In 1998, NASA started a program to track near-Earth objects. In 2005, Congress ordered NASA to find all asteroids greater than 140 m (459 ft) in diameter. By 2013, NASA had discovered 9,610 near-Earth objects, although most are not large enough or close enough to threaten human civilization.

The U.S. Department of Defense tracks more than 22,000 objects of at least 0.05-m diameter, mostly artificial junk that could damage satellites but would not survive Earth's atmosphere. NASA has counted fewer than 1,300 near-Earth asteroids that measure up to 30 m in diameter, still too small typically to survive Earth's atmosphere but large enough to devastate much of a city. Their atmospheric collision frequency is about once every 100 years.

Less than 2,200 near-Earth objects measure 30 to 100 m in diameter, with an estimated future impact frequency of once every 1,000 years. NASA estimates 25,000 near-Earth asteroids of 100 m (328 ft) or larger, of which it has identified about 25%. Less than 2,400 of identified near-Earth asteroids measure 100 to 300 m in diameter.

By 2013, NASA counted 1,381 *potentially hazardous asteroids*, defined by an "earth minimum orbit intersection distance" closer than about 7,480,000 km (4,650,000 mi) (closer than most near-Earth objects) and a diameter larger than about 150 m (500 ft). A meteorite of 150 m would devastate human civilization, although such an event should occur only once every 10,000 years.

NASA estimated about 900 near-Earth asteroids that it classified as large—larger than 1,000 m (1,094 yd) in diameter. A meteorite of such size could devastate a continent directly and cause a climatic change that would kill most flora and fauna globally. Future impact frequency is about once every 500,000 years by NASA's estimates.

The largest near-Earth asteroids are less than 16 mi (25 km) in diameter. The meteorite that impacted Earth 65 million years ago (around the end of the dinosaurs) and caused extinction of at least 75% of current species measured more than 9 mi (15 km) in diameter.

RETURNS Near-Earth objects could collide with the 3,000 human-manufactured Earth-orbiting satellites, thereby interrupting the transmission of radio signals, the Global Positioning System (GPS), surveillance of global weather and human activities, and surveillance of the cosmos. About 60 nations and government consortia own and operate satellites; commercial and academic operators own and operate some too. The U.S. government is the biggest single user of GPS; it has invested at least $43 billion in GPS infrastructure, equipment, and services alone.

Earth is orbited by plenty of junk left over from objects launched into space by humans. These objects travel very fast, so even specks of dust are energetic enough to puncture other artificial materials. Artificial satellites are difficult to repair and must eventually become junk themselves.

Satellites take about 10 years to procure and are useful for about 30 years, after which they must be maintained in orbit, dismantled in space, or allowed to fall back to Earth in a controlled descent. Uncontrolled satellites are major hazards. For instance, in February 2009, a disabled Russian military satellite collided with a U.S. commercial satellite, leaving about 10,000 pieces in space. Officially, this was an accident, but it illustrates the risks associated with malicious use of satellites as weapons, although, under international law, weapons are not permitted in space.

Some satellites have been destroyed in space by missiles launched from Earth.

- On September 13, 1985, a U.S. military aircraft (F-15) launched a Vought ASM135 missile that downed an old U.S. satellite as it was entering Earth's atmosphere.

- On January 11, 2007, China destroyed an old weather satellite with an Earth-launched missile, leaving about 3,000 pieces in a high orbit.

- On February 20, 2008, a U.S. Aegis cruiser launched a SM3 antiballistic missile against an old military satellite.

Satellites destroyed in space disintegrate into many more hazards. Disabled artificial satellites fall to Earth as large hazards, although their controllers try to direct their descent at a shallow angle so that they burn up in space or fall over an unpopulated area of the earth.

Most natural cosmic objects do not orbit Earth or are deflected by Earth's gravitational fields. If near-Earth objects collide with the Earth, most burn up in the atmosphere or break up into fragments that miss human habitation. (Most of the Earth's surface is uninhabited; most of it is water.) Every day, around 100 T of meteors hit the atmosphere, but most are smaller than sand and burn up long before humans on the surface of the Earth would notice them.

The most devastating meteor in living memory exploded in 1908, fortunately in a remote area of Siberia. It measured 50 to 100 m and exploded in the air with 1,000 times more energy than the atomic bomb that the United States dropped over Hiroshima in 1945. (Meteors do not contain or cause radioactive material.) The meteor's blast devastated an area of more than 800 square miles (500,000 ac; 2,000 sq km), felled 80 million trees, and damaged windows more than 125 mi (200 km) away.

The largest recorded meteor since 1908 exploded in the air above the city of Chelyabinsk, 1,000 mi east of Moscow in Russia, with a population of about 1.1 million, on February 15, 2013. This meteor was around 17 m (55 ft) in diameter. Most meteors of this size explode due to increasing friction with the thickening atmosphere. This meteor exploded about 20 mi (30 km) above the city. Fortunately, its fragility was enhanced by stress fractures, probably caused by the collision that knocked it out of its home in the cosmic meteor belt. The meteor had shed parts before it exploded. Its final explosion spread debris over an area wider than the city and caused a sonic blast similar to that from a small nuclear weapon. Its meteorites impacted the Earth more than 75 mi from Chelyabinsk. The blast shattered materials as strong as bonded bricks in more than 3,000 buildings and injured more than 1,200 residents; for the most part, people were hurt by the blast or shattered glass as they were looking at the visual signature of the explosion before the blast reached them. (The interval was as long as minutes for most people.)

CONTROLS Earth's gravitational field deflects most near-Earth objects. A meteor just large enough to survive the atmosphere and cause devastation is practically impossible to predict even hours before impact, a shorter time period than would be required to evacuate a city. A meteor's actual flight time within the Earth's atmosphere is measured in seconds. Current antiaircraft systems would not deflect meteors out of the atmosphere and would produce more hazardous objects.

A collision with an object large enough to threaten human civilization should be predictable within several years of the collision. In theory, asteroids could be destroyed or deflected deliberately, but no authority has invested in any such plan. With current technology, a heavy enough spacecraft (weighing a few tons) could be launched into space and placed close enough to an asteroid to change its course sufficiently, just by the spacecraft's gravitational field, to divert the asteroid outside of the small window into Earth's gravitational pull. NASA has planned but not programmed an Asteroid Redirect Mission, which, sometime in the 2020s, could launch a robot to capture a relatively small, slow asteroid and redirect it into a lunar orbit, where astronauts could visit it.

Comparing the Future of Wildfire Risks and Flooding Risks in the United States

Jessica Block and Sally Thompson

Wildfire Risks

Our current urbanization in this environment has tipped the ecological balance of the past into a different climatological system of rainfall, wind, seasons, and thus fire seasons. Recent studies confirm that climate change will increase the frequency and severity of wildfires in the coming decades. Climate change not only compounds this vulnerability to fire, it induces a greater level of uncertainty. Now our biggest challenge to adapting to this new regime is that the environment is changing faster than we can understand it. Experts from disparate fields disagree about how best to mitigate the risks ahead. Conservationists work to restore forests to their native vegetation while government agencies focus on protecting life and property at the cost of ecological preservation. Megafires pose a threat to national security because they take an enormous toll on our economy. But regardless of the perspective, we are all increasingly vulnerable.

While we as a species attempt to survive in the midst of these ever-changing dynamics,

we are also making great advancements in technology. We are now able to monitor our environment in time and space at better resolutions than ever before. Citizens are sensors with smartphones, cameras, and mobile Internet. The prevalence of these tools means we have an opportunity to observe and then respond to changing conditions faster than ever imagined. Technology is giving us a chance to adapt in real time and to live with this new regime. Most importantly, it facilitates a common understanding of how the world is changing between those who agree and disagree with climate change. My hope is that technology will give us a chance to change the conversation—to stop arguing about how we got here and to create solutions, solutions that not only make our cities more secure but maintain a planet on which we can and want to live.

Source: Courtesy of Jessica Block.

Jessica Block is staff research associate at the California Institute for Telecommunications and Information Technology at the University of California, San Diego.

Flooding Risks

Good infrastructure is one component of the solution. The other is social resilience. How do you build social resilience? Mechanisms like comprehensive insurance programs, functional

(Continued)

(Continued)

early-warning systems, effective response teams and government follow-through, and supportive neighborhoods . . .

Unfortunately, this also means that communities that are impoverished or have other social problems have an even greater risk of floods. Often these communities are in risky locations and have greater exposure to the flood hazard. This is multiplied by lack of funds to maintain infrastructure, lower household incomes to buy insurance or rebuild, and less funding for local emergency response crews. For these reasons, a recent study suggested that poor farming communities in the Sacramento-San Joaquin Delta (in California) have the greatest flood risks in the USA—the combination of aging infrastructure, big rivers, flat landscapes, and high social vulnerability.

Climate change may add another burden to flood-prone communities, for example, in California. Research indicates changes in the Sierra Nevada mountain range's snow line could result in generally smaller snowpacks, which could reduce the overall risk of catastrophic spring flooding. But if more spring precipitation falls as rainfall rather than snow, flood risks will increase. This means that, in some basins, flood risk is decreasing while, in others, it may be increasing by about 5 to 10% from today. Other research suggests that rainfall will become more variable in California—more droughts and more events of intense rainfall—and we don't yet know what that will mean for flood risks.

Source: Courtesy of Sally Thompson.

Sally Thompson is an assistant professor in surface water hydrology in the Department of Civil and Environmental Engineering at the University of California, Berkeley.

CHAPTER SUMMARY

This chapter has reviewed the definitions, trends, distribution, and returns of

- Natural hazards and threats in general

- Climate change in general

- Weather events in general

- Droughts and heat waves

- Storms, hurricanes, cyclones, and typhoons

- Tornadoes

- Floods

- Geological and geomorphic hazards (such as subsistence)

- Seismic hazards (mostly earthquakes)
- Volcanic hazards (such as ejected lava or ash)
- Fires (both human-caused and wild)
- Cosmic hazards (such as solar storms and meteors)

KEY TERMS

Artificial Earth-orbiting satellites *278*
Asteroid *278*
Biodiversity *234*
Blowup *264*
Climate *230*
Climate change *231*
Comet *278*
Cosmos *276*
Crown fire *264*
Cyclone *239*
Drought *237*
Dry movement *253*
Earth movement *253*
Earthquake *254*
Fire *264*
Flood *237*
Focus *258*
Geological hazards *253*
Geomagnetic storms *276*

Geomorphic hazards *253*
Ground fire *264*
Hazard *218*
Heat wave *237*
Human-caused *236*
Human-made threat *218*
Hurricane *239*
Intensity *260*
Lava *263*
Magma *263*
Magnitude *258*
Meteor *278*
Meteorite *278*
Moment magnitude scale *258*
Natural hazard *218*
Natural threat *228*
Natural risk *218*
Near-Earth object *278*
Nor'easter *242*
Precipitation *233*

Rapid-onset hazards *220*
Richter scale *258*
Seismic *254*
Shielding *277*
Slow-onset hazards *220*
Solar flare *276*
Solar storm *276*
Solar wind *276*
Spot fire *264*
Storm *239*
Storm surge *239*
Subsidence *253*
Threat *218*
Tornado *248*
Tsunami *255*
Typhoon *239*
Volcano *263*
Weather *221*
Wet movement *253*
Wildfire *264*

QUESTIONS AND EXERCISES

1. What is the difference between human-caused and other natural threats?

2. Why do natural risks tend to be underestimated?

3. Why are some natural risks increasing?

4. In what ways are slow-onset and rapid-onset hazards riskier?

5. Why does the United States suffer the costliest disasters?

6. Why do more people die during natural disasters in the developing than the developed world?

7. How else are natural disasters different in the developing world compared to the developed world?

8. How do natural risks in the developing world affect the developed world?

9. Within any society, why do some people face disproportionate natural risks?

10. What is predictable about solar storms?

11. How are geomagnetic risks controlled?

12. What is the difference between a comet, asteroid, meteor, and meteorite?

13. How can the risks from cosmic objects be controlled?

14. What is the difference between geological, geomorphic, seismic, and volcanic hazards?

15. How do humans increase geological risks?

16. How do seismic events cause harm?

17. Where are seismic risks highest?

18. What is the difference between earthquake magnitude and intensity?

19. How would you explain the contradictory distribution of deaths and economic costs due to seismic events?

20. How does volcanic harm compare with purely seismic harm?

21. What are three common causes of fires?

22. Where are different forms of fire ignition more likely?

23. What sorts of vegetation and climates suffer more wildfires?

24. Why has wildfire frequency changed over time?

25. How does global climate change affect wildfire risk?

26. How has the wildfire threat to natural ecology changed?

27. How are wildfire risks controlled?

28. What is the difference between weather and climate?

29. What is the difference between climate change and global warming?

30. Why are weather risks increasing?

31. Why are weather risks distributed differently within the developed and developing worlds?

32. In what ways does climate change cause harm?

33. Why is climate change difficult to control?

34. What causes floods?

35. How are floods controlled?

36. What is the difference between a storm, tropical depression, hurricane, and cyclone?

37. How do storms cause harm?

38. What is the difference between a hurricane and a tornado?

39. Where do most tornados occur?

40. What is the difference between a drought and a heat wave?

41. How is climate change affecting the risks associated with droughts and heat waves?

PART III

PROVIDING SECURITY

7

EMERGENCY MANAGEMENT

In the following passage, Richard Serino, deputy administrator of the U.S. Federal Emergency Management Agency (FEMA), describes the management of the terrorist attack on the marathon in Boston, Massachusetts, on April 15, 2013.

As the medical incident commander in Boston for more than 35 mass casualty incidents and for all of Boston's major planned events, including the Boston Marathon, I can tell you that the fact that the response was so well executed wasn't an accident—it was a result of years of planning and coordination. It was no accident that not a single hospital in the city was overwhelmed with patients in the aftermath of the bombings. It was no accident that patients were appropriately triaged and transported in an orderly manner to the appropriate hospital based on their needs. And it was no accident that a Medical Intelligence Center was fully staffed and operating on race day to keep track of patients, coordinate resources, and share information with the medical community throughout the region. All of these are tangible results of disaster planning that has gone on in Boston for more than 20 years. I'm here today to discuss, in part, how FEMA played an important role in making the people on the ground more prepared for that day. . . .

This incident also demonstrated how FEMA's approach to National Preparedness helped to empower and strengthen the whole community by giving its members the right tools and information they needed to be prepared. The National Preparedness System (NPS) is the instrument that the Nation employs to build, sustain, and deliver the core capabilities that work toward the National Preparedness Goal. FEMA requires grantees—which include both the Commonwealth of Massachusetts and the City of Boston—to implement the NPS and establish a whole community

Learning Objectives and Outcomes

At the end of this chapter, you should know

- How to understand and define emergencies

- How to assess emergencies

- How emergencies are managed in the United States

- How to define and assess capacity and capability

- How to define and assess vulnerability

- How to define and assess exposure

- How to communicate information about emergencies

approach to homeland security and emergency management, making them more prepared should an event like this occur. As a result of the NPS, the whole community plans better, organizes better, equips better, trains better, and exercises better, resulting in improved national preparedness and resilience. And this was evident in Boston. (*Lessons learned*, 2013)

EMERGENCIES

An **emergency** is an event that demands immediate response. Emergencies might be known by other words, such as **issue** or **incident**. In general use, an *issue* is "an important topic for debate or resolution" (FrameNet, 2012, n.p.) while an *incident* is either "an occurrence" or "a disruptive, usually dangerous or unfortunate event" (FrameNet, 2012, n.p.). Emergencies, issues, and incidents are useful to separate from other events because they require further action, while other events can be ignored.

An **event** is an occurrence in time or "a thing that happens or takes place" (FrameNet, 2012, n.p.). Events include accidents, wars, attacks, structural failures, etc. For the U.S. Department of Homeland Security (2009), an *incident* is

> an occurrence, caused by either human action or natural phenomena, that may cause harm and may require action. Incidents can include major disasters, emergencies, terrorist attacks, terrorist threats, wild and urban fires, floods, hazardous materials spills, nuclear accidents, aircraft accidents, earthquakes, hurricanes, tornadoes, tropical storms, war-related disasters, public health and medical emergencies, and other occurrences requiring an emergency response. (p. 110)

Catastrophe and **disaster** are often used interchangeably, but many insurers and reinsurers differentiate *natural catastrophes* from *man-made disasters*. The U.N. International Strategy for Disaster Reduction (ISDR, 2009) defines *disaster* as "a serious disruption of the functioning of a community or a society involving widespread human, material, economic or environmental losses and impacts, which exceeds the ability of the affected community or society to cope using its own resources" (p. 9).

Local, state, and federal governments can declare an emergency. In the United States, the president declares a *federal emergency*—meaning that federal assistance is needed to supplement state and local efforts, but this event might be known by other terms, including disaster or catastrophe. The Stafford Act, or the Disaster Relief and Emergency Assistance Act of 1988, defines a **major disaster** as

> any natural catastrophe (including any hurricane, tornado, storm, high water, wind-driven water, tidal wave, tsunami, earthquake, volcanic eruption, landslide, mudslide, snowstorm, or drought), or, regardless of cause, any fire, flood, or explosion, in any part of the United States, which in the determination of the President cases damage of sufficient severity and magnitude to warrant major disaster assistance under the Act to supplement the efforts and available resources of states, local governments, and disaster relief organizations in alleviating the damage, loss, hardship, or suffering caused thereby. (U.S. Federal Emergency Management Agency, 2013, p. 2)

ASSESSING EMERGENCIES

Emergencies must be assessed by their returns, as explained in the first subsection. These returns can be judged subjectively or by objective correlates, as explained in subsequent subsections.

Returns

Emergencies are assessed mainly in terms of their returns. The returns of an event are the changes experienced by an affected entity. The holders of the risk or those exposed to the risk, such as investors or victims, experience the event, or are affected by the returns. The term *returns* includes many other concepts used by the U.S. government, such as impacts, consequences, and costs and benefits.

SUBJECTIVELY JUDGING RETURNS Correlates are things that vary together, such as sunshine and sunburn. We are forced to choose a correlate when the subject is too difficult to measure directly.

Objective correlates are collected without subjective involvement. Judgmental correlates are subjectively coded, meaning somebody (the coder) must make a judgment as to what the code should be.

DEFINITION

BOX 7.1

Synonyms of Returns From Emergencies

Impact

The impact is "the amount of loss or damage that can be expected from a successful attack on an asset. Loss may be monetary, but may include loss of lives and destruction of a symbolic structure" (U.S. Government Accountability Office [GAO], 2005c, p. 110).

Consequence

For the U.S. Department of Homeland Security (2009), the consequence is "the effect of an event, incident, or occurrence" (p. 109). "Consequences mean the dangers (full or partial), injuries, and losses of life, property, environment, and business that can be quantified by some unit of measure, often in economic or financial terms" (U.S. Federal Emergency Management Agency, 1992, p. xxv). The consequence is

the expected worse case or reasonable worse case impact of a successful attack. The consequence to a particular asset can be evaluated when threat and vulnerability are considered together. This loss or damage may be long- or short-term in nature. (U.S. GAO, 2005c, p. 110)

Cost and Benefit

For the U.S. government, a cost is "input, both direct and indirect," while a benefit is the "net outcome, usually translated into monetary terms; a benefit may include both direct and indirect effects" (U.S. GAO, 2005c, p. 110).

Generally, objective correlates are preferred over subjective measures because subjectivity implies bias. Yet subjective judgments are attractive where the authority lacks time or opportunity to measure the objective correlates. For instance, at the start of the emergency, before the returns are clear or before observers could access the emergency, some judgment must be made subjectively.

Returns can be assessed judgmentally on ordinal scales. A judgmental ranking could range from, say, 1 to 5, low to high, or mild to severe. The World Economic Forum (2013) asks respondents to estimate the impact of a possible event on a purely numerical 5-point scale (1–5) (p. 45). Similarly, the consequences of terrorism have been coded from 1 to 5 (Greenberg, Chalk, Willis, Khilko, & Ortiz, 2006). The risk management standard issued by Australia, New Zealand, and the International Organization for Standardization (ISO, 2009) uses a 5-point ordinal scale from 1 to 5, or insignificant, minor, moderate, major, or catastrophic respectively. The U.S. Department of Defense (DOD) standard, which has been used in civilian government and the commercial sector, uses a 4-point scale of negative consequences by three different dimensions (see Table 7.1).

The U.N.'s Threat and Risk Unit standardized a 5-point scale of impacts by three dimensions (see Table 7.2).

OBJECTIVELY MEASURING RETURNS Returns can also be estimated in terms of many objective correlates. The subsections below collect typical objective correlates: official responses and economic, human, environmental, and territorial returns.

Official Responses. The emergency can be measured in terms of the official responses, such as whether the response was local, state, or federal. Public Safety Canada recommends at least rating the extent to which hierarchical levels or jurisdictions are affected or required in response (see Table 7.3).

Table 7.1	The U.S. DOD's Standard Scale of Impacts		
Catastrophic	Death	System loss	Severe environmental damage
Critical	Severe injury or occupation illness	Major system damage	Major environmental damage
Marginal	Minor injury or occupational illness	Minor system damage	Minor environmental damage
Negligible	Less than minor injury or occupational illness	Less than minor system damage	Less than minor environmental damage

Source: U.S. Government Accountability Office (1998, p. 7).

Table 7.2 The U.N.'s Standard Scale of Impacts

Critical	Death or severe injury	Total loss of assets	Loss of programs and projects
Severe	Serious injury	Major destruction of assets	Severe disruption to programs
Moderate	Non–life-threatening injury and high stress	Loss or damage to assets	Some program delays and disruptions
Minor	Minor injuries	Some loss or damage to assets	Minimal delays to programs
Negligible	No injuries	Minimal loss or damage to assets	No delays to programs

Source: U.N. Department of Peacekeeping Operations & Department of Field Support (2008).

Table 7.3 The Canadian Government's Rating of the Magnitude of Response to an Emergency

Rating	Response Magnitude
None	None
0	Some local general response but no specialized response
1	Some local specialized response and surveillance and monitoring from federal authorities
2	Multiregional general response and notification from federal authorities
3	Multifunctional, multiregional specialized response and notification from federal authorities
4	Multifunctional, multijurisdictional specialized response and mobilization from federal authorities
5	Multifunctional national and international specialized response and rapid mobilization from federal authorities

Source: Public Safety Canada (2013, p. 32). *All Hazards Risk Assessment Methodology Guidelines, 2012–2013,* page 32, http://www.publicsafety.gc.ca/cnt/rsrcs/pblctns/ll-hzrds-ssssmnt/index-eng.aspx#ahra_business, 2012–2013. Reproduced with the permission of the Minister of Public Safety and Emergency Preparedness Canada (2015).

This rating would be modified by the following periods of response:

- 1 week (add 0.5)

- 1–3 weeks (add 1.0)

- 3–10 weeks (add 1.5)

- 2–8 months (add 2.0)

- 8–24 months (add 2.5)

- 2–6 years (add 3.0)

- 6–20 years (add 3.5)

Human Returns. Human returns are the changes experienced by human beings. Typically, human returns are measured as deaths, injuries, disability-adjusted life years (see Definition, Boxes 7.2 and 7.3), economic value, and changes of situation.

Economic Value. A life lost or injured has financial value in insurance and the tort system (although insurance or legal liability would not be engaged in every case). The economic value of a particular fatality can be calculated from standardized "schedules" or from past inputs into the person, such as the sunk cost of education, and lost future outputs, such as lost earnings (see Comparative Perspectives, Box 7.4).

Many medical authorities (such as the American Medical Association) and government authorities issue standard "schedules" for assessing the economic worth of injuries for use by adjusters in insurance claims, employers in compensation of injured employees, and judges in tort cases. The first calculation normally expresses the impairment locally on the body, specific to the part of the body (down to the finger or toe or organ), the scale of the impairment, and the type of injury. Multiple impairments are then combined and expressed as the resulting impairment to the whole body. This overall impairment is combined with the occupation of the victim and the age of the victim according to prescribed codes and formulae. The final product of all this is normally a "rating" of the victim's *final permanent disability rating* or *physical impairment for employment* on a scale from 0% (no reduction of earning potential) through progressively more severe partial disability to 100% (permanent total disability).

Changes of Situation. **Changes of situation** include forced migration or displacement from normal place of residence, homelessness, loss of work, separation from family, loss of rights, and injustice. For instance, we might assess the returns of an insurgent campaign in terms of the number of persons who escape by emigration, lose their homes due to insurgent attacks, or are enslaved by the insurgents.

ECONOMIC RETURNS Emergencies can be measured by the economic costs of damages, the direct economic losses (such as reduced trade), indirect economic gains and losses (such as increased transaction costs due to damaged communications), and flow changes, such as the flow of goods and services that will not be produced or delivered due to damages to productive assets or infrastructure (see Comparative Perspectives, Box 7.5).

DEFINITION

BOX 7.2

Measures of Human Returns

Deaths

Deaths (fatalities) are normally counted as a cardinal number. They can also be measured as **mortality rate** (deaths per unit population) or **death frequency** (deaths per unit time).

In the context of emergencies, **mass casualty** tends to mean at least five dead and **high casualty** tends to mean at least 15 dead.

Death is one of the severest human returns, but a fixation on deaths can underestimate other serious returns, such as injuries, disabilities, loss of life expectancy, psychological stress, health costs, and injustices.

Injuries

An **injury** is any damage to the body. The term **wound** implies a puncture wound or an injury due to violence. An injury could cause death, but normally we measure deaths and survivable injuries separately.

Injuries can be measured as a rate, as a frequency, by number on the body, and on a scale (normally described by *severity*). For

instance, the Canadian government recognizes a high degree of injury as "severe harm that affects the public or compromises the effective functioning of government following a disruption in the delivery of a critical service" (Canadian Translation Bureau, 2015).

Injuries can be categorized by location on or in the body, medical cause (for instance, toxic or traumatic), or event (for instance, road traffic accident or sports).

Injuries, like deaths, have economic value in the tort system and health system (see below).

DALYs (see also Definition, Box 7.3)

Disability-adjusted life years (DALYs) are the years of healthy life lost across a population due to premature mortality or disability caused by some event or threat. The DALY is a useful measure because it places two separate measures (deaths and injuries) on the same dimension, helping to equate the returns. For instance, one source might affect few people but kill most of them while another source severely disables everyone it affects but kills few of them directly.

Financial or monetary measures are attractive because they are **fungible**, meaning that they are easily converted into other forms. Insurers and reinsurers tend to measure the financial cost of insured claims and to regard the sum of insured and uninsured losses as the *total economic losses*. For instance, in 2012, Swiss Re Group coded events as natural catastrophes or man-made disasters if their total losses breached $90.9 million or their associated insured-property claims reached at least $45.8 million (or $18.3 million for shipping claims or $36.6 million for aviation claims).

The returns can also be measured in terms other than the financial costs (for instance, by the scale of the items, area, or population affected). For instance, over 2 days in 1871, a great fire in the city of Chicago burnt more than 2,000 acres of urban land, destroyed 28 mi of road, 120 mi of sidewalk, 2,000 lampposts, and 18,000 buildings and cost more than $200 million in property damage.

Official Definitions and Measures of DALYs

The World Health Organization (WHO) calculates the DALYs for a disease of injury as the sum of

- the years of life lost (YLL) due to premature mortality in the population (calculated from the number of deaths at each age multiplied by a standard life expectancy of the age at which death occurs), and

- the years lost due to disability (YLD; the product of the frequency of incident cases in that period, the average duration of the disease, and the severity of the disability on a scale from 0—the code for perfectly healthy—to 1—the code for death; years lost in young or old age are discounted nonuniformly by around 3%) (WHO, 2009, p. 5).

This method remained unchanged from 1990 until 2012, when the Global Burden of Disease

Study (World Health Organization, 2015) adapted the method.

- The YLL and YLD are summed, as before.

- The YLL are calculated similarly, except they are calculated from age-, sex-, country-, and time-specific estimates of mortality by cause, multiplied by the standard life expectancy at each age.

- The YLD are calculated as prevalence of disabling conditions by age, sex, and cause, weighted by new disability weights for each health state, without any discount or weighting by age.

The Canadian government prescribes the consolidation of the impacts on people in terms of DALYs and prescribes conversion of estimated DALYs into an *impact rating* from 0 to 5 (see Table 7.4).

Table 7.4 The Canadian Government's Rating of the Impact on People by DALYs

Impact Rating	Total DALYs (Injuries and Fatalities)	Equivalent Adult Fatalities
None	0	0
0.0	40	1
0.5	120	3
1.0	400	10

(Continued)

(Continued)

Impact Rating	Total DALYs (Injuries and Fatalities)	Equivalent Adult Fatalities
1.5	1,200	30
2.0	4,000	100
2.5	12,000	300
3.0	40,000	1,000
3.5	120,000	3,000
4.0	400,000	10,000
4.5	1,200,000	30,000
5.0	4,000,000	100,000

Source: Public Safety Canada (2013, p. 27). *All Hazards Risk Assessment Methodology Guidelines, 2012–2013,* page 27, http://www.publicsafety.gc.ca/cnt/rsrcs/pblctns/ll-hzrds-ssssmnt/index-eng.aspx#ahra_business, 2012–2013. Reproduced with the permission of the Minister of Public Safety and Emergency Preparedness Canada (2015).

COMPARATIVE PERSPECTIVES

BOX 7.4

Official Compensation for Terrorism

Since 1984, the U.S. government has offered financial compensation (in the form of money or tax relief) for deaths and injuries suffered by resident victims of crime, usually to the value of a few tens of thousands of dollars. In 1996 (following mass-casualty terrorism bombing of the federal office in Oklahoma City in 1995), this offer was extended to resident victims of terrorism, even if abroad at the time. Victims of terrorism on September 11, 2001, were compensated under an additional federal scheme, whose payouts far exceeded payouts by charities or insurers. From all sources, the seriously injured and the dependents of each victim killed received $3.1 million per victim on average, except emergency responders, who received $4.2 million on average. Payouts varied with projected lifetime earnings (Dixon & Kaganoff Stern, 2004).

Canadian Schemes for Assessing Economic Losses

The Canadian government prescribed an ordinal scale to rank total economic impacts by total estimated economic losses (see Table 7.5).

Table 7.5 The Canadian Government's Rating of the Impact on the Economy	
Impact Rating	Economic Loss (Canadian Dollars)
None	None
0.0	$10 million
0.5	$30 million
1.0	$100 million
1.5	$300 million
2.0	$1 billion
2.5	$3 billion
3.0	$10 billion
3.5	$30 billion
4.0	$100 billion
4.5	$300 billion
5.0	$1,000 billion

Source: Public Safety Canada (2013, p. 30). *All Hazards Risk Assessment Methodology Guidelines, 2012–2013*, page 30, http://www.publicsafety.gc.ca/cnt/rsrcs/pblctns/ll-hzrds-ssssmnt/index-eng.aspx#ahra_business, 2012–2013. Reproduced with the permission of the Minister of Public Safety and Emergency Preparedness Canada (2015).

The Canadian government has published a useful scheme for judgmentally assessing direct economic losses by

- buildings,
- infrastructure,
- machinery and equipment,
- residential housing and contents, and
- raw materials.

It prescribes a judgmental assessment of the indirect economic losses by

- production or service provision losses due to the paralysis of productive activities;

- higher operational costs due to destruction of physical infrastructure and inventories or losses to production and income;

- lost production due to linkage effects, such as when suppliers cannot find alternative markets to their lost markets;

- additional costs incurred due to the need to use alternative means of production or provision of essential services; and

- costs of required government responses to the emergency.

These indirect economic losses can be mitigated by indirect benefits, primarily

- the shift in consumer demand or spending on alternative products or services;

- the change in the productivity of assets, such as when a flood waters and nourishes productive land;

- labor reallocation, such as when workers are more productive to compensate for lost productive capacity; and

- reconstruction activity, such as the products and services required during repair and reconstruction.

Source: Public Safety Canada (2013, pp. 72–73). *All Hazards Risk Assessment Methodology Guidelines, 2012–2013,* pages 72–73, http://www.publicsafety.gc.ca/cnt/rsrcs/pblctns/ll-hzrds-ssssmnt/index-eng.aspx#ahra_business, 2012–2013. Reproduced with the permission of the Minister of Public Safety and Emergency Preparedness Canada (2015).

ENVIRONMENTAL RETURNS Natural environmental damage can be assessed in economic terms when agriculture or some other economically productive use of the area is affected. Otherwise, an environmental regulator or assessor refers to statutory scales of value or legal precedents before seeking to impose a fine on or compensation from the perpetrator. Biologists and geographers may assess environmental damage in lots of nonfungible direct ways, such as animals killed, species affected, and the area of land or water affected. The land area is the most fungible of these measures (see Comparative Perspectives, Box 7.6).

The Canadian government would add another 0.5 to the magnitude if the sum value of the natural environmental damage was 9 after summing as many of the following criteria that might apply:

- Loss of rare or endangered species (value: 2)

- Reductions in species diversity (value: 1)

- Loss of critical or productive habitat (value: 2)

- Transformation of natural landscapes (value: 0.5)

BOX 7.6

Canadian Assessment of Natural Environmental Harm

After a natural disaster, the Canadian government uses the area affected to modify the ranking of the magnitude of official response (see Table 7.3), where a damaged area of 400 sq km would raise the ranking of official response by 1.0 (see Table 7.6).

Table 7.6   The Canadian Government's Modification of Consequences Magnitude (Table 7.4) by Geographical Area Affected

Extent Rating	Area Damaged (up to x number of sq km)
0.0	50
+0.5	150
+1.0	500
+1.5	1,500
+2.0	5,000
+2.5	15,000

Source: Public Safety Canada (2013, p. 33). *All Hazards Risk Assessment Methodology Guidelines, 2012–2013*, page 33, http://www.publicsafety.gc.ca/cnt/rsrcs/pblctns/ll-hzrds-ssssmnt/index-eng.aspx#ahra_business, 2012–2013. Reproduced with the permission of the Minister of Public Safety and Emergency Preparedness Canada (2015).

- Loss of current use of land resources (value: 1)

- Loss of current use of water resources (value: 2)

- Environmental losses from air pollution (value: 0.5)

- Duration of environmental disruption

  o 3–10 weeks (value: 0.5)

  o 2–8 months (value: 1)

  o 8–24 months (value: 1.5)

  o 2–6 years (value: 2)

  o 6–20 years (value: 2.5)

Source: Public Safety Canada (2013, pp. 35–39). *All Hazards Risk Assessment Methodology Guidelines, 2012–2013*, pages 35–39, http://www.publicsafety.gc.ca/cnt/rsrcs/pblctns/ll-hzrds-ssssmnt/index-eng.aspx#ahra_business, 2012–2013. Reproduced with the permission of the Minister of Public Safety and Emergency Preparedness Canada (2015).

TERRITORIAL OR GEOPOLITICAL INSECURITY Separate from an assessment of harm to a natural environment, we may need to assess declining security of a geopolitical unit, such as a sovereign territory, city, or province (see Table 7.7).

This magnitude score would be modified by duration.

- 1 hour (subtract 2)

- 1–3 hours (subtract 1.5)

- 3–10 hours (subtract 1)

- 0.5–1 day (subtract 0.5)

- 3–10 days (add 0.5)

- 20 days to 1 month (add 1)

COMPARATIVE PERSPECTIVES

Canadian Assessment of Territorial Insecurity

In the context of a loss of territorial control or security, assess the area affected (see Table 7.7), the duration, and the population density affected (Public Safety Canada, 2013, pp. 39–41).

Table 7.7 The Canadian Government's Ranking of Territorial Loss or Insecurity	
Extent Rating	Area Damaged (up to x number of sq km)
0.0	50
+0.5	150
+1.0	500
+1.5	1,500
+2.0	5,000
+2.5	15,000

Source: Public Safety Canada (2013, p. 40). *All Hazards Risk Assessment Methodology Guidelines, 2012–2013,* page 40, http://www.publicsafety.gc.ca/cnt/rsrcs/pblctns/ll-hzrds-ssssmnt/index-eng.aspx#ahra_business, 2012–2013. Reproduced with the permission of the Minister of Public Safety and Emergency Preparedness Canada (2015).

- 1–3 months (add 1.5)

- 3–12 months (add 2)

- 1–3 years (add 2.5)

- 3–10 years (add 3)

- More than 10 years but not permanent (add 3)

- Permanent (add 3.5)

It would also be modified by population density.

- 0.1 persons per km (subtract 1)

- 0.3 persons per km (subtract 0.5)

- 3 persons per km (add 0.5)

- 10 persons per km (add 1)

- 30 persons per km (add 1.5)

- 100 persons per km (add 2)

Source: Public Safety Canada (2013, pp. 40–41). *All Hazards Risk Assessment Methodology Guidelines, 2012–2013,* pages 40–41, http://www.publicsafety.gc.ca/cnt/rsrcs/pblctns/ll-hzrds-ssssmnt/index-eng.aspx#ahra_business, 2012–2013. Reproduced with the permission of the Minister of Public Safety and Emergency Preparedness Canada (2015).

EMERGENCY MANAGEMENT

Definition

Emergency management is any attempt to control the risks or respond to the events associated with emergencies. FEMA defines emergency management as "the process through which the Nation prepares for emergencies and disasters, mitigates their effects, and responds to and recovers from them" (FEMA, 2008, p. 57). This is based on the Post-Katrina Emergency Management Reform Act of 2006, which defines emergency management as

> the governmental function that coordinates and integrates all activities to build, sustain, and improve the capability to prepare for, protect against, respond to, recover from, or mitigate against threatened or actual natural disasters, acts of terrorism or other man-made disasters.

Most emergency management practices attempt to control or reduce the negative effects that would arise from a potential event. The strategy of controlling the negative effects is known

DEFINITION

Synonyms of Emergency Management

Protection

For the U.S. DHS (2009), **protection** is the

> actions or measures taken to cover or shield from exposure, injury, or destruction. In the context of the NIPP [National Infrastructure Protection Plan], protection includes actions to deter the threat, mitigate the vulnerabilities, or minimize the consequences associated with a terrorist attack or other incident. (p. 110)

Preparedness

For U.S. Federal Emergency Management Agency (1992), **preparedness** is "those activities, programs, and systems that exist prior to an emergency that are used to support and enhance response to an emergency or disaster." For U.S. DHS (2009), *preparedness* is the

> activities necessary to build, sustain, and improve readiness capabilities to prevent, protect against, respond to, and recover from natural or manmade incidents. Preparedness is a continuous process involving efforts at all levels of government and between government and the private sector and nongovernmental organizations to identify threats, determine vulnerabilities, and identify required resources to prevent, respond to, and recover from major incidents. (p. 110)

Contingency and Scenario Planning

The term **contingency planning** literally means planning to meet different contingencies

(future issues), although it is sometimes used to mean preparedness (for instance, in Heerkens, 2002, p. 150).

For the U.N., *contingency planning* is "a management tool used to ensure that adequate arrangements are made in anticipation of a crisis" (U.N. Office for the Coordination of Humanitarian Affairs [OCHA], 2004, p. 7) or "a management process that analyses specific potential events or emerging situations that might threaten society or the environment and establishes arrangements in advance to enable timely, effective, and appropriate responses to such events and situations" (U.N. ISDR, 2009, p. 7). For the Humanitarian Practice Network (2010), *contingency planning* is "a management tool used to ensure adequate preparation for a variety of potential emergency situations" (p. xv) while **scenario planning** is "forward planning about how a situation may evolve in the future, and how threats might develop [and] reviewing the assumptions in plans and thinking about what to do if they do not hold" (p. xviii).

Mitigation

For the U.S. government, **mitigation** is "any sustained action taken to reduce or eliminate the long-term risk to human life and property from hazards" (Blanchard, 2008, p. 724), "ongoing and sustained action to reduce the probability of or lessen the impact of an adverse incident" (U.S. DHS, 2009, p. 110), or "the capabilities necessary

BOX 7.8

to reduce loss of life and property by lessening the impact of disasters" (U.S. DHS, 2011, p. 9).

Resilience

The U.S. DHS (2009) defined **resilience** as "the ability to resist, absorb, recover from, or successfully adapt to adversity or a change in conditions" (p. 111).

For the U.N., *resilience* is

> the ability of a system, community or society exposed to hazards to resist, absorb, accommodate to and recover from the effects of a hazard in a timely and efficient manner, including through the preservation and restoration of its essential basic structures and functions. . . . the ability to "resile from" or "spring back from" a shock. (U.N. ISDR, 2009, p. 24)

Resilience is the "adaptive capacity of an organization in a complex and changing environment" (International Organization for Standardization, 2009, p. 11).

Response

U.S. emergency management has separated **response** as a "phase" of emergency management before recovery.

> [Response is the] activities that address the short-term, direct effects of an incident, including immediate actions to save lives, protect property, and meet basic human needs. Response also includes the execution of emergency operations plans and incident mitigation activities designed to limit the loss of life, personal injury, property damage, and other unfavorable outcomes. As indicated by the situation, response activities include applying intelligence and other information to lessen the effects or consequences of an incident; increasing security operations; continuing investigations into the nature and source of the threat; ongoing surveillance and testing processes; immunizations, isolation, or quarantine; and specific law enforcement operations aimed at preempting, interdicting, or disrupting illegal activity, and apprehending actual perpetrators and bringing them to justice. (U.S. DHS, 2009, p. 111)

Recovery

Response might overlap **recovery**. The U.S. DHS (2009) defined recovery as

> the development, coordination, and execution of service- and site-restoration plans for affected communities and the reconstitution of government operations and services through individual, private sector, nongovernmental, and public assistance programs that identify needs and define resources; provide housing and promote restoration; address long-term care and treatment of affected persons; implement additional measures for community restoration; incorporate mitigation measures and techniques, as feasible; evaluate the incident to identify lessons learned; and develop initiatives to mitigate the effects of future incidents. (p. 111)

by seven other terms that are highly synonymous but rarely admit their common objective or the existence of other synonyms and are often poorly defined. These seven terms are as follows: protecting the targets, preparing to defend or protect against the threat, planning for contingencies, mitigating the negative returns, building resilience against disruption, responding to the event, or recovering from the event (see Definition, Box 7.8).

FEDERAL STRUCTURE

Before 1979, federal emergency management was shared between the Federal Preparedness Agency and the Federal Disaster Assistance Administration, with military assistance from the Defense Civil Preparedness Agency (against nuclear warfare) and the U.S. Army Corps of Engineers (against floods).

The Disaster Relief Act (1974) enhanced funding for federal insurance against disasters, through the Federal Insurance Administration. The Department of Housing and Urban Development administered the Federal Insurance Administration and the Federal Disaster Assistance Administration.

In 1978, President Jimmy Carter declared an environmental emergency when pollutants leaked from a landfill in Love Canal, near Niagara, New York. The landfill had been used from 1942 to 1952; as water levels rose, pollutants, including dioxin, escaped into developed areas and the Niagara River. The discovery exposed decades of local and federal neglect and flaws in the structure of local and national responsibilities. On June 19, 1978, Carter sent Congress a Reorganization Plan (Number 3) that created a Federal Emergency Management Agency, which would report directly to the president. A partial nuclear meltdown at a power station in Three Mile Island, Pennsylvania, in March 1979, for which the existing agencies seemed unready, helped to justify Carter's executive order of March 31.

In 1979, FEMA replaced and absorbed six agencies or administrations: the Federal Preparedness Agency from the General Services Administration; the Federal Disaster Assistance Administration and the Federal Insurance Administration from the Department of Housing and Urban Development; the National Fire Prevention Control Administration from the Department of Commerce; the Federal Broadcast System from the Executive Office of the President; and the Defense Civil Preparedness Agency.

The terrorist attacks of September 11, 2001, prompted the largest restructuring of the U.S. government since 1947. The George W. Bush administration's *National Strategy for Homeland Security* specified the following relevant objectives for the proposed Department of Homeland Security:

- Integrate separate federal response plans into a single all-discipline incident management plan

- Create a national incident management system

- Improve tactical counterterrorism capabilities

- Enable seamless communication among all responders

- Prepare health care providers for catastrophic terrorism

- Augment America's pharmaceutical and vaccine stockpiles

- Prepare for chemical, biological, radiological, and nuclear decontamination

- Plan for military support to civil authorities (U.S. Office of Homeland Security, 2002, p. x)

The DHS absorbed FEMA as a directorate, effective March 2003. Until that time, the director of FEMA had been a member of the president's cabinet, but now he reports to the secretary of homeland security. FEMA suffered more political appointees and cuts in its budget and hemorrhaged professional emergency managers. The poor federal response to Hurricane Katrina in August 2005 exposed just how unprepared FEMA was to respond to national emergencies.

Katrina was the deadliest hurricane (more than 1,200 dead, mostly in and around New Orleans, Louisiana) in the United States since 1928 and the costliest since Hurricane Andrew in 1992 (or the costliest since 1926 if adjusted for inflated money value, population, and housing value). Katrina was certainly a large and unusually vectored storm, but underprepared local and federal authorities poorly mitigated its harmful effects.

The New Orleans Police Department had suffered years of poor personnel retention and scandals and proved unready for the emergency, particularly as measured by police officers reporting for duty and by crime. The New Orleans Police Superintendent Eddie Compass later resigned.

The U.S. Army Corps of Engineers held primary responsibility for the material protection of New Orleans against floods, but key levees failed. Later, a civil court found the corps responsible; however, they maintain sovereign immunity from civil liabilities.

The personnel at the Federal Emergency Management Agency had been discontented since being demoted from an independent agency to a directorate of the Department of Homeland Security. (FEMA operated with less than 85% of required staff for more than one year before Katrina.) FEMA misassessed the risks and implemented insufficient responses to Hurricane Katrina.

FEMA's Director Michael D. Brown and Deputy Director Patrick Rhode "had little or no prior relevant emergency-management experience before joining FEMA," concluded a U.S. Senate investigation after Katrina, which also described Brown as "insubordinate, unqualified, and counterproductive" (*National emergency management*, 2006). The Senate criticized President George W. Bush, too, for underpreparedness. The president had voiced public confidence in Brown's responses but later distanced himself, while his supporters complained that Brown had reacted slowly to the White House's warnings. After vicious accusations and counteraccusations between people loyal to Michael Brown and to the president, Brown finally resigned.

The Post-Katrina Emergency Management Reform Act (2006) gave FEMA more responsibilities and autonomy within the DHS. The restructured FEMA's next equivalent test was Hurricane Sandy, which landed in the United States on October 29, 2012, after killing around 100 people in the Caribbean. It killed more than 110 people and knocked out power to 8.5 million people across 10 American states. These costs were severe but were appropriately assessed and mitigated by official preparations. The consequences of Sandy could have been more severe than those of Katrina. (Sandy was the largest Atlantic hurricane on record in terms of wind span and coincided with amplificatory moon tides and weather.) But Sandy (about $50 billion) cost less than half as much as Katrina had cost ($108 billion). Days in advance, federal, state, city, and local officials coordinated their advice to the public and their preparations. In preparation for Sandy, FEMA led nearly 60 federal agencies, operated more than 60 interagency disaster-recovery centers in the affected states, and sent more than 7,000 personnel. Utility companies from unaffected states arrived under a collective agreement to help during emergencies. The U.S. military flew in hundreds of vehicles to help to restore power. The Internal Revenue Service helped aid groups acquire tax-exempt status. On November 14, 2012, President Barack Obama made a public statement that fairly summarized the collective response. "The response hasn't been perfect, but it's been aggressive and strong and fast and robust" (Naylor, 2012, n.p.). By December, during a severe snowstorm, about 130,000 people in the states of New York and New Jersey still remained without power; thousands of homes and businesses remained without power in late January 2013, when another unusually severe cold front hit. The governors of New Jersey and New York requested nearly $80 billion in federal aid; in January 2013, the U.S. Congress approved over $60 billion ($9.7 billion for immediate relief from flooding, followed by $17 billion for general relief, $5.4 billion for aid through FEMA directly to individuals and local communities for rebuilding, and $33.6 billion for long-term rebuilding). The total federal aid was equivalent to more than half of the federal spending cuts agreed to days before and was larger than the annual budgets of many states (Caruso, 2013).

Process and Planning

The federal agencies of the 1970s explicitly emphasized an **all-hazards approach**—meaning readiness to manage any emergency. They generally agreed on four phases of emergency management:

1. mitigation,
2. preparedness,
3. response, and
4. recovery.

In 1979, the National Governors' Association (NGA) Disaster Project published the first statement of Comprehensive Emergency Management, in which all authorities were recommended to develop the capacity to manage all phases of all types of emergency. NGA and FEMA formally adopted the recommendations. In 1980, the Comprehensive Environmental Response, Compensation, and Liability Act (called the Superfund Law) was passed.

In 1983, FEMA adopted an Integrated Emergency Management System that included "direction, control and warning systems which are common to the full range of emergencies from small isolated events to the ultimate emergency—war" (Giuffrida, 1983, p. 9). Passage of the Robert Stafford Disaster Relief and Emergency Assistance Act of 1988 established that the federal government would share the costs of preparing for emergencies with state and local governments.

FEMA's management of Hurricane Hugo in 1989, Hurricane Andrew in 1992, and flooding in the Midwestern United States in 1993 was recognized as poor. (The Government Accounting Office was the highest nonpartisan authority to report so.) In 1993, President Bill Clinton appointed FEMA's first professional emergency manager as director. (James Lee Witt had served as director of emergency management for Arkansas.) Witt reoriented FEMA from emergency response to risk reduction. By 1997, FEMA had seven directorates: Mitigation; Preparedness; Response and Recovery; the Federal Insurance Administration; the United States Fire Administration; Information Technology Services; and Operations Support.

> This system worked very well in the 1990s when the United States had the most sophisticated and efficient emergency management system in the world. This system effectively responded to hundreds of major natural disasters across the country and successfully managed the federal response to the Oklahoma City bombing [1995] and the September 11 attacks in New York City and at the Pentagon. (Bullock, Haddow, & Coppola, 2013, p. 618)

The 9/11 Commission recommended an incident command system (ICS), based on a wildfire-fighting ICS (FIRESCOPE ICS). An ICS specifies the interdepartment structure that should be adopted in response to different events. On February 23, 2003, President Bush signed Homeland Security Presidential Directive 5, which called on the DHS to establish an ICS. On March 1, 2004, the DHS, with help from other departments at the federal, state, and local levels, produced a final national incident management system (NIMS), with five main components:

1. an ICS,

2. a prescription for standardized and interoperable communications and information management,

3. standards of preparedness before the event,

4. a Joint Information System to deliver a unified message to the public, and

5. the NIMS Integration Center (NIC), under the secretary of homeland security, to integrate and develop best practices, to educate stakeholders in best practices, and to certify skills and equipment.

As soon as 2002, outsiders published concerns that the homeland security mission was diverting FEMA from its core mission and competencies. In March 2004, former director Witt testified to a joint hearing of two House subcommittees on government reform that FEMA should be removed from the DHS and returned directly under the executive. He stated, "FEMA, having lost its status as an independent agency, is being buried beneath a massive bureaucracy whose main and seemingly only focus is fighting terrorism while an all-hazards mission is getting lost in the shuffle" (Corn, 2005).

As verified by the Government Accountability Office in subsequent years, FEMA suffered low morale, high turnover of senior personnel, and more political appointees. Other authors noted that FEMA's mission was dissimilar to counterterrorism and contributed to "mission distortion within the DHS" (Gaines & Kappeler, 2012, p. 34). The breadth of homeland security and the political emphasis on counterterrorism were unjustified by the greater natural risks. For instance, from 9/11 through 2007, FEMA recorded four terrorist attacks in the United States, 105 hurricanes, 78 tornados, and five earthquakes. Certainly, the obsession with counterterrorism contributed to a neglect of integrated emergency management.

> Responding effectively to harmful events after they occur means anticipating the variety of ways that future events might unfold. The criticism in the aftermath of 9/11 is that although the government has tightened airport security, it has paid less attention to securing ports and harbors, which are other potentially vulnerable venues. Preparation in the aftermath of a harmful event must include thinking outside the box. Perhaps more damaging criticism was evidenced in the response to and aftermath of Hurricane Katrina [in 2005], with the suggestion that efforts to anticipate future terrorist attacks had moved resources away from other realms of potential security threats such as hurricanes. (Gibbs Van Brunschot & Kennedy, 2008, p. 16)

In March 2006, the DHS inspector general issued a report that called for a more inclusive approach (*all-hazards preparedness*) to security and risk management.

> The response to Hurricane Katrina demonstrated that DHS' efforts to protect and prepare the nation for terrorist events and natural disasters have not yet translated into preparedness for all hazards. State emergency management staff we interviewed said the majority of DHS preparedness grants are spent on terrorism preparedness, which has not afforded sufficient support or funding for natural hazards preparedness. However, a July 2005 Government Accountability Office report said that while some DHS grants have prescriptive requirements focused on terrorism, most of the grant funding is applicable to all-hazards preparedness. Many preparedness measures funded by DHS first responder grants can serve both means, and federal and state emergency managers need to adopt an all-hazards approach. (U.S. Department of Homeland Security, 2006, p. 135)

The Post-Katrina Emergency Management Reform Act of 2006 ordered an all-hazards approach.

> In carrying out the responsibilities under this section, the Administrator shall coordinate the implementation of a risk-based, all-hazards strategy that builds those common capabilities necessary to prepare for, protect against, respond to, recover from, or mitigate against natural disasters, acts of terrorism, and other manmade

disasters, while also building the unique capabilities necessary to prepare for, protect against, respond to, recover from, or mitigate against the risks of specific types of incidents that pose the greatest risk to the Nation. (Title VI, Section 503)

The DHS's next lexicon (Masse, O'Neil, & Rollins, 2007) defined *all-hazards* as a "grouping classification encompassing all conditions, environmental or manmade, that have the potential to cause injury, or death; damage to or loss of equipment, infrastructure services, or property; or alternately causing functional degradation to societal, economic or environmental aspects." The DHS has retained this definition (U.S. Department of Homeland Security, 2009, p. 109).

In 2007, FEMA revised its four-phase approach to emergency management to read "all-hazards emergency management."

- Prevent
  - Detect terrorist threats
  - Control access
  - Eliminate threats

- Protect
  - Protect physical or cyber assets and systems
  - Mitigate risks to human and animal health

- Respond
  - Evaluate incident
  - Minimize impact
    - Manage incident
    - Respond to hazard
    - Implement protective actions
    - Conduct search and rescue
  - Care for public

- Recover
  - Assist public
  - Restore environment
  - Restore infrastructure

After 9/11, the Federal Response Plan (1992) was updated as the National Response Plan (NRP, 2004), but after Hurricane Katrina (2005), it developed once again into a revised NRP (2006) and, finally, the National Response Framework (NRF). The draft NRF was released in September 2007, but its final version appeared on January 22, 2008, to address criticism of its neglect of state or local involvement.

The NRF specifies how emergencies and major disasters can be declared. A local authority can appeal to the state governor, who, in cooperation with regional staff from FEMA, could appeal to the president for help. FEMA's regional administrator would evaluate the request and make a recommendation to FEMA's administrator, who would recommend a decision through the secretary of homeland security to the president. Following a presidential declaration, FEMA would determine those agencies required; they would be notified by the National Operations Center (DHS) and would send personnel to the National Response Coordination Center and the National Infrastructure Coordinating Center, as appropriate.

CAPACITY AND CAPABILITY

Capacity is a fundamental concept in managing emergencies because we need to have capacity before we can respond. This section defines capacity and explains the fungibility of different capacities, how capacity is traded with capability, and how capacity (and thence security) tends to distribute inequitably.

Definitions

Capacity is the potential to achieve something. Different capacities include the potentials to, for instance, acquire capabilities or deliver performance. A **capability** is something we can use to achieve something. *Performance* is our actual delivery of something.

THE FUNGIBILITY OF CAPACITY Since capacity is the potential for something, it must be converted into something else to be useful, but different forms of capacity are fungible into some things but not others. When we identify capacity, we should also define what the capacity might be converted into because capacities might be useful for one thing but not another. For instance, one organization's capacity for self-defense is different from another organization's capacity for investigation of crime.

Financial capital is the most fungible form of capacity since it can be spent on the defenses or actions that would control risks or counter threats. Within political units, economic capacity is the focus because the economy can be a source of revenues, technologies, and expertise that could be converted into other things. Declining, unstable, or inequitable economies suggest incapacity. For instance, in September 2012, the World Economic Forum surveyed more than 1,000 experts on global risks. Those experts ranked potential wealth gaps (severe income disparity) followed by unsustainable government debt (chronic fiscal imbalances) as the top two global risks, mostly because these risks suggest potential incapacity for controlling other risks, such as climate change (the third-ranked global risk) (Howell, 2013).

Some capacity remains somewhat fungible even after conversion into more specialized forms. For instance, military organizations are required for defense against major violent threats, against which their capabilities must be highly specialized, but most are utilized effectively as emergency responders too (for instance, to rescue citizens from natural disasters).

By contrast, some capacities are so particular that they cannot be converted into much else. For instance, a state's built infrastructure, such as an airport, is expensive and practically not fungible. In an emergency, a road could be closed to road traffic and temporarily used to store assets or to accept aircraft, but it is of no use as a power station. The underlying land can change use, but the infrastructure built on the land usually must be demolished before a change of use, and little material would be reusable.

TRADING CAPACITY AND CAPABILITY Increased capacity suggests the potential for a capability, but capacity and capability are not the same; capacity needs to be converted or translated into capability. Being wealthy enough to acquire something is not the same as having acquired something. Strategically, we should convert some capacity into capabilities that would help us respond to an emergency. However, we would not convert all our capacity. Instead, we would want to retain some capacity in case we discover that we are underprepared for some emergencies. Risks often change. Thus, the achievement of security is an imperfect trade-off between capacity and capability—between capacity reserved against emerging risks and capacity converted into controls on current risks.

Self-satisfaction about our capacity would be regrettable if we were to fail to convert that capacity into a required control on some intolerable risk, perhaps because we had failed to realize the risk or the control. For instance, before 9/11, the U.S. government certainly failed to adequately control the increasing risks associated with religious terrorism, even though many persons within and without the U.S. government had warned of increasing trends toward religiosity, lethal intent, capability, lethality, and anti-Americanism in terrorism (see, e.g., Hoffman, 2001). After 9/11, the U.S. government converted colossal capacity into counterterrorist, homeland security, defense, and military capabilities. Less capacity would have been required to control the risks when they were emerging than after they had emerged.

THE DISTRIBUTION OF CAPACITY In theory, incapacity suggests insecurity. In practice, small declines in capacity can lead to dramatic, nonlinear declines in security. In absolute terms, people without sufficient capacity do not have the potential to counter anything. Incapacity tends to correlate with exposure, vulnerability, and other concepts suggestive of insecurity, and these things tend to be highly interrelated. People who are poor or marginalized are more likely to be exposed to threats by living or working in dangerous areas, to lack defenses against threats, to lack the capacity to change their situation or recover from threats, and to lack official support. For instance, very poor people cannot afford to live except in infertile or highly hazardous areas where they cannot build food reserves or protect themselves against natural disasters, and such areas may be too remote from central official services to expect help.

Relative incapacity suggests a dramatic, nonlinear jump in the negative returns of an event. People with capacity can acquire the various controls that dramatically lower the risks, so when a negative event, such as an earthquake, occurs, negative returns are controlled to survivable levels. Conversely, people with incapacity cannot acquire any of those controls, so when the same event occurs for them, the negative returns are many times higher; they suffer a disaster or catastrophe.

Consequently, for some people, their exposure, vulnerability, and incapacity interact as very high risks of many types while, for others, the risks are less numerous and lower in magnitude. Normally, risk does not distribute linearly across the population; instead, one large part of the population faces much greater risks than the other part (often a privileged minority) (Wisner, Blaikie, Cannon, & Davis, 2004, pp. 11–13).

Without outside help, the gap between those with capacity and those without tends to be stable or even grow because negative risks most affect those without capacity and thereby reduce their capacity further. Consequently, many governments advocate interventions to improve the capacity of the deprived, particularly at the time of any intervention to recover from a negative event. "There is a strong relationship between long-term sustainable recovery and prevention and mitigation of future disasters. Recovery efforts should be conducted with a view towards disaster risk reduction" (Public Safety Canada, 2013, p. 78).

VULNERABILITY

In addition to assessing our capacity to respond to emergencies, we should assess our vulnerability to emergencies. This section defines vulnerability and introduces methods for assessing vulnerability.

Defining Vulnerability

Vulnerability essentially means that the target can be harmed by the threat. For instance, I would be vulnerable to a threat armed with a weapon that could harm me. The threat would cease if I were to acquire some armor that perfectly protects me from the weapon or some other means of perfectly countering the weapon.

Vulnerability is routinely conflated with exposure. In general use, vulnerability is "the state of being exposed to or likely to suffer harm" (FrameNet, 2012, n.p.). The Humanitarian Practice Network (2010) defined *vulnerabilities* as "factors that increase an organization's exposure to threats, or make severe outcomes more likely" (p. 42). However, it is useful to differentiate vulnerability and exposure (see the following section). Essentially, vulnerability means that we are undefended against the threat while exposure means we are subject to the threat.

Some definitions of vulnerability conflate risk. For instance, the Humanitarian Practice Network (2010) defined vulnerability as "the likelihood or probability of being confronted with a threat, and the consequences or impact if and when that happens" (p. 28), but this sounds the same as risk.

The U.S. Government Accountability Office (2005c) defines *vulnerability* as "the probability that a particular attempted attack will succeed against a particular target or class of targets" (p. 112) or (under *vulnerability assessment*) the "weaknesses in physical structures, personal protection systems, processes or other areas that may be exploited" (p. 112). The GAO used this definition in a dispute about assessments by the Department of Homeland Security of the vulnerability of physical assets (GAO, 2008a). The Department of Homeland Security (2009) defines *vulnerability* as "a physical feature or operational attribute that renders an entity open to exploitation or susceptible to a given hazard" (p. 112). In the context of cybersecurity, the GAO (2005a) defines *vulnerability* as "a flaw or weakness in hardware or software that can be exploited, resulting in a violation of an implicit or explicit security policy" (p. 10).

The DOD (2010) defines *vulnerability* as "the susceptibility of a nation or military force to any action by any means through which its war potential or combat effectiveness may be reduced or its will to fight diminished" or "the characteristics of a system that cause it to suffer a definite degradation (incapability to perform the designated mission) as a result of having been subjected to a certain level of effects in an unnatural (man-made) hostile environment" (p. 262).

Assessing Vulnerability

This section introduces different schemes for assessing vulnerability by the target's defenses; the gap between the target's defenses and a particular threat; and the gap between the target's defenses and standard defenses.

DEFENSES As a correlate of invulnerability, we could measure the target's defenses. For instance, the Humanitarian Practice Network (2010) prescribes measuring our strengths as "the flip-side of vulnerabilities" (p. 42).

We could measure our defensive inputs by scale or value. For instance, the defensive inputs along a coastline could be measured by spending on all defenses, total concrete poured as seawalls, or total length of barriers at the site.

Preferably, we should measure the outputs—the actual defensive capabilities and performance—although this is usually more difficult than measuring inputs. The ideal measures of outputs are practical tests of defensive function. For instance, official authorities often send agents to attempt to pass mock weapons through baggage screening systems in airports as tests of airport security.

TARGET–THREAT GAP ANALYSIS More particularly, we should identify a real threat (or imagine a real hazard as an activated threat) and compare our defensive capacity against the threat's offensive capacity. This sort of assessment is often termed a **gap analysis**, since it looks for a gap between our defensive capacity and the threat's offensive capacity. For instance, we should be alarmed if we learn that a threat with a heavy-caliber firearm has targeted a building that is not fortified against such a firearm.

TARGET–STANDARD GAP ANALYSIS In practice, we are often uncertain about any particular threat. Consequently, we usually measure our vulnerability to some standardized notional threats, such as chemical explosive weapons of a certain type or size (see Comparative Perspectives, Box 7.9).

EXPOSURE

Separate to our vulnerability, we should assess our exposure to the hazards that could cause emergencies. This section defines exposure and suggests strategies to assess exposure.

COMPARATIVE PERSPECTIVES

U.S. Diplomatic Vulnerability Assessments

The U.S. Department of State effectively measures the gap between the security standards and the actual security of overseas missions. The standards for overseas security are set by the Overseas Security Policy Board, chaired by the assistant secretary for diplomatic security, with representatives from U.S. government agencies that have a presence overseas. Each year, the Bureau of Diplomatic Security creates the Diplomatic Security Vulnerability List, which ranks sites according to their vulnerability. The Bureau of Diplomatic Security's Threat Investigations & Analysis Directorate determines the security environment threat ratings (established May 2008) (GAO, 2009b, pp. 5–7).

Definition

Exposure often is treated as synonymous with vulnerability, but *exposure* implies that we are subject to the threat while *vulnerability* implies our lack of defenses against the threat. We are subject to the threat if we coincide with or are discovered by the threat in ways that allow the threat to target us.

FrameNet (2012) defines the verb *to expose* as to "reveal the true, objectionable nature of" (n.p.) something. In general use, *risk* is sometimes used as a verb to imply our voluntary exposure to some threat (as in, "I risked discovery by the enemy."). Risk is also used as a verb in front of some valued object representing what the actor has to lose (as in, "I risked my savings on that bet.") (Fillmore & Atkins, 1992, pp. 97, 100–101). This use of the verb risk helps explain the dual meanings of exposure in the frame of risk: exposure to the threat; and what we have to lose. In military contexts, exposure implies that we are under observation by a threat, but in financial contexts, exposure implies the things that could be lost. Thus, unfortunately, one word is used routinely with two different meanings, which I will term **threat exposure** (the more military context) and **loss exposure** (the more financial context).

Here, we will focus on threat exposure (the target's revelation to the potential threat). If the hazard could not reach us or find us, we would not be exposed, whatever our vulnerability. This is a profound insight because if we were confident that we were not exposed to a certain hazard, we would not need any defenses against that hazard (although we would need to be ready to acquire defenses if the hazard were about to discover or reach us). For instance, if we were confident that a communicable disease had been quarantined perfectly, we would not be justified in ordering mass immunization against that disease. We would not be exposed, so we would not need defenses.

Essentially, any control of access is an attempt to control the potential target's exposure. Access controls include any attempt to manage the entry of actors or agents into some domain (for instance, by demanding identification of permitted persons before entry into a building or a password before access to some digital environment). As long as the access controls work perfectly, everything inside the perimeter remains unexposed to external threats, even though the perimeter would remain exposed. For instance, after 9/11, under new regulations, airline cockpit doors were supposed to be locked during flight, stopping the pilot's exposure to any threat in the passenger cabin during flight. The pilot remains vulnerable to the sorts of weapons (small knives, fists, and tear gas) used on 9/11, unless the pilot is equipped with a firearm, body armor, and a gas mask. (Some cockpit crew are certified to carry firearms.) But the pilot is not exposed to any of these things as long as he or she remains on the other side of the door. Passengers in the passenger cabin would remain exposed to any threat in the passenger cabin, but their vulnerability would be reduced if joined by an armed air marshal prepared to defend them.

Assessing Exposure

For assessing exposure, we should measure exposure by area coincident with a particular hazard or threat, exposure by time, or some combination thereof.

EXPOSURE BY AREA Someone's exposure to a threat could be defined by the space known to be coincident with that threat. For instance, crime tends to concentrate in certain areas (sometimes known as **hot spots**), perhaps because of local de-policing, a self-segregated community, or some accident of history. (Perhaps some criminal gang is led by someone with family there.) Someone's exposure to crime in that area increases as he or she spends more time traveling through, working in, or living in that same area. This repeated exposure helps to explain repeat victimization. Someone who becomes a victim of crime in a high-crime area and who does not move or change his or her behavior is just as likely to be a victim in the future (and past victimization may harm a person's capacity to avoid future crime). One study suggests that 10% of the space in which any crime occurs experiences 60% of crime, 10% of offenders are responsible for about 50% of offenses, and 10% of victims suffer about 40% of crimes (Kennedy & Gibbs Van Brunschot, 2009, pp. 69–72).

We could measure the number or value of targets exposed. We could measure exposure spatially (such as the target area as a proportion of the total area or the target area's length of border or coastline as a proportion of total border or coastline) or in terms of flows (the number or scale of ports of entry, migrants, or trade).

EXPOSURE BY TIME We are exposed in time whenever the threat is coincident with us or knows where we are and can target us at that time. We could measure our exposure in time in either absolute terms (such as days exposed) or proportional terms (such as the fraction of the year). We could make the measure judgmental; for instance, one judgmental scheme assigns a value between 1 and 5 to correspond respectively with rare, quarterly, weekly, daily, or constant exposure (Waring & Glendon, 1998, pp. 27–28).

Natural threats are often cyclical or seasonal and predictable in duration, allowing us to calculate the proportion of time when we would be exposed if we were to reside in the area where a natural hazard occurred, such as a hurricane zone that experiences a hurricane season. If we knew that a threat was current, we could calculate the duration of our exposure if we were to travel through the area where the threat was active. Some of our behaviors allow us to calculate the duration of our exposure. For instance, we could calculate the time we spend traveling by

BOX 7.10

Other Measures of Exposure

The U.N. ISDR (2009) noted that

> [m]easures of exposure can include the number of people or types of assets in an area. These can be combined with the specific vulnerability of the exposed elements to any particular hazard to estimate the quantitative risks associated with that hazard in the area of interest. (p. 15)

Similarly, the Humanitarian Practice Network (2010) prescribed asking which persons travel through or work in the most exposed areas, which sites are most exposed to the threats, and which assets are most exposed to theft or damage (p. 42).

automobile as a measure of our exposure to road traffic accidents. Similarly, we could calculate the time we spend traveling or residing in an area as a measure of our exposure to crime in that area (see Comparative Perspectives, Box 7.10).

COMMUNICATING EMERGENCIES

Communication of your management of emergencies is useful for external confidence and transparency as well as a necessary vehicle in compliance with external reviews, monitors, and audits.

The subsections below discuss some visual ways to communicate risk. The most common are risk scales or ladders, risk matrices, heat maps, risk radars, and risk maps.

Risk Scales or Ladders

You can communicate the risk of emergencies via explicit **risk scales** (sometimes called **risk ladders**) with 3 points or 5 points. Military and diplomatic sites traditionally have advertised 3-point *threat levels* at different physical sites, but they essentially mean risk levels. More practical still are *response levels*, which indicate the set of escalating controls in response to escalating risks.

However, even 5-point scales have been criticized for communicating too little information to be useful. At the same time, they have also been criticized for suggesting more certainty or precision than was justified.

The Homeland Security Advisory System or *homeland threat level* was first released by the newly established U.S. Office of Homeland Security in late 2002. This scale included the levels *severe*, *high*, *elevated*, *guarded*, and *low*, which were colored red, orange, yellow, blue, and green, respectively. The George W. Bush administration changed the level 17 times from 2002 through

2006 but never below elevated, prompting complaints that the administration was holding the level artificially high for political reasons and causing subordinate authorities to control risks inefficiently. The first homeland security secretary, Tom Ridge, later recalled that the administration had pressured him to raise the level before the national election in 2004 (Ridge & Bloom, 2009). Meanwhile, state and local authorities complained that the level was not specific enough. At first, these authorities ordered increased security whenever the level rose, but without more information, they could not know where to reallocate resources. (In March 2003, the U.S. Conference of Mayors estimated that cities alone were spending $70 million every week on additional homeland security measures due to heightened levels.) They demanded more intelligence so that they could control the specific risk by, for instance, ordering an increased police presence around the railway system if the intelligence suggested an increased threat to trains. In practice, intelligence was preferable to any abstract threat level. Most consumers were issued only the homeland threat level; since this changed between one of the three highest levels for poorly justified reasons, consumers became neglectful.

For this and other reasons, in 2009, a bipartisan panel recommended reducing the number of levels from five to three, but the scale was not replaced until April 2011, when the DHS implemented the National Terrorism Advisory System (NTAS), which occasionally and temporarily issues a statement specifying an elevated terrorist threat or an imminent terrorist threat, each with a specified date of expiration. The default option is no statement of threat. Effectively, the NTAS is a 3-point scale but is never communicated on any scale. Instead, each statement is issued as a single-page document describing the threat.

Risk Matrices

Risk matrices are the most recognizable way to communicate risk thanks to their simplicity and frequent use, although matrices typically oversimplify the data on which they are based and often use misleading scales or risk levels.

Conventional risk matrices are formed by two dimensions: returns and likelihood. A fair and transparent matrix should have symmetrical scales on each dimension and should admit that the risk in each cell is a product of these dimensions. This mathematical consistency produces risk levels each with a definite order and clean boundaries. For instance, Table 7.8 shows a simple risk matrix with symmetrical 3-point scales on each dimension and with risks calculated as products of the scales.

Table 7.8 A Simple Risk Matrix With Symmetrical Scales and Mathematically Correct Products			
High likelihood (3)	*Medium risk (3)*	*Medium-high risk (6)*	*High-high risk (9)*
Medium likelihood (2)	*Low-medium risk (2)*	*Medium risk (4)*	*Medium-high risk (6)*
Low likelihood (1)	*Low risk (1)*	*Low-medium risk (2)*	*Medium risk (3)*
	Low impact (1)	**Medium impact (2)**	**High impact (3)**

The Australian/New Zealand and ISO standards (Australian and New Zealand Joint Technical Committee, 2009) introduced a risk matrix with symmetrical 5-point dimensions (each scale is numbered 1 to 5, although the qualitative explanations are poorly differentiated) and four risk levels that are consistent with the risk scores produced from the dimensions. Subsequently, the U.N.'s Threat and Risk Unit chose a risk matrix with symmetrical 5-point dimensions and six risk levels (see Table 7.9).

Unfortunately, many risk matrices assign risk levels that are not mathematically justified and are misleading. For instance, Table 7.10 shows a risk matrix with four discrete qualitative risk levels but does not show that these levels are mathematically irregular and overlapping: acceptable risks (1–3); risks subject to review (2–5); undesirable risks (6–9); and unacceptable risks (10–20). These risk levels effectively overstate the impact and understate the likelihood; some risks were placed in a higher level when the impact is high and the likelihood is low rather than when the likelihood is high and the impact is low. This may have been deliberate, such as to acknowledge the layperson's overvaluation of high-impact over high-likelihood events of the same risk level, but the reasons should be explained.

Communicators who want risks to be interpreted consistently should use risk ladders or matrices that are symmetrical and assign risk levels that are congruent with the mathematics. Consumers should check for these things or ask the communicator to explain any divergence.

Additionally, communicators should use media consistently because the inconsistencies are confusing and often traceable to quantitative or qualitative mistakes.

The risks in a risk matrix can be represented by dots, each placed in a cell corresponding with the risk's associated likelihood and returns, where each dot's size or color corresponds with the risk's

Table 7.9 The U.N.'s Standard Risk Matrix

Critical impact (5)	Low (5)	Medium (10)	High (15)	Critical (20)	Critical (25)
Severe impact (4)	Low (4)	Medium (8)	High (12)	High (16)	Critical (20)
Moderate impact (3)	Negligible (3)	Low (6)	Medium (9)	High (12)	High (15)
Minor impact (2)	Negligible (2)	Low (4)	Low (6)	Medium (8)	Medium (10)
Negligible impact (1)	No determinable risk (1)	Negligible (2)	Negligible (3)	Low (4)	Low (5)
	Unlikely (1)	**Moderately likely (2)**	**Likely (3)**	**Very likely (4)**	**Certain or imminent (5)**

Source: U.N. Department of Peacekeeping Operations & Department of Field Support (2008).

Table 7.10	A Risk Matrix With Asymmetrical Dimensions and Risk Levels				
Catastrophic impact (4)	*Risk subject to review (4)*	*Undesirable risk (8)*	*Unacceptable risk (12)*	*Unacceptable risk (16)*	*Unacceptable risk (20)*
Critical impact (3)	*Risk subject to review (3)*	*Undesirable risk (6)*	*Undesirable risk (9)*	*Unacceptable risk (12)*	*Unacceptable risk (15)*
Marginal impact (2)	*Risk subject to review (2)*	*Risk subject to review (4)*	*Undesirable risk (6)*	*Undesirable risk (8)*	*Unacceptable risk (10)*
Negligible impact (1)	*Acceptable risk (1)*	*Acceptable risk (2)*	*Acceptable risk (3)*	*Risk subject to review (4)*	*Risk subject to review (5)*
	Improbable (1)	**Remote likelihood (2)**	**Likely to occur sometime (3)**	**Probable (4)**	**Likely to occur frequently (5)**

Source: Based on U.S. Government Accountability Office (1998, p. 8).

rank. Such displays are called sometimes *oil stain plots* or **heat maps** (although I and others use *heat map* to describe another display described in the following section).

Risks can be plotted within a matrix to show how risks have changed over time. A particular risk could be plotted in the same matrix twice: at an earlier point in time and a later point in time. If the risk level has changed in that time, an arrow between the plots can represent the change. The change might be due to controls on the risk; in this case, some users have referred to the matrix as a *control effectiveness map*.

HEAT MAPS A *heat map* is a matrix on which we can plot risks by two actionable dimensions, usually risk owner and risk category. The level of risk can be indicated by a color (say, green, yellow, and red) or a number (say, from 1 to 3) in the cell formed where the risk's owner and category intersect. Such heat maps are useful for drawing attention to those owners or categories that hold the most risks or largest risks and thus need higher intervention or those who hold fewer or smaller risks and have capacity to accept more risk.

RISK RADARS Risk radars are segmented, concentric circles that normally are used to represent time (circles further from the center represent time further into the future) and risk categories or risk owners (each segment of the pie would represent a different category or owner). Risk radars are useful for drawing attention to risks whose control is most urgent.

Moving outward from the center circle (which normally represents the present), each concentric circle would represent some interval of time further into the future (say, an interval of 1 year). Segments or arcs of the concentric circles can be delineated to differentiate risk by category or owner, depending on whether the categories or owners were most salient. Each risk's level or rank can be represented by a distinct color or number.

SPATIAL MAPS Some risks are usefully plotted in space by their real geographical locations through **spatial maps**. For instance, if we operate or are based in different areas, the risks to or the security of our operations and bases can be plotted on a map of these areas. Vehicles or assets in transit move through areas with different risks. Some security and risk managers, such as coast guards and navies, use software to monitor the locations of assets as large as oil tankers in real time.

FINAL CASE STUDY

How Do We Address the Complexities of Emergency Management?

Thad Allen

In the period since the Cold War, the concept of emergency management has evolved from a doctrine of civil defense and emergencies services delivered locally at the state or municipal level to a more comprehensive layer approach. The current emergency-management framework is best seen as a social ecosystem that attempts to unify participants under a *whole of community* effort. Yet while our recognition of the need for unity of effort has grown, so has the complexity of events that face us. The challenge to emergency management today and looking forward is the need to address two key challenges: complexity and coproduction.

Complexity as a risk aggravator remains an elusive concept in thinking about emergency management. My embrace of this concept stems from my personal involvement in the 9/11 response in New York Harbor, Hurricane Katrina, the Haitian Earthquake, and the Deepwater Horizon oil spill. In my view, we are seeing increasing frequency of events of greater complexity. By complexity, I mean those elements that confound and vex existing doctrine, policy, and operating procedures. Complexity can be related to the scale of an event in terms of geographical span, population density, concentration and age of infrastructure, or the interaction of all of these or more. Complexity can also result from the increased intersection of the natural and built (man-made) environments. As a result of the Great Flood of 1927, the Mississippi River was transformed into a navigation channel that severed the river from the delta that it had replenished for centuries. In these situations, the complexity of the event creates challenges to existing operating procedures and doctrines. When this happens and there is no attempt to scale the response through unity of effort (horizontally and vertically) across government and the private sector, the public are harsh judges, and the media becomes their voice.

To the extent that complexity is the challenge, coproduction is an answer. The concept of coproduction assumes that complex events (wicked problems, black swans) cannot be adequately addressed by a single government agency, private-sector firm, or not-for-profit organization or the military. Resources, legal authorities, capability, capacity, or competency restricts each. The key to effective coproduction of outcomes lies in a thorough understanding of the basic legal authorities and jurisdictions of all participants, the development of a common understanding of the problem and its complexity, and a commitment to unity of effort. This is easier said than done.

During Hurricane Katrina, the assumption was that we were dealing with a hurricane. In actuality, the problem was more complex. My definition for what happened in New Orleans was the equivalent of a weapon of mass effect that resulted in a loss of continuity of government. It took over one week to understand that pouring resources into the area was not effective until the elements of government that would command and control resources were reestablished without presuming the legal authorities of the mayor and governor.

In the Deepwater Horizon response, complexity was driven by the environmental conditions. The well was 45 mi offshore and in 5,000 ft of water with no human access. There was no question of legal authority as the well was outside state waters. There was political complexity based on the desire of state and local governments to mount their own responses in what was clearly a regional problem and, therefore, a federal responsibility. Finally, in the hurricane, Mother Nature was the protagonist. In the oil spill, there was a responsible party. The need to simultaneously hold British Petroleum (BP) accountable for the event and insure they responded as required by law created severe concerns among political leaders who questioned the legal framework. The frustration of political leaders who wanted to hold BP accountable created significant tension in directing them to cap the well and clean up the oil.

In addressing any complex problem or crisis in the current environment, leaders would be well advised to suspend assumptions on doctrines and procedures to insure the needed actions are being taken. Once the problem is correctly understood to the extent the available information and conditions allow, there is no effective response that is not coproduced. Unity of effort must be the North Star.

Thad Allen is a leader in Booz Allen Hamilton's business at the Departments of Justice and Homeland Security, focusing on emergency management, critical-infrastructure protection, cybersecurity, emergency communications, and maritime security. He is a national thought leader in homeland security, maritime policy, law enforcement, and national resiliency. Known for his expertise in bringing together diverse parties to address major challenges and create unity of effort, Mr. Allen completed a distinguished career in the U.S. Coast Guard as its 23rd commandant in 2010. Mr. Allen's crisis leadership experience includes responses to the Deepwater Horizon oil spill in the Gulf of Mexico, Hurricanes Katrina and Rita, the Haitian earthquake, and port security operations in New York Harbor following the September 11 attacks. He is a fellow in the National Academy of Public Administration and a member of the Council on Foreign Relations. Mr. Allen also currently serves as a director of the Coast Guard Foundation and Partnership for Public Service. He is a 1971 graduate of the U.S. Coast Guard Academy. He holds a master's degree in public administration from The George Washington University, from which he received the Alumni Achievement Award in 2006. He also holds a master's degree in science from the Sloan School of Management at the Massachusetts Institute of Technology.

CHAPTER SUMMARY

This chapter has

- Defined emergency

- Showed how to assess emergencies in terms of returns, impacts, consequences, and costs and benefits

- Explained how to assess emergencies judgmentally on an ordinal scale

- Explained how to assess emergencies objectively by their official responses and human, economic, environmental, and territorial or geopolitical returns

- Defined emergency management

- Explained how the U.S. federal government is structured for emergency management

- Explained the process of and how to plan for managing emergencies

- Defined capacity and capability

- Defined vulnerability

- Defined exposure

- Explained how to communicate emergencies

KEY TERMS

All-hazards approach *304*
Benefit *288*
Capability *308*
Capacity *308*
Catastrophe *287*
Change of situation *291*
Consequence *288*
Contingency planning *300*
Correlate *288*
Cost *288*
Death frequency *292*
Disability-adjusted life year
   (DALY) *292*
Disaster *287*
Emergency *287*
Emergency management *299*
Event *287*

Exposure *312*
Fungible *292*
Gap analysis *311*
Heat map *317*
High casualty *292*
Hot spot *313*
Impact *288*
Incident *287*
Injury *292*
Issue *287*
Judgmental correlate *288*
Loss exposure *312*
Major disaster *287*
Mass casualty *292*
Mitigation *300*
Mortality rate *292*
Objective correlate *288*

Preparedness *300*
Protection *300*
Recovery *301*
Resilience *301*
Response *301*
Returns *288*
Risk ladder *314*
Risk matrix *315*
Risk radar *317*
Risk scale *314*
Scenario planning *300*
Spatial map *318*
Threat exposure *312*
Vulnerability *310*
Wound *292*

QUESTIONS AND EXERCISES

1. What is the difference between an emergency and other events?

2. Why is it important to make a distinction between returns and events?

3. What are the advantages of judgmental over objective measures of returns?

4. What are the differences between a death count, death rate, and death frequency?

5. Identify a real disaster or catastrophe. Use the Canadian government's rating of the impact on people to measure the human returns.

6. Why are DALYs useful?

7. Choose a real disaster or catastrophe and use the Canadian method for assessing its economic returns.

8. Identify an environmental disaster. Use the Canadian method to assess the environmental returns.

9. Identify a state that has experienced changes in its territorial or geopolitical control. Use the Canadian method to assess these changes.

10. Explain the consequences of FEMA's shift to an *all-hazards approach* to emergency management.

11. What is the difference between capacity and capability?

12. When would we not want to convert capacity into capability?

13. Why would an authority be mistaken to assess its preparedness by its capacity?

14. Why might capacity be distributed unfairly?

15. What is the difference between vulnerability and exposure?

16. Explain three categorical ways to assess vulnerability.

17. Practically, what could you measure to assess vulnerability and exposure of a target?

18. Explain when would you prefer to communicate risk by a scale, matrix, heat map, radar, or spatial map.

19. How might you assess any potential biases in risk matrices?

8

SITE SECURITY

On the night of November 8, 2007, two teams of armed men entered an official nuclear research center near Pelindaba, South Africa, where hundreds of kilograms of weapons-grade highly enriched uranium were being stored. The site's guards chased off one team while the other team of four armed men disabled the detection systems at the perimeter, cut through the electric fence, and proceeded to the emergency control center, where they shot a worker who raised the first alarm in the chest. The attackers fled the way they had come, with a stolen laptop computer from the control room, after they had spent 45 minutes inside the perimeter already. None of the attackers was captured or identified, although officials suspected that they had received help from an insider. South African officials publicly blamed local organized criminals, but a later leak suggests that they secretly blamed Chinese agents (Bunn, 2014, p. 174; Fitsanakis, 2015).

The Y-12 National Security Complex near Oak Ridge National Laboratory, Tennessee, is the United States' primary facility for processing and storing weapons-grade uranium and developing related technologies. On July 28, 2010, three peace activists, including an 82-year-old nun, cut the outer fence and reached a building where highly enriched uranium was stored. They splashed blood on the outer walls and revealed banners denouncing nuclear weapons before guards reached them. The site was shut down for 2 weeks during a review of security, after which several officials were dismissed or reassigned.

SCOPE AND DEFINITIONS

A **site** is a defined space. **Site security** is the security of a defined space. (This is known less accurately as **physical security**.) The North Atlantic Treaty Organization (NATO) and the U.S. Department of Defense (DOD) define *physical security* as "physical measures designed to safeguard personnel, to prevent unauthorized access to equipment, installations,

Learning Objectives and Outcomes

At the end of this chapter, you should be able to understand how to

- Manage site security
- Assess targets
- Manage access controls
- Manage passive perimeters
- Conduct surveillance and countersurveillance
- Manage security engineering

material, and documents, and to safeguard them against espionage, sabotage, damage, and theft" (NATO, 2008, p. 2-P-4; DOD, 2010, p. 191).

ASSESSING TARGETS

This section explains targets, site location, and how to evaluate the attractiveness of targets to threats.

Defining Target

A **target** is the object of a risk or plan. The **threat** is the subject whose actions cause harm to the object. In the semantic frame for *risk*, two types of object are routine: a human victim ("the individual who stands to suffer if the harm occurs") or "a valued possession of the victim" (Fillmore & Atkins, 1992, p. 82).

The North Atlantic Treaty Organization (2008) defines a *target* as "the object of a particular action, for example a geographic area, a complex, an installation, a force, equipment, an individual, a group or a system, planned for captures, exploitation, neutralization or destruction by military forces" (p. 2-T-2). The U.S. Department of Defense (2010) defines a *target* as "an entity or object that performs a function for the adversary considered for possible engagement or other action" (p. 241).

Location

Geographically or topographically, some sites face less risk or are easier to secure, such as those sites that are higher than the floodplain, remote from urban crime, or protected by intervening authorities. On the other hand, such sites may be more valuable, in which case they are more likely to attract challengers.

Sometimes a site is given without choice, but if possible, careful choices should be made about the location. The Humanitarian Practice Network (2010) notes that "site protection starts with site selection" (p. 181) and recommends sites

- with low natural risks,

- with few human hazards (such as criminals),

- with good public services or at least contractors who can provide the same,

- with positive externalities (such as nearby sites with good security capacity), and

- with natural perimeters (such as a river or street) but

- without concealed approaches (such as overgrown, dry riverbeds or dark alleyways) and

- without negative externalities (such as gathering places for protesters).

Sites can be mobile or temporary, such as when operators must set up temporary camps during emergencies or humanitarian operations. These camps tend to be close to the threat that displaced the persons in the first place, so sometimes the camps are exposed to traveling threats, such as a flood or any human threats who want to harm the displaced groups. Some operations must move camp daily for a period when threats are in pursuit or the environment is intolerably hazardous due to natural hazards, unexploded ordnance, or other factors.

Targets Attractive to Threats

In some way, targets must be attractive to threats. Sites need to be secure because of their inherent value and the value of things within them. Some sites are valuable in themselves or accommodate other things of value. For instance, even desolate land in a downtown area is valuable depending on allowable potential uses. Illegal occupancy or contamination of such land would lower its value or prevent the owners from exploiting the value, so owners are forced to take measures to control access to valuable land even when desolate.

Built structures represent sunk costs and are of systemic value to wider operations. At the same time, built structures are vulnerable to destruction by sustained vandalism, occasional arson, or explosive devices. More valuable material parts, such as copper pipes, attract thieves.

Structures accommodate valuable stores or equipment or secret or proprietary information that attracts thieves or vandals. Structures accommodate operational activities and associated personnel and thus attract threats intent on interrupting operations or punishing operators.

The activities or resources at different sites may represent critical nodes on which wider systems depend. For instance, a production site likely depends on a logistics site, a power supply, the residences where personnel live away from work, the transport vehicles that carry supplies to consumers and users or carry personnel from residences to offices, and the infrastructure on which transport vehicles travel.

We could assess the demand side by asking what sort of targets the threat demands. For instance, certain criminals target certain types of people, such as the more accessible, vulnerable, wealthy, different, or provocative types (from the threat's perspective). For rare threats like terrorists, we could review their rhetorical threats (as contained in the threat's speeches and policy statements). We could even measure the threat's focus on a particular target by measuring the proportion of this content that is focused on one target relative to other targets. This would be a more objective measure than simply asking people for their judgments of whether the group is a threat. An objective measure is useful because it might contradict or confirm our judgments.

Relating to the threat's demand for targets, we should measure the supply of such targets in an area of concern (sometimes called the **attractor terrain**). For instance, if we were concerned about potential targets for political terrorists, we could count the number of political representatives for the area or the value or size of official sites. If we were concerned about the potential targets for religious terrorists, we could count the number of religious sites in the area.

Authorities often seek to measure the scale or value of a socioeconomy in an area as a measure of all targets, although such a measure would capture the vulnerability, exposure, and capacity to respond to a threat, not just attractor terrain. A separate suggestion for measuring the potential targets of terrorism is to measure population, socioeconomic development (demographic characteristics, labor force demands, education, health services, production, and income), city development, and net trade (exports less imports) (Rusnak, Kennedy, Eldivan, & Caplan, 2012,

p. 170). These sorts of measures could be combined mathematically in a single quotient (see Figure 8.1 for an example).

Figure 8.1 A Formula for Target Risk (T_{iv}) Using Simple Measures of Exposure and Threat

$$T_{iv} = (T_i / T_v) / ((^N\Sigma_{=1} T_I) / (^N\Sigma_{n=1} T_V))$$

n = individual target area

N = total area

T_v = value of target area

T_V = value of total area

T_i = crime incidents per target area

T_I = crime incidents across total area

Source: Based on Rusnak et al. (2012, p. 169).

A useful categorical list of criteria by which a terrorist could select a target includes eight categories, remembered by the mnemonic EVIL DONE.

1. Exposed

2. Vital

3. Iconic

4. Legitimate

5. Destructible

6. Occupied

7. Near

8. Easy (Clarke & Newman, 2006)

Given the resources, we should research the particular threat's intent and capability in relation to particular targets. Consider the simple, notional scenario below, which I will present as a series of logical steps in analysis.

1. Terrorist group *T* has the intent to harm our organization.

2. Terrorist group *T* is based near our organization's site *S*. Thus, we should consider that site *S* is exposed to *T*.

3. Terrorist group *T* currently does not have the capabilities to penetrate the defenses of site *S*, so *S* is exposed, but the 100 employees within are not vulnerable.

4. If terrorists were to discover attack method *M*, the defenses at site *S* would fail, and all 100 employees would be vulnerable.

Terrorists often pretend to live by political ideals but are more likely to attack private rather than official targets due to the exposure of private targets. From 1970 to 2008, 40% of terrorist attacks struck private citizens and property (22%), businesses (16%), or the news media (2%); another 17% of terrorist attacks struck transport, utilities, educational institutions, and religious or other mass sites; 43% of terrorist attacks struck national government (14%), military (14%), police (12%), or diplomatic (3%) sites (Global Terrorism Database). In the last decade, attacks on private citizens and property have increased in absolute and proportional terms.

ACCESS CONTROLS

The section explains how to control access to a site. The subsections below cover the scope of such controls, assessments of access controls, known bypasses of access controls, guards, emergency services and quick-reaction forces, gates, and emergency refuges.

Scope

Access controls are attempts to manage the entry of actors or agents into some domain, for instance, by demanding identification of permitted persons before entry into a building. Most physical security and crime prevention within a site depends on preventing unauthorized access or use. Access controls also can be used to prevent unauthorized persons or items from leaving. Most thefts from sites seem to be by authorized users of the site, not unauthorized visitors. In case a visitor commits a crime while on site, a controlled exit gives an opportunity to at least record information about the time of exit that would be useful to the investigation.

Analytically, all access controls are attempts to control exposure. Perimeter barriers include walls, fences, or ditches that restrict access from the outside to the inside. The perimeter has points of controlled access where the visitor must negotiate a human guard, lock, or identity check before access. If these access controls were to work perfectly in preventing all threats from access to the inside, nothing on the inside would be exposed to threats unless it were to leave the perimeter. Thus, given perfect access controls, only the perimeter and any assets on or outside the perimeter would need to be defended. Good access controls are more efficient than whole-of-site invulnerability.

The U.S. DOD (2012b) defines *access control* as "any combination of barriers, gates, electronic security equipment, and/or guards that can limit entry or parking of unauthorized personnel or vehicles" (p. 42). "At a minimum, access control at a controlled perimeter requires the demonstrated capability to search for and detect explosives" (p. 43).

Assessing Access Controls

In assessing our site security, we should judge exposure, vulnerability, and resilience. Exposure can be measured as the inverse of the effectiveness of controls on a threat's access to the interior while bearing in mind that security comes at the expense of convenience. We could measure vulnerability by judging how prepared we are to defend against the threat. We should measure resilience by judging our capacity to control the negative returns of any attack and to operate despite an attack.

Table 8.1 shows a published attempt to judge a site's exposure (as access) and the site's controls on the returns of any attack.

Friendly personnel can be employed to pretend to be threats in order to test the access controls. The ultimate test of the controls is a real unauthorized attempt at access, but the ultimate compliment to good access controls is that nobody attempts unauthorized access.

Table 8.1   A Scheme for Judging Exposure in Terms of Access Controls and Controls on the Returns

Score	Exposure		Resilience
	Access to Certified Personnel or to Positions Where Attacks Can Be Carried Out	Screening, Surveillance, or Inspections to Detect Attacks	Engineering Controls on Attack Consequences
1 (low)	Limited	Invasive	No controls
2	Limited	Invasive	No controls
3	Controlled	Semi-invasive	No controls
4	Controlled	Noninvasive	Limit consequences
5 (high)	Free	None	Prevent consequences

Source: Based on Greenberg, Chalk, Willis, Khilko, and Ortiz (2006).

BYPASSES OF ACCESS CONTROLS

Unfortunately, access controls are not perfect, and they can be bypassed. Technology or human guards could fail, allowing access to the wrong people or simply not detecting whomever should not be allowed. Malicious actors could develop fake identifications that fool guards or electronic readers. For instance, in February 2013, Pakistani immigration authorities detained three persons who admitted that they had purchased their diplomatic passports from officials for 2 million rupees each. Pakistani investigators believe that between July 2010 and February 2013, corrupt officials illegally sold at least 2,000 diplomatic passports.

Disguises could fool guards into neglecting access controls. For instance, insurgents in Iraq and Afghanistan often wear police or military uniforms during attacks on official sites. For instance, on September 14, 2012, a carefully prepared attack by Taliban insurgents on Camp Bastion in Afghanistan culminated with a penetration of the perimeter by attackers on foot wearing U.S.

military uniforms. On June 25, 2013, four Taliban suicide bombers drove inside the perimeter of the presidential palace in Kabul in vehicles similar to those used by coalition forces, with coalition uniforms, fake badges, and vehicle passes. They were able to bluff their way past two security checkpoints before guards stopped them, and they killed themselves and three guards.

Relatives have been known to share identifications in order to fool access controls after one relative has been denied access or freedom to travel. Unfortunately, some malicious actors have abused exceptions to access controls granted on religious or cultural grounds. For instance, at least one of the attempted suicide bombers on the London underground train system on July 21, 2005, escaped from London to Birmingham in a **burqa** (a full body covering), although he was soon arrested there. Sometime in the last days of 2005, one of the murderers of a policewoman fled Britain in a **niqab** (face veil) with his sister's passport to Somalia (although 2 years later he was extradited from there). On December 30, 2012, a non-Muslim British woman wore a niqab as a disguise in a shopping center before throwing acid in the face of a former friend. On September 14, 2011, armed insurgents dressed in burqas occupied an unfinished high-rise building from where they fired on the U.S. embassy in Kabul, Afghanistan. Some of the armed men who attacked the Westgate Premier Shopping Mall in Nairobi, Kenya, on September 21, 2013, had entered in burqas.

Guards might be too lazy or disgruntled to enforce compliance with the access controls or could be bribed by material incentives or seduced by ideological appeals. Guards who help outsiders are examples of **insider threats** (people inside the site who are threats to the site). For instance, from November 2009 to August 2011, a U.S. citizen with top-secret security clearance was employed as a contracted guard at the U.S. consulate in Guangzhou, China, which had been completed only in 2011 at a cost of $1.5 billion. In August 2012, he pled guilty to conspiracy to sell access to Chinese officials so that they could plant surveillance devices.

Many guards have been bribed to allow items or persons access for smuggling purposes and have justified their actions as harmless. However, they may not realize that they could be allowing in weapons intended for use against the site and even its guards.

Malicious actors can bypass access controls by finding less controlled routes. For instance, on November 26, 2008, armed terrorists landed in Mumbai by small boats rather than use public transport. They went on to murder more than 160 people, including many on public transport and roads. Similarly, private boats are regularly used to smuggle drugs and people past the strict access controls into the United States from Mexico to the Californian coast.

Private planes can be used to bypass the much more robust controls on access into and out of airports via commercial aircraft. Private planes have been used not only to smuggle cargo but also as weapons that can bypass controls on weapons. For instance, on January 5, 2002, a 15-year-old boy flew a stolen light plane into a Bank of America building in Tampa, Florida, killing himself and leaving a note supporting the 9/11 attacks. On February 18, 2010, an American man flew a private plane into an Internal Revenue Service office in Austin, Texas, killing himself and one other person.

Unmanned aerial vehicles (UAVs) are more available than manned aircraft, although their carrying capacity and operating range are usually much inferior. The operation of UAVs is normally subject to stricter domestic controls, but violations are more difficult to observe because of their small size and ease of operation from the ground. The smallest radio-controlled model aircraft can seem like harmless toys to the operator, but they are hazardous to persons, other vehicles, overhead electrical power cables, and other infrastructure.

Regulatory authorities are trying both to loosen restrictions on less hazardous economically useful and socially useful operation of UAVs while investing more in enforcement of current restrictions on hazardous uses. For instance, in April 2014, Britain's Civil Aviation Authority completed its first criminal prosecution of a person for flying a UAV within 50 m of a structure and within restricted airspace. The guilty man's model aircraft had flown low over a heavily trafficked bridge near a nuclear submarine base in Barrow-in-Furness. Its on-board camera recorded video footage that proved crucial in the prosecution.

UAVs have been used to gather intelligence on or protest against sensitive sites. For instance, on October 30, 2014, the French interior minister announced a judicial investigation into reports that UAVs had flown into the restricted air space over seven nuclear power plants in France that month (Labbe & Rose, 2014).

Additionally, terrorists have considered using UAVs to carry weapons or as guided missiles. For instance, in September 2011, FBI agents arrested Rezwan Ferdaus (then aged 26 years) for a plot to attack targets in Washington, DC, with various weapons, including model aircraft packed with explosives, although these were developed under the partial control of agents posing as coconspirators. In November 2012, he was sentenced to 17 years in prison.

GUARDS

Guards are the personnel tasked with controlling access. Guards, at least those working around the perimeter, are more exposed than are personnel within the perimeter, so guards need different capabilities. Consequently, the guards could be justifiably equipped with arms and armor against the threats while the personnel on the inside would not need the same equipment so long as the access controls work perfectly.

Resources and laws often restrict the capabilities that can be acquired, carried, and used, and any acquisition implies additional training and liabilities. Portable arms include sticks or batons, irritant chemical sprays, weapons that discharge an electrical charge, and handguns. Attacks dogs are common alternatives to carried weapons. Portable defensive technologies include vests and helmets made with materials resistant to kinetic attack. Cheap personal-barrier protections against communicable diseases and toxic materials include latex or rubber gloves and facemasks. Kinetic-resistant materials would be required against sharp materials. Fire-resistant materials are required against incendiary devices. Short sticks are useful for inspecting the contents of bags and vehicles. Extended mirrors are useful for viewing the underside and interior compartments of vehicles. Systems for inspecting other personnel include magnetic metal detectors, chemical-explosive detectors, and explosives detection dogs.

Good access controls do not necessarily deter malicious actors with strong intent but at least keep the attacks on the perimeter. A successful control on access prevents exposure of the interior and its assets and persons. However, other assets or persons must expose themselves to the threat in order to perform the control. So long as the guards are performing their role, the guards are more exposed but less vulnerable; the personnel on the inside are more vulnerable but less exposed. For instance, on April 16, 2010, a Republican terrorist group forced a taxi driver to drive a vehicle with an explosive device up to the gate of a British military base (Palace Barracks in Holywood,

Northern Ireland), where it detonated, causing considerable destruction and few injuries around the gate, fortunately without killing anyone.

The perimeter's controllers remain exposed so long as they continue to control access (and do not run away). Consequently, most guards are harmed while preventing unauthorized access. For instance, on August 15, 2012, an unarmed guard was shot in the left forearm while apprehending an armed man attempting to enter the Family Research Council in Washington, DC, with admitted intent to kill as many staff as possible. On February 1, 2013, a suicide bomber detonated inside a built access point for staff of the U.S. Embassy in Ankara, Turkey, killing himself and a Turkish guard but nobody inside the perimeter.

Unfortunately, absent perfect diligence during the procurement of guards and perfect leadership of guards, some guards tend toward inattention or even noncompliance, sometimes for corrupt reasons. For instance, all of us have probably experienced a guard who did not pay proper attention to our credentials before permitting our access. More alarmingly, some smuggling is known to occur via airport personnel who take bribes in return for placing items in aircraft without the normal controls. The human parts of the countersurveillance system need careful monitoring and review. Consequently, much of day-to-day physical security management can seem more like personnel management and leadership.

> Too often, however, guards are ineffective because they are untrained, poorly instructed, poorly paid, poorly equipped and poorly managed. It is not uncommon to find a bed in the guardhouse of aid agency compounds, virtually guaranteeing that the guard will fall asleep on duty. During the day guards might be busy doing other things, and may be distracted. When hiring guards, provide clear terms of reference and make these part of the contract. (Humanitarian Practice Network, 2010, p. 188)

Guards are hazards in the sense that they could become threats, perhaps activated with the weapons and the access provided to them for their work, perhaps colluding with external threats. In theory, properly vetted guards are trustworthy guards, but vetting is imperfect and should include periodic monitoring in case the initial conditions change. Responses to distrust of guards should include banning the guards from the interior of the perimeter, close supervision, random inspections, and covert surveillance of their activities, perhaps including their activities while off duty.

Site managers might reject local guards as untrustworthy or just for difficulties of linguistic or cultural translation. Multinational private-security providers proliferated during the rapid growth in demand in the 2000s, particularly in Iraq. Providers might not have any loyalties to local threats and might boast impressive prior military experience, but they might also offer new negative risks arising from insensitivity to local culture and a heavy military posture (see Box 8.1).

EMERGENCY SERVICES AND QUICK-REACTION FORCES

Most sites rely on police and other public security personnel as their ultimate guards. In fact, most private actors have no guards of their own and rely entirely on public services, good neighbors, or their own resources for protection. Private actors with their own guards must make choices

BOX 8.1

The U.S. Diplomatic Mission in Benghazi, 2012

Local security personnel are usually cheaper and more available than foreign personnel, but their effectiveness might not justify their cheapness. For instance, in 2012, the U.S. mission in Benghazi, Libya, had agreed that a local militia (the 17th February Martyrs Brigade) would provide guards and a quick-reaction force.

Although the February 17 militia had proven effective in responding to improvised explosive device (IED) attacks on the Special Mission in April and June 2012, there were some troubling indicators of its reliability in the months and weeks preceding the September

attacks. At the time of Ambassador Stevens' visit, February 17 militia members had stopped accompanying Special Mission vehicle movements in protest over salary and working hours. (Accountability Review Board for Benghazi, 2012, p. 5)

By further request, dated September 9, 2012, the mission requested three members of the quick-reaction force to reinforce the guards on site. However, during the attack of September 11, the guards fled and the militia did not reinforce, after which the invaders killed the ambassador and three others.

about when to involve public authorities. For instance, if guards repeatedly disturb actors trying to enter a perimeter without authorization, the guards could ask the police to temporarily increase the frequency of their visits to that perimeter. Unless the area is exceedingly corrupt or unstable, if external actors commit any crimes, the guards should call in judicial authorities. Consequently, site security managers should liaise with public authorities, and public authorities should cooperate in site security.

In addition to temporary increases in the number of guards, we should consider allocating personnel to respond to an emergency. In military terminology, such a force is often termed a **quick-reaction force**. (A quick-reaction force is sometimes categorized as threat interdiction rather than an access control but is usefully discussed here.) In areas with functioning public governance, public security personnel act as the final force in response to any emergency that the site's own guards cannot handle. In areas without reliable local security forces, the site would be forced to arrange for its own quick-reaction force. For instance, an embassy, as sovereign territory, may deploy any personnel and weapons it wants within its perimeter, but most embassies reach formal agreements with local authorities for local security forces to respond to emergencies at the embassy. In case local authorities fail in their duties, other personnel are prepared to deploy to the aid of diplomatic missions or posts in need. In areas where local security forces are unreliable, diplomatic missions from different countries might reach agreements on mutual aid during an emergency.

GATES

Gates are the switchable barriers at the access control point. Gates are active barriers in the sense that they can switch between open and closed. By default (at least during higher risk periods), gates should be closed; if a visitor is permitted entry, the gate would be opened. This seems like an obvious prescription, but consider that gates are often left open because of complaints about disruption to traffic or simple laziness on the part of the guards rather than because the risk level justifies the gate being left open.

The subsections below consider portable, antivehicle, multiple, and containment gates.

Portable Gates

In an emergency, a **portable gate** can be formed with available portable materials such as rocks, drums, or trestles that can be moved by the guards. Vehicles and human chains can be used as gates, but these are valuable assets to expose. Sometimes gates are extremely portable, such as cable or rope, which are adequate for indicating an access control but are not substantial enough to stop a noncompliant visitor. More repellent but still portable materials include barbed wire and razor wire mounted on sticks that the guards can handle without harm.

Sometimes, when the risk is sufficiently elevated or guards or gate materials are short, the sites of access are closed and perhaps reinforced with more substantial materials, in which case they act effectively as passive barriers (see the section below).

Vehicle Gates

Separate to pedestrian gates, your site might need **vehicle gates** that can control vehicles. In prepared sites, gates normally consist of barriers that can be raised and lowered or swung out of the way on hinges or that slide on rails. More substantial barriers to vehicles could be formed by filling drums or boxes with earth, rocks, or concrete while keeping the item light and handy enough to be removed whenever the guards permit. As portable vehicle barriers, guards could deploy spikes. A caltrop is easily improvised with four spikes so that at least one spike presents upward however it falls; some systems consist of a belt of spikes that collapses into an easy package when not needed. One-way exits can be created with spikes that are hinged to fall away when a vehicle exits but to present if a vehicle attempts to enter. These spikes would disable most pneumatic tires, but some vehicles have solid tires, pneumatic tires with solid cores, or pneumatic tires designed to deflate gracefully, permitting the vehicle to run for some distance (more than enough distance for a suicidal driver to reach any target within a typical perimeter). More substantial vehicle gates consist of bollards or plates that are raised in front of the visiting vehicle and are retracted when permitted.

Multiple Gates

Some access control points must include **multiple gates**—several gates or gates with controls on more than one type of threat. For instance, a gate might be specified to be robust enough at a low height to stop an energetic vehicle from crashing through but also tall enough to discourage a pedestrian from climbing over the gate. Sometimes gates are placed in series so that the visitor must negotiate one gate successfully before the visitor is permitted entry through the next gate (see Box 8.2). The traffic is sometimes slowed by passive barriers, such as bumps in the road or fixed vertical barriers staggered across the road, which the vehicle must negotiate at a slow speed; these passive barriers slow traffic in case guards need time to close a gate or take offensive action against the driver. However, such measures add costs and inconvenience, so they may not be justified when the risks are low.

Containment Areas

Sometimes designers must consider a **containment area** within which visitors of all types can be contained before further access is permitted. Containment areas should be established in the areas between where people, supplies, and mail arrive and where they are accepted inside the perimeter. Supplies often arrive in large packages that could contain hidden threats; the smallest mailed packages could contain hazardous powders or sharp materials. Moreover, these items usually are transported within large vehicles that themselves could contain threats. For security reasons, delivery areas should be remote from the interior, but for commercial reasons, the delivery area should be close to the point of demand. An attractive compromise is a dedicated area for deliveries, close to but outside the perimeter so that vehicles can make their deliveries without the delays and transaction costs associated with accessing the interior. The delivery or unloading area should be a contained area in which items can be inspected for threats before allowance into another area where they can be sorted and labeled for their final destination within the perimeter. The interface between the contained delivery area and the main sorting space should be strengthened against blast or forced human entry and provided with access controls. For small, quiet sites, perhaps a single room would be sufficient for storage of deliveries at peak frequency.

EMERGENCY REFUGES

Within the perimeter, the site security manager could construct a further controlled area as an **emergency refuge** from threats that breach the perimeter. Such areas are sometimes called **refuges**, **citadels**, **safe havens**, **panic rooms**, or **safe rooms**. They are differentiated by extra controls on access, fewer access points, and access points that are controlled solely from within.

Some safe areas are supplied in prefabricated form, the size of a standard shipping container for quick and easy delivery to the user.

U.S. Man-Traps

The December 6, 2004, attack on the U.S. consulate in Jeddah, Saudi Arabia, provides a specific example of how Diplomatic Security adjusts its security procedures. According to State, the attackers gained entry into the U.S. consulate by running through the vehicle access gate. While Diplomatic Security had installed a device to force vehicles to stop for inspection before entering a compound, it did not prevent the attackers from entering the compound by foot once the barrier was lowered. To correct that vulnerability, Diplomatic Security has incorporated "**man-traps**" in conjunction with the vehicle barriers at vehicle entry points at most high and critical threat posts, whereby, when the barrier is lowered, the vehicle enters a **holding pen**, or "man-trap," for inspection before a second barrier in front of the vehicle opens into the compound. (U.S. Government Accountability Office [GAO], 2009b, pp. 13–14)

BOX 8.2

In theory, a safe area could be constructed anywhere with normally available construction materials to a standard that would disallow entry to anybody unless equipped with substantial military-grade explosives.

> It should be easily and quickly accessible, and preferably located in the core of the building. Alternatively, an upper floor can be converted into a safe area by installing a grill on the staircase, which is locked at night. Safe rooms should have a reinforced door, a telephone or other means of communication (preferably un-interruptable [from outside]) in order to call for help, and a list of key contact numbers, plus a torch or candles and matches. Consider storing a small quantity of water, food and sanitary items in the safe room as well. The purpose of a safe room is to protect people, not assets. Putting everything in the safe room is only likely to encourage robbers to make greater efforts to break in. Leave them something to steal, if not everything. (Humanitarian Practice Network, 2010, p. 187)

Structures could be built proof against the largest aircraft-delivered explosives and radiological, chemical, and biological threats, but they would become very expensive and are not typical of safe areas. Consequently, most safe areas should be regarded as truly short-term emergency solutions to an invasion of the perimeter pending rescue from outside the site.

However, such structures are vulnerable to any outside restriction of supplies of air, water, or food unless the protected area is equipped with substantial reserves of water and food and is sealed. Outside air could be filtered and conditioned by a system that also produces a slight air overpressure inside the structure. Absent such equipment, fire and smoke are easy weapons for outside threats to use against those trapped within a safe area. Even if the safe area itself is not flammable, the occupants could be suffocated or poisoned by smoke from burning materials placed against the safe area's apertures or vents. For instance, on September 11, 2012, U.S. Ambassador Chris Stevens was killed by smoke inhalation inside the safe room at the diplomatic site in Benghazi, Libya. Consequently, a system for filtering incoming air, with baffles to ingress of threats (such as grenades), and for generating an overpressure of air inside the structure (in combination with hermetic seals on all apertures) now seems required. Such a system became standard in military fortifications around World War II and is not prohibitively expensive.

PASSIVE PERIMETERS

This section defines passive perimeters and describes the material barriers, human patrols and surveillance, and sensors.

Scope

The **perimeter** is the outer boundary of a site. The perimeter is controlled more passively than the access points, usually in the sense that passivity implies less human interaction and more material barriers. Passive perimeters can be designed to block vehicles, persons, and animals (rogue and diseased animals are more common in unstable areas) and can be equipped with sensors that alert guards to any attempt to pass the barrier.

Material Barriers

Material barriers do not necessarily involve humans but are composed of other materials. Natural barriers include dense or thorny vegetation, rivers, lakes, oceans, mud, and steep ground. Even a wide expanse of inhospitable terrain can be considered a barrier. Indeed, most international borders have no barriers other than natural barriers.

Discrete artificial barriers include ditches, fences, walls, stakes, wire, and stacked sandbags, rocks, or earth. Artificial barriers include more deliberate weapons, such as sharpened stakes, metal spikes, broken glass, hidden holes, landmines, and even toxic pollutants, biological hazards, and pathogens.

The U.S. DOD (2008b) prescribes a chain-link fence of 2.75 in. diameter cables, taller than the average man, with barbed-wire strands at the top as a barrier against pedestrians. As barriers against vehicles, it prescribes either

- concrete bollards (no more than 4-ft apart, each 3-ft above ground and 4-ft below ground in a concrete foundation, each consisting of 8-in. diameter of concrete poured inside a steel pipe 0.5-in. thick) or

- a continuous concrete planter (3-ft above ground, 1.5-ft below ground, 3-ft wide at base, with a trough at the top for planting vegetation as disguise or beautification). (pp. 4-7–4-9)

Human Patrols and Surveillance

Barriers are passive if they imply no necessary human in the system (once they have been constructed), but guards are still important to the prevention of any breach of the barrier. No barrier can perfectly prevent access, but a guard could prevent someone cutting through, climbing over, tunneling under, or otherwise passing a barrier. Thus, barriers should not be considered entirely inanimate controls and should be used with periodic human patrols and inspections.

Human patrols may vary with the risk level. For instance, the U.S. Department of State has prescribed varying perimeter patrols according to threat level (see Table 8.2).

Humans can guard perimeters on foot or from towers overlooking the perimeter. Towers imply more oversight but also a more sedentary posture on the part of the guards, so a good policy is to rotate guards between towers and ground duties. Towers also encourage some authorities to unwarranted reductions in personnel. For instance, on September 14 and 15, 2012, the Taliban penetrated the perimeter of Camp Bastion near an unmanned tower. Thirteen of the camp's 24 towers were unmanned despite at least 21 penetrations of the fence over the previous 2 years, including at least one occupation of a guard tower. Since the attack, all the towers were manned (U.K. House of Commons, Defence Committee, 2014, pp. 3, 11–13).

Surveillance technologies can help to extend the scope of the guard's control of the perimeter, as described in the next section.

Table 8.2   The U.S. Department of State's Prescribed Changes in Perimeter Patrol Requirements by Threat Level

Threat Level	Perimeter Patrol Requirements
Critical	24-hr foot patrol at official facilities and residences for the ambassador, deputy chief of mission, principal officers, and Marines. Guards are to be armed unless prohibited by law.
High	24-hr foot patrol at official facilities and residences for the ambassador, deputy chief of mission, principal officers, and Marines.
Medium	12-hr foot patrol of perimeter during the day and at residences at night, where required, to supplement host-country support at official facilities.
Low	No provision for foot patrol of official facilities' perimeters.

Source: U.S. Department of State (2006).

SURVEILLANCE AND COUNTERSURVEILLANCE

This section describes the scope of surveillance, the practice of countersurveillance at a site, surveillance technologies in general, surveillance of communications, and surveillance in poor light.

Surveillance

Surveillance is systematic observation of something. Surveillance is an activity open to both malicious actors and guards. Malicious actors often survey potential targets before choosing a target, then survey the target in order to plan an attack, and survey the target again in order to train the attackers. In turn, guards should be looking to counter such surveillance.

For the U.S. DOD (2010), surveillance is "the "systematic observation of aerospace, surface, or subsurface areas, places, persons, or things, by visual, aural, electronic, photographic, or other means" (p. 456).

Countersurveillance

Countersurveillance is "watching whether you are being watched" (Humanitarian Practice Network, 2010, p. xvi). Energetic guards, by discouraging loitering or suspicious investigation of the site's defenses, can disrupt malicious surveillance before an attack can be planned. For instance, in March 1999, the U.S. State Department's Bureau of Diplomatic Security introduced the concept of "surveillance-detection teams" at most diplomatic posts. These teams look for terrorist surveillance of diplomatic sites and operations (U.S. GAO, 2009b, p. 13).

Also, surveillance can be useful to the investigation after an attack. Television cameras that record images of a site are less deterrent than guards but more useful for investigators because their images are usually more accurate than human memories and more persuasive as evidence during criminal prosecutions.

Be careful not to underestimate the audacity of threats to the most secure sites. For instance, in September 2010, British officials ordered trees to be cut down around the headquarters of the British Security Service (MI5) in Northern Ireland, inside Palace Barracks, a secure military site. Four surveillance cameras were found hidden among the tree branches. On September 26, 2012, Irish police arrested two men suspected of spying on the operational headquarters of the Irish police (Garda Síochána) in Dublin. One of the suspects was recognized as a known member of the Real Irish Republican Army, a terrorist group, by police officers passing through the hotel opposite the headquarters. Police officers searched the suspect's hotel room, where they found parabolic microphones and digital cameras.

The Humanitarian Practice Network (2010) describes five steps in the typical attack on a site:

1. Initial target selection

2. Preattack surveillance

3. Planning the attack

4. Rehearsing the attack

5. Executing the attack (p. 194)

It recommends the following five countersurveillance activities:

1. Identify likely observation posts and point them out to staff

2. Instruct guards to patrol the potential observation points

3. Instruct staff to look out for behaviors that indicate external surveillance, such as loitering or frequent passes by the same vehicle or person

4. Build relationships with neighbors and ask them to report suspicious behavior

5. Vary routines and routes into and out of the site (pp. 194–195)

Surveillance Technologies

Surveillance technologies are the technologies that assist people with surveillance. They can be as simple as binoculars or even the optical sights on weapons (although the latter can be provocative). Remote television cameras allow guards to more efficiently and securely watch sites. Radar devices can be used to track vehicles out of visual range. Range finders can be used to measure the ranges of targets within line of sight. (Range finders can be as simple as handheld prismatic or laser-based instruments.) Unmanned aerial vehicles (UAVs) can be launched to film targets further away. Earth-orbiting satellites can take images more routinely, although from higher up.

Most of these technologies are available in cheap and portable forms for the poorly resourced user or for temporary sites. A small robotic camera, a remote-control interface, and display screen can be packaged inside a briefcase. Radar devices can be packaged inside something the size of standard luggage yet still offer a range over miles. Prismatic range finders are cheap and satisfactory for most uses short of long-range gunnery; laser range finders are more accurate. UAVs, too, can be small enough to be carried and launched from one hand. Commercial satellites can provide images that can be printed or stored digitally in a handheld form.

Passive barriers can be made more active if equipped with sensors, such as video cameras (see Box 8.4), trip wires, or lasers that detect movement or infrared or thermal sensors that detect body heat, although motion or heat sensors can be triggered by false positives such as harmless animals. Still, a guard dog is the best combined sensor/nonlethal weapon available to the human guard on foot.

Surveillance of Communications

Scanning for two-way radio traffic near a site makes sense because the short-range of such traffic and the lack of a service provider implies irregular motivations. Organized actors often use two-way radio communications during surveillance and attacks; cheap and portable scanners can search likely bandwidths for traffic, although a linguist would be required to translate foreign languages. However, the threats could use coded signals to defeat even a linguist.

Scanning for private telephone traffic is technically possible but is more legally restricted and implies more false positives. An organization usually faces few restrictions on tapping the e-mail systems, telephones, and radios that the organization itself provides to employees or contractors. In fact, organizations often secretly intercept employee e-mails in search of noncompliant behaviors. Judicial authorities with probable cause can seek legal powers to seize any communications device.

Malicious actors can avoid such observation by avoiding the organization's communications systems. Indeed, terrorists now routinely use temporary e-mail accounts, unsent draft messages with shared access, temporary cell/mobile telephones, text messages that are deleted after one reading, coded signals, and verbal messages to avoid surveillance of their communications.

Surveillance in Poor Light

In poor light conditions (nighttime, dust storms, cloudy weather), observers can turn to artificial sources of light for illumination, such as electric lamps. Indeed, **artificial light** is considered a key technology in countering nighttime crime in urban areas. The perimeters of sites, or at least the access points, are often artificially lit. Access points should be lit artificially and guards should carry battery-powered lamps.

Infrared filters block visible light but permit infrared radiation, which occupies a range neighboring the visible-light range, so artificial lights with infrared filters (**infrared lights**) can be used to illuminate targets without the target being aware (unless the target were equipped with infrared sights). Passive infrared sights (available since the 1950s) rely heavily on active infrared

BOX 8.4

Closed-Circuit Television

Closed-circuit television (CCTV) essentially refers to cameras that transmit images electronically to some remote monitor. (The term was developed as a distinction from television that is broadcast on an open network.) CCTV cameras remain attractive for material reasons despite their limitations. Cameras are much cheaper than human employees. Juries often prefer camera-captured images as evidence over human testimony, and studies show that human witnesses are often mistaken when they claim to identify others as the perpetrators. However, their use can be challenged on ethical, legal, and effectiveness grounds.

Britain is often given as the country with the most CCTV units deployed, most of them deployed since the mid-1980s in response to urban crime and terrorism. By the early 2000s, Britain had more than 4 million cameras, and by 2007, it had more than 25% of the world's CCTV cameras. Ten thousand had been installed in London alone. Certain parts of the United States boast similar densities. For instance, more than 500 had been installed in Times Square, New York City, by 2007.

Cameras deter some crime, and their images can be used as evidence of crime during the investigation or prosecution of criminals. However, most cameras have narrow fields of view and poor resolution. Some cameras are dummies, some are not operable some of the time, and some recorded images are not saved up to the time when investigators realize that they are needed. Most cameras are passive, although some cameras can be controlled remotely, and a few can even react automatically to certain target behaviors (such as the erratic circular walking as the criminal ponders the target). Criminals would not be deterred if they knew how to avoid cameras or hide their identity or realized that not all cameras are recording effectively. Even perfect images of criminals do not necessarily lead to the identification of a criminal. Evidence from Britain suggests that only 20% of the crimes captured on CCTV actually lead to an arrest. In Britain, CCTV cameras are installed in almost every public space, but some evidence suggests that cameras abate crimes only inside mass car-parking structures. Meanwhile, law-abiding citizens are increasingly concerned about privacy violations via cameras (Kennedy & Gibbs Van Brunschot, 2009, pp. 14–19).

illumination (usually from electrically powered infrared searchlights), which, in turn, is easily detected by passive infrared sights. Infrared images are higher in resolution than thermal and intensified visible-light images, although infrared images are monochrome. Infrared systems also remain much cheaper than those later alternatives.

Like infrared sights, **thermal imagers** (deployed since the 1970s) detect radiation in the infrared range of the electromagnetic spectrum. Thermal imagers focus on the narrower range associated with temperature and do not rely on active illumination. As long as the target's temperature is sufficiently distinct from background temperature and is not obscured by dampening materials, it can be distinguished through a thermal imager.

However, thermal images are not as high in resolution as actively illuminated infrared images. Moreover, thermal signatures can be dampened. Intervening materials can totally obscure the thermal signature, so targets can hide from enemy thermal imagers in much the same ways they hide from illumination by visible light (i.e., behind structures, forested or urban areas, inclement weather, or the appropriate type of smoke). Since glass and transparent plastic materials permit visible light but not infrared radiation, targets can use these materials to obscure themselves from thermal imagers without obscuring visible light. Human beings give off an easily detectable infrared signature in the open but can hide behind hotter objects or nonconductive materials. Automotive engines are hotter than humans, but engine compartments can be dampened and will equalize with background temperatures within 30 minutes or so of turning off the engine (and parking outside of sunlight).

Thermal imagers can see through light fog and rain but are confused by thick fog (whose water droplets refract light in unpredictable ways). They can see through most types of battlefield smoke, but modern forces can lay smoke that is chemically configured to obscure infrared signatures.

The lenses of thermal imagers are expensive and easily damaged by a fingernail, dust, or sand, so they are normally covered by a protective cover when not in use, unlike a cheap, robust, and always-available infrared filter. Like image intensifiers, thermal imagers are easily dazzled by laser weapons. Some cheap handheld laser pointers are sufficiently powerful to dazzle thermal imagers from a range of about 1 mile.

Image intensifiers (deployed since the 1980s) are vacuum tube–based devices that intensify visible light. Like thermal imagers, they are less reliant than are infrared sights on active illumination, but they are expensive (most are confined to major military platforms) and can be disabled by pulse lasers.

SECURITY ENGINEERING

Built structures accommodate people, stores, equipment, and operational activities and are part of the material protective system at a site. The design and construction of buildings and other structures to be more secure is a technical area sometimes termed **security engineering**.

The subsections below describe how to materially protect the site by setback or standoff construction, blast barriers, barriers to kinetic attack, and protective glass.

Setback or Standoff

The most effective way to materially improve invulnerability within the perimeter is to increase the **setback** or **standoff**—meaning the distance between the perimeter and the site's assets, such as the buildings, although this ideal is often retarded by urban constraints, material limitations, or desires for accessibility.

The effectiveness of setback can be appreciated from the many recent attacks on sites using substantial explosive devices outside the perimeter without killing anyone inside the perimeter (such as the van bomb that detonated on the road outside the military headquarters in Damascus, Syria, on September 25, 2012) compared to similar devices that penetrated the target building in the days of lax attention to setback. (On October 23, 1983, a suicidal vehicle-borne explosive device exploded inside the lobby of the U.S. Marine Corps barracks in Beirut, killing 242.)

The standoff distance can be engineered simply with winding access routes or access controls along the access route. Passive barriers can be used to increase this standoff distance. Passive barriers to vehicles can be as unobtrusive as raised planters for trees or benches, as long as they are substantial enough to defeat moving vehicles. Setback can be achieved urgently by closing roads outside the perimeter. For instance, after Egyptian protesters invaded the U.S. embassy in Cairo on September 11, 2012, Egyptian authorities stacked large concrete blocks across the ends of the street.

The U.S. DOD (2012b) recommends at least 5.5 m (18 ft) between structures and a controlled perimeter or any uncontrolled vehicular roadways or parking areas or 3.6 m (12 ft) between structures and vehicular roadways and parking within a controlled perimeter. Reinforced-concrete load-bearing walls can stand as little as 4 m (13 ft) away from vehicles only if human occupancy of the building is relatively light and the perimeter is controlled. (An *inhabited building* is "routinely occupied by 11 or more DoD personnel and with a population density of greater than one person per 430 gross square feet (40 gross square meters)" [p. 45].) The same walls would need to stand 20 m (66 ft) away from the perimeter in the case of primary gathering buildings or high-occupancy housing. (*Primary gathering buildings* are "routinely occupied by 50 or more DoD personnel and with a population density of greater than one person per 430 gross square feet" [p. 46]. *Billeting* is "any building . . . in which 11 or more unaccompanied DoD personnel are routinely housed" [p. 42]. *High-occupancy family housing* is "family housing with 13 or more units per building" [p. 45].)

The DOD issues different standards for standoff distances according to the building material, occupancy, and perimeter. For instance, containers and trailers that are used as primary gathering places during expeditionary operations are supposed to stand at least 71 m (233 ft) away from a perimeter, although fabric-covered structures (which generate fewer secondary projectiles under blast) could stand 31 m (102 ft) from the perimeter.

The DOD no longer endorses a previous standard (2007) that physical security managers might remember in an emergency if they are unable to access the current standards: high-occupancy and primary gathering buildings were supposed to stand 25 m or no less than 10 m (33 ft) away from vehicle parking or roadways or trash containers within the perimeter; other inhabited buildings were supposed to stand 25 m away from an uncontrolled perimeter and 10 m away from vehicles and trash containers within the perimeter; and low-occupancy buildings were allowed to be closer still.

The Department of State's standard, since 1985, for diplomatic buildings is a 30-m (100-ft) setback, although many diplomatic buildings remain substandard due to the constraints of available land and demands for higher occupancy in dense central urban areas. A full U.S. embassy requires about 15 acres of land even before setback is factored in.

Where setback is not possible, buildings need to be hardened above standard, which is very expensive, or have the standards waived. For instance, in 2009, U.S. officials sought waivers from State Department standards in order to build a consulate in Mazar-e-Sharif in northern Afghanistan. The officials signed a 10-year lease and spent more than $80 million on a site currently occupied by a hotel. The setback distance between the buildings and the perimeter was below standard; moreover, the perimeter shared a wall with local shopkeepers and was overlooked by several tall buildings. Following a revealing departmental report in January 2012, the site was abandoned before the consulate was ever established.

Setback is specified mostly as a control on blast, but firearms can strike from further away, particularly from elevated positions. For instance, in Kabul, Afghanistan, on September 13, 2011, insurgents occupied an unfinished high-rise building overlooking the U.S. embassy about 300 yd away. With assault rifles and rocket-propelled grenades they wounded four Afghan civilians inside the U.S. perimeter before Afghan forces cleared the building the next day.

In suburban locations, diplomatic missions typically have more space but are more remote from urban stakeholders. Sometimes diplomatic missions are established in suburban and rural locations with plenty of space but with exceptions to the security standards given their ongoing temporary status, the constraints of surrounding private property, and diplomatic goals of accessibility to locals. For instance, the small U.S. mission in Benghazi was noncompliant with the standards at the time of the devastating attack of September 11, 2012, which killed the ambassador and three other federal employees. In fact, it was little more than a small private villa on lease.

Blast Barriers

Blast barriers are material barriers required to baffle and reflect blast; often they are incorporated into the barriers to vehicles and humans too.

Specialized blast walls are normally precast from concrete and designed for carriage by standard construction equipment and to slot together without much pinning or bonding. They can be improvised from sandbags, temporary containers filled with earth (some flat-packed reinforced-canvas bags and boxes are supplied for this purpose), vehicles filled with earth, or simply ramps of earth. Stacked hard items of small size do not make good blast barriers because they collapse easily and provide secondary projectiles.

The most effective and available blast barriers are actually other complete buildings. Any structure will reflect or divert blast waves. Buildings present layers of load-bearing walls. The first structure to be hit by blast will absorb or deflect most of the energy that would otherwise hit the second structure in the direction of blast, so the ideal expedient is to acquire a site with buildings around the perimeter that are not needed and can be left unoccupied to shield the occupied buildings on the interior of the site. However, this ideal sounds expensive in material terms and also implies extra burdens on the guards who must ensure that malicious actors do not enter the unoccupied structures. This is why setback usually specifies an uncovered space between perimeter and accommodation. However, advantages would remain for the site security manager who acquires a site surrounded by other built sites with sufficient security to keep blast weapons on the outside of them all. Indeed, this is one principle behind placing a more valuable site in the center of an already-controlled built site.

Barriers to Kinetic Threats

Kinetic threats are projectiles and other missiles that might be thrown or propelled by chemical explosives. Typical walls, even typical load-bearing walls in the largest buildings, are not proof against projectiles fired from some portable firearms. Typical wood-framed and -paneled structures can be perforated by the bullets from any small arms. Typical masonry walls will defeat a few bullets from light assault firearms but will not resist larger caliber projectiles of the sort fired from a sniper's rifle or heavy machine gun. Indeed, damage from multiple rounds of such caliber would cause masonry walls to fail. Armor-piercing bullets, although rare outside of major militaries, would pass cleanly through typical masonry.

Reinforcing rods will dramatically increase the tensile (shear) strength of masonry and concrete, effectively holding the matrix together despite the stresses caused by blast or the damage caused by projectiles. Additionally, concrete is a harder material than clay or mud brick. A typical load-bearing wall in reinforced concrete (6-in. thick is standard in the United States) is not quite proof against typical firearms. To resist ubiquitous 7.62-mm bullets (as fired by most assault rifles since Soviet proliferation of the AK-47), reinforced concrete needs to be 0.15 m (7 in.) thick while reinforced masonry needs to be 0.20 m (8 in.) thick (U.S. DOD, 2008b). Few bullets would perforate such a thickness, but bullets can disintegrate into small ductile parts that flow through apertures (such as cracks) from the outside to the inside, even flowing around corners.

To defeat better equipped threats or mixed threats (such as blast followed by kinetic attack), the walls should be much thicker. The standard U.S. embassy has walls 0.76 m (2.5 ft) thick. During World War II, the standard thickness of military fortifications was 2 m (6.5 ft) if mostly buried or 3.5 m (11.5 ft) if fully exposed.

These standards assume that the material was constructed correctly, which would be a bad assumption in unstable areas where contractors or laborers are less incentivized or regulated to deliver to standards. For example, the reasons that the State Department's inspector gave for condemning the U.S. consulate in Mazar-e-Sharif, Afghanistan, in January 2012 included the poor materials (sun-dried mud bricks and untreated timber) and construction techniques used for the nascent perimeter wall.

Inspectors should watch out for the following:

- The correct materials (Cement and steel-reinforcing rods are expensive materials that are most likely to be substituted.)

- The correct curing and hardness (Concrete is normally allowed to cure for 28 days before further construction, although it can be considered about 80% cured after 7 days; wet curing for 90 days would double the hardness.)

- Proper reinforcing and strength (The rods should be made of a mild steel or similarly tough substitute. The rods should be tied or hooked together. Their matrix should be sufficiently dense, and they should be undisturbed during pouring of the wet concrete.)

Protective Glass

Glass is a frequent material in windows, doors, and surveillance systems (see above). However, it is usually the most fragile material in a built structure, so it is easiest for actors to break when attempting to access it. Moreover, when glass fails, it tends to shatter into many sharp projectiles, although species are available that shatter into relatively harmless pieces. **Protective glass** is any specialized species of glass that offers superior protection against projectiles or fewer hazards when shattered. Shatterproof and bulletproof species are essentially laminated plastic and glass sheets; more sheets and stronger bonds imply less fragility.

Glass can be minimized by designing buildings with fewer and smaller apertures. Glass should be acquired in shatterproof or bulletproof species where human break-ins or small arms attacks are sufficiently likely. Laminated sheets of glass and plastic are useful for protecting guards who must have line of sight in exposed locations in order to perform their duties. Pieces of such material can be set up even in temporary or emergency sites, where no built structures are present.

SITE SECURITY SERVICES

Security services can be hired from commercial providers. For the Humanitarian Practice Network (2010), these services range from **soft security** (consultancy, training, and logistical support) to **hard security** (guards and close protection) (p. xvii).

FINAL CASE STUDY

Trends in Terrorist Attacks on Sites

FEMA

Terrorist tactics may shift to exploit vulnerabilities, including those against active shooter–type attacks and screening for concealed weapons. Terrorist tactics tend to favor attacks that avoid effective countermeasures and exploit vulnerabilities. For example, recent suicide operations have targeted countries' lack of experience and capability to respond to simultaneous and well resourced attacks, like those in Mumbai, or suicide shooters, like the Fort Hood attack. Both of those attacks featured tactics that resemble "active shooters," a situation in which police are generally trained to cordon off an area and wait for paramilitary response units, like SWAT teams. In Mumbai, this paradigm was exploited by terrorists who laid siege to entire areas, carried supplies to extend the length of time they could operate, and attacked response teams.

These sorts of attack methods have lower consequences than catastrophic chemical, biological, radiological, or nuclear (CBRN) attacks or improvised explosive device attacks, but have a higher probability of succeeding. In addition, these types of tactics are hard to distinguish from traditional disasters. Responders to the first World Trade Center attack and Oklahoma City Bombing believed they were responding to accidents, while responders to plane crashes in New York City since September 11 have believed they were responding to terrorist incidents. Responding to conventional terrorist attacks can also be complicated for first responders, due to the possibility that secondary devices may be targeted at them. (U.S. Federal Emergency Management Agency, 2011, p. 2)

Fortunately, sites do not need to rely on private security but can build their own capacity with official help. In recent decades, public authorities have made available officials as advisers on private security, at least to major sites in or near populous areas.

For instance, the Department of Homeland Security places private-security advisers in local communities across the United States. Similarly, the Federal Bureau of Investigation is the main sponsor of local chapters of InfraGard, which advise local businesses on criminal threats and security. For American private operators overseas, since 1985, the U.S. Department of State has administered the Overseas Security Advisory Council (OSAC) to improve the exchange of information on security between the federal government and private businesses operating overseas. More than 100 cities around the world have OSAC councils. Within the Bureau of Diplomatic Security (also established in 1985), the Threat Investigations and Analysis Directorate (since 2008), through OSAC, supplies selected information to the private sector overseas and classified information to diplomatic sites.

CHAPTER SUMMARY

This chapter has explained

- The scope of site security

- Assessing risks by defining the target, the site location, and the attractiveness of targets to threats

- Access controls, including the scope of access controls, how to assess them, how they are bypassed, guards, emergency services and quick-reaction forces, gates, and emergency refuges

- Passive perimeters, including their scope, the material barriers, and human patrols and observation

- Surveillance, countersurveillance, surveillance technologies, surveillance of communications, and surveillance in poor light

- Security engineering, including construction setback from the perimeter, blast barriers, barriers to kinetic attacks, and protective glass

- Site security services

KEY TERMS

QUESTIONS AND EXERCISES

1. In what ways could a site's geographical location alter its exposure and vulnerability to specific risks as well as its capacity to respond?

2. Why is it important to implement exit controls along with access controls?

3. What are the best criteria to assess our access controls?

4. How might malicious actors bypass passive barriers and manned access controls?

5. What are the advantages and shortcomings of using guards for site security?

6. What new risks arise from reliance on a private quick-reaction force rather than local police or military forces?

7. Why would we want multiple gates at the point of access?

8. Why would we want a containment area at the point of access?

9. What are the limitations of a refuge?

10. In what ways can humans enhance passive material barriers?

11. Outline five critical components of a countersurveillance strategy.

12. How might countersurveillance disrupt potential attacks on the site?

13. What are the advantages and disadvantages of setback as material protection?

14. Give some examples of improvised blast barriers.

15. Why is reinforced concrete a useful material for resisting kinetic attack?

16. What two threats are blocked by protective glass?

national cross-sector CIKR protection and refines resiliency programs. As part of this collaboration, SSAs work with public and private-sector partners to develop and implement appropriate information-sharing and analysis mechanisms, which enhance sector security. In addition to working with private-sector partners to implement the National Infrastructure Protection Plan, SSAs cooperate with other federal, state, local, tribal, and territorial entities. Tables 9.2 and 9.3 list the federal agency and the corresponding sector for which it bears responsibility.

Sectors diverge in the degree of their planning. Some plans are more comprehensive and thorough than others. DHS presumes there to be an uneven evolution process at work among the various sectors, their councils, and the sectoral plans. As they evolve, DHS anticipates updates and annual implementation reports will reveal that the gaps in the level of protection between the sectors will close. The same process will help the government identify existing gaps, hopefully, so that the task of securing the most critical infrastructure and key resources will mature (U.S. GAO, 2007). These expectations may be somewhat wishful, according to critics, since participation is voluntary. Adding to the complexity is that each sector has inherent design features. They differ

Table 9.2 Sector-Specific Agency Responsibilities	
Federal Department/Agency	**Sector**
Department of Homeland Security	Chemical
	Commercial facilities
	Communications
	Critical manufacturing
	Dams
	Emergency services
	Information technology
	Nuclear reactors, materials, and waste
Department of Homeland Security and General Services Administration	Government facilities
Departments of Homeland Security and Transportation	Transportation
Department of Defense	Defense industrial base
Department of Energy	Energy
Department of Treasury	Financial services
Departments of Agriculture and Health and Human Services	Food and agriculture
Department of Health and Human Services	Health care and public health
Environmental Protection Agency	Water and wastewater systems

Source: U.S. White House (2013a).

in functionality, the openness of their systems, and the sophistication of their operating models. However, they connect through a shared interoperability. The failure of mutually supporting functions and distributed networks can have catastrophic consequences in the event of a coordinated multipronged attack.

Table 9.3   Infrastructure Sectors and Responsibilities

Sector	Description of Responsibility
Agriculture and food	Provides for the fundamental need for food. The infrastructure includes supply chains for feed and crop production. Carries out the postharvesting of the food supply, including processing and retail sales.
Banking and finance	Provides the financial infrastructure of the nation. This sector consists of commercial banks, insurance companies, mutual funds, government-sponsored enterprises, pension funds, and other financial institutions that carry out transactions.
Chemical	Transforms natural raw materials into commonly used products benefiting society's health, safety, and productivity. The chemical sector produces more than 70,000 products that are essential to automobiles, pharmaceuticals, food supply, electronics, water treatment, health, construction, and other necessities.
Commercial facilities	Includes prominent commercial centers, office buildings, sports stadiums, theme parks, and other sites where large numbers of people congregate to pursue business activities, conduct personal commercial transactions, or enjoy recreational pastimes.
Communications	Provides wired, wireless, and satellite communications to meet the needs of businesses and governments.
Critical manufacturing	Includes metal, machinery, electrical-equipment, and transportation equipment manufacturing, which is crucial to the economic prosperity and continuity of the United States.
Dams	Manages water retention structures, including levees, more than 77,000 conventional dams, navigation locks, canals (excluding channels), and similar structures, including larger and nationally symbolic dams that are major components of other critical infrastructures that provide electricity and water.
Defense industrial base	Supplies the military with the means to protect the nation by producing weapons, aircraft, and ships and providing essential services, including information technology and supply and maintenance.
Drinking water and water treatment systems	Provides sources of safe drinking water from more than 53,000 community water systems and properly treated wastewater from more than 16,000 publicly owned treatment works.
Emergency services	Saves lives and property from accidents and disaster. This sector includes fire, rescue, emergency medical services, and law enforcement organizations.

Sector	Description of Responsibility
Energy	Provides the electric power used by all sectors and the refining, storage, and distribution of oil and gas. The sector is divided into electricity and oil and natural gas.
Government facilities	Ensures continuity of functions for facilities owned and leased by the government, including all federal, state, territorial, local, and tribal government facilities located in the United States and abroad.
Information technology	Produces information technology and includes hardware manufacturers, software developers, and service providers as well as the Internet as a key resource.
Nuclear reactors, materials, and waste	Provides nuclear power, which accounts for approximately 20% of the nation's electrical-generating capacity. The sector includes commercial nuclear reactors and nonpower nuclear reactors used for research, testing, and training; nuclear materials used in medical, industrial, and academic settings; nuclear-fuel fabrication facilities; the decommissioning of reactors; and the transportation, storage, and disposal of nuclear materials and waste.
Public health and health care	Mitigates the risk of disasters and attacks and also provides recovery assistance if an attack occurs. The sector consists of health departments, clinics, and hospitals.
Transportation systems	Enables movement of people and assets that are vital to our economy, mobility, and security with the use of aviation, ships, rail, pipelines, highways, trucks, buses, and mass transit.

Source: Compiled with data from the U.S. Government Accountability Office (2007).

The Partnership Structures

The voluntary arrangement between private-sector owners and operators and their government counterparts, according to the NIPP, "has been and will remain the primary mechanism for advancing collective action toward national critical infrastructure security and resilience" (U.S. DHS, 2013a, p. 10).

The government sees these as partnerships where the Department of Homeland Security is the key actor. In this role, DHS has wide-ranging responsibilities for leading and coordinating the overall national critical-infrastructure protection effort. This coordination with infrastructure stakeholders is considered critical in fulfilling the government's responsibility and mandate to preserve public safety, assure the continuance of commerce, and provide national security.

In its role as lead coordinating agency, DHS helps make certain that critical infrastructure within and across the 16 infrastructure sectors is secure by attempting to set uniform policies, approaches, guidelines, and methodologies.

▶ Energy: One of the National Critical Infrastructure Sectors

Source: iStockphoto.com/Bumann.

Furthermore, the government views the NIPP as a base plan that serves as a blueprint for how DHS and appropriate stakeholders might collaborate in implementing risk management standards across sectors in an integrated, coordinated manner.

Meanwhile, critical-infrastructure sectors attempt to work across jurisdictions and geographic boundaries to establish stable and representative partnerships. According to NIPP literature, the critical-infrastructure partnership structure is the means by which stakeholders strive to meet collective-security goals. The Critical Infrastructure Partnership Advisory Council (CIPAC), established by DHS in 2006, is "a mechanism to support the sectors' interests to jointly engage in critical infrastructure discussions and to participate in a broad spectrum of activities" (U.S. DHS, 2013a, p. 38). The CIPAC organizes forums to support discussions on critical-infrastructure issues. In its advisory role, the CIPAC hopes to build consensus positions that result in formal recommendations to the federal government. Its efforts span an arc of infrastructure sectors, jurisdictions, and specifically defined geographical areas.

The CIPAC engages partnership councils, which involve sector coordinating councils (SCC), government coordinating councils (GCC), and cross-sector partnership councils. The critical infrastructure is a highly and intrinsically complex environment. Therefore, in order to achieve a semblance of coherent strategy and framework for collaboration, the assemblage of partner advisory bodies is equally complex. The collection includes a broad variety of organizational structures, governance constructs, operating models, and large-scale distributed networks. Furthermore, despite their specificity and area of concentration, these councils function interdependently with one another. This interdependence is key to a functioning critical-infrastructure environment and, hence, policy formulation. To attempt to maintain strategic and operational seamlessness, national partnership structures regularly convene with government and private-sector stakeholders for planned programs. Under such fosterage, participants learn about and contribute to issues relating to

- strategic planning,

- risk management,

- program evaluation,

- sector-specific metrics development,

- advancements in information sharing,

- research and development activities, and also

- take part in training and exercises programs.

As described in the 2013 National Infrastructure Protection Plan, the sector and cross-sector partnership structure includes the following government and private sector advisory bodies.

Sector Coordinating Councils (SCCs)—Self-organized, self-run, and self-governed private sector councils consisting of owners and operators and their representatives, which interact on a wide range of sector-specific strategies, policies, activities, and issues. SCCs serve as principal collaboration points between the government and private sector owners and operators for critical infrastructure security and resilience policy coordination and planning and a range of related sector-specific activities.

Critical Infrastructure Cross-Sector Council—Consisting of the chairs and vice chairs of the SCCs, this private sector council coordinates cross-sector issues, initiatives, and interdependencies to support critical infrastructure security and resilience.

Government Coordinating Councils (GCCs)—Consisting of representatives from across various levels of government (including Federal and SLTT), as appropriate to the operating landscape of each individual sector, these councils enable interagency, intergovernmental, and cross-jurisdictional coordination within and across sectors and partner with SCCs on public-private efforts.

Federal Senior Leadership Council (FSLC)—Consisting of senior officials from the SSAs and other Federal departments and agencies with a role in critical infrastructure security and resilience, the FSLC facilitates communication and coordination on critical infrastructure security and resilience across the Federal Government.

State, Local, Tribal, and Territorial Government Coordinating Council (SLTTGCC)—Consisting of representatives from across SLTT government entities, the SLTTGCC promotes the engagement of SLTT partners in national critical infrastructure security and resilience efforts and provides an organizational structure to coordinate across jurisdictions on State and local government guidance, strategies, and programs.

Regional Consortium Coordinating Council (RC3)—Comprises regional groups and coalitions around the country engaged in various initiatives to advance critical infrastructure security and resilience in the public and private sectors.

Information Sharing Organizations—Organizations including Information Sharing and Analysis Centers (ISACs) serve operational and dissemination functions for many sectors, subsectors, and other groups, and facilitate sharing of information between government and the private sector. ISACs also collaborate on a cross-sector basis through a national council. (U.S. DHS, 2013a, p. 12)

Fusion Centers—Although the FBI is the primary government agency charged with counter intelligence responsibilities, the Office of Intelligence Analysis works to coordinate all elements of the intelligence community and between state and local authorities. Additionally, there are state and major regional area **fusion centers**, which are intelligence-gathering stations at the sub-federal level. These organizations vary in size and competency. Their missions are all similar: to pursue, disrupt, and identify precursor crime and activity relative to emerging terrorist threats, they also work with private sector personnel and public safety officials on critical infrastructure protection, disaster recovery, and emergency response events.

The **Homeland Infrastructure Threat and Risk Analysis Center (HITRAC)** is the DHS infrastructure-intelligence fusion center. It serves as a joint intelligence center that brings together the analysis from the intelligence community, infrastructure specialists, and law enforcement.

Despite these noble attempts, the partnership structure has been cumbersome and less efficient than hoped. The government's emphasis upon **public–private partnerships** is still underdeveloped and wrought with tensions. This is particularly the case with respect to cybersecurity (Sommer & Brown, 2011, p. 6). There are many assessments that contend that, regardless of the effort, partnerships between government and private entities have been difficult to establish and maintain. Claims persist that these arrangements between government and industry are still as confusing and uncoordinated as they are meant to be collaborative. The security clearance process is often attributed with hampering the information-sharing machinery between government and industry entities. Complementing the government's covetous approach to intelligence, private firms are loath to hand over precise internal information for fear of compromising sensitive market-intelligence data or exposing management to potential liability.

BOX 9.2

Homeland Infrastructure Threat and Risk Analysis Center (HITRAC)

HITRAC conducts integrated threat and risk analyses for CIKR sectors. HITRAC is a joint fusion center that spans both the Office of Intelligence and Analysis (I&A)—a member of the Intelligence Community—and IP. As called for in section 201 of the Homeland Security Act, HITRAC brings together intelligence and infrastructure specialists to ensure a sufficient understanding of the risks to the Nation's CIKR from foreign and domestic threats. HITRAC works in partnership with the U.S. Intelligence Community and national law enforcement to integrate and analyze intelligence and law enforcement information in threat and risk analysis products. HITRAC also works in partnership with the SSAs and owners and operators to ensure that their expertise on infrastructure operations is integrated into HITRAC's analysis.

HITRAC develops analytical products by combining threat assessments based on all source information and intelligence analysis with vulnerability and consequence assessments. The combination of intelligence and practical CIKR knowledge allows DHS to provide products that contain strategically relevant and actionable information. HITRAC coordinates closely with partners outside the Federal Government through the SCCs, GCCs, ISACs, and State and Local Fusion Centers to ensure that its products are accessible and relevant to partner needs.

As part of its Infrastructure Risk Analysis Partnership Program (IRAPP) initiative, in 2008, HITRAC launched the NY State IRAPP in coordination with the NY State Office of Homeland Security in order to assist the state with building the capability to develop a State Risk Profile.

Source: National Academy of Sciences (2010); U.S. Department of Homeland Security (2006).

Prior to 9/11, information sharing between the private sector and government was inhibited by distrust, legal concerns, and bureaucratic inertia. Both sectors have conflicting agendas. The private sector feels it has a right to information on specific threats to their operations. Government reticence to turn over this information is based upon concerns of compromising sources or investigations. On the other hand, the government requires data, which the private sector fears could not only make them vulnerable to attack, market risk, and legal liability but also the threat of future regulatory action (Moteff, 2010).

With an understanding of these divergent motives and missions between the public and private sectors, Congress passed the **Critical Infrastructure Information Act** of 2002. The legislation recognized that the private sector was reluctant to pass commercial, sensitive, and revealing target information to the federal government in case that information passed into the

▶ Information Sharing

Source: iStockphoto.com/alengo.

public domain, so the act protected critical-infrastructure information from public release, including protections against claims under the Freedom of Information Act, state and local disclosure laws, and civil litigation. In 2006, DHS issued its final rule on the handling of this protected information. In 2011, the Protected Critical Infrastructure Information Management System (administered by the Infrastructure Information Collection Division within the Office of Infrastructure Protection) reached full operation. DHS defines **critical-infrastructure information (CII)** as information that is not customarily in the public domain and is related to the security of critical infrastructure or protected systems. CII consists of records and information concerning any of the following:

- actual, potential, or threatened interference with, attack on, compromise of, or incapacitation of critical infrastructure or protected systems by either physical or computer-based attack or other similar conduct (including the misuse of or unauthorized access to all types of communications and data transmission systems) that violates Federal, State, or local law, harms interstate commerce of the United States, or threatens public health or safety;

- the ability of any critical infrastructure or protected system to resist such interference, compromise, or incapacitation, including any planned or past assessment, projection, or estimate of the vulnerability of critical infrastructure or a protected system, including security testing, risk evaluation thereto, risk management planning, or risk audit; or

- any planned or past operational problem or solution regarding critical infrastructure or protected systems, including repair, recovery, reconstruction, insurance, or continuity, to the extent that it is related to such interference, compromise, or incapacitation. (S. Am. 4901, 2002)

The Economics of Securing the Critical Infrastructure

Of the number of barriers to creating a seamless and comprehensive critical-infrastructure security environment, a few key concepts are central to the dilemma. Much of the challenge arises from an aversion to regulation and the reticence of private firms to invest in security. Security investment does not directly convert into earnings. Put simply, security is a difficult business case. In many instances, the actual loss of an asset due to theft, sabotage, or electronic exfiltration is a more acceptable cost of doing business than the investment to defend against the loss. Generally, without a strong enforcement regime or some way to recover the cost, there is little incentive for companies to invest in their own security and contribute to the greater national defense.

Government does not mandate as it once did because of a decades-long and fractious political debate over its appropriate role. The years of deregulation and privatization have put a considerable inventory of public-good assets in private hands and, over time, have exacerbated the commerce-versus-security dilemma. Therefore, national defense, the textbook example of a public good, is mostly in the form of a private asset. In the meantime, incremental and ad hoc upgrades to the commercial infrastructures leave the country more vulnerable to terrorist attacks and natural disasters.

As our systems become more automated, they also become more complex and interconnected (Jarmon, 2014). Hence, the threat of **cascading failure** increases. Modern industrial societies today are highly dependent on a relatively small number of giant utilities, which, in turn, are highly dependent upon industrial control systems. Electricity, oil and gas, water, and sewage— including pipelines, refineries, generators, and storage depots—are some of the sectors mentioned above that are particularly vulnerable. Other sectors are less susceptible.

As rare as large-scale disasters are, they pose a serious risk and have some history of occurrence. The potential for economic loss could be catastrophic. In the North American energy sector alone, the real assets are worth over a trillion dollars. Four to over five billion dollars represent the total in control systems. Because of the prevailing economic wisdom and the lack of pressure from a rigorous legal mandate, these investments most likely will be replaced and upgraded only after full depreciation for tax purposes (Anderson & Fuloria, 2010).

In the meantime, the main design features of utility control systems are reliability and ease of use. Therefore, the security element is not a high priority. Moreover, costs drive business decisions. Most critical infrastructure operates on two or more separate networks in order to shield the system from inadvertent virus contagion or electronic attack. However, engineers often connect control systems to the Internet as a cost-reduction method. Private networks are expensive in large-scale environments and can incur exponential increases naturally.

In the United States, Sarbanes-Oxley imposes indirect pressure, but security enforcement mostly rests on internal risk management strategies and policies. This brand of volunteerism brings into focus some other systemic problems. Not only are there limited incentives and financial resources available within most businesses to address security needs, there is also a general dearth of qualified staff. Limited budgets reflect back on demand in the labor market. Although this demand is rapidly increasing, the educational system is not turning out enough highly qualified and formally trained personnel.

BOX 9.3

Less Vulnerable Infrastructure Sectors

Rail systems escape threat better than other large-scale industrial environments. A deterrent to a cyber attack is the built-in resilience of rail-system networks. Rail systems have a rather loose dependency on information and communications technology (ICT). Much of the rail transportation industry depends on manual technology to perform functions critical to its operations. (Because of the manual alternative, the U.S. railroad system might be the most resilient industry in the infrastructure sector. An outage or disruption of service at a command and control center might be neutralized by the deployment of field crews or having function controls transferred to laptops.) For an attack to be successful in this environment, it would most likely be a result of a large-scale, multipronged assault affecting multiple targets. Such an event might include several infrastructure industries. Hence, the greatest threat to a rail system comes from neglect and sub-standard maintenance.

Knowledge and appreciation of control systems and their security risks is at a premium because of a scarcity of talent. Management of existing and future operations demands a highly educated workforce with wide-ranging skill sets and expertise. (Edward Snowden, who claimed he earned $200,000 a year as a computer expert, dropped out of high school and took computer courses at a local community college without earning a degree.) It usually also means having the ability to get a security clearance. New regulations can impose further demands beyond the technical capability of legacy systems and staff. Add to these influencers the increasing sophistication of tools used by hackers and the emission rate of malware. Some estimates claim that in 2012, a new version of malware was released every 8 seconds (Husick & Turzanski, 2012). Therefore, the threat of disaster increases exponentially each year.

In a Cambridge University study, Ross Anderson and Shailendra Fuloria made some observations on the economic costs of security relative to national critical infrastructure. In several industrial countries, they noted, levels of investment differed as did the scale and scope of regulation. However, in these industries, the pressure comes from the major companies themselves, whose security regime and risk management strategies are self-imposed. Most government standards are voluntary and the security framework is, generally, self-regulating. It is mainly through the contracting process with vendors where security requirements are established and put in place. As a rule, because security is considered a cost center, enterprise metrics involve limitations on security investments. Financial and legal responsibility depend upon how the enterprise management team deems its social responsibility for external, large-scale systematic failures. Beyond a certain point, the government is expected to take over.

It must also be remembered that as opposed to classical military theory in the past, in the case of today's arena of asymmetric conflict, the advantage is with the attacker, not the defender. It is no longer easier to defend than attack. In the previous era of warfare, the defense staked out its perimeter and concentrated its forces at the most appropriate points along the barricade. Now, however, in protecting the critical infrastructure, the defender must shield itself from

Figure 9.2   Increase in Internet Traffic

In 2012 | 2 billion users
         | 12 billion devices

As the number of people with access to the Internet rises, total Internet traffic is expected to more than double from the 2012 level by 2017.

Source: U.S. Department of Homeland Security (2014).

Economics of Security

We suggest that a useful way to view this is *the large externalities of correlated failure* [simultaneous targeted attacks or untargeted systemic failures]. If a small terrorist group—a latter-day Timothy McVeigh—were to blow up a single oil refinery, that might cost $1bn: say $500m of damage and $500m of lost profits during rebuilding. The oil company and its insurers could surely cope. However, if a more organised terrorist group—say al-Qaida—were to blow up six oil refineries, then chaos and petrol rationing would ensue, with significant damage to the economy.

For example, Britain suffered a strike by fuel-tanker drivers in 2001 that caused major disruption for weeks; the loss of six oil refineries might have a comparable impact but for a year or more, leading to social costs in the tens or even hundreds of billions. The oil company does not internalise the social costs of this, so will make the fence high enough only for a $1bn single-incident loss. If the additional risk of a $100bn multiple incident loss is to be dealt with, the state may have to step in.

(In passing, we note that the argument for state intervention is similar in some respects to the case for financial regulation. The isolated failure of a single bank would be of little consequence; it's the risk of correlated failure that rightly worries governments. And correlated failures impose large externalities; Lehman's collapse may have cost its CEO Dick Fuld a few hundred million dollars, but it could cost the world economy over a trillion dollars.) (Anderson & Fuloria, 2010, pp. 58–59)

BOX 9.4

assault along an immense and dispersed target set. In contrast, the attacker needs only to center its efforts on a small set of targets, of its own choosing and selection based upon the potential to cause the most damage. Seeking a security administration with total vulnerability coverage is prohibitively expensive, particularly in the case of such open systems as surface transportation.

Lastly, and perhaps ultimately, private firms mostly cooperate on a voluntary basis and, therefore, are under no mandate to comply with government regulation. Their first priority is to turn profits and provide returns for shareholders. As long as large swathes of the critical infrastructure are under private ownership and the political environment has little tolerance for regulation, the conflict between government and the private entity remains. While the government's duty is with the public's health and security, the corporation's main responsibility is to the stockholder. Because of these conditions and distinctions, the friction exists.

Unfortunately, in many places today, the national infrastructure suffers from overuse, underinvestment, neglect, and obsolescence. In 2003, officials claimed overgrown trees coming in contact with high-voltage lines caused the outage of more than 100 power plants in Michigan, Ohio, New York, and Canada. The grid failure affected 50 million, covered a 9,300-sq-mi area and had an estimated economic toll of between six and 10 billion dollars. The incident exposed the fear of many experts that the nation's electronic infrastructure was intolerably weak. The U.S. electrical-power grid, according to Gilbert Bindewald of the Department of Energy, "was never holistically designed" and "developed incrementally in response to local load growth" (Bindewald, 2009). The same might be said for much of the national infrastructure, which includes transportation and communication networks, water- and waste-treatment systems, and health care.

Because the private sector owns most of the critical infrastructure, questions concerning responsibility of a public good arise. Over 85% of these assets are in private hands. If it breaks or is destroyed, who is accountable for its restoration? It is easy to say that the onus is with the owner. However, many contend that since the threat and risks are shared, so should the responsibility. Experts also estimate that the critical infrastructure is substandard in its quality and investment. In many cases, upgrades in their design, construction, and security are overdue. The strength of the nation depends upon the efficiency of its critical infrastructure and its ability to secure it. These are also highly strategic targets for terrorists, competitor state actors, and any entity that seeks to weaken or disrupt the national economy. These same assets are also highly vulnerable to natural catastrophes and unintended human error. The topic of critical infrastructure is at the core of any discussion on homeland security.

In the meantime, the national critical infrastructure is as diverse as it is complex. The networks, varied organizational structures, and service modes are interdependent and often involve multinational ownership. As mentioned above, making this constellation of connections and mechanisms more elaborate and Byzantine is its arc of mutually supporting functions that span cyberspace, the physical world, and various levels of governance with simultaneously overlapping and conflicting laws and regulations. The national infrastructure is not only a prime element in the country's daily routines and global industrial competitiveness but also an important factor in its role and economic influence in international relations.

SUPERVISORY CONTROL AND DATA ACQUISITION SYSTEMS

Perhaps one of the primary areas of vulnerability in the United States is the **supervisory control and data acquisition systems**, or **SCADA** systems. SCADA systems are computer systems that automate, monitor, moderate, and control industrial-plant functions and critical infrastructure. The technology is ubiquitous. Public and private infrastructure processes and operations that operate over SCADA include

- water treatment and distribution,
- wastewater collection and treatment,
- oil and gas pipelines,
- electrical-power transmission and distribution,
- wind farms,
- civil-defense warning systems, and
- large-scale communication systems.

A simple flaw is that these systems were not initially designed to be secure either. The designers sought a scalable computer environment that was easy to operate, robust, open, and had the ability to link together decentralized facilities. The use of standardized technologies and open solutions was more compatible with the Internet's growth and the increased number of connections between SCADA systems. Secure proprietary networks offered less of an advantage under this expanding environment.

As with the original Internet, as mentioned above, security was not an early concern. Data is sent "in the clear," or over open pathways that rely on the Internet and often require no authentication (National Research Council of the National Academies, Committee on Science and Technology for Countering Terrorism, 2002). Security mostly relies upon **commercial off-the-shelf (COTS) components**, which served as "patches," rather than holistic solutions. By using COTS, enterprises avoid the cost and delays of an overall system-development process. They are useful as not only security patches but also can increase capacity. In defense of their usage, sometimes COTS are simply more practical. Their installation requires no extended period of suspended services. Frequent updates may be unfeasible for control systems in certain instances. Entire upgrades sometimes take months of advance planning and require suspension of operations. Therefore, the justification for installing security patches may be driven by economic considerations or market demands (Jarmon, 2014).

However, patching has several known downsides. In addition to the drawback of being merely a mélange of staggered security solutions, patch updates may violate manufacturer certification (Cárdenas et al., 2009). The use of COTS under certain conditions might open the operator up to litigation. Also, when industrial controllers and SCADA software systems are replaced and updated, hardware may be compromised (Husick & Turzanski, 2012). Patched SCADA systems may be more cost effective, but they are also attractive targets for malicious hackers, criminals, or potential terrorist agents looking to exploit security gaps. Their vulnerability, criticality to infrastructure operations, and the general awareness of the lack of security used in their design and support make them a tempting objective.

Proprietary networks, on the other hand, offer much superior security than Internet-based systems. These proprietary protocols provide extra fail-safe because they are familiar to only a few expert programmers and are physically separate from the networks used for communication, Web surfing, and document sharing. Although most critical infrastructure runs on two or more separate networks in order to protect the system from inadvertent virus contagion or intentional electronic attack, it can still be susceptible to failure. One reason is that there exists **Web-based translation software** that can convert proprietary protocols into other computing languages (Salkever, 2003). Hacker tools such as these are quite accessible and can compromise the advantage of running separate networks to control plant, energy, and transportation operations.

▸ Command and Control Systems
Source: NASA.

SCADA manages the physical elements of the network as well as soft elements. Physical damage that might result in the destruction of infrastructure may have longer term consequences. Network equipment has to be rebuilt and its components remanufactured from scratch (National Research Council, 2002). The frailty of the entire system is further compounded by the unintended ironies of an open Internet. According to the National Research Council's Committee on Science and Technology for Countering Terrorism, these vulnerabilities are widely known, and details on system exposure are accessible to all on the World Wide Web. In the committee's 2002 report, it states,

> Product data and educational videotapes from engineering associations can be used to familiarize potential attackers with the basics of the grid and with specific elements. Information obtained through semiautomated reconnaissance to probe and scan the networks of a variety of power suppliers could provide terrorists with detailed information about the internals of the SCADA network, down to the level of specific makes and models of equipment used and version releases of corresponding software. And more inside information could be obtained from sympathetic engineers and operators. (p. 141)

Stephen Flynn, in his 2007 book, *The Edge of Disaster*, discloses in one example how hazardously bound national security is to the national power grid. In citing a 2006 report in the Baltimore *Sun*, Flynn discusses a fear by the NSA that the installation of two of its supercomputers would overload an already stressed power grid. The agency concluded that, if conditions go unmitigated, the longest period of time the electrical infrastructure could forestall a collapse of the system was 2 years. It would take between 18 and 30 months to design and procure equipment, obtain permits, and build a new power station.

The U.S. electrical-power grid is a service environment of constant change and uncertainty. The system's complexity, decentralized flow control, and fluctuating dynamic of consumer usage contribute additional challenges to security. A sudden drop in voltage, either because of uncontrolled demand or the result of false information inserted into SCADA, could cause collapse. The absence of flow control and the lack of any large-scale storage capacity make the electric-power grid unique, vulnerable, and "the ultimate just-in-time production process" (Bindewald, 2009). The same features that propel and permeate commercial life are the symptoms of a deficient immunity to a cyber attack. Today, the power grid is decentralized, aging, susceptible to blackouts, reliant on SCADA, and under increasing demand due to the expanding digital economy (Bindewald, 2009).

The best solutions are long-term. They involve using alternative energy sources and changing the supply mix, putting a greater emphasis on conservation methods, and creating a more holistic and smarter grid. Meanwhile, networks remain under attack as hackers and hacker tools become more sophisticated. Detection tools for finding hacker malware exist. However, some intrusions go unexposed, and once inside a system, an attacker can establish a foothold and expand his control for future exploitation.

In 2012, there were several reports involving major power outages by Internet-enabled intrusions (Anonymous, 2012). The 2003 power blackouts, which occurred in the northeast United States, opened up a national discussion about the grid's vulnerability to hacker activity. Official explanation maintains that overgrown trees coming in contact with high-voltage lines led to system failure. However, many in the intelligence community speculate that China or agents working in collaboration with the PLA (Peoples Liberation Army) caused the outage that became the greatest blackout in North American history (Harris, 2008). Those who doubt that natural phenomena were involved suggest the PLA gained access to one of the networks controlling electric-power systems. Some electronic snooping may have inadvertently interacted with a widespread computer virus and put the system over the edge by disrupting the communication lines used to manage the power grid (Harris, 2008). Officially, no foreign government has been accused of any involvement. Yet whether an ill-timed event or an event by intention, the incident compelled one industry analyst to opine "that security for the nation's critical electronic infrastructures remains intolerably weak" and the incident confirms "that government and company officials haven't sufficiently acknowledged these vulnerabilities" (Harris, 2008, n.p.).

In 2004, another cyber attack, dubbed **Operation Code Red**, disabled Amtrak (Husick, 2011). The virus, initially released in 2001, affected more than 225,000 computer systems worldwide at that time and defaced websites with the message, "Hacked by Chinese" (Associated Press, 2001). In 2008, a 14-year-old schoolboy in Poland was able to hack into the communications system and manipulate the tram system as if it was "a giant train set." The teenager converted the television remote control in his home into a device that could manipulate all the junctions along the operating line and maneuver the trams. Four trams derailed and 12 people were hospitalized as a result of his actions. In 2008, another outage raised speculation of Chinese hacker activity. A power failure cut off three million utility customers along Florida's east coast. Florida Power & Light blamed human error. However, there are some inside government and industry who contest the official explanation. They further argue that hackers working in China have been mapping and analyzing the U.S. critical infrastructure for years in preparation for a possible cyber conflict.

In summary, there are many examples where the manipulation of the computer code could have a devastating effect on critical infrastructure. There are many possible actors, and at the same time, the conflict is asymmetrical and symmetrical. In addition to state and nonstate actors, the threat matrix includes natural disasters, system overloads, obsolescence, and sustained neglect.

THE INFRASTRUCTURE ASSET INVENTORY AND RISK ASSESSMENT

Across the United States, over $1 billion of daily investment goes to infrastructure by one form or another. Yet despite this commitment of resources, the apparatus is frail. Not only has age and neglect contributed to the obsolescence of much of the infrastructure but demographic changes have too (Kolasky, 2014). The range of assets and the expanse of U.S. territory give the task of identifying and categorizing the facilities, functions, and systems that support the society an almost epic sweep. It is a Herculean undertaking to build a comprehensive database of critical-infrastructure assets, collect information about their vulnerability, and prioritize assets and protective and support resources and measures. The migration of physical control to information and communications technology and the morphing attack surface make such labor perhaps Sisyphean. Nevertheless, following the attacks on 9/11, under the guidance of DHS, owners, operators, and other stakeholders of the critical infrastructure began such a process.

Over time, DHS's ability to coordinate this activity developed slowly but continued stridently. Initially, the U.S. Office (October 2001) and Department (November 2002) of Homeland Security developed assessments of risk that were corrupted by the need for a quick method for allocating to lower authorities a surge in federal dollars for homeland security. Until late 2003, DHS simply assumed that the population of an area was directly related to its risk; consequently, a large but remote and rural area received more inputs than a less populous area with an exposed urban concentration, border, port, and financial center.

In March 2003, the same timeframe as the announcement of Operation Iraqi Freedom, DHS launched **Operation Liberty Shield**. It was the national plan to defend the infrastructure and ensure continuous commerce. The program saw its mission as hardening border controls, increasing public-health preparedness, securing the transportation network, readying federal response resources, and creating better protection for the critical infrastructure and key assets (U.S. Department of Homeland Security, 2006, pp. 4–5).

Originally, 160 assets or sites made a list of items deemed critical to the nation based on their vulnerability to attack and potential consequences. They included an array of chemical and hazardous-materials sites, nuclear power plants, energy facilities, business and finance centers, and others. By the end of the year the list grew to 1,849.

Eventually, Operation Liberty Shield evolved into the **National Asset Database**. As of January 2006, the bank contained over 77,000 entries (Moteff, 2010). Its usefulness, however, comes under criticism. While DHS apparently made progress on the reliability of the information contained in the database, it continued to draw skepticism for including thousands of assets that many believe have more local importance than national importance. There is some confusion as to what the National Asset Database is meant to be. Critics of the database assume it is a continuation of DHS's list of high-priority sites. DHS asserts that it is an inventory of assets from which critical assets may be drawn.

In the grandest of estimates, the number of potential physical-infrastructure targets for terrorists has been estimated in the millions (Gaines & Kappeler, 2012, p. 55). Having relied on states and industries to provide much of the data without consistent coding rules, the data betrayed stark incongruities. Some of the assets were irregular and small events, such as local parades and petting zoos, presumably captured under old listings of gatherings of people as critical assets but ignored by most states and industries. Indiana had 8,000 assets in the database, more than California, Texas, and New York. California reported the Bay Area Rapid Transit System as a single asset whereas New York City reported 739 subway stations as assets. North Dakota reported more banking assets than New York reported.

By 2011, DHS counted 4.5 million sites where hazardous materials are manufactured or stored; 2,200,000 mi of pipelines for liquid and natural gas, operated by more than 1,300 companies; 5,300 power stations, including 66 nuclear power stations and 104 reactors); 160,000 mi of high-voltage transmission lines; 16,000 wastewater treatment systems; 79,000 dams; 591,000 bridges, 3,900,000 mi of public roads; 208 million automobiles; 15.5 million trucks, of which 42,000 are rated for carriage of hazardous materials, across 1.2 million trucking companies; 10 million drivers licensed for commercial vehicles, including 2.7 million licenses for hazardous materials carriage; 120,000 mi of mainline railways; 15 million passengers on railways per day; 25,000 mi of commercial waterways; 361 ports; 19,576 general airports, including heliports; 211,450 general aviation aircraft; 459 federalized commercial airports; and 255 million mobile telephones.

In 2005, the GAO urged further development of official assessment of threats to critical infrastructure. The DHS subsequently assessed the "attractiveness" of the target area to the threat as part of a threat assessment. When measuring the vulnerability of a particular geographic area, DHS measured the total number of international visitors (more simply, a measure of hazards) and the total miles of designated waste isolation pilot plant (WIPP) route. When measuring the vulnerability of a particular asset of national infrastructure, DHS judged the capacity of a potential threat to harm the asset. The DHS counts military bases and other defense-related sites, assets of national infrastructure, and population when measuring vulnerability and consequence. Over the next 3 years, DHS tried another three formulations of risk—effectively different formulations of threat, vulnerability, and consequences, although these were not settled until 2007. Section 550 of the DHS Appropriations Act of 2007 granted the Department of Homeland Security the authority to regulate chemical facilities that "present high levels of security risk." In concurrence, DHS issued the Chemical Facility Anti-Terrorism Standards (CFATS), which defined the chemical facilities that would be determined by DHS to be high risk and what the DHS would do in response.

By 2007, DHS, by its own reckoning, had assessed the vulnerability of assets within surface transportation modes (mass transit, freight rail, and highway infrastructure) and conducted over 2,600 vulnerability assessments on every critical-infrastructure sector through the Comprehensive Review (CR) program the Buffer Zone Protection Program and the Site Assistance Visit Program (Masse, O'Neil, & Rollins, 2007; U.S. GAO, 2005a, 2008a). Even then, its measurements actually conflated other concepts. In its regional risk assessments, DHS admitted that its concepts of *vulnerability* and *consequences* overlapped. Its measurements of an area's vulnerability (by population, economy, infrastructure, etc.) hardly measured vulnerability (which means absence of protection) but measured potential targets or losses—something closer to *exposure*—which was not explicitly captured by DHS analysis at all.

In practice, the DHS's *vulnerability and consequence index* measured an expanse of things that could be considered correlates of vulnerability, exposure, and consequences (returns). The vulnerability and consequence index was a product of four indices: the national infrastructure index (a count of higher assets), the national-security index (a count of the military bases and other defense-related sites and of international border crossings), the population index (a count of the population, including visitors and commuters, and a measure of population density), and the economic index (either gross metropolitan product or the state's share of gross domestic product). In actuality, these indices measure the potential range of returns or exposure; they do not measure any explicit defenses or controls, such as the number of police personnel or health professionals. Therefore, these formulations did not explicitly measure vulnerability, although some measures (such as the number of military personnel) capture some military types of defenses.

In June 2008, GAO (2008a) recommended "that the Secretary of DHS . . . formulate a method to measure vulnerability in a way that captures variations across states and urban areas and apply this vulnerability measure in future iterations of the risk-based grant allocation model" (p. 5). The relevant centers of excellence within DHS, FEMA, and the Office of Intelligence & Analysis agreed that the current methodology for determining vulnerability was not optimal.

FEMA's Grant Directorate allocated its resources to smaller jurisdictions by effectively measuring the gap between the jurisdiction's capability to prevent and respond to various types of disasters and a target level of capability (FEMA called this the Cost-to-Capability Initiative) (GAO, 2008b). In 2009, FEMA published a draft of its *Target Capabilities List User Guide*, which

▶ Inventorying Critical Infrastructure

Source: Photo by Robert Raines on Flickr.

was populated with *credible targets* as identified by officials and industries within the different classes of asset. It aimed to "provide more user-friendly, accessible, and credible capacity targets" (U.S. FEMA, 2009, p. 3).

DHS prioritizes certain targets; "prioritization is the process of using risk assessment results to identify where risk-reduction or -mitigation efforts are most needed and subsequently determine which protective actions should be instituted in order to have the greatest effect" (U.S. DHS, 2009, p. 110). Priority targets fall into one of two tiers:

1. Tier 1 facilities and systems are those that if successfully destroyed or disrupted through terrorist attack would cause major national or regional impacts similar to those experienced with Hurricane Katrina or the September 11, 2001, attacks.

2. Tier 2 facilities and systems are those that meet predefined, sector-specific criteria and that are not Tier 1 facilities or systems. (U.S. DHS, 2009, pp. 111–112)

Aside from axiomatic language, DHS has no established and proven method for assessing risk. Quantifying the vulnerability, threat, and consequences over the vast array of potential targets may be impossible. Not only is the set of potential targets enormous, but also, the functional interdependence of these assets makes the calculus of risk assessment that much more tortuous. The threat is an all-hazards one, the asset information is subject to change, and the continuum of historical rhythms is oblique. Past incidences are not statistically helpful for predicting future events. It is also impossible to forecast which targets are of interest to terrorists, particularly in the case of lone actors or entrepreneurs whose actions might not appear rational by our own group standards. DHS's current risk-assessment formulas might provide some approximation of the risk environment, however, a definitive model for evaluating risk and setting prioritization processes seems out of reach.

DEFINITION

BOX 9.6

Infrastructure Risk Assessment

Initially, advice on assessing risks to infrastructure looked little different from any risk assessment.

Assessing risks for specific assets—such as community water systems or chemical plants on navigable waterways—is defined by two conditions: (1) probability, the likelihood, quantitative or qualitative, that an adverse event would occur;

and (2) consequences, the damage resulting from the event, should it occur. Thus, the most severe risks are those that have both the greatest probability of occurring and would cause the greatest damage. Actual risk reflects the combination of the two factors. Risks may be managed by reducing the probability, the consequence, or, where possible, both. (U.S. GAO, 2005b, pp. 24–25)

The disadvantage in infrastructure security is that unless diverse collections of critical components fall under broad panoply protection, our entire interdependent infrastructure systems might be compromised or forced to fail. The reliability of individual parts, mechanisms, and sectors is not enough (Brown, Carlyle, Salmerón, & Wood, 2006). This disadvantage is expensive. The openness of the infrastructure system can make redundancy costly, such as in the case of rail networks, bridges, and tunnels.

Investment decisions are not only inhibited by cost but also by the lack of historical data. The difficulty of projecting cascading financial costs and political fallout from an overreaction is impossible to assess. The infrastructure was designed and created to enable commerce and to be as cost-effective as possible. Security was and still is an inferior concern. Despite the reordering of national-security interests and the new realities of the post–Cold War era, commercial stimulus and tax incentives are weak or nonexistent. As noted above, the state is the insurer of last resort. A list of collateral costs that have a cascading effect include

- police and first responder operations,

- reconstruction costs,

- the impact on insurance markets,

- extended health care costs,

- the strain on alternative infrastructure,

- future investment in security, and

- damages due to market panic and political instability, particularly if the event is terrorist induced.

Finally, among the attacker's list of advantages, they have the benefit of access to information while choosing the time and place of their attack. "Governmental agencies have produced Web sites that offer much useful information to citizens and terrorists alike. While many Web sites have been redesigned to reduce access to potentially dangerous information, exceptions abound" (Brown et al., 2006, p. 543). As science advances and intersects with breakthroughs in ICT, the threat vector takes on a new potency and threat of misuse. This general availability of material and expertise in the manufacture of weapons of mass destruction or mass disruption increases with time, rather than restrains. The skills and tools for malicious activity are becoming more easily attained owing to advancements in life-sciences research and computer science and the intersection with the globalization process and evolution of information and communications technology.

The U.S. infrastructure is enormous, complex, and, in many areas, aging or obsolete. From its beginnings, it was intended to be cost-effective and enabling to commerce. Security was not a primary concern. However, since the end of the Cold War and due to the processes of globalization, the infrastructure system vulnerabilities have surfaced with alarming starkness and urgency. Privatization and lax regulation, which have accelerated economic growth and the creation of wealth, have come at the cost of security. Despite the threat to the national economy and national security, there is still little motivation for amending infrastructure protection through government mandate or revised business models that promote enterprise security alongside profit incentives.

Following the attacks on 9/11, the Department of Homeland Security became the primary coordinating agency for infrastructure protection. Through a series of strategic plans, presidential policy directives, and separate initiatives, DHS worked to establish a core set of uniform policies, approaches, guidelines, and methodologies for infrastructure protection. The National Infrastructure Protection Plan is the blueprint for national policy to defend the nation's critical infrastructure and key resources. Despite periodic revivals, it remains mostly a complicated document of recommendations, which span an array of industry sectors, jurisdictions, and government agencies for the purpose of leading and coordinating the overall national critical-infrastructure protection effort. DHS's wide-ranging responsibilities come with expected bureaucratic obstructionism. Its attempt to harness the resources, people, and commitment of a vast assortment of separate but interdependent components is as complex as the critical infrastructure itself.

To help organize the effort to protect the nation's critical infrastructure, DHS identifies 16 industrial sectors as critical. Working with DHS agencies, sector-specific plans are drawn in collaboration with public and private-sector partners to develop and implement appropriate information-sharing and analysis mechanisms, which enhance sector security. Other federal, state, local, tribal, and territorial entities participate with private-sector representatives in a sectoral and cross-sector partnership structure. The arrangement includes an array of councils that are self-governing and whose participation is voluntary.

The range of assets and the span of the U.S. infrastructure make an onerous task of identifying and categorizing the facilities, functions, and systems that are vital to economic and social life. From an initial list of 160 assets or sites that were on the list of the National Asset Database in 2003 (based on their vulnerability to attack and potential consequences), the number of potential physical-infrastructure targets for terrorists is now estimated in the millions. Without a standard methodology or consistent coding rules, states and industries provide much of the data randomly and according to parochial and separate assessments. The result is an irregular collection of infrastructure components and a system of risk measurement open to criticism. Analysis of such a large and diverse infrastructure merits a meticulous, optimizing set of decision support tools, which, as of yet, have been underdeveloped.

Furthermore, partnerships between government and the private sectors have been difficult to establish and maintain. The partnership structure is more of a scattered contraption of voluntary participation whose recommendations have little regulatory force. Both industry and government maintain proprietary control over sensitive data, and therefore, the goals of efficient and actionable information-sharing programs and mechanisms go partially fulfilled. The natural conflict between frictionless commerce and security oftentimes surfaces.

Meanwhile, the supervisory control and data acquisition systems, which monitor and manage the industrial-plant functions and critical infrastructure, are aging and under increasing demand due to the expanding digital economy. There is a serious underinvestment in our network of roads, water supply, energy grid, inland waterways, wastewater systems, and communities. If the United States continues to lag in this area, in the future, it could put itself at greater risk. Not only does the United States depend upon its critical infrastructure to compete economically but also to affirm its unique and hegemonic standing in world affairs.

How Could Terrorism Complicate Matters?

Bansari Saha

Although the cost of the August 2003 blackout did not prove devastating for our $15 trillion economy, it is important to keep in mind that a terror-induced blackout could prove significantly more costly and have potentially debilitating impacts on the affected region as well as the entire country. As the economy tries to recover from a severe recession, a sabotage-related shock that could affect such a huge area of the country could significantly increase the cost burden and prove fatal for the recovery. Some of the added costs from a terrorism-related transmission grid attack would be as follows.

- *Damage to equipment.* A terrorist attack could not only lead to a transmission grid malfunction but also to significant damage to the equipment, resulting in higher costs and more time required for repair and replacement.

- *Hangover effect.* In the simulation referenced above, the most significant economic burden was borne by the tourism industry as people became nervous and avoided travel even after electricity was fully restored. A similar blackout caused by a terrorist attack would lead to substantially higher costs to the hotel, airline, and other service industries that are directly impacted by tourism. At the risk of sounding alarmist, it is important to remember that the economic costs of the blackout would have been significantly higher had it been caused by a terrorist attack.

The need is even greater now to think about the critical-infrastructure assets, the electric-transmission grid, and ways to improve its security and reliability. Here are some of the areas of critical-infrastructure protection that need further study:

- Understand the level of dependencies between different parts of the transmission grid so that we can establish protection priorities and strategies in line with the recommendations of the White House report.

- Study the need for increased redundancy in our transmission infrastructure, and build it by making greater investment in reserve equipment. Increased generation will improve the reliability of the whole network and reduce its vulnerabilities.

- Identify critical equipment stockpiles so there is minimal delay in recovery and restoration, and analyze ways to standardize equipment and increase component interchangeability. This is another area highlighted by the White House report on critical-infrastructure protection.

- Increase distributed generation, such as through promoting combined heat and power technologies (commonly called cogeneration technologies) to relieve transmission bottlenecks.

(Continued)

(Continued)

- Analyze the risks faced by these critical facilities as well as the steps we can take for the accrual of physical protection of our nation's assets so that we are better prepared to guard against such attacks.

Bansari Saha is a senior manager at ICF International. Dr. Saha is one the senior economists at ICF supporting public and private-sector clients in understanding the economic effects of public policy decision-making. His work focuses on issues related to energy and the environment and their relationship to our infrastructure. Dr. Saha holds a PhD in economics.

CHAPTER SUMMARY

This chapter has explained

- How infrastructure policy adapts to the threat

- The variance in the definitions of infrastructure

- What the sector-specific categories of the critical infrastructure are

- How the framework and partnership structure for interaction between the private sector and government operates in practice as opposed to policy

- The obstacles underlying successful information sharing between government and industry

- The supervisory control and data acquisition (SCADA) systems and their vulnerability

- The economic threat to homeland security from the costs of the cascading loss due to infrastructure destruction and/or disruption

- How ownership rights and responsibilities of critical-infrastructure assets conflict

- The impact of terrorism and its potential to intensify public fear and impact on infrastructure policymaking

KEY TERMS

QUESTIONS AND EXERCISES

1. What is the definition of critical infrastructure?

2. What are the 16 sector-specific industries that compose the critical infrastructure?

3. How does the U.S. government work to organize the private sector's participation in critical-infrastructure protection?

4. Why is the private sector so important to the security of the critical infrastructure?

5. Over what issues do government and private interests sometimes clash?

6. How might a terrorist attack on a critical-infrastructure target have greater impact than a natural occurrence and why?

7. What are the cascading errors of an attack upon the critical infrastructure and what is meant by "a system's failure to close down gracefully"?

8. What are the advantages and disadvantages of using commercial-off-the-shelf (COTS) patches to secure network systems?

9. What is meant by "being sent in the clear" when referring to ICT with respect to SCADA, and how is this an issue for discussion on infrastructure security?

10. Why is security investment described as a "difficult business case"?

11. What are resilience and redundancy, and how do these terms relate to a discussion on infrastructure security?

INFORMATION, COMMUNICATIONS, AND CYBERSECURITY

The following is a warning from an outgoing secretary of homeland security:

> Our country will, for example, at some point, face a major cyber event that will have a serious effect on our lives, our economy, and the everyday functioning of our society. While we have built systems, protections and a framework to identify attacks and intrusions, share information with the private sector and across the government, and develop plans and capabilities to mitigate the damage, more must be done, and must be done quickly. (U.S. Department of Homeland Security, 2013c, n.p.)

SCOPE AND DEFINITIONS

Information

Information is any knowledge communicated or recorded. **Data** are discrete items of information. A **communication** is anything that transfers information between two entities. **Information security** includes the security of information in all its forms, of which the most important conventional categories are verbal and cognitive forms, hard material forms (including paper documents and artifacts), information technology (IT), information and communications technology (ICT), industrial control systems (ICSs) and cyber physical systems (CPSs), and cyberspace (essentially electronically networked information and ICTs).

The subsections below define IT and ICT; ICS, CPS, and SCADA; and cyberspace.

IT and ICT

Information technology normally refers to any electronic or digital means of holding or communicating information. Some

Learning Objectives and Outcomes

At the end of this chapter, you should be able to understand

- The scope of information, information and communication technologies, and cyberspace

- The sources of attacks, such as thieves

- The vectors for these attacks, such as social interaction

- The actual malicious activities, such as access to private information, espionage, and sabotage

- How information and cyberspace are secured

authorities prefer to refer to **information and communications technology** (ICT) in order to bring more attention to communications technologies, such as radios, telephones, and e-mail.

ICS, CPS, and SCADA

The systems that control external processes are often known generically as *industrial control systems* or *cyber physical systems*. Literally, an **industrial control system** is any system that controls industrial processes, such as a mechanical switch that allows a pipe to empty of fluid, but today these systems are mostly used to refer to electronic controls of anything.

Cyber physical systems join "computational and physical resources," such as a computer that monitors and adjusts the performance of an automobile engine (Applegate, 2013, p. 1).

A **supervisory control and data acquisition system (SCADA)** "collects data from remote systems and relays it to a central computer in what is usually a closed loop requiring little in the way of human intervention" (Reveron, 2012, p. 13).

These systems are used to control access, heating and cooling systems, water management systems, power stations, road traffic, air traffic, emergency responses, and IT and ICT, so potential sabotage of them is of increasing concern (see the section below on sabotage).

Cyberspace

In recent decades, information and communications technology have tended to be conflated inaccurately with cyberspace. **Cyberspace** is a lax term but best refers to digitally networked information and information technologies, such as computer terminals and servers but increasingly also mobile devices such as mobile telephones connected to remote computers or hard drives (servers) via a digital network. The two main types of digital network are the **Internet,** or **World Wide Web**, which is normally open to anyone, and organizational **intranets**, which are normally restricted.

The U.K. Ministry of Defence (MOD) (2010) describes the following historical growth of cyberspace:

- The personal-computer era from 1980 to 1990, when information proliferated on desktop computers

- The first-Web era from 1990 to 2000, when information moved on to the World Wide Web

- The second-Web era from 2000 to 2010, when the Web became more social

- The third-Web era since 2010, when the Web connected knowledge (the *semantic Web*)

- Some future fourth-Web era, when some metaweb will connect intelligence (p. 138)

From 2007 to 2013, global Internet users doubled to around 2.27 billion. From 2011 to 2016, global network connections should rise from 10.6 billion to around 18.9 billion. The total number of connected devices should rise from around two billion in 2011 to 31 billion in 2020 (Negroponte, Palmisano, & Segal, 2013, p. 8).

The United States certainly has the most personal computers in use and hosts the most valuable websites, service providers, and online businesses. China, the most populous country, has the second largest national population of personal computers and the largest national population of mobile-telephone subscribers. India and Russia follow with the next largest populations of mobile-telephone subscribers but much fewer people have personal computers there. Japan, Australasia, Western European countries, and Canada are densely populated with mobile telephones and personal computers. The regional leaders include Brazil in South America, Mexico in Central America, and South Africa in Africa.

SOURCES OF ATTACKS

All attempts to access, manipulate, or change information ultimately have human sources; some of the attempts may be automated, but ultimately, even automation has human sources. These **human sources** include official actors (such as spies), profit-oriented organized criminals, terrorists, commercial competitors, ideologically motivated **hackers** (including campaigners for political and Internet freedoms), inquisitive and curious people, and journalists. Another key categorization is between external and internal threats (those without or within the target organization).

Some of the categories above overlap and some are defined more by their **vectors** than motivations. (Vectors are described later.)

The U.S. Department of Homeland Security (DHS, 2013b) defines *cyber threats* as "any identified efforts directed toward accessing, exfiltrating, manipulating, or impairing the integrity, confidentiality, security, or availability of data, an application, or a federal system, without lawful authority" (p. 1).

The U.S. GAO (2005a) reviewed data from the FBI, Central Intelligence Agency (CIA), and the Software Engineering Institute before publishing the following list of sources.

- Hackers break into networks for the thrill of the challenge or for bragging rights in the hacker community. While remote cracking once required a fair amount of skill or computer knowledge, hackers can now download attack scripts and protocols from the Internet and launch them against victim sites. Thus, while attack tools have become more sophisticated, they have also become easier to use. According to the Central Intelligence Agency, the large majority of hackers do not have the requisite expertise to threaten difficult targets such as critical U.S. networks. Nevertheless, the worldwide population of hackers poses a relatively high threat of an isolated or brief disruption causing serious damage.

- **Bot-network operators** are hackers; however, instead of breaking into systems for the challenge or bragging rights, they take over multiple systems in order to coordinate attacks and to distribute phishing schemes, spam, and malware attacks. The services of these networks are sometimes made available on underground markets (e.g., purchasing a denial-of-service attack, servers to relay spam or phishing attacks, etc.).

- **Criminal groups** seek to attack systems for monetary gain. Specifically, organized crime groups are using spam, **phishing**, and **spyware/malware** to commit **identity theft** and online fraud. International corporate spies and organized crime organizations also pose a threat to the United States through their ability to conduct industrial **espionage** and large-scale monetary theft and to hire or develop hacker talent.

- Foreign intelligence services use cyber tools as part of their information-gathering and espionage activities. In addition, several nations are aggressively working to develop information warfare doctrine, programs, and capabilities. Such capabilities enable a single entity to have a significant and serious impact by disrupting the supply, communications, and economic infrastructures that support military power—impacts that could affect the daily lives of U.S. citizens across the country.

- The disgruntled organization insider is a principal source of computer crime. Insiders may not need a great deal of knowledge about computer intrusions because their knowledge of a target system often allows them to gain unrestricted access to cause damage to the system or to steal system data. The insider threat also includes outsourcing vendors as well as employees who accidentally introduce malware into systems.

- Phishers [are] individuals, or small groups, that execute phishing schemes in an attempt to steal identities or information for monetary gain. Phishers may also use spam and spyware/malware to accomplish their objectives.

- Spammers [are] individuals or organizations that distribute unsolicited e-mail with hidden or false information in order to sell products, conduct phishing schemes, distribute spyware/malware, or attack organizations (i.e., denial of service).

- Spyware/malware authors [are] individuals or organizations with malicious intent [that] carry out attacks against users by producing and distributing spyware and malware. Several destructive computer viruses and worms have harmed files and hard drives, including the Melissa Macro Virus, the Explore.Zip worm, the CIH (Chernobyl) Virus, Nimda, Code Red, Slammer, and Blaster.

- Terrorists seek to destroy, incapacitate, or exploit critical infrastructures in order to threaten national security, cause mass casualties, weaken the U.S. economy, and damage public morale and confidence. Terrorists may use phishing schemes or spyware/malware in order to generate funds or gather sensitive information. (p. 5)

Cybersecurity experts at the Sandia National Laboratories in New Mexico noted that the assessment of threats "remains immature. This is particularly true in the dynamic and nebulous domain of *cyber* threats—a domain that tends to resist easy measurement and, in some cases, appears to defy *any* measurement" (Mateski et al., 2012, p. 7; emphasis in original). They identified seven "semi-descriptive labels" of cyber threats that "reinforce preconceived notions regarding motivation and resources" (Mateski et al., 2012, p. 11).

- Nation state.

- Organized criminal.

- "A *cyber terrorist* uses Internet-based attacks in terrorist activities, including acts of deliberate, large-scale disruption of computer networks."

- Hacker.

- "A **hacktivist** uses computers and networks as a means of protest to promote social, political, or ideological ends."

- "A **script kiddie** uses existing computer scripts or code to gain unauthorized access to data, but lacks the expertise to write custom tools."

- **Malicious insider** (Mateski et al., 2012, pp. 7, 11)

The subsections below describe the four main categories of **source**: profit-oriented criminals, insider threats, external threats, and nation-states.

Profit-Oriented Criminals

Of an international sample of data breaches in 2012, 75% were driven by financial motives. This proportion fell to around 55% in 2013, but this fall might be attributed to a relative surge in **cyber espionage**. When **profit-oriented criminals** target private individuals, they may request money while posing as someone else, such as a friend in need, a charity, a potential business

COMPARATIVE PERSPECTIVES

BOX 10.1

Official Method of Threat Assessment

In 2007, the Risk and Vulnerability Assessment Program (part of the Federal Network Security Program, which assists federal executive agencies in assessing cyber risks, inside DHS) and the Sandia National Laboratories cooperatively developed an operational threat assessment (OTA), which includes a scheme (known as the *generic threat matrix*) for judging the relative scale of each threat on an ordinal scale "without assigning a label (with its preconceived notions) [such as *hacker*] to a specific threat." It assigns a threat level from 1 (most threatening) to 8 (least threatening) for each of seven dimensions (see Table 10.1). It also allows for consideration of three *threat multipliers*: outside monetary support; assets, such as the equipment and accommodation to dedicate to the attack; and superior technology.

Table 10.1 A Suggested Scheme for Assessing Cyber Threats

	Commitment			Resources			
Threat Level	Intensity	Stealth	Time	Technical Personnel	Cyber Knowledge	Kinetic Knowledge	Access
	"the diligence or persevering determination of a threat in the pursuit of its goal"	"the ability of the threat to maintain a necessary level of secrecy throughout the pursuit of its goal"	"the period of time that a threat is capable of dedicating to planning, developing, and deploying methods to reach an objective"	"the number of group members that a threat is capable of dedicating to the building and deployment of the technical capability in pursuit of its goal"	"the theoretical and practical proficiency relating to computers, information networks, or automated systems"	"the theoretical and practical proficiency relating to physical systems, the motion of physical bodies, and the forces associated with that movement"	"the threat's ability to place a group member within a restricted system—whether through cyber or kinetic means—in pursuit of the threat's goal"
1	High	High	Years to decades	Hundreds	High	High	High
2	High	High	Years to decades	Tens of tens	Medium	High	High
3	High	High	Months to years	Tens of tens	High	Medium	Medium
4	Medium	High	Weeks to months	Tens	High	Medium	Medium
5	High	Medium	Weeks to months	Tens	Medium	Medium	Medium
6	Medium	Medium	Weeks to months	Ones	Medium	Medium	Low
7	Medium	Medium	Months to years	Tens	Low	Medium	Low
8	Low	Low	Days to weeks	Ones	Low	Low	Low

Source: Adapted from Mateski et al. (2012, pp. 16–23).

partner, or a potential seller or supplier. Some criminals break into the victim's computers, encrypt the victim's data, and demand a fee in return for decryption key. These attacks are sometimes called **ransomware** (Verizon Enterprise Solutions, 2013, pp. 4, 29; 2014, p. 9).

Some profit-oriented criminals are phishing for information that would allow them to steal the target's identity for profit. Normally they are looking for identities in order to take control of financial assets. Even if the victim loses no financial asset, they face at least opportunity costs in restoring the security of their identity. More than 1.5 million people a year suffer the theft of their identity for an annual economic loss estimated at $1 billion (U.N. Office of Drugs and Crime [ODC], 2010a, p. 17).

Of the organizations whose data were hacked in 2012, 37% of breaches affected financial organizations, and 24% affected retail organizations and restaurants (Verizon Enterprise Solutions, 2013, pp. 3–4). Some of the largest banks and official departments have been hacked for profit. For instance, in July 2007, malware nicknamed "Zeus," which had been downloaded mainly from phishing e-mails and fake websites, was identified after it had stolen information from the U.S. Department of Transportation. Zeus was designed to harvest login credentials stored on the target computer and to capture keystrokes during the user's logins. Zeus was also backdoor malware, meaning that it could take commands from its controllers, who remotely upgraded it and changed its missions. In June 2009, Prevx (a commercial security service provider) reported that Zeus had compromised more than 74,000 File Transfer Protocol accounts across dozens of websites, including websites owned by the Bank of America and the U.S. National Aeronautics and Space Administration. Thousands of login credentials were stolen from **social media** offered by Facebook, Yahoo, and others. In July 2010, Trusteer, another security service provider, reported that Zeus had captured information on credit cards issued by 15 U.S. banks. (Trusteer did not name the banks.) On October 1, 2010, the FBI announced that it had discovered an international criminal network that had used Zeus to steal around $70 million from U.S. targets. Arrests were made in the United States, Britain, and Ukraine. Around 3.6 million computers had been infected in the United States, perhaps millions more internationally (Cox & Golomb, 2010).

In 2007, TJX Companies admitted that 45 million credit card numbers were exposed to hackers who had accessed databases over a period of 3 years. In 2009, Heartland Payment Systems admitted that malware had penetrated the servers that processed 100 million credit card transactions per month, but they did not know the actual number of credit cards compromised.

On May 9, 2013, prosecutors in New York unsealed indictments against eight men accused of being the local team of a global cyber thieves. Since October 2012, hackers broke into computer networks of financial companies in the United States and India and eliminated the withdrawal limits on prepaid debit cards before withdrawing tens of millions of dollars from ATMs in more than 20 other places around the world. First, hackers breached an Indian firm that processes credit card transactions for MasterCard debit cards issued by Rakbank, an institution in the United Arab Emirates, then they withdrew $5 million in 4,500 ATM transactions. Second, hackers breached a MasterCard processor in the United States that handled transactions for prepaid debit cards issued by the Bank of Muscat in Oman, then they withdrew $40 million in 36,000 transactions over a 10-hr period.

In the largest cyber theft yet, hackers penetrated the systems of more than 100 banks and other financial institutions across 30 nations, transferring money into accounts digitally, inflating account balances digitally, and prompting cash machines to dispense cash physically in front of accomplices. The thefts started in late 2013 but were not revealed until February 2015 by a company called in to investigate. It estimated a total theft around $900 million, although it had only seen evidence for about one third of that. The theft persisted undetected because the thieves limited individual thefts to mere thousands of dollars (the largest theft was worth $10 million) and changed account balances to disguise the transaction (Kaspersky Lab, 2015).

The USA PATRIOT Act of October 2001 provides authority to prosecute fraud involving American credit cards even if abroad. In July 2010, U.S. President Obama's administration published a draft *National Strategy for Trusted Identities in Cyberspace* to improve the security of personal identities in cyberspace. Its principal immediate measure was to demand only minimal necessary information to be transferred during any cyber transaction. In April 2011, the final version was released; this provided guidelines for voluntary compliance (U.S. White House, 2011a).

Insider Threats

Insider threats are personnel who are employed, authorized, or granted privileges by the organization but who harm the organization in some way. The U.S. Readiness Team (US-CERT, 2013) defines a *insider threat* as

> a current or former employee, contractor, or business partner who has had authorized access to an organization's network, system, or data and intentionally exceeded or misused that access in a manner that negatively affected the confidentiality, integrity, or availability of the organization's information or information systems. (n.p.)

The National Counterintelligence and Security Center (n.d.) defines an insider threat as "a person with authorized access to U.S. Government resources, to include personnel, facilities, information, equipment, networks, and systems, [who] uses that access to harm the security of the United States" (n.p.).

ICTs have given insiders more capacity to steal data. For instance, Dongfan Chung, an engineer who transferred secrets to China, mostly relating to military aircraft and space shuttles, had hidden 250,000 pages of paper documents with sensitive information under his home by the time he was arrested in 2006. Almost twice as much information would fit on one compact disc (U.S. Office of the National Counterintelligence Executive [ONCIX], 2011, p. 2). In January 2010, Bradley Manning, a soldier of private rank in the U.S. Army then assigned as an intelligence analyst to a base in Iraq, stole the largest amount of restricted data ever leaked from one source— more than 260,000 U.S. diplomatic cables and more than 500,000 military reports about or from Iraq and Afghanistan. He downloaded all the information on to digital media, which he carried out of the secure facility. In March 2010, he started to leak documents to the website WikiLeaks. He was betrayed to the FBI in May by a hacker to whom Bradley had described his activities in an online forum. His correspondence included this damning revelation of the information security: "Weak servers, weak logging, weak physical security, weak counter-intelligence, inattentive signal analysis . . . a perfect storm" (Bennett, 2011, n.p.).

Most insider threats who release sensitive information are carelessly rather than maliciously noncompliant with the access or transfer controls. Even the most senior employees can be noncompliant. For instance, on November 9, 2012, General David Petraeus resigned as U.S. director of central intelligence after revelations of his affair with Paula Broadwell, a former U.S. Army intelligence officer (and his biographer). Her harassing e-mails to another woman prompted a criminal investigation that unearthed her privileged access to Petraeus's private and classified information, partly through a Web-based e-mail account that they had shared in an attempt to communicate privately (Miller & Nakashima, 2012).

A public-private survey in the United States in 2007 found that 31% of electronic-crime perpetrators in the United States were insiders. Sixty percent of them were thieves; 40% of them intended to sabotage IT, of which very few (2% of all cases) sabotaged for financial gain, while most were seeking vengeance against an employer or colleague. Almost all of the sabotage was of IT from inside the IT industry.

A survey in 2013 of nearly 10,000 executives at large organizations found that 31% estimated the likeliest threats as current employees, 27% blamed former employees, 16% blamed current service providers, consultants, or contractors, 13% blamed former providers, 12% blamed suppliers or business partners, and 10% blamed information brokers. Only 50% of these organizations reported any formal plan for responding to insider threats, and only 18% reported that their management of insider cyber threats was "extremely" effective (PricewaterhouseCoopers, 2013).

Verizon's analysis of a sample of international data breaches in 2012 found that insiders were involved in only 14% of breaches, most of them deliberate and financially motivated. Twenty-nine percent of breaches involved social engineering, and 76% exploited weak or stolen credentials, in all of which insiders must be implicated, however accidentally (Verizon Enterprise Solutions, 2013, pp. 4, 21).

Insiders could be intrinsically inspired or directed by external actors, perhaps unknowingly (the external actor could trick the internal threat into thinking that they are acting on behalf of the same employer) or knowingly (the insider could accept a bribe to traffic information). The U.S. Computer Emergency Readiness Team drew attention to the increasing role of external actors in insider threats after finding that half of insider threats from 2003 to 2007 in the United States had been recruited by outsiders, including organized criminals and foreign governments. US-CERT also found more crimes perpetrated by the employees of business partners that had been granted privileges inside the organization. New mergers and acquisitions also increase the chance of insider threats (Cappelli, Moore, Trzeciak, & Shimeall, 2009, p. 6). Germany's Federal Office for the Protection of the Constitution estimates that 70% of all foreign economic espionage involves insiders (U.S. ONCIX, 2011, p. B1).

Information security experts prescribe more monitoring and training of compliance but also suggest that about 5% of employees will not comply despite the training. Most training is formal, but most people are better at recalling than applying formally trained knowledge. More experiential training would help the employees to become more self-aware of their noncompliance, but even so, some people are not inherently compliant or attentive. In order to catch the very few people who are chronically noncompliant, the organization is forced to monitor them increasingly obtrusively, which is restricted by ethical and legal obligations and the material challenges; in a large organization, monitoring most people most of the time would be prohibitively expensive, legally risky, and would raise the employees' distrust and stress. In many jurisdictions, dismissal of employees is difficult. At the same time, the risks of an insider threat are increasingly great. By 2010, some companies had added to employment contracts an agreement that noncompliance would be a dismissible offense (after two or three breaches, say). Nondisclosure agreements (in which the employee promises not to release sensitive information, even after separation) became commonplace in the 1990s.

OFFICIAL ADVICE FOR MANAGING INSIDER THREATS The U.S. Office of the National Counterintelligence Executive suggests the following cycle for managing insider risks.

1. Assure insider security, by for instance, checking the backgrounds of new hires and reaching nondisclosure agreements.

2. Assure information security, by for instance, imposing controls on the insider's access to and transfer of information, particularly around the time when the employee separates.

3. Control external travel or contacts with external hazards.

4. Train insiders in secure behaviors and promote awareness of their behaviors.

5. Analyze insider behaviors and respond to issues.

6. Audit and monitor insider behaviors and their management. (ONCIX, 2011, p. A4)

U.S. CERT recommended the following 16 practices for controlling insider risks.

1. Consider threats from insiders and business partners in enterprise-wide risk assessments.

2. Clearly document and consistently enforce policies and controls.

3. Institute periodic security awareness training for all employees.

4. Monitor and respond to suspicious or disruptive behavior, beginning with the hiring process.

5. Anticipate and manage negative workplace issues.

6. Track and secure the physical environment.

7. Implement strict password and account management policies and practices.

8. Enforce separation of duties and least privilege.

9. Consider insider threats in the software development lifecycle.

10. Use extra caution with system administrators and technical or privileged users.

11. Implement system change controls.

12. Log, monitor, and audit employee online actions.

13. Use layered defense against remote attacks.

14. Deactivate computer access following termination.

15. Implement secure backup and recovery processes.

16. Develop and insider incident response plan. (Cappelli et al., 2009, pp. 27–31)

External Threats

External threats cause harm to an organization without being employed by the organization or without authorized access to internal information or domains.

External threats are more numerous than insider threats because external actors are more numerous and less directly controlled. One database suggests that external threats made up about 90% of all cyber intruders in 2004 and 2013, although changes in sources and methods had suggested that internal threats and external threats were almost equal in 2007 (Verizon Enterprise Solutions, 2014, p. 8). Of data breaches in 2012, external actors were involved in 92% of them, insiders 14%. Of the external actors, 55% were organized criminals, 21% were state affiliates, 13% unknown, 8% unaffiliates, 2% activists, and 1% former employees (Verizon Enterprise Solutions, 2013, pp. 3, 17, 19). A survey in 2013 of business executives found that 55% of organizations evaluate the security of third parties with which the organization shares data or network access, and only 22% reported that they planned with third parties how to respond to incidents (PricewaterhouseCoopers, 2013).

Practically, any commercial or public relationship involves some compromise of the boundary between internal and external actors. For instance, when the organization outsources services, such as Internet services, to an external actor, the external actor is granted privileged information about the organization's network. Some competitors may pretend to be potential clients or business partners in order to gain information that is then useful for developing some competitive product or service. For instance, in the 2000s, some French, German, and Japanese companies complained that Chinese partners developed high-speed electric railways from information gathered from bids for unawarded contracts as well as from supplied but patented technologies (see Box 10.2).

When the organization procures anything externally, the resulting supply chain is exposed to malicious actors. For instance, official procurers worry about buying computers from abroad where foreign intelligence services could plant malware on the computers to spy on official users. In theory, malicious actors could sabotage acquisitions in more traditional ways, such as by planting an explosive device inside a delivered package. (These risks—potential espionage or sabotage—are separate from traditional commercial risks, such as a supplier's nonperformance—its failure to deliver something on the schedule or with the capabilities specified.) Official procurers also worry about external ownership of their supply chain, where an external actor could steal intellectual property (in addition to the more traditional supply chain risk of simply interrupting supply).

External threats may access information or plant malware after procurement, during the deployment, configuration, and integration of some procured hardware, such as when external actors are employed to train users in their new hardware or to set up the new hardware for use. External actors could distribute malware through the software acquired for the hardware or through peripheral devices. Periodic maintenance, servicing, and upgrades are also opportunities for external malicious intervention. A final opportunity for the malicious actor in the life cycle of the hardware is during the organization's retirement or deletion of the hardware from service or use. The hardware is often sent for disposal without proper removal of the information contained therein. (Many operating systems do not entirely delete files when ordered to delete them.) Insiders may contribute to this risk by selling hardware to external actors or by diverting hardware to their friends and family rather than obeying orders to destroy it.

Nation-States

Nation-states are sovereign political units. They are much less numerous than private actors (the United Nations has 193 member states; the human population numbers over seven billion), yet the average national-state government has more capacity than the average private actor. (In between are commercial corporations, some of which are wealthier than most governments.)

Chinese Gathering of French Proprietary Information Around 2011

BOX 10.2

In January 2011, a French news magazine (*Le Parisien*) published a leaked French intelligence document that describes three Chinese techniques for gathering foreign proprietary information: lamprey, mushroom factory, and reverse counterfeiting.

The **lamprey technique** advertises for commercial bids on large projects, such as infrastructure. After Western companies bid, they are urged to offer more information in order to secure a contract. After several rounds of rebidding, the competing bidders are summarily informed that the project has been shelved, but Chinese developers then use the information to develop their own alternative. For instance, TGV of France was the leading bidder on a multibillion dollar tender to build China's high-speed train. As part of the process, the French embassy in Beijing organized a 6-month training course for Chinese engineers.

A few months after the course, China revealed its own high-speed train remarkably similar to the TGV and Germany's ICE train.

The **mushroom factory** involves manipulation of a joint venture between a foreign company and a local Chinese firm. After the foreign company has transferred enough technology, the Chinese company divests a new company outside of the joint venture to offer the same technology. For instance, Danone, the French dairy and drinks group, alleged that the Chinese drinks producer, Wahaha, divested their joint venture.

Reverse counterfeiting means stealing technology but accusing the victim of counterfeiting. For instance, in 1996, Schneider Electric of France patented a hook in its fuse box. Its Chinese rival, Chint, started building the same hook and took Schneider to court in China for copying its design, and Schneider was ordered to pay a fine worth 330 million yuan.

We seem to face a mismatch between sovereign capacity and common perceptions of sovereign capacity. For instance, a survey in 2013 of nearly 10,000 executives at large commercial organizations found that only 4% blamed foreign nation-states while 6% blamed foreign organizations or entities for their information security incidents (PricewaterhouseCoopers, 2013).

Verizon found that of more than 600 breaches that occurred in 27 countries in 2012, more than 75% of those breaches could be sourced to someone in an identifiable country, although only 19% of data breaches were attributed to state-affiliated actors. Most of the sources were not affiliated with any state and were acting privately. Forty different countries were represented. Brazil, Colombia, Germany, Armenia, and the Netherlands were each the source of about 1% of breaches, with Russia at 5%, Bulgaria 7%, the United States 18%, Romania 28%, and China 30%. Almost all of the breaches were financially motivated, except the Chinese-sourced breaches, which were almost all espionage. Chinese sources accounted for 96% of all espionage cases in the data set (Verizon Enterprise Solutions, 2013, p.3).

Less than 10 of the nearly 200 sovereign governments in the world are commonly cited as having most of the capacity or intent for cyber attacks. Official capacity for cyber attacks is usually assigned to intelligence or military agencies. U.S. intelligence and security agents often categorize **foreign intelligence services** (FISs) and **foreign intelligence and security services** (FISSs) separately from other threats, operationally meaning any foreign official threat short of positive identification as a particular service or agency. In recent years, U.S. officials referred to **advanced persistent threats** (APTs) as code for national threats in general, Chinese threats in particular.

Unofficially, some U.S. officials have stated that about 140 FISSs target the United States, of which about 50 have serious capacity to harm the United States and five or six are severe threats. The commonly identified national cyber threats are China, Russia, Israel, Iran, North Korea, and France. (The sources are not necessarily official; they could be private activists, private actors with official support, or disguised official actors.)

Some officials have issued accusations on the record.

- On April 12, 2011, the Director of Intelligence at U.S. Cyber Command, Rear Admiral Samuel Cox, told subordinates that "a global cyber arms race is underway" and at least six countries have offensive cyber-warfare capabilities that they are using to probe U.S. military and private computer networks.

- In February 2013, Janet Napolitano, U.S. Secretary of Homeland Security, said, "There are a number of countries that we see attacks emanating from—and again they can be just individuals who are located in the country—but three that are I think of special concern would be Iran, Russia, and China" (Epatko, 2013).

- Director of National Intelligence James R. Clapper Jr., in a prepared statement to the U.S. Senate Armed Services Committee on January 31, 2012, stated that "Russia and China are aggressive and successful purveyors of economic espionage against the United States. Iran's intelligence operations against the United States, including cyber capabilities, have dramatically increased in recent years in depth and complexity. . . . these three countries will remain the top threats to the United States in the coming years" (Clapper, 2012, p. 8).

National threats have more capacity for using information and communications technologies as vectors for their phishing. The victims are often unwilling to reveal events because of the commercial impacts (in the case of commercial victims) or the bureaucratic or political impacts (in the case of official victims), so the true frequency of these attacks is underestimated.

Largely anonymous and anecdotal reports suggest that APTs will research a particular organization over weeks before attacking as widely and repeatedly as possible before the different attacks are recognized as threatening, which could take days. The attacks are conducted in campaigns with multiple methods, cumulatively penetrating deeper into a target's defenses, despite frequent failures. Human skills are more important than the technological tools: The sources gather much of their information by phishing and social engineering through direct communications with the targets and by adapting to the defenses. The attacks themselves are usually e-mails to executives, usually tailored to the target person by pretending to be someone whom the target knows or by attaching malware disguised as something of interest to the target (such as a document about the oil industry sent to an oil industry executive).

Mandiant (2013), a cybersecurity provider, describes the following activities within the APT *attack life cycle*:

1. Initial external reconnaissance

2. Initial compromise (access) inside the target's secured domain

3. Establishing a foothold inside the domain

4. Escalating privileges

5. Internal reconnaissance

6. Movements laterally within the domain

7. Maintaining presence and perhaps returning to Step 4

8. Ending the mission (p. 27)

APTs are countered by the following:

1. Preparing human targets to spot suspicious communications

2. Preparing real-time threat management software that can detect the APT's more sophisticated and stealthy malware and network traffic

3. Legally prosecuting the sources

4. Deterrence or retaliation (p. 27)

ACCESS VECTORS

While the ultimate sources of all attacks are human actors, most attacks are vectored by some sort of material or communication. Sandia National Laboratories identified a number of **attack vectors**, where each is "an avenue or tool that a threat uses to launch attacks, gather information, or deliver/leave a malicious item or items in those devices, systems, or networks" (Mateski et al., 2012, p. 23).

The subsections below describe these vectors and their controls: printed documents, malware, databases, webpages, social interaction, social media, postal communications, telephone communications, e-mail, removable and mobile digital media, cloud computing, wired networks, and wireless networks.

Printed Documents

Printed documents are any materials with information printed on them in ink. They are ubiquitous; they include maps, plans, photographs, letters, notes, books, and other texts. In the 1970s and 1980s, futurists forecasted the imminent demise of anything but digital information, but still we use printed information, in part because digital information is less secure than they had hoped, in part because electronic screens still do not offer higher resolution. (Higher resolutions imply more information and less stress on the human eye.)

In 2012, the U.S. Government Business Council asked federal officials and contractors to choose the media that represented their "biggest security concern for 2012"; they were more concerned about paper documents than digital documents.

- Paper documents (91%)

- E-mail (89%)

- Digital text and documents (77%)

- Transitory content (68%)

- Digital audio and video (53%)

- Paper drawings and charts (47%)

- Social media (42%)

- Film (24%)

- Microfiche and microfilm (24%)

- Other (6%) (Jackson, 2013a)

The loss of information on paper is normally due to a failure to control social transfer or physical access. As an example of the risks of unsecured information on paper, consider the masses of paper found by rebels, activists, and journalists inside abandoned official sites in Iraq in 2003, in Libya during the revolution against Muammar Gaddafi in 2011, and in Syria since the revolution against Bashar al-Assad since March 2011. Some of these documents revealed surprising cooperation between western governments, commercial suppliers, and autocrats, contrary to official policy. Other information revealed operational and personal secrets. For instance, militants, looters, and journalists picked up paper documents, including security protocols, information about personnel, contracts with commercial providers and militia, and diplomatic messages from the

U.S. diplomatic outpost in Benghazi, Libya, after U.S. personnel and allies had abandoned the post following an armed attack overnight on September 11–12, 2012.

Malware

Malware is software that is harmful. For the U.S. GAO (2005a), malware is "software designed with malicious intent, such as a virus" (p. 8). A **computer virus** is a

> program that infects computer files, usually executable programs, by inserting a copy of itself into the file. These copies are usually executed when the infected file is loaded into memory, allowing the virus to infect other files. Unlike the computer worm, a virus requires human involvement (usually unwitting) to propagate. (p. 8)

A **worm** is an "independent computer program that reproduces by copying itself from one system to another across a network. Unlike computer viruses, worms do not require human involvement to propagate" (p. 8).

Malware is sometimes created by accident or for fun but is usually developed or exploited for malicious objectives. One expert noted

> that the current trend is that there is now less of a propensity to make the user aware of the presence of malicious code on a computer, and more of a will to have the code run silent and deep so that the attacker can remotely control the target's computer to launch massive attacks or exfiltrate data from a sensitive network. (Yannakogeorgos, 2011, p. 261)

Commercial software itself has become more complicated, increasing the chance of inherent flaws or of vulnerabilities to attack. In 2005, the U.S. National Institute of Standards and Technology estimated 20 flaws per 1,000 lines of software code; Microsoft Windows 2000 (a computer operating system) had 35 million lines (U.S. GAO, 2005c, pp. 9–10). U.S. officials once estimated that 80% of successful intrusions into federal computer systems are vectored through flawed software (Wilson, 2003, p. 6).

Verizon's analysis of 621 breaches of mostly commercial data across 27 countries found that 40% were vectored by malware, such as spyware, compared to 52% by hacking, such as stolen credentials. These malware arrived by

- direct installation (74%),

- e-mail attachment (47%),

- unknown means (10%),

- website (8%),

- e-mailed link (5%),

- remote injection (3%), and

- another malware's download.

These malware acted as

- spyware (75%),

- backdoors (66%),

- data exporters (63%),

- stored-data capturers (55%),

- command and control (51%),

- downloader (51%),

- password dumper (45%),

- rootkit (39%),

- adminware (18%),

- random access memory scraper (17%),

- control disabler (9%),

- app data capturer (4%), and

- client-side attacker (4%). (Verizon Enterprise Solutions, 2013, pp. 24, 27–28)

Malware continues to proliferate at exponential rates. Panda Security reports that 20% of all malware was created in 2013. In that year, Kaspersky Lab detected 315,000 new malicious files per day, up from 200,000 per day in 2012 (Lyngaas, 2014).

Databases

A **database** is a collection of data. Almost everybody provides sensitive information that is held on some other organization's media—sensitive information such as ethnicity, gender, sexuality, religion, politics, trade-union membership, birth, death, marriage, bank account, health care, and crimes (either perpetrator or victim). The growth of bureaucratic capacity and digital communications has encouraged wider handling of more data. One British authority estimated that such sensitive information about the average adult Briton is held in around 700 databases (U.K. Information Commissioner's Office, 2006, p. 7). ICTs have made the holding of data easier but also exposed more data to cyber attack. The Privacy Rights Clearinghouse estimated that in 2011, 30.4 million sensitive records were exposed by just 535 cyber intrusions in the United States that year. A survey of thousands of executives globally in 2013 found that each of their organizations had experienced 3,741 computer security incidents on average; the worst impacts were on data privacy, including compromised employee records (35% of respondents), compromised customer records (31%), loss or damage of internal records (29%), and client or employee identity theft (23%) (PricewaterhouseCoopers, 2013).

The U.S. ONCIX (2011) gives this advice on managing data:

- Get a handle on company data—not just in databases but also in e-mail messages, on individual computers, and as data objects in web portals;

categorize and classify the data, and choose the most appropriate set of controls and markings for each class of data; identify which data should be kept and for how long. Understand that it is impossible to protect everything.

- Establish compartmentalized access programs to protect unique trade secrets and proprietary information; centralize intellectual property data—which will make for better security and facilitate information sharing.

- Restrict distribution of sensitive data; establish a shared data infrastructure to reduce the quantity of data held by the organization and discourage unnecessary printing and reproduction. (p. A4)

Webpages

A **webpage** is a document that can be accessed through cyberspace and presented on a computer screen. Most Internet activity involves online searches, browsing, and e-mail. Visiting the associated webpages exposes the user to malware, particularly if the user downloads or is misled into visiting a webpage resembling a login page, where the threat gathers the user's passwords and other access keys. Websense Security Labs (2013b) found that from 2012 to 2013, the number of malicious Web links increased by 6 times globally and by 7.2 times in the United States alone. Eighty-five percent of these malicious Web links were found on compromised legitimate hosts. Ninety-two percent of spam e-mails contain potentially malicious Web links. The increase is probably mostly due to increased use of shortened Web links in social media; shortened Web links redirect you to the ultimate destination. Although shortened Web links can be legitimate efforts to make the destination easier to communicate, they can be used to disguise the ultimate destination (pp. 4–14, 27).

The user can spot malicious Web links by checking that the actual destination matches the declared destination. (The real destination is revealed when the mouse cursor hovers over the link.) Users should not enter their credentials into unknown webpages or webpages whose address does not look the same as normal. (A fake website cannot have exactly the same address as the real website.) Some addresses can be replaced by shorter alternatives for the convenience of the user, but these shortened addresses can be used by threats to redirect to malicious sites.

Users tend to underestimate the insecurity of their online activities. Unlike the typical software on an intranet or other organizationally secured domain, Web-based applications are designed to be accessible and easy to use more than secure. Some sites and browsers, by default, place information packets known as *cookies* on the user's computer. Legitimately, these cookies are used by the site to recognize the user; illegitimately, they can upload information back to the site that the user has not authorized. Some of this information may be used for purposes that the user finds useful, such as more targeted advertising, but often it leads to unwanted advertisements or can be sold to third-party marketers, including **spammers**—people who send you information you never requested and do not want. Worse, cookies can be vectors for malware. In December 2013, leaked documents from the U.S. National Security Agency (NSA) suggested that the NSA and Britain's General Communications Headquarters (GCHQ) had used commercial cookies to track the online activities associated with individual persons, whatever device or browser they were using to access the Internet (Soltani, Peterson, & Gellman, 2013).

Most webpages use scripts to perform functions, such as placing cookies or running advertisements. Some of these scripts can be exploited by external threats who insert malicious scripts, such as scripts that surreptitiously gather login credentials. At the user's end, script-blocking extensions can be added to the Web browser. Otherwise, a malicious script is free to download malware, leaving the user with the difficult and sometimes impossible task of discovering and removing the malware.

Programming languages also are exploitable if not properly programmed. For instance, Structured Query Language (SQL, pronounced "sequel") is used by websites to manage data. A **SQL injection (SQLi)** inserts malicious code to access or alter the data. These data could include your login credentials and private information associated with your profile. These vulnerabilities are impossible for the user to control except by avoiding or at least minimizing use of such websites. Since SQLi cannot normally exploit your data unless you are logged into the data set, you can limit your exposure by logging on as rarely as possible and by logging off as soon as possible. Closing your browser does not always log you off automatically; you should always refuse options to stay logged in indefinitely.

Social Interaction

Most harmful leakage of privileged information arises from a **social interaction**, such as when people talk too loosely about private information or are verbally persuaded to give up information to somebody who is not whom they pretend to be. Similarly, most unauthorized access to digital information is gained socially, albeit through digital media. ICTs (especially mobile telephones and Internet-based communications) have enabled more remote communications that users tend to treat casually.

Many people release information unintentionally through careless rather than deliberate social interactions. The threat could use any and all of the following seven activities.

1. **Shoulder surfing** is the term used to describe threats who surreptitiously watch you using your credentials to access some secure domain, such as an automated cash dispenser or personal computer.

2. **Tailgating** describes threats who follow closely behind you in order to pass through a door that was released by your credentials or who follow you onto a computer system while you are still logged in.

3. **Dumpster diving** describes threats who search through trash and rubbish looking for documents that could reveal other people's credentials. The threat could use such information to pose as you or as a pretext for opening a social interaction with you.

4. The threat could contact you pretending to be someone you know, such as a client or colleague (known as *phishing* or **spear phishing**).

5. The threat could pretend to be you in order to persuade a third party, such as your bank, to release information about you (known as **spoofing**, *scamming*, or **pretexting** in American English, or **blagging** in British English).

6. The threat could bribe someone to release information about you.

7. The threat could blackmail you or someone you know.

Of these routes to information, the route that has become much easier through digital technologies is phishing. Phishing can be used as a means to any end, including sabotage, but is commonly defined and discussed as a form of espionage. More than 95% of state-affiliated espionage identified by Verizon in 2012 employed phishing.

Of 621 commercial-data breaches identified in 2012, 13% resulted from insider misuse or abuse of their privileges, 29% leveraged social interactions, 35% involved physical access, and 76% exploited weak or stolen credentials. Only 2% of the 621 breaches were attributable to human error, such as inadvertent sharing with a threat, but 48% of more than 47,000 other incidents, such as lost devices, were attributable to human error.

The social interactions included

- phishing (77%),

- bribery (12%),

- extortion (4%),

- pretexting (3%),

- influence (2%), and

- unknown (2%) (Verizon Enterprise Solutions, 2013, pp. 4, 24–25, 34).

Sometimes the most senior officials are guilty of such carelessness. For instance, on October 24, 2013, Michael Hayden, formerly Director of the Central Intelligence Agency (2006–2009) and of the National Security Agency (1999–2005), was sitting in a regular seat on an Amtrak train, speaking by mobile telephone to a journalist off the record or on background, but he was overheard by another journalist (Tom Matzzie) in a nearby seat, who tweeted about Hayden's "disparaging" comments about the Obama administration's handling of the CIA's covert activities and the NSA's role in making the president's Blackberry phone more secure.

In practice, the most senior executives and officials are the primary targets. They are likely to hold the most valuable data, they are likely to have the most privileges, and their work tends to distract them from security. Verizon found that executives were the most likely targets of malicious social interactions, followed by managers (Verizon Enterprise Solutions, 2013, p. 35).

Social Media

Social media are ICTs on which personal users release information about themselves or subscribe to information from other users. The most used social websites are Facebook, LinkedIn, and Twitter. Some sites specialize in sharing photographs, videos, and audio files, some in romantic connections, some in professional connections, some in social games.

According to leaked official documents, the U.S. and British governments have been concerned since at least January 2007 that terrorists could use online games to train and to communicate. Apparently, U.S. and British officials have been operating in massively multiplayer online games (MMOGs) in order to survey such threats, although reportedly with little success (Mazzetti & Elliott, 2013). Some official actors, such as the Iranian government, have developed official forms of social media in an effort to impose control on or gain information from social media.

Social media are exposed to anyone who browses the same sites. Some software is available to scrape information from the social media associated with a person's name. Social media encourage users to expand their social network but unguardedly or superficially. Many social media allow anonymous discussions and postings. Generally, users tend to behave more anonymously but revealingly when online. Users of social media may believe that their information is restricted to their friends, but some social media allow anybody to view information on anybody else, store such information in insecure domains, or even sell such information. Some social media promise not to sell information or to prevent access to the posted information except to the user's "friends," but the friends, as defined by the user and the site, likely include casual acquaintances; indeed, users, in pursuit of a larger count of online "friends," often agree to "friend" anyone who asks. Social media contribute to their cumulative online presence, from which threats might gather enough information to steal the individual's identity.

Some very important persons and officials have been careless on social networks. For instance, in November 2012, a Belgian newspaper published an investigation into how many employees of the Belgian state security service listed their employer on Facebook or LinkedIn. Several French users of LinkedIn had listed their employer as France's external intelligence agency. American journalists found more than 200 users of LinkedIn listing the Central Intelligence Agency as their employer.

Users are likelier to be revealing of personal and professional information when they are looking for another job or romantic partner. For instance, official employees, after leaving official employment or when seeking another job, have been known to distribute online photographs of themselves inside secured domains, of their official credentials, and of themselves with important persons as evidence for their professional qualifications.

Additionally, the privacy and accuracy of information is less protected legally when online than offline, encouraging rampant online slander, defamation, **misinformation**, and abuse, including online bullying. Private citizens face practically no criminal legal restrictions on online behavior. The tort system is usually a waste of time for claimants or victims; the few cases that have been heard in civil or criminal court usually fail to clarify responsibility or harm. In practice, cyber information and misinformation are controlled by users and hosts, motivated mostly by their intrinsic ethics and external commercial pressures, not the law. In the United States, the Communications Decency Act of 1996 makes clear that Internet service providers and online hosts are not responsible for the content of posts from outside parties, although the positive implication of this clarity is that hosts are free to moderate or delete content without legal liability.

Traditionally, public concern has been raised over juvenile use of social media where adults (probably pretending to be other juveniles) could groom them for abuse, such as by asking them to share intimate information or even to meet in the real world. Some social media are supposed to be reserved for juveniles, but any adult could register as a user. In any social media, juveniles routinely disclose their own identities or the identities of other juveniles, in contrast to most news media, where journalists normally follow codes of ethics that prohibit revelations of juvenile identities, even when juveniles are accused of crimes. Juveniles are capable of undermining such regimes. For instance, in February 2013, users of online forums on a website devoted to issues in Fairfax, Virginia, revealed the names of three male high-school students who had been arrested for allegedly making videos of themselves having sex with several girls during a news embargo on those same names. More worrying, juveniles are quite capable of exploiting each other and adults by online bullying, slander, and defamation. Adults are disadvantaged against juvenile threats because juveniles are protected in ways that adults are not but are not equally accountable.

Adult users, too, can be exploited sexually in similar ways (posting of intimate information or grooming for sexual exploitation). The average adult, being wealthier and in possession of more valuable information than the average juvenile, is more likely to be exploited financially or professionally. In pursuit of friends, employers, or romantic partners, individual users tend to post online information that they would not reveal offline, commonly including their sexuality, age, address, profession, and hobbies. In communicating through social media with supposed friends, they may discuss private information such as their health or romantic partners. They may also reveal plans, such as foreign travel, that encourage thieves to target their homes. They also may be persuaded to send money to strangers or agree to meet people in the real world who turn out to be robbers or worse.

Users who want to use social media but also to preserve privacy are advised to avoid posting anything except what they want to and expect to become freely available. They should not use open information, such as their pet's name, in their log-in names or passwords.

Postal Communications

Postal communications are material that is physically transported by some provider. Post can be intercepted; postal deliverers have been bribed to divert mail; threats can also seize the mail from the container into which it has been posted or delivered before it is picked up by the deliverer or the recipient. Some private actors, such as unscrupulous journalists, commercial competitors, jealous romantic partners, participants in legal disputes, and stalkers, are incentivized to intercept communications. Common thieves also steal mail in pursuit of financial checks and credit cards or information that helps them to steal personal identities. Official investigators may also intercept mail in pursuit of evidence for crimes.

Nevertheless, **postal mail** remains ubiquitous despite some replacement by ICTs. The increasing use of electronic means of transacting business has reduced the use of paper transactions, but increasing interception of the electronic means suggests that electronic means are not perfect replacements. Meanwhile, official and criminal actors have demonstrated that private information is more effectively and efficiently gathered digitally than through the mail.

Some people, including activists, businesspersons, diplomats, profit-oriented criminals, and terrorists, have returned to verbal and postal communications since uncovering more revelations in the 2000s of the insecurity of their digital and electronic communications. For instance, al-Qaeda's most senior staff switched back to traditional communications in the early 2000s after discovering that some of their e-mails, mobile telephones, and satellite telephones had been occasionally intercepted during the 1990s. However, as a result of these precautions U.S. intelligence eventually identified a courier whose movement led them to the hiding place in Pakistan of Osama bin Laden, where he was killed by U.S. special operations forces on May 2, 2011.

Similarly, official authorities continue to use couriers because of concerns about electronic and digital espionage. For instance, the U.S. Bureau of Diplomatic Security (part of the Department of State) operates a courier service for the carriage of classified materials in diplomatic pouches (which international law treats as sovereign territory) between diplomatic sites at home and abroad. In 2008, the service employed 98 couriers and delivered more than 55,000,000 lbs of classified diplomatic materials (U.S. GAO, 2009b, p. 6).

Telephone Communications

A **telephone** is an ICT that converts a verbal conversation into some electronic signal for transmission to another ICT. Increasing use of ICTs implies increasing exposure to interception of our communications. Telephones have been commercially available for more than 100 years. In the last two decades, mobile (wireless) telephones and Internet-based alternatives have become accessible to the majority. The Internet offers effective telephone replacement technologies, such as Voice over Internet Protocol (VoIP), of which the most well-known carrier is Skype. Around 3.5 billion people, or half the global population, own a mobile telephone, whose mobility encourages more use of both voice communications and text messages. Americans alone sent 188 billion text messages in 2010. Most of the global population has access to a mobile telephone through a family member or close friend. Five billion users are in the developing world, where mobile telephones are more valuable because of the poor availability of other forms of communication. Africa is the fastest-growing mobile market. The top national investors in ICTs are the United States, China, Japan, Britain, and Russia (in that order). Internationally, most telephonic and Internet traffic is routed through the U.S. and Europe (Negroponte et al., 2013, p. 9).

Telephones can be used for phishing or **phone scamming**. A variation of phishing is **vishing**, in which the threat e-mails or mails the target with an invitation to call a given telephone number on the pretext of a prize, settling a tax bill, confirming credentials, or something similar. Most people underestimate their exposure; new technologies encourage more spontaneous and casual communications. Of the social interactions that led to data breaches identified by Verizon, 3% involved telephone conversations and 1% involved text messages. These numbers are much lower than for e-mailed phishing attacks (79%), but the information gathered by telephone may be more valuable or of a different quality than could be gathered by e-mail (Verizon Enterprise Solutions, 2013, p. 35).

Without interacting directly with any of the parties to a communication, the threat could surreptitiously hack the voice mail or text messages. A telephone conversation is fleeting and not recorded by default, but voice mails and texts are stored until the user deletes them. Many service providers allow remote access to voice mails and texts through a third-party telephone or website, perhaps after passing some control on access, such as by typing in a personal identification number (or password). Many users do not change whatever default password was issued with a particular telephone or by a particular provider, so a threat (hacker) could access private voice mail using a third-party telephone or computer and a known default password. The hacker could call the provider and pretend to be the user in order to reset the password. The hacker could configure another telephone to pretend to have the same telephone number as the target's telephone. The hacker could also bribe an employee of the service provider to reveal confidential information.

Mobile communications pass wirelessly, so they are more difficult to physically tap than are wired communications. Nevertheless, the threat can use cheap technology to intercept wireless communications if the threat knows the user's telephone number and is proximate to the target. A mobile or cellular telephone, like any telephone, can be tapped directly if the threat can physically access the device and place a bugging device within it.

Smartphones (telephones that run software) can be infected through Internet downloads or an open Bluetooth portal with malware that records or allows a remote threat to listen in on the target's conversations. Sophisticated threats can remotely turn on a target's mobile telephone and use it as a bugging device without the target even realizing that the telephone is on; the only full defense is to remove the battery, although later generations of cell-phone technology reduce the risk.

The growth of computer hacking tends to obscure the inherent exposure of telephones to hacking or tapping, which is more likely where the government controls the service or where the service providers are open to corruption. Most democracies do not allow official access except with a court order granted to official investigators who can show probable cause of a severe crime, although such controls are easy to evade or forget in emergencies. Some officials, encouraged by loose political oversight, have allowed unwarranted taps, while private detectives have illegally tapped telephones or obtained data from a corrupt service provider.

Confidential information includes the parties to a private conversation, not just the content of the conversation. Internet and telephone service providers hold data on the location and other party in every communication made or received. Most democracies have strict legal controls on the storage and use of such data. For instance, European Union law requires providers to retain such data for at least 6 months and no more than 24 months and not to record content.

Concerned users should add **access controls** to their telephones, such as passwords, before the telephone can be used. They should check and delete their voice mails and text messages frequently. They could choose to prevent access to their voice mails and texts except with a passcode entered from their own phone. They could remove the battery from their mobile telephone except when they need to use it. They could also use temporary telephones that expire or can be discarded regularly. They could avoid smartphones or Bluetooth devices or at least eschew any access to the Internet from such devices. If they need to use such devices, they should procure security software and keep it up to date. They could avoid personal ownership of communications technology entirely—an extreme solution but one that more officials are adopting.

These controls may sound severe to casual users of current communications devices, but many official organizations and some highly targeted corporations now ban their employees from using or carrying smartphones, Bluetooth, or third-party devices—at least when inside secure domains or during the discussion of any organizational information. In addition, many malicious actors, such as terrorists, avoid such devices after revelations of how easily counterterrorist authorities can use them for spying.

U.S. OFFICIAL SURVEILLANCE OF TELEPHONE COMMUNICATIONS The U.S. Supreme Court has held that the Fourth Amendment of the Constitution, which protects against unreasonable search and seizure, extends to the interception of communications and applies to all conversations where an individual has a reasonable expectation of privacy. But the court has also allowed warrantless collection of metadata relating to private communications and has allowed warrantless search and seizure of electronic devices at the borders.

Under its charter, the U.S. Central Intelligence Agency is not allowed to gather intelligence on U.S. citizens at home, but from 1961 to 1971, the CIA spied on domestic anti–Vietnam War groups, communists, and leakers of official information. Both the CIA and NSA intercepted private telephone communications during that time. In 1972, the CIA tracked telephone calls between Americans at home and telephones abroad.

The Foreign Intelligence Surveillance Act (FISA) of 1978 criminalizes unauthorized electronic surveillance and prescribes procedures for surveillance of foreign powers and their agents (including U.S. citizens) inside the United States. The Foreign Intelligence Surveillance Court (FISC) issues the warrants for such surveillance. The FISA allows official investigators to request from a FISC an order authorizing interception of communications in order to prove foreign espionage or **terrorism**, but officials must certify to the court "probable cause to believe" that such crimes are being committed and that "the purpose for the surveillance is to obtain foreign intelligence information."

The FISC declined just 11 of nearly 34,000 surveillance requests made by the government from 1979 through 2012. Although officials often point out that they make requests that they expect to be approved, others interpret the figures as evidence for redundancy (Perez, 2013).

Although the FISA legislation and the FISC were born out of a concern over privacy abuses by federal law enforcement officials, both are clearly designed to favor the government and the issuance of investigative warrants, not to protect citizens' privacy and liberty interests. If the attorney general (AG) decides that an emergency situation exists, he or she is authorized to begin a program of surveillance without a FISC warrant. The AG must, however, inform the court of the operation within 72 hrs. If a member of the FISC rejects a search application, the decision can be appealed to the United States Foreign Intelligence Surveillance Court of Review. Based on existing information, the rejection of a warrant application by the FISC is a rare happening, and more often than not, warrant applications are modified and issued by the court rather than being rejected (Gaines & Kappeler, 2012, p. 102).

Title III of the Omnibus Crime Control and Safe Streets Act of 1968 (also known as the Wiretap Act) prohibits the unauthorized, nonconsensual interception of "wire or oral communications" by the government or private parties. (The Electronic Communications Privacy Act of 1986 extended this protection to electronic communications.) Title III establishes procedures for obtaining warrants to authorize wiretapping by government officials and regulates the disclosure and use of authorized intercepted communications by investigative and law enforcement officers.

> A judge may issue a warrant authorizing interception of communications for up to 30 days upon a showing of probable cause that the interception will reveal evidence that "an individual is committing, has committed, or is about to commit a particular offense" listed in § 2516. (18 U.S.C. § 2518[3])

A law enforcement or investigating officer may use, disclose to another law enforcement or investigating officer, or disclose during testimony information obtained in authorized wiretapping, provided the use or disclosure "is appropriate to the proper performance of the official duties of the officer making or receiving the disclosure" (18 U.S.C. § 2517).

Any federal official who "receives information pursuant to this provision may use that information only as necessary in the conduct of that person's official duties subject to any limitations on the unauthorized disclosure of such information" (18 U.S.C. § 2517).

After the terrorist attacks of September 11, 2001 (9/11), the U.S. executive and legislature substantially enhanced official powers to intercept private telecommunications. The USA PATRIOT Act of October 26, 2001,

- extended the laws on pen-register devices (which record the telephone numbers that a particular telephone calls) and trap-and-trace devices (which record the sources of incoming telephone calls) to electronic communications (essentially permitting officials to access the records of e-mail sources and destinations whenever they could access telephone records),

- redefined stored voice mail as stored e-mail rather than a telephone conversation,

- added terrorist and computer crimes to the list of offenses covered by the Wiretaps Act,

- eliminated previous requirements for officials to prove that the suspect is "an agent of a foreign power,"

- extended FISA's coverage to U.S. citizens without foreign controllers,

- allowed a FISA order whenever gathering foreign intelligence is a "significant purpose" rather than just "the purpose,"

- eliminated the need for court orders to identify the particular instrument or places where the surveillance can occur (effectively permitting "roving" surveillance of a particular target), and

- allowed the sharing between federal agencies of intelligence gathered under any FISA court order.

Some officials acted beyond even these new powers. For instance, between 2002 and 2006, the FBI sent more than 700 demands to service providers for records of telephone use, often using misleading language and including false claims of emergency. Information on the use of more than 3,500 telephone numbers may have been gathered improperly, although later, investigators from the Department of Justice could not be sure because of sketchy record-keeping by the FBI. (The department published its report in January 2010.)

No official was prosecuted. Instead, on February 12, 2008, the U.S. Senate approved new rules for government interceptions of telephone calls and e-mails and granted retroactive immunity from lawsuits for telecommunications companies that had cooperated with the federal government. In 2012, anonymous officials told journalists Greg Miller and Ellen Nakashima of the *Washington Post* that Internet and telephone service providers rarely turn down official requests for information, with or without a warrant. On the record, U.S. Representative Adam B. Schiff (a member of the House of Representatives' Permanent Select Committee on Intelligence) said that "the expansive data that is available electronically now means that when you're looking for one thing, the chances of finding a whole host of other things is exponentially greater" (Miller & Nakashima, 2012, n.p.).

The USA PATRIOT Act extended FISA's scope from foreign powers to terrorists. The Protect America Act of August 2007 removed the warrant requirement if the individual is "reasonably believed" to be corresponding with someone outside the United States. It expired on February 17, 2008, but the FISA Amendments Act of July 2008 extended the same amendment. On May 26, 2011, President Barack Obama signed the USA PATRIOT Sunset Extension Act, which extended for 4 years the provisions for roving wiretaps and searches of business records. The FISC is known to have approved all warrant requests in 2011 and 2012. In December 2012, Congress reauthorized FISA for another 5 years.

On October 4, 2001, before the USA PATRIOT Act was introduced, President George W. Bush secretly authorized the NSA to collect domestic records of telephone, Internet, and e-mail use with one foreign node, without court oversight, whenever investigators believed that any party could be linked with al-Qaeda. The business records provision of the Patriot Act was used to further authorize these actions. Inevitably, investigators became casual in their allegations of an al-Qaeda link. In May 2006, anonymous sources revealed to journalists that the NSA, without warrants, had made an effort to log a majority of the telephone calls made within the United States since 9/11 in an effort to trace telephone numbers used by al-Qaeda. *USA Today* reported that the NSA had "been secretly collecting the phone call records of tens of millions of Americans, using data provided by AT&T, Verizon and BellSouth" and was "using the data to analyze calling patterns in an effort to detect terrorist activity" (Cauley, 2006, n.p.). In 2007, the Bush administration admitted that the NSA was monitoring a broader population than authorized. Since 2006, the FISC has approved warrants to service providers every 3 months; Congress was informed. The most recent FISC order to Verizon was published by the *Guardian* newspaper on June 5, 2013. Senator Diane Feinstein, the chair of the Senate's Intelligence Committee, confirmed the 3-month renewals back to 2006.

Former NSA contractor Edward Snowden leaked more documents from June 2013 on that described various programs by the NSA to collect metadata on telephone communications, usually from the digital infrastructure carrying these communications rather than by intercepting the communications themselves. On June 12, 2013, the head of the NSA, General Keith Alexander, testified before the Senate Appropriations Committee that metadata was "critical" to unraveling "dozens" of terrorist plots at home and abroad, although he specified only two cases.

1. Alexander claimed that foreign phone calls suggested that a potential terrorist was residing in Colorado and that in 2009, the FBI used the data to identify Najibullah Zazi, an Afghan American who later pleaded guilty to planning suicide attacks in New York City.

2. Alexander claimed that the PRISM program had identified Pakistani-American David C. Headley and that telephone metadata provided "corroborating evidence" for his role in a terrorist attack in 2008 in Mumbai, India. He was arrested in 2009 and sentenced in January 2013.

However, on December 18, 2013, the U.S. President's Review Group on Intelligence and Communications Technologies concluded that the NSA activity "was not essential to preventing attacks" and that much of the evidence it did turn up "could readily have been obtained in a timely manner using conventional [court] orders" (Clarke, Morell, Stone, Sunstein, & Swire, 2013, p. 104).

On January 13, 2014, the New America Foundation reported that of 225 jihadis charged with terrorism inside the United States since 9/11, NSA phone metadata programs "had no discernible impact on preventing acts of terrorism" (Bergen, Sterman, Schneider, & Cahall, 2014, n.p.). In 60% of cases, traditional law enforcement and investigative methods initiated the case. In 28% of cases, the method of initiation was unclear. Phone metadata provided evidence to initiate only one case, involving a San Diego cab driver, Basaaly Moalin, who, in February 2013, was convicted of sending money to a terrorist group in Somalia, with three coconspirators. In 12 cases, the plot was not prevented by any method (Bergen, Sterman, Schneider, & Cahall, 2014).

In December 2013, Snowden revealed new documents suggesting that the NSA can easily decrypt the wireless encryption technology A5/1 used in 2G (second-generation) phones—80% of cell phones (Timberg & Soltani, 2013). Later releases suggest that in April 2010, NSA and GCHQ formed the Mobile Handset Exploitation Team, which stole encryption keys from the largest manufacturer (Gemalto) of SIM cards (2 billion per year) by hacking into its computer network. GCHQ penetrated authentication servers that handle communications between a phone and the provider's network. GCHQ claimed to manipulate billing servers to hide actions against an individual user. These capabilities suggest that NSA and GCHQ can intercept and decrypt communications borne on later generations of cell phone technology (3G, 4G, and LTE) (Scahill & Begley, 2015).

E-mail

E-mail or electronic mail is a digital communication sent via some computer network. According to estimates published in 2013, 3.9 billion e-mail accounts existed around the world, of which 2.9 billion (76%) were personal/individual accounts and 929 million (24%) were commercial/business accounts. The commercial/business accounts sent or received nearly 100 billion messages per day in 2013 and were expected to vector 132 billion messages per day by 2017 (Radicati & Levenstein, 2013, pp. 2–3). Unfortunately, 78.4% of e-mail traffic is illegitimate (unwanted advertising or *spam*, false requests for information or other resources, unauthorized transmissions of information, etc.), according to samples in 2013 (Websense, 2013b, pp. 4, 24–26).

The ease of e-mail and the easy attachment of files to e-mail has improved communications but also increased the leakage of sensitive information. E-mails are prolific, users are casual in their use, and service providers tend to hold data on every e-mail ever sent, including user-deleted e-mails. "Email systems are often less protected than databases yet contain vast quantities of stored data. Email remains one of the quickest and easiest ways for individuals to collaborate—and for intruders to enter a company's network and steal data" (U.S. ONCIX, 2011, p. A3). E-mail is a vector for sensitive information in three main ways, as described in the subsections below: external phishing, unauthorized access to stored e-mail, and insider noncompliance with controls on the release of information.

PHISHING E-MAILS Network applications, such as organization-wide e-mail, are exposed to phishing attacks (for definitions of phishing, see the section above on social engineering). Of the social interactions that led to data breaches analyzed by Verizon, 79% involved e-mails, compared to 13% in person and 3% by telephone. Websense Security Labs (2013b) found that in 2012, about 70% of e-mails contained Web links, any of which could be used to phish, while another 1.6% of e-mails attempted to phish directly, and 0.4% had malware attached (p. 27).

If the threat could identify the e-mail address of a target within the network, the threat could send an e-mail that pretends to request information legitimately or it could persuade the target to click on a website or download malware that steals information from the target's computer. The infected computer could infect the whole network, perhaps by sending a similar e-mail to everyone else on the network.

Some e-mail attachments are more persuasive than others, but vulnerability to this vector seems inevitable given enough e-mails (particularly if the e-mails differ). Each new e-mail from the same source might suggest to some recipients that the source must be legitimate. Most people are simply inattentive most of the time, so while they might ignore a clearly phishing e-mail one time, they might absentmindedly click on it another time. Experimentally, researchers have shown that an attacker needs to send just three e-mails to the same target for a better than 50% chance that the target will click on the link. After 10 e-mails, the chance passes 90%. With more e-mails, the chance approaches inevitability (Verizon Enterprise Solutions, 2013, pp. 35–36). Another blind phishing study found that more than half of users accessed corporate e-mail from outside the corporate network, such as at home, thence outside of the corporation's network security. In both 2012 and 2013, two thirds of phishing e-mails were sent on Mondays and Fridays, when recipients are most likely to be distracted from security (Websense, 2013b, pp. 25–26).

ACCESS TO STORED E-MAIL Hackers can hack into e-mail accounts after discovering passwords or by bribing service providers. For instance, in February 2013, a website published information received from a hacker identified only as "Guccifer," who had downloaded e-mails and attached photographs sent between former President George W. Bush and his family, including information about their e-mail addresses, home addresses, mobile-telephone numbers, and photographs of his father, former President George H. W. Bush, receiving hospital treatment.

E-mailers increasingly must worry about official interception of e-mails, particularly in authoritarian countries where governments routinely search for dissidents but also in democracies, where, since 9/11 particularly, officials and service providers have become more cooperative in their access of private e-mails. Official investigators cannot practically differentiate in advance what particular e-mail they may be looking for, and service providers prefer not to search for such an e-mail. Consequently, they tend to access the user's entire e-mail account. "You're asking them for emails relevant to the investigation, but as a practical matter they let you look at everything," said one anonymous former federal prosecutor. "It's harder to do [be discriminate] with e-mails, because unlike a phone, you can't just turn it off once you figure out the conversation didn't relate to what you're investigating," said a former chief (Michael DuBose) of the Department of Justice's Computer Crime and Intellectual Property Section (quoted in Miller & Nakashima, 2012, n.p.).

Much of this official vigor is justified as counterterrorism, but in the process, rights and freedoms are degraded. For instance, in April 2013, the judge at the U.S. military tribunal court at Guantanamo Bay, Cuba, revealed that digital files owned by defense counsels' official computer networks had been inexplicably deleted and that unrelated mining of data held by prosecutors revealed that prosecutors had access to around 540,000 e-mails between defense counsels and alleged terrorist clients, which should enjoy attorney–client privileges. Defense counsels were ordered to stop using U.S. official networks, and current legal proceedings were postponed.

Concerned users of e-mail could use the few e-mail service providers (such as HushMail) that promise encrypted e-mail and more access controls. They could use temporary e-mail accounts. (For instance, terrorists are known to have deployed, after agreeing with their handlers, a list of anonymous e-mail accounts, one for each day of deployment.) Users could agree to share a single e-mail account, in which they write up their messages as draft e-mails that the recipient would delete after reading, without either user needing to send an e-mail. (Sent e-mails tend to be stored on a server, even after the user has ordered deletion.) Sophisticated users could convert a digital image into characters, into which they could type a message before converting it back into a digital image. (Terrorists are known to have achieved this method.) Users could avoid e-mail in favor of text messages, which are less likely to be archived than e-mails. Users could avoid both e-mail and text messages in favor of old-fashioned verbal messages or hand-delivered written messages, although these have separate risks.

NONCOMPLIANT USERS E-mail can be hacked maliciously, but most unauthorized access of information through e-mail is due to noncompliant releases of information by the legitimate user of that e-mail. Phishers could encourage such release, for instance, by pretending to be a colleague asking for information, but insiders could e-mail sensitive information on a whim, such as when they want to share a story for amusement or complaint, without realizing that they are violating privacy.

A study by MeriTalk (2012) reported that the U.S. federal government sends and receives 1.89 billion e-mails per day—the average federal agency sends and receives 47.3 million e-mails each day. Forty-eight percent of surveyed federal information managers reported that unauthorized information leaked by standard work e-mail, more than by any other vector, 38% by personal e-mail, and 23% by Web-based work e-mail. Forty-seven percent wanted better e-mail policies, 45% reported that employees did not follow these policies, and only 25% of them rated the security of their current e-mail system with an *A* grade.

E-mail can be encrypted before it leaves the internal network, but encryption can be used to hide unauthorized information as it leaves through the e-mail gateway. Eighty percent of federal information security managers were concerned about the possibility of unauthorized data escaping undetected through encrypted e-mails, 58% agreed that encryption makes detection of such escapes more difficult, and 51% foresaw e-mail encryption as a more significant problem for federal agencies in the next 5 years (MeriTalk, 2012).

Removable Media Devices and Mobile Devices

Removable media devices and **mobile devices** are digital devices that can be carried in one hand and plugged into other digital devices, such as plug-in Universal Serial Bus (USB) *flash-memory* or *stick drives* and mobile telephones. They can be used as vehicles for unauthorized removal of information out of a secured domain and as vectors for malware into a secured domain. In response to MeriTalk's survey of July 2012, 47% of federal information managers reported that unauthorized data left their agency on agency-issued mobile devices (almost as many who reported that it left in e-mail), 42% on USB drives, and 33% on personal mobile devices. In February 2011, a survey of private-sector information technology and security professionals revealed that 65% do not know what files and data leave their enterprise. According to a March 2011 press report, 57% of employees save work files to external devices on a weekly basis (U.S. ONCIX, 2011, p. A3).

Mobile devices, especially smartphones, are particularly exposed to malware downloaded within apps (application software) or automated connections.

> The migration of increasingly powerful mobile devices into the workplace was a major concern for administrators [in 2012] who had to find ways to manage and secure the devices and control access to sensitive resources. Malware for the devices continued to grow, especially for Androids, and even legitimate applications have proved to be leaky, buggy, and grabby . . . The predictions [for 2014] are not comforting. They include death by internet-connected devices and the use of emerging Near Field Communications [NFC] in smartphones for large-scale fraud and theft. The first

phones using NFC already are on the market, and proof-of-concept attacks to control or disrupt internet-enabled medical devices have been publicly demonstrated. (Jackson, 2013a, p. 20)

Bluetooth technology—normally used to wirelessly connect a telephone to an earpiece or mouthpiece or car-based speaker or microphone—can be intercepted by practically any other Bluetooth device, unless the target user switches off the device. The Bluetooth device can be used to directly listen in on the user's conversations, not just their telephone conversations. Bluetooth devices tend to have very short ranges (a few yards), but a threat could get within such ranges within a restaurant or other public space and these ranges can be amplified.

Spaces can be secured by disallowing entry to any digital devices. This is a common regulation for sensitive compartmentalized information facilities (SCIFs) and conference rooms. However, people may forget more innocuous devices on their person, such as key fobs, pens, cigarette lighters, and apparel, inside which recording or tracking devices can be hidden. Such items may be provided to the target as corporate gifts or in commercial transactions.

Cloud Computing

Cloud computing involves access from remote terminals to shared software or data. For instance, you might store documents on a remote server, which you access only when needed or from multiple terminals. Effectively, all large organizations store most of their information on remote servers to which access is granted to authorized users.

Cloud computing is attractive in economic terms. In recent years, information managers have sought to reduce the financial overhead associated with distributed data centers by moving to cloud computing, where more information and applications are held on remote servers and only accessed by individual terminals when users require. Cloud computing also helps users to share information, collaborate on projects, and back up their information.

Cloud computing improves security in the sense that information and applications can be gathered more centrally and distributed only when properly demanded. However, centralization of data creates a single point of failure, and shared code implies more vulnerability to malware inside the system.

When surveyed in 2013, 47% of business executives reported that their organizations use cloud computing, but only 18% include the cloud in their security policies (PricewaterhouseCoopers, 2013, p. 29).

Commercial organizations have led cloud computing, but official organizations also value the efficiencies and collaborative opportunities. Official interest in cloud computing has led to official development of particular security technologies and systems. For instance, in 2005, the U.S. Office of the Director of National Intelligence (ODNI) launched Intellipedia using wiki technology. In 2008, the ODNI created A-Space, a website where cleared analysts from different agencies could share information. In 2012, the DNI approved a proposal by the chief information officers from five intelligence agencies to develop a cheaper, more secure cloud over the next 5 years (the Intelligence Community Information Technology Enterprise, or ICITE).

Similarly, the U.S. DOD intends to transition from more than 1,500 data centers to one cloud that would be secure against the most sophisticated foreign state-sponsored attacks. In 2011, DOD announced its Mission-oriented Resilient Clouds program and scheduled testing of a system for 2015. The projects include redundant hosts, diverse systems within the system, and coordinated gathering of information about threats.

Wired Networks

Wired networks are systems of devices that communicate electronically through wires or cables rather than wirelessly. In theory, any digital network could be tapped. Wired networks must be tapped inside the network, either by malware or a hard device between or on the cables. In the 19th century, telegraph cables were tapped by placing electromagnetic sensors on the outside of the cables. In the 20th century, some countries placed large taps on the large telegraph cables and, later, the telephone and digital cables, laid by national telecommunications companies, governments, and militaries. Some of these cables were tapped at the bottom of oceans, some at their intersections on land. This basic technology can be used to tap any electrical signals but cannot tap fiber-optic signals, which became prevalent in the later 20th century.

A more accurate and direct tap is placed between two cables or between the computer and a cable. Such a tap on the Internet or intranet cable could read all data between the computer and other computers. Some taps contain software that also records all keystrokes (inputs through the keyboard into the computer); these taps are also known as **key loggers** or **key grabbers**, although this term could refer to malware too, not just hardware. Key loggers include hardware, such as a device plugged in between a keyboard and the terminal or between a computer and its Internet connection cable. Hardware key loggers are undetectable by the computer's software but are detectable visually, at least by someone who knows what a typical computer's hardware should look like.

These taps can be disguised as electrical power strips, electrical air fresheners, electrical power transformers, or interfaces to connect incompatible interfaces. These disguises provide enough space for the addition of a wireless or cellular-telephone communication device so that the captured data can be transmitted wirelessly.

Wireless Networks

A **wireless network** is a system of devices that communicate electronically through radio, infrared, or some other transmission that does not require a wire or cable. Wireless networks are less exposed to a hard tap but more exposed to wireless interception. Since wireless traffic is broadcast, no one needs to join the network just to record the traffic; one would need to break into the nodes in order to read the traffic. Criminals sometimes drive around or walk around purposefully searching for insecure networks (known as **war driving**).

This exposure is more likely for public networks, such as at hotels and cafes, where access controls are low so that guests can use the network temporarily using their personal computers. Malicious actors could dwell in such spaces waiting for a high-value target to use the same network. If the target's security is poor, the threat could observe the target's wireless communications and even access the target computer itself.

Private networks, such as a network that a family would set up within a household, become public when households forget to set any access controls (as simple as a password), share their password with the wrong people, or forego any password on the common assumption that nobody would be interested enough to attack a home network. Since households increasingly work online, bank online, and send private digital communications from home networks, the exposure could include professional information, personal identities, financial assets, and intimate private information. Sometimes holders assume that their wireless network is too short-range or remote for anyone else to access, but a skilled threat only needs minutes of proximate access to do harm. Directional antennas can collect traffic from further away.

Criminals sometimes access other private networks to conduct additional criminal activity on a network other than their own so that they are less traceable, such as accessing child pornography or redirecting traffic to pay-per-view websites.

MALICIOUS ACTIVITIES

The two preceding sections respectively described the human sources of malicious activities and the vectors for malicious activities. A **malicious activity involving information** is any unauthorized interaction with information. Malicious activities are much older and more extensive than the spectacular cybercrimes that grab attention from popular media. Three main categories are identified here:

1. *Invasions of information privacy and freedom*—the personal control of what information to keep private and what information to share

2. *Espionage*—the collection of privileged information

3. **Sabotage**—changing digital data and information or disrupting or damaging a target through cyberspace. Some sabotage might be equated with or include **cyber terrorism**, which is the use of cyberspace to terrorize, although cyber terrorism could be achieved through misinformation as well as sabotage.

Information Privacy and Freedom

New technologies have democratized information and challenged official control of information but have also eroded privacy and enabled easier surveillance. The subsections below explain international governance of ICTs, international governance of data privacy, and U.S. governance of privacy.

INTERNATIONAL GOVERNANCE OF ICTS In 1865, leading states agreed that the International Telegraph Union would govern the international interoperability of telegraph communications and the associated commercial and economic flows. This union took on the governance of telephone and wireless radio communications too, becoming the International Telecommunication Union (ITU), based in Geneva, Switzerland. Its activities include governing the international sharing of the radio spectrum, assigning incoming telephone dialing codes to different countries, and standardizing technical performance and interoperability. In 1950, it became an agency of the United Nations, representing all member nations of the U.N. and concerned organizations. In 1988, the members of the ITU agreed to major changes, mostly in response to new technologies, primarily those related to the Internet, and signed the International Telecommunications Regulations (ITRs) treaty.

In 1988, the U.S. DOD established the Internet Assigned Numbers Authority (IANA) to assign Internet protocol (IP) addresses and related systems. In 1998, the Internet Corporation for Assigned Names and Numbers (ICANN) was established by the Department of Commerce as a nonprofit organization headquartered in Playa Vista, California, to take over IANA's responsibilities. The United States continues to boast the base for ICANN and the most valuable IP addresses, websites, and Internet-based companies.

In November 2001, the Council of Europe, with the support of Canada and Japan, agreed to a Convention on Cybercrime (also known as the Budapest Convention) that aligned national laws and efforts to counter cybercrime. It requires signatories to cooperate in the investigation and prosecution of crimes, although a signatory could opt out if the request were to infringe on national sovereignty, security, or similar critical interests. For immediate signatories, the convention came into force in July 2004. For the United States, it entered into force in January 2007 (following ratification in August 2006). By the end of 2013, 40 states had ratified the convention, but the major nonsignatories include Russia and China. Russia opposes a provision that would allow foreign investigators to work with network service providers and operators without involving Russian officials.

In May 2011, the U.S. White House (2011a) published the *International Strategy for Cyberspace*. The strategy proposed to use diplomacy, defense, and development "to promote an open, interoperable, secure, and reliable information and communications infrastructure" (p. 8). Its goals included

- protecting freedom of expression,

- promoting innovation and protecting intellectual property,

- supporting the multistakeholder model,

- preventing cyber attacks and crime, and

- enabling military operations.

The strategy called on U.S. officials to concentrate their efforts in eight areas:

1. International standards and open markets

2. Network defense

3. Military alliances and cooperative security

4. Internet governance

5. International development and capacity building

6. The support of Internet freedom and privacy

7. Law enforcement

8. Extending the reach of the Convention on Cybercrime

Some countries have complained about U.S. leadership. In September 2011, China, Russia, Tajikistan, and Uzbekistan cosigned a letter to the U.N. General Assembly that called for an "international code of conduct" and "norms and rules guiding behavior" for countries overseeing the Internet. China, Russia, and several Arab countries have called for more U.N. control over the Internet and more controls on online misinformation and threats to privacy. On May 31, 2012, Google, Microsoft, Verizon, and Cisco jointly warned a U.S. congressional hearing that these foreign calls threaten Internet freedoms and their business.

In December 2012, the World Conference on International Telecommunications met in Dubai to revise the ITRs of 1988. The U.S. delegation (the largest) proposed a treaty that it justified mostly to preserve nonprofit, nongovernmental control of Internet content and to safeguard freedom of information.

After the United States had submitted its proposal, Russia proposed intergovernmental governance of the Internet (replacing ICANN), more national control of data trafficking, and controls on unwanted advertising (spam), which it claimed would make the Internet more efficient, secure, and truthful. Russia's proposal drew support from China and some Arab states, for a total of about 10 states explicitly committed.

The United States and others argued that Russia's proposed regulations could be used by individual governments to censor information or punish individuals or organizations. The delegations negotiated a proposed treaty that placed some of Russia's proposals in a nonbinding part and was about 80% agreeable to the U.S. delegation, but the United States and others opposed the remainder. The United States, Canada, most European countries, and some other states (for a total of 55) refused to sign the treaty and thus remained bound by only the ITRs of 1988, but 89 states supported it and thus set up an alternative regime (the ITRs of 2013).

A nongovernmental task force of official and industry representatives agreed with U.S. opposition to the new ITRs but faulted the United States for not achieving a single regime in U.S. interests.

> In the United States, a lack of a coherent vision, the absence of appropriate authority to implement policy, and legislative gridlock are significant obstacles to global leadership. The United States should act affirmatively to articulate norms of behavior, regulation, and partnership or others will do so. . . .
>
> Some of the signatories [of the ITRs of 2013] are authoritarian regimes that fear the free flow of information and are happy to paint Washington's opposition to the ITU as self-serving, designed to protect US influence and the market position of American technology companies. Yet a significant number that signed did so because they lack cyber security or other technical expertise, have a long history of dealing with the ITU, and see it as a credible partner. (Negroponte et al., 2013, pp. 4–5, 14)

The task force recommended alternative venues for Internet governance, particularly smaller, more agile, U.S.-led regional and functional groups, such as the Global Counterterrorism Forum and the Major Economies Forum on Energy and Climate. These alternatives could inform the ITU but would also increase divergence between a U.S.-led group and the rest of the world (Negroponte et al., 2013, pp. 59–60).

In May 2013, the ITU returned to the same issues at the fifth meeting of the ITU's World Telecommunication/ICT Policy Forum. In 2014, the ITU rewrote its constitution and elected a new secretary-general.

INTERNATIONAL GOVERNANCE OF DATA PRIVACY The International Covenant on Political and Civil Rights (ICCPR) was written in 1966 and came into force in 1976. Article 17 states that "no one shall be subjected to arbitrary or unlawful interference with his privacy, family, home or correspondence, nor to unlawful attacks on his honor and reputation." It states also that "everyone has the right to the protection of the law against such interference or attacks."

On October 24, 2013, at the U.N. headquarters in New York, diplomats from Brazil and Germany, whose elected leaders and officials had been victims of espionage by the U.S. NSA, according to documents leaked since the summer, and diplomats from some other Latin American and European countries started to negotiate a draft resolution that calls for extending the privacy rights contained in the International Covenant on Civil and Political Rights to cyberspace. Brazil and Germany put the draft resolution to the U.N. General Assembly's human rights committee on November 27, 2013. A draft of the resolution called on states "to respect and protect the right to privacy" and asserted that the "same rights that people have offline must also be protected online, including the right to privacy." It also requested that in 2014, the U.N. High Commissioner for Human Rights would present to the U.N. General Assembly a report on the protection and promotion of the right to privacy. In March 2015, its Human Rights Council reaffirmed the right to privacy in the digital age and created, for three years, a Special Rapporteur on the right to privacy (U.N. Office of the High Commissioner for Human Rights, 2015).

The International Organization for Standardization (ISO) and the International Electrotechnical Commission (IEC) have led international standards for information security, including expectations for technical and organizational controls on unauthorized or unlawful processing of personal data (see, e.g., ISO/IEC 17799:2005 and ISO/IEC 27001:2005).

U.S. GOVERNANCE OF PRIVACY The United States passed a Freedom of Information Act (FOIA) in 1966. This allows for individuals to receive information held by the federal government unless such release would violate national security, law enforcement, commercial privileges, or the privacy of others. Within the United States, most states have passed FOIAs allowing for private access to information held by state governments with similar restrictions.

The U.S. FOIA of 1966 has been amended several times by new laws, the first of which was the Privacy Act of 1976, which obliges federal protection of information about private individuals, except as mandated for law enforcement and other vital activities. It also allows for private individuals to access and amend information about them. The Privacy Act of 1976 was updated by the Computer Matching and Privacy Protection Act of 1988, which extends protections to IT and ICT.

Unlike the European Union and most European states, the United States has not passed a law comprehensively defining how private actors should protect data but has passed legislation protecting certain types of data, such as health data, which is protected mainly by the Health Insurance Portability and Accountability Act of 1996 (HIPAA). U.S. criminal laws against economic espionage and protections of intellectual property were strong already while its strong civil laws against defamation and slander help to control misuse of private information.

All in all, organizations within U.S. jurisdictions face severe legal and commercial risks for violating data privacy, even if they might be incentivized by commercial advantages. For instance, in 2005, the U.S. Federal Trade Commission accused an American consumer data broker (ChoicePoint Incorporated) of improperly securing confidential data from theft; the broker admitted that the personal financial records of more than 163,000 consumers in its database had been compromised and agreed to pay $10 million in civil penalties and $5 million in consumer redress; millions of dollars were wiped off its stock-market value.

The main U.S. effort against violations of privacy has aimed to raise awareness. For instance, in October 2009, President Obama declared the first national cybersecurity awareness month due to "our Nation's growing dependence on cyber and information-related technologies, coupled with an increasing threat of malicious cyber attacks and loss of privacy" (U.S. White House, 2009).

While the United States has long-standing policies in favor of freedom of information, it is one of many states with at least the capacity to collect private information and to control information. Current capacity was most exposed in the summer of 2013 by Edward Snowden, a contracted employee of the National Security Administration, who released to journalists secret documents describing surveillance programs by the NSA and foreign partners (such as Britain's General Communications Headquarters) that many governments, professional interest groups, and privacy advocacy groups have condemned. For instance, Reporters Without Borders usefully summarized the implications in its annual report of March 2014, after most of the leaks had been reported.

> The NSA and GCHQ have spied on the communications of millions of citizens including many journalists. They have knowingly introduced security flaws into devices and software used to transmit requests on the Internet. And they have hacked into the very heart of the Internet using programs such as the NSA's Quantum Insert and GCHQ's Tempora. The Internet was a collective resource that the NSA and GCHQ turned into a weapon in the service of special interests, in the process flouting freedom of information, freedom of expression and the right to privacy. The mass surveillance methods employed in these countries, many of them exposed by NSA whistleblower Edward Snowden, are all the more intolerable because they will be used and indeed are already being used by authoritarian countries such as Iran, China, Turkmenistan, Saudi Arabia and Bahrain to justify their own violations of freedom of information. (Reporters Without Borders for Freedom of Information, 2014, pp. 3–4)

Espionage

The subsections below review the scope of espionage, the costs of cyber espionage, the history of cyber espionage against the United States, and alleged espionage by the United States, China, Russia, and Syria.

SCOPE *Espionage* is the collection of privileged information. Any information may be subject to espionage, down to the personal level, such as information about personal health or finances. Most of the information that attracts professional spies is official or commercial.

Espionage is commonly depicted as international, but as the sections above on the sources of attacks and activities suggest, official authorities continue to gain capacity and incentives for espionage on private actors too. For instance, in February 2013, a U.S. military lawyer acknowledged that microphones had been hidden inside fake smoke detectors in rooms used for meetings between defense counsels and alleged terrorists at the U.S. detention center at Guantanamo Bay, Cuba. The U.S. military said the listening system had been installed before defense lawyers started to use the rooms and was not used to eavesdrop on confidential meetings. The government subsequently stated that it had removed the system.

In a world of increasing cyber espionage, espionage continues in old-fashioned ways that are easily neglected, such as surreptitiously recording or eavesdropping on private conversations. As shown above, any digital media (including telephones, Bluetooth devices, and computers) with a recording or imaging device can be used to surreptitiously spy. Recording devices can be hidden inside other items, such as buttons and keys.

Cyber espionage normally involves use of a computer network to access information. Some attempts to physically or digitally bypass access controls are detectable by protective software, but as the section on vectors illustrates, a threat could use many vectors to bypass such controls. Verizon found that 95% of all state-affiliated espionage started with phishing (Verizon Enterprise Solutions, 2013, p. 34). Once a threat has gained the user's identification and password, it should be able to log in to a controlled space, such as a personal computer, e-mail account, or online directory, within which the threat can browse for information. *Snooping and downloading* describes such unwanted access within the controlled space (Yannakogeorgos, 2011, p. 259).

Malware that is used for espionage is better known as *spyware*. *Eavesdropping* and *packet sniffing* are "techniques [that] refer to the capturing of data-packets en route to their destinations without altering information" (Yannakogeorgos, 2011, p. 258). A **packet sniffer** is "a program that intercepts routed data and examines each packet in search of specified information, such as passwords transmitted in clear text" (U.S. GAO, 2005a, p. 8). *Key loggers* record keyboard strokes on a computer.

THE COSTS OF CYBER ESPIONAGE The returns of cyber espionage are difficult to calculate because of commercial and official secrecy about the actual frequency and harm of such espionage. Globally, the cyber theft of intellectual property costs as much as $500 billion per year. The costs of cyber espionage to the United States range from $25 billion (0.1% of GDP) to $125 billion (0.5% of GDP) (Negroponte et al., 2013, pp. ix, 38).

In the United States, ONCIX (2011) reported that the negative returns of cyber espionage were "large but uncertain" (p. 3). Academic estimates varied too greatly to be useful (from $2 billion to $400 billion per year). ONCIX (2011) was prepared to state that in the previous two years, foreign threats had attempted to steal technologies that had "cost millions of dollars to develop and represented tens or hundreds of millions of dollars in potential profits" (p. 1).

In 2012, Scott Borg, Chief Economist at the U.S. Cyber Consequences Unit (an independent, nonprofit research organization) told a journalist that the annual loss of intellectual property and investment opportunities were worth $6 billion to $20 billion per year to the United States alone. In 2013, the same journalist received expert estimates of U.S. national economic losses due to cyber espionage worth 0.1% to 0.5% of U.S. gross domestic product per year—equivalent to $25 billion to $100 billion (Nakashima, 2012, 2013).

U.S. targets are mostly in the energy, finance, information-technology, aerospace, and automotive industries. Companies tend to deny victimization for fear of negative effects on share value or customer confidence. For instance, the 27 largest U.S. companies that reported cyber attacks also claimed no major financial losses. However, the Director of the National Security Agency, General Keith Alexander, reported that American companies had lost $250 billion in stolen information and another $114 billion in related expenses. He described foreign cyber espionage as the "greatest transfer of wealth in history" (Negroponte et al., 2013, p. 17). Evidence presented in criminal prosecutions since 2005 suggest that Motorola lost $600 million worth of proprietary data, DuPont suffered $400 million in harm from the theft of chemical formulae, Dow Chemical suffered $100 million in harm from the theft of research on insecticides, and Valspar lost $20 million worth of paint formulae to espionage (equivalent to one eighth of its profits in 2009, when the insider was arrested) (ONCIX, 2011, pp. 1, 3).

THE UNITED STATES AS A TARGET OF CYBER ESPIONAGE In the early days of the Internet, individual hackers and spies achieved some spectacular penetrations of U.S. official information at a time when digital security was unprofessional. Such penetrations would be more difficult today without more advanced skills, but generally, the skills and vectors have not changed fundamentally. For instance, in 1986, an audit discovered a discrepancy in a telephone bill at the Lawrence Berkeley National Laboratory, California; this led to the discovery of the theft of U.S. classified research on nuclear warfare and the Strategic Defense Initiative (an anti–ballistic missile program). The theft had proceeded for 2 years via malware nicknamed the "Cuckoo's Egg." Eventually, the source was traced to Hannover and caught after a trap was set up in an online forum promising secrets held at the university there. The source betrayed himself as Marcus Hess; he turned out to be an East German agent working for the Soviet intelligence service.

In February 1998, U.S. authorities detected simultaneous intrusions into the Department of Defense's secure domains, targeting financial, medical, and logistical information. Initially, the U.S. government suspected Iraq; at that time, the United States was preparing to escalate against Iraqi obstruction of U.N. inspectors of the Iraqi nuclear-weapons program. The administration under President Bill Clinton considered a military response, but eventually, authorities traced the source through a network of private hackers to a primary trainer and controller (Ehud Tenenbaum, then aged 19) in Israel.

Attacks on American cyber infrastructure seem to be increasing at a rapid linear rate, with almost 9 times as many private reports in 2012 as in 2006, although some of the increase might be explained by increased reporting rather just increased attacks (see Table 10.2).

Privately reported attacks on private infrastructure run at a much lower rate than officially reported attacks on official infrastructure. In 2010, automated sensors (collectively they make up a system known as EINSTEIN 2) in U.S. federal civilian cyberspace recorded 5.4 million intrusions, or more than 450,000 per month. In 2012, U.S. Cyber Command reported that attacks on U.S. computer networks had increased 17-fold from 2009 to 2011.

Most of these count as economic espionage directed at the commercial sector, where the true frequency is typically not counted by anybody outside of the affected organization. For instance, in February 2010, NetWitness reported that since late 2008, malware planted by phishing e-mails had infected 75,000 computers at nearly 2,500 companies in the U.S. The sources were mostly in Eastern Europe. In October 2011, the Office of the National Counterintelligence Executive reported to Congress,

Foreign economic collection and industrial espionage against the United States represent significant and growing threats to the nation's prosperity and security. Cyberspace—where most business activity and development of new ideas now takes place—amplifies these threats by making it possible for malicious actors, whether they are corrupted insiders or foreign intelligence services (FIS), to quickly steal and transfer massive quantities of data while remaining anonymous and hard to detect. (p. i)

ONCIX judged that foreign espionage would focus on information and communications technology, natural resources, military technologies, clean energy, health care, pharmaceuticals, and other technologies in rapidly growing sectors. The National Counterintelligence Executive Robert Bryant said at a news conference that cyber espionage is "a quiet menace to our economy with notably big results. . . . Trade secrets developed over thousands of working hours by our brightest minds are stolen in a split second and transferred to our competitors" (quoted in Nakashima, 2011). The report of October 2011 accused (in order) China, Russia, Israel, and France of using their official intelligence services to steal such secrets. In January 2013, the *National Intelligence Estimate* (a classified document partly leaked to the press) also identified China, Russia, Israel, and France as most aggressively spying for economic gain.

Table 10.2	Cyber Incidents Involving American Cyber Infrastructure as Reported to the U.S. Computer Emergency Readiness Team
2006	5,503
2007	11,911
2008	16,843
2009	29,999
2010	41,776
2011	42,854
2012	48,562

Source: U.S. Government Accountability Office (2013, n.p.).

ALLEGED U.S. ESPIONAGE

Against Europe. In 2010, the German government assessed the United States and France as Germany's primary economic espionage threats "among friends."

In 2011, France's Central Directorate for Domestic Intelligence described the United States and China as the leading hackers of French businesses (ONCIX, 2011, p. B2).

In October 2011, Symantec (a cybersecurity company) reported discovery of a new malware (Duqu, a derivative of Stuxnet) in the computer networks of some European manufacturers of industrial control systems. (As described in the section on sabotage, Stuxnet is malware used by the United States, with Israeli help, as the United States confirmed in 2012, to spy on and sabotage the Iranian nuclear program.)

In May 2012, Hungarian analysts at CrySyS and Russian analysts at Kaspersky Labs announced their discovery of another Stuxnet-derivative (*Flame*, *Flamer*, or *Skywiper*) that had been active for 5 to 8 years. Flame is a large and sophisticated malware (about 20 MB of code) that is designed to spy and has the capacity to sabotage. It records keystrokes, screenshots, video through the computer's camera, audio through the microphone, and data from wireless and Bluetooth peripherals and exfiltrates the data via five encryption methods, three compression methods, and five file formats.

In November 2012, anonymous sources within the French network and information security agency (ANSSI) told French journalists of their discovery of malware similar to Flame on the intranet of the French president's office, probably planted by U.S. sources in the final weeks of the presidency of Nicolas Sarkozy before the presidential election of April 2012. The malware had been placed by a webpage pretending to be the intranet's login page, which appeared when employees clicked on a link contained within phishing e-mails. The sources had e-mailed the employees through Facebook after friending them from fake Facebook accounts.

In June 2013, the *Guardian* newspaper of London reported several stories, using documents supplied by Edward Snowden, about the interception of telephonic and cyber communications passing from Europe through Britain to North America. Other reports described deliberate bugging of the communications used by foreign officials visiting the G20 conference in London in 2009. Both the NSA and Britain's GCHQ were implicated in this espionage.

One of the earlier stories described CIA espionage in Switzerland. Edward Snowden told the *Guardian* that his loyalties first turned when, on assignment in support of U.S. intelligence activities based in the U.S. embassy there, he observed CIA officers getting a Swiss banker drunk and encouraging him to drive home in his car. When the banker was arrested for drunk driving, his recruiter offered to help in return for the banker collecting intelligence on the Swiss banking system, which was a target for the NSA too. These activities were presumably a part of long-standing U.S. efforts to counter the evasion of U.S. taxes by Americans placing money in Swiss bank accounts. On June 19, 2013, the Swiss Parliament's lower house bounced back to the upper house legislation to help the United States to identify tax evaders (the U.S. Foreign Account Tax Compliance Act) until, on September 10, it finally approved the act.

On October 21, 2013, the French newspaper *Le Monde*, citing documents provided by Edward Snowden, reported the NSA had recorded 70.3 million French phone calls between December 10, 2012, and January 8, 2013. The NSA's program, code-named US-985D, used a variety of collection methods, including spoken keyword recognition software that activated the recording of a phone call. Among the targets were terrorism suspects, European Union officials, French political representatives and officials, French businesspeople, and French telecommunications and e-mail providers. The French government called in the U.S. ambassador to explain the program. French Foreign Minister Laurent Fabius described the program as "totally unacceptable." The next day, President Obama and French President François Hollande spoke by telephone to discuss the issue; Obama did not deny the collection.

On October 23, 2013, *Der Spiegel* revealed that its investigations, shared with German authorities, suggest that the NSA had intercepted the mobile telephone calls made by the German Chancellor, Angela Merkel. That day, she telephoned U.S. President Obama to demand an explanation. She told journalists that such espionage between friends would be unacceptable. Spokesmen for the U.S. administration said that the president had reassured her that the United States was not and would not intercept her communications, but the spokesmen declined to state that her communications had not been intercepted in the past. That weekend, *Der Spiegel* reported that the NSA had tapped Merkel's phone since 2002, before she became chancellor, until shortly before a visit to Germany by Obama in June 2013. Later reports suggested that Merkel's predecessor, Gerhard Schröder, had been tapped since 2002. On November 5, 2013, the *Independent* newspaper of London reported, citing documents leaked by Snowden, historical reports, and photographs, that the U.S. and British embassies in Berlin each have signals collection systems hidden within structures atop their roofs. The British embassy had been built in 2000, so any such system there could not be a legacy of the Cold War. The German government called in Britain's ambassador to explain the report.

On October 24, 2013, the *Guardian* reported on a document, dated October 2006, suggesting that the NSA had asked U.S. diplomats and other officials to share their knowledge of the telephone numbers used by foreign officials. The collected telephone numbers included those used by 35 premiers, presumably mostly European.

On October 28, 2013, anonymous officials from the White House claimed that it was unaware of NSA espionage directed against foreign premiers until summer 2013, when it ordered the operation to end, but now knew that the operation had been active since 2002. On the same day, Senator Dianne Feinstein (Democrat from California), the head of the Senate Intelligence Committee, said that the committee had not been properly informed of the operation and would "initiate a major review into all intelligence collection programs" (Wilson & Gearan, 2013, n.p.).

> With respect to NSA collection of intelligence on leaders of U.S. allies—including France, Spain, Mexico and Germany—let me state unequivocally: I am totally opposed. Unless the United States is engaged in hostilities against a country or there is an emergency need for this type of surveillance. I do not believe the United States should be collecting phone calls or emails of friendly presidents and prime ministers. The president should be required to approve any collection of this sort. (Wilson & Gearan, 2013, n.p.)

During the week *Der Spiegel* had revealed that the NSA was monitoring an international bank transfer system (Swift), the European Parliament voted to suspend a transatlantic bank data sharing agreement in response. The European Commission (the EU's executive) publicly backed proposals that would require U.S.-based companies to seek permission before handing over EU citizens' data to U.S. intelligence agencies. The European Commission also called on the United States to establish a legal right for European citizens anywhere to sue for redress in American courts when they believe that their privacy rights have been violated by either the U.S. government or U.S. companies. In the following week (from October 28), the European Union sent a nine-member delegation to Washington for meetings with U.S. diplomatic, trade, and other officials but first warned that the United States must restore confidence or risk scuttling a major transatlantic free-trade pact. "Friends and partners do not spy on each other—that is simply a principle" (Wilson & Gearan, 2013, n.p.), said the head of the delegation and vice president of the European Commission, Viviane Reding, on October 28.

Meanwhile, on October 28, the Spanish newspaper *El Mundo* reported, again citing documents provided by Edward Snowden, that the NSA had collected metadata on 60 million telephone calls in Spain from December 10, 2012, to January 8, 2013. The Spanish Foreign Ministry stated that such collection was improper between friends and demanded an explanation (Wilson & Gearan, 2013).

On February 17, 2014, Angela Merkel announced a plan to develop European cyber networks so that they would not pass through American jurisdictions.

Against China. In 2012, the National Computer Network Emergency Response Technical Team/Coordination Center of China (CNCERT or CNCERT/CC), part of the Ministry of Industry and Information Technology (MIIT), identified more than 73,000 foreign servers acting as command or control of malware in China, 56.9% more than in 2011, and most of these servers were in the United States (Asia Pacific Computer Emergency Response Team, 2012, p. 51; CNCERT/CC, 2012, pp. 4–5). In February 2013, China announced that in 2012, foreign hackers, 62% of them based mainly in the United States, had attacked two Chinese military websites on average 144,000 times per month. China's top Internet security official said that he had "mountains of data" pointing to extensive U.S. hacking aimed at China, but it would be irresponsible to blame the U.S. government for such attacks. He called for greater cooperation to fight private hacking (Jones, 2013).

In June 2013, revelations by Edward J. Snowden, a contracted employee at the NSA, included the revelation that the NSA had been hacking China for 15 years, including official, commercial, and academic servers. Some of the documents revealed that the NSA had obtained millions of text messages from the servers used by Chinese providers of mobile-telephone communications (Lam & Chen, 2013; Rapoza, 2013). The Chinese Ministry of National Defense accused the United States of hypocrisy for opposing Chinese cyber espionage while conducting cyber espionage against China, listing operational details of specific attacks on computers, including IP addresses, dates of attacks, and whether a computer was still being monitored remotely. A Chinese Defense Ministry spokesman, Col. Yang Yujun, said,

> To, on the one hand, abuse one's advantages in information technology for selfish ends, while on the other hand, making baseless accusations against other countries, shows double standards that will be of no help for peace and security in cyberspace. (Buckley, 2013, n.p.)

Against North Korea. The NSA and its allies expanded their cooperative cyber espionage on North Korea since at least 2010, mainly aimed at countering North Korea's own espionage. Malware placed then or since proved critical to the gathering of the evidence that persuaded the Obama administration that North Korea was responsible for hacking Sony Pictures in November 2014, although somehow the malware were not sufficient to warn the United States of the attack in advance (Sanger & Fackler, 2015).

Elsewhere. Other national official sites known to have been penetrated by similar cyber attacks include Canada's Ministry of Finance and the Australian Prime Minister's Office.

In September 2013, a newspaper, citing documents leaked by Edward Snowden, reported that the NSA was gathering metadata on billions of e-mails, phone calls, and other Internet traffic flowing through Brazil, including the communications of Brazil's President, Dilma Rousseff, Brazilian officials, and a state-run oil company, Petrobras. Rousseff canceled her state visit to the United States and demanded an official explanation.

In October, Brazil demanded clarifications from the Canadian government about reports that Canada's Communications Security Establishment (CSEC) had collected metadata on phone calls and e-mails from and to Brazil's Ministry of Mines and Energy. The next month, the Canadian Broadcasting Corporation revealed top-secret documents suggesting that the Canadian administration, led by Prime Minister Stephen Harper, allowed the NSA to cooperate with Canadian equivalents to spy on foreign attendees at the G8 and G20 summits in Toronto in June 2010. One NSA briefing note described U.S. operational plans and noted that they were "closely coordinated with the Canadian partner" (Weston, Greenwald, & Gallagher, 2013).

On October 19, 2013, the German newsmagazine *Der Spiegel* reported, citing documents provided by whistle-blower Edward Snowden, that an NSA program, code-named Operation FLATLIQUID, had intercepted the e-mail communications of Mexican President Peña Nieto, several members of the Mexican cabinet, and civil servants. The country's Ministry of Foreign Affairs stated that, if true, the NSA's actions would be both "unacceptable and illegal" and "run contrary to good relations between neighbors" (Fitsanakis, 2013, n.p.).

ALLEGED CHINESE ESPIONAGE Of international data breaches attributable to state-affiliated actors in 2012, most were Chinese. About one fifth of all breaches in the data set were Chinese state attempts to steal intellectual property. About 96% of the espionage cases were Chinese; the other 4% were of unknown origin. "This may mean that other threat groups perform their activities with greater stealth and subterfuge. But it could also mean that China is, in fact, the most active source of national and industrial espionage in the world today" (Verizon Enterprise Solutions, 2013, pp. 3, 19).

In late 2007, Japan's Ministry of Economy, Trade, and Industry reported that a survey of manufacturing companies found that more than 60% of them reported economic espionage involving China. In 2008, South Korea reported that half of economic espionage is traced to China (US ONCIX, 2011, p. B1). In 2008, Britain's Center for the Protection of National Infrastructure, part of the Security Service (MI5), distributed to hundreds of financial service providers and banks a "restricted" document entitled "The Threat from Chinese Espionage." It warned that agents of the Chinese People's Liberation Army and the Ministry of Public Security had approached British businesspeople—particularly from defense, energy, communications, public-relations, and international-law industries—at trade fairs and exhibitions with gifts of USB drives and cameras that contained malware.

Michelle Van Cleave was National Counterintelligence Executive (NCIX) from 2003 to 2006. She stated,

> One of the first things I did when I assumed my role as head of US counterintelligence was to read all of the damage assessments. I was astounded at the extent to which we had suffered serious, serious losses. One example: the Chinese, by espionage, acquired all of the design information of US nuclear weapons currently in our inventory. We know they have that information, we still don't know how they got it. (Taylor & Rudin, 2012, n.p.)

In April 2009, the DOD announced that hackers had stolen 1.5 TB of data relating to the developmental F-35 Joint Strike Fighter. Most anonymous sources blamed the Chinese, which was apparently confirmed in March 2012 by an executive from BAE Systems, the design authority, who said that Chinese sources had access to the program's information for 18 months. In 2011, China revealed its own stealth fighter, superficially identical to the F-35.

In fiscal year 2009–2010, U.S. courts tried seven cases under the Economic Espionage Act of 1998, of which six were linked to China. In the four fiscal years 2010 to 2013, the U.S.

Department of Justice indicted around 100 individuals and corporations for transferring protected information to China, according to court records, excluding the indictments that remain sealed.

In December 2010, Richard A. Clarke (Special Adviser to the President on Cybersecurity and Cyberterrorism from 2001 to 2003) told the Foreign Policy Research Institute that Chinese agents were "regularly breaking into American companies and stealing anything of value. We know of some 3,000 US companies that have been hacked, including Google and Cisco, whose source codes were stolen. It is a serious threat to our economy" (Rubin, 2010, n.p.). He continued to say that the Chinese have "established cyberwar military units," created networks of private hackers, "laced US infrastructure with logic bombs," and developed "the ability to disconnect all Chinese networks from the rest of the global internet" (Rubin, 2010, n.p.).

Since May 2007, a group of unknown cyber spies placed malware on the computer networks and mobile devices at official organizations and scientific research sites, mostly in Eastern Europe and Central Asia but also in Western Europe and North America. Some of the exploits were employed against Tibetan activists and military-commercial energy-sector targets in Asia outside of China, suggesting that the sources are Chinese. Some of the malware was written by Russian-speaking authors, and most of the attacks were routed through Russia and Germany, but the targets included Russian official sites, suggesting that Russian hackers were employed by foreign controllers. The ultimate source remains unknown because more than 60 domain names and several servers were used to hide the ultimate controller. Kaspersky Lab, a security company founded in Russia, was alerted in October 2012 and reported in January 2013, using the term *Rocra* or *Operation Red October* to label the malicious campaign. The malware was placed via phishing e-mails, with the malware hidden inside Microsoft Excel and Word files, which appeared as advertisements for a second-hand car or other attractive items. The malware was designed to harvest e-mails, extract online browsing history, extract saved passwords, record keystrokes, capture screenshots, and harvest information from whatever USB drives and mobile phones were connected to the target computer, among other tasks, as well as standby for new tasks triggered by the remote controller.

Starting in November 2009, employees of U.S. companies from the energy sectors, particularly oil and petrochemicals, were subjected to offline social engineering, phishing e-mails, and network exploitation. In February 2011, McAfee (another cybersecurity company) traced malware (that it called *Night Dragon*) to an Internet protocol address in China and found that the sources had exfiltrated information on sensitive competitive proprietary operations and the financing of oil and gas field bids and operations.

In January 2010, more than 30 corporations, including Google, claimed that they had suffered cyber attacks mostly from sources in China. VeriSign iDefense blamed the Chinese government for intrusions into Google's networks. Google subsequently accused China of stealing its source code. Also in 2010, Mandiant reported that information was extracted from the corporate networks of a U.S. Fortune 500 manufacturing company while it was negotiating to acquire a Chinese firm, which probably used the information to attain a better deal.

In November 2010, private-sector participants, especially those doing business in China, told a conference organized by ONCIX that they had lost information on clients, prices, mergers and acquisitions, and finances to cyber espionage.

In May 2011, Google revealed that Gmail accounts held by U.S. and South Korean officials and Chinese dissidents had been phished. In June, the U.S. secretary of state asked the FBI to investigate attacks on Gmail accounts held by U.S. diplomats. In December 2012, the FBI investigated a foreign attack on the private computers held by the former chairman of the Joint Chiefs of Staff (Admiral Mike Mullen), the latest in a series of otherwise unnamed retired officials targeted. In 2012, the Department of Justice started a program to train 100 prosecutors to prosecute criminal cases related to cyber espionage sponsored by foreign governments. The Department of State also elevated the issue of Chinese cyber espionage to its strategic security dialogue with China.

Another case of phishing with both commercial and national-security implications occurred in March 2011, when phishing e-mails were sent to users of the SecurID system. (Most users use the small hardware token, which produces a new number every 60 s that the user adds to their password when logging in remotely.) The e-mails included malware hidden inside an attached spreadsheet file titled "2011 Recruitment Plan." Where the malware was downloaded, it harvested credentials and information about the user and technology. The SecurID system was well used in U.S. official organizations and their classified contractors. Shortly thereafter, Lockheed Martin, one of these contractors and a user of SecurID tokens, was penetrated. RSA, the owner of SecurID, and Lockheed Martin claimed that they lost no data, and no other organization admitted to a harmful attack, but anonymous officials told journalists that China had used SecurID secrets to penetrate systems used by holders of SecurID systems. U.S. officials blamed all these attacks on Chinese sources.

In October 2011, ONCIX reported to Congress that

> Chinese actors are the world's most active and persistent perpetrators of economic espionage. US private sector firms and cybersecurity specialists have reported an onslaught of computer network intrusions that have originated in China, but the IC cannot confirm who was responsible. (p. i)

In November 2011, the House of Representatives Permanent Select Committee on Intelligence started an investigation into the threats posed by Chinese telecommunications companies doing business in the United States. On October 8, 2012, it reported on two particular Chinese companies, Huawei and ZTE.

> During the investigation, the Committee received information from industry experts and current and former Huawei employees suggesting that Huawei, in particular, may be violating United States laws. These allegations describe a company that has not followed United States legal obligations or international standards of business behavior. The Committee will be referring these allegations to Executive Branch agencies for further review, including possible investigation.

> In sum, the Committee finds that the companies failed to provide evidence that would satisfy any fair and full investigation. Although this alone does not prove wrongdoing, it factors into the Committee's conclusions below. Further, this report contains a classified annex, which also adds to the Committee's concerns about the risk to the United States. The investigation concludes that the risks associated with Huawei's and ZTE's provision of equipment to U.S. critical infrastructure could undermine core U.S. national-security interests. (Rogers & Ruppersberger, 2012, pp. v–vi)

In January 2013, the U.S. DOD released a declassified version of the Defense Science Board's report on *Resilient Military Systems and the Advanced Cyber Threat*, which warned that U.S. DOD was not secure against a peer cyber threat.

> The cyber threat is also insidious, enabling adversaries to access vast new channels of intelligence about critical U.S. enablers (operational and technical; military and industrial) that can threaten our national and economic security. Current DoD actions, though numerous, are fragmented. Thus, DoD is not prepared to defend against this threat . . . With present capabilities and technology it is not possible to defend with confidence against the most sophisticated cyber attacks. (U.S. Defense Science Board, 2013, p. 1)

In late May 2013, leaks of the classified version revealed that the threat of most concern was China and that, allegedly, Chinese cyber espionage had collected classified designs of the most advanced defense systems, including the PAC3 (an advanced Patriot anti–ballistic missile system), the Terminal High Altitude Area Defense (the U.S. Army's anti–ballistic system of systems), the U.S. Navy's Aegis anti–ballistic missile system, the U.S. Navy's Littoral Combat Ship, the F-35 Joint Strike Fighter, the F/A-18 fighter aircraft, the U.S. Marine Corps' V-22 Osprey transport aircraft, and the Black Hawk helicopter.

On May 6, 2013, the DOD released a report on *Military and Security Developments Involving the People's Republic of China* that explicitly stated that most cyber espionage appears "to be attributable directly to the Chinese government and military" (p. 36).

In February 2013, the DNI disseminated its classified *National Intelligence Estimate*, which, according to anonymous leaks to news media, identified China as the source of most cyber espionage. In March 2013, the U.S. President's National Security Adviser, Thomas Donilon, used a public speech to urge China to curb its cyber activities.

On January 30, 2013, the *New York Times* revealed the results of an investigation, lasting months, in partnership with a security provider (Mandiant), into attacks on its computers and on the computers held privately by some of its journalists, resulting in external access to all user passwords. the *New York Times* and Mandiant blamed Chinese military sources that were searching for the newspaper's sources for a story, published in October 2012, on the Chinese premier's private wealth. Mandiant soon reported that it had linked China's military to cyber attacks on nearly 150 organizations since 2006 and had identified a long-standing APT (external experts designated it as *APT1* and attributed attacks to it back to 2006) as a Chinese military unit in Shanghai, which uses more than 1,000 servers and 832 Internet protocol addresses for its attacks. APT1 had attacked 141 companies, of which 115 were based in the United States; five in Britain; three each in Israel and India; two each in Canada, Taiwan, Singapore, and Switzerland; and one each in Japan, Belgium, France, Luxemburg, Norway, United Arab Emirates, and South Africa. Mandiant categorized these companies across 20 major industries, of which the top 10 most represented were (in order) IT, aerospace, public administration, telecommunications and satellites, scientific research and consulting, energy, transportation, construction and manufacturing, international organizations, and engineering services.

> As with other APT groups, spear phishing is APT1's most commonly used technique. The spear phishing emails contain either a malicious attachment or a

hyperlink to a malicious file. The subject line and the text in the email body are usually relevant to the recipient. APT1 also creates webmail accounts using real peoples' names—names that are familiar to the recipient, such as a colleague, a company executive, an IT department employee, or company counsel—and uses these accounts to send the email. (Mandiant, 2013, p. 28)

Sometimes APT1 created new e-mail accounts using the name of an employee within the target organization in an effort to deceive another employee. Usually, the attached malware was disguised. For instance, some of the executable .zip files contained malware but were disguised as documents with .pdf extensions by adding the letters *pdf* just before the extension, by turning the executable's icon into the symbol associated with a real .pdf extension, and by adding an innocuous file name (such as "updated_office_contact"). Sometimes APT1 was ready to interact dynamically with the target if the target were to reply to the e-mail with skepticism. In one case, an American target replied with skepticism about the attachment, but the threat responded within minutes with nominal confirmation of the attachment's legitimacy. If the target were to download the malware, usually the target would be unaware of anything malicious. The malware could be configured to search for certain information and send it back to the threat automatically. Some malware (a *backdoor*) could be configured to accept commands from the threat; for instance, the threat could analyze some stolen documents for valuable information and decide to command the backdoor to gather other documents that refer to the same information. APT1's backdoors were able to modify and create executable programs; modify the system registry; capture screenshots, keystrokes, and mouse movements; harvest passwords; and shut down the target system, among other things.

ALLEGED RUSSIAN ESPIONAGE In 2008, a German insider threat was convicted of economic espionage for passing helicopter technology to the Russian Foreign Intelligence Service (SVR) in exchange for just $10,000. The insider communicated with his Russian handler through anonymous e-mail addresses. Germany's Federal Office for the Protection of the Constitution estimated that Russia uses cyber espionage to steal research and development worth billions of dollars from Germany's energy, information-technology, telecommunications, aerospace, and security sectors.

The director-general of the British Security Service (MI5) publicly stated that Russia is targeting the U.K.'s financial system. In 2009, a Russian automotive company bribed executives at South Korea's GM-Daewoo Auto and Technology to pass thousands of computer files on car engine and component designs (ONCIX, 2011, p. B2).

In June 2010, the FBI arrested 10 Russians who were spying for the SVR. They had been tasked to collect information on the U.S. economy and steal U.S. technology, mostly through intelligence gathered through human interactions (HUMINT), although they communicated with their controllers through encrypted e-mail. More Russian cyber activities have emerged with intent to sabotage than to spy, but the rate of Russian cyber espionage must be underestimated.

In October 2011, ONCIX reported to Congress that

> Russia's intelligence services are conducting a range of activities to collect economic information and technology from US targets. . . . Motivated by Russia's high dependence on natural resources, the need to diversify its economy, and the belief that the global economic system is tilted toward US and other

Western interests at the expense of Russia, Moscow's highly capable intelligence services are using HUMINT, cyber, and other operations to collect economic information and technology to support Russia's economic development and security. (pp. i, 5)

The actors could intend to acquire information for diplomatic advantage; they could even use this information to embarrass the target. For instance, on February 6, 2014, a digital recording of a telephone conversation was posted online in which U.S. Assistant Secretary of State Victoria Nuland made disparaging remarks about the E.U. to the U.S. ambassador to Ukraine during increasing U.S.–Russian tensions over Russian intervention in Ukraine. A White House spokesman claimed Russian involvement in the leak.

ALLEGED SYRIAN PHISHING Syrian sources emerged as sophisticated phishers during the civil war (since March 2011), mostly directing phishing against Syrian rebels and dissidents, sometimes against news media or governments that appear to favor the rebels. On August 29, 2011, multiple Syrian Twitter accounts distributed tweets that offered a link to Facebook for a "fascinating video clip showing an attack on Syrian regime" but actually linked to a fake Facebook page, where the threat captured the target's login credentials before redirecting the target to the real Facebook home page.

Sabotage

The subsections below describe the scope of cyber sabotage, review the vectors and activities, and describe past U.S., Chinese, Russian, Iranian, North Korean, and Syrian attacks.

SCOPE *Sabotage* is intentional disruption or damage of something material; sabotage may end up killing people, but murder is not necessary to sabotage. Where sabotage is meant to harm, it may be labeled terrorism, but terrorism is not necessarily the same as sabotage; *terrorism* is activities that terrorize, whether intended or not.

Cyber sabotage is vectored through or affects cyberspace. **Offensive cyber warfare** is ill defined but is mostly about sabotage, although it must include cyber espionage and some defensive activities too. The term **cyber warfare** is normally used in the context of international conflict, but cyber warfare has been waged between governments, insurgents, and terrorists.

Cyber sabotage is less frequent than cyber espionage but riskier by certain measures because of the great harm that cyber sabotage could cause. Cyber sabotage can disrupt private access to the Internet, damage private computers, and cause damage to infrastructure on a national scale.

Malicious cyber activities became of national concern by the mid-1980s. Since then, they have become much more common with increasing access to the skills and technology. In 2005, the U.S. Department of Commerce's National Institute of Standards and Technology estimated 30 to 40 new attack tools being posted on the Internet every month.

VECTORS AND ACTIVITIES Malware can be configured to damage or destroy digital systems or the other systems controlled by the infected digital networks.

Definitions of Malware Used to Sabotage

A **Trojan horse** is "a computer program that conceals harmful code. A Trojan horse usually masquerades as a useful program that a user would wish to execute" (U.S. GAO, 2005a, p. 8). A Trojan horse is

> stealthy code that executes under the guise of a useful program but performs malicious acts such as the destruction of files, the transmission of private data, and the opening of a back door to allow third-party control of a machine. (Reveron, 2012, p. 8)

A **logic bomb** is "a form of sabotage in which a programmer inserts code that causes the program to perform a destructive action when some triggering event occurs, such as

terminating the programmer's employment" (U.S. GAO, 2005a, p. 8) or "camouflaged segments of programs that destroy data when correct conditions are met" (Reveron, 2012, p. 8).

Viruses, worms, and Trojan horses each could inject malicious code into other software, potentially causing the software to malfunction or to execute destructive actions, such as deleting data or shutting down the computer. A **rootkit** is especially stealthy because it modifies the computer's operating system or even its kernel (core) (Yannakogeorgos, 2011, p. 261).

Software tampering or **software diddling** is "making unauthorized modifications to software stored on a system, including file deletions" (Denning, 1998, pp. 33–34).

As described in the subsections below, cyber sabotage is achieved mainly by redirecting domain names, denying Internet service, or sabotaging control systems.

DOMAIN NAME SYSTEM ATTACK A **Domain Name System (DNS) attack** causes a domain name to redirect incorrectly. Nearly all servers that publish content to the Internet are identified by a numeric address. Numbers are difficult to remember, so in the 1980s providers agreed on a Domain Name System. It acts as a directory system, automatically translating domain names into server addresses. DNS allows you to type letters, such as www.sagepub.com, into your browser rather than the associated numerical address.

DENIAL OF SERVICE A **denial-of-service (DOS) attack** aims to disrupt Internet sites, principally by overloading the servers that provide the information on the site. The attacks are strengthened by using multiple sources to deliver the malicious traffic, a technique known as **distributed denial of service** (DDOS). Typically, malware is delivered by virus or worm, shutting down servers from the inside or taking over a network of computers (a **botnet** of **zombie** computers) so that they send requests for information that overwhelm the servers. An attacker would use a botnet in most cases but also could recruit colleagues or volunteers. Collectively, these attacks have been categorized as *jamming* or *flooding attacks* (Yannakogeorgos, 2011, p. 260).

Most DOS attacks are aimed at particular organizations, but some have wider implications. In November 1988, a worm known as Morris brought 10% of systems connected to the Internet to a halt. In 2001, the Code Red worm shut down or slowed down Internet access from millions of computer users.

Denial-of-service attacks have become easier with increased availability of Internet bandwidth and technical skills. Cloud-hosting structures give attackers more processing power and more digital space in which to hide their activities.

SABOTAGE OF CONTROL SYSTEMS Sabotage could be directed against anything, but in theory, the most efficient and effective forms of sabotage would be directed against or through the industrial **control systems** and cyber physical systems that control more hazardous materials or processes, such as road traffic, air traffic, heart beats, automobile brakes, sewage, weapons, electrical power, and nuclear and radiological materials.

Some of these systems are fully automated without outside communication, but most will accept communications of some form, if only a manual input through some interface connected directly to the systems. The physical interface may be the only access control. "Unfortunately, like other information technologies, most were originally designed with little or no security, or security has been added after the fact. Many of these systems rely on the security-through-obscurity concept rather than building security into the design process" (Applegate, 2013, p. 2). Most of these systems are connected to an intranet. Sometimes these systems are open to attacks via the Internet.

National Cyber Sabotage

The subsections below describe alleged U.S., Chinese, Russian, Iranian, North Korean, and Syrian cyber attacks.

U.S. ATTACKS The United States, China, Russia, Israel, India, and France (in order) are six countries often listed with the most "sophisticated cyber–national security capabilities" (Reveron, 2012, p. 15). This section examines U.S. cyber sabotage. The subsections below describe the structure of U.S. cyber sabotage, U.S. strategy, U.S. attacks on Iran, and U.S. attacks on China.

Structure. The U.S. Department of Defense discussed cyber war first in 1977; in 1981, it began planning for cyber offensives. In 1991, the United States made its first attempt to use malware as part of its war against Iraq (Reveron, 2012, p. 13).

Under the administration of President Bill Clinton (1993–2001), the national security adviser, the secretary of defense, and the Joint Chiefs of Staff all strongly advocated real-world covert action and cyber warfare against Iraq, particularly around a false concern that Iraqi hackers had penetrated the Department of Defense in February 1998, and against the financial assets of al-Qaeda, particularly after al-Qaeda's terrorist bombings of the U.S. embassies in Kenya and Tanzania (August 1998). The two secretaries of the treasury in that period (Robert Rubin from 1995 to 1999 and Lawrence Summers from 1999 to 2001) opposed such responses for fear of undermining international norms and destabilizing international finance.

In 1997, the secretary of defense authorized the National Security Agency (established in 1952 mainly for signals intelligence) to conduct computer network attacks (CNAs), meaning

BOX 10.4

Private and Experimental Cyber Attacks

In March 1997, a teenager in Worcester, Massachusetts, used Internet access to disable controls systems at the local airport control tower. In the 2000s, several countries reported that their national power grids, air-traffic control systems, and nuclear installations had been penetrated, although the relative roles played by malicious actors or bugs in the system are difficult to separate, particularly because officials often deny any issue for fear of alarming the public or alerting the attackers to their performance (U.N. Office of Drugs and Crime, 2010a).

Over three months in 2000, a former worker on a sewage control system in Queensland, Australia, hacked into the system and released more than 264,000 L of raw sewage at different locations, polluting the environment. He was eventually sentenced to two years in jail.

In August 2006, two striking traffic engineers logged into a road traffic management center using their manager's identity and caused gridlock at an airport, a freeway ramp, and other key intersections. They were eventually charged with seven felonies between them and sentenced to community service and to pay fines.

In January 2008, in Łódź, Poland, a 14-year-old boy rewired a television remote control to control wireless switch junctions on the city's tram system. His actions caused the derailment of four trams, resulting in minor injuries to more than a dozen passengers. This was the first cyber attack to cause injuries directly.

Experimentally, in 2007, the U.S. Department of Energy, sponsored by the Department of Homeland Security, hacked into a modeled control system for an electrical power plant and altered a generator's operating cycle so that it shook itself to death within 30 s.

In 2008, medical researchers warned that implantable cardioverter defibrillators and pacemakers with electronic circuits theoretically could be accessed wirelessly and interrogated for private information or reprogrammed to harm the patient. In 2012, another researcher demonstrated this practically by hacking into a pacemaker and reprogramming it to deliver a deadly 830-V shock. At that time, such implants still were not encrypted and could be accessed wirelessly from a range of up to 12 m.

In 2010, researchers demonstrated that they could connect a computer into the on-board diagnostics ports in automobiles and take control of the on-board computer that controls automobile performance and, thus, directly control the locks, brakes, and the engine, independent of driver controls and automated controls. Later, they demonstrated that they could take control wirelessly through cellular radio, Bluetooth, audio compact-disc players, navigation systems, and emergency communications. Given the high frequency of automobile accidents and the ease with which attackers could disguise the real cause, automobiles might have crashed in the past due to cyber attacks but have been counted as accidents (Applegate, 2013).

"operations to disrupt, deny, degrade or destroy" information in target computers or networks "or the computers and networks themselves." In March 2003, the NSA conducted cyber attacks that, together with air attacks, shut down the Iraqi electrical grid during the invasion of Iraq.

What Is the Risk of Cyber Sabotage to the United States?

The United States suffers the most cyber attacks because it is the most valuable economy, politically important, a commercial and technological leader, and highly connected digitally. For most of the same reasons, the United States probably perpetuates plenty of cyber attacks, which critics have pointed out as drivers of foreign retaliation.

The United States officially is most concerned about the potential to cause material or physical harm through cyber attacks on the national infrastructure. The frequency of attacks on American cyber infrastructure alone has increased nearly 8 times from 2006 to 2012 (see Table 10.2), and the Government Accountability Office continues to rate cyber critical infrastructure as high risk, with an effective forecast of increasing risk. They note,

> As computer technology has advanced, federal agencies and our nation's critical infrastructures— such as power distribution, water supply, telecommunications, and emergency services have become increasingly dependent on computerized information systems and electronic data to carry out operations and to process, maintain, and report essential information. The security

of these systems and data is essential to protecting national and economic security, and public health and safety. Safeguarding federal computer systems and the systems that support critical infrastructures—referred to as cyber critical infrastructure protection (cyber CIP)—is a continuing concern. Federal information security has been on GAO's list of high-risk areas since 1997; in 2003, GAO expanded this high-risk area to include cyber CIP. Risks to information and communication systems include insider threats from disaffected or careless employees and business partners, escalating and emerging threats from around the globe, the ease of obtaining and using hacking tools, the steady advance in the sophistication of attack technology, and the emergence of new and more destructive attacks. Cyber threats and incidents are increasingly prevalent. Threats to systems supporting critical infrastructure and government information systems are evolving and growing. (U.S. Government Accountability Office, 2013, p. 184)

In 2005, a new military command (Joint Functional Component Command–Network Warfare) was established, administered by Strategic Command but led by the NSA director. In October 2009, this became Cyber Command. (It nominally achieved operational status in May 2010.) The U.S. Air Force claims cyberspace as its third domain (in addition to air and space), but the U.S. Navy created the Fleet Cyber Command (10th Fleet).

Over the summer of 2013, Edward Snowden revealed to journalists documents, some of which described the NSA's Office of Tailored Access Operations (TAO), which had been hacking foreign devices for 15 years. According to former NSA officials interviewed by journalists, TAO's mission is to collect information from computers, telecommunications systems, e-mail, and text messages. The documents included a classified budget authorization that reported 231 offensive cyber operations by the United States in 2011; these attacks were focused on computer networks in Russia, China, Iran, and North Korea. The budget authorization stated that the operations proceeded by placing "covert implants" (malware) in computers, routers, and firewalls on tens of thousands of machines every year, with plans to expand those numbers into the millions (Aid, 2013; Ingersoll, 2013).

The budget request for fiscal year 2014 raised the budget for computer-network warfare by 20% to $4.7 billion. Cyber Command will raise its personnel from 900 to 4,900 employees. By 2015, Cyber Command will employ 13 offensive teams at home and another 27 within the combatant commands (Negroponte et al., 2013, p. 35).

Strategy. In March 2005, the *National Defense Strategy* (which is released by the secretary of defense) described cyberspace as a new theater of operations. It stated that in "rare instances, revolutionary technology and associated military innovation can fundamentally alter long-established concepts of warfare" (U.S. Department of Defense, 2005, p. 3).

In June 2008, the *National Defense Strategy* estimated that nonstate actors "can attack vulnerable points in cyberspace and disrupt commerce and daily life in the United States, causing economic damage, compromising sensitive information and materials, and interrupting critical services such as power and information networks" (U.S. Department of Defense, 2008a, p. 7).

In February 2011, the *National Military Strategy* (which is the responsibility of the military Joint Chiefs of Staff) estimated that cyber threats were growing due to weak international norms against malicious use of cyberspace, the challenges of attribution, the low barriers to entry, and the ease with which offensive capabilities can be developed relative to the challenges of developing defensive capabilities.

In July 2011, Cyber Command announced DOD's first *Strategy for Operating in Cyberspace.* The strategy has five goals or components.

1. Treat cyberspace as an operational domain, in addition to the four existing domains (land, sea, air, and space)

2. Develop *active defense* (new defenses and operating concepts for DOD networks)

3. Partner with DHS and the private sector to support critical infrastructure

4. Cooperate internationally

5. Leverage talent and innovation in research and development

On May 31, 2011, U.S. officials warned publicly that cyber attacks could be treated as acts of war. On September 18, 2012, U.S. Cyber Command hosted a public conference, at which the U.S. State Department's legal adviser, Harold Koh, announced that

- the United States has adopted and shared through the U.N. 10 principles, including the position that international law applies in cyberspace;

- cyber attacks can amount to armed attacks triggering the right of self-defense;

- a cyber operation that results in death, injury, or significant destruction would probably be seen as a use of force in violation of international law; and

- cyber attacks that cause a nuclear-plant meltdown, open a dam above a populated area, or disable an air-traffic control system resulting in plane crashes are examples of activity that probably would constitute an illegal use of force.

In 2012, the U.S. government completed a legal review that concluded that the president could order a preemptive strike if the United States were to gather credible evidence of an imminent major cyber attack. New strategic defense guidance identified one of the primary missions of U.S. armed forces as operating effectively in cyberspace.

In October 2012, President Obama reportedly signed Presidential Policy Directive 20, which specified the principles and processes of cyber operations. In leaked excerpts, the thresholds for kinetic retaliation were written as follows:

> Significant Consequences: Loss of life, significant responsive actions against the United States, significant damage to property, serious adverse U.S. foreign policy consequences, or serious economic impact on the United States.

> U.S. National Interests: Matters of vital interest to the United States to include national security, public safety, national economic security, the safe and reliable functioning of "critical infrastructure," and the availability of "key resources." (U.S. White House, 2012, p. 3)

Reportedly, cyber operations outside a war zone would require the President's permission (Negroponte et al., 2013, pp. 35–36; Reveron, 2012, pp. 8–9).

U.S. Attacks on Iran. In summer 2010, Iran blamed the United States and Israel for malware (known as *Stuxnet*) that had damaged more than 1,000 of the 6,000 centrifuges at an Iranian uranium-enrichment plant. Stuxnet had been used to spy for a longer period. In June 2012, after a newspaper investigation, U.S. officials confirmed that the NSA and its Israeli equivalent had produced Stuxnet. Stuxnet was supposed to disable the centrifuges gradually without alerting the Iranians and apparently continued to operate despite discovery. Stuxnet and its derivatives spread through shared printer networks and are backdoor malware that allow controllers to adapt and upgrade them. In February 2012, the Iranian Fars News Agency quoted an Iranian intelligence officer as saying that 16,000 computers in Iran had been infected by Stuxnet.

> The Stuxnet worm was more complex than any previously discovered piece of malware. It contained four Windows zero-day exploits and was able to propagate itself through USB flash drives, network shares, a remote procedure call (RPC) vulnerability or a print spooler vulnerability. Stuxnet was also the first piece of malware ever identified to include a programmable logic controller (PLC) root kit. Stuxnet spread itself via Microsoft Windows but appeared to target a specific PLC, the Siemens S7-300 system, and only if that PLC was attached to two specific types of variable-frequency drives which had to be spinning between 807 to 1210 Hertz. Once these and other specified conditions had been met, the Stuxnet worm would periodically modify the frequency of the variable frequency drives to 1410 Hertz and then to 2 Hertz and then to 1064 Hertz while simultaneously masking these changes from attached monitoring systems.

The Stuxnet is known to have infected at least 120,000 Microsoft Windows systems worldwide, however, it is only known to have damaged systems in the Fuel Enrichment Plant in Natanz, Iran [including] more than 1,000 centrifuges used in Iran's nuclear fuel enrichment program. (Applegate, 2013, p. 8)

U.S. Attacks on China. On August 25, 2013, China announced that it had suffered the largest cyber attack in its history. DDOS attacks had interrupted many servers responsible for sites with a .cn domain name. CloudFlare's Chief Executive, Matthew Prince, said the company observed a 32% drop in traffic for the thousands of Chinese domains on the company's network during the attack compared with the same period 24 hrs earlier (Mozur, 2013; Roney, 2013).

CHINESE ATTACKS U.S. officials often talk about China as the most severe national cyber threat to the United States, but almost all cases are cases of espionage rather than sabotage, although some officials admit that the United States is reticent to admit any cases of sabotage for fear of revealing to the sources the effectiveness of the attack.

Chinese sources are possibly responsible for a series of cyber attacks on U.S. infrastructure, particularly the electrical power system. In January 2003, the Slammer worm was used to shut down for hours the safety monitoring system at the Davis-Besse nuclear power plant in Ohio; fortunately, operations had been suspended months earlier due to a physical fault in the reactor. This attack was probably a probe of security. U.S. officials did not reveal it to the public until after a possible attack on the electrical grid in August. On August 14, 2003, about 55 million people across Ontario, Canada, and eight U.S. states in the Northeast and Midwest experienced an unprecedented outage of electrical power lasting up to 2 days. More than 100 power plants had shut down at some point during that period. For months, an official explanation was lacking, although officials generally downplayed concerns about terrorism or cyber sabotage; one contributory cause was the Blaster computer worm, which degraded communications between data centers used to manage the electrical grid (Wilson, 2003, p. 3). Eventually, after many contradictory explanations by officials from both countries, officials blamed trees that short-circuited power transmission lines during high demand and identified a fault in software that had been designed to alert operators to electrical overloading. These cumulative faults were not officially blamed on a cyber attack, but journalists reported that anonymous officials had admitted that the faults were caused by malware from official Chinese sources; enough former officials have given the story credence to suggest that it not just another conspiracy theory. In 2008, the U.S. intelligence community reported that in fiscal year 2007–2008 hackers had accessed computers used to control the electrical grid, "in at least one case causing a power outage that affected multiple cities" (Yannakogeorgos, 2011, pp. 258–259).

In April 2009, journalists reported anonymous official claims that China had hacked the air-traffic control system used by the U.S. Air Force. In May 2009, the Department of Transportation's Office of the Inspector General published a *Review of Web Applications Security and Intrusion Detection in Air Traffic Control Systems*, which found that hackers had penetrated air-traffic control systems in Alaska, penetrated Federal Aviation Administration (FAA) network servers, and accessed personal information from 48,000 current and former FAA employees.

In early 2013, U.S. officials claimed that hackers based in China had accessed the computers of a company that monitors more than half of the oil and gas pipelines in North America, perhaps to spy on the system, perhaps to plant malware that could be triggered later as sabotage (Negroponte et al., 2013, p. 37).

RUSSIAN ATTACKS In May 2007, Russian hackers paralyzed the Estonian banking system and some telecommunications, news, and government websites during a dispute between the Estonian and Russian governments over a former Soviet war memorial on Estonian territory.

In August 2008, during a short kinetic war between Russia and Georgia over the pro-Russian region of South Ossetia, Russian hackers disrupted Georgian websites and tried to silence a Georgian blogger by disrupting his social media, using widely available toolkits including DoSHTTP and BlackEnergy to implement distributed denial of service attacks. Similar attacks against Estonia had greater consequences because of Estonia's greater reliance on the Internet.

In November 2008, malware attacked the secure cyberspace controlled by United States Central Command. These attacks were traced to Russian hackers, although the United States did not blame the Russian government.

Since Russian intervention in Ukraine's civil war in February 2014, more cyber attacks have targeted the Ukraine and the United States from sources in Russia. In March 2014, Russia helped to interrupt communications between the Crimean peninsula and the rest of Ukraine during ethnic Russian protests for separation and Russian occupation. Separatists in Ukraine and Russian citizens hacked official Ukrainian websites and communications, especially those passing through Russian infrastructure. Some protesters took over facilities owned by the Ukrainian telecommunications service provider and shut down nodes that carried both Internet and telephone communications. Russian military forces cut wired communications into Ukrainian military facilities. Meanwhile, Russian warships offshore jammed radio and mobile-telephone communications. These attacks did not cause a complete collapse of Ukrainian communications as Ukraine had prepared reasonable defenses and redundancy against prior Russian probes. Additionally, the Ukrainian government has come under attack from a Russian cybercrime gang known as Quedagh (Gilbert, 2014). JPMorgan Chase saw 76 million of its accounts compromised in a related attack; Russian sources probably chose the target for its involvement in U.S. sanctions against Russia (Goldstein, Perlroth, & Sanger, 2014).

IRANIAN ATTACKS Anonymous U.S. officials have blamed Iran for DDOS attacks on U.S. corporate websites since December 2011. In August 2012, for 2 days on, 2 days off, 2 days on, Iranian attackers attempted to disrupt the websites of companies in the Middle East, such as Aramco in Saudi Arabia, that participated in the embargo on Iranian oil. More seriously, malware (nicknamed *Shamoon*) damaged 30,000 computer hard drives belonging to Aramco, knocking out part of the company's network for 2 weeks. The attackers routed their activities though the servers owned or operated by major U.S. telecommunications companies. On October 18, 2012, U.S. Defense Secretary Leon E. Panetta told a meeting of Business Executives for National Security in New York that the Shamoon attack was "probably the most destructive attack that the private sector has seen to date" (Pincus, 2012, n.p.).

In the week of September 17, 2012, the websites of U.S.-based banks were slowed by major DDOS attacks. On September 21, the chairman of the Homeland Security and Governmental Affairs Committee, Senator Joseph I. Lieberman, publicly blamed Iran, where banks were suffering stronger U.S. and European sanctions. Similar attacks occurred in October 2012, January 2013, and March 2013. A group calling itself the Izz ad-Din al-Qassam Cyber Fighters claimed responsibility, but U.S. officials claimed that this group was at least tolerated by the Iranian government. In February 2013, U.S. banks submitted their annual financial reports to the Securities and Exchange Commission; 19 banks reported that they had suffered a denial of service attack or malicious intrusion within the previous year (Negroponte et al., 2013, p. 17).

NORTH KOREAN ATTACKS North Korea is not well connected to the Internet, except through its government, which had established an official hacking unit by 1994, which now employs perhaps 6,000 people, with the help of accomplices or assets placed predominantly in China and Malaysia (Sanger & Fackler, 2015).

In July 2009, U.S. and South Korean government and commercial websites, including those of the Secret Service, Treasury Department, Federal Trade Commission, New York Stock Exchange, Nasdaq, and *Washington Post*, were among the targets of a DDOS attack attributed to North Korea. Around 166,000 computers in 74 countries were recruited as a botnet for the attack in 2009.

In early 2011, South Korea blamed North Korea for similar DDOS attacks that disrupted South Korean and U.S. official websites and banking websites.

On March 20, 2013, around 32,000 computers at six South Korean banks and broadcasters were shut down by malware. South Korean authorities traced the malware to an Internet protocol address in China, which they characterized as a ghost site for North Korean attackers. In the previous weeks, North Korea had threatened to cancel its armistice with South Korea in response to the U.N. Security Council's vote, with Chinese support, in favor of increased sanctions on North Korea after another underground test of a nuclear weapon.

The most valuable known case of cyber sabotage on U.S. soil occurred on November 24, 2014, when malware propagating on the intranet of Sony Pictures Entertainment overwrote all data on hard drives, including the master boot records. Sony's e-mail and other systems were down for a week while the hackers progressively posted online stolen movies, embarrassing internal e-mails, and privileged information about employee salaries. North Korea was blamed; Sony had planned to release (on Christmas Day) a comic film about two American journalists recruited by the CIA to assassinate the North Korean leader. On December 1, the FBI warned other corporations, in a limited release, of the malware and stated that parts of its code contained text in the Korean language (Finkle, 2014). Threats, with the same signature ("Guardians of Peace"), against movie theaters prompted the five largest distributors to announce, on December 17, that they would postpone their showings. Sony indefinitely canceled its release of the film, which had cost $44 million to produce and $35 million to promote up to that point, although, after criticism, it eventually chose to release the movie on schedule, initially only online (Barnes & Cieply, 2014).

SYRIAN ATTACKS Since at least 2010, the Syrian Electronic Army (SEA) has attacked dozens of websites and social media accounts. The Syrian Electronic Army is a signature of attackers who remain anonymous, but they use a website registered by the Syrian Computer Society, which was run by Bashar al-Assad from 1995 until he became president of Syria in 2000. Its early targets included the official biographical webpages for U.S. President Barack Obama and Secretary of State Hillary Clinton.

Its activities became more targeted after a civil war broke out in Syria (since March 2011). On September 26, 2011, the Syrian Electronic Army explicitly took over the homepage of Harvard University and posted opposition to U.S. policy toward Syria. On August 28, 2012, Syrian hackers posted stories about rebel atrocities on Amnesty International's Livewire blog, which previously has posted concerns about Syrian regime abuses of human rights.

On February 28, 2013, the Qatar Foundation's Twitter and Facebook accounts started posting confusing messages. (Qatar has strongly supported the rebels since early in the civil war.) On March 22, 2013, the Syrian Electronic Army explicitly took over the Twitter feeds from BBC Arabic Online, BBC Weather, and BBC Ulster Radio and sent messages characterizing the BBC as biased. On March 17, 2013, it posted similar messages on the Twitter feed and website for Human Rights Watch. On April 15, it took over National Public Radio's website and Twitter feeds in order to criticize NPR's coverage of the Syrian Civil War. On April 20, hackers defaced four Twitter accounts owned by CBS News with a long string of messages that accused the United States of supporting terrorism in Syria as part of a larger plot to impose a one-world government.

On August 27, the Syrian Electronic Army redirected the website for the *New York Times*, limiting access to the *Times'* news pages for nearly 48 hrs. It also attacked Twitter; users reported problems seeing images, such as profile pictures. The attackers were able to disrupt the websites by phishing the records of an Australian firm, Melbourne IT, which registers domain names and stores directory records for those websites. The hackers altered the information on these records, which caused the domain names to misdirect. In some cases, users were also redirected to a page with what appeared to be the SEA's logo.

On October 28, 2013, the Syrian Electronic Army briefly hijacked President Obama's Twitter and Facebook accounts, causing updates to redirect to a YouTube video titled "Syria facing terrorism." The SEA exploited the URL shortener used to promote Organizing for Action, an organization that promotes Obama's health care law.

PROVIDING SECURITY

The sections above, in reviewing the sources, vectors, and activities associated with attacks on information, have provided much advice on countering these things. This (final) section presents advice for higher managers in providing information security in general and cyber and communications security in general.

Information Security

Advice on securing information has been swamped with advice on securing digital information alone, but information security must have a wider scope than digital information. Well-established advice separates information security by three components:

1. **"Protective security,"** meaning "passive defenses" against attempts to collect your information or information on you, defenses such as controlling access to, transfer of, communication of, and travel with information of certain classifications

2. **"Detection and neutralization** of intelligence threats," meaning an "active defense by eliminating the opponent's offensive intelligence threat"

3. **"Deception,"** meaning "deceiving or confusing" the threat (Herman, 1996, pp. 166–170)

The Humanitarian Practice Network (2010) recommends the following minimum policy on information security:

1. Define sensitive information

2. Define who is authorized to handle sensitive information

3. Define how the sensitive information is to be

   a. stored,

   b. communicated,

   c. transported,

   d. made unsensitive, or

   e. destroyed. (p. 154)

A more detailed strategy for information security involves

- defense of the secure domain by

  ○ controlling physical access, such as by restricting the persons who are allowed to enter the physical spaces where information is stored or accessed,

  ○ controlling digital access, such as by restricting who may use a computer network,

  ○ controlling the transfer of information between domains, such as by forbidding the carriage of papers or digital media out of the secure domain, and

  ○ establishing *firewalls*, essentially filters or gates to information, permitting information or requesters that pass some rule-based criteria,

- redundancy, by duplicating critical parts of the operation, such as the power sources, workers, and sites (although full redundancy would be unnecessary and expensive),

- backups, in case the primary source or asset is lost, of

  ○ data,

  ○ network and processing capacity,

  ○ personnel,

- o processes, and
- o critical service providers and suppliers

- planning for future contingencies, and

- testing the network against modeled contingencies (Suder, 2004, pp. 196–197).

The SANS Institute (2013) publishes 20 "Critical Security Controls":

1. Maintain an inventory of authorized and unauthorized devices

2. Maintain an inventory of authorized and unauthorized software

3. Monitor the secure configurations of hardware and software

4. Routinely assess and remediate vulnerability

5. Maintain defenses against malware

6. Maintain the security of application software

7. Control access to wireless networks

8. Maintain the capability to recover data

9. Assess and train security skills

10. Maintain the security of network devices such as firewalls, routers, and switches

11. Control network ports, protocols, and services

12. Control administrative privileges

13. Defend the perimeter

14. Maintain, monitor, and analyze security audits

15. Control access on the basis of a need to know

16. Monitor and control user accounts

17. Prevent loss of data by installing access controls and encrypting mobile hard drives

18. Manage incidents, such as insider non-compliance and external breaches

19. Secure network engineering, such as security zones and segmented networks

20. Test the system with penetration tests (pentests) and red team exercises

PricewaterhouseCoopers (2013) recommended the following 10 "essential safeguards" for effective information security:

1. A written security policy

2. Back-up and recovery/business continuity plans

3. Minimum collection and retention of personal information, with restrictions on physical access to personal data

4. Strong technology safeguards for prevention, detection, and encryption

5. Accurate inventory of where personal data of employees and customers is collected, transmitted, and stored, including third parties that handle that data

6. Internal and external risk assessments of privacy, security, confidentiality, and integrity of electronic and paper records

7. Ongoing monitoring of the data-privacy program

8. Personnel background checks

9. An employee security awareness training program

10. Require employees and third parties to comply with privacy policies (p. 34)

Verizon's advice for securing data is as follows:

- Eliminate unnecessary data and keep tabs on what's left.

- Ensure essential controls are met and regularly check that they remain so.

- Collect, analyze, and share incident data to create a rich data source that can drive security program effectiveness.

- Without deemphasizing prevention, focus on better and faster detection through a blend of people, processes, and technology.

- Regularly measure things like "number of compromised systems" and "mean time to detection" in networks. Use them to drive security practices.

- Evaluate the threat landscape to prioritize a treatment strategy. Don't buy into a "one size fits all" approach to security.

- If you're a target of espionage, don't underestimate the tenacity of your adversary. Nor should you underestimate the intelligence and tools at your disposal. (Verizon Enterprise Solutions, 2013, p. 5)

In the event of a breach, Verizon recommends analyzing each breach using what it calls the A4 Threat Model.

- Actors: Whose actions affected the asset

- Actions: What actions affected the asset

- Assets: Which assets were affected

- Attributes: How the asset was affected (Verizon Enterprise Solutions, 2013, pp. 14–15)

CYBERSECURITY

This book does not have space for a full review of the technical provisions of cybersecurity, although many technical provisions are described below following a description of particular threats. The subsections below review access controls, defensive measures, and deterrence.

Access Controls

Access controls are the measures intended to permit access into certain domains or to certain information by the appropriate users but to deny access to anyone else. Increasingly, cybersecurity experts advocate the *least privilege principle*, according to which users are granted only the permissions they need to do their jobs and nothing more.

Access controls on authorized users normally consist of a system that demands an authorized username and password. These data are much more likely to be compromised at the user end of the system than the server end. The servers normally hold the users' passwords in an encrypted form (a **password hash**—a number generated mathematically from the password). When the user attempts to log in, the server generates a hash of the typed password that it compares to the stored hash. If they match, the server permits access.

The hash is difficult to crack, but some national threats have the capacity, particularly in the United States, through which most of the world's telecommunications pass. Since at least 1976, some specialists have raised suspicions that the National Security Agency inserted a backdoor into the Data Encryption Standard, issued by the National Bureau of Standards. Over the summer of 2013, former NSA contractor Edward Snowden revealed documents describing NSA's exploitation of a vulnerability in the random number generator used for generating cryptographic keys, which was specified by the U.S. government's own National Institute of Standards and Technology (NIST). The vulnerability allowed the NSA to discover the keys being generated. In September, NIST reopened public review of the publications containing the specification. In December, the NIST opened a formal review of the process by which it generates crypto standards. The vulnerable random number generator is the Dual Elliptic Curve Deterministic Random Bit Generator (Dual EC_DRBG). The relevant standards are as follows:

- SP800-90A, Recommendations for Random Number Generation Using Deterministic Random Bit Generators

- SP800-90B, Recommendation for the Entropy Sources Used in Random Bit Generation

- SP800-90C, Recommendations for Random Bit Generator Constructions (Jackson, 2013b)

Future technologies promise better encryption but also better decryption (U.K. MOD, 2010, p. 140).

Most threats are admitted to a secure space by some action on the part of the user. The user may be noncompliant with a rule (such as "do not share your password") but much of the user's work activity (such as communicating by e-mail or attending conferences) implies inherent exposure to threats. Consequently, most cybersecurity managers, having implemented controls on access to or transfer of information, focus their attention on improving the user's compliance with secure behavior.

In theory, the advice is mostly simple (such as "use only allowed software," "do not download from untrusted sources," and "keep your security system updated"). Such advice relies too heavily on users (Yannakogeorgos, 2011, p. 261). Consequently, as many of the controls on software use and updates as possible should be automated so that user fallibility is removed from the risks.

User fallibility would still remain when users are granted user-controlled access, which is inherent to most work today, such as access to e-mail, data, and software. Almost all user access to such things proceeds given an authorized password, but passwords are fallible. As people use the Internet more, they use their identity across more sites, usually without varying their password. The average American holds passwords to 30 to 40 websites, of which he or she logs in to about 10 websites per day. Most Americans use a single password for all sites. Sixty percent of all passwords are less than five characters long. More than 80% of passwords use whole words, such as real names. Phishers could gather enough information, such as the target's favorite pet or their spouse's name, in the public domain to guess such simple passwords. Even easier to gather would be information about the target's first school or mother's maiden name, which are typical answers to questions that serve as back-door access in case the user forgets their password. Some surprising websites have been hacked in these ways. For instance, Stratfor sells information and analysis on current international and national-security issues, mostly to paid subscribers who access the information online. In December 2011, Anonymous (a hacking group) stole information on thousands of subscribers, including their credit card numbers, from Stratfor's servers, claiming that access passwords were easy to guess. Stratfor apologized to clients and promised improved security, but in February 2012, Anonymous stole some of Stratfor's e-mails with its clients.

Threats may place spyware on the target's computer in order to record the target's keystrokes, which will include their typed identities and passwords. Some malware can be designed to search for stored passwords. Users should avoid using a more exposed terminal, such as a terminal lent by a stranger or in an Internet café, but if forced to use a strange terminal, such as when away from the home or office, they could avoid using the keyboard by pasting their identity word and password after copying it from a file held on a USB drive (although USB drives are exposed to malware on the terminal).

A few online services (typically online banking websites, specialized web-based e-mail applications, and online access to organizationally controlled e-mail or data) require the user to change his or her password periodically, disallow whole words or common terms (such as *password*), or specify inclusion of numbers or unusual characters in the password.

Additionally, more services are requiring more than one step of identity verification. For instance, a website could ask for a password followed by an answer to one of many demographic questions. Users may be required to carry a piece of hardware that displays a periodically randomized number that only the remote server would recognize.

Some access controls include software that looks for abnormal behavior, such as attempted log ins from foreign countries or at untypical times of the day, or that will block access completely, pending further checks, if somebody attempts more than once to access without the correct identification.

Ultimately, any system of using and storing a typed password is personally and mathematically fallible, so digital-security managers are looking for more physical checks of identity, primarily hardware that can recognize biometric signatures, such as fingerprints, irises, and skin chemistry. Some computers and peripherals already include digital readers of fingerprints and other biometric data, and some border controls include machines that read biometric data.

Defense

Defense is important for preventing illegitimate access and for minimizing illegitimate access. Eliminating all illegitimate access is an unrealistic goal given legitimate demands for quicker or easier access, but even allowing for some illegitimate access, the security system can control the risk by detecting the access as early as possible in order to limit threatening exploitation. Verizon's data suggests that a breach starts with access that takes from seconds to hours to achieve in 84% of cases. By contrast, the victim's discovery of the breach usually takes months (62% of cases), even years (4% of cases), after which containment typically takes days (41% of cases), weeks (14% of cases), or even months (22% of cases). Thanks to better defenses, the time before compromise has increased over the last decade, but the time before discovery also has trended upward (Verizon Enterprise Solutions, 2013, p. 49; 2014, p. 12).

In general, private actors can provide minimal cybersecurity via the following defensive measures:

- monitoring insiders for noncompliant communication of information;
- analyzing incoming traffic for potential threats;
- consulting experts on threats, subscribing to documents issued by hacking supporters, and monitoring online forums for hackers;
- automated intrusion-detection systems;
- automated intrusion-prevention systems;
- automated logs of anomalous behaviors or penetrations and regular audits of these logs;
- firewalls (effectively, rule-based filters of traffic or gates to information, permitting information or requesters that pass some rule-based criteria);
- antivirus software;
- antispam software; and
- monitoring for security patches.

Systems with more bandwidth, processing power, or on-demand access to a cloud are less vulnerable to denial of service attacks. Operating systems can be configured to disable services and applications not required for their missions. Network and application firewalls can be designed to block malicious packets, preferably as close to the source as possible, perhaps by blocking all traffic from known malicious sources. Prior intelligence about the threats, their domains, and their IP addresses can help to prevent attacks.

System managers should coordinate between Internet service providers, site-hosting providers, and security vendors. Contingency planning between these stakeholders before an attack can help during management of the response. Some stakeholders treat an attack as an incident triggering a business continuity plan or human-caused disaster response plan.

Deterrence

Increasingly, officials are seeking to use **deterrence** as well as defense, to punish as well as to prevent, although this is usually an option that must involve a judicial authority or a government. For instance, on May 31, 2011, U.S. officials first warned publicly and officially that harmful cyber attacks could be treated as acts of war, implying military retaliation. On September 18, 2012, U.S. Cyber Command hosted a public conference at which the State Department's legal adviser, Harold Koh, stated that the United States had adopted and shared through the U.N. 10 principles, of which the most important implications included

- international law applies in cyberspace;

- cyber attacks can amount to armed attacks triggering the right of self-defense; and

- cyber attacks that result in death, injury, or significant destruction, such as a nuclear-plant meltdown, a dam opened above a populated area, or a disabled air-traffic control system resulting in place crashes, would constitute a use of force in violation of international law.

The U.N. has considered outlawing first strikes in cyberspace, just as international law forbids first strikes in the physical world by states. However, this legal deterrence is still an incomplete solution.

> This approach certainly makes sense given that the United Nations is organized around the nation-state concept, but it can have little effect on contemporary vulnerabilities to the Internet, where many threats emanate from small groups and nonstate actors. Security challenges in cyberspace are another indication that traditional nation-state approaches to national security cannot address contemporary challenges like those in cyberspace. Furthermore, there is an inherent deniability of Internet-based attacks, which makes any agreement extremely difficult to monitor or enforce. (Reveron, 2012, p. 10)

THE STRUCTURE OF U.S. CYBERSECURITY

The official structure of U.S. cybersecurity is examined below by the criminal-justice authorities, military and defense authorities, the Department of Homeland Security, interagency authorities, and critical-infrastructure authorities.

Criminal Justice Authorities

The Department of Justice (DOJ) is the highest U.S. authority for prosecuting cybercrimes. It administers the Federal Bureau of Investigation (FBI), which is the highest investigative authority. The FBI has a Cyber Crime Division, with local hi-tech crime squads in major cities, such as San Jose, California. The FBI leads the investigation if the issue involves cyber espionage or terrorism. The U.S. Secret Service, administered by the Department of Homeland Security, leads criminal investigations into most other cybercrimes. Its core department is the Electronic Crimes Task Force, with units based in major cities.

Other federal investigative authorities involved in investigating cybercrimes, particularly involving intellectual-property violations, include the Immigration & Customs Enforcement Agency (DHS), the Internal Revenue Service, and the Postal Inspection Service.

These federal authorities work with local, state, and foreign law enforcement partners and commercial stakeholders. Local authorities may form interagency task forces. The main federal criminal code of use in prosecuting cybercrimes is Section 1030, although this is too long and complex to describe here.

Abroad, the Secret Service posts foreign liaison officers. The DOJ has two Intellectual Property Law Enforcement Coordinators—one in Bangkok, Thailand, the other in Sofia, Bulgaria. The DOJ is the U.S. representative in the 24-7 Network, a voluntary international network of national points of contact, which around 50 countries have joined. The 24-7 Network is effectively a list of points of contact in each of these countries for use whenever one country needs to request foreign judicial intervention to preserve data that could be useful to investigators. This request is normally considered informal, ahead of a slower, more formal request, usually under the auspices of a mutual legal assistance treaty. A **mutual legal assistance treaty** is a bilateral treaty that specifies how one country could request assistance from the other country and how the other country should act. The United States does not have mutual assistance treaties with most countries.

The highest authority devoted to countering foreign intelligence is the Office of the National Counterintelligence Executive, although ONCIX is a coordinating authority, not a judicial authority. (In 2001, the office replaced the center that had been established in 1994.)

Military and Defense Authorities

Established in 1952, the National Security Agency has been the lead U.S. defense authority for signals intelligence and eventually for cyber warfare. The NSA and the Defense Information Systems Agency share responsibilities for the security of U.S. military networks. Strategic Command (since 1992) is the leading unified military command with cybersecurity responsibilities (included within "freedom of action" in cyberspace). Since 2005, Strategic Command has administered and the NSA Director has led a network warfare command that became, in October 2009, Cyber Command.

The DOD is the designated sector-specific agency for the Defense Industrial Base Sector, one of the 16 critical-infrastructure sectors identified by the Department of Homeland Security (see Chapter 9). In June 2011, the DOD launched the Exploratory Cybersecurity Initiative as an experiment in sharing official assessments of cyber threats with 20 private-sector providers of services to the DOD and the defense industrial base, although DHS took the lead later in 2011. In 2012, DOD's Chief Information Office established a cybersecurity information-sharing program in Arlington, Virginia, to help the DOD and eligible companies to share secure information (Magnuson, 2014).

Department of Homeland Security

In 1998, President Bill Clinton signed Presidential Decision Directive 63, which created an authority under the President to "eliminate any significant vulnerability to both physical and cyber attacks on our critical infrastructures, including especially our cyber systems" (U.S. White House, 1998, n.p.).

Since March 2003, the Department of Homeland Security, under the secretary of homeland security, has led cybersecurity in U.S. civilian government and critical infrastructure. Its National Protection and Programs Directorate, led by an undersecretary, established the National Cybersecurity Division (NCSD) in June 2003.

Within the National Cybersecurity Division, the Computer Emergency Readiness Team is the lead authority for cybersecurity within the federal civilian government, for coordinating with lower levels of government and with foreign governments, and for coordinating with private operators. It invites private citizens and organizations to send in information about cyber threats and disseminates information about known cyber threats through the National Cyber Alert System to voluntary consumers. It also issues security guidance as cybersecurity preparedness. The Industrial Control Systems Cyber Emergency Response Team (ICS-CERT) provides onsite support to owners and operators of critical cyber infrastructure.

Since 2004, the EINSTEIN program system has alerted US-CERT to intrusions into the federal civilian cyberspace. By 2012, EINSTEIN 2 had been deployed to 15 of 19 departments and agencies and to four providers, although the DHS needs a memorandum of agreement before deploying EINSTEIN on any network. By then, US-CERT was developing EINSTEIN 3, with capacity to automatically defeat intrusions. However, some have criticized EINSTEIN as too focused on exploits, rather than other cyber threats. While EINSTEIN focuses on incoming network traffic, the Continuous Diagnostics & Mitigation (CDM) program scans the end points of that traffic, such as servers and workstations, for vulnerabilities. CDM produces data that can be used to improve EINSTEIN's monitoring (Lyngaas, 2014).

Throughout its first years, DHS was under considerable scrutiny. The U.S. GAO (2005a) identified in law and policy 13 cybersecurity-related roles and responsibilities for DHS:

1. Develop a national plan for critical infrastructure protection, including cybersecurity.

2. Develop partnerships and coordinate with other federal agencies, state and local governments, and the private sector.

3. Improve and enhance public/private information sharing involving cyber attacks, threats, and vulnerabilities.

4. Develop and enhance national cyber analysis and warning capabilities.

5. Provide and coordinate incident response and recovery planning efforts.

6. Identify and assess cyber threats and vulnerabilities.

7. Support efforts to reduce cyber threats and vulnerabilities.

8. Promote and support research and development efforts to strengthen cyberspace security.

9. Promote awareness and outreach.

10. Foster training and certification.

11. Enhance federal, state, and local government cybersecurity.

12. Strengthen international cyberspace security.

13. Integrate cybersecurity with national security. (n.p.)

The U.S. GAO (2005a) found that DHS had initiated many efforts to fulfill these responsibilities but also found that DHS had "not fully addressed any of the 13 responsibilities, and much work remains" (n.p.), mostly because DHS had not resolved its organizational issues.

The GAO, the National Security Telecommunications Advisory Committee, and an industry–government working group all found that the National Cybersecurity Division had underperformed, in part because of high personnel turnover, and recommended the colocation, integration, and interoperability of the existing structures for responding to incidents of cyber and communications insecurity.

In 2006, Congress created the Office of Cybersecurity and Communications to replace the NCSD, still reporting to the National Protection and Programs Directorate. In March 2008, the office established the National Cybersecurity Center to coordinate the six largest federal cyber centers and private-sector operators with the Office of Intelligence and Analysis.

Effective November 2009, these units were placed under the National Cybersecurity and Communications Integration Center (NCCIC) in Arlington, Virginia. This center leads the real-time monitoring of cybersecurity and leads national responses to cyber issues, in partnership with the Departments of Defense and Justice and the FBI. Its operational elements include the US-CERT, the Industrial Control Systems CERT, and the National Coordinating Center for Telecommunications and Cyber Exercises.

The National Cybersecurity & Communications Integration Center also took over the National Coordinating Center for Telecommunications (NCC), which had been established in 1983 and had been directed mainly by the president or the National Security Council. The NCC is the lead authority for managing the security of emergency communications. The NCCIC also absorbed the National Communications System—a federal office established in 1963, when the primary threats related to nuclear warfare; it was dissolved in 2012.

In September 2010, the DHS tested its first National Cyber Incident Response Plan, which would coordinate all federal, state, and local authorities and private owners and operators in response to a national cyber emergency, by hosting a regular exercise (Cyber Storm). In November 2010, the federally funded Multi-State Information Sharing and Analysis Center opened the Cyber Security Operations Center to help the federal government to share information with state and local authorities. The Joint Agency Cyber Knowledge Exchange allows officials to share information directly at the unclassified and classified levels.

DHS has struggled to attract and retain cybersecurity experts and to coordinate its own departments, although it seems to be doing better in recent years (Lyngaas, 2014). Yet it continues to attract critics, diplomatically summed up by a task force commissioned by the Council on Foreign Relations, which said,

> Many in the private sector and Congress are skeptical of DHS's emerging role as the primary civilian lead on several aspects of U.S. government cybersecurity. Some have questions whether DHS has the administrative and technical capabilities to fulfill such a role. Critics question whether DHS has the strength to bring together all the agencies needed to coordinate information sharing and reach out to the private sector. Although NCCIC has recently gone through an internal reorganization, leadership turnover continues to be high, pointing to continued institutional turmoil. DHS and NCCIC will have to take steps to reassure the public and private sectors that they are capable of taking the lead on many cyber issues. (Negroponte et al., 2013, p. 47)

In practice, DHS is the lead but not sole authority, leaving plenty of redundancy and cross-purposes in the rest of civilian government.

> Coordination problems continue to bedevil the interagency process. Organizational change is important for supporting all three pillars of digital policy: alliances, trade, and governance. Within the State Department, Internet issues are divided among the Office of the Cyber Coordinator, Bureau of Economic and Business Affairs, and Bureau of Democracy, Human Rights, and Labor. Across the entire U.S. government at least fourteen government bureaus, divisions, and departments collaborate with international agencies and organizations on cyberspace issues. This not only leads to coordination and messaging problems but makes it difficult for those outside of the United States without great knowledge of the workings of cyber policy to know with whom to interact. (Negroponte et al., 2013, p. 48)

The task force recommended raising the director of the NCCIC to undersecretary or deputy secretary rank, as is the director of the National Counterterrorism Center, and raising the State Department's cyber coordinator to an assistant secretary. (The office would rise to a bureau.)

Interagency Authorities

In late 2007, the George W. Bush administration commissioned a nonpartisan think tank to form the Commission on Cybersecurity for the 44th Presidency. It reported in December 2008, as President-elect Barack Obama was forming his administration. The report stated that

> America's failure to protect cyberspace is one of the most urgent national security problems facing the new administration . . . Weak cybersecurity dilutes our

investment in innovation while subsidizing the R&D of foreign competitors. In the new global competition, where economic strength and technological leadership . . . [are] as important to national power as military force, failing to secure cyberspace puts us at a disadvantage. (Center for Strategic & International Studies, 2008, p. 7)

Meanwhile, in January 2008, Bush had authorized (by National Security Presidential Directive 54 and Homeland Security Presidential Directive 23) a Comprehensive National Cyber Security Initiative worth $30 billion, although most of the information was classified.

In May 2009, President Obama announced plans for a national strategy for information security, a cybersecurity coordinator within the national-security staff, stronger relationships between public and private sectors, more research into cybersecurity, and more awareness of cybersecurity.

In June 2010, the Cybersecurity Local Partners Access Plan allowed cleared owners and operators access to intelligence at local fusion centers. In March 2010, the Secretary of Homeland Security, Janet Napolitano, launched the National Cybersecurity Awareness Challenge, which called on the public and private-sector companies to submit ideas to enhance cybersecurity. In July, seven of more than 80 proposals were selected to inform the National Cybersecurity Awareness Campaign.

The DHS relies mainly on the NSA for identification and investigation of major cyber threats. In 2010, the NSA and DHS signed a Memorandum of Agreement that allows NSA to give to DHS access to any capabilities that DHS might require in fulfilment of its cybersecurity responsibilities. In 2010, the DHS, DOD, and the Financial Services Information Sharing & Analysis Center launched a pilot program to share information about financial services cybersecurity. In October 2010, the DHS and DOD agreed to align their protection of civilian and military networks and to embed DOD cyber analysts within DHS while DHS would send legal personnel to NSA.

In June 2011, the DOD launched the Exploratory Cybersecurity Initiative as an experiment in sharing official assessments of cyber threats with 20 private-sector providers of services to the DOD and the defense industrial base. In late 2011, the DHS Office of Cybersecurity and Communications joined the program as lead operator, which became the Joint Cybersecurity Services Program. In May 2012, the federal government extended the program from pilot to ongoing. By 2013, it was known as the Enhanced Cybersecurity Services program and was being extended to owners and operators of all critical infrastructure. The information includes indicators of the threats: their Internet protocol, domain, and e-mail addresses and any known files or strings sent by these threats.

Critical Cyber Infrastructure

In April 2012, the newly retired Executive Assistant Director of the FBI's Criminal, Cyber, Response, and Services Branch, Shawn Henry, publicly advised the private sector to admit more self-reliance, saying,

> I know a lot of companies have suffered, and they are going to want to see somebody come in and assist them. It won't be the US government . . . so it's going to have to be the private sector. (Nakashima, 2012, n.p.)

In summer 2012, political representatives from both major parties sponsored a bill that would establish standards for the cybersecurity necessary to protect critical infrastructure, such as water and electricity distribution systems. President Barack Obama and his military and national-security officials supported the bill. On August 2, 2012, U.S. senators voted 52 to 46 in favor of the bill, short of the two thirds majority necessary to send the bill to a final vote. On August 8, the president's counterterrorism adviser, John "Jack" O. Brennan, told the Council on Foreign Relations that "if Congress is not going to act on something like this, then the president wants to make sure that we're doing everything possible . . . Believe me, the critical infrastructure of this country is under threat" (DeYoung, 2012, n.p.). On September 7, a newspaper revealed that the White House had drafted an executive order establishing a Cybersecurity Council to set voluntary standards for the private sector, led by the DHS with representatives from the director of national intelligence and the Departments of Defense, Energy, Treasury, Commerce, and Justice. On October 25, the Secretary of Homeland Security, Janet Napolitano, said that the administration was prepared to issue an executive order if Congress failed to legislate in November and noted that the DHS had observed increasing cyber attacks on critical infrastructure. However, the U.S. Chamber of Commerce stated that "executive action is unnecessary and opposes the expansion or creation of new regulatory regimes" (Beauchesne, 2013, n.p.) and threatened to track how lawmakers voted on the bill.

On February 12, 2013, President Obama signed an executive order ("Improving Critical Infrastructure Cyber-security") that directed the National Institute of Standards & Technology (NIST) to lead the development of a cybersecurity framework—a set of voluntary security standards, including the sharing of information within each of the 16 critical-infrastructure sectors identified by DHS, that would be agreeable to both the federal government and the private companies in charge of infrastructure. The executive order expected private companies to comply voluntarily and did not envision any legislated compliance; it ordered agencies to develop incentives for voluntary participation. The target companies include those that own or manage cyberspace or critical infrastructures, such as electrical power stations, whose safety or functionality could be affected by malicious actions in cyberspace. The cybersecurity framework is supposed to specify standards for the security of computer networks and communications across infrastructure, with additional standards for particular sectors, such as nuclear energy.

That night, President Obama justified his executive order to Congress and called for more legislation in his annual State of the Union address.

> We cannot look back years from now and wonder why we did nothing in the face of real threats to our security and our economy. And that's why, earlier today, I signed a new executive order that will strengthen our cyber defenses by increasing information sharing, and developing standards to protect our national security, our jobs, and our privacy. . . . But now Congress must act as well, by passing legislation to give our government a greater capacity to secure our networks and deter attacks. This is something we should be able to get done on a bipartisan basis. (U.S. White House, 2013b, n.p.)

At the end of October 2013, the NIST released its draft framework for public comment until December 13. The final framework was released in February 2014. DHS is charged with implementing the framework. The financial-services sector, some state and local governments, and the Department of Defense already had implemented sector-specific cybersecurity centers (Magnuson, 2014).

A Perspective on Cyber Readiness

Melissa E. Hathaway

The decision to pursue ICT-enabled economic-development strategies has been embraced by most countries around the world. Today, countries are provisioning near ubiquitous communications to every household and business and pursuing a development and modernization agenda to nurture their information society into the digital age. Initiatives like e-government, e-banking, e-health, e-learning, next-generation power grids, air-traffic control, and other essential services are at the top of most countries' economic agendas. These initiatives are being pursued to increase productivity and efficiency, enhance workforce skills, drive innovation, and deliver gross domestic product (GDP) growth. Some estimates offer that when 10% of the population is connected to the Internet, the GDP should grow by 1 to 2% (World Economic Forum, 2009). Moreover, governments and businesses that embrace the Internet and ICTs recognize it will enhance their long-term competitiveness and societal well-being and potentially contribute up to 8% of GDP (Dean, DiGrande, Field, & Zwillenberg, 2012). Recent reports go even further and suggest that the opportunity surrounding the modernization of industrial systems (e.g., electrical power grids, oil and gas pipelines, factory operations, etc.) represents a 46% share of the global economy over the next 10 years (Evans & Annunziata, 2012, p. 13).

Nations cannot afford to ignore this economic opportunity, particularly in today's stagnant economic climate. Yet, the Internet's ability to deliver positive economic growth can only be sustained if its core infrastructure is accessible, available, affordable, secure, interoperable, resilient, and stable. The threats to our connected society are outpacing our defenses and GDP growth is being eroded every day. Put simply, our cyber *insecurity* is a tax on growth.

For example, it is estimated that the Group of Twenty (G20) economies have lost 2.5 million jobs to counterfeiting and piracy and that governments and consumers lose 125 billion USD annually, including losses in tax revenue (Frontier Economics, 2011, p. 3). The United States estimates the annual impact of international intellectual-property (IP) theft to the American economy at $300 billion. This approximates to 1% of its GDP (National Bureau of Asian Research, 2013). Furthermore, research by Toegepast Natuurwetenschappelijk Onderzoek (TNO), an independent research organization in the Netherlands, has shown that cybercrime costs Dutch society at least 10 billion euros per annum, or 1.5 to 2% of their GDP. This loss is almost equal to the Netherlands' economic growth in 2010 (Hathaway, 2013). There are other estimates conducted by the United Kingdom and Germany that indicate similar losses. No nation can afford to lose even 1% of its GDP to illicit cyber activities.

Moreover, while many governments around the world champion the benefits of fast, reliable, and affordable communications in terms of GDP growth, job creation, access to information, and the ability to innovate, few of them are measuring the exposure and costs of less resilient critical services, disruption of service(s), e-crime, identity theft, intellectual-property theft, fraud, and other activities exploiting the ICT hyperconnectivity in terms of GDP loss.

Measuring the declining gains may force governments to better align their national-security agendas with their economic agendas and invest in the derivative value of both. Bringing transparency to the economic losses may spark national and global interest in addressing the economic erosion. Global leaders can alter their current posture by leveraging policy, law, regulation, standards, market incentives, and other initiatives to protect the value of their digital investments and preserve the security of their connectivity.

Global leaders must recognize that no country is cyber ready. Until now, there was no methodology to evaluate any country's maturity and commitment to securing the cyber infrastructure and services upon which their digital future and growth depend. The Cyber Readiness Index (CRI) represents a new way of examining this problem (Hathaway, 2013). It challenges the conventional thinking about cybersecurity, showing that it must be married to the debate and desire for economic prosperity. The CRI identifies the essential elements of a stronger security posture that can defend against the GDP erosion. Adopting a security framework and knowing cyber readiness level is essential to realizing *full* potential of the Internet economy and our digital future.

Melissa E. Hathaway is president of Hathaway Global Strategies LLC and a senior advisor at Harvard Kennedy School's Belfer Center. She served in two U.S. presidential administrations, where she spearheaded the Cyberspace Policy Review for President Barack Obama and led the Comprehensive National Cybersecurity Initiative for President George W. Bush. Ms. Hathaway is a frequent keynote speaker on cybersecurity matters and regularly publishes papers and commentary in this field.

CHAPTER SUMMARY

This chapter has

- Defined

  ○ information,

  ○ IT and ICT,

  ○ ICS and CPS, and

  ○ cyberspace

- Introduced official categories of attackers, such as hackers

- Shown an official method for assessing threats

- Described the four main categories of sources:

  ○ profit-oriented criminals,

  ○ insider threats,

  ○ external threats, and

  ○ nation-states.

- Described the typical access vectors and their controls:

  ○ printed documents,

  ○ malware,

  ○ databases,

  ○ webpages,

- ○ social interaction,
- ○ social media,
- ○ postal communications,
- ○ telephone communications,
- ○ e-mail,
- ○ removable digital media and mobile devices,
- ○ cloud computing,
- ○ wired networks, and
- ○ wireless networks.
- • Defined and described the typical malicious activities, including

- ○ illegitimate access of private information,
- ○ espionage, and
- ○ sabotage.
- • Shown how to provide information security in general
- • Shown how to provide cybersecurity by
  - ○ controlling access,
  - ○ defense, and
  - ○ deterrence.
- • Described how cybersecurity is structured in the United States

KEY TERMS

QUESTIONS AND EXERCISES

1. Give examples of information outside of cyberspace.

2. What is the difference between ICT and cyberspace?

3. What was Sandia National Laboratories' warning about conventional categorization of the sources of cyber attacks?

4. What differentiates the objectives of most criminals when they acquire private information?

5. Describe the known motivations and intentions of insider threats.

6. What is the relationship between insider and external threats?

7. How could a commercial relationship become an external threat?

8. Describe the opportunities for external threats during the life cycle of an item of ICT.

9. How can APTs be especially countered?

10. What is an access vector?

11. What is an access control?

12. What is the difference between a computer virus, worm, and Trojan horse?

13. By what four main social interactions could a threat obtain private information about you?

14. How could visiting a webpage be harmful?

15. How does social media enable

 violations of privacy?

 abuse?

16. Describe the similarities and differences in risks for juveniles and adults.

17. When are people likely to be most revealing of private information through social media?

18. Why is postal communication useful to a comprehensive information security plan?

19. When are officials more likely to intercept private telephone communications?

20. How can threats intercept telephone communications?

21. How can you reduce the insecurity of your personal telephone communications?

22. How can you reduce the insecurity of your personal e-mail?

23. What are the three main ways in which e-mail is a vector for unauthorized access to information?

24. Why are mobile devices vectors?

25. What are the security advantages and disadvantages of cloud computing?

26. Under what circumstances are wireless networks likely to be less secure?

27. What is the international dispute about the governance of the Internet?

28. What is the difference between a logic bomb and denial of service?

29. Why have DOS attacks become easier?

30. How can DOS attacks be countered?

31. Why should an organization define its sensitive information?

32. Give an example of a nondigital activity that would help to provide cybersecurity.

33. How could a threat acquire your password?

34. How could a website encourage more secure passwords?

35. Give examples of two-step access controls.

11

MARITIME SECURITY

Less than 25 mi from Sicily on the Italian mainland is the port of Gioia Tauro. The Italian crime group 'Ndrangheta wields significant influence at the port and in the city. Gioia is the chief Mediterranean transshipment site for cargo, and law enforcement officials believe that 80% of Europe's cocaine trade passes through the port. Hence, the port facility is ripe for illegal exploitation by many unlawful sources.

In October 2001, port workers noticed a harsh grating sound reverberating off the stacks of cargo containers. When they followed the trail of noise to its source, they found in one container a stowaway who was using a rasp to widen the ventilation holes from the inside. The container included a bed, toilet, heater, and water supply. The stowaway, Rizik Amid Farid, an Egyptian national with a Canadian passport, was also carrying two cell phones, a laptop computer, airport security passes and a mechanic's certificate valid at JFK, O'Hare, L.A. International and Newark airports. His temporary housing had been loaded onto a vessel in Port Said, Egypt, and scheduled to be transshipped to Rotterdam before reaching its final destination in Canada. He was arrested, detained, and released after posting bail. Unfortunately, the chances of collecting further information about his purpose, the details about his mode of transportation, or his connection with other individuals or organizations were lost when he disappeared following his arraignment. Farid claimed he was seeking refuge in Canada. The ease of his access to the cargo container network and contraband materials raised obvious alarms for security officials.

In assessing the threat to homeland security in terms of direct economic and commercial cost, many experts agree the greatest exposure is along the maritime supply chain. Not only does the maritime supply chain have the greatest number of potential breach points, its ports are located at centers of population flows, communication nodes, and transportation hubs. It is an

Learning Objectives and Outcomes

At the end of this chapter, you should be able to understand

- Maritime security by risk distribution and category

- Port security

  - Scope and complexity of the threat to port security
  - Potential for trade disruption

- Cargo and container security

  - The uniqueness, ubiquity, and threat harbored by the cargo container
  - Safe and trusted shippers

- The Maritime Transportation Security Act—programs and details

  - Layered defenses
  - Technology and strategies
  - Cooperation and interoperation initiatives

- Maritime terrorists attacks—motives, modes, and overall risk

  - List of terrorist groups with maritime capability
  - Opportunities versus likelihood

(Continued)

environment open to exploitation and the possibility of significant economic or political impact is ever present.

In this chapter, we will discuss the vulnerabilities to the maritime supply chain and the potential impact on homeland security. The chapter will also examine the threat to the port facilities and container transport systems as well as the security measures in place to mitigate these risks. Finally, we will assess the motives and strategies of terrorist and criminal groups and how countermeasures, geographic locations, and socioeconomic demands vary.

(Continued)

- Strategic choke points and their potential for impact on global commerce
  - Geographic distribution and regional impact
- Maritime crime and piracy
  - Geographic distribution
  - Costs
  - Countermeasures

SCOPE AND DEFINITIONS

An open trading system is essential to the global economy and national security, yet the maritime transportation system has the greatest number of breach points and the potential for the most serious damage. The growth of Asian and Pacific economies will compound the problems. The planet's seas are vast and undergoverned.

In this chapter, we discuss not only the scope and complexity of the threat to maritime security but also the levels of risk. There are different risk categories distributed over a vast maritime environment. They involve the open sea-lanes, geographic bottlenecks, and the unit of cargo container. To counter the threat, security regimes at various jurisdictional levels deploy a layered array of security programs and protocols. As they read this chapter, students will learn how these efforts interoperate as well as where they fail to contain the gaps and, at times, even clash.

Geography

The **maritime domain** refers to the parts of the world covered by water. Water covers more than two thirds of the world or 139,768,200 sq mi. Nominally, different areas of this water are known or designated, sometimes arbitrarily and indistinctly, as the oceans, seas, lakes, rivers, and related terms.

The *oceans* are the saline waters forming the larger parts of the world's surface. In order of size, they are the Pacific, Atlantic, Indian, Southern (Antarctic), and Arctic Oceans.

The *seas* are saline waters partly or wholly contained by land, such as the Mediterranean Sea, which joins with the Atlantic Ocean, and the Red Sea, which joins with the Indian Ocean.

A *lagoon* is a body of water only partially separated from a sea or ocean by land, usually a sand bank or reef, which the sea or ocean routinely crosses.

An *estuary* is the area where a river and a sea or ocean meet; the area is more operationally defined as being subject both to the tides and saline water from the sea or ocean and to the downflow and freshwater from the river.

The *littoral* area is defined by geographers and biologists normally as the area from around high tide to the edge of the continental shelf. The **continental shelf** is the flooded edge of a continent before the underwater terrain slopes down more dramatically. The continental shelf can stretch just a few dozen miles out to sea or hundreds of miles. In economics, politics, and military operations, the littoral area is some coastal area, such as a special customs zone, a local authority, or an area of operations for invading amphibious military forces and their naval and aerial supporting forces. Economic, political, and military littoral areas have no consistent definition but can extend dozens of miles out to sea and inland.

A *lake* is any body of water completely surrounded by land, except for any connecting river. Lakes are distinguished from ponds only by size; naming conventions normally refer to lakes as larger than ponds. Lakes are normally freshwater, but inland lakes can sometimes salinate while some freshwater lakes are named seas.

Rivers are flows of freshwater. Sometimes rivers can be cut off or stagnate like lakes or dry out for periods of time, but fresh rain or a release of groundwater can restart the river. Streams and other synonyms are differentiated mostly by size.

A *strait* is a natural narrow channel between larger bodies of water. Synonyms include *channel* and *pass*; the implication of *strait* is greater importance, usually economic or military. A *canal* is an artificial channel.

Distribution of Risks

Maritime-security management is most often focused on the oceans because they are the largest, least regulated, and most hazardous areas of water. In fact, most of the world's water is legally designated as **high seas**—beyond the jurisdiction of any one state. However, operating on the high seas requires great capital before acquisition of the ship, its equipment, and mariners while operating such a ship requires great technical skills too, so such operations are out of reach of most nonstate actors.

Smaller areas of water, such as the seas, or parts contained within land, such as rivers and lakes, or parts within easy reach of land, such as straits, tend to be better regulated but more exposed to land-based hazards, such as pirates. Proximity to land is no guarantee of effective human regulation and capacity. Moreover, some littoral areas are riskier for natural reasons, such as susceptibility to cyclones or hurricanes or to particular diseases.

Thus, the actual risks at any place reflect the local natural risks, local human risks, local human capacity, and remote interest and capacity to intervene. For instance, the beaches of Somalia are beautiful and washed by one of the warmer, calmer oceans (the Indian Ocean) but crossed by pirates, smugglers, terrorists, and tropical diseases without systematic national or international control. The North Sea is one of the deepest, coldest, and stormiest seas but within the range of the emergency services of eight well-developed neighboring countries.

Finally, some areas of water are well within the range of the services of neighboring countries, but these countries contest their jurisdiction in these waters or lack capacity to secure these waters against nonstate threats, such as pirates. These contests are intensified when the waters contain something of value, such as relatively concentrated fish, trade, or fossil fuels. For instance, the waters between East Asia and Southeast Asia are contested by several states, contain a major sea line of communication (SLOC), and cover reserves of fossil fuels.

Proximity to land implies increased exposure to land-based threats, such as pirates and terrorists. Choke points and bottlenecks imply increased exposure to and increased effectiveness of malicious attacks. Local trade or a SLOC imply more frequent or valuable targets. A **sea line of communication** is a route well traveled by ships; the phrase is used mostly to describe a concentrated trade route or a route for military reinforcement or supply. Sometimes, straits, canals, and the like are identified by their **choke points** or **bottlenecks**—areas where a threat could more easily interrupt the flow, perhaps because the water is narrower or shallower at that point.

Shipping is not evenly distributed across the world's oceans. Most ships follow predictable routes due to the predictability of markets, ports, and coastlines. Thus, shipping routes present both access and choke points. A detailed discussion of terrorist choke points appears later in the chapter. Below is a list of 11 bottlenecks, which strategically and historically are the most notable. (see Map 11.1).

1. The Panama Canal in Panama is an artificial link between the Pacific and Atlantic Oceans.

2. The Strait of Magellan off Chile is the quickest ice-free natural link between the Pacific and Atlantic Oceans.

3. The only natural link between the Atlantic and Indian Oceans is south of the Cape of Good Hope, South Africa.

4. Shipping crosses between the Atlantic Ocean and Mediterranean Sea through the Strait of Gibraltar.

5. Shipping between the Mediterranean and Caspian Seas must travel through the Bosporus, Turkey.

6. The quickest route between Europe and the Indian Ocean is via the Suez Canal, Egypt. This canal artificially links the Mediterranean and the Gulf of Aden. Transits of the canal declined in the later 2000s due to increased piracy in the Gulf of Aden.

7. The Gulf of Aden narrows at the Bab-el-Mandeb passage between Yemen and Djibouti. By 2006, 3.3 million barrels of oil per day transited these straits (U.N. Office on Drugs and Crime [UNODC], 2010a, p. 198).

8. The Gulf of Aden remains a narrow stretch of water between Yemen and the Horn of Africa.

9. Most oil from the Middle East is shipped out of the Persian/Arabian Gulf via the Strait of Hormuz between Iran and Qatar.

10. Most shipping between the Indian Ocean and South China Sea must travel through the Malacca Strait between Malaysia and the Philippines.

11. Shipping between Southeast Asia and Australasia generally travels between Indonesia and Australia.

Types of Risks

Maritime risks include potential theft of cargo, damage to cargo, sabotage of vessels, sabotage of ports and related infrastructure, smuggling and trafficking, accidental release of hazardous materials, accidental collisions, illegal immigration, maritime terrorism, and maritime piracy.

International Maritime Laws and Regulations

The Convention for the Suppression of Unlawful Acts Against the Safety of Maritime Navigation (SUA), agreed in Rome on March 10, 1988, defines unlawful acts against ships, such as

- the seizure of ships by force;

- acts of violence against persons on board ships; and

- the placing of devices on board a ship which are likely to harm.

The Convention obliges contracting governments either to extradite or prosecute alleged offenders.

The 2005 Protocol to the SUA Convention broadens the offenses to include

- when the purpose of the act, by its nature or context, is to intimidate a population, or to compel a Government or an international organization to do or to abstain from any act;

- uses against or on a ship or discharging from a ship any explosive, radioactive material or BCN (biological, chemical, nuclear) weapon in a manner that causes or is likely to cause death or serious injury or damage;

- discharges, from a ship, oil, liquefied natural gas, or other hazardous or noxious substance, in such quantity or concentration that causes or is likely to cause death or serious injury or damage;

- uses a ship in a manner that causes death or serious injury or damage;

- transports on board a ship any explosive or radioactive material, knowing that it is intended to be used to cause, or in a threat to cause, death or serious injury or damage for the purpose of intimidating a population, or compelling a government or an international organization to do or to abstain from doing any act;

- transports on board a ship any BCN weapon, knowing it to be a BCN weapon;

- any source material, special fissionable material, or equipment or material especially designed or prepared for the processing, use or production of special fissionable material, knowing that it is intended to be used in a nuclear explosive activity or in any other nuclear activity not under safeguards pursuant to an IAEA (International Atomic Energy Agency) comprehensive safeguards agreement; or

(Continued)

(Continued)

- transports on board a ship any equipment, materials or software or related technology that significantly contributes to the design, manufacture or delivery of a BCN weapon, with the intention that it will be used for such purpose.

The Protocol for the Suppression of Unlawful Acts Against the Safety of Fixed Platforms Located on the Continental Shelf, agreed in Rome on March 10, 1988, specifies the following offenses:

a) seizes or exercises control over a fixed platform by force or threat thereof or any other form of intimidation; or

b) performs an act of violence against a person on board a fixed platform if that act is likely to endanger its safety; or

c) destroys a fixed platform or causes damage to it, which is likely to endanger its safety; or

d) places or causes to be placed on a fixed platform, by any means whatsoever, a device or substance which is likely to destroy that fixed platform or likely to endanger its safety; or

e) injures or kills any person in connection with the commission or the attempted commission of any of the offences set forth in subparagraphs (a) to (d).

The 2005 amendment broadened the offenses to include

- when the purpose of the act, by its nature or context, is to intimidate a population, or to compel a Government or an international organization to do or to abstain from doing any act; or

- uses against or on a fixed platform or discharges from a fixed platform any explosive, radioactive material or BCN weapon in a manner that causes or is likely to cause death or serious injury or damage; or

- discharges from a fixed platform, oil, liquefied natural gas, or other hazardous or noxious substance, in such quantity or concentration, that it causes or is likely to cause death or serious injury or damage; or

- threatens, with or without a condition, as is provided for under national law, to commit an offence.

A new article includes the offenses of unlawfully and intentionally injuring or killing any person in connection with the commission of any of the offenses; attempting to commit an offense; participating as an accomplice; or organizing or directing others to commit an offense.

Any of these risks have direct commercial and economic implications; potentially, some of the returns include a temporary shutdown of global logistics and thence of national economies. Some of these risks have implications for society and politics at the national level, including slow-onset risks, such as potential harm to individuals and societies from illegal drugs. Others are rapid-onset risks, such as potential terrorist attacks via shipped weapons or personnel.

The International Maritime Organization's **International Convention for the Safety of Life at Sea** (SOLAS) requires all internationally voyaging passenger vessels or vessels of 300 GT or more to

E.U. Legislation on Maritime Security

- Regulation (EC) No 725/2004 of the European Parliament and of the Council of March 31, 2004, on enhancing ship and port-facility security

- Directive 2005/65/EC of the European Parliament and of the Council of October 26, 2005, on enhancing port security

- Report from the European Commission to the Council and the European Parliament on transport security and its financing (COM/2006/0431 final)

- European Commission Regulation (EC) No 324/2008 of April 9, 2008, laying down revised procedures for conducting commission inspections in the field of maritime security

- European Commission Decision of January 23, 2009, amending Regulation (EC) No 725/2004 of the European Parliament and of the Council as far as the IMO Unique Company and Registered Owner Identification Number Scheme is concerned

- European Commission Recommendation of March 11, 2010, on measures for self-protection and the prevention of piracy and armed robbery against ships (2010/159/EU)

carry an **Automatic Identification System (AIS)**, which automatically sends (by radio) information about the vessel to other ships and any interested shore-based agencies (see below under Maritime Transportation Security Act of 2002). The class of vessel affected includes more than 40,000 vessels.

Additionally, many countries, including the United States, China, India, and those of the European Union, require other classes to fit an approved AIS device for safety and national-security purposes. The U.S. Coast Guard completed a Nationwide AIS by 2014. In 2010, the E.U. ordered most commercial vessels operating on inland waterways to use an AIS Class A device. The E.U. also ordered fishing vessels over 15 m in length to do the same by 2014.

However, vessel crews can turn this system off. For instance, in June 2012, a Russian vessel carrying attack helicopters to Syria turned off its AIS after its insurer removed coverage while the vessel was transiting the North Sea without declaring its cargo. (The insurer probably had been tipped off or pressured by the British government, which opposed arms imports by Syria.)

PORT SECURITY

Scope

Ports as small as village harbors handle commercial trade of one sort or another, at least fish or tourists, but most concern is expressed over busy commercial ports with capacity to handle standard shipping containers and to service container ships and large passenger ships. Around 6,500 such ports across 225 states and dependent territories service around 112,000 merchant vessels that carry containers internationally (Chalk, 2011b, p. 88). The busiest ports are generally in the northern hemisphere, in East Asia, Southeast Asia, the eastern coast of South Asia, the southern Middle East, Egypt, Greece, Italy, Spain, Germany, the eastern and western coasts of the United States, and Central America.

Impact

Interruptions to these major ports could have national and international implications. In 2002, the consulting company Booz Allen Hamilton sponsored a simulation of an interruption to all American seaports for 12 days, which estimated a cost to the United States of $58 billion in lost revenue alone (GAO, 2008c, p. 8). However, many experts familiar with this exercise and this estimate believe, even at that time, the numbers to be unreasonably conservative. In addition to the ripple effect and financial impact of a port closing, other issues arose. At the time of the simulation, organizers and participants in the exercise acknowledged that while various powers had the unilateral authority to declare facilities and services closed down, there is no mechanism in place to coordinate the restoration of these offices, either operationally or legally. Because these facilities are in private ownership, the issues as to which state authority or corporate concern has jurisdiction and responsibility over such matters becomes Byzantine.

▶ Standard Shipping Containers in Port

Source: Container Security Initiative, 2006–2011 Strategic Plan; iStockphoto.com/36clicks.

As another example of how intensely the maritime supply chain intertwines with the economy, a 10-day labor lockout in 2002 at the Port of Los Angeles/Long Beach cost U.S. commerce $1 billion per day. The pause of operations also hurt foreign economies, particularly in Asia (Blumenthal, 2005, p. 12). These numbers are an insufficient benchmark, however. They only reflected pure economic costs without the impact of market panic, political volatility, and the price of higher investment in security. Some observers claim that a single terrorist attack on a prime container port could trigger a global recession. In the event of a terrorist attack, the political fallout alone might be destabilizing (*A review to assess progress*, 2004).

CARGO SECURITY

Scope

Maritime vessels carry over 99% of transoceanic trade. Only a relative fraction is conveyed by air transport. States with long coastal borders tend to depend most on oceanic trade. For instance, Britain, Japan, and South Korea each import or export by ship more than 90% of their trade by value or 95% by weight.

More than 90% of global cargo moves in shipping containers. At any time, 12 million to 15 million containers are in use, and the number of containers in operation is expected to increase to 30 million over the next 20 years (Williscroft, 2003). In 2011, the equivalent of more than 300 million containers were handled around the world. Approximately 10.7 million containers arrived in U.S. ports that year (U.S. GAO, 2012, p. 1). The loading and unloading process is highly automated. Computers

BOX 11.3

U.S. Maritime and Port Security

By 2011, DHS counted 12,383 mi of coastline, 25,000 mi of commercial waterways, and 361 ports. The Coast Guard (administered by DHS since January 2003) prioritized 55 ports for the Port Security Assessment Program. The TSA (under DHS since March 2003) administers grants to ports, totaling more than $235 million in 2011 for the 52 riskiest port areas.

The U.S. Coast Guard (USCG) leads maritime-security activities, including ensuring the safe operation and flow of maritime traffic; rescue at sea; the protection of natural resources, environmental areas, and fishing; the interdiction of illicit traffic (mostly illegal drugs and immigrants), countering maritime terrorism, and keeping the marine environment open for military use. It administers the National Targeting Center, which assesses risks from incoming vessels and containers and supports risk-reduction activities. Maritime Intelligence Fusion Centers are located in Norfolk, Virginia, and Alameda, California. The Coast Guard has established **area maritime-security committees** in all U.S. ports to coordinate federal, state, and local authorities, port authorities, and private operators. By authority of the **Maritime Transportation Security Act** of 2002, the Coast Guard commands maritime safety and security teams (MSSTs) (each about 75 persons) that can deploy rapidly by helicopter in response to a terrorist attack on a port or vessel. By 2006, two MSSTs had been created, although one (at Anchorage, Alaska) was deleted in 2011.

Under the Marine Transportation Security Act of 2002, the International Ship and Port Facility Security Code (ISPS) requires large foreign vessels and ports to manage their security in compliance with Customs and Border Protection (CBP) standards.

The **International Port Security Program** (IPSP) facilitates the exchange of information between the USCG and foreign official partners and allows for reciprocal regulations of U.S. exports into foreign ports.

In November 2002, the Department of Commerce and the U.S. CBP launched Operation Safe Commerce to research and test technologies and methods for improving security in maritime commerce. It closed in 2004 after giving more than $200 million in grants to U.S. and foreign ports, including Los Angeles, Long Beach, Seattle/Tacoma, and New York/New Jersey.

The SAFE Port Act of October 2006 ordered DHS to ensure the security of maritime transport and ports and to create a plan for mitigating the economic consequences of a terrorist attack on a major port. In October 2007, the TSA started credentialing workers at the Port of Wilmington, Delaware, under the Transportation Worker Identification Credential program. By the end of 2011, nearly 2 million workers had been enrolled at more than 165 enrollment centers, and more than 1.8 million workers had received cards.

choreograph container movements as cargo is discharged from vessels and outgoing cargo is simultaneously loaded with the aid of preprogrammed container cranes. Despite the efficiencies built into the processing of throughput, in 2003, the Organisation for Economic Co-operation and Development (OECD) estimated worldwide cargo theft at $30 billion to $50 billion per year. This number has been consistent for the past decade. The more alarming threat is that, via compromise, vessels and hazardous cargoes could be used as weapons or weapon-delivery systems, aimed directly at the local level and generating cascading economic consequences beyond their immediate target. Because they can be stolen, hijacked, held to ransom, and used for smuggling or trafficking and they can carry hazardous materials, cargo containers are a matter of considerable concern.

Anyone can lease a container box and fill it with 65,000 lbs of cargo. Frequently, the items inside the container appear on documents in the most generalized terms and descriptions. Intermediary operators, or consolidators, know only what their customers allow them to know about their shipments (Flynn, 2004b).

Manifest records can be inaccurate, corrupted, or falsified. Efforts for transparency, hence, can be thwarted intentionally or through mishap. Because of their commoditization and the defects in audit management, shipping containers are an obvious method for inserting WMDs into the global supply chain and/or any targeted territory. "Containers can be just as efficient for smuggling undeclared merchandise, illegal drugs, undocumented immigrants, and terrorist bombs as for moving legitimate cargo" (Levinson, 2006, p. 7).

Various programs are in place to improve the transparency of the maritime supply chain while, at the same time, accommodating the demands of the modern global economy, whose volume of trade and throughput at world ports grows every year. However, the entire body of programs, initiatives, protocols, and networks, which attempts to create a single organic security design around the maritime supply chain, is not without vulnerabilities. Most of the "ecosystem" does not include inland container traffic or account for the system of import controls of other U.S. agencies, such as the Department of Agriculture, Food and Drug Administration, or Environmental Protection Agency (McLaury, 2007). Additionally, many ports around the world are not party to major maritime-security agreements. There is also a lack of consistency of best-practices norms, technological sophistication, and infrastructure quality standards throughout the network of international port facilities.

▶ Standard Containers Being Embarked

Source: Container Security Initiative, 2006–2011 Strategic Plan; Photo by James Tourtellotte.

The international maritime supply chain is a web of transport routes that intersect at thousands of points and among as many intermediaries. Amid the webbing of international affairs and global commerce is this stateless, anarchic realm—beyond the jurisdictional reach and control of politicians, law enforcement authorities, intelligence agencies, and international regimes. It is an environment open to exploitation by terrorists and criminals. The major concern for authorities is that terrorists will not only exploit this potential successfully but also do so with dramatic economic and political effect. Seaports pose a particularly serious risk as high-valued targets because they lie at the heart of our economic and societal vital intersections. Also important is the fact that the circulatory system of the global supply chain is also the inventory warehouse of the just-in-time manufacturing process. Should an attack at a major intermodal juncture of the transportation system occur, the disruption could be disabling to international trade and the world economy.

The challenge and complexity of protecting the global supply chain rests upon cargo-container security. At the core of the commercial and technological revolution in the global marketplace and its environment of frictionless trade is this dull assembly of wood and aluminum. The shipping container, despite its lack of sophistication, is arguably a main reason for the transformation of the world economy. Its standard dimensions, ubiquity, and inexpensiveness have changed our conception of the geographic economy in much the same manner as the Internet has redefined distance. By making shipping cheap, it has made capital more mobile, facilitated just-in-time manufacturing, extended the enterprise, and created new market centers as it has eliminated or forced the decline of old ones. This revolution in the transportation industry made possible disaggregated production schemes, allowing for firms to gain economies of scale and more highly organized inventory and asset management control (Jarmon, 2014). The same benefits it has endowed global commerce can be shared with crime and terrorism.

Map 11.1 Major Trade Routes, Container Traffic—2007 (Million Tons)

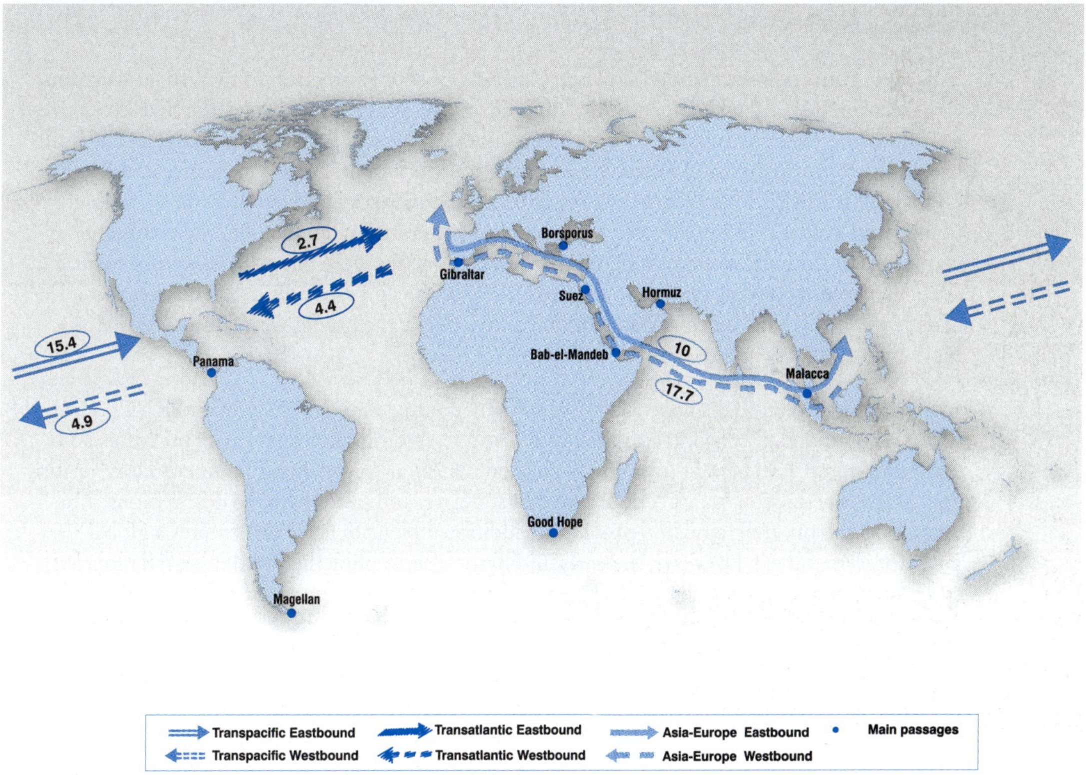

2.7
4.4
15.4
4.9
Panama
Magellan
Gibraltar
Borsporus
Suez
Hormuz
Bab-el-Mandeb
10
17.7
Malacca
Good Hope
Transpacific Eastbound
Transpacific Westbound
Transatlantic Eastbound
Transatlantic Westbound
Asia-Europe Eastbound
Asia-Europe Westbound
Main passages

Source: U.N. Conference on Trade and Development (2008). *From Review of Maritime Transport 2008* by the UNCTAD Secretariat. Copyright © 2008 United Nations. Used by permission of the United Nations.

MARITIME CARGO AND CONTAINER SECURITY

As described by subsections below, initiatives to secure cargo and cargo shipping include certification of safe traders, manifest rules, the Container Security Initiative, the Smart Box Initiative, port inspections, and various regimes, international agreements, grant programs, and cooperative exercises.

Safe and Trusted Traders

The U.S. **Customs-Trade Partnership Against Terrorism (C-TPAT)** came into existence in November 2001; it was formalized into law with the SAFE Port Act in October 2006. It is administered by the **Customs Border Protection** agency within the DHS. Initially, C-TPAT was a response to the events of 9/11 by government and the private sector in an attempt to rebound from the catastrophe. The program urges businesses (such as importers, carriers, brokers, port authorities) to voluntarily ensure compliance, internally and within their supply chains, with U.S. security standards. In return, shippers can expect fewer inspections and other benefits. The program has no regulatory authority; therefore, responsibility by members to maintain standards is self-regulating. The foundation of the program is an honor system. In turn for agreeing to a minimum standard of security measures, private-sector firms receive certification status and member privileges.

This same concept has expanded through Customs Border Protection to the World Customs Organization (WCO). As a capacity-building effort, the program known as the **SAFE Framework** effectively extends C-TPAT beyond the sphere of U.S.-bound trade. In 2005, the World Customs Organization established the Framework of Standards to Secure and Facilitate Global Trade (SAFE Framework) as a set of broad security standards to provide a baseline of technical guidance for enhancing security and facilitating trade. In 2006, the terms and conditions of Authorized Economic Operator (AEO) status were put into document form. For firms that are involved in international trade, AEO is the corresponding designation to C-TPAT certification. C-TPAT certification automatically affords the holder AEO status. As of 2011, more than 10,000 companies had enrolled in C-TPAT.

In general, an established shipper has already implemented many of the practices C-TPAT and SAFE recommend. By enrolling in the program and agreeing to these security measures and standards, companies benefit from the likelihood that their shipments will undergo less scrutiny and, hence, a reduction in inspection time, fewer delays, and faster paths to destinations. The creators of the program aimed to provide an additional security layer as it creates a global "fast lane" for its members. However, the early and hasty rush to implementation created inherent program vulnerabilities. The C-TPAT's earlier manpower shortages and lack of coordination produced a lenient certification and validation process. Membership requirements were lax and often depended upon a firm's financial condition, which may not be an indicator of future intent, events, conditions, or transfers of ownership. Because the benefits of being C-TPAT or SAFE certified means negligible or no inspection time for the shipper, a potential and systemic risk exists. A legitimate maritime commercial service with C-TPAT or SAFE certification would be a deadly cover for any group seeking to launch a well-coordinated and devastating attack. Terrorist groups have a history of using shipping vessels to move assets. In addition, other C-TPAT and SAFE members become targets of terrorists seeking to launch an attack, particularly if a disgruntled or willing worker within the shipper's enterprise is involved. Although the validation and certification procedures have become more rigorous, the earlier control and monitoring lapses still harbor a potential threat to the present regime.

Manifest Rules

In October 2003, the United States first implemented the **24-Hour Advance Manifest Rule,** which mandates all sea carriers (except for bulk carriers and approved break-bulk cargo) to submit specified information about the cargo to the United States through the Sea Automated Manifest System before loading cargo intended for a U.S. port. Importers file 10 additional data elements electronically to U.S. authorities. This information includes the manufacturer; seller; consolidator; buyer name and address; ship

▶ Port Security

Source: U.S. Department of Homeland Security (2014); U.S. Customs and Border Protection (2012).

name and address; container-stuffing location; importer record number; consignee record number; country of origin of goods; and the Commodity Harmonized Tariff Schedule number. The 24-Hour Rule, also known as the **10 Plus 2 Program**, means that importers must submit their data no less than 24 hrs prior to the loading of containers from the port of exit.

CBP risk assessments are produced from a rule-based system known as the Automated Targeting System (ATS) at the National Targeting Center in Virginia. The National Targeting Center's Automated Targeting System employs a computer model to review and evaluate documentation on all containers scheduled to arrive in the United States. Using manifest data, historical patterns, and intelligence reports, ATS assigns risk levels to cargo. Depending upon the resultant scores, containers may be selected for further document review and possible inspection. The U.S. CBP can order the carrier not to load the cargo if it is assessed as too risky ahead of a local inspection. Additionally, foreign ships must send information about the cargo, passengers, crew, and voyage to the U.S. Coast Guard 96 hrs before arrival in a U.S. port. If the Automated Targeting Center rates the vessel as high risk, the Coast Guard can be ordered to board the vessel before it enters port. The Coast Guard can also inspect vessels randomly.

In 2010, the E.U. announced its own 24-Hour Advance Manifest Rule, effective from 2011. It demands 24-hrs notice before cargo is loaded aboard any vessel that will enter the E.U. across deep seas, 2 hrs before short-sea shipments arrive in an E.U. port, and 4 hrs before break-bulk cargo arrives in an E.U. port. An **Entry Summary Declaration** (ENS) is the statement of goods and transportation vehicle submitted electronically before arrival to entry customs office with the purpose of making a risk analysis of the cargo entering into the E.U. Customs Territory. It bans the use of generic terms, such as agricultural products, equipment, and chemicals, and requires the shipper to specify the source type, sector use, or precise substance name of the material. If the language on the ENS is too vague, the shipper may have their cargo seized and held for physical examination.

Screening, Scanning, and Inspecting

A layered defense for cargo security means a process of *screening*, *scanning*, and physical *inspection* or de-vanning. The terms *screening* and *scanning* are often confused in the literature.

Screening refers to the use of analytic tools and algorithm theory methodology to sort out suspicious cargo based upon rule-based, risk-scoring methods. In addition to isolating high-risk containers, the technology identifies changes in data patterns and aids intelligence in gathering.

Scanning is nonintrusive inspection of cargo using sensor and imaging technology. Cargo may be pulled aside randomly or as a result of a high-risk score. As the container passes through a detection device, gamma readings expose anomalies.

Inspection technically means the physical entry and investigation of the container's contents. It is also referred to as "vanning" and "de-vanning." Port inspections usually involve a 5–7% inspection rate. Many experts claim that if inspection levels went above that rate, world commerce would come to a halt.

Container Security Initiative

In January 2002, the U.S. government announced the **Container Security Initiative** (CSI) to ensure containers overseas by committing overseas ports to U.S. security standards. CSI is a risk-based program designed to increase the security of containers shipped to the United States from around the world. It deploys a system of enhanced and advanced technology and intelligence-gathering tools for converting information into, what it hopes will be, actionable analysis. At the same time, the program's objective is to facilitate growth and development within the international trade community through bilateral arrangements (Jarmon, 2014). The U.S. CBP administers the program, but foreign personnel provide most of the security, sometimes with U.S. agents based at foreign ports. Local officials could identify high-risk cargos for themselves; U.S. intelligence contributes to some of those assessments. Additionally, U.S. officials could ask foreign officials to screen high-risk containers as assessed from the United States. Low-risk and prescreened containers gain rapid entry into the United States.

Under this program, the largest world ports host CSI teams of U.S. customs agents, which are multidisciplinary units from within the Customs and Border Protection and U.S. Immigration and Customs Enforcement agencies. Agents identify and inspect high-risk containers bound for the United States before they are loaded onto vessels. A CSI team generally consists of three specialist categories: targeters, intelligence analysts, and special agents. The program is a series of bilateral agreements with foreign governments. It involves intelligence sharing and a mutual aim of enhanced counterterrorism preparedness that spans international borders. However, much of the program's success depends upon the reliability of intelligence and efficient staffing balances across CSI ports (Stana, 2005, p. 20).

By 2003, 18 foreign ports had joined; by 2008, 58 had joined; this remained the total in 2013. These 58 ports account for 85% of all U.S.-bound containers, or around 8 million

Map 11.2 Container Security Initiative Ports

There are currently 58 foreign ports participating in CSI, accounting for 85% of container traffic bound for the United States.

Source: U.S. Customs Border Protection (2012).

containers per year, of which about 45,500 containers are screened in the foreign port (equivalent to about two containers per port per day). About 2% of all inbound containers were screened in 2008, but the proportion dropped to 0.5% in 2011. Despite CSI, about 10% of containers are screened after arrival in the United States, almost all of them (99%) for gamma radiation. Fifteen percent of all inbound containers originate in a port outside of CSI. It is important to note that diplomatic relations and issues are critical and, at times, out of CSI's control (Stana, 2005). Local government officials, however, can deny inspection if, after review, they feel further diligence is unwarranted. In these cases, CSI's recourse is to place a

▸ Spectrographic Scanning

Source: Department of Homeland Security.

domestic hold on the cargo. When the shipment eventually arrives at its U.S. destination, it will be subject to inspection by U.S. authorities. The European Union and many countries have opposed the Container Security Initiative as a nontariff barrier to trade and worry about bad U.S. intelligence or U.S. political biases causing harm to certain trade without improving security.

In 2006, the DHS and Department of Energy launched the Security Freight Initiative (SFI) to counter nuclear and radiological terrorism through shipped containers. All U.S. ports and 75 foreign ports (as of 2013) have U.S.-supplied radiation portal monitors in order to screen containers destined for U.S. shores. Honduras and Pakistan joined the SFI immediately, followed by Britain, Hong Kong, and Singapore. The 9/11 Commission Act of 2007 ordered all inbound containers to be scanned overseas by x-rays and for gamma radiation by July 2012, but many officials soon predicted that this target was unreasonable. In May 2012, the Homeland Security Secretary Janet Napolitano extended by another 2 years the exemption for all foreign ports, claiming that scanning of all inbound containers would cost $16 billion. Some experts conclude that perhaps 10% of inbound containers could be scanned without disrupting trade flows. The legislation, known as Public Law No. 110-53, Implementing Recommendation of the 9/11 Commission Act (2007), would eventually require 600 ports around the world to scan containers bound for the United States. Over 1,400 radiation portal monitors (RPMs) have been deployed thus far. However, the initiative raised protest from foreign governments and representatives from commerce. The objections range from it being an unnecessary expense and impediment to trade to fears over a perceived attempt by the United States to impose its hegemony ("Are US security measures going too far?" 2007; Watkins, 2007). The uncertain probability of detection, the tribulation of false alarms, the risk of being defeated or compromised, and excessive cost stoke many experts' fears of system failures and inefficiency.

The feasibility of 100% scanning is still largely unconfirmed. A 2012 GAO report noted that the Secure Freight Initiative experienced safety and logistical problems. The technology attempts to integrate images and radiological signatures of scanned containers onto a computer screen for observation by analysts. The images can be reviewed remotely from sites within the United States. However, at the pilot ports Qasim, Pakistan, Puerto Cortes, Honduras, and Southampton, U.K., poor image quality and equipment breakdowns created frustrations (Caldwell, 2012b, p. 16). Since one of SFI's purposes was to determine the feasibility of 100% scanning of U.S. inbound container traffic, these problems may have confirmed the predictions of the programs' critics.

As the program expanded and the technology upgraded, new complications arose. At the larger ports with higher transshipment volumes, the officials complained that costs increased and port efficiencies declined. Another criticism contended that equipment deployment and technical recommendations are often vendor-driven rather than merit-based (Massey, 2007). Logistics and security experts also contend that 100% scanning may even be inconsistent with risk-based strategies, which are the basis of the layered security approach. The inconsistencies of false reads, lack of benchmarks, and other corruptive influences undermine the logic-based methodology of the filtering analysis of high-risk cargo and other forms of contraband. Furthermore, the variance of host nation examination practices, performance measures, resource constraints, technological limitations, and the physical features of foreign ports have created additional obstacles (Caldwell, 2012b, p. 46). As of 2013, the SFI program has shriveled to a single port and plans to continue with the cost–benefit and feasibility study have halted due to a lack of funding.

Smart Box Initiative

In 2003, the CSI spawned the Smart Box Initiative, which developed new containers that include an internationally approved mechanical seal that attaches to the container's hinges and records

Table 11.1	The Program Components of the United States' Layered Approach to Maritime Security
Customs Trade Partnership Against Terrorism	Cooperative security agreement between the U.S. government and the private sector that requires businesses to establish security guidelines for member organizations and commercial partners. Participants receive preferential treatment and benefits in return. The WCO's SAFE Framework recognizes C-TPAT certification.
Container Security Initiative	A working network of bilateral agreements between the United States and foreign governments to prescreen cargo prior to shipment bound for U.S. territory. Using risk-based computer models, intelligence sources, and commercial history, suspected cargo is identified and targeted for possible detainment and inspection.
Secure Freight Initiative	At participating foreign ports, optical-scanning technology, nonintrusive radioactive imaging, and passive radiation detection equipment scan and identify cargo containers for anomalies regarding documentation records and radiation readings. (The program has been reduced due to technical flaws and feasibility concerns.)
The 10 Plus 2 Program	A requirement of the SAFE Port Act of 2006 that U.S. importers submit information to customs authorities at least 24 hrs prior to loading at the port of exit.

or signals any attempt to open the door after sealing. Some have signaling devices; some are able to record the container's movements using GPS. The seals are commercially available to U.S. standards. Users gain privileges such as quicker routing through ports. However, the choice of product type, sophistication, and effectiveness of cargo seals is often driven by cost. Tamper-resistant and tamper-evident seals cost several dollars. Those with GPS transponders or radio frequency identification may be several hundred. Seals costing only a few cents can be easily defeated with a simple utensil and, unfortunately, are the most common. These simple "bolts" offer little protection and can be removed and reattached quickly without much indication of any tampering. It takes a highly trained eye with a reasonable cause, based on suspicion or ex ante, to detect whether a container has been compromised (Jarmon, 2014).

Inspections at Port

Cargo security authorities can inspect containers afloat or ashore randomly but mostly respond to intelligence, tip-offs, and automated inspections. Most inspections are conducted at the exit from the port. At U.S. ports, cargo is pulled aside randomly or because of its suspicious nature. The container then passes under the detection tower or arm of a mobile nonintrusive inspection vehicle (NII). These vehicles are also known as Vehicle and Cargo Inspection Systems (VACIS) and use gamma detectors to spot anomalies. After conferring with lab analysis, suspect containers are pulled and sent to on-site container evaluation facilities (CES) for full vanning and de-vanning inspection. As well, the U.S. CBP deploys large nonintrusive x-ray inspection systems and nuclear-radiation portal monitors, through which a truck can drive. For intrusive inspections, fiber-optic cameras can be pushed through apertures into the container without opening its door. Most intrusively, a container can be unloaded and opened for a full intrusive inspection with handheld detection systems, by explosives detection dogs, and by hand.

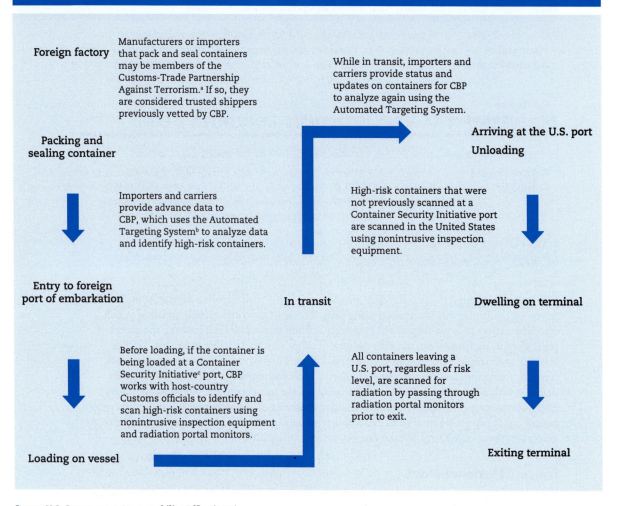

Figure 11.1   Maritime Supply Chain

Foreign factory
Manufacturers or importers that pack and seal containers may be members of the Customs-Trade Partnership Against Terrorism.[a] If so, they are considered trusted shippers previously vetted by CBP.

Packing and sealing container

Importers and carriers provide advance data to CBP, which uses the Automated Targeting System[b] to analyze data and identify high-risk containers.

Entry to foreign port of embarkation

Before loading, if the container is being loaded at a Container Security Initiative[c] port, CBP works with host-country Customs officials to identify and scan high-risk containers using nonintrusive inspection equipment and radiation portal monitors.

Loading on vessel

While in transit, importers and carriers provide status and updates on containers for CBP to analyze again using the Automated Targeting System.

In transit

Arriving at the U.S. port

Unloading

High-risk containers that were not previously scanned at a Container Security Initiative port are scanned in the United States using nonintrusive inspection equipment.

Dwelling on terminal

All containers leaving a U.S. port, regardless of risk level, are scanned for radiation by passing through radiation portal monitors prior to exit.

Exiting terminal

Source: U.S. Government Accountability Office (2012).

Notes:

a. The Customs-Trade Partnership Against Terrorism is a voluntary program designed to improve the security of the international supply chain while maintaining an efficient flow of goods. Under this program, CBP officials work in partnership with private companies to review their supply chain security plans to improve members' overall security.

b. The Automated Targeting System is a mathematical model that uses weighted rules to assign a risk score to arriving cargo shipments based on shipping information. CBP uses the Automated Targeting System as a decision support tool in targeting cargo containers for inspection.

c. The Container Security Initiative places CBP staff at participating foreign ports to work with host country customs officials to target and examine high-risk container cargo for weapons of mass destruction before they are shipped to the United States. CBP officials identify the containers that may pose a risk for terrorism and request that their foreign counterparts examine the contents of the containers.

Inspections at port are heavily biased toward nuclear radiation. Technical and feasibility concerns of SFI aside, U.S. capacity to detect nuclear and radiological material at the ports of entry has improved dramatically in recent years. The GAO agreed with the DHS that

> the likelihood of terrorists smuggling a WMD into the United States in cargo containers is low, [however,] the nation's vulnerability to this activity and the consequences of such an attack—such as billions of losses in U.S. revenue and halts in manufacturing production—are potentially high. (Caldwell, 2012b, p. 1)

MARITIME TRANSPORTATION SECURITY ACT

In the track and turbulence of the 9/11 attacks, the U.S. Congress passed the Maritime Transportation Security Act (MTSA) of 2002, PL 107-295. (The 2010 updated proposed legislation died in committee.) Concern for port security by government officials and security experts was high. A year prior to the attacks on New York and Washington, the Interagency Commission on Crime and Security in U.S. Seaports warned of the vulnerability of U.S. ports and the threat to global commerce if a large-scale event were to occur (Frittelli, 2003). The legislation raised broad policy issues, such as the impact of maritime security on commerce; the approach between overall port security standards versus site-specific standards; shared cost ownership among taxpayers, local authorities, and facility users; and the creation of an international security regime implemented through some arrangement of unilateral agreements, multilateral agreements, international trade agreements, and U.S. subsidization of underdeveloped foreign infrastructure. In addition to C-TPAT, CSI, ATS, SFI, the 24-Hour Rule, and the Smart Box Initiative discussed above, various other strategies, programs, and initiatives evolved from congressional hearings, government research, and expert consultation.

As part of these efforts, in 2005, a Homeland Security Presidential Directive (HSPD-13) instructed the Department of Defense and the Department of Homeland Security to draft the *National Strategy for Maritime Security*. The paper, published in September 2005, "aimed to align all federal government maritime security programs and activities into a comprehensive and cohesive national effort involving appropriate federal, state, local, and private sector entities" (Caldwell, 2012a, p. 29). The presidential directive put forth a national strategy based upon the pillars of eight interlinked implementation plans. These plans attempted to create a broad security strategy while forming a framework of mutually supportive mechanisms that addressed specific issues at the same time. They included the following:

- A plan that achieved and addressed domain awareness

- Integration of global maritime intelligence

- Implementation of an (interim) Maritime Operational Threat Response Plan

- An international outreach and coordination strategy

- A Maritime Infrastructure Recovery Plan

- A Maritime Transportation System Security Plan

- A domestic outreach plan

However, not included in *National Strategy for Maritime Security* were recommendations for establishing success measurements, risk management, and investment strategies for strategic and financial support. These implementation plans still lack direct funding. Nevertheless, the MTSA and a national strategy for maritime security continue to provide policy guidance through various mechanisms, programs, and initiatives—despite shortcomings.

In order to assist in creating prevention, protection, response, and recovery procedures in the event of crises, MTSA required the U.S. Coast Guard to develop *area maritime-security plans* (AMSPs). Appropriate government and private-sector entities contributed to the design and communication/ coordination methods of these AMSPs. By mandate, they are updated every 5 years. Periodic, existing forums allow the USCG and port stakeholders to review present plans and exchange recommendations for improvements. Forty-three geographically defined port areas come under AMSP direction. The individual plan recommendations differ at each facility, and more often lately, proposals have been made to establish some standards that would limit the variance.

In support of the AMSPs, *port security exercises* occur routinely (every 18 months) to test preparedness by identifying strengths and weaknesses of current disaster plans. Command and control structures also come under scrutiny and evaluation. Designated to lead and participate in these exercises are the Coast Guard captain of the port and the members of the area maritime-security committee, which includes key port stakeholders. Participation or active management of an exercise is required annually. An action report is drafted after each exercise and submitted for review. An accounting of results and a description of lessons learned form the content of the report. The data include recommendations for an improvement plan process that identifies, monitors, and disseminates information for implementation of improvements to the existing framework. Incident response, decision-making authority, communication, coordination, and resource allocation are the areas generally evaluated. Reports are due within 21 days of the exercise or operation for entry in the appropriate database.

Maritime-facility security plans also provide improvement recommendations. The MTSA requires port facilities to develop and implement their own security plans, which they must submit for approval to DHS and which are subject to the U.S. Coast Guard for administration. The Coast Guard conducts at least two inspections of each facility annually. Inspections may be unannounced, and their purpose is to verify compliance with the facility's own security plan. Although the facilities design these plans to suit their specific site needs and to address their express threats, in 2007, the GAO found deficiencies in one third of all those inspected. These inspections also include offshore energy facilities and, therefore, extend beyond U.S. territorial waters.

The Port Security Grant Program (PSGP) assists domestic ports with federal funding in order to ease the financial burdens of implementing security measures. The MTSA administers the grant program through FEMA with consultation of the Coast Guard. Grant awards are based upon risk within a field of three separate categories: Group I—highest risk, Group II—next highest risk, and Group III. A fourth category, simply called "All Other Port Areas," offers funding to those sites that fail to meet the criteria of the other risk groups. Among the costs covered by the grants are purchases of equipment, employee training, and other expenses related to port-wide risk management, resilience and recovery efforts, and enhancing maritime domain awareness.

Worldwide, maritime shipping is an industry of 8 to 10 million people working for as many as 40,000 freight forwarders and buying agents. An extremely diverse international labor force provides the pool of employees. Ports of call are often drop-off or pick-up terminals for

Table 11.2   The 20 Biggest Suppliers of Officers and Ratings in 2010

Country	Number of Officers Supplied	Percentage of World Market Share Officers	Country	Number of Ratings Supplied	Percentage of World Market Share Ratings
Philippines	57,688	9.2	China	90,296	12.1
China	51,511	8.3	Indonesia	61,821	8.3
India	46,497	7.5	Turkey	51,009	6.8
Turkey	36,734	5.9	Russia	40,000	5.4
Ukraine	27,172	4.4	Malaysia	28,687	3.8
Russia	25,000	4.0	Philippines	23,492	3.1
United States	21,810	3.5	Bulgaria	22,379	3.0
Japan	21,297	3.4	Myanmar	20,145	2.7
Romania	18,575	3.0	Sri Lanka	19,511	2.6
Poland	17,923	2.9	United States	16,644	2.2
Norway	16,082	2.6	India	16,176	2.2
Indonesia	15,906	2.5	Honduras	15,341	2.1
United Kingdom	15,188	2.4	Cambodia	12,004	1.6
Canada	13,994	2.2	Vietnam	11,438	1.5
Croatia	11,704	1.9	Italy	11,390	1.5
Myanmar	10,950	1.8	Ukraine	11,000	1.5
Bulgaria	10,890	1.7	Pakistan	9,327	1.2
Vietnam	10,738	1.7	France	9,316	1.2
Greece	9,993	1.6	Egypt	9,000	1.2
South Korea	9,890	1.6	United Kingdom	8,990	1.2
World	624,062	100.0	World	747,306	100.0

Source: Compiled by UNCTAD on data supplied by BIMCO in *Manpower Update* (2010) as cited in OECD (2003). From *Review of Maritime Transport 2011* by The UNCTAD Secretariat. Copyright © 2011 United Nations. Used by permission of the United Nations

"temporary seamen" wishing to navigate the world as persons seeking a better life or out to fulfill more sinister missions. Over 1,370,000 seafarers staff the international merchant fleet. This vast labor force moves freely around the globe with relatively liberal travel rights and minimal identification documents. Abetting their movement is a black market for falsified seafarer certificates and identity documents (OECD, 2003). Illegal immigrants are aware of the lax procedures and often pose as seamen in order to bypass the more stringent controls applied to other types of passengers (Greenberg, Chalk, Willis, Khilko, & Ortiz, 2006).

As a result of these pressures, MTSA also requires DHS to control access to secure port areas by unauthorized personnel. Through the Transportation Worker Identification Credential (TWIC) program, unauthorized and unescorted personnel who do not have official biometric identification cards or the approval of a sanctioning authority are denied the right of entry to MTSA-regulated, secured facilities. Eligible employees apply and are granted ID cards from the U.S. Coast Guard and the Transportation Security Administration (TSA) after undergoing background checks. As of 2012, data from the TSA calculates that it has activated over 2 million TWIC cards. Most recent accounts from the Coast Guard (2010 through 2011) report that 2,509 facilities and 12,908 vessels fall under MTSA regulation and are subject to TWIC implementation (Greenberg et al., 2006, p. 34). The GAO, however, reported that a greater than anticipated number of applicants and employee population has overwhelmed the demand for access control technology. Inefficiencies have developed as the pressures mount to facilitate trade flow and, at the same time, enhance security performance standards.

Making matters worse, the black market is a source for falsified seafarer certificates and identity documents (OECD, 2003). The actors involved in the movement of goods through the maritime-transportation chain include an international cast of regulatory agencies, liability regimes, operators of various transportation modes, port authorities, freight integrators, and legal frameworks. Interaction is complex and unsystematic (Jarmon, 2014). As world maritime trade grows, the labor force expands.

Despite the Transportation Worker Identification Credential program, the U.S. government still has no control over foreign seafarer-credentialing practices. Typically, over 5 million entries by seafarers (mostly foreign) from cargo and cruise ships occur annually in the United States. Alien crew members can gain illegal entry into the United States with fraudulent identification. Therefore, a key concern is the exploitation opportunities from lax practices and corruption that might allow a terrorist admittance onto U.S. territory. In order to address the threat, the U.S. State Department reviews all seafarers' application for visas. The Coast Guard and CBP conduct seafarer enforcement and compliance operations that include vessel boarding and inspection. These *controls over foreign seafarers*, as they are referred, are regulatory responsibilities under the MTSA. Upgrades and improvements plans to the process continue to proceed. They include expanding electronic verification of foreign seafarers, further limiting the discrepancies between USCG and CBP databases, and enhancing information sharing between agencies.

The threat from the millions of small vessels that ply U.S. waterways is the concern of the Small Vessel Security Activities program. In 2008, DHS released its *Small Vessel Security Strategy* to help mitigate the threat by and to the small-vessel fleet. The document identifies the following four scenarios involving terrorist use of small vessels in an attack with potentially grave consequences:

- A waterborne improvised explosive device

- A means of smuggling weapons into the United States

- A means of smuggling humans (terrorists)

- A platform for conducting an attack that uses a rocket or other device that would allow attackers to evade capture or defensive fire because of its distance from the target

Small vessels could be used as platforms for a radiological attack. In order to mitigate the risk, DHS works to address the specific issues related to small-vessel transport. The number of small vessels and volume of traffic, the obstacles in identifying suspicious activity, and the difficulty in providing resources for the stricken area in an effective and timely manner are the main challenges. For testing solutions, DHS works with the **Domestic Nuclear Detection Office** (DNDO). The DNDO is the primary agency within DHS charged with implementing domestic nuclear-detection efforts and coordinated response to radiological and nuclear threats. It is also responsible for global nuclear-detection efforts and developing a reporting architecture. In performing its tasks, the DNDO partners with international governments, private-sector entities, and federal, state, and local authorities to achieve its aims. In particular, DNDO works with the Coast Guard to install and test nuclear-detection instruments at local ports. The program establishes security zones at ports and inland waterways. It provides escorts for vessels that might be targeted for attack and port-level vessel tracking for small vessels with radars and cameras. The DNDO also works within the Small Vessel Security Activities program to develop community outreach initiatives.

The **Maritime Security Risk Analysis Model** (MSRAM) is the Coast Guard's primary tool for managing and assessing risk to maritime infrastructure. Sites such as oil refineries, chemical plants, passenger terminals, cruise ships, and cargo vessels compose a list of more than 28,000 potential maritime targets, which MSRAM evaluates. Attack modes, target options, and potential consequences determine the degree of risk from terrorist attack. The model cannot factor in complex scenarios involving more than one facility at a time. Adaptive adversaries and systemic impact are other factors that challenge the limits of the model's capability. However, it is still an important risk management assessment tool, and progress has been made to refine the model to help set risk prioritization within ports and drive resource allocation. The methodology also assists DHS to determine investment and administer the Port Security Grant Program.

Area maritime-security committees (AMSC) consist of key stakeholders who are in a position to recommend defense and mitigation strategies against an attack. Because of their involvement in port operations these committee members understand the risks and can identify vulnerabilities of the critical port infrastructure. The committee assesses appropriate factors and disseminates findings and information to other stakeholders. Ports span local jurisdictions and, therefore, facilitate information sharing. As creations of a sprawling partnership of private- and public-sector concerns, AMSCs cross local, state, and federal boundaries and are a central source of information in developing prevention and response strategies. The nation's 361 ports fall within 43 maritime-security areas, each with its own AMSC. In addition to representatives from agencies of the various levels of government, AMSCs also include personnel from industry groups, organized labor, trade associations, shipyards, commercial fishing operations, trucking and railroad companies, yacht clubs, and maritime exchanges. This diverse array offers up consensus opinions that, hopefully, convert into effective policy guidance. The type of knowledge sharing includes information on threats, vulnerabilities, and suspicious activities and data about Coast Guard strategy. Because of its success, new members to AMSCs are given priority in the security clearance process so that these committees can expand their membership and role as an effective counterterrorism tool.

Interagency operation centers (IOCs) are locations where intelligence sharing, vessel tracking, and information exchange concerning program implementations and other maritime-security activities occur. They can be either physical facilities or virtual ones. IOCs showed promise during the early stages as the Department of Justice, Department of Defense, and DHS all participated in the development of the initial prototypes. Vessel boarding, cargo inspections, and enforcement of port security zones are aided by the capabilities and force-multiplier effect of these IOCs.

Generally speaking, they are centers to improve maritime domain awareness and operational coordination among all port partners, which include law enforcement, every level of government, and private-sector stakeholders. The Safe Port Act mandated the creation of IOCs, and the Coast Guard Authorization Act of 2010 further required that a physical colocation facility be provided (when practical) for meetings with Coast Guard officials. The Coast Guard Authorization Act also called for a deployment of information management systems at IOCs. In compliance with the legislation, the Coast Guard implemented a web-based information management and -sharing system called WatchKeeper in 2005. The collection of real-time operational information allows for not only continuous streams of information about maritime activity but also facilitates involvement by participating agencies to assist in operational decision making and planning.

Vessel tracking of large cargo ships is a means of monitoring maritime activities and risk without disruption of maritime trade. The MTSA required an Automatic Identification System (discussed above) for tracking and locating vessels of certain sizes while in U.S. territorial waters. Eventually, long-range automated tracking systems were mandated by a revision to the MTSA and are in development to monitor the movement of vessels in the high seas. Existing onboard radio equipment and data communication systems transmit vessel identification and positioning information to authorities and rescue forces in the event of emergencies. Such vessels are, generally, 300 GT or more. Smaller craft are not compatible with these systems, however.

As a result of cost-sharing arrangements between the Coast Guard and port entities, port operators and other port entities implement these tracking systems for their own logistical benefit. The system allows security entities to identify potential suspicious cargo as commercial shippers gain better control over their asset and inventory management. The arrangement allows the U.S. Coast Guard and various port entities to interoperate and reduce the incidence of information duplication and hone analysis of maritime situational awareness. As a result, high-risk vessels are more identifiable and the security risk associated with them is reduced. Therefore, vessel tracking has been a positive example of how security measures can also assist in creating not only a safer global supply chain but also a more efficient one. It is also a case study for future private–public partnerships.

The Automated Targeting System (ATS), mentioned above, is a rule-based computerized model that assists CBP officers in identifying suspicious cargo containers for inspection. This technology not only isolates high-risk containers but also identifies changes in patterns of data and creates risk-scoring methods to aid intelligence gathering as well as cargo-screening methodology (Jarmon, 2014). In the after effects of the attacks on New York and Washington, DC, the major security concern was the threat that a terrorist group might attempt to smuggle a weapon of mass destruction using a cargo container. As a decision support tool, ATS has been using data from the 10 Plus 2 Rule, which includes customs entry information, cargo manifest, and vessel stowage details. Over time, the system has been refined. In addition to targeting high-risk containers for inspection, system managers also seek to constantly improve the quality and timeliness of manifest information and have implemented a national-targeting training program. CBP also engages the services of consulting firms to conduct external peer reviews.

A system of radiation portal monitors to detect and identify radioactive emissions from containers loaded on ships and trucks at seaports and land border crossings is known as the **Advanced Spectrographic Portal Program** (ASP). These advanced monitors were expected to replace many of the current devices in use at ports of entry for primary scanning. Handheld monitors used in secondary scanning were also considered for replacement. The DNOD was developing the technology at a considerable expense. The upgraded machines cost approximately 2.5 times more than the current monitors. The GAO estimates that the total cost of the program will be $2 billion (Caldwell, 2012a, p. 43). In return, the CBP argued that the technological upgrade would result in more accurate readings and more vibrant trade flow due to the reduced time spent on secondary inspections. However, the trial period revealed serious flaws. In 2012, DHS cancelled the program after spending $280 million on research and development. Until funding is revived and a technological breakthough occurs, the ASP program remains moribund.

The **Megaports Initiative** was established in 2003 by the U.S. Department of Energy to detect and interdict the smuggling of nuclear and radiological material through foreign ports. Selected overseas seaports received detection equipment and personnel training for scanning cargo containers, regardless of their destination. The aim of the program was to not only prevent the use of nuclear or radiological material against the United States but also its allies. Using a system called the Maritime Prioritization Model, the DOE ranks and selects seaports according to their appeal to smugglers based upon port security conditions, volume of cargo throughput, proximity to sources of nuclear material, and geographic location relative to U.S. territory.

Unfortunately, as with the ASP, the program was plagued by technical difficulties. False reads, technical challenges due to installation and maintenance issues, climatic conditions, and variances of individual port configurations posed problems. Host port officials complained about the plan's inability to conform to the physical layout of their port and its stacking patterns. Together, these obstacles lead to unnecessary delays and losses of revenue, according to foreign port authorities. The Megaport Initiative also lacks a long-term plan for prioritizing strategic investment and criteria for future deployment, which the U.S. General Accountability Office recommends the DOE consider. Funding for expansion was cut in December 2012, leaving the Megaports Initiative with 42 ports, rather than 100.

Mutual Recognition Arrangements (MRA) are reciprocal agreements that allow supply chain security practices and programs valid in one country to be recognized and accepted by the customs authority in another country. As with the agreement between C-TPAT and the WCO's SAFE Framework, these MRAs hope to create a more secure supply chain while satisfying the global economy's demand for frictionless trade. Greater efficiency results from a reduction in the redundancy of cargo container examinations and a streamlining of security requirements throughout the global supply chain. As of July 2012, the United States has six signed MRAs that include the European Union, Canada, Japan, Australia, New Zealand, and Switzerland.

The C-TPAT program has become a model for business-to-customs programs around the world. This fact, plus the recognition that the United States cannot create an efficient and successful maritime-security regime without the cooperation of international partners, has formed a reality and demand environment for a global framework for standards governing customs and business relationships. Critical information on customs examination procedures and practices of states outside these mutual-recognition agreements is often vague or lacking. These situations include even those countries where there is a CSI presence. Therefore, expanding the overall MRA program is a gradual ordeal and requires a rigorous data collection process.

The International Port Security Program is in place to address and assess the discrepancies and inconsistencies of port security measures between different foreign ports. The U.S. Coast Guard works with its counterpart agencies in other countries to conduct visits and assessments of world ports. The International Maritime Organization's (IMO) International Ship and Port Facility Security Code is the benchmark for evaluating a country's counterterrorism measures. These evaluations occur at least once every 3 years. Participants exchange observations and recommendations. As discussed above, an effective global maritime system depends upon international cooperation and a system of recognized best-practices standards in order to implement a comprehensive and consistent framework. If in developing countries there appears to be substandard port security as well as a lack of financial resources for technology upgrade and training, the Coast Guard works with other U.S. federal agencies and international organizations to secure funding. The World Bank Group has also put aside funds, managed privately, for infrastructure investment and development in economically distressed regions.

BOX 11.5

Entities Created by Maritime Transportation Security Act of 2002

- National Strategy for Maritime Security

- Area maritime-security plans

- Port security exercises

- Marine-facility security plans

- Port Security Grant Program

- Control over foreign seafarers

- Transportation Worker Identification Credential

- Vessel security plans

- Small-vessel security activities

- Maritime Security Risk Analysis Model

- Area marine-security committees

- Interagency operation centers

- Vessel tracking

- Automated Targeting System

- Advanced Spectrographic Portal Program

- Container Security Initiative

- Megaports Initiative

- Secure Freight Initiative

- Customs-Trade Partnership Against Terrorism

- Mutual-recognition agreements

- International Port Security Program

MARITIME TERRORISM

The following subsections summarize maritime terrorism attacks and terrorist flows by sea.

Maritime Terrorism Attacks

Maritime terrorism is rare but is potentially catastrophic to the international economy and has encouraged wide-ranging and expensive international legal and material responses.

The few cases of maritime terrorism allow for more attention to imaginative estimates of new maritime terrorism in the future, including nuclear weapons landed in shipping containers, nuclear irradiation of ports, large ships sunk across harbor entrances or sea lines of communication, deliberate leakage of a hazardous chemical, or destruction of the pipelines or terminals in the distribution of fossil fuels. However, these would be very difficult for a nonstate actor to achieve.

Compared to land-based terrorist attacks, maritime terrorism is far less common. Yet despite its infrequency, the threat is a very serious issue for global commerce. An attack on a major world port could have devastating potential. Estimates of the actual number of ports vary. They number in the thousands. Worldportsource.com puts the total at 4,764; other sources estimate the number to be around 6,500 (Chalk, 2011b, p. 88). However, the top 10 ports handle more than the next 40 ports in terms of tonnage and throughput. With maritime trade concentrated in so few seaports and the existence of key natural choke points around the world, the possibility of severe economic and human disruption is frightfully real.

Choke Points

Naturally formed straits and manmade canals are narrow bodies of water connecting larger ocean masses. Around the world, approximately 200 straits or canals form links within the maritime supply chain. For centuries, the most strategic passageways have been protected by international law defending the rights of access by all nations. In 1982, the Law of Sea Conventions further assured international access for nations to sail through straits and canals and extended these rights to aviation carriers.

Only several are considered strategic choke points. If constricted or closed, any of these bottlenecks would most certainly cause an international incident and economic chaos. Seven key choke points pose such threats. They vary according to their geographic and natural features and by the uniqueness of their political environments. Although their risks may not be uniform, the impact on world trade would be equally severe if any one of them became impassable (see Map 11.3).

The Strait of Malacca is one of the most important strategic passages in the world. Approximately 90,000 ships pass through the strait each year. Thirty percent of the world's trade, two thirds of the world's liquefied-gas transport, and 80% of Japan, South Korea, and Taiwan's oil imports transit through the strait. If the passage through the Strait of Malacca were to be lost, redirected cargos would be forced to spend an additional 2 days at sea. The estimated cost would amount to $8 billion per year.

The Strait of Hormuz forms a strategic link between the oil fields of the Persian Gulf, the Gulf of Oman, and the Indian Ocean. It is a geographic choke point and a main artery for the transport of oil from the Middle East. Due to the sizable amount of tanker and containership traffic, movement in the Persian Gulf is highly constrained in both directions. Iran and Oman are the countries nearest to the Strait of Hormuz and share territorial rights over the waters. Because of its strategic importance, Iran has periodically threatened to close the strait in order to impress upon the world its political clout in the region.

The Suez Canal crosses the Isthmus of Suez in northeastern Egypt to connect the Mediterranean Sea with the Gulf of Suez, an arm of the Red Sea. It functions as a shortcut for ships between both European and American ports and ports located in southern Asia, eastern Africa, and Oceania. The canal has the capacity to accommodate up to 25,000 ships per year (about 78 per day) but handles about 20,000, which roughly accounts for 15% of the global maritime trade. The 103-mi-long Suez Canal is located entirely within Egypt, and it is the only sea route between the Red Sea and the Mediterranean Sea (Rodrique, Comtois, & Slack, 2013).

The Strait of Bab el-Mandab ("the gate of tears") controls access to the Suez Canal. The strait is 20 mi (32 km) wide and is divided into two channels. The sizable amount of tanker traffic makes navigation difficult along the narrow channels. A closing of this strait would have serious consequences, forcing a detour around the Cape of Good Hope. The flow through this strait provides for the means of access between the Red Sea and the Gulf of Aden, since no flow takes place through the Suez Canal.

The Bosporus represents a passage of growing strategic importance, particularly since the collapse of the Soviet Union. Much of the vast oil reserves of the Caspian Sea transits through the Black Sea and the Bosporus to reach external markets of the Mediterranean and beyond. Oil transiting through the Bosporus has grown substantially in recent years with the exploitation of oil fields around the Caspian Sea. Nearly 2.8 million barrels per day were transiting through the passage in 2003. Thus, the future growth of petroleum trade through the Bosporus raises questions and, perhaps, poses potential problems for the energy markets and the global economy.

Map 11.3   Global Choke Points and Oil Routes

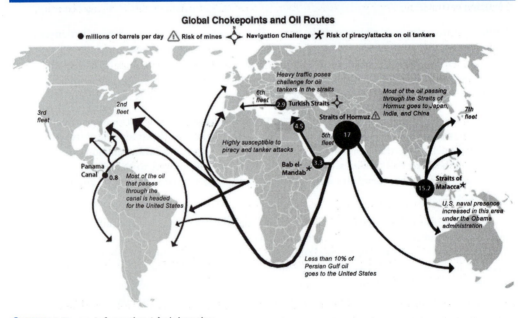

Source: U.S. Energy Information Administration.

The Panama Canal links the East and the West Coast of the United States and joins the Atlantic and Pacific Oceans across the Isthmus of Panama. Its strategic importance is, therefore, obvious. More than one million vessels transited the canal, carrying 8,100,000,000 T of cargo. The canal handles about 5% of the global seaborne trade and about 12% of the American international seaborne trade.

Gibraltar is a peninsula between the Atlantic Ocean and the Mediterranean Sea. Gibraltar represents an obligatory passage point between these two bodies of water. There are two ways to force all shipping to go around Africa to the south. Close either the Suez Canal or the Strait of Gibraltar, and no ship can go from the Indian Ocean to the Atlantic Ocean without going around Africa.

Attack Likelihood, Modes, and Motives

There are many ports around the world. Yet despite this constellation of ports, the vastness of the seas, volume of traffic, immense size of the labor force, strategic choke points, and the unlimited number of attack scenarios, the number of maritime incidents is comparatively very low. Less than 1% of all global terrorist attacks between 1997 and 2007 involved maritime targets (Parfomak & Frittelli, 2007, p. 26). Since the 2002 attack on the M/V *Limburg*, maritime attacks are generally fairly small in nature, consisting largely of bombings near port facilities or suspicious activities involving barges (Nincic, 2012). Most of the danger surrounds the potential of small vessels rather than large seagoing ships. Among the commonly recognized attack conditions is the use of unmanned light craft laden with explosives, suicide boats, and even water-borne flotsam used to conceal channel mines. Terrorists historically prefer simplicity to complexity. Therefore, the planning, coordination, and expertise generally required for conducting a large-scale attack using a high-seas tanker or cargo ship inhibits the potential for these types of assaults. The Small Vessel Security Activities program discussed above is the direct effect of the small-vessel threat. One reason for the relatively low incidence of a terrorist sea attack is that there are inherent operational difficulties in launching a successful assault. Some of the challenges include the following obstacles.

1. Land targets are more numerous and accessible compared to maritime targets.

2. Sea surveillance is less impeded by natural features, man-made structures, or other human effects as opposed to land obstructions and, therefore, open to exposure and interdiction.

3. Any coordinated terrorist attack by sea is subject to uncontrollable factors such as currents, tides, climatic conditions, and proximity and accessibility to land.

4. Navigational skills, ship handling, and other special training may be required in a maritime attack.

5. Attack preparation, training, and weapons testing at sea is more open to surveillance and discovery by authorities.

6. The cascading effects of death and damage may not reverberate with the same force at sea as on land with higher populations and concentrations of economic assets.

Yet despite these complications, maritime attacks must be viewed as serious risks. The potential for a terrorist group to achieve its aims of destruction, economic disruption, and political chaos via an attack on a maritime target is very real. Regardless of the fact that land-based targets are more generously arrayed and less protected, maritime targets abound. Significant targets, such as the choke points discussed above, are located at precarious intersections of political and economic stability. Therefore, an attack upon one of these targets is an attack at the heart of a regional economy, its political system, and, at the same time, an iconic structure. The confluence of the effects would have global consequences.

Although maritime terrorism may be either politically or economically motivated, currently, economic gain rather than terrorism for political gain now accounts for all maritime hijacking incidents (Nincic, 2012). However, maritime capabilities exist among several well-known terrorist groups. The U.S. State Department identifies 10 terrorist organizations that have maritime capability and have either used these resources in the past and/or have the potential for future exploits.

- Al-Qaeda
- Abu Nidal Organization
- Abu Sayyaf Group
- Basque Fatherland and Liberty
- Hamas
- Hezbollah
- Jemaah Islamiya
- Lashkar e-Tayyiba
- Palestine Liberation Front— Abu Abbas Faction
- Liberation Tigers of Tamil Eelam (inactive)

Attack scenarios are numerous and opportunities for a maritime strike are almost limitless because of the hundreds of millions of on-loading, off-loading, and handlings of cargo every year. The number of objectives is an imposing assortment of calamitous events. Human casualties, economic loss, political chaos, media impact, and environmental spoilage are some of the possible outcomes. The threat of maritime attacks and terrorism is significant. As noted above, the low incidence of maritime attacks does not mitigate the threat. The concentration of trade flow through a handful of choke points, the range of opportunities and breach points, and the fleet of containers, vessels, and actors in maritime security must also influence policymaking. The impact from a single incident could have enormous foreseen and unforeseen repercussions.

Terrorist Flows by Sea

As already noted, terrorist attacks afloat are rare, but maritime smuggling of terrorist personnel and weapons is common, particularly in and around countries with long insecure maritime borders, such as

- Burma, Thailand, Cambodia, Vietnam, Malaysia, the Philippines, and Indonesia in Southeast Asia;
- Sri Lanka and India;
- Tanzania, Kenya, Somalia, Eritrea, Sudan, Egypt, Saudi Arabia, Yemen, and Oman in East Africa and Arabia;
- West Africa from Senegal to Congo; and
- the Caribbean and the Gulf of Mexico from the southern states of the United States to Venezuela.

Most terrorist smuggling in these areas does not directly lead to a maritime terrorist attack but could smuggle weapons, persons, or money that enable other terrorist attacks.

Table 11.3 Scope of Maritime Terrorists Attacks

Dimensions	Example Characteristics	
Perpetrators	• Al-Qaeda and affiliates • Islamists unaffiliated • Foreign nationalists	• Disgruntled employees • Others
Objectives	• Mass casualties • Port disruptions	• Trade disruptions • Environmental damage
Locations	• Over 360 U.S. ports • 165 foreign trade partners	• Nine key bottlenecks
Targets	• Military vessels • Cargo vessels • Fuel tankers • Ferries or cruise ships	• Ship channels • Port area populations • Port industrial plants • Off-shore platforms
Tactics	• Explosives in suicide boats • Explosives in light aircraft • Ramming with vessels • Ship-launched missiles • Harbor mines	• Underwater swimmers • Unmanned submarines • Exploding fuel tankers • Explosives cargo ships • WMDs in cargo ships

Source: Congressional Research Service.

Table 11.4 Maritime Terrorism Risks

Maritime Terrorism Scenario	Potential Human Consequences	Potential Economic Consequences	Potential Social Consequences
Sinking or disabling a ship in a channel or port	Tens of injuries and deaths among the crew	Tens of millions of dollars in life and injury compensation, repair, and replacement; hundreds of millions of dollars in lost cargo; billions of dollars in short-term business disruption and augmented security	Loss of human capital and changes in consumer behavior
Hijacking a ship and using it to destroy infrastructure	Injuries and deaths among the crew; several hundred civilian casualties	Tens of millions of dollars in repair and replacement; tens of millions of dollars in damaged infrastructure; hundreds of millions of dollars in life and injury compensation	Loss of human capital and changes in consumer behavior

(Continued)

Table 11.4 (Continued)

Maritime Terrorism Scenario	Potential Human Consequences	Potential Economic Consequences	Potential Social Consequences
Using a shipping container as a delivery device for a conventional bomb	Several hundred injuries and deaths	Millions of dollars in damaged infrastructure; millions of dollars in destroyed property; hundreds of millions of dollars in life and injury compensation; $1 billion in short-term business disruptions; billions of dollars in augmented security	Loss of human capital
Using a shipping container as a delivery device for a radiological dispersion device	Tens to hundreds of injuries and deaths	Hundreds of thousands of dollars in contaminated or damaged infrastructure; millions of dollars in contaminated or damaged property; hundreds of millions of dollars in life and injury compensation; billions of dollars in augmented security; tens of billions of dollars in long-term macroeconomic effects	Loss of human capital, changes in consumer behavior, and political consequences
Using a shipping container as a delivery device for a nuclear weapon	50,000–1,000,000 deaths	Billions of dollars in damaged or contaminated infrastructure; tens of billions of dollars in short-term business disruptions and augmented security; hundreds of billions in life and injury compensation, contaminated or damaged property, and long-term macroeconomic effects	Loss of human capital, changes in consumer behavior, and political consequences

Source: Greenberg, Chalk, Willis, Khilko, and Ortiz (2006). Reprinted with permission from RAND Corp.

BOX 11.6

Past Terrorist Attacks at Sea

- From October 7 to October 10, 1985, Palestinian Liberation Front terrorists hijacked an Italian cruise ship (MS *Achille Lauro*) in the Mediterranean on its way from Alexandria to Port Said. They killed a Jewish-American passenger after their demands for the release of 50 Palestinians from Israeli detention and to dock in Tartus, Syria, were unmet. After 2 days of negotiations in Port Said, the hijackers agreed to leave the ship in exchange for safe conduct to Tunisia in an Egyptian commercial airliner, but U.S. fighter aircraft forced the aircraft to land at a U.S. base in Sicily. After a tense standoff between Italian and U.S. authorities, the former took the hijackers into custody and eventually convicted them but allowed their leaders, who had met the aircraft in Egypt, to leave, against U.S. wishes.

- On January 3, 2000, al-Qaeda-sponsored suicide bombers attempted to bring their explosives-laden boat alongside the USS *The Sullivans* (a guided-missile destroyer) while it was visiting Aden Harbor, Yemen, but their boat sank. On October 12, 2000, other bombers detonated explosives on a boat alongside the USS *Cole* (another guided-missile destroyer) in Aden, killing 17 and injuring 39 U.S. sailors.

- On October 23, 2000, two passenger ferries were attacked in the waters of Sri Lanka. Members of the Liberation Tigers of Tamil Eelam (LTTE) used two small crafts armed with explosives to sink one target and seriously damage the second. The attack also resulted in approximately 250 dead and 300 wounded.

- On October 30, 2001, the LTTE struck again in the coastal waters, attacking the oil tanker *Silk Pride*. Five assault crafts took part in the attack inflicting serious damage. Despite the intense blaze, all 25 crew members were rescued.

- On October 6, 2002, near Aden, a suicide explosive boat struck a large French-flagged oil tanker (*Limburg*) off Aden, where it was about to pick up more crude oil after leaving Iran with nearly 400,000 barrels of crude oil. One crewman was killed, and 12 crewmen were injured. A fire broke out, and around 90,000 barrels leaked, but the explosion failed to perforate the inner of the tanker's double walls, so the ship was eventually towed to safety. Insurers tripled their premiums on ships calling

at Aden, and the flow of containers through Aden's terminal fell 93% and caused port revenue to fall $3.8 million per month (Chalk, 2011b, p. 87). Al-Qaeda claimed responsibility.

- On February 27, 2004, Abu Sayyaf Group planted a bomb on the Superferry-14 out of Manila, the Philippines, in an attempt to extort money from the commercial operator, but the small explosion started a fire that killed 118 people and almost sank the ship. In October 2005, the European Commission introduced a new regulation for ship and port security, including new rules (effective July 2007) for the security of domestic ferries.

- On April 24, 2004, Yemeni members of al-Qaeda executed a suicide attack on the Khor Al-Amaya oil terminal in the Persian Gulf. The terrorists used a single small craft loaded with explosives to kill two crew members, wound four onshore security guards, and inflict $40 million in financial losses.

- On January 29, 2010, Israel reported that improvised explosive devices in floating barrels, launched from off shore, had drifted on the coast. They were probably launched by Palestinian Islamic Jihad and Popular Resistance Committees against Israeli patrol vessels.

- On July 28, 2010, a suicide explosive boat struck an oil tanker in the Strait of Hormuz en route to Japan from Qatar. The ship's outer structure was damaged but not perforated, and the true cause was not confirmed for 2 weeks. A new jihadi group, Abdulla Azzam Brigades, claimed responsibility.

Maritime Piracy

Maritime piracy is much riskier than maritime terrorism because maritime piracy is much more frequent and imposes routine costs. The subsections below define and describe the scope of

Past Terrorism on Land Enabled by Maritime Smuggling

- The explosives used in the bombing of the U.S. embassies in Kenya and Tanzania in 1998 probably were imported by a vessel controlled by al-Qaeda.

- On December 14, 1999, an al-Qaeda terrorist (Ahmed Ressam, an Algerian living in Montreal, Canada) drove a car loaded with explosives on to a ferry from Vancouver. He was arrested at Port Angeles, Washington state, after a search by U.S. customs officials called by a suspicious border agent. Ressam probably planned to bomb Los Angeles international airport around the new year of 1999–2000.

- Khalid Sheikh Mohammed, who was arrested in Pakistan in March 2003 before transfer to U.S. detention sites, reportedly told interrogators that he had prospected the shipping of explosives into the United States, hidden in a container of personal computers from Japan.

- In March 2004, the same week of the commuter-train bombing in Madrid, a suicide attack at the Israeli port of Ashdod killed ten Israelis. The *Jerusalem Post* reported that Palestinian operatives might have imported the weapons from Gaza in an undetected, hidden compartment of a shipping container.

- On November 26, 2008, armed terrorists from Pakistan-based Lashkar-e-Taiba landed at the port in Mumbai, India, by private boat, from where they proceeded to kill 101 people at the railway station, a synagogue, from passing cars, and at a hotel.

- Palestinian groups outside of Israel probably have smuggled items into Israel by direct landings from boats and by dropping floating containers offshore, from where they would drift on shore. These containers are probably mostly portable and easily hidden, but some may be as large as barrels, similar to those dropped as sea mines in 2010.

- On September 13, 2011, armed men used a boat from Somalia to access a bungalow on Kiwayu Island, Kenya, near the border with Somalia. Officials suspected that the attackers were affiliated with al-Shabaab, a Somalia-based jihadi terrorist group, but it denied this. A British couple was vacationing at the bungalow. The attackers shot dead David Tebbutt and took his wife Judith hostage to a hideout in Somalia. On March 21, 2012, she was released after her family paid a ransom.

maritime piracy, pirate operations in practice and their geographical distribution, the costs and the frequency of maritime piracy over time, and the practices of counterpiracy.

SCOPE AND DEFINITIONS *Maritime piracy* is any attempt to board a vessel in order to steal or extort for profit. The U.N. effectively separates maritime theft from extortion.

> The term "piracy" encompasses two distinct sorts of offences: the first is robbery or hijacking, where the target of the attack is to steal a maritime vessel or its cargo; the second is kidnapping, where the vessel and crew are threatened until a ransom is paid. (U.N. Office of Drugs and Crime, 2010, p. 193)

The International Maritime Organization's Maritime Safety Committee Circular of 1993 categorized maritime piracy three ways:

1. Low-level armed robbery or assault

2. Medium-level armed robbery and assault

3. Major criminal hijacks

Piracy and terrorism are increasingly intertwined: Terrorists sometimes turn to piracy as one means to fund terrorism; many pirates in Nigeria, Somalia, and Southeast Asia have the ideological predilection to fund jihadi terrorism or to engage in it themselves (Luft & Korin, 2004).

PIRATE OPERATIONS Pirates generally operate in full view of foreign shipping, including navies, while searching for targets. Their small boats are difficult to identify on the open ocean, are difficult to distinguish from fishing vessels, and are not actually committing any crime until they attack.

Pirates generally use small, fast boats (*skiffs*; each carrying half a dozen men) to attack ships within 50 nmi of shore; they generally need a larger boat for operating further off shore. A *mothership* normally tows a fast boat that carries the attackers. Despite the term mothership, it is not a large vessel, just a small boat carrying a dozen or two dozen men, often powered by small engines and sails, indistinguishable from fishing boats until the attack starts. Sometimes motherships tow more than one fast boat or cooperate with each other. Multiple fast ships will confuse the target's crew, whose visibility and room for evasion is limited. The attackers are armed with ubiquitous Soviet-manufactured automatic firearms and rocket-propelled grenades. An attack is normally completed within 30 min.

Pirates are often controlled from shore. Since the 1990s, pirates have used satellite telephones to communicate from ship to shore. They also use commercially available navigation equipment that can direct them anywhere, given a target coordinate and information about current position from the Global Position System. The coincidence of pirates with valuable vessels in more remote seas suggests that some are tipped off by employees with access to the vessel's coordinates (UNODC, 2010, p. 198).

Most successful piracy ends in theft and resale of the cargo, the crew's possessions, the vessel's portable items, or sometimes the vessel itself (in the case of small craft). West African pirates target fuel cargo for illegal sale through the developed infrastructure of Nigeria. Off the Horn of Africa, which lacks Nigeria's infrastructure, most pirates aim at holding a large ship, cargo, and crew for ransom. Pirates target vessels that can be held ransom for large amounts of money. These tend to be large container and tanker ships; small yachts suggest wealthy owners who could be held for ransom, although they are more likely to outpace pirate motherships, given sufficient warning. Shippers can negotiate with the hijackers via the hijacked vessel's communications systems or the pirate's satellite telephones. Ransoms are normally paid in cash and delivered physically to the hijackers by an intermediary. Sometimes the ransom is dropped by parachute from an aircraft. Rarely, the pirates will accept payment to a trusted third party. The pirates normally honor agreements to release their prizes for ransom, but they usually release a vessel, cargo, and crew only after stripping them of anything valuable and portable. The vessel and cargo may be damaged, too, during the attack, the subsequent thievery, or long periods under hijack without proper maintenance.

GEOGRAPHICAL DISTRIBUTION Pirates are naturally attracted to any of the choke points or bottlenecks described earlier but tend to concentrate in five areas. (see Map 11.4).

1. Measured over the last couple decades, the most concentrated piracy has occurred in the Gulf of Aden and off the Horn of Africa. About 10% of shipping passes through these seas, although some shippers have chosen the less risky but slower route around the Cape of Good Hope between the Indian and Atlantic Oceans. According to the International Maritime Bureau, the number of pirate attacks off the Horn of Africa doubled from 111 in 2008 to 217 in 2009 and peaked in 2010 but fell to 237 in 2011 and to 75 in 2012, thanks to sustained counterpiracy. Nevertheless, Somali pirates still held eight ships and 127 hostages at the end of 2012. Somalia is the main national source of the pirates in these seas.

2. About 10% of shipping passes the Gulf of Guinea off West Africa. Piracy there is less frequent than off the Horn of Africa but more successful now, thanks to international attention on Somalia. In 2012, West African pirates attacked ships 62 times and threatened 966 sailors, compared to 851 in Somali waters. West African pirates hijacked 10 ships and took 207 new hostages, of which five were killed, according to the International Maritime Bureau. Nigeria is the largest and most populous state in West Africa and the main national source of pirates in the region.

3. In the early 2000s, most piracy risks were concentrated in the seas between Vietnam, Indonesia, and Malaysia, particularly the Malacca Straits between Malaysia and the Philippines, where about 50% of shipping passes. In 2012, 81 pirate attacks were reported in Southeast Asia, 31 in the rest of the Far East.

4. The Caribbean Sea and the sea off Panama is a hazardous and poorly policed area rife with short-range piracy.

5. The Bay of Bengal is another poorly policed area, opening up on the Indian Ocean. Bangladesh is the main national source there.

COSTS From 2003 to 2008, the global economic cost of piracy was $1 billion to $16 billion per year. From 2009 to 2012, it was somewhere between $7 billion and $12 billion per year. Most of these costs relate to controlling the risks rather than the direct costs of pirate attacks. In controlling the risks, shippers pay additional costs, such as insurance, armed guards, antiboarding materials, defensive weapons, extra fuel costs due to higher speeds and evasive routes in riskier waters, and the extra operational costs of longer journeys to avoid riskier waters.

The cost of ransoms is difficult to calculate because shippers and pirates tend to underreport. In 2010, the reported average and median ransoms were around $4 million to $5 million, with a high

Somali Piracy

BOX 11.8

Pirates from one of the world's poorest countries, Somalia, are holding to ransom ships from some of the richest, despite patrols by the world's most powerful navies. Almost all piracy in the Gulf of Aden and off the Horn of Africa originates in Somalia, a failing state since the 1980s. Central government finally collapsed in 1991, leaving an independent state of Somaliland to the north, an effectively autonomous province of Puntland, and a failed state of Somalia in the southwest, where Somalia's capital and largest port, Mogadishu, is located. In 2012, international forces secured Mogadishu and drove south, but most of the nominal territory of Somalia remains insecure.

Somali pirates numbered about 1,400 as of 2009. They are concentrated in Puntland and south-central Mudug. The lowest ranked pirates are easily replaced with recruits from the majority destitute population, which includes 40,000 internally displaced Somalis. A pirate earns somewhere from $6,000 to $10,000 for each $1 million in ransom paid. Available data suggests that about 30% of ransoms go to the pirates, 10% to local militia, 10% to local elders and officials, and 20% to the financier. The period of hijack ranges from 6 days to 6 months, with an average around 2 months. Ransoms total somewhere between $50 million and $100 million. From 2008 to 2009, insurance premiums for vessels in these waters jumped from $20,000 to $150,000.

In 2004, the International Maritime Board warned all vessels to travel further than 50 nmi off the Somali coast. In 2005, it raised the specification to 100 nmi. By 2006, some Somali pirates were operating as far as 350 nmi from Somalia, into the Red Sea and the Indian Ocean.

From 2007 to 2008, piracy shifted from mainly southern Somali waters to the Gulf of Aden. By 2009, some Somali pirates were attacking ships more than 1,000 nmi from Somalia.

Some shippers accepted the risks of operating closer to shore in return for faster journeys while the World Food Program continued to ship 30,000–40,000 MT of food aid every month into the Horn of Africa. (By late 2008, 43% of Somalis were dependent on food aid, of which 95% arrived by sea.) In late 2008, the World Food Program required naval escorts from European Union or Canadian forces while some Somali pirates consented to honor humanitarian aid (such cargos would garner lower ransoms anyway) (UNODC, 2010).

Since December 2008, the European Union Naval Force Somalia (EU NAVFOR – Atalanta) and the North Atlantic Treaty Organization's Combined Task Force 151 have been the main international antipiracy forces off Somalia, but they patrol more than 1,000,000 sq mi of ocean. Somali pirates now operate in a total sea space of approximately 2,500,000 sq nmi (about the size of the continental United States). Nevertheless, relative to prior enforcement, naval impact was great; up to August 2009, they seized or destroyed 40 pirate vessels and rendered 235 suspected pirates. The Indian Navy extended its patrols from the Indian Ocean into the Gulf of Aden. Since January 2009, the Chinese Navy has maintained at least two frigates in the Gulf of Aden. By 2012, up to 30 vessels from 22 navies were patrolling the Gulf of Aden.

These naval forces operate with fewer restrictions on the use of force than their

(Continued)

(Continued)

predecessors. In November 2008, an Indian warship in the Gulf of Aden destroyed a pirate mothership. In April 2009, French marines rescued four French hostages from their yacht and detained three pirates, although one hostage was killed. On April 12, 2009, U.S. Navy personnel shot to death three pirates and freed the captain of the *Maersk Alabama* from a lifeboat under tow. In December 2009, an Indian navy helicopter with marines helped to deter hijackers from boarding a Norwegian ship. In January 2012, U.S. forces freed a Danish hostage.

Meanwhile, states have agreed on international responses beyond naval force. In December 2008, the U.N. Security Council Resolution 1851 established the International Contact Group on Piracy off the Coast of Somalia, chaired by the United States in 2013 and the E.U. in 2014.

Also in December 2008, the U.S. National Security Council issued the Partnership and Action Plan for Countering Piracy Off the Horn of Africa and established the Counter-Piracy Steering Group, co-led by the Departments of State and Defense, with representatives from the Departments of Justice, Homeland Security, and Treasury and the U.S. Maritime Administration and the U.S. Agency for International Development. The U.S. Partnership and Action Plan has included a Maritime Security Sector Reform framework.

The Contact Group now boasts 62 states and 31 international organizations and maritime trade associations as participants. The members volunteer to any of five working groups. Working Group 1 (chaired by Britain) promotes international military coordination and the development of regional capacity for maritime security. Working Group 2 (Denmark) works on legal issues. Working Group 3 (South Korea) helps to develop commercial shipping's awareness and protections. Working Group 4 (Egypt) works on public awareness and support for counterpiracy. Working Group 5 (Italy) coordinates the countering of pirate financing. The Contact Group claims a "marked reduction" in piracy; successfully pirated ships off Somalia fell from 47 in 2009 and 2010 to 25 in 2011 and five in 2012.

Local stabilization and capacity building are solutions to the root causes or enabling conditions of piracy in Somalia. On April 23, 2009, a European donor conference raised $160 million for security sector reform in Somalia. In February 2012, Britain hosted an international conference on the future of Somalia, which reiterated that force alone could not solve the problem and advocated for more support of local communities. In August 2012, central authorities in Mogadishu adopted a new provisional constitution, legislature, and president and, with international military support, started to expand their control outside the capital.

of $9.5 million. By 2012, the average and median were about the same, but the high had reached $12 million. Ransoms totaled around $135 million in each of 2011 and 2012.

Delivering the ransom and recovering the vessel is costly in itself. In some cases, shippers have procured a light aircraft to drop the ransom on the ship or near the pirates' base. The ship must be recovered, cleaned, and repaired. The cargo may be spoiled. In the worst cases, all is lost. For instance, on July 8, 2013, the Malaysian-flagged and -owned M/V ALBEDO, which in November 2010 had been pirated with 15 crewmen aboard, sank at anchor off the coast of Haradhere, Somalia.

Map 11.4 World Maritime Piracy, 2008–2009

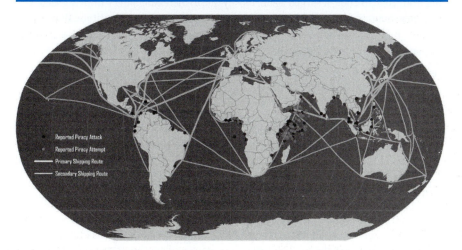

Source: Rodrique et al. (2013); ICC International Maritime Bureau; encoding by William Moreto. Reprinted with permission from Dr. Jean-Paul Rodrigue, Department of Global Studies and Geography, Hofstra University.

Note: Boundaries depicted on map may not be fully recognized international boundaries.

The human costs are confined to the few crew who are unfortunately killed or detained. Fortunately, these rates have declined in recent years but are still terrible for those directly affected. In 2011, eight crew members were killed, 802 crew members were taken hostage afloat on 45 vessels, and 15 were kidnapped (taken ashore). In 2012, six were killed, 585 taken hostage on 28 vessels, and 26 kidnapped. In 2013, one was killed, 304 taken hostage on 12 vessels, and 36 kidnapped. In 2014, 442 were taken hostage. If the crew are lucky enough to survive their abduction, they likely will need rest, treatment, and compensation, although the flexibility of crew contracts often leaves the shipper with few obligations (ICC International Maritime Bureau, 2015, p. 11).

FREQUENCY Piracy is an underreported problem because of the shipper's desire to hide vulnerability and costs from stakeholders. Worldwide frequency of piracy increased in the early 1990s, mostly due to increased sources from China and Indonesia. In the late 1990s, austerity, competition, and automation encouraged ship owners to reduce crews and defenses. Piracy peaked in 2000 and remained high in that decade (around 350 to 450 events per year, according to the International Maritime Organization). Official reactions to 9/11 encouraged states to divert resources away from counterpiracy to counterterrorism. Many states declined into further instability during that decade. Pirates found their environments more permissive and also found weapons and equipment more accessible (Chalk, 2009). Global incidents peaked at 445 in 2010, a peak last seen in 2003, although still short of the peak of 469 in 2000. The frequency then declined as official and commercial focus returned. The International Maritime Bureau reported 439 vessels attacked and 45 hijacked in 2011, 297 attacked and 28 hijacked in 2012, 264 attacked and 12 hijacked in 2013, and 245 attacked and 21 hijacked in 2014.

In the 1990s, sources surged most rapidly from Indonesia; sources surged in Bangladesh, India, and Malaysia too. Piracy dropped by half in 2005, thanks to international responses in Southeast Asia and South Asia, but from 2008 to 2009, it surged again, mostly due to increasing piracy from Somalia, a persistent failed state. Sources surged in Nigeria too (data source: International Maritime Bureau).

Counterpiracy

Countermeasures include stricter laws and law enforcement, naval enforcement, defensive options for ships, and activities to counter the wider pirate networks, as explained in the subsections below.

LEGAL RESPONSES International norms and laws have proscribed maritime piracy for a long time, including the Paris Declaration of 1856, the Geneva Convention of 1958, the U.N. Convention on the Law of the Sea of 1982, and the Convention for the Suppression of Unlawful Acts Against the Safety of Maritime Navigation (SUA) of 1988, which allows any state to detain, extradite, and prosecute maritime terrorists and pirates. One-hundred-and-fifty countries are party to SUA.

While the norms and laws are strong on paper, they are difficult to enforce in practice. International law constrains an outside state's right to intervene. Mackubin Owens (2009) has argued that "a sovereign state has the right to strike the territory of another if that state is not able to curtail the activities of *latrunculi* (Latin for 'little robbers' but also refers to pirates and other outlaws)" (n.p.), but no state has exercised this right in decades.

Pirates are based in unstable or weakly governed areas where the judicial system tends to be weak. For instance, international authorities still regard Somalia as unable to try pirates properly. Outside states can prosecute pirates, but democracies, which have been most engaged in countering piracy at the source, have honored human-rights legislation or the detainee's claims of asylum to the extent that most pirates have been released after arrest without any indictment. For instance, for many years, European naval forces were advised by home governments that rendition to states around the Indian Ocean, each of which had unreliable human rights, would violate the European Human Rights Act.

Even if the judiciary is strong, practical difficulties remain. Pirates are difficult to prosecute unless caught in the act. Witnesses are difficult to bring to court. Sailors are keen to return to work, particularly because most are not compensated for their time as hostages or in court; most sailors are from developing countries and spend most of their time at sea without a mailing address. Given the diverse nationalities of sailors and pirates, the court often requires as many translators as witnesses.

In the late 2000s, outside states started to act more responsibly. In late 2008, France started to send pirates for prosecution in France. In March 2009, Kenya agreed to try pirates in return for help from the European Union with judicial reform. In September 2010, international naval forces handed over to Kenya nine Somali citizens who had hijacked a vessel, MV *Magellan Star*, in the Gulf of Aden. In June 2013, a Kenyan court sentenced each of them to 5 years in prison.

In April 2009, after U.S. naval forces shot to death a gang of pirates holding the crew from the U.S.-flagged *Maersk Alabama*. One lone pirate was captured and brought to New York to face trial. In February 2011, he was sentenced to 33 years in prison. By March 2012, the United States had prosecuted 28 Somali pirates. The United States, like many states, maintains that the flag state should prosecute the pirate but has arranged for Somali pirates to serve out their sentences in Somalia, thanks to international military support of a new provisional constitution and government in Somalia in 2012.

During the February 2012 London Conference on Piracy and Somalia, Britain pledged more than $1 million and found staff from the British Serious Organized Crime Agency to establish a Regional Anti-Piracy Prosecutions and Intelligence Coordination Centre (RAPPICC) in the Seychelles. The temporary offices opened on June 1, 2012, the permanent building in January 2013, including a fusion center for coordinating international judicial information and enforcement and a 20-person detention facility for conducting interviews. By 2013, more than 1,000 pirates were in detention in 20 countries, of which most had been or would be convicted.

▶ Port Security

Source: Container Security Initiative, 2006–2011 Strategic Plan; U.S. Customs and Border Protection.

NAVAL ENFORCEMENT Ships are supposed to travel through national waters patrolled by national coast guards or international shipping lanes patrolled by multinational naval forces. The main international naval force is the **Combined Maritime Forces**, operationally commanded from U.S. Naval Support Activity Bahrain, commanded by a U.S. Navy vice admiral, who also serves as commander of U.S. Navy Central Command and the U.S. Navy Fifth Fleet, with a British Navy commodore as deputy commander. Other staff roles are filled from personnel from member nations.

At of the end of 2013, the Combined Maritime Forces included 29 member nations (Australia, Bahrain, Belgium, Canada, Denmark, France, Germany, Greece, Italy, Japan, Jordan, South Korea, Kuwait, Malaysia, the Netherlands, New Zealand, Norway, Pakistan, the Philippines, Portugal, Saudi Arabia, the Seychelles, Singapore, Spain, Thailand, Turkey, the United Arab Emirates, the United Kingdom, and the United States).

The Combined Maritime Forces form three principle combined task forces: CTF-150 (maritime security and counterterrorism), CTF-151 (counterpiracy), and CTF-152 (Arabian Gulf security and cooperation). However, these CTFs are small—around half a dozen warships—while their area of operations is vast—about 2,500,000 sq mi—and their operations are curbed by law and the practicalities of proving piracy.

Nevertheless, CTF-151 sometimes can identify pirates. For instance, on October 11, 2013, Somali pirates exchanged gunfire with a supertanker; on October 14, the same pirates attacked a Spanish fishing vessel. CTF-151 tracked the pirates over 500 mi away with signals intelligence, arrested nine men, and sank their two small boats. International naval counterpiracy surged in 2009 off Somalia in response to new international forums and national commitments, but even there, the area of operation is vast and the forces are small.

The Gulf of Aden is a well-patrolled channel, although highly exposed to pirates in the Indian Ocean and Horn of Africa. The narrow channel through the Straits of Hormuz is easiest to patrol, although the threats there are more military and terrorist than pirate. The Straits of Malacca have a well-patrolled channel and are tightly contained by Malaysian and Indonesian land but exposed at either end to traffic from the India Ocean and South China Sea. Other oceans with pirates are barely patrolled at all.

SHIP DEFENSES

Requirements. Vessels, even in international waters, must comply with regulations and guidance referred to, in American English, as **best management practices**. Issued by international authorities, national authorities, trade associations, or owners, their intent is to specifically prevent piracy. The U.N. International Maritime Organization is the highest authority. It requires all vessels of 500 GT or larger to acquire a Ship Security Alert System, which allows the crew to send a covert signal to shore in case of piracy. The U.N. Office on Drugs and Crime is also effectively involved.

Some vessels are required to obey national regulations and guidance, particularly if they are to take the national flag or travel into national waters. The U.S. Coast Guard has issued a Maritime Security Directive that is more rigorous than any international regulation. The U.S. Maritime Administration (MARAD, part of the Department of Transportation) issues area-specific advice. The U.S. Merchant Marine Academy trains midshipmen in counterpiracy.

The best defense for smaller vessels is to outpace the pirate vessels. The larger ships, despite their bulk, are more vulnerable; their crews are surprisingly small and have become smaller with more automation and reliability over the last 2 decades. Ship owners are incentivized to keep their costs down and have traditionally acquired for their ships no defenses against pirates.

> Some in the shipping industry have been unwilling to make basic investments that would render their crews and cargoes less vulnerable to attack. Approximately 20 percent of all ships off the Horn of Africa are not employing best management practices or taking proper security precautions. Unsurprisingly, these 20 percent account for the overwhelming number of successfully pirated ships. We have intensified our efforts to encourage commercial vessels to adopt best management practices. (Shapiro, 2012, n.p.)

Defeating Boarders. Behavioral best management practices include

- seeking secure national waters or internationally designated shipping lanes;

- traveling at full speed through high-risk areas (ships otherwise operate at much less than full speed in order to save fuel and prevent wear);

- reporting location and progress to military authorities;

- seeking a naval escort; and

- forming a convoy with other vessels.

Closed-circuit television cameras can be installed to monitor areas of the ship that are otherwise invisible to the aboard crew. Additional lookouts on bridge wings help to spot threats on the sides. The ship could change course rapidly to prevent pirates coming alongside or to capsize the pirate vessel, although large vessels have little agility to change course significantly within the minutes that an attack might last.

The bridge should be armored against small arms so that the crew can keep the ship under full control during the attack. Crew should be provided with body armour and helmets. Side ladders or nets should be taken up once the vessel is underway, although pirates could launch grappling hooks. Physical barriers such as razor wire or electric wire are cheap and can prevent pirates from climbing from the sides onto the deck. Locked entryways could prevent entry, although pirates could shoot off the locks, and any such defense could be considered a provocation that encourages the pirates to be trigger-happy. A *citadel* or *refuge* (usually the engine room) could be provided with extra access controls; it could be provided with master ship controls and emergency supplies so that the crew could continue to control the ship's movements even after pirates come aboard, although pirates still can steal from open areas.

Fighting Back. Preparations to defeat an attack are more expensive and controversial. Large vessels already carry water dischargers for cleaning or fighting fires that could be turned on pirates, although operators would be exposed to the pirate's weapons unless protected behind some sort of shield. Some water cannons have been installed closer to the sides of the ship, behind protection from where they can be brought to bear on pirate ships alongside. Heated water has proved most effective at deterring pirates. Slippery foam could hinder the pirate's attempts to board. Acoustic guns are additional nonlethal options. In December 2008, the Chinese crew of *Zhenhua 4* fought off pirates with fire hoses and incendiary devices improvised from fuel containers.

Increasingly, operators are willing to hire armed guards for high-risk vessels. These personnel are best armed with high-powered, large caliber firearms and scopes with which they can outrange the typical assault rifles carried by pirates. Body armour helps to protect them while they are targeting the pirates. Usually, the visible presence of prepared, armed personnel deters pirates. Otherwise, the guards can escalate by firing warning shots to demonstrate their greater capabilities at long range. Night-vision equipment helps to maintain their superior range at night, although pirates increasingly use the same equipment.

The U.S. government has effectively encouraged private operators to acquire armed guards.

> The reality is that international naval forces simply might not be there to respond. The problem of piracy is one that can't simply be solved by national governments. Therefore, we have also supported industry's use of additional measures to ensure their security—such as the employment of armed security teams. To date, not a single ship with Privately Contracted Armed Security Personnel aboard has been pirated. *Not a single one.* . . . At the State Department, we have encouraged countries to permit commercial vessels to carry armed teams. However, we do note that this is a new area, in which some practices, procedures, and regulations are still being developed. We are working through the Contact Group and the International Maritime Organization or IMO on these issues. For instance, we have advised that armed security teams be placed under the full command of the captain of the ship. The captain then is in control of the situation and is the one

to authorize the use of any force. Last September [2011], we were encouraged to see language adopted by the IMO that revised the guidance to both flag States and ship operators and owners to establish the ship's master as being in command of these teams. (Shapiro, 2012, n.p.)

As of 2015, no vessel with armed guards has been hijacked. However, increased use of force deters some pirates while prompting others to be vengeful or trigger-happy. On April 14, 2009, Somali pirates announced by radio, "If they have started killing us, we have decided to take revenge and kill any American or French crew of passenger members of ships we capture fishing in our seas" (Nincic, 2012, n.p.). In 2010, Somali pirates attacked two U.S. warships. On February 22, 2011, pirates shot to death four U.S. hostages on their yacht after the U.S. Navy detained two pirate negotiators.

Countering the Wider Networks. The U.N., the Contact Group, and states agree that they must reduce the enabling conditions of piracy, not just the pirates at the point of attack, by stabilizing the countries where they are based, building local capacity to counter piracy, and pursuing the wider network of people who control, support, benefit from, or finance piracy. The United States has led funding for such initiatives.

> Our approach to combating piracy has also taken on new dimensions. In the effort to combat piracy, we are now targeting pirate ringleaders and their networks. While expanding security and prosecuting and incarcerating pirates captured at sea is essential, we also recognize that the pirates captured at sea are often low-level operatives. Their leaders and facilitators are ashore in Somalia and elsewhere relatively unaffected. After an intensive review of our strategy, Secretary Clinton last year approved a series of recommendations which, taken together, constitute a new strategic approach. A focus on pirate networks is at the heart of our strategy. (Shapiro, 2012, n.p.)

The current U.S. counterpiracy strategy emphasizes

- a multilateral approach (cooperating with other governments to enforce international law and build local capacity),

- military enforcement of international law,

- making the private sector more aware of best management practices,

- judicial prosecution of pirates and related criminals,

- stabilizing the areas where pirates proliferate, and

- targeting the wider pirate networks. (Kelly, 2012)

SUMMARY

In summary, maritime commerce is the major form of conveyance of the global economy and source of concern for security authorities. Maritime trade transport amounts to 80% to 90%

of world trade (OECD, 2003, p. 7; Flynn, 2004a, p. 84). The sea-borne supply chain has the greatest number of breach points and the potential for the most serious damage. The more critical the port, the more likely it is to be located at the intersection of vital transportation and communication hubs and high-population centers. For many reasons, ports can be prime targets for terrorist attacks. Moreover, the vast, unmonitored, and undergoverned areas of the maritime system are another reason terrorists might find maritime targets attractive.

The seas cover 130,000,000 mi of the earth's surface. No sole state or hegemon is powerful enough to command it. The international maritime supply chain is a complex web of sea-lanes that intersect at thousands of points. The maritime labor force offers an international cast of seafarers, facilitators, cargo handlers, port workers, and intermediaries. Within this matrix of global commerce is this stateless, transnational space, often beyond the jurisdictional reach and control of politicians, law enforcement authorities, intelligence agencies, and international regimes and conventions. It is an environment open to exploitation by terrorists and crime. The major security concern is that terrorists will not only exploit this potential successfully but also do so with dramatic economic and political effect. Therefore, ports can be either gateways into foreign territory, targets for terrorists, or loci of plunder and points of entry for contraband for both terrorists and criminals. Attack scenarios are multiple and varied.

In order for a security strategy and framework to be successful, it must not only neutralize the vulnerabilities but also enable commerce. The uniformity, velocity, and anonymity of containerized traffic make the dilemma more formidable. The cargo container offers terrorists an opportunity to inflict catastrophic damage to the commercial infrastructure or exploit it in criminal ways. As the volume of trade increases precipitously and tensions increase in various places around the Earth, there seems to be little positive outlook for any abatement of the risk and challenge to legitimate authorities to keep pace. This is particularly true as trafficking becomes more profitable and the underground trade routes become more durable.

These conditions oftentimes lend themselves to a global maritime trade system that serves illicit activity as much as it serves legitimate players. Part of the dilemma is that an open trading system is essential to national-security policies as it is to those who seek to undermine legitimate interests. The growth of Asian and Pacific economies will only compound future problems. Shipping along the Asian Pacific is densely concentrated along the coasts and through straits before letting out to open ocean transit. A denser, less insulated web of commerce allows for more leakage between legitimate and illegitimate actors and cargo (Jarmon, 2014). These trends culminate with a scenario that is ripe with opportunity for both sides of the law.

In order to address the systemic dilemma of effective security and trade facilitation, the United States relies on the layered approach to maritime security. Programs such as the Customs-Trade Partnership Against Terrorism, Automated Targeting System, Container Security Initiative, and the 24-Hour Advanced Manifest Rule are a sweeping filtering regimen of screening, scanning, and intrusive and nonintrusive inspection to identify and isolate potentially dangerous cargos. Augmenting the core strategy is a list of programs and initiatives that establish funding mechanisms, interoperational and cooperation activities, worker verification processes, multinational agreements, vessel-tracking systems, and required planning, training, and preparedness exercises.

Although the incidence of maritime terrorism is low, the opportunities are many, and the threat is serious. A high-impact incident at a major port, particularly if it is at one of the key strategic choke points, could have devastating consequences on a regional economy and possibly the global system. These are great enticements for any terrorist group seeking to spread destruction and panic and/or to exploit a political opportunity. Politically motivated maritime attacks have become rare. Economic gain has become the driver of criminal activity at sea. As the trend grows, antipiracy measures become more a serious issue for maritime security.

Obstacles to prosecuting a war against piracy are substantial. The laws pertaining to sovereign rights allow corrupt states to harbor pirates and even support their activity. Pursuing, apprehending, and trying pirates across international boundaries and jurisdictional divides is problematic in an environment lacking effective global governance. The current strategy is to urge private operators to invest in their own security by installing defense weapons, such as water cannons, and hiring **privately contracted armed security**. Meanwhile, governments work to attack the source causes of piracy. This means not solely focusing upon the point of attack but also attempting to stabilize the conditions within frail and corrupt states where piracy finds safe harbor and expands. Countering the wider networks that enable piracy is an evolving solution but also a longer term one.

FINAL CASE STUDY

How Can Container Security Be Improved?

Stephen Flynn

Americans remain exposed to the possibility that a ship, truck, or train will one day import a 40-ft cargo container in which terrorists have hidden a dirty bomb or nuclear weapon.

Both the Bush and Obama administrations maintain that they have in place satisfactory safeguards for managing this risk. Importers are required to report the contents of their containers to customs inspectors 1 day before the boxes are loaded on ships bound for the United States. The Department of Homeland Security's National Targeting Center then reviews the data, checking against other intelligence to determine which boxes may pose a threat. A fraction of a percent of the containers destined for the United States are inspected at cooperating foreign ports, with other containers that are deemed to be a high risk inspected after they have entered the United States. More than 95% of containers are released into the

U.S. economy without anyone subjecting their contents to a nonintrusive inspection.

This approach has two serious flaws. First, it presumes that the U.S. government has good enough counterterrorism intelligence to reliably discern which containers are suspicious and which are not. But the ongoing terrorist threat demonstrates that officials often lack such specific tactical intelligence. And supporting customs inspectors, who must make the first assessment of risk, is not a priority for the intelligence agencies. Inspectors must rely on their experience in spotting anomalies—a company that claims to be exporting bananas from Latvia, for example.

Second, determined terrorists can easily take advantage of the knowledge that customs inspectors routinely designate certain shipments as low risk. A container frequently makes 10 or more stops between its factory of origin and the vessel carrying it to American shores. Many of the way stations are in poorly policed parts of the world. Because name-brand companies like Wal-Mart and General Motors are widely known to be considered low risk, terrorists need only to stake out their shipment routes and exploit the weakest points to introduce a weapon of mass destruction. A terrorist cell posing as a legal shipping company for more than 2 years or a terrorist truck driver hauling goods from a well-known shipper can also be confident of being perceived as low risk.

So what needs to be done? We need to harness new technologies that are capable of routinely scanning the contents of containers and securely transmitting those images to inspectors in importing jurisdictions who are operating remotely. This can be done for all outbound goods by embedding this technology within maritime terminal operations within global ports.

Even in the face of the worst-case scenario whereby a terrorist group succeeds in shipping a dirty bomb in a box, the database of these images could help to safeguard the resilience of the global trade system. It accomplishes that by serving as a kind of black box that provides officials with an invaluable forensic tool for identifying how and where security was breached. That information could help prevent politicians from reacting spasmodically to close ports and border crossings, thereby freezing the entire global container system after an incident.

An additional goal should be to find ways to ensure that terrorists do not breach containers before shipments arrive at loading ports. Sensors should be installed inside containers in order to track their movements, detect any infiltration, and discern the presence of radioactive material. Where boxes are loaded, certified, independent inspectors should verify that companies have followed adequate protocols to ensure that legitimate and authorized goods are being shipped.

Taken together, these recommendations will require new investments and an extraordinary degree of international cooperation. But increased container security will not only help the United States prevent terrorism, it will also help all countries reduce theft, stop the smuggling of drugs and humans, crack down on tariff evasion, and improve export controls. What's more, such a program would require a tiny faction of the capital that would almost certainly be lost if the global container-shipping system were shut down after an attack.

Container security is a complex problem with enormous stakes. American officials insist that existing programs have matters well in hand. But we cannot afford to take these perky reassurances at face value while the same officials fail to embrace promising technologies and approaches.

Dr. Stephen Flynn is a professor of political science and founding director of the Center for Resilience Studies at Northeastern University. In 2014, he was appointed to serve as member of the Homeland Security Science and Technology Advisory Council. Before joining the faculty at Northeastern University, Dr. Flynn served as president of the Center for National Policy. Prior to that he spent a decade as a senior fellow for national security studies at the Council on Foreign Relations.

This chapter has

- Described the scope of maritime security
  - Vastness of the seas and lack of governance
  - Immensity of trade and ubiquity of the cargo container
  - Array of breach points in the maritime supply chain
  - Sizeable and expanding labor force

- Described port security
  - Layered approach to maritime and port security
  - Legislation, programs, and multinational accords

- Described cargo security, including
  - safe, trusted shippers,
  - manifest rules,
  - container security,
  - smart boxes, and
  - inspections at ports.

- Reviewed maritime terrorist attacks

  - Modes of attack and motives
  - Consequences of an attack on a strategic choke point
  - Frequency and likelihood compared to land-based attacks
  - Challenges and appeal to terrorists in launching a maritime attack

- Reviewed maritime terrorist flows

- Defined maritime piracy

- Explained how piracy works in practice

- Assessed the costs of piracy

- Reviewed the frequency of piracy

- Explained the geographical distribution of piracy

- Explained how to counter piracy, principally by

  - legal responses,
  - naval enforcement,
  - ship defenses, and
  - countering the wider networks.

KEY TERMS

QUESTIONS AND EXERCISES

1. What are the features and attributes of the maritime supply chain that make it open to exploitation by terrorists groups and criminal organizations?

2. What are the distinctions in screening, scanning, and inspection, and how do they work to create a layered security approach to maritime trade?

3. What are the strengths of the C-TPAT program and the SAFE Framework, and what are their vulnerabilities?

4. Identify the primary maritime choke points and explain what threat they harbor for the global economy.

5. The Container Security Initiative is part of the layered security scheme. What are the diplomatic issues it raises? What is meant by *cascading events* when discussing the potentials of a major terrorist incident?

6. Despite the broad range of targets and opportunities to launch a maritime terrorist attack, why have there been so relatively few?

7. Why would a terrorist group consider a maritime attack as opposed to an attack against a land-based target?

8. What is the definition of piracy, and what are the two types according to objectives?

9. What is the difference between the Container Security Initiative and the Smart Box Initiative?

10. What is the difference between maritime terrorist attacks and flows?

11. Why did maritime piracy increase in the years after 2000?

12. Why are the Gulf of Aden and the Indian Ocean the riskiest territories with respect to piracy?

13. Why are the known costs of piracy underestimated?

14. Why are laws against piracy difficult to enforce?

15. Why is naval enforcement of counterpiracy practically difficult?

16. What are the dilemmas and trade-offs in preparing a ship against piracy?

17. What do officials mean when referring to "countering a wider network"?

12

AVIATION SECURITY

On September 11, 2001, terrorists sponsored by al-Qaeda hijacked four planes and killed almost 3,000 people, most of them in the World Trade Center, New York. The event exposed inferior air security authorities, procedures, and technologies in America than in other developed countries. From foundation in late 2001 through 2010, the U.S. Transport Security Administration (TSA) spent roughly $14 billion in more than 20,900 transactions with dozens of contractors. Sometimes, the contracts were unambiguously regrettable, as illustrated by the brief acquisition of unproven explosives chemical sniffers ("puffers"). In 2009, the U.S. Government Accountability Office (GAO, 2009a) stated that the TSA had "not conducted a risk assessment or cost–benefit analyses, or established quantifiable performance measures" (p. 22) on its new technologies. "As a result, TSA does not have assurance that its efforts are focused on the highest priority security needs" (p. 22). Nevertheless, spending on technology remained high. For 2011, the TSA required $1.3 billion for airport screening technologies.

SCOPE

Aviation refers to artificial flight. **Civilian aviation** covers commercial transportation of cargo by air, commercial carriage of passengers by air, privately owned and operated aircraft, and all associated infrastructure, such as airfields and service and support facilities.

About 28,000 flights take off from the United States per day, accounting for half of global commercial air traffic. In a year, commercial flights carried about 600 million people and 10,000,000 T of air freight within the United States or between the United States and another country.

- In 2011, DHS counted as aviation infrastructure: 19,576 general airports (including heliports), 211,450 general aviation

Learning Objectives and Outcomes

At the end of this chapter, you should be able to understand

- The scope of aviation security

- The threats to aviation

- How to provide aviation security

aircraft, 599 airports certified to serve commercial flights—including 459 federalized commercial airports (Guam is most remote to the continental United States).

- At the 459 federalized airports, 43,000 Transportation Security Officers and 450 Explosives Detection Dogs from the U.S. TSA work at more than 700 security checkpoints and 7,000 baggage screening points.

- In 2006 (the last year for which numbers are available), the TSA screened 708,400,522 passengers on domestic flights and international flights coming into the United States. This averages out to over 1.9 million passengers per day. (Newsome, 2014, p. 322)

HAZARDS AND THREATS

The threats to aviation are categorized below as accidents, thefts, sovereign states, and terrorism.

Accidents

Air accidents make up a specialized subject across engineering, industrial psychology, and policy science, for which this book has insufficient space, but the risks of air accidents should be acknowledged here as low. Compare this to road traffic accidents: Air safety is rigorously regulated and inspected, whereas individual car owners and drivers effectively regulate their own safety, outside of infrequent and comparatively superficial independent inspections. Consequently, an average aircraft flight is much less likely to cause fatality than an average car journey. According to data from the U.S. Centers for Disease Control, fatalities compute at about 0.00001 per flight. In 2013, three billion passenger journeys suffered just 210 fatalities—a rate of 0.00000007 per flight. Yet the fatalities of air travel seem large because an aircraft typically carries more passengers than a car carries.

Air accidents, like any accidents, can be caused by some sort of material failure or human error, most of which are well understood by now, although impossible to eliminate entirely (at least in a cost-effective way).

Unmanned Aerial Vehicles

Hazards to aircraft include other aircraft, birds, weather, and foreign objects (such as airborne volcanic ash). A more recent and uncertain hazard is the unmanned aerial vehicle (UAV), whose technologies and regulations are still evolving rapidly. Since the 1990s, UAVs have become accessible and useful enough as to become routine acquisitions by official actors, from law enforcers to emergency managers, particularly for surveillance but also for carriage or military attacks. Some of these UAVs are as large as passenger aircraft and can loiter in the air for days.

UAVs tend to have higher accident rates than manned aircraft due to the difficulties of piloting aircraft remotely, the potential for failure in the remote link, and the nonreactiveness of a UAV on a preprogrammed or default flight plan. UAVs are generally restricted from altitudes or areas occupied by manned aircraft, but faulty or poorly controlled UAVs could stray into the path of manned aircraft. Moreover, UAVs could be deliberately directed into other aircraft.

More concern is being raised about privately operated UAVs than official UAVs. Toy remote-controlled aircraft are cheap enough and easy enough to operate as to be accessible to almost anyone. They typically measure only a few feet in diameter and weigh less than 10 lbs but could catastrophically damage a cockpit or engine. Currently, in the United States, UAVs can be legally operated under 400 ft and at least 5 mi from restricted airspaces. Regulations on their use are being relaxed in pursuit of the economic or social benefits, such as a real-estate agent who wants to survey property from the air. In 2012, the U.S. Congress passed a law ordering the Federal Aviation Authority (FAA) to integrate UAVs into national airspace, although the FAA expects to take years to resolve the issue. From June 1 through November 19, 2014, the United States recorded 175 instances of commercial pilots reporting UAVs in restricted airspace (almost one instance per day), including 25 instances of UAVs within a few seconds or feet of crashing into passenger aircraft. These instances usually occur at low altitudes during taking off or landing at commercial airports, sometimes at altitudes of thousands of feet (Whitlock, 2014). France has seen more alarm over UAVs being used to observe restricted sites, including at least 13 nuclear-power stations from October 2014 to January 2015 and five tourist sites in Paris overnight on February 24–25, 2015 (BBC News, 2015).

Thefts

Aviation is a high-capital form of transportation and is used to carry high-value items, so thieves are attracted particularly to air cargo and infrastructure (at least the portable items).

For instance, on February 18, 2013, eight armed men cut a hole in the perimeter fence around Brussels airport, Belgium, and drove onto the runway in two cars with flashing lights mimicking police cars. From a Swiss-bound aircraft, they stole diamonds worth around $50 million. On September 30, 2013, 10 armed men entered the cargo terminal at Sao Paulo airport, Brazil, detained two guards, and stole computers worth an estimated $800,000.

Sovereign Threats to Civilian Aviation

A *sovereign state* is an independent political unit, also known as a nation-state, so a **sovereign threat** is one caused by or sourced from a nation-state. Air travel is covered by many international laws, some of which guarantee rights of travel that conflict with national sovereignty (see Box 12.1). Ultimately, a sovereign could close its airspace to anyone, although this threat is more credible if the state is militarily or diplomatically powerful enough to get away with it.

Sovereign interference could be either beneficent or malicious. Interference with aviation could be advantageous against airborne terrorism or invaders, but it also allows for illegitimate interruptions to international flows of travelers and cargo for selfish advantage, such as when a state diverts a plane carrying a foreign diplomat during an unrelated diplomatic dispute (see Box 12.2).

Some sovereign interventions are accidental, such as accidental military responses to legitimate civilian aircraft, including airliners that have been shot down with the loss of everybody on board (see Box 12.2). Some interventions should be considered deliberate state terrorism. Some interventions result from deliberate political linkage of issues, such as when a state obstructs air cargo on national-security grounds, though the real reason is some other diplomatic dispute with the carrier's home government.

International Laws on Aviation Security

- Convention on Offenses and Certain Other Acts Committed on Board Aircraft, signed in Tokyo on September 14, 1963

- Convention for the Suppression of Unlawful Seizure of Aircraft, signed at The Hague on December 16, 1970

- Convention for the Suppression of Unlawful Acts against the Safety of Civil Aviation, signed at Montreal on September 23, 1971

- International Convention Against the Taking of Hostages, adopted by the General Assembly of the United Nations on December 17, 1979

- Protocol for the Suppression of Unlawful Acts of Violence at Airports Serving International Civil Aviation, supplementary to the 1971 convention, signed at Montreal on February 24, 1988

Malicious Actors

Malicious actors could attack airports, commercial aircraft in the air, or the ancillary systems in between. Usually the attacks are violent in a kinetic sense, but increasingly, they are conducted in cyberspace. For instance, Estonia and Georgia have accused Russia of cyber attacks on its civil-aviation traffic control systems during unrelated diplomatic disputes.

Malicious actors include sovereign states but are typically terrorists, insurgents, and other nonstate actors in opposition to the official authority that owns or regulates the target.

Passengers use ground transport more frequently, and most cargo is carried in ships, so rationally, terrorism would be more cost-effective if it targeted ground or maritime transport, yet terrorists like to target passenger airliners (see Box 12.3). Attacks on passenger airliners offer catastrophic direct effects, great human harm (one airliner could carry 850 passengers), and major indirect economic effects. Airliners are symbols of globalization and material development, which some terrorists, particularly jihadi terrorists, oppose. Additionally, airliners are mostly produced, owned, operated, and used in the West.

PROVIDING AVIATION SECURITY

The provision of **aviation security** includes the international and national legal regimes for protecting aviation, which are very mature and well enforced now, and the technical standards and regulations for ensuring the aircraft against technical or accidental failure.

Otherwise, as described in subsections below, aviation security is focused on screening the cargo, passenger luggage, footwear, liquids, clothing, and the human body for weapons; controlling human access; preventing metallic weapons; securing the aircraft during the flight against human threats aboard the aircraft; and countering antiaircraft weapons.

Major Incidents of Sovereign Interference With Civilian Aviation

On September 1, 1983, a Soviet fighter shot down Korean Air Lines Flight 007 en route from New York City to Seoul via Anchorage after it had strayed into Soviet airspace over the Sea of Japan, west of Sakhalin Island. All 269 passengers and crew aboard were killed.

On July 3, 1988, the U.S. Navy guided-missile cruiser USS *Vincennes* (CG-49) shot down Iran Air Flight 655 while flying in Iranian airspace over Iran's territorial waters on its usual flight path from Bandar Abbas, Iran, to Dubai, United Arab Emirates. All 290 on board, including 66 children and 16 crew, perished. The ship's crew had mistaken the flight for an attack plane.

On October 10, 2012, about 19 months into the Syrian Civil War, Turkish military aircraft intercepted a Syrian airliner from Moscow to Damascus with 30 passengers on board as it entered Turkish airspace on suspicions that it was carrying weapons. Turkey claimed to find Russian military communications and missile parts. Hours earlier, Turkey had ordered all Turkish civilian aircraft to cease flights through Syrian airspace, apparently to prevent Syrian retaliation. Russia protested on behalf of Russian passengers. On October 14, Syria and Turkey closed airspaces to each other.

On July 2, 2013, Italy, France, and Portugal prevented the passage from Russia to Bolivia of Bolivian President Evo Morales's official plane, suspecting that an American fugitive, Edward Snowden, formerly a contractor working for the U.S. National Security Agency, was on board. It was grounded in Vienna, where Austrian authorities boarded the plane without discovering Snowden. Bolivian Vice President Álvaro García Linera said the plane was "kidnapped by imperialism."

Major Terrorist Attacks on Aviation

- On December 21, 1988, a small explosive device, hidden in luggage, exploded on Pan Am Flight 103 over Lockerbie, Scotland, on its way from Frankfurt via London to New York, killing all 259 aboard and 11 on the ground. The bomb had probably been loaded on to the plane in Frankfurt from a connecting flight from Malta. Investigators accused two employees of Libyan Arab Airlines, whom Libya surrendered for trial in 1999; only Abdel Basset Ali al-Megrahi was convicted by a Scottish court in 2001. (He was freed in 2009 on compassionate grounds relating to cancer, although he did not die until May 2012.) Libya reached a civil-international legal settlement in 2002 but always claimed that its officials had been acting without government orders.

- On March 9, 1994, the Irish Republican Army launched four improvised mortar shells from the back of a car parked at a hotel near the perimeter of London Heathrow Airport. Some impacted on the apron between two runways. On March 12, a similar attack was launched from woods on the perimeter. On March 13, another was launched from scrubland. None of the 12 projectiles exploded, but each was filled with high explosive. After each attack, the runways were closed during the searches for the projectiles and the launch areas.

- In 1994, Ramszi Yousef and Khalid Shaikh Mohammed, both primary members of al-Qaeda, then in the Philippines, planned to bomb 12 U.S. airliners in a single 48-hr period as they flew from the Far East to the United States. They also planned to fly a hijacked plane into the headquarters of the Central Intelligence Agency. (They called the collective plans the Bojinka plot.) On January 6, 1995, an explosive fire in a private apartment led to police arrests of the bomb makers.

- On September 11, 2001 (9/11), terrorist attacks caused the destruction of four airliners, the collapse of both towers of the World Trade Center in New York, and the destruction of part of the Pentagon building in Washington, DC. These events are normally considered one attack; it caused the greatest loss of life to any terrorist attack ever—just under 3,000 people. September 11 remains the costliest terrorist attack in history: The direct material cost was about $22 billion, including insured damage to property ($10 billion), insured interruption to business ($11 billion), and insured event cancellation ($1 billion). The human deaths of 9/11 (nearly 3,000) and disabilities were unprecedented; they amounted to just under $5 billion in insured lives and workers' compensation. The human effects of 9/11 amounted to just under $10 billion in lost earnings. All in all, the insured losses from 9/11 amounted to $40 billion—about twice as much as the last costliest event for insurers, Hurricane Andrew, but much smaller than the

next, Hurricane Katrina in 2005 (more than $40 billion in insured losses and $100 billion in total losses and more than 1,800 dead). On top of insured losses, the federal government spent $8.8 billion in aid in response to 9/11. (It would spend $29 billion in aid in response to Katrina.)

- On December 22, 2001, Richard Reid, a British-Jamaican convert to Islam, attempted to detonate a bomb hidden in his shoe on an airliner from Paris to Miami. Sajid Badat, another British-born citizen, had withdrawn from a similar attack but was convicted on terrorism charges.

- On November 28, 2002, al-Qaeda terrorists fired two SA-7 surface-to-air missiles at an Israeli charter flight leaving Mombasa, Kenya, but the missiles failed to engage at such short range. (Also, they may have been confused by unadmitted antimissile systems on the aircraft.) The same day, a suicide vehicle bomb killed 13 others at a hotel in Mombasa.

- On August 9, 2006, British police arrested 29 people in connection with a plot to bomb airlines bound for North America with explosives improvised from commercially available liquids. Eleven of those arrested were convicted later, of which only eight were convicted in connection with the plot and not on the most serious charges.

- In 2007, four men (three from Guyana, of which one was naturalized in the United States, and one from Trinidad and Tobago, all converts to Islam) were arrested after telling an informer that they planned to blow up fuel tanks at John F. Kennedy Airport, New York.

- In 2009, four men (three U.S. citizens, one Haitian immigrant, all converts to Islam) were

(Continued)

(Continued)

arrested in New York after implementing a plot to bomb a synagogue and shoot down aircraft, all with fake weapons provided by FBI informers.

- On Christmas Day, 2009, a Nigerian man (Umar Farouk Abdulmutallab) attempted to detonate explosives hidden in his underwear while aboard a commercial flight. He had been prepared by al-Qaeda in the Arabian Peninsula.

- Overnight on May 22–23, 2011, 15 Pakistani Taliban fighters struck a naval air base in Mehran, Pakistan, killing 18 members of the military and destroying two American-made surveillance aircraft before they were killed.

- In April 2012, U.S. and foreign intelligence learned that al-Qaeda in the Arabian Peninsula was developing an improved device to bomb an airliner. On May 7, 2012, the United States revealed that within the previous days, it had taken control of the device after it had left Yemen for some other Middle Eastern country (probably Saudi Arabia).

- On December 15, 2012, an unknown number of men from the Pakistani Taliban attacked the perimeter of the airport in Peshawar, Pakistan, with rockets, a vehicle-borne explosive device, and small arms. At least nine people were killed, including five attackers.

- On June 10, 2013, seven Afghani Taliban fighters attacked the military side of Kabul International Airport, Afghanistan. Two fighters detonated suicide explosive vests, while the other five opened fire with small arms and rocket-propelled grenades from an overlooking building. All were killed. Two Afghan civilians were wounded.

- Overnight on June 8–9, 2014, 10 men from the Islamic Movement of Uzbekistan, armed with small arms and explosives, attacked the airport at Karachi, the largest in Pakistan. By dawn, at least 39 were dead, including the attackers. On June 10, gunmen on motorbikes fired on the airport security base.

Cargo

Air cargo or **air freight** is anything carried by air other than human passengers. The security of air cargo is addressed below via its scope, the threats, and the controls.

SCOPE Global air freight is worth about $100 billion per year. Due to increased security after 9/11, air freight costs rose about 15% from 9/11 to January 2002 (according to the World Bank).

Security measures have always focused more on passenger than freight aircraft because terrorists have attacked more passenger than cargo planes, even though rationally they could more efficiently damage the economy by shutting down air freight. (See above for reasons why terrorists prefer to attack passenger aviation.)

The security of air cargo is an issue for passenger aviation too, since most passenger aircraft also carry cargo, usually smaller, faster mail while bulk items travel in dedicated cargo planes. In the United States, about 80% of air cargo is carried by cargo-only domestic flights, 20% by passenger flights. About 3,500,000 MT per year travels as cargo on U.S. domestic and international passenger flights.

THREATS The most frequent illegal activities relating to air cargo relate to smuggling and trafficking, including banned drugs, exotic and protected animals and plants, banned animal products, firearms, and gems.

Sometimes, smuggling exposes how easily large and animated items can be carried as air cargo without discovery. Indeed, people sometimes travel in air freight as a cheaper form of travel or in order to avoid **access controls**. These noncompliant passengers are known as **stowaways**. For instance, in 2003, a young man sealed himself into a box that was carried as air freight from New York City via Niagara Falls and Fort Wayne, Indiana, to his parent's home in Dallas through the hands of several commercial haulers, without discovery.

Of more concern than private stowaways are hidden explosives that could cause a catastrophe that destroys an aircraft or the storage area, kill personnel or (if an aircraft is destroyed in the air) people on the ground, and disrupt air transport, with huge economic consequences. A small device, smaller than a briefcase, would be small enough to hide inside the typical large freight containers and still threaten the aircraft catastrophically, although the blast would be mitigated by surrounding cargo. The larger containers on dedicated cargo planes are of concern for the carriage of weapons of mass destruction that would be too heavy or easily detected to be loaded as passenger luggage on a passenger flight.

In recent years, terrorists have attempted to mail devices that were designed (probably using a timed detonator) to explode in mid-air over the destination country. In October 2010, after a tip-off derived from a multinational intelligence operation directed against al-Qaeda in the Arabian Peninsula and American-exile Anwar al-Awlaki, East Midlands Airport in England and Dubai Airports discovered explosives hidden inside printer toner cartridges on UPS and FedEx flights respectively, both mailed from Sanaa, Yemen, to addresses in the United States and configured to detonate over the U.S. East Coast. On October 30, 2010, Britain banned all air cargo from Yemen and Somalia. On the same day, the U.S. DHS banned all air cargo from Yemen. Later, on November 9, it banned all air cargo from Somalia and all high-risk cargo on passenger planes.

In October and November 2010, a Greek anarchist group mailed bombs to various embassies and foreign leaders, including two that were intercepted at Athens International Airport before being loaded as air freight.

In March 2011, Istanbul Atatürk Airport discovered a dummy bomb inside a wedding cake box that had arrived on a UPS flight from London. British police arrested a Turkish man on suspicion of a hoax. On June 17, 2011, the British Department for Transport banned UPS from screening air cargo at some facilities in Britain until it could meet British security requirements.

CONTROLS Since 9/11, all cargo is supposed to be screened before loading onto passenger aircraft within or inbound to the United States. (This is the same rule as for passenger baggage.) Cargo on nonpassenger aircraft faced lighter controls for several years after 9/11 so that most air cargo was practically not inspected during transport. Effective October 2003, the U.S. Customs and Border Protection agency has required electronic submission of the manifest if the plane originates abroad, at least 8 hrs before an air courier boards, or 12 hrs before any air cargo is loaded abroad. The 9/11 Commission Act of 2007 required the TSA to screen 50% of cargo on cargo-only flights by February 2009 and 100% by August 2010. TSA screens all packages from Afghanistan, Algeria, Iraq, Lebanon, Libya, Nigeria, Pakistan, Saudi Arabia, Somalia, and Yemen.

Businesses generally oppose more security because of the costs and the delays to commercial flows. Many commodities and raw materials must travel quicker or more sensitively than routine inspections would allow. Consequently, officials have focused on acquiring technologies that allow quicker, nonintrusive inspections or intelligence that enables more targeted inspections. In 2009, the TSA piloted (at Houston) a Pulsed Fast Neutron Scanner (which can differentiate materials at the molecular level), but the unit cost $8 million, and the funding covered just a few months of operating costs.

Luggage

Before 9/11, much checked **luggage** (passenger items intended for the hold, separate from the passenger cabin) was not inspected or screened at all, although higher risk airlines (such as the Israeli and Jordanian national airlines) screened all luggage for explosives and temporarily passed all luggage through a pressure chamber before loading onto aircraft (because some explosive devices had been improvised with detonators triggered by changes in pressure as the aircraft climbed into the air).

After 9/11, the United States ordered a rate of 100% inspection of anything loaded onto passenger aircraft, including checked luggage, involving at least x-ray screening for explosives. Initially, the promise was 100% manual inspection, but that promise fell away given the burden. Information on the true rate of manual inspection remains guarded.

Metallic screening is less important for checked luggage than for carry-on baggage because the passenger has no access to the hold, so any metallic weapons hidden there would be an issue of trafficking rather than hijacking.

Human-Access Controls

Before 9/11, controls on human access to airports were lax since friends and families were in the habit of seeing off the passenger at the gate of the aircraft, while airports appreciated the extra business. The **human-access controls** mainly started at the gate of the flight. (Baggage would be separated or screened earlier.)

Human-access controls became stringent after 9/11. In most cases, only ticketed passengers or airport or airline personnel can pass the controls from the land side to the air side (where passengers and aircraft are prepared). The United States maintained a database (the no-fly list) of people forbidden from flying into or within the United States; convicted terrorists were uncontroversial targets, but many people found that they were forbidden to fly because they had names similar to someone of concern. A new redress system soon cleared up most of the complaints, but sometimes the explanation was lacking, and the false positive was fixed only after years of complaints.

Despite post-9/11 measures, some people have managed to access flights illegitimately. For instance, on June 24, 2011, a Nigerian man flew from New York to Los Angeles with a boarding pass for the same flight of the previous day, a student card, and a police report about his stolen passport. He was arrested 5 days later when he tried the same trick from Los Angeles to Atlanta. He was found to be carrying several stolen boarding passes.

Air-side personnel are hazardous in that they could exploit more trusting controls on their access. For instance, from 2007 to 2010, Rajib Karim, a Bangladeshi-British male working for British Airways as a computer specialist, conspired with American-exile Anwar al-Awlaki to blow up a U.S.-bound plane. On March 18, 2011, he was sentenced to 30 years in jail.

Air-side personnel may unwittingly attack aviation. For instance, air-side workers are known to have taken money to place items, such as illegal drugs, aboard aircraft or take them off aircraft without the proper screening. While they may be loath to place weapons aboard an aircraft for terrorist purposes, a threat could pretend to be placing contraband rather than a bomb.

Air-side access controls can be exploited too. For instance, cargo and supplies are delivered to airports at delivery sites with a short space between the land side and air side. Many airports require personnel at such sites to check the credentials of deliverers and to keep the air side closed while the land side is open, but sometimes, due to carelessness or to promote air flow during hot weather, both sides are left open, and unauthorized personnel are left to walk around without being challenged.

Metallic-Weapons Screening

Magnetic and x-ray scanners became routine in the 1970s, mainly to spot metallic weapons, such as knives and firearms, that could be used to hijack planes. On 9/11, terrorists evaded these controls by carrying small knives (*box cutters*) and by traveling in a sufficiently large group per plane to intimidate passengers. At the time, conventional wisdom and official advice was to avoid confronting hijackers. After 9/11, authorities banned knives of any size and even banned the airlines from issuing metallic cutlery. However, cynics pointed out that the regulations permitted glass bottles that could be smashed to produce sharp weapons and wooden objects that could be combined and sharpened as weapons. Soon enough, metallic cutlery returned to airlines without any recorded use as a weapon.

Despite extra controls since 9/11, metallic weapons or fake weapons have been used inside the cabin for old-fashioned hijackings. For instance, on November 27, 2002, a schizophrenic Italian man used a fake bomb to hijack an Air Italia flight from Bologna to Paris. On February 17, 2007, a man used two pistols to hijack a Spanish flight from Mauritania to the Canary Islands. On April 24, 2011, a Kazakh man used a knife to attempt a hijack of an Air Italia flight from Paris to Rome but was restrained by crew.

In addition, threats can carry weapons into the land side of the airport before confronting the access controls. For instance, on November 1, 2013, Paul Anthony Ciancia (aged 23) entered Los Angeles International Airport, Terminal 3, and approached the boarding pass checkpoint, where he pulled a Smith & Wesson assault rifle from his bag and shot to death TSA screener Gerardo Hernandez. He wounded another two screeners and a passenger before police wounded him and took him into custody. They found a handwritten note in Ciancia's bag describing his intent to harm TSA employees.

Footwear Screening

Al-Qaeda evaded the enhanced access controls by hiding explosives in the sole of a large training shoe (as worn by Richard Reid in December 2001), after which some authorities required passengers to place their shoes through x-ray screening devices. However, implementation is inconsistent, with some airports allowing some shoes to remain on the feet while others insist on all footwear being screened.

Liquids Screening

Terrorists have planned to use liquid explosives to be prepared on the flight using materials carried aboard without alerting the screeners. According to the plot intercepted in August 2006, the main component would have been hydrogen peroxide, hidden inside commercially available bottles whose tops remained sealed because the terrorists had replaced the contents using syringes stuck through the plastic sides. A detonator would have been disguised as the battery inside a disposable camera. Another disposable camera could have served as the electrical ignition source. Intelligence during the planning stage led to arrests that prevented the plot of August 2006 from being finalized, but under the regulations of the time, the materials probably would have passed the access controls.

The initial solution was to ban liquids entirely from passing through the access controls (although passengers could purchase more from the secure area of the airport). This led to long lines as baggage and persons were inspected manually and some farcical confrontations (such as intrusive inspections of colostomy bags, breast milk, and hand creams) before screening technology was adjusted to better detect liquids, agents aligned their activities, and the public became more familiar with the new regulations. Soon, the rules were adjusted to allow liquids in small containers, although cynics have pointed out that enough terrorists traveling with enough small containers could carry enough materials to make the same explosive device that had been planned in August 2006.

In 2009, the TSA procured 500 bottled-liquid scanners in a $22 million contract with a commercial supplier. It deployed more than 600 of the scanners to airports nationwide in 2011 and 1,000 by 2013. These scanners are used to screen medically required liquids.

In February 2014, the U.S. DHS warned airlines that terrorists might conceal explosives in toothpaste tubes and cosmetic containers in order to disrupt the Winter Olympics in Sochi, Russia. The TSA temporarily banned liquids, gels, aerosols, and powders from carry-on passengers flying to Russia.

Clothing Screening

Since 9/11, authorities have demanded more screening of passengers and their clothing by x-ray and evolved systems but are opposed by passengers who prefer to remain covered on personal, cultural, or religious grounds.

Thick or outer garments are usually passed through explosive detection systems—conveyer-fed machines, often described inaccurately as x-ray machines but using evolved technology in order to differentiate explosive materials. However, they are unlikely to differentiate small amounts, as could be distributed thinly within the lining of heavy clothing, or trace amounts, as left behind when someone handles explosives. Some suppliers have offered handheld electronic devices for detecting the chemical traces, but these are ineffective unless practically touching the person. From 2004 to June 2006, the U.S. TSA acquired 116 full-body explosives sniffers (*puffers*) at 37 airports, despite poor tests of effectiveness. They were deleted because of poor detection and availability rates, after a sunk cost of more than $30 million.

Since 2009, the TSA's systems for detecting explosives have included small tabletop machines (explosives trace detection machines) for detecting explosive residues on swabs. In February 2010, TSA announced that these machines would be deployed nationwide. These machines are used mainly for random or extra inspections of clothing worn by the passenger.

Explosives detection dogs are the best sensors of explosives, although they are hazardous to some people and have short periodic work cycles, so they could not screen lines of people efficiently or effectively. They are used mostly for random patrols on the land side.

Body Screening

Body imagers produce an electronic image of the person's body underneath their clothes and can be configured to reveal items hidden between the body and clothing. They are quicker than a manual inspection (about 30 s to generate the scan and inspect the image, compared to 2 min for a pat down) but are expensive and violate common expectations of privacy and health security.

Body imagers come in two main technologies: **backscatter x-ray systems** and **millimeter wave systems**. Backscatter units are less expensive but still costly (about $150,000 per unit at the time of first acquisition). They use a flat source/detector, so the target must be scanned from at least two sides. (The system looks like a wrap-around booth, inside of which the passenger stands facing one side.) Many passengers are understandably reluctant to subject themselves to a backscatter x-ray, having been told to minimize their exposure to x-rays except for medical purposes. Additionally, health professionals have disputed official claims that the energy emitted by a scan is trivial. Meanwhile, reports have emerged that backscatter images do not adequately penetrate thick or heavy clothing; some entrepreneurs have offered clothing to shield the body from the energy, casting doubt on their effectiveness at their main mission.

Millimeter wave systems produce 360-degree images, so they are quicker, and their images are more revealing, but they are more expensive, their health effects are less certain, and their revealing images are of more concern for privacy advocates. Authorities claim that software is used to obscure genitalia, but obfuscation of genitalia would obscure explosives hidden in underpants.

Operators generally keep the images and the agent hidden inside a closed booth and promise not to record any images. However, these measures do not resolve all the ethical and legal issues. For instance, British officials admitted that child pornography laws prevented scans of people of under 18 years of age.

Backscatter imagers have been available commercially since 1992. They have been deployed in some U.S. prisons since 2000 and in Iraq since 2003 but at no airports before 2007. The United States conducted a trial of one at a Phoenix airport in February 2007, then deployed 40 at 18 airports before 2010. The United States also donated four to Nigeria in summer 2008. Britain tested one at London Heathrow Airport in 2007. By then, officials already realized preferences for millimeter wave systems. The Netherlands trialled three millimeter wave systems at Schipol airport in 2007. Canada used one for a trial period in fiscal year 2008. Britain tried some at Manchester beginning in December 2009.

Body imagers of all types were deployed slowly and restrictively because of privacy, health, and cost issues. In 2009, the GAO faulted the TSA for poor cost–benefit analysis; the agency's plan to double the number of body scanners in coming years would require more personnel to run and maintain them, an expense of as much as $2.4 billion. Until 2010, all of the deployed machines were used for secondary inspections only, as a voluntary alternative to a manual inspection, which itself was occasional.

After the new controls on outer clothing and liquids, terrorists planned to hide explosives in underpants (as worn by Umar Farouk Abdulmutallab in December 2009). He passed screeners and boarded an aircraft to the United States but failed to detonate catastrophically (although he burnt himself), probably because damp had degraded the explosive.

Within days of this attack, U.S., British, and Dutch governments required scans of all U.S.-bound passengers or a manual inspection of the outer body (*pat downs*). Within one year, more than 400 body-imaging machines had been deployed at 70 of the 450 airports in the United States. Today, some of these major airports require all passengers to pass through imaging machines or opt-out in favor of a manual inspection, although cynics noted that the requirement was sometimes abandoned during heavy flows of passengers.

After years of more access controls and delays at airports, passengers rebelled most against body imagers and intrusive pat downs. Certainly some of the inspections were farcical or troubling, such as an agent inspecting a baby's diaper or making contact with an adult's genitalia during a pat down. In November 2010, private citizens launched "We Won't Fly," essentially an online campaign against excessive access controls, including a National Opt-Out Day on Thanksgiving 2010, although few passengers opted out on America's busiest travel day. Polls showed that the public disliked the new procedures but also thought them necessary. Meanwhile, in November 2010 and repeatedly in subsequent months, U.S. Representative Ron Paul (Republican from Texas) introduced a bill, the American Traveler Dignity Act, to hold officials accountable for unnecessary screenings.

Although officials would not admit that procedures can change due to public pressure rather than changes in threat, in fact, security is an evolving balance between commercial and popular and official requirements. Universal body imagers and pat downs probably represented the high tide of controls on access to passenger aviation. From January 2011, the TSA tested a new millimeter wave software for 6 months at three airports, including Reagan National, on the promise of less violations of privacy with the same detection of weapons. On July 20, 2011, the TSA announced that the new software would be installed on 241 millimeter wave units at 41 airports. Information on the full distribution, use, and effectiveness of units remains guarded.

Cockpit Security

The **cockpit** is the aircraft's compartment housing the pilot or pilots. Before 9/11, cockpit security was poor; pilots on long flights were in the habit of allowing other staff to visit the cockpit with refreshments and of inviting select passengers to view the cockpit. On 9/11, hijackers burst into cockpits and overpowered flight crews. After 9/11, national and commercial regulations specified that cockpit doors were to be locked during flight from the inside, although pilots must open the cockpit occasionally to use toilets or to accept refreshments from cabin crew.

Cockpits contain their own hazards in the sense that pilots could take control of the plane with suicidal or murderous intent, in which case, a locked cockpit door gives a false sense of security and even can be used by pilots to prevent outside intervention (see Box 12.4).

BOX 12.4

Alleged Malicious Pilots of Passenger Planes

On December 19, 1997, a SilkAir passenger plane from Jakarta in Indonesia to Singapore crashed in Sumatra, killing all 104 aboard after a steep dive. The U.S. National Transportation Safety Board concluded that the dive was initiated deliberately by the pilot; the cockpit voice recorder showed that the pilot had left the cockpit just before the recorder was disabled.

On October 31, 1999, an EgyptAir passenger plane bound from Los Angeles to Cairo crashed into the Atlantic, killing all 217 people on board. The U.S. National Transportation Safety Board concluded that probably a suicidal copilot had flown the plane into the sea. The cockpit voice recorder showed that the copilot had waited for the pilot to leave for the toilet before initiating a dive while praying to God. The pilot, on returning from the toilet, failed to regain control.

On February 17, 2014, the copilot of an Ethiopian Airlines passenger plane bound for Rome took control of the plane, activated a transponder indicating a hijack, and was permitted to land in Geneva, Switzerland, where he claimed asylum.

On March 8, 2014, someone aboard a Malaysia Airlines flight, shortly after leaving Kuala Lumpur for Beijing, disabled all transponders and communications before turning the aircraft off course. It flew for hours in the wrong direction before crashing into the southern Indian Ocean off western Australia, killing all 239 aboard.

On March 23, 2015, a Germanwings flight crashed in the French Alps, killing all 150 people on board. Citing information from the voice recorder, French prosecutors alleged that the copilot flew the plane into the ground while the pilot was locked out of the cockpit.

Cabin Security

The **cabin** is the compartment in the aircraft housing the passengers.

The Federal Air Marshal Program deploys officers with concealed weapons on commercial aircraft in case of hijackings. At the time of 9/11, perhaps 33 air marshals were active, according to press reports, primarily on international flights. The number was expanded rapidly after 9/11 but remains secret—perhaps in the thousands. The TSA, which administered the marshals since 2005, admits that only about 1% of the 28,000 daily flights—or about 280 flights per day—have an air marshal aboard.

Some cabin crew are trained in self-defense, although not armed in case they could be disarmed by a passenger and have their arms used against them. Some cockpit crew are armed and trained in self-defense.

Passengers have proven to be most effective guardians of cabin security. Before 9/11, officials and the industry advised passengers not to confront hijackers in case they retaliated, but after 9/11, that conventional wisdom was reversed. On 9/11, the fourth plane to crash did so after passengers attempted to take control of the cockpit, having heard reports from colleagues, friends, and family on the ground that the other three hijacked planes had been flown into buildings. Passengers overpowered Richard Reid in December 2001 and Umar Farouk Abdulmutallab in December 2009 after they tried to detonate their explosives.

COUNTERING ANTIAIRCRAFT WEAPONS

Antiaircraft weapons could be used to shoot down aircraft in flight. These weapons are categorized as small arms, rocket-propelled grenades, cannons, and guided missiles.

Small Arms

Small arms bullets, normally of calibers from 5 mm to 8 mm, are rarely catastrophically destructive to large aircraft, except when the discharge is from within a pressurized compartment at high altitude. In theory, bullets fired from without could incapacitate a pilot or engine, but bullets of these calibers usually leave small holes without destroying anything critical; this is true for wings, cabins, even fuel tanks. (Forget whatever you've seen in movies.) They are so unstable that they do not typically reach above 1,000 ft, where they are easily deflected by wind. Bullets must be around 15-mm caliber before they can carry any useful explosive charge. This would leave a larger hole, but even this is unlikely to be catastrophic unless, again, the aircraft is pressurized at high altitude, in which case the attacker would need to be firing from another aircraft, not the ground.

Rocket-Propelled Grenades

Rocket-propelled grenades are as portable as small arms but are even less accurate, although the self-destruct timers could be shortened so that the grenade would explode at a predictable altitude near the target. This altitude is below most flight paths but, in theory, could threaten any aircraft as it takes off or lands. Helicopters at low altitude and slow speed are most exposed. Such threats are most profound in peacekeeping, counterinsurgency, and counterterrorism operations, which rely on helicopters for logistics, transport, surveillance, and fire support. In 1993, Somali militia reconfigured their rocket-propelled grenades to explode at the low altitude used by U.S. military helicopters in support of ground operations. On one day in October 1993, they brought down two U.S. UH-60 Blackhawk helicopters that were providing support to U.S. special-operations forces on the ground in Mogadishu. On August 6, 2011, a rocket-propelled grenade struck the aft rotor of a U.S. Chinook (a twin-rotor transport helicopter) while it was transporting special operations west of Kabul, Afghanistan, killing all 38 people on board.

Cannons

Projectiles of less than 15-mm caliber are not energetic enough to harm aircraft at normal flying altitudes. Automatic cannons (15–40 mm) fire projectiles with sufficient energy and explosive content at an automated rate to be catastrophically destructive at altitudes up to several thousand feet, just enough to threaten light aircraft at cruising altitudes. These weapons are specialized military weapons and are not man-portable, but some can be transported by ordinary pickup trucks, and many have fallen into the hands of malicious actors.

GUIDED MISSILES

Scope

Guided missiles are rocket-propelled projectiles guided on targets by infrared sensors or radar. **Man-portable air defense systems (MANPADS)** are essentially shoulder-launched antiaircraft missiles, usually guided by infrared. MANPADS are portable enough to be carried on the shoulder or hidden in an automobile yet have sufficient destructiveness to bring down any plane, although they do not reach airliner cruising height. A MANPAD, with launcher, weighs from 28 to 55 lbs (13–25 kg) and measures 4 to 6.5 ft (1.2–2 m) in length and about 3 in. (72 mm) in diameter. The missile is launched at about twice the speed of sound and reaches an altitude around 15,000 ft (4.57 km). No helicopter can cruise above this altitude; airliners cruise above this altitude but are exposed during their long approaches before landing and after taking off before reaching cruising altitude.

Large radar-guided surface-to-air missiles (SAMs), as must be carried by large specialized automobiles, have been deployed since the 1950s. These are severe threats to all aircraft at almost any practical altitude; the smallest can strike at around 50,000 ft (15.2 km) while most airlines cruise at around 35,000 ft (10.7 km). Unlike most MANPADS, SAMs are guided by radar. Some are guided by large radar systems that must be carried on separate vehicles. Such missiles are too cumbersome and detectable to be of much use to terrorists, but they could be procured and operated by nonstate actors wherever official controls are so weak as to allow for these actors to acquire these systems in operable condition and to train with them.

Proliferation

Hundreds, perhaps thousands, of MANPADS remain unaccounted for. In the 1980s, the U.S. Central Intelligence Agency supplied about 500 FIM-92 Stinger missiles to Afghanistan's mujaheddin fighters in response to the Soviet invasion. Some were expended there, some were bought back, and some leaked to other countries.

Hundreds of Soviet-made MANPADS leaked from Libya during the civil war there in 2011. In September 2012, an anonymous U.S. official claimed that 100 to 1,000 from Libyan sources were still unaccounted for and that Egyptian terrorists and Somali pirates had acquired some. On September 22, 2012, progovernment Libyan militiamen overran an Islamist militia (Rafallah al-Sahati) base in Benghazi and discovered MANPADS.

When civil war broke out in March 2011 in Syria, rebels overran many Syrian military stores of MANPADS. In late summer 2011, videos showed Soviet-produced SA-14 MANPADS in rebel hands. By November 2012, Syrian rebels had about 40 MANPADS, according to Western and Middle Eastern intelligence. At least some were supplied by the Qatari government. (U.S. and Western European governments officially support the rebels with only nonlethal material.) The space affected by these missiles has expanded with the expansion of jihadi insurgents from Syria into central Iraq in June 2014.

Another hot spot of proliferation is eastern Ukraine, where since February 2014 pro-Russian rebels have acquired MANPADS and SAMs from former official Ukrainian stocks. Ukraine alleges that Russia has supplied more directly.

Past Use

More than 40 civilian aircraft have been hit by MANPADS from 1970 through 2011, resulting in 28 crashes and more than 800 fatalities. All occurred in conflict zones. Almost all targets were cargo aircraft, delivering freight to peacekeepers, counterinsurgent forces, or unstable authorities. The count is an underestimate because some smaller aircraft disappear without a full explanation and some authorities may be unwilling to admit such a loss during a counterterrorist or counterinsurgency campaign.

In November 2002, al-Qaeda's agents attempted to use two Soviet-produced SA-7 MANPADS to shoot down an Israeli commercial passenger aircraft departing Kenya. This attack failed probably because the range was too short for the missiles' sensors to lock onto the target, although rumors persist that the target was equipped with an unadmitted antimissile system.

Since then, al-Qaeda seems to have considered antiaircraft weapons against very important persons. According to documents captured during the U.S. operation to kill him in May 2011, Osama bin Laden ordered his network in Afghanistan to attack aircraft carrying U.S. President Obama and General David H. Petraeus (then commander of the International Security Assistance Force in Afghanistan) into Afghanistan.

Pro-Russian rebels in eastern Ukraine have downed several Ukrainian helicopters and small fixed-wing aircraft since March 2014. On June 14, 2014, they used a MANPAD to down a large Ukrainian military transport plane as it was coming in to land at Luhansk, killing 49. On July 14, they used a SAM to down a smaller transport plane, this one at 21,000 ft (6.4 km), killing three. On July 17, they used a SAM to bring down a Malaysia Airlines–operated Boeing 777 from Schipol to Kuala Lumpur cruising at 33,000 ft (10 km), with the loss of all 298 on board. At that time, Ukrainian and international air authorities had closed airspace in that area below 32,000 ft.

Hot spots are increasingly likely wherever states are losing control of their own territory and military stocks. For instance, on January 17, 2015, the French Aeronautical Information Service ordered French airliners to fly at least 24,000 ft over Pakistan. On January 29, the European Aviation Safety Agency generalized the advice.

Given the increasing success of insurgencies, we should expect further proliferation for at least years if not decades. Worse, we should expect more malicious interest in SAMs as malicious actors tire of the limited usefulness of MANPADS and capture military stocks from failed states.

Countering Guided Missiles

As areas of threat arise, air transport authorities could divert aircraft or insist on higher cruising altitudes, but local solutions do not control the global risk.

Military air forces commonly acquire countermissile technologies as simple as flare dispensers. (Flares confuse any heat sensor on the missile.) Some civilian carriers have deployed the same, such as the U.S. president's official planes and Israel's national airline. These flares burn for a short period of time without necessarily diverting the missile's sensor from the larger heat signature emanating from the aircraft's engines.

In January 2004, DHS initiated the C-MANPADS program, which developed (via contracts) a system (marketed as Guardian) that uses an automated laser to confuse the missile's sensor. In September 2006, FedEx started a full operational trial. On November 5, 2014, Israel announced adoption of a similar system (Flight Guard) across its airliners. However, these systems would not affect a radar-guided missile, such as most SAMs.

Richard Clarke has advocated more widespread acquisition, arguing that such technology would cost about $1 billion to acquire across U.S. airliners while a single downed airliner would cost the U.S. economy about $1 trillion in economic disruption (Clarke, 2008).

In fiscal year 2003, the U.S. State Department started a program to counter MANPADS, mostly activities to prevent acquisition by terrorists, insurgents, or other nonstate actors and to reduce accidental explosions in stores. The department engaged 30 countries, focusing on the Near East, North Africa, and the Sahel. The State Department claims that the program led to the reduction of over 33,000 MANPADS in 38 countries and the improved security of thousands more MANPADS. In fiscal year 2012, the State Department distributed $9.3 million through the program.

Two Forecasts of Aviation Terrorism

FEMA and Jeffrey C. Price

1. An additional tactic that terrorists have adopted to exploit vulnerabilities is to find new, seemingly innocuous places to conceal weapons, explosives, and other dangerous materials. Richard Reid concealed explosives in his shoes in December 2001, terrorists planned to conceal liquid explosives in soft drink containers, Umar Farouk Amdulmutallab concealed explosives hidden in his underwear in December 2009, and bombs were found in toner cartridges flown from Yemen in October 2010. In each case, screening and other countermeasures were altered to try to reduce their vulnerabilities to these types of attacks. Drug smugglers and customs enforcers have engaged in a similar process where concealment methods evolve as new countermeasures are put in place. As terrorist concealment tactics evolve, this may force emergency managers and first responders to reconsider screening procedures during special events.

Terrorist groups will still pursue opportunities to inflict mass casualties. For example, terrorists continued to target commercial aircraft despite the employment of enhanced security measures at airports. The tactics favored by terrorists have become more lethal over time, a trend which could continue. (U.S. Federal Emergency Management Agency, 2011, p. 2)

2. We often get accused of being reactive, instead of proactive in the aviation industry, but the fact of the matter is we actually have to be both. If we are only proactive by trying to predict the next thing, then we have failed to account for what has already occurred. This is just what occurred on 9/11; we kind of gave up on the fact that hijackings could even happen, and that is exactly what occurred. So when you get hit, when there is the new bomb, the new hijack threat, the new active shooter threat, you have to react because until you do, those types of attack will continue. But you also have to be proactive and realize the bad guy is evolving as well. That is something we have done much better since 9/11. There have been a lot more policies and procedures in place and more proactive activities trying to predict the next threat.

The next attack probably will not look like the last attack. It probably will not be pocket knives and box cutters because that was the last attack. I think that if there is going to be another hijacking, it is going to be employees and insiders or with access. I think they will have weapons like firearms, not knives. For all of the passengers who want to rise up, it is one thing to go against a guy with a box cutter; it is another thing entirely to go against a guy with a submachine gun. It is a possibility that these will be smuggled in by people within the industry. Employee access has been a big issue. For example, workplace violence took down Pacific Southwest Airlines Flight 1771 back in 1987. There have been incidents of people dressed as customs agents and security guards that accessed aircraft. A lot of your major terrorist attacks—TWA 847 and Pan Am 103—have had an employee as some part of the attack, whether they facilitated or were the hijacker. I believe hijacking is still on the table as an option of attack. I think we will see more active shooters because it seems to be the trend these days. It can very much screw up an airport as an attack. The brand new risks are going to be the asymmetrical threats, such as cyber attacks and drones, but particularly the cyber attacks.

Jeffrey C. Price is a professor of aviation at the Metropolitan State University of Denver and the owner of Leading Edge Strategies, an aviation management training company. He is also the lead author of *Practical Aviation Security: Predicting and Preventing Future Threats* (now in its second edition) and *Airport Operations, Safety and Emergency Management*. Jeff has been a professional aviation-management trainer for the past decade, teaching and authoring the American Association of Airport Executives' ACE-Security program and the Certified Member program. Jeff Price was the director of Jefferson County Airport, the second-largest general aviation airport in Colorado. He previously served as the assistant security director at Denver International Airport and in airport operations at Stapleton International Airport. He is a commercially certificated pilot and holds a bachelor's degree in professional pilot from MSU Denver and a master's in curriculum and instruction from Colorado Christian University. He is currently working on his doctorate in educational psychology at Capella University.

Source: Courtesy of Jeffery Price.

CHAPTER SUMMARY

This chapter has

- Described the scope of civilian air transport security

- Described aviation accidents

- Described aviation thefts

- Reviewed sovereign threats to civilian aviation

- Described aviation terrorism

- Explained how to improve aviation security via

  - cargo screening,
  - passenger luggage screening,
  - human-access controls,
  - metallic-weapons screening,
  - footwear screening,
  - liquids screening,
  - clothing screening,
  - body screening,
  - cockpit security,
  - cabin security, and
  - countering antiaircraft weapons.

KEY TERMS

Access controls *509*
Air cargo *508*
Air freight *508*
Aviation *502*
Aviation security *505*
Backscatter x-ray system *513*

Body imager *513*
Cabin *516*
Civilian aviation *502*
Cockpit *515*
Explosives detection dog *513*
Human-access controls *510*

Luggage *510*
Man-portable air defense system
    (MANPAD) *517*
Millimeter wave system *513*
Sovereign threat *504*
Stowaway *509*

QUESTIONS AND EXERCISES

1. In what ways are sovereign threats to aviation greater than terrorist threats?

2. Why are terrorists focused on civilian aviation?

3. In what ways are cargo-only flights more or less risky than passenger flights?

4. In what ways does checked luggage need different screening than carry-on luggage?

5. In what ways can air-side personnel pose risks?

6. How have terrorist passengers evaded controls on explosives?

7. Why are body imagers controversial?

8. For critics of screening technology, what is the alternative?

9. How is security provided against human threats already aboard a flight?

10. Why are MANPADS of more concern than other antiaircraft weapons?

13

GROUND TRANSPORT SECURITY

On November 26, 2008, 10 men, acting under the orders of Lashkar-e-Tayiba—a terrorist group based in Pakistan—hijacked a fishing trawler and killed the crew before landing in small boats in Mumbai on the western coast of India. They divided into four teams and, using annotated maps and photographs, proceeded to different targets: a railway station, cinema, restaurant, residential complex, hospital, Jewish center, and two large hotels popular with wealthy and Western visitors. Along the way, they fired on locals from hijacked taxis and a police car, and left improvised explosive devices behind in two of the vehicles that killed around five people. They replenished themselves from prepositioned caches and stayed in contact with their handlers in Pakistan using cell phones. Two terrorists, armed with automatic rifles and hand grenades, killed 58 people at the railway station. Three terrorists survived inside the Taj Mahal Hotel until November 29, at which point they had killed 166 people and wounded more than 300. The terrorists were under orders to die fighting. All were killed except one who was taken alive while fleeing the railway station.

SCOPE

Ground transportation is anything that physically carries passengers or other items across the ground. Most ground transportation is by **road** and **railway** (**railroad**) transportation; it includes pedestrian and animal carriers, which tend to be more important in developing countries.

Maritime and aerial forms of transportation tend to be more secure because they are less coincident with malicious actors (at least between ports or stations) and have more restrictive controls on access (at least at ports and stations), but they are more expensive up front (even though they are usually cheaper to operate in the long term). Short-range aviation (primarily helicopters and small fixed-wing aircraft) offers accessibility and speed, but it is much more expensive to operate and is exposed to short-range ground-to-air weapons.

Learning Objectives and Outcomes

At the end of this chapter, you should be able to understand

- The scope of ground transport

- The threats and hazards to ground transport

- How to provide ground transport security

Road transportation is commonplace and will remain commonplace because of private favor for the accessibility and freedom of roads, even though road transport is expensive (at least operationally, over longer distances), suffers frequent accidents, and is extensively exposed to malicious actors.

Railways are more efficient and safer than roads, but some authorities cannot afford the up-front investment, in which case they invest in roads and bus services, even though these are more operationally costly and harmful in the long term. Railway lines are often more important economically and socially at local levels and in larger, less developed countries, where the railway is the only way to travel long distances or through rough terrain (short of using slow animals or expensive off-road vehicles or aircraft).

In insecure or underdeveloped areas, road transportation is often the only means of transportation after the collapse of the infrastructure required for aviation and railway alternatives. Consequently, road transportation becomes more important in unstable or postconflict areas, even though road transport remains very exposed to threats with simple weapons and skills.

Sometimes, road transportation is the only option for routine communications, such as in the mountainous areas of Afghanistan and Pakistan, where the poor weather, thin air, and insurgent threats discourage use of even helicopters. Indeed, some of these areas are so underdeveloped as to stop automobiles altogether, leaving pedestrians and equines (primarily donkeys) as the only reliable routine means of communications between bases and the most remote official and military outposts.

THREATS AND HAZARDS

The main categories of threats and hazards to ground transport are accidents and failures; thieves, robbers, and hijackers; and terrorists and insurgents.

Accidents and Failures

Rail travel is less risky than road travel; compared to car journeys, trains travel longer distances, cheaper, with fewer accidents or breakdowns. For instance, from 2008 through 2010, the European Union (E.U.) suffered one fatality in more than 6,400,000,000 km (4,000,000,000 mi) travelled per passenger by train compared to one fatality in 225,000,000 km (140,000,000 mi) travelled per passenger by car. Railway accidents are almost as rare as airline accidents but tend to be as spectacular and memorable, helping to explain popular inflation of railway risks over road risks. For instance, on July 24, 2013, a high-speed train derailed traveling too fast on a curve near Santiago de Compostela in Galicia, Spain, killing more than 80 passengers. Spain's high-speed network had not suffered any fatalities since introduction in 1992; Spain's railways as a whole had suffered a rate of just six fatalities per year in previous years. In the whole of 2011 (the last year for which data are available), across the E.U.'s 27 countries and more than 500 million residents, 1,183 people died in incidents on the railways, of which 98% were pedestrians or car drivers, not railway passengers (Laursen, 2013).

North America does not have nearly as intensive a passenger rail network as the E.U. but permits more hazardous freight on its railways. U.S. railroads carry one million barrels of crude oil per day but spilled just 2,268 barrels of crude oil from 2002 to 2012, much less than were spilled by pipelines or watercraft. However, increased carriage of oil may be raising the risk. For instance, on July 7, 2013, a train with 72 cars of crude oil from North Dakota ran out of control and derailed in downtown Lac-Mégantic, Quebec, Canada, causing a fire that killed 13 people. Lower casualty, less spectacular events are much more frequent. Thirteen people were killed every 5.7 days by trains in the United States during 2014; the 827 deaths that year were the highest since 2007. Of these, about 255 were nonpassengers struck by trains—the highest rate since records began in 1964. The increase is partly attributable to increased freight traffic. About 575 deaths in 2014 were caused by freight trains, partly by increased urban penetration and trespassing. Declining infrastructure and careless operation contribute to a risk that is difficult for nontechnicians to assess but are suspected as factors in the derailment that killed seven and injured more than 200 passengers in Philadelphia on May 12, 2015 (Lavelle, 2015).

In the developed world, most mechanical journeys are by car, so more people are harmed in or by cars than in or by trains, aircraft, or watercraft. For various behavioral and mechanical reasons, car travel is inherently more hazardous. Road traffic accidents (RTAs) kill and injure passengers and pedestrians, disrupt traffic, damage vehicles, and sometimes damage infrastructure. Accidents are associated with increased other risks, particular in unstable areas, such as theft from disabled vehicles and passengers, insurgent or terrorist attacks on first responders, and stress and illness.

Most accidents are collisions between a single vehicle and another object, with some damage or harm but without fatality, but accidents are frequent and the rate of fatalities in cars is very high as a whole compared to other transport risks and even criminal risks. In 2014 (the safest year on American roads to date), automobiles killed 32,675 Americans, an average of 90 persons per day. Twice as many Americans die in road traffic accidents than are murdered. The risks increase with voluntary behaviors, such as reckless driving, telephone use, or intoxication (U.S. National Highway Traffic Safety Administration, 2015).

Car travel seems less risky when the measures capture our more frequent exposure to car travel: In 2014, the United States observed 1.08 fatalities per 100,000,000 mi traveled by car. This rate is declining slightly despite increasing road traffic. Nevertheless, even though people take more road journeys than air journeys, road traffic is more deadly than air travel, both absolutely and as a rate per miles traveled. Road travel kills more than 600 times more Americans than air travel kills.

In developing countries, accidents run at much higher rates. Road traffic accidents kill 0.020% of low- and 0.022% of middle-income country residents per year globally (2004), 0.016% of Americans per year (2010), and 0.006% of Britons per year (2010). While the risks have fallen in the developed world, the risks are growing in the developing world as development correlates with more car use but less rapid development of the controls on accidents. In these areas, risk averseness, regulations, and law enforcement tend to be weak, so simple controls are not required or enforced, such as seat belts (which reduce the chance of death in a crash by 61%), collision-triggered air bags, energy-absorbing structures, and speed restrictions. Globally, the DALYs (disability-adjusted life years) lost to road traffic injuries increased by 34% from 1990 to 2010. More than 90% of road traffic deaths occur in low- and middle-income countries. In fact, in the developing world, RTAs kill more people than typhoid, malaria, and AIDS/HIV combined (WHO, 2009, p. 26).

The rate of RTAs tends to increase rapidly in more unstable or conflictual environments, where public capacity and risk sensitivity dissipates further. Some risky behavior may be justified to avoid other risks (such as by speeding through an area where insurgents operate). External threats can cause accidents indirectly (such as when an insurgent attack distracts a driver who then crashes the automobile).

Thieves, Robbers, and Hijackers

Parked vehicles, stores, refueling sites, and delivery sites are exposed to opportunistic thieves and vandals. If thieves focus on the infrastructure, they can steal construction materials and equipment if left unattended, the lamps and electrical cables used in lighting or signals, and in extreme cases, may steal metals (which are easily sold for scrap) from bridges, hatches and other coverings, and cables.

Vehicles may be stopped by malicious actors who want to hijack the vehicle for its own value or to kidnap a passenger for ransom. In unstable areas, roads are easily blocked or vehicles are intercepted while in transit, sometimes by corrupt public officers in search of bribes.

Terrorists and Insurgents

Official vehicles and their cargos or passengers are normally more secure in their bases, so terrorists and insurgents are incentivized to attack official targets on the roads. They can also attack unofficial targets in pursuit of further instability or to directly harm certain out-groups. Roads are pervasive (even if those roads are materially poor by the standards of the developed world), so the network as a whole is readily exposed to terrorists and insurgents.

In recent decades, terrorists and insurgents have attacked transportation in four main ways:

1. Interrupting traffic in general by comparatively easy attacks on the infrastructure, such as blowing holes in the road surface, digging into the side of the road or railway embankment in order to cause subsidence, destroying bridges, flooding low-lying routes, causing earth or rocks to slide onto a route, or blocking the route with debris

2. Attacking critical logistical convoys, usually on the road at a remote distance from well-protected bases

3. Attacking bases

4. Killing people who use or operate the system

   a. Attacks on private citizens discourage their use of the system. They are most exposed and concentrated on mass transit. The trend to more religious and intransigent terrorism is associated with more attacks on mass transit. Most obviously, most terrorist groups in Northern Ireland have formally accepted peace since the Provisional Irish Republican Party agreed to a ceasefire in 1994, but some zealots refused peace and attacked more mass transit, albeit sometimes with the pretense of attacking official targets. For instance, on the evening of November 20,

2013, a masked man boarded a bus in Londonderry, Northern Ireland, placed an improvised explosive device behind the driver's seat, and told the driver to take the bus to a local police station. She drove a short distance before alerting the police, who later confirmed that the device was viable.

b. Attacks on the operating personnel degrade the transport system as a whole. For instance, on September 17, 2012, a suicide bomber rammed a car into a minivan carrying foreign aviation workers on their way to the airport in Kabul, Afghanistan, killing 10. This attack further discouraged foreigners from using the roads and from taking jobs in the aviation system.

(Continued)

prevented his device from exploding on a train along with the others. He killed himself and 13 others. Two weeks later, two Somalis, one Ethiopian, and one Eritrean-born British citizen attempted to copy the 7/7 attacks, but their devices failed to explode. Like the bombers in Madrid, the British bombers were all first- or second-generation immigrants and Muslims (one was a convert), some with probable terrorist training abroad. The Spanish bombers used dynamite procured illegitimately from miners while the British bombers used liquid explosives produced from hydrogen peroxide.

On July 28, 2005, an explosion on an express train leaving Jaunpur, Uttar Pradesh, India, for Delhi, killed 13 and injured more than 50.

On July 11, 2006, seven bombs within 11 min across seven trains in Mumbai, India, planted by Lashkar-e-Taiba (an Islamist terrorist group based in Pakistan) killed 209 and injured more than 700 people.

On November 20, 2006, an explosion on a train between New Jalpaiguri and Haldibari in West Bengal, India, killed five.

On February 18, 2007, bombs detonated on the Samjhauta Express Train soon after leaving Delhi in India for Lahore in Pakistan, killing 68 and injuring more than 50 people. The main perpetrator was probably Lashkar-e-Taiba.

In 2006, Lebanese authorities arrested Assem Hammoud on evidence gathered in cooperation with the Federal Bureau of Investigation (FBI) that he was plotting with Pakistani terrorists for suicide attacks on trains between New Jersey and New York.

In 2009, Najibullah Zazi, a childhood immigrant to the United States from Afghanistan, and two high school friends (one another immigrant from Afghanistan, the other from Bosnia) were arrested close to implementing a long-planned al-Qaeda–sponsored plot to blow themselves up on subway trains in New York.

On November 27, 2009, a high-speed train was derailed by a bomb near the town of Bologoye on its way between Moscow and Saint Petersburg, causing 27 deaths and about 100 injuries.

On April 22, 2013, Canadian authorities arrested a Tunisian immigrant and an ethnic Palestinian immigrant for an alleged plot, sponsored by al-Qaeda, to derail a train between Toronto and New York.

PROVIDING GROUND TRANSPORT SECURITY

Ground transport security can be improved by improving the security of the transportation infrastructure, navigation, communications, the vehicle's survivability, mobility, and escorts and guards.

Ground Transport Infrastructure Security

Ground transport infrastructure includes the roads, railways, service and support sites and systems, and the fuels and electrical power demanded. Infrastructure security includes protecting infrastructure from malicious attack, preventing accidents and injuries on the system, and preventing failures of infrastructure.

Any transport system needs a secure base, so haulers or passenger services need to secure the sites (see Chapter 8) at which vehicles are stored, maintained, fueled, and loaded. The system benefits from some redundancy so that one insecure node, such as a fueling station, does not incapacitate the whole system. The routes need to be regularly maintained and patrolled. Local civilians should be encouraged to report malicious actors and activities. Clearing debris and vegetation from the sides of routes would help to remove the potential hiding places for thieves and attackers. Where official capacity declines, users might contract with their own maintainers and guards.

Road Security

In the United States, in the 2000s, road traffic accidents were declining in frequency but terrorism was salient, so new government capacity focused on reducing malicious threats, such as weaponization of materials carried on the roads. These initiatives are primarily administered by the Department of Homeland Security, or DHS. The Transportation Security Administration (TSA) was established in November 2001 under the Department of Transportation but moved to DHS in March 2003.

In 2011, DHS counted in America 3,900,000 mi of public roads, 208 million automobiles, 15.5 million trucks (of which 42,000 are rated for carriage of hazardous materials) across 1.2 million trucking companies, and 10 million drivers licensed for commercial vehicles (including 2.7 million licenses for hazardous-materials carriage). The Department of Transportation administers the Research and Special Programs Administration; this includes the Office of Hazardous Materials Safety, which issues guidance and regulations for the security of hazardous materials during carriage. In 2005, the Office of Screening Coordination and Operations (later the Screening Coordination Office), also within DHS, started checking the backgrounds of commercial drivers before granting a hazardous-materials endorsement for their commercial driving licenses. In 2006, this requirement was extended to drivers crossing from Mexico and Canada. Meanwhile, the TSA started the Trucking Security Program, which included 5-year projects

- for developing plans to manage highway emergencies,

- to recruit and train drivers and officials for managing hazardous materials and emergencies, and

- to establish a Highway Information Sharing and Analysis Center.

The program allocated grants to truckers worth $4.8 million for the first 2 fiscal years (2005–2006), $11.6 million in 2007, $25.5 million in 2008, and $7 million in 2009, before termination in 2010.

Meanwhile, critics of the government's focus noted that road traffic accidents make up a much greater risk than terrorism, and their long decline was ending. Critics also noted that the infrastructure was aging with little funding for replacement. (The greatest surge in road building was in the 1960s.) Infrastructure failures are very rare, although the risk seems to be increasing. For instance, in 2008, a bridge carrying the Interstate 35W highway across the Mississippi River in Minneapolis, Minnesota, collapsed, killing 13 and injuring around 100.

Railway Security

Railway systems are more critically exposed in the sense that a malicious actor could easily damage a line, thereby interrupting communications between two points, short of alternative lines between the same two points. As long as the threats can counter the repairers and whatever forces are sent to protect them, small damage would disable a system. This is not just an issue for developing countries with low capacity for repairing and defending railway systems. For instance, in the 2000s, British railway operators and transport police were forced to invest heavily in patrols, fencing, and security cameras after a surge in sabotage and theft of railway infrastructure, usually sabotage by pranksters and errant juveniles who rolled boulders onto tracks or threw stones at driver's cabs or passenger compartments but also organized criminals who lifted trailer-loads of copper cables (used in electrical systems), timber sleepers, or steel tracks from open storage.

In March 2003, the DHS announced Operation Liberty Shield to improve railway security. It asked

- state governors to allocate additional personnel from police or national-guard forces at selected rail bridges,

- railroad operators to increase security at major facilities and hubs, and

- Amtrak to align its security measures with private operators.

The Department of Transportation asked private operators to increase surveillance of trains carrying hazardous materials.

The Rail Security Act (April 2004) authorized an increase in funding for the Rail Security Grant Program from $65 million to $1.1 billion and ordered DHS to assess the vulnerability of the national rail system. Together, the DHS and the Association of American Railroads identified more than 1,300 critical assets. The results were used to inform the distribution of grants and to develop 50 changes to operating procedures, such as physical access, cybersecurity, employee screening, and cargo tracking. A full-time Surface Transportation Information Sharing and Analysis Center (ST-ISAC) was created at the association with clearance for top-secret intelligence. A rail police officer joined the FBI's National Joint Terrorism Task Force.

The TSA provided explosives detection dog teams to the top 10 passenger rail agencies under the Transit and Rail Inspection Pilot (TRIP) program. Phase I (at New Carrollton, Maryland) evaluated technologies for screening passengers and baggage before boarding the train. Phase II (Union Station, Washington, DC) evaluated the screening of checked baggage and cargo prior to loading. Phase III (aboard a Shore Line East commuter car in Connecticut) evaluated technologies to screen passengers and baggage during transit. In fiscal year 2011, the DHS launched the Freight Rail Security Program ($10 million appropriated), which invited railroad carriers of toxic inhalation hazards (TIH) to apply for funds to acquire trackers in their cars and invited owners of railroad bridges to apply for funds to install access controls and monitoring systems at such bridges.

By 2011, DHS counted 120,000 mi of mainline railways and estimated 15 million passengers on railways per day.

NAVIGATION

Navigation is the process of discovering one's position or planning one's way. Good navigation saves time in transit and thus reduces exposure to the risks in the system and reduces wear to the system. Navigation is also important to avoiding and escaping particular threats. Users of the transport system should be advised how to avoid natural hazards. In unstable or high-crime areas, drivers and passengers should be trained to evade malicious roadblocks, hijackers, and other threats. The best routes of escape and the places to gather in an emergency should be researched and agreed in advance of travel.

Personnel should have access to suitable maps marked with the agreed bases, other safe areas (such as friendly embassies), escape routes, and rendezvous locations. Compasses are useful acquisitions for each person and automobile. Where the budget allows, each vehicle could be acquired with an electronic navigation system, although in case this system fails, the personnel should be trained to read a paper map too. (A **Global Positioning System** [GPS] triangulates locations with data sent from Earth-orbiting satellites; an inertial guidance system, using motion and rotation sensors, plots movements based on the vehicle's altitude and speed.)

COMMUNICATIONS

Vehicles should be equipped with radio or telephone communications so that passengers can communicate with emergency services or a base in case of any emergency while in transit. Vehicles can be equipped with tracking technology in case a vehicle is hijacked or the passengers otherwise lose communications. **Trackers** are electronic units that wirelessly communicate their location; they are simple and cheap enough to be widely used to track vehicles in commercial operations. Some trackers can be configured to communicate with a base if they sense that the vehicle has been involved in an accident or the driver has been away from the vehicle outside of the programmed scheduled. Passengers, too, can be equipped with trackers, usually in their clothing or mobile phones.

VEHICLE SURVIVABILITY

Typically, vehicle manufacturers and users must fulfill some obligations for the safety of vehicles in terms of their reliability and the passenger's survivability during an accident. The vehicle's survivability under malicious attack is a dramatically more challenging requirement. The subsections below explain why the requirement has increased, how to improve resistance to kinetic attacks, how to improve blast resistance, how to control access to vehicles, the balance between overt survivability and stealth, and the personal aid equipment that should be carried.

Requirement

The demand for more survivable vehicles has risen dramatically in response to increased terrorism and insurgency. For instance, prior to the terrorist bombings of U.S. embassies in

Kenya and Tanzania in 1998, the U.S. diplomatic service provided around 50 armored vehicles for chiefs of mission at critical and high-threat posts. Thereafter, the service prescribed at least one armored car for every post. By 2009, the service had acquired more than 3,600 armored vehicles worldwide, including 246 vehicles for chiefs of mission (U.S. Government Accountability Office [GAO], 2009, pp. 13, 24). Meanwhile, as insurgencies in Afghanistan and Iraq grew in quantity and quality, operators there realized requirements for more survivable vehicles of all types, from the smallest liaison vehicles to large force protection vehicles and logistical vehicles. The period of most rapid acquisition of armored vehicles was in 2007.

The North Atlantic Treaty Organization (NATO) long ago agreed upon standards of protection for military vehicles that are widely used to define the survivability of all vehicles (see Table 13.1). The standard (STANAG 4569) specifies five protection levels. Most available vehicles do not meet Level 1 (the lowest protection level), most of the military armored vehicles (including wheeled and tracked armored personnel carriers) that were acquired through the Cold War do not surpass Level 1, most armored vehicles fall within Level 2, a few of the larger wheeled vehicles (normally six- or eight-wheeled) fall within Level 3, including the mine-resistant ambush protected vehicles that were widely acquired in the 2000s, light tanks and infantry-fighting vehicles lie within Level 4, and only main battle tanks surpass Level 5.

No armor is proof against all threats, and uncomfortable trade-offs must be made among protection, mobility, and expense.

Resistance to Kinetic Attack

Automobiles are not proof against portable firearms, despite popular culture's depiction of bullets bouncing off a car's panels and windows. Automobiles can be armored reliably against firearms but at great cost, financially and in weight. The extra load implies that the automobile's motor and running gear should be upgraded too; survivability includes capacity to escape and evade, so the vehicle is often upgraded for more rugged off-road travel and for crashing through barriers (hence the term **ruggedized**). The limousines acquired to carry the U.S. president are supposed to cost more than $1.5 million and weigh 8 T each.

Armor is any material meant to prevent external penetration. The armor materials traditionally include hardened steel plates. Hardness is best for defeating projectiles, so it is best on upper surfaces. However, tougher steel is preferred for surviving blast without cracking, so it is best as flooring. Hardness and toughness are normally antagonistic properties; the correct physical balance is achieved by chemically and physically producing materials that are both unusually hard and tough or by layering hard and tough materials. Other hard materials include certain species of aluminum, ceramics, and titanium that deliver superior protection for the same weight of steel. Hard materials can be layered on top of other materials so that the outer materials defeat hard projectiles while inner materials resist blast. Windows and other apertures should be minimized and filled with impact-resistant laminates of glass and plastics and provided with shutters made from a harder material.

Armor can be improvised from scrap materials, but these tend to be mild steels that give a false sense of security. (They are easily punctured or broken.) Armor can be improvised from sandbags; the sand should be as fine as possible since larger pieces are more likely to become projectiles. Keeping the sand wet increases its capacity to absorb energy and also dampens the chemical

Table 13.1 NATO's Standard Vehicle Protection Levels

| STANAG 4569 Level | Projectile Defeated | | | | Blast Defeated | Artillery Shell Fragments Defeated | Estimated Minimum Armor Steel Thickness (mm) |
	Caliber (mm)	Projectile	Range (m)	Muzzle Velocity (m/s)			
1	7.62	Lead core	30	833	Fragmentation grenade, landmine, or submunition	—	10
2	7.62	Steel core	30	695	Blast mine of 6 kg under running gear (2a) or center (2b)		15
3	7.62	Tungsten carbide core	30	930	Blast mine of 8 kg under running gear (3a) or center (3b)		30
4	14.5	Tungsten carbide core	200	911	Blast mine of 10 kg under running gear (4a) or center (4b)	155-mm caliber high-explosive shell at 30 m	40
5	25	Discarding sabot	500	1,258	As above	As above except at 25 m	60

explosive. Rubber mats and belts help to contain flying dirt while retaining the flexibility to survive blast without tearing. However, all these materials add weight. Ideally, sandbags should be more than one layer deep, but most vehicles lack internal capacity and load-bearing capacity for more than one layer. If the sandbags cannot be placed around all sides, they should prioritized around crew positions and wheel wells. (Ground explosives are most likely to be detonated by wheels.)

Liquids can be used to protect; water is physically resistant to projectiles and also dampens explosives and fuels before they can fully combust. Water inside pneumatic tires helps to dampen explosives detonated under the wheel. Less volatile fuels can be used as protection. Diesel fuel is not naturally flammable except under high pressure or temperature or when agitated; most military vehicles are diesel fueled, and some incorporate their fuel tanks into their protection against projectiles. At the same time, fuel tanks should be armored against hot fragments and separated from crew compartments.

Bar armor or **slat armor** is a particular physical defense against rocket-propelled grenades, which are normally detonated by an electrical signal running from the point of the projectile to the explosive at the base. A rocket that impacts between bars or slats, if they are arranged with the proper separation, will be crushed, damaging its electrical circuit before it can detonate. Bar/slat armor is attached to the outside of a vehicle's vertical surfaces, resembling an outer cage.

Blast Resistance

Vehicles can be designed and constructed to be dramatically more survivable against blast, which is typically produced by chemical explosives hidden on or in the ground. This blast resistance was the main capability offered by a class of vehicles known as **mine-resistant, ambush-protected vehicles (MRAPs)** in the U.S. military or **heavy, protected patrol vehicles** in the British military, which were urgently required in Afghanistan and Iraq from the mid-2000s. From 2005 to 2009 alone, the U.S. military urgently ordered more than 16,000 MRAPs. The U.S. Army's National Ground Intelligence Center's Anti-Armor Incident Database suggests that a MRAP vehicle reduced interior deaths compared to an armored Humvee by between 9 times (Afghanistan) and 14 times (Iraq) (based on data for the average number of troops killed per explosive attack on each vehicle, 2005 to 2011).

However, MRAPs are more than 4 times more expensive than replaced vehicles and about twice as heavy, larger, slower, less mobile, and more burdensome to sustain. Their size meant that often they could not fit in confined urban areas or on narrow roads while their weight often caused roads or bridges to collapse. Their height contributes to higher rates of rollovers (such as when roads collapsed and a vehicle tumbled into a ravine). Often they were confined to good roads (where insurgents could more easily target them). In 2009, the U.S. military required, especially for Afghanistan, another 6,600 vehicles of a smaller more mobile class of blast-resistant vehicle, designated **MRAP all-terrain vehicles (M-ATVs)**. Also in 2009, the British required a similar class that they called light protected patrol vehicle. By mid-2012, around 27,000 MRAPs and M-ATVs had been produced in response to urgent orders, of which 23,000 had been deployed to Afghanistan and Iraq.

In practice, most operators and situations require all classes of vehicle. MRAPs should patrol and escort on the good roads and in the spacious urban areas, but M-ATVs are required for poorer terrain. However, MRAPs and M-ATVs each remain imperfect trade-offs; M-ATVs proved insufficiently survivable for some roles, so more than 6,000 of them were upgraded to be more resistant to blast from beneath.

Areas facing blast should be made from tougher materials and can be filled with energy-absorbing materials or constructed to collapse gracefully (although these materials tend to reduce interior space). Higher ground clearances increase the distance between ground-based blast and the vehicle's interior, although tall vehicles tend to roll easier and to be more difficult to hide. The bottom armor of the vehicle should be v-shaped so as to deflect blast to the sides and should contain the automotive parts so that they do not separate as secondary missiles. Monocoque hulls (where the same structure bears all loads and attachments) eliminate some of the potential secondary missiles associated with a conventional chassis. Wheel units should be sacrificial, meaning that they separate easily under blast without disintegrating further, taking energy away from the vehicle interior without producing further secondary missiles. The interior passenger compartments should be separated from the automotive and engine compartments. Interior passengers should be seated on energy-absorbing or collapsible materials or suspended from the roof to reduce the energy transmitted from below into the passengers' bodies. Footrests and foot pedals also should be energy absorbing without separating as secondary missiles. (Otherwise, they would transmit energy that could shatter the legs.)

Access Controls

Vehicles need apertures for human ingress, egress, and visibility, but apertures increase the interior's exposure to sudden ingress of projectiles, human attackers, and thieves. Vehicles should be secured from unauthorized access by specifying locks on all doors and hatches, and windows constructed from a puncture-resistant material. Door and hatch hinges should be designed and constructed to be resistant to tools. In hot environments or prolonged duties, crews will tend to leave doors and hatches open for ventilation, where they can be surprised, so an air-conditioning system should be specified. Rules on closing and locking hatches and leaving at least one guard with a vehicle should be specified and enforced.

When civilian vehicles are converted to armored versions, some minor upgrades may be forgotten. For instance, on February 15, 2011, two U.S. Immigrations and Customs Enforcement agents were shot (one killed) inside an armored civilian vehicle in northeastern Mexico after the driver was forced off the road by armed threats (probably robbers targeting an expensive vehicle). Unfortunately, the vehicle was configured to automatically unlock the doors when the driver put the transmission in park (a typical safety feature in ordinary cars), but this allowed the threats to open a door. During the struggle to close and relock the door, the window also was lowered, through which the threats fired some bullets. Once the door and window were secured, the vehicle survived all further bullets (around 90), but the harm to the two agents was already done.

Operators face a choice between complying with external requests to stop and ignoring such requests in case they have malicious intent disguised as official duties or requests for assistance. For instance, on August 24, 2012, in Mexico City, two U.S. agents (probably from the U.S. intelligence community) were wounded by some of around 30 bullets fired by Mexican federal police during a chase after the Americans refused a checkpoint, probably influenced by the event in 2011. They were driving in a ruggedized, armored vehicle, but its rear wheel and some of its apertures did not survive the bullets. A Mexican passenger was unharmed.

Stealth

Operators face a choice between armored, ruggedized vehicles and **stealthy** vehicles that do not attract as much attention. Some operators have very contrasting preferences in the trade-off between visible deterrence or defense and stealth, with some operators insisting on traveling everywhere alone in randomly hailed taxis and others insisting on traveling nowhere without visibly armed escorts and armored vehicles. Some operators like to hire local vehicles that resemble the average local vehicle and to remove any branding from their vehicles while others prefer to procure more robust and armored vehicles, even though they stand out from most other vehicles. Commercial interests, home-funder requirements, and local laws may force operators to display their branding in specialized vehicles, whatever the cost in stealth.

Personal-Aid Equipment

The automobile should be equipped as appropriate to the particular threats, but a minimal set of equipment would include **first-aid kits** (essentially immediate-medical-response kits, perhaps including blood ready for transfusion, a defibrillator, and oxygen) and **personal-survival kits** (firefighting equipment, drinking water, food, fuel, and pedestrian-navigation equipment).

Mobility

Survivable vehicles are normally acquired with **run-flat tires**, which are pneumatic tires with solid or rigid cores, which will continue to run for dozens of miles after a puncture. The pneumatic tire may be reinforced with a tear- and puncture-resistant material. Given a sudden change in threat level, pneumatic tires can be replaced with solid rubber tires, which cannot be punctured (although they can be chipped), or tires filled partly with water, which helps to dampen chemical blast, although their extra weight and reduced flexibility transfer more vibration and wear to the vehicle.

Armoring the vehicle and adding equipment implies an added load, which implies a need for upgraded running gear to permit running over rougher grounds and inferior roads in case the vehicle needs to escape threats on superior roads. The U.S. president's limousines offer excellent armor protection around a voluminous passenger compartment, but they do not offer good off-road capabilities. On March 23, 2011, the president's spare limousine for his official visit to Ireland grounded on a small hump in the gateway leaving the U.S. embassy in Dublin and was temporarily abandoned in front of crowds of spectators and journalists. Most civilian armored vehicles are based on chassis designed for off-road use while military armored vehicles are based on more specialized platforms.

Still, procurers must trade expense and mobility against survivability, so survivable vehicles tend to be very expensive with short life cycles. For instance, as of October 2009, 914 (32%) of U.S. diplomatic armored vehicles were in Iraq, each at a procurement cost of about $173,000 with a life cycle of just about 3 years due to Iraq's difficult terrain (U.S. GAO, 2009).

Increased survivability implies increased risks associated with accidents and reduced mobility. Increased armor and equipment imply reduced internal space and more heat stress, biomechanical stress, and acceleration injuries. Reduced mobility implies that the vehicle is restricted to the best terrain, helping threats to target the vehicle. Increased protection also implies more separation between the passengers and locals on the ground, thereby alienating locals and interrupting opportunities for local engagement and intelligence.

ESCORTS AND GUARDS

Guards can ride in vehicles, but guards can be provocative to external threats and are hazards that may be activated as insider threats, perhaps by external bribes or ideologies.

Road convoys can be escorted by police or military vehicles or by privately contracted armed and armored vehicles that should deter attackers, but these escorts can also draw attention to convoys that would otherwise blend in to routine traffic. Operators from different companies or authorities can cooperate by choosing to travel at the same time with shared escorts. They could also choose to follow a better protected convoy, although if they failed to notify the other convoy in advance its escorts might interpret followers as threats.

Escorts may be subject to ethical standards, regulations, or laws issued by the home organization or local authorities, but in unstable areas, escorts may be reckless and uncontained. In Afghanistan, Iraq, and Libya, police and military forces have a reputation for a mix of absenteeism and reckless violence. Private-security contractors were not subject to local or coalition military laws or to professional or industry standards of behavior, so they developed a reputation for varied performance, such as reckless driving in order to reduce exposure to attackers on the roads and shooting to death other drivers who approached too quickly (as a suicide bomber would approach). Contractors were supposed to reduce the overall costs and inflexibility of military security, but when the security situation deteriorated, some refused to work unless accompanied by military escorts.

Beyond Protection: The Case for Resilience in Surface Transportation

Michael Dinning

Protection of our surface transportation systems, including rail, highway, intermodal freight, pipeline and public transportation, is critical to our economy and our way of life. Security and emergency managers play critical roles in keeping the system moving safely. To do this requires a collaborative, multimodal, risk-based approach that addresses all hazards and increases transportation resilience.

Enhancing transportation operations. Security measures do not always have to present bottlenecks and incur extra costs but can be designed to increase durability, throughput, and efficiency. To accomplish this, security systems must be designed and implemented in collaboration with transportation operations managers and other stakeholders. Security technologies can be integrated into transportation processes in ways that contribute directly to the bottom line. Take the following examples:

Video cameras can provide situational awareness to detect, assess, and respond to security incidents and also to assist operations managers in assessing demand and optimizing service. They can also provide risk managers with powerful evidence to reduce false accident and damage claims.

Secure technologies for identifying travelers and vehicles can expedite movement of

(Continued)

FINAL CASE STUDY

(Continued)

passengers and freight at borders, ports, and other transportation facilities as part of risk-based screening programs.

Nonintrusive screening of cargo can detect contraband and stolen goods and can increase revenues by facilitating enforcement of customs-duty payments.

Ensuring system resilience. The surface transportation system is so vast and open that protection from all threats is not always possible. Security strategies are needed that not only reduce vulnerabilities but also minimize the consequences of incidents. Security managers must collaborate with a wide range of other organizations to design and implement multimodal strategies to increase transportation resilience and reduce risks from any hazard. Transportation resilience strategies must include three elements:

- Transportation infrastructure must be **robust**. Bridges and other transportation infrastructure designs can be hardened, not only to resist explosives and other physical attacks but also to reduce costly damage from earthquakes, flooding, and vehicle impacts.

- The transportation system must be **redundant**. Regional transportation emergency plans must identify alternative facilities and networks for both passenger and freight transportation. These plans must consider substituting one mode of transportation for another and must take into account multimodal connections. For example, a resilient airport will be of little use if surface transportation access is unavailable.

- Surface transportation systems must be able to **adapt** to disruptions from deliberate attacks and other events and to recovery quickly. Embedded sensors and intelligent transportation-system technologies increase situational awareness and allow operators to monitor and respond. These tools can facilitate collaborative decision making where operators work together to minimize the impacts of disruptions. Transportation recovery plans, involving both the public and private sectors, must be developed during the regional planning process to ensure that infrastructure can be rebuilt to be more resilient than before.

Reducing cybersecurity risks. Transportation systems must be resilient to cyber as well as physical risks. Every mode of transportation is increasingly dependent on information technology and cyber-physical control systems, and these systems are connected with the Internet and wireless networks in ways that present new risks. Transportation system designers, operators, and managers must work with security specialists to

- Understand the potential vulnerabilities and risks of both traditional IT systems and control systems that are critical to safety and transportation operations. Mobile devices, remote network access, GPS, and digitally connected vehicles or autonomous vehicle operations present potential vulnerabilities.

- Develop risk mitigation plans to protect against, detect, and rapidly recover from cyber attacks or failures.

Separating safety and mission-critical systems from less critical systems and passenger-infotainment systems is a way to reduce risks. Efforts to mitigate cybersecurity vulnerabilities must be coordinated with physical security measures to reduce risks from hybrid attacks.

- Have a well-exercised strategy for responding to and recovering from disruptions to IT systems, communications networks, and control systems. Transportation organizations should have downtime procedures that employees are able to use if critical IT or control systems fail. Collaborative information-sharing and analysis capabilities with other organizations will enhance incident response and should be part of daily operations.

- Instill a culture of cybersecurity and resilience throughout the organization. Employees and stakeholders must understand how their actions can reduce cyber risks. Transportation systems should strive for a level of awareness with all users and stakeholders similar to what has been achieved for fire safety, where everyone, from designer to user, understands and practices risk mitigation behavior.

The surface transportation system is subject to an ever-changing set of challenges and risks. Both passenger and freight transportation are truly multimodal and are integral parts of our economy. Collaborative approaches are essential to reduce surface transportation risks in all modes of transportation and to increase overall transportation system resilience.

Michael Dinning has served as director of transportation logistics and security at Volpe National Transportation Systems Center, leading programs to mitigate cyber and physical security risks and to introduce innovative situational awareness and logistics management systems. He now coordinates multimodal initiatives at Volpe. These efforts include freight transportation, big data in transportation, cyber-physical systems, multimodal payment systems, transportation resilience, and other cross-cutting issues. Dinning facilitates collaboration within Volpe and with industry, academia, and government agencies.

CHAPTER SUMMARY

This chapter has

- Described the scope of ground transport security,

- Described the threats and hazards to ground transport, including

  o accidents and failures,

  o thieves, robbers, and hijackers, and

  o terrorists and insurgents.

- Explained how to improve the security of ground transport via

  o the infrastructure,

  o navigation,

  o communications,

  o vehicle survivability, including resistance to kinetic projectiles, resistance to blast, access controls, stealth, and personal aid equipment,

  o mobility, and

  o escorts and guards.

KEY TERMS

Armor *532*
Bar armor *534*
First-aid kit *536*
Global Positioning System *531*
Ground transportation *523*
Ground transport infrastructure *528*

Heavy, protected patrol vehicle *534*
Mine-resistant, ambush-protected vehicle (MRAP) *534*
MRAP all-terrain vehicle (M-ATV) *534*
Navigation *531*
Personal-survival kit *536*

Railroad *523*
Railway *523*
Road *523*
Ruggedized *532*
Run-flat tire *536*
Slat armor *534*
Stealthy *535*
Tracker *531*

QUESTIONS AND EXERCISES

1. Describe different modes of ground transportation and why they become more or less important as an area becomes less stable or developed.

2. What compound risks arise from road traffic accidents?

3. Describe the three main ways in which terrorists and insurgents target ground transportation.

4. Describe routine activities necessary to secure the ground transport infrastructure.

5. How could you prepare for ground navigation in case of an emergency?

6. Explain why a vehicle's resistance to kinetic attacks can be antagonistic to blast resistance.

7. Describe the trade-off between a vehicle's overt survivability and stealth.

8. Describe the trade-off between a vehicle's survivability and mobility.

9. Describe the positive and negative risks of vehicle escorts and guards.

14

BORDER SECURITY

In 2006, the Department of Homeland Security launched the Secure Border Initiative (SBI) to safeguard the U.S. borders with Canada and Mexico. It was an overarching program designed to link the four governmental operating arms responsible for border security: Customs and Border Protection (CBP), Immigration and Customs Enforcement (ICE), the Transportation Security Administration (TSA), and the Coast Guard. The goal is an integrated system with a common infrastructure of personnel, technology, and rapid response. A further aim was to allow these agencies to function seamlessly to secure the borders by enforcing national immigration laws. A central component of the grand design was SBInet. **SBInet** was the advanced-technology program to increase detection capabilities. Its deployment involved the construction of a virtual fence, laden with remote surveillance camera systems, thermal-imaging devices, ultralight detectors, sensors, and unmanned aerial vehicles.

From the beginning, SBInet was beset with difficulties. The primary government contractor, Boeing, consistently missed deadlines, and the government routinely responded by lowering expectations. Yet the project pressed on despite the projection by the Government Accountability Office (GAO) that at a rate of 28 mi every 4.5 years, the entire virtual fence would not be fully deployed until 2330—320 years from the time of its report (McCutcheon, 2010). When the program was finally cancelled in 2010, one reporter wrote, "You could almost hear a collective sigh of relief" (Aitoro, 2011, n.p.). In explaining how a program with this degree of scope, attention, and importance was allowed to continue along such an errant path, a former director at the GAO remarked, "It's hard to re-direct an iceberg once it's headed in the wrong direction" (Aitoro, 2011, n.p.).

The iceberg is an apt metaphor in a discussion on U.S. border security strategy. The issues are not merely confined to the topic of homeland security. Immigration policy, civil rights, and international relations are subject matter that form the immense scope of relevant themes. The pace of management change and

Learning Objectives and Outcomes

At the end of this chapter, you should be able to understand

- The scope of border security

- The nature and trends in immigration

- The threats, hazards, and how border security risk is managed

- The role of Customs and Border Protection (CBP)

- The role of Immigration and Customs Enforcement (ICE)

- The role of Citizenship and Immigration Services (CIS)

- The role of the U.S. Coast Guard

- The social cost of illegal immigration

- The economic cost of restricted immigration

policy implementation, furthermore, can be glacial under any of these areas alone. When the task is to harmonize terrains, the results are often inconsistent at best, conflicting at worst.

In Chapter 14, we will look at the policy and structure in place to secure the borders while trying to enable the daily routines of commerce and ordinary life. Much has already been mentioned in the previous chapters on maritime, aviation, and ground security. Through this section's pages, we discuss the threats, organization, and countermeasures to secure the nation's immediate crossing as well as the complex issues that affect development and implementation of policy.

SCOPE

The United States has 5,525 mi of border with Canada and 1,989 mi with Mexico. The maritime border includes over 12,000 mi of shoreline (95,000 if internal coasts are included). Over 4,000 ports and terminals dot the map, and approximately 120 million travelers pass through several hundred airports. According to the CBP, more than 500 million people cross the borders into the United States every year. In addition, 118,129, 875 vehicles and 25.3 million cargo containers enter the United States annually. The value of trade transiting over and through U.S. borders in 2012 was $2.3 trillion (*Measuring outcomes*, 2013). Therefore, border security policy takes on a vast array of issues that not only involve personnel resources, funding priorities, and jurisdictional overlap but also economic, legal, political, and diplomatic concerns.

The transport network is basically an open landscape, and its vastness challenges our employee pool and financial capacity to secure it. In order to stop the flow of potential terrorists on to the territory of the United States, the national strategy is to "push out the borders." The approach not only seeks to control the threat of terrorism, it also is an effort to interdict against the trafficking of narcotics and other contraband before they reach the United States.

However, as discussed in Chapter 2, many of these programs raise the uncomfortable issue of *American exceptionalism*. This is the notion embedded within U.S. defense policy that justifies the right to act unilaterally in quest of national self-interest. The defense of the borders through programs that give priority to U.S. inbound cargo, the monitoring of finances, profiling, stationing armed agents at foreign ports, and the creation of extralegal expediencies, such as the Guantanamo detention camp, has drawn criticism from foreign allies and critics at home.

Meanwhile, the United States is, as it has always been, a nation of immigrants. The diversity that arriving populations bring with them has been a major contribution to the *American experiment*. This population segment has added to social and scientific advancement and will always be a source of innovation and national identity. However, as more people converge upon the United States to invest their lives and seek opportunity, others come looking to exploit the system through crime or political violence. The access routes are the same for both.

Over the past 50 years, the immigrant population grew significantly. In 1960, there were 9.7 million foreign-born people living in the United States. By 2011, that number increased by more than 300%. The U.S. population currently includes nearly 40 million foreign-born citizens and other residents. Broken down by immigration status, the foreign-born population in 2011 was composed of 15.5 million naturalized U.S. citizens, 13.1 million legal permanent residents, and 11.2 million unauthorized migrants (Malik & Wolgin, 2015). During this time period, the major

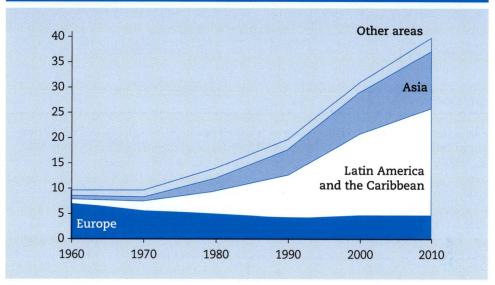

Figure 14.1 Foreign-Born Population by Region of Birth, 1960 to 2010 (Numbers in Millions)

Source: U.S. Census Bureau, Census of Population, 1960 to 2010, and the America Community Survey, 2010.

Note: Other areas include Africa, Northern American, Oceania, born at sea, and not reported.

region of origin has shifted markedly. Previously, Europeans accounted for most of the immigrant flow to the United States. Today, Latin America and Asia are the main sources of immigration.

Human migration is increasing worldwide. At present, the largest migration in history is occurring. The debt trap in the developing world is driving people to seek opportunities in urban centers and in industrialized countries. In addition, climate change forces populations subject to food and water shortages to abandon their homes for the sake of their own survival. **Climate migrants'** numbers may reach as many as 200 million as the demand for basic necessities and world population increases (Gaines & Kappeler, 2012). These trends will raise the number of people seeking better futures in the United States.

These developments are pressuring the debate on immigration reform and demands on border enforcement agencies. As the process moves forward, Congress funds border security piecemeal while spending millions of dollars in workforce hours holding hearings.

Border threats may separate into *actors* and *goods*. Threatening goods include weapons, particularly weapons of mass destruction and their precursor parts and matériel. Smuggling weapons out of the United States is also outlawed. Illegal drugs, counterfeit products, and products brought into the United States illegally and/or with potentially harmful effect, such as animals and plant life that could have environmental consequences or might endanger the food supply, are other prohibited items. Under the category of banned traffic are persons carrying serious communicable diseases.

Table 14.1 Legal Permanent Resident Flow by Region and Country of Birth, Fiscal Years 2010 to 2012 (Countries Ranked by 2012 LPR Flow)

Region and Country of Birth	2012		2011		2010	
	Number	Percent	Number	Percent	Number	Percent
REGION						
TOTAL	1,031,631	100.0	1,062,040	100.0	1,042,625	100.0
Africa	107,241	10.4	100,374	9.5	101,355	9.7
Asia	429,599	41.6	451,593	42.5	422,063	40.5
Europe	81,671	7.9	83,850	7.9	88,801	8.5
North America	327,771	31.8	333,902	31.4	336,553	32.3
Caribbean	127,477	12.4	133,680	12.6	139,951	13.4
Central America	40,675	3.9	43,707	4.1	43,951	4.2
Other North America	159,619	15.5	156,515	14.7	152,651	14.6
Oceania	4,742	0.5	4,980	0.5	5,345	0.5
South America	79,401	7.7	86,096	8.1	87,178	8.4
Unknown	1,206	0.1	1,245	0.1	1,330	0.1
COUNTRY						
TOTAL	1,031,631	100.0	1,062,040	100.0	1,042,625	100.0
Mexico	146,406	14.2	143,446	13.5	139,120	13.3
China, People's Republic	81,784	7.9	87,016	8.2	70,863	6.8
India	66,434	6.4	69,013	6.5	69,162	6.6
Philippines	57,327	5.6	57,011	5.4	58,173	5.6
Dominican Republic	41,566	4.0	46,109	4.3	53,870	5.2
Cuba	32,820	3.2	36,452	3.4	33,573	3.2
Vietnam	28,304	2.7	34,157	3.2	30,632	2.9
Haiti	22,818	2.2	22,111	2.1	22,582	2.2
Colombia	20,931	2.0	22,635	2.1	22,406	2.1
South Korea	20,846	2.0	22,824	2.1	22,227	2.1

Region and Country	2012		2011		2010	
of Birth	Number	Percent	Number	Percent	Number	Percent
Jamaica	20,705	2.0	19,662	1.9	19,825	1.9
Iraq	20,369	2.0	21,133	2.0	19,855	1.9
Burma	17,383	1.7	16,518	1.6	12,925	1.2
El Salvador	16,256	1.6	18,667	1.8	18,806	1.8
Pakistan	14,740	1.4	15,546	1.5	18,258	1.8
Bangladesh	14,705	1.4	16,707	1.6	14,819	1.4
Ethiopia	14,544	1.4	13,793	1.3	14,266	1.4
Nigeria	13,575	1.3	11,824	1.1	13,376	1.3
Canada	12,932	1.3	12,800	1.2	13,328	1.3
Iran	12,916	1.3	14,822	1.4	14,182	1.4
All other countries	354,270	34.3	359,794	33.9	360,377	34.6

Source: U.S. Department of Homeland Security, Computer Linked Application Information Management System (CLAIMS), Legal Immigrant Data, Fiscal Years 2010 to 2012.

Banned persons, or **threat actors**, include potential terrorists, transnational criminals, and unauthorized migrants. The first two types were discussed in Chapters 3 and 4. Unauthorized migrants are types of people that, if not in the category of criminal or terrorist, are coming to the United States for personal opportunity, family connections, or for survival due to political or economic conditions in their place of origin. However, they enter the United States in violation of its laws and amid the debate and argument by some Americans that, if unchecked, pervasive immigration might become a burden on society.

The **Immigration and Nationality Act** (INA) is the basic body of immigration law. It was created in 1952 and amended many times. The INA of 1990, among other things, increased the limits on legal immigration to the United States and revised all grounds for exclusion and deportation. It also prohibits the admission of any alien with a history of involvement in terrorist activity considered likely to engage in terrorist activity or who is a representative of a terrorist organization that endorses or advocates terrorist activity. In addition to terrorists and certain criminals, the INA bans aliens on grounds of health-related issues, aliens who raise certain foreign-policy concerns, aliens considered likely to become a public burden, certain employment-based immigrants without a labor certification, and aliens arriving at an illegal time or place or not in possession of a valid unexpired visa or other valid entry document (Rosenblum et al., 2013, pp. 6–7). While immigration reform efforts stall in Washington, the INA remains the legislation that establishes the level and preference system for admission of immigrants to the United States.

Border Security

Types of Threat Actors		
Terrorists	Transnational Criminals	Unauthorized Migrants
Motivation—Ideological: achieve socially transformative change or narrower specific ends. Typically not focused on controlling turf or underground markets but reacting to particular grievances.	*Motivation*—Profit driven: create and maintain illicit wealth and prestige. Defend criminal markets and turf. Stave off enemies, including law enforcement, other state actors, and rival criminal groups.	*Motivation*—Personal opportunity: seeking to improve economic circumstances, avert dangerous conditions in home country, lured by family connections.
Means—Propaganda and violence with symbolic features. Justify violence in moral terms by insisting on the restoration of justice in an unjust society. Propaganda used to raise support and attract recruits.	*Means*—Engaged in violence and corruption during the exploit of illegal markets. Use violence to intimidate officials, innocent victims, and rivals and to protect operations. Tend to act in obscurity and may use propaganda to vilify rivals.	*Means*—Illegal entry or visa overstay. Apart from immigration related offences and the use of fraudulent documents to obtain employment, most never commit criminal offenses. May become involved in transnational crime during the course of their migration or while seeking employment.

Source: Rosenblum, Bjelopera, and Finklea (2013, p. 10).

BOX 14.1

RISK MANAGEMENT AND ASSESSMENT

Following the attack on 9/11, U.S. policy on border security reflected the outrage and fears the catastrophe stirred among the public and in government. The USA PATRIOT Act gave law enforcement new investigative powers, which at times tested fundamental civil rights assumptions in the courts. DHS and advocates of all-inclusive border security threat coverage may once have had the support of adopting an "all of the above" approach after September 11, 2001 (Rosenblum et al., 2013, p. 1). However, over time, operational and financial realities forced the Department of Homeland Security and many in Congress to consider more fiscally prudent options. Effective enforcement strategy also meant regularly assessing the threat matrix and evolutions in technology in order to align policy with functional cost–benefit analysis. Because threat actors change their tactics in reaction to law enforcement efforts and tendencies, border security policy should be evolutionary and risk-based. This requires evaluating the likelihood of threats and their potential for harm against the availability of resources and the threshold capacity for acceptable loss. DHS defines risk management approach to border security as follows.

▶ Immigration, Border Security, and Citizenship

Source: U.S. Department of Homeland Security (2014); U.S. Citizen and Immigration Services.

> In general, DHS's border enforcement strategy, like its overall approach to homeland security, is based on risk management, which DHS defines as "the process for identifying, analyzing, and communicating risk and accepting, avoiding, transferring, or controlling it to an acceptable level considering associated costs and benefits of any actions taken." In short, the goal of risk management is to target enforcement resources to specific threats in proportion (1) to the gravity of the associated risk, and (2) to the cost-effectiveness of the enforcement response. (Rosenblum et al., 2013, p. 2)

The USA PATRIOT Act required the Department of Homeland Security to develop risk assessment formulae. Some vehicles for putting risk management practices into action are the Automated Targeting System (ATS), the rule-based cargo-screening system discussed in Chapter 12, and intelligence and law enforcement databases, such as the National Targeting Center. FEMA administers many funding and grant programs to high-risk geographic areas based upon DHS determination of the level of threat and effectiveness of response.

DHS also works beside academia, with the intelligence community, and with other federal agencies to develop quantitative models to assess the risks of possible terrorist attacks using chemical, biological, radiological, or nuclear (CBRN) weapons. These models often use *event trees* to simulate and estimate the likelihood and potential of various attack scenarios. Factors and projected outcomes run into the millions of possibilities and are captured by the following models:

- **Bioterrorism Risk Assessment** (BTRA)

- **Chemical Terrorism Risk Assessment** (CTRA)

- **Radiological and Nuclear Terrorism Risk Assessment** (RNTRA)

- **Integrated Terrorism Risk Assessment** (ITRA)

Pursuant to its responsibilities under the Patriot Act, DHS produced two documents to define, communicate, and promote risk management practices and convey a common grasp of the approach. The **Risk Lexicon** and *Risk Management Fundamentals* put forth a foundation for conducting risk assessments and risk management alternatives across the spectrum of DHS components and partner organizations (Rosenblum et al., 2013, p. 15). DHS's risk management process involves six steps: (1) define the decision-making context; (2) identify potential risks; (3) assess and analyze risks; (4) develop alternatives; (5) decide upon and implement risk management strategies; and (6) evaluate and monitor outcomes (U.S. DHS, 2010, p. vii).

Risk management requires developing risk assessment models. Standard risk estimates of the likelihood of a threat or other harmful event and the potential consequence of the threat are the component elements of an actionable assessment model. *Likelihood* and *consequence* are the prime integrants. The likelihood-times-consequences framework is used for estimating risk of CBRN attacks and for allocating resources and funding of the grant programs described above. However, the use of these metrics in border security is incomplete, mainly because an understanding of the full range of threats at U.S. borders is still partial.

The ability to calculate the likelihood that an event will occur depends much on historical trends. These are, obviously, more useful tools when attempting to interdict against common crimes such as smuggling and drug trafficking, which have a record of past frequencies. However, if defending against an event in connection with a CBRN attack or any plot to use WMD material, analytic predictions about expected frequencies is a more difficult calculus. In these cases, quantitative predictions about the probability of a future incident can be illusive. In order to make more informed predictions about anticipated events, risk management needs to rely on subject matter experts and intelligence analysis to expand capability when historical data is insubstantial. Factors such as operational competencies, organizational structure, and political or economic motivation are valuable insights when historical trends are lacking. Definition, Box 14.2 itemizes key concepts of risk assessment. They are applicable in all situations relative to homeland security and are used frequently in modeling exercises.

The U.S. border is a critical intersection for transnational commercial and human flow. Because of the strategic and geographic expansiveness of border threats, policy formulation and execution is complex. Furthermore, border policy extends well beyond the area of the border region. As discussed above, border security policy can overlap, clash, or complicate jurisdictional authority, diplomatic relations, and human and civil rights, as well as rights of privacy. In the face of these complications, collaboration is essential for success.

BORDER SECURITY: KEY AGENCIES

Before September 11, 2001, the authority over border security was a fragmented arrangement whose responsibility fell under an assortment of federal departments, the chief agencies being the Immigration and Naturalization Service within the Department of Justice; the Customs Service in the Treasury Department; Animal and Plant Health Inspection Service of the

Understanding Risk: Key Terms

Consequence: Effect of an event, incident, or occurrence (p. 10)

Likelihood: Chance of something happening, whether defined, measured or estimated objectively or subjectively, or in terms of general descriptors (such as rare, unlikely, likely, almost certain) frequencies, or probabilities (p. 20)

Risk: Potential for unwanted outcome resulting from an incident, event, or occurrence as determined by its likelihood and he associated consequences (p. 27)

Risk Management: The process of identifying, analyzing, assessing, and communicating risk and accepting, avoiding, transferring or controlling it to an acceptable level at an acceptable level (p. 30)

Scenario: Hypothetical situation comprised of a hazard, an entity impacted by that hazard, and associated conditions including consequences when appropriate (p. 33)

Threat: Natural or man-made occurrence, individual, entity, or action that has or indicates the potential to harm life, information operations, the environment, and/or property (p. 36)

Source: U.S. DHS (2010).

Department of Agriculture; and the Coast Guard, which was then part of the Department of Transportation. The creation of the Department of Homeland Security reorganized government and entrusted the responsibility of border security to four main agencies under one federal department: DHS. They are Customs and Border Protection, Immigration and Customs Enforcement, the Transportation Security Administration, and the Coast Guard, which are all accountable to the Office of Policy at DHS. Through this managerial structure, these bureaus report directly to the secretary of Homeland Security and undersecretaries. The aim of the reorganization is to add efficiency to the policy design process and make certain DHS policies and regulations conform across the department. Listed in Table 14.2 are the agencies with their corresponding missions.

Although these four bureaus have the main responsibility for border security, the overall mandate remains scattered over many other federal agencies also involved in the strategic task of securing U.S. borders. Despite not being central to their missions, the contribution of these agencies is also important. They include such organizations as the Federal Bureau of Investigation, Drug Enforcement Agency, Centers for Disease Control and Prevention, and Central Intelligence Agency as well as state and local responders from jurisdictions along the Canadian and Mexican borders.

Table 14.2 Agencies in Charge of Border Security

Bureau	Responsibility
Bureau of Customs and Border Protection (CBP)	Patrols the border and conducts immigration, customs, and agricultural inspections at ports of entry
Bureau of Immigrations and Customs Enforcement (ICE)	Investigates immigration and customs violations in the interior of the country
Transportation Security Administration (TSA)	Responsible for securing the nation's land, rail, and air transportation networks
United States Coast Guard	Provides maritime and port security

Source: Nuñez-Neto (2008, pp. 2–6).

Customs and Border Protection (CBP)

CBP can be considered the law enforcement arm of DHS. It is the largest federal law enforcement agency of the United States. It has a workforce of more than 45,600 sworn federal agents and officers charged with regulating and facilitating international trade, collecting import duties, and enforcing U.S. regulations relative to trade, customs, and immigration (Nuñez-Neto, 2008, pp. 2–3).

Simply and broadly stated, its mission is to prevent terrorists and terrorist weapons from entering the country, provide security at U.S. borders and ports of entry, apprehend illegal immigrants, stem the flow of illegal drugs, and protect American agricultural and economic interests from harmful pests and diseases. It provides this through the frontline responders whose job is to interdict in immigration and customs violations. This *line watch* is one of the most central activities of border security.

Detection, prevention, and apprehension of terrorists, undocumented aliens, and smugglers of aliens at or near the land border are under the jurisdiction of CBP. These operations employ various methods and means of surveillance. They involve responding to electronic-sensor television systems, aircraft sightings, and using covert observation positions to detect intrusions. CBP agents must also rely on investigative skills and professional experience in pursuing leads, assessing conditions, and interpreting simple physical evidence, such as following tracks and markings, which might lead to suspects. Other major activities are routine traffic checks, traffic observation, city patrols, and transportation checks. CBP also works with other government agencies gathering intelligence and providing analysis.

To accomplish its tasks, CBP maintains and utilizes several databases. In addition to the Container Security Initiative discussed in Chapter 11, CBP also administers the **U.S. Visitor and Immigrant Status Indicator Technology (US-VISIT)** program. US-VISIT requires all incoming nonimmigrant aliens to submit to a biometrics scan of 10 fingerprints and a series of photographs, mostly through overseas consular offices. The identifications are checked with watch lists of known or suspected terrorists and criminals. Upon entry into the United States, travelers have their fingerprints scanned again in order to verify their identities. The aim is to prevent document fraud

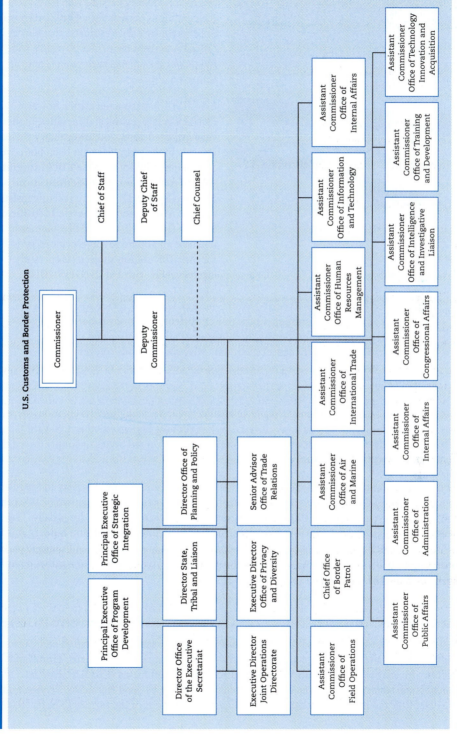

Figure 14.2   CBP Organizational Chart

U.S. Customs and Border Protection

- Commissioner
  - Chief of Staff
  - Deputy Chief of Staff
  - Chief Counsel
- Deputy Commissioner
  - Principal Executive Office of Program Development
  - Principal Executive Office of Strategic Integration
  - Director Office of the Executive Secretariat
  - Director State, Tribal and Liaison
  - Director Office of Planning and Policy
  - Executive Director Joint Operations Directorate
  - Executive Director Office of Privacy and Diversity
  - Senior Advisor Office of Trade Relations
  - Assistant Commissioner Office of Field Operations
  - Chief Office of Border Patrol
  - Assistant Commissioner Office of Air and Marine
  - Assistant Commissioner Office of Public Affairs
  - Assistant Commissioner Office of Administration
  - Assistant Commissioner Office of Internal Affairs
  - Assistant Commissioner Office of International Trade
  - Assistant Commissioner Office of Congressional Affairs
  - Assistant Commissioner Office of Human Resources Management
  - Assistant Commissioner Office of Intelligence and Investigative Liaison
  - Assistant Commissioner Office of Information and Technology
  - Assistant Commissioner Office of Training and Development
  - Assistant Commissioner Office of Internal Affairs
  - Assistant Commissioner Office of Technology Innovation and Acquisition

Source: Department of Homeland Security.

▶ Unmanned Aerial Vehicle

Source: U.S. Customs and Border Protection.

and to also identify persons who have overstayed the conditions of their visit. The Government Accountability Office estimates that border officials intercept over 100,000 people with fraudulent documents each year (Gaines & Kappeler, 2012).

US-VISIT has attracted critics, however. Detractors cite technical difficulties, higher than expected costs, and lower than anticipated returns. In the past, there has been both overlap and incompatibility with the FBI's **Integrated Automated Fingerprint Identification System** (IAFIS). DHS more recently insists that the **Automated Biometric Identification System** (IDENT), US-VISIT's biometric database and home to fingerprint records for over 108 million subjects, is currently interoperable with IAFIS (DHS, 2010).

> Automated biometric entry-exit systems such as US-VISIT face some of the greatest roadblocks to implementation. For systems to work properly, data collection must be comprehensively required of all who enter and exit, but for a system to accurately capture exit data that corresponds to every entry, extensive investments in exit processes and border infrastructure are necessary. (Koslowski, 2011, p. 20)

Despite its flaws, the program may already be an effective deterrent. Since its creation, there has been a noticeable decline of visa applications. It is not yet fully known whether US-VISIT has helped to actively dissuade undesirables from coming to the United States or simply forced them to use alternative methods of entry.

The men and women of CBP are responsible for enforcing hundreds of U.S. laws and regulations. As a matter of routine, they welcome nearly one million visitors, screen more than 67,000 cargo containers, arrest more than 1,100 individuals, and seize nearly 6 T of illicit drugs daily. The Border Patrol patrols the 6,000 mi of Mexican and Canadian international land borders and 2,000 mi of coastal waters surrounding the Florida Peninsula and the island of Puerto Rico. Over various terrain, in remote regions and isolated communities, and regardless of weather conditions, CBP agents work ceaselessly.

Bureau of Immigration and Customs Enforcement (ICE)

While CBP is border security's law enforcement arm, the Bureau of Immigration and Customs Enforcement is the investigative arm. The bureau has two primary components: Homeland Security Investigations and **Enforcement and Removal Operations** (ERO). ICE is the bureaucratic result of the merger of the Customs Service, the Federal Protective Service, and the detention and removal functions and intelligence operations of the former INS. Its 20,000 employees track money, materials, and suspicious persons who might act or be in support of terrorist or criminal activity. In addition to having a presence in all 50 states and being charged with the investigation and enforcement of over 400 federal statutes within the United States, the bureau also maintains attaché offices in 47 foreign countries (U.S. ICE, n.d.).

Another contrast with CBP is that while Customs and Border Protection focuses on activity and threats to the United States at its borders, ICE's mission is investigating and preventing threats from materializing on the interior of the country. Therefore, the agency is concerned with uncovering evidence and threats from WMDs, political violence, and individuals who may harbor those threats. As part of its mandate, ICE is also responsible for the collection and analysis of strategic and tactical intelligence data relative to infrastructure protection. ICE also polices and secures more than 8,800 federal facilities nationwide via the Federal Protective Service.

An important part of border security is deterrence through the enforcement of U.S. immigration laws. Thus, the investigative work of ICE involves exposing smuggling operations of illegal drugs, hazardous material, and aliens. It also concentrates its operations on benefit fraud and work site immigration violations (Nuñez-Neto, 2008, p. 4). In addition to seeking to deter illegal immigration through apprehension and deportation, the bureau enforces laws against employers who hire undocumented aliens as well. Many employers are lax, either unintentionally or otherwise, when verifying the right-to-work status of their employees. A noted case that became well publicized in 2008 was when ICE investigators found illegal aliens employed at the home of Michael Chertoff, then secretary of homeland security (Hsu, 2008). The business owner of the company that supplied the workers paid a fine of $22,800 and claimed to be driven out of business by the excessive penalty.

ICE's Enforcement and Removal Operations directorate is responsible for the removal of aliens who are deemed to pose a threat to national security or public safety. To conduct its mission, ERO's workforce includes law enforcement personnel and also medical professionals to provide screenings and administer physicals and health care during periods of detainment. As fair and effective as efforts appear to be, deportation is a contentious issue for policymakers and advocates for immigration reform. Many claim that current policy is ineffective and subject to the whims of politicians and the media. The traditional strategy recommends (1) workplace enforcement for "harvesting" illegal aliens for removal and deportation, (2) lengthy detention as a disincentive, and (3) mass removals of aliens in order to disrupt employment trends (Gaines & Kappeler, 2012). The failure of these approaches is attributed to the consequences of high costs of incarceration, an abundant labor pool of aliens willing to take work many Americans find unacceptable, and the demand for labor by U.S. employers. According to a U.S. Immigration and Customs Enforcement (n.d.) fact sheet, a typical day in the ERO includes but is not limited to the following activities:

- ERO managed 6 Service Processing Centers, oversaw 7 contract detention facilities, and housed aliens in over 240 facilities under intergovernmental service agreements.

- The average length of stay in an ERO detention facility was approximately 27 days.

- ERO housed an average of 34,260 illegal aliens in these various facilities nationwide.

- ERO personnel managed over 1.71 million aliens in the various stages of immigration removal proceedings.

- ERO processed 1,305 aliens into detention centers. The intake process includes an initial health care screening that is completed within 12 hours of arrival at the facility, followed by a comprehensive health assessment that includes a physical examination and the completion of a detailed medical history within 14 days of arrival. . . .

- Health care personnel saw 44 detainees for urgent care, and there were 46 emergency room or off-site referrals.

- ERO responded to 250 calls placed by detainees, family members, and community stakeholders received through the ICE Community and Detainee Helpline. . . .

- ERO removed 1,120 aliens from the United States to countries around the globe, including 616 criminal aliens. . . .

- Thirty seven aliens were removed via commercial airlines and 788 aliens were removed via government aircraft.

- Thirty one children were placed with the Office of Refugee Resettlement in the Department of Health and Human Services.

- ERO officers arrested 471 convicted criminal aliens through its enforcement efforts. (pp. 1–2)

Removal and deportation can also have harsh consequences on the families and communities of those affected. Children who are legal citizens can be separated from parents and left without supervision. Families may be left destitute and without a means or likelihood of financial support. Options such as crime or poverty become the only prospects available. In effect, the effort to address one perceived burden on society only contributes to others. In an attempt to ease some of the repercussions of incarceration, ICE established its **Alternatives to Detention (ATD) Program**. Rather than incur the financial and social burden of incarceration, there is the option to be released on bond, recognizance, or under monitoring conditions. Proponents say the program has saved the taxpayer billions and has been a more humane way of coping with the troublesome social problems.

With approximately 11 million unauthorized aliens working in the United States, DHS relies on a range of tools to help enforce laws and protect the homeland. **E-Verify** is a computerized Internet-based system created by the U.S. Citizenship and Immigration Service (USCIS) to check the work status of foreign employees. Employers and foreign employees must register. The registry compares information from an employee's Form I-9, Employment Eligibility Verification, to data from the U.S. Department of Homeland Security and Social Security Administration records to confirm employment eligibility. The service is free and USCIS claims the system is in use by over 500,000 employers.

In the past, users have complained of accuracy problems regarding data. As of 2009, the GAO reported over a 97% accuracy rate on the records of over eight million workers. However, the

Alternatives to Detention Program

The use of detention for immigration enforcement has grown dramatically in recent years. In fiscal year (FY) 2011, the Department of Homeland Security's Immigration and Customs Enforcement (ICE) **detained an all-time high number of 420,000 individuals** at a cost of nearly **$166 per person per day**. For context, in FY 1994 the federal government detained fewer than 82,000 migrants. Immigration detention is a civil authority, despite the use of penal institutions. The sole purpose of immigration detention is to ensure compliance with immigration court proceedings and judicial orders.

For many migrants in ICE custody, detention is not legally required. In these cases, ICE has the discretion to decide whether a person should be detained, released, or placed into an alternative to detention (ATD) program. Historically, ICE has not always exercised this discretion, resulting in the needless detention of hundreds of thousands of people, and costing taxpayers billions of dollars. Recently, ICE developed and deployed a risk assessment tool to make informed detention decisions

based on individual circumstances. However, because current appropriations language requires ICE to maintain 34,000 daily detention beds, individualized detention decision may be overridden by the requirement to meet a detention quota.

ATDs are a proven and highly cost-effective approach for ensuring that individuals appear at immigration proceedings. There are a range of options that ICE can utilize to encourage compliance. Some options, like release on recognizance or bond, carry little to no cost. More intense forms of supervision and monitoring, such as enrollment in an ATD program, cost around **$22 per person per day**. Compared to the billions spent each year on detention operations, ATDs represent a smarter, cheaper, and more humane way to ensure compliance with U.S. immigration laws. ATDs may also be more appropriate for detainees with certain vulnerabilities. Of particular concern are asylum seekers, torture survivors, the elderly, individuals with medical and mental health needs, and other vulnerable groups.

Source: Lutheran Immigration and Refugee Service (2013, p. 1; emphasis in original). Reprinted with permission from Lutheran Immigration and Refugee Service.

same report warned of a system vulnerability to identity theft and employer fraud (U.S. GAO, 2010). E-Verify is another example of the tools and policy guidance that affect border security. As with most, improvements have been made, yet challenges exist. The same assessment about the administrational, operational, economic, and legal issues of border security can also be said of immigration reform.

Transportation Security Administration (TSA)

Since the events of September 11, 2001, the need for security was exposed, and the attempts to address those needs have been epic. On a similar scale, the dilemma of integrating security with a commercial system that thrives on the unhindered movement of goods and citizens has been as Herculean. The U.S. government created the Transportation Security Administration to help resolve these two virtually irreconcilable forces. Security clashes directly with the circulation of frictionless trade. Hence, the Aviation and Transportation Security Act (ATSA, PL 107-71) created the TSA within the Department of Transportation with the mission of providing security while enabling commerce. The TSA's stated purpose is to defend the United States' air, land, and rail transportation systems while ensuring the interchange of commerce and the free movement of people. In addition to airports, railway stations, and seaports, this includes other public-transportation facilities, the inland waterway, highways, and pipelines.

With its creation, the legislation also established a federal baggage screener workforce and required screening of checked baggage by explosive detection systems. It also appreciably expanded the **Federal Air Marshal Service** (FAMS). TSA ultimately transferred to DHS as did FAMS. (Before 2006, FAMS was under the authority of ICE; since then, it has been part of the TSA.) Prior to the creation of the TSA, airline carriers conducted passenger and luggage screening. That responsibility now resides with the federal government through the TSA. The agency ensures air cargo security and oversees security procedures at over 450 airports. These tasks include limiting access to restricted areas, establishing airport security perimeters, and conducting background checks for airport personnel. FAMS places undercover armed agents in airports and on flights to detect, deter, and prevent hostile acts aimed at U.S. air carriers, airports, passengers, and crews.

TSA's workforce includes 50,000 transportation security officers who screen millions of passengers each day. Among these ranks are TSA explosives specialists, behavior detection officers, trained explosives detection canine teams, and thousands of federal air marshals deployed on domestic and international flights. In the course of its operations, the TSA employs risk-based intelligence methods and various detection and access control tools. Several examples include the following:

- Advanced imaging technology machines at airports nationwide to detect prohibited, illegal, or dangerous items

- Millimeter wave technology (three-dimensional imaging using electromagnetic waves) that automatically detects potential threats using a standardized outline of a person for all passengers in order to identify anomalies. The system was tested and being used on the New York City Staten Island Ferry to screen for explosives.

- The Biometric Transportation Worker Identification Credential to provide over two million maritime workers access to secure areas of ships and maritime facilities without the need of an escort

According to the TSA website, TSA personnel, routinely and during the course of its existence,

- Screen more than 1.8 million passengers a day to prevent guns from getting on planes (nationwide, TSA detected over 1,500 guns in 2012 alone)

- Screened more than four billion checked bags for explosives since its inception

- Conduct 100% air cargo screening on domestic and international-outbound passenger aircraft

- Conduct daily background checks on over 15 million transportation-related employees working in or seeking access to the nation's transportation system

- Conducted thousands of Visible Intermodal Prevention and Response operations in collaboration with local law enforcement and other security officials

- Instruct pilots in the use of firearms and provides members of the flight crew with self-defense training

- Support the allocation of $2 billion to mass-transit security in federal grant money, including system security enhancements for Amtrak since 2005

▶ Full Body Scanners

Source: iStockphoto.com/EdStock.

TSA's layered defense approach to security has several notable components. Similar to CBP's trusted shipper concept of the Customs-Trade Partnership Against Terrorism is the TSA's Known Shipper Management System (KSMS). The program only applies to air transportation, where shippers qualify for special status if they comply with a range of security requirements. Although the Known Shipper program predates 9/11, the KSMS claims to provide a systematic approach to assessing risk by facilitating the verification of known-shipper status.

KSMS functions in concert with the Indirect Air Carrier Management System (IACMS). This management system and application applies to freight forwarders wishing to receive TSA approval to tender cargo utilizing an indirect air carrier certification. IACMS is not intended for use by individual shippers. The Indirect Air Carrier Management System is a management system used to approve and validate these indirect air carriers (IACs). The system allows TSA to assess and capture pertinent information regarding IACs throughout the country. Despite reported complaints about the certification process, the program grows. TSA claims it processes approximately 150 new IAC applications and 350 certification renewals monthly (U.S. TSA, 2013).

Another example of TSA's layered approach is the Surface Transportation Security Inspection workforce program. The program positions 175 inspectors in 54 field offices throughout the nation to conduct surveys and inspections of freight rail operations. Inspectors focus on the areas of highest risk in the freight rail industry. The inspection program verifies implementation of voluntary security measures, conducting vulnerability assessments and checking operators for regulatory compliance. In the event of a need for emergency planning and response, these inspectors act as local liaisons to rail carriers and other government agencies as well.

As part of its partnering and layered-defense strategy, the TSA works with the rail industry also through its **Corporate Security Review Program** (CSR). Over a period of time, TSA worked closely with the railroad carriers to determine the level of security throughout the industry. Collaboratively, with industry representatives, TSA issued security guidelines and recommended measures to improve rail freight security. Of particular concern is the risk associated with the rail

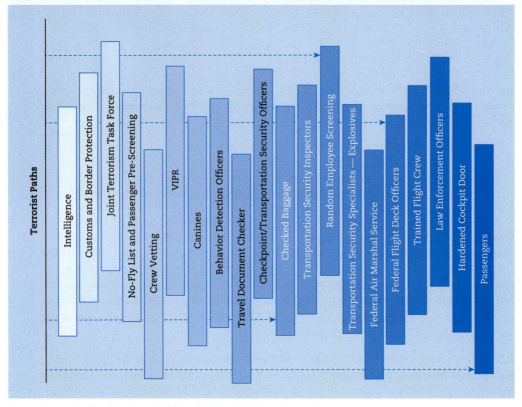

Figure 14.3 Layers of U.S. Aviation Security

Terrorist Paths

Intelligence

Customs and Border Protection

Joint Terrorism Task Force

No-Fly List and Passenger Pre-Screening

Crew Vetting

VIPR

Canines

Behavior Detection Officers

Travel Document Checker

Checkpoint/Transportation Security Officers

Checked Baggage

Transportation Security Inspectors

Random Employee Screening

Transportation Security Specialists — Explosives

Federal Air Marshal Service

Federal Flight Deck Officers

Trained Flight Crew

Law Enforcement Officers

Hardened Cockpit Door

Passengers

Source: Transportation Security Administration.

transportation of toxic-inhalation hazardous materials. The CSR program not only assesses how a carrier's security plan addresses the transportation of hazardous materials but also reviews and evaluates the effectiveness of the plans in the following areas:

- communication of security plan,
- audit of security plan,
- cybersecurity,
- protection of critical assets,
- security awareness training,
- personnel security, and
- threat assessment.

The above are a few examples of how TSA conforms to the general homeland security strategy of layered defense and extending the defenses through the formation of partnerships. In the absence of another high-impact event, success has, so far, been the outcome of these efforts. One case example occurred in 2008, when a man named Kevin Brown walked into the Orlando Airport and caught the attention of a plainclothes behavior detection manager. Mr. Brown exhibited behavior that raised the suspicions of the manager and several other trained behavior specialists. The TSA officers intercepted his checked baggage before they went to screening. When officials searched his bags, they found the ingredients to build a bomb. Brown didn't make it to the checkpoint, and his bags never left the lobby. He was intercepted and taken into custody by the Orlando police, searched at curbside by the Orange County bomb squad, and turned over to the FBI (CBS News, 2008).

The above account describes the ideal scenario of TSA's strategy materializing into action and resulting in success. The happy ending validated TSA's investment in personnel training, a layered-defense approach, and its partnership with local and federal law enforcement. Although aviation is a prime target for terrorists, attacks on rail and mass transit in other parts of the world demonstrate the vulnerability and attraction mass-transit targets pose for those who want to cause mass casualties and panic. Approximately 11.3 million people travel by mass transit each weekday, and security must contend with the realities of an open transit system. This requires a risk-based strategy that visualizes a whole picture beyond the airport, building, or checkpoint environment. While waiting for the next breakthrough in anomaly detection, sensor technology, or algorithmic methods in intelligence gathering, TSA must be content with spreading the layers of security outward beyond the immediate point of attack and building partnerships with other agencies and jurisdictions.

United States Coast Guard (USCG)

The Coast Guard came under the jurisdiction of the Department of Homeland Security in 2002 as a separate agency. In concert with CBP and the TSA, it forms the law enforcement triad of homeland defense. While CBP protects the border areas and the TSA oversees the security of federal buildings and the aviation, surface, and pipeline routes of the interior, the U.S. Coast Guard secures the country's maritime regions. The Coast Guard's mission of countering terrorist threats and intercepting the flow of contraband, illegal-drug, and human traffic extends its security domain to the nation's ports and waterways, along the coast, and in international waters. In fulfilling their duties, Coast Guard crews routinely appraise, board, and inspect commercial ships as they approach U.S. waters.

The Coast Guard also ensures that marine transportation remains open for the supply of the U.S. military and the transfer of assets and personnel between all armed services. For this responsibility, which is a key role in national security, it maintains a high state of readiness. The Coast Guard mission basically divides into homeland security and non–homeland security groupings.

The Coast Guard also has a history of challenges, including problems identifying its workforce needs. It found it particularly difficult stretching and balancing resources between homeland security responsibility and its traditional law enforcement and marine-safety missions. Determining critical skills and defining suitable staffing levels to fulfill the new array of missions posed specific obstacles (Caldwell, 2010). The need to develop metrics in identifying new priorities, setting appropriate budgets, designing performance indicators, and allocating personnel

Table 14.3 Coast Guard Homeland Security and Non–Homeland Security Missions

Missions	Primary Activities and Functions of Each Coast Guard Mission
Ports, waterways, and coastal security	Conducting harbor patrols, vulnerability assessments, intelligence gathering and analysis, and other activities to prevent terrorist attacks and minimize the damage from attacks that occur
Defense readiness	Participating with the Department of Defense in global military operations Deploying cutters and other boats in and around harbors to protect Department of Defense force mobilization operations
Migrant interdiction	Deploying cutters and aircraft to reduce the flow of undocumented migrants entering the United States via maritime routes
Drug interdiction	Deploying cutters and aircraft in high–drug-trafficking areas Gathering intelligence to reduce the flow of illegal drugs through maritime transit routes
Aids to navigation	Managing U.S. waterways and providing a safe, efficient, and navigable marine transportation system Maintaining the extensive system of navigation aids Monitoring marine traffic through vessel traffic service centers
Search and rescue	Operating multimission stations and a national distress and response communication system Conducting search-and-rescue operations for mariners in distress
Living marine resources	Enforcing domestic fishing laws and regulations through inspections and fishery patrols
Marine safety	Setting standards and conducting vessel inspections to better ensure the safety of passengers and crew aboard commercial vessels Partnering with states and boating safety organizations to reduce recreational-boating deaths
Marine environmental protection	Preventing and responding to marine oil and chemical spills Preventing the illegal dumping of plastics and garbage in U.S. waters Preventing biological invasions by aquatic-nuisance species
Other law enforcement (foreign fish enforcement)	Protecting U.S. fishing grounds by ensuring that foreign fishermen do not illegally harvest U.S. fish stocks

Missions	Primary Activities and Functions of Each Coast Guard Mission
Ice operations	Conducting polar operations to facilitate the movement of critical goods and personnel in support of scientific and national-security activity
	Conducting domestic ice-breaking operations to facilitate year-round commerce
	Conducting international ice operations to track icebergs below the 48th north latitude

Source: Data compiled from Caldwell (2010, pp. 26–27).

resources was thrust upon the Coast Guard by the events in September 2001. Not only was it asked to "build the machine while they were using it," the Coast Guard needed to look beyond the current environment and set long-term strategy marks for distributing human resources and other assets across a range of new missions.

In overview, the Coast Guard reflects the changing times in national homeland security. On various occasions, it has been an armed service, a member of the intelligence community, a law enforcement agency, and a humanitarian organization. It assumes an important role in the homeland security strategy of pushing out borders. To that end, it conducts security assessments at overseas ports to assess security and antiterrorism measures. It also assures compliance with the International Ship and Port Facility Security (ISPS) code, at times denying entry to vessels that do not conform to standards and, on other occasions, helping foreign countries to meet standards. It screens manifests for advance arrivals that may be on a watch list. Through the CoastWatch program, the Coast Guard partners with CBP in managing a database of 30.7 million crew and passenger records. It also helps protect arctic regions and has a CBRNE unit to work with DHS's **Domestic Nuclear Detection Office** and U.S. Special Operations Command. It has one of the most diverse mission sets in DHS, which requires the Coast Guard to build and maintain partnerships at many official levels and jurisdictions. To be effective, it must, as well, form collaborations with enterprises and organizations outside government.

SUMMARY

In the post–Cold War era, borders have lost their magical presence as control points. They come under pressure from the global economy, transnational crime, and mass migration. The events in September of 2001 proved to Americans that their national borders were not inviolate. As the battle fronts moved from remote parts of the world onto U.S. territory, border security became

▶ U.S. Coast Guard

Source: U.S. DHS (2014); U.S. Customs and Border Protection.

a central issue, not only in respect to national defense but also with respect to vibrancy of routine commerce and civil and human rights. Restrictions on the movement of goods and people posed an infringement on trade and the right of privacy. The U.S. strategy of pushing out its borders also drew criticism from opponents to U.S. hegemony in the United States and abroad.

With the creation of the Department of Homeland Security, responsibility for border security mostly fell upon four main bureaus: CBP, ICE, TSA, and the U.S. Coast Guard. All but the Immigration and Customs Enforcement agency are law enforcement organs. ICE is the investigative arm. Whether in law enforcement or in investigative operations, border security has become increasingly dependent upon technology. It uses various sensors and anomaly detection tools, unmanned aerial vehicles, and advanced weaponry to harden the borders. In order to intercept terrorist plots and staunch the flow of illegal immigration and contraband, authorities rely on advanced software and algorithm methodology to manage risk and create predictive tools for intelligence-gathering, analysis, and interdiction operations. These elements create a complex environment around border security formulation.

Tensions arise between regulation versus voluntary compliance, between the hardness of security regimes and the enablement of commerce, and between the public good of national defense and the traditions of civil and human rights. The contention spills out into debates over budgets, foreign policy, foreign affairs, the role of government, and immigration reform. As the arguments rage on, mass world migration intensifies, technology advances, and the world becomes a more interconnected and—often—more perilous place.

FINAL CASE STUDY

How Does Immigration Policy Impact Political and Economic Cost Effectiveness?

Rey Koslowski

The challenge of effective border control in the United States has grown dramatically over the past few decades. Each year, over 400 million travelers enter the country through official entry points, and hundreds of thousands of people cross the border illegally. Forced by enormous political pressure to stop illegal immigration and, especially since September 11, 2001, to prevent the entry of potential terrorists, the U.S. government has devoted ever more resources to enforcing its border policy. These resources have funded a range of innovations in border systems and technologies designed to screen passengers more effectively at official entry points while preventing people from crossing borders between these entry points.

Efforts to prevent entries at unauthorized locations have focused primarily on the U.S.–Mexico land border, where the overwhelming majority of unauthorized entries occur, and included the construction of physical fencing; an extraordinary array of radars, ground sensors, and unmanned aerial vehicles designed to detect border crossers and dispatch border agents to apprehend them; and a five-fold increase in the number of agents deployed at the southwest border over a period of less than two decades. Some of the policies have been difficult to implement, however. In particular, one of the most ambitious recent attempts to create a virtual fence at the southwest border—a high tech marriage of camera towers, sensors, and aerial surveillance known as SBInet—proved too expensive, vulnerable to technical failures, and insufficiently sensitive to the requirements of border control agents on the ground and was subsequently cancelled.

Substantial spending on securing the United States' physical borders has pushed up costs and risks for migrants attempting to cross the border and has undoubtedly reduced illegal immigration to some extent. But virtual fence technologies have their limits. This is because, in order to be effective, they must be backed up with sufficient personnel to apprehend border crossers after they are detected. Hiring additional agents is expensive, but smugglers can engage decoy border crossers to tie up these personnel at relatively low costs. Indeed, one by-product of border controls has been the increasing sophistication of smugglers trying to facilitate illegal entry, including by diverting flows to less accessible areas or by circumventing enforcement measures at official ports of entry. In other words, border management programs must follow a constantly evolving and moving target, but doing this can be extremely costly.

The challenge of managing ports of entry has also grown, spurring the creation and development of automated screening technologies, integrated databases to give immigration officials access to law enforcement information and monitor entries and exits, and systems to collect more data on travelers before they reach the country. These systems aim to provide more intensive screening and to facilitate international trade and the movement of people, leveraging new technologies to accomplish both goals.

Congress has a history of setting immigration enforcement goals that are not always realistic or feasible, even with the billions of dollars that lawmakers have been willing to appropriate for the purpose. However, political support remains strong for US-VISIT entry–exit capability and for high levels of border patrol agents supported with virtual-fence technologies. These policies have, to date, met varying levels of success in reducing illegal immigration, and it is far from clear whether they have been worth their extraordinary cost or whether resources could be more productively employed elsewhere. Given that illegal immigration is essentially a function of labor demand, more persistent efforts to prosecute law-breaking employers could probably do much more to reduce illegal immigration than increasing the already high spending on border fences, physical or virtual.

Source: Courtesy of Mark Schmidt.

Rey Koslowski is an associate professor of political science and public policy in the Rockefeller College of Public Affairs and Policy and an associate professor of infomatics in the College of Computing and Information at the University of Albany (SUNY). He is also a nonresident fellow at the Migration Policy Institute.

CHAPTER SUMMARY

This chapter has

- Defined the range and scale of border security and border security policy

- Discussed the trends in immigration

- Discussed the threats, hazards, and how border security risk is managed

- Examined the role and organization of Customs and Border Protection (CBP)

- Described the role of Immigration and Customs Enforcement (ICE)

- Described the role of Citizenship and Immigration Services (CIS)

- Described how the United States Coast Guard fits organizationally and functionally within the border security framework

- Discussed the social and economic costs of illegal immigration and restricted immigration

KEY TERMS

QUESTIONS AND EXERCISES

1. Over the past 50 years, what are the trends in immigration to the United States with respect to growth and countries of origin?

2. What are some of the factors driving human migration worldwide?

3. Why is the U.S. approach to border security, unofficially referred to as "pushing out the borders," often criticized as another term for *American exceptionalism*?

4. What are the categories of border threats?

5. What are the categories of border threat actors?